VICEROY'S COURT
GUARDROOM

SECTION AT C

SECTION LOOKING EAST

THE LIFE OF SIR EDWIN LUTYENS

Sir Edwin Lutyens
A drawing by Sir William Rothenstein, 1922 (*National Portrait Gallery*)

THE LIFE OF SIR EDWIN LUTYENS

CHRISTOPHER HUSSEY

Antique Collectors' Club

© Country Life 1950
an imprint of Newnes Books
a division of Hamlyn Publishing Group Ltd.

World copyright reserved
ISBN 0 907462 59 6

First published 1950 by Country Life Ltd.
Special edition 1953
This reprint first published in 1984 for
the Antique Collectors' Club by
the Antique Collectors' Club Ltd.
Reprinted 1989

All rights reserved. No part of this publication may be reproduced, stored in a retrieval system or transmitted in any form or by any means electronic, mechanical, photocopying, recording or otherwise, without the prior permission of the publishers.

British Library CIP Data

Hussey, Christopher
    The Life of Sir Edwin Lutyens. Special ed.
    1. Lutyens, *Sir* Edwin
    2. Architects — Great Britain — Biography
    I. Title
    720'.92'4   NA997.L8

Printed in England by
the Antique Collectors' Club Ltd.
5 Church Street, Woodbridge, Suffolk

CONTENTS

Preface to the Special Edition   xi

Author's Preface   xv

Introduction   xvii

PART I. 'AS FAITH WILLS'

Chapter I	Sources	3
II	Surrey Picturesque	11
III	The Casket	36
IV	Betrothal	61
V	Romantic Architect	77
VI	The High Game	118
VII	29 Bloomsbury Square	143
VIII	Flood Tide	185

PART II. IMPERIAL ARCHITECT

	Overture	237
Chapter IX	The Delhi Planning Commission	245
X	The Evolution of Viceroy's House	290
XI	*Vishvakarman*	326
XII	First War Years	333
XIII	Cenotaph	359

PART III. 'SO FAITH FULFILS'

	Interim Portrait	399
Chapter XIV	Delhi Rising	405
XV	The Twenties	432
XVI	Queen Anne's Gate	461

CONTENTS

Chapter XVII	The Finishing of Viceroy's House	495
XVIII	Cathedral	524
XIX	As Light Fell Short	553

Conclusion: Lutyens and the Architecture of the Future 583

Index 591

LIST OF PLATES

Sir Edwin Lutyens: a drawing by Sir William Rothenstein — *frontispiece*

1. Chinthurst Hill, Surrey — 15
2. The Hut, Munstead Wood — 16
3. Ruckmans, Oakwood Park, Surrey — 16
4. Munstead Wood seen from the south — 33
5. Munstead Wood: the gallery on the north side — 33
6. Munstead Wood: the sitting-hall and staircase — 34
7. Sullingstead, Hascombe, Surrey: detail of the entrance side — 34
8. The Casket: designed for Lady Emily Lutyens, 1896 — 51
9. Designs (actual size) of 'The Little White House' — 52
10. Sketch of The Casket — 52
11. The Inn, Roseneath, Dunbartonshire — 69
12. Crooksbury, Farnham, Surrey — 69
13. Crooksbury: the Fig Court — 69
14. Deanery Garden, Sonning — 70
15. Le Bois des Moutiers, Varengeville — 70
16. Deanery Garden: the Court — 70
17. Orchards, Godalming, Surrey: the entrance — 79
18. Orchards, from the garden — 79
19. Goddards, Abinger, Surrey — 79
20. Grey Walls, Gullane, E. Lothian — 80
21. Tigbourne Court, Witley, Surrey — 80
22. Marsh Court, Stockbridge, Hampshire: entrance (east) front — 81
23. Marsh Court: sunk garden and north-west corner — 81
24. The hall at Marsh Court — 81
25. Little Thakeham, Sussex: the garden front — 82
26. Little Thakeham: the entrance side — 82
27. Lindisfarne Castle, Holy Island, Northumberland — 91
28. Lindisfarne: the staircase to the gallery — 91
29. Monckton House, Singleton, Sussex: south aspect — 92
30. Daneshill, Basing, Hampshire: entrance (north) front — 92
31. New Place, Shedfield, Hampshire: garden front — 92
32. Buckhurst Park, Sussex: additions made in 1902–3 — 109
33. Ashby St. Ledgers, Northants: the east front and sunk garden — 109
34. Cottages at Ashby St. Ledgers — 110

LIST OF PLATES

35. Lambay, Co. Dublin, from the south-east	110
36. Lambay Island, from the air	111
37. Lambay: the approach through the rampart	111
38. Nashdom, Taplow, Buckinghamshire	112
39. Papillon Hall, Leicestershire: the round court	112
40. Gardens at Hestercombe, Somerset	129
41. Hestercombe: the Orangery	129
42. Folly Farm, Sulhampstead, Berkshire	130
43. Folly Farm: a corner of the 1912 addition	130
44. Folly Farm: the hall	130
45. Middlefield, Shelford, Cambridgeshire	131
46. Dormy House, Walton Heath, Surrey	131
47. Heathcote, Ilkley, Yorkshire	132
48. The Doric Order as handled at Heathcote	132
49. Great Maytham, Rolvenden, Sussex	149
50. Temple Dinsley, Hertfordshire: the new wing	149
51. Competition design for London County Hall	150
52. The Salutation, Sandwich, Kent	150
53. 'Mr. E. L. Lutyens exhorting his young men'	183
54. 'Lut' in 1906: caricature by the Hon. Paul Phipps	183
55. E. L. Lutyens. About 1897	183
56. Stages in the evolution of St. Jude's Church, Hampstead	184
57. Hampstead Garden Suburb: Erskine Hill and the Free Church	201
58. St. Jude's Church, Hampstead Garden Suburb	201
59. Renishaw Hall, Derbyshire: ante-room to ballroom	202
60. Howth Castle, Dublin: an added tower	202
61. Howth Castle: the chapel	202
62. Johannesburg: the Rand Regiments' Memorial, original full scheme	211
63. Castle Drogo, Drewsteignton, Devon	212
64. Castle Drogo, from the air (*Photo by Aerofilms Ltd for Country Life*)	212
65. Castle Drogo: lower flight of the great staircase	213
66. Castle Drogo: the scullery	213
67. Castle Drogo: looking down the upper flight of the great staircase	213
68. Castle Drogo: granite steps in the garden	214
69. Castle Drogo: the private staircase	214
70. Castle Drogo: the south end	223
71. Castle Drogo: the east side	223
72. King Edward VII Memorial: proposed design for Piccadilly site	224
73. Dublin Municipal Art Gallery: design of, 1913	224
74. The New Delhi Planning Commission, 1913 (*Photo: S. H. Evans*)	241
75. Delhi and its environs: map	242
76. Perspective drawing of the approach to Viceroy's House	291
77. Plan of the western, official quarter of New Delhi, as carried out	291
78. Ednaston Manor, Derbyshire: the south, east, and entrance (west) fronts	292
79. Viceroy's House, New Delhi: the approach through Viceroy's Court	301
80. The east front from opposite the south-east wing	301

LIST OF PLATES

81.	Two detail sketches of Viceroy's House	302
82.	The ascent to the portico	302
83.	Viceroy's House: the south court	303
84.	The south court at upper basement level	303
85.	The Secretariats, inclined way to Government Court, and Viceroy's House: aerial view from the east (*Photo: Crown Copyright*)	304
86.	Viceroy's House: the north court	313
87.	Viceroy's House: the open staircase court	313
88.	The inclined way to Government Court between the Secretariats	314
89.	Movable sketch diagram demonstrating the above aspect	314
90.	The screen to Viceroy's Court	314
91.	Viceroy's House: north side	331
92.	The Jaipur Column: diploma drawing	331
93.	Design for the Theosophical Society's Headquarters, Gordon Square	331
94.	Sketch by Lutyens of a Brahmin bull	332
95.	Elephants at the corners of the north ascent to Viceroy's Court	332
96.	Viceroy's House: lower basement colonnade	349
97.	Junction of retaining wall of Viceroy's Court and South Secretariat	349
98.	Lower basement of Viceroy's House	349
99.	Miss Gertrude Jekyll: portrait by William Nicholson	350
100.	Ursula Lutyens: portrait by William Nicholson	350
101.	The Stone of Remembrance ('War Stone')	383
102.	Design for proposed temporary war shrine in Hyde Park	383
103.	First sketches for the Cenotaph	384
104.	Portrait sketch by Edmund Dulac, 1922	401
105.	Portrait by Augustus John, about 1920 (*Photo: Ernest Brown and Phillips Ltd*)	401
106.	Lutyens in his sixties: four snapshots	402
107.	New Delhi: the Military Secretary's house	403
108.	Lutyens and his bearer, Persotum	403
109.	With E. V. Lucas	403
110.	Air view of New Delhi looking west	404
111.	The All India War Memorial Arch (*Photo: Kinsey Bros*)	404
112.	Viceroy's House from the north-east, December 1921	421
113.	Secretariats and Council Chambers, *c.* 1926	421
114 and 115.	A picture letter for the children	422–3
116 and 117.	Two typical comic drawings for children	424
118 and 119.	'Ghastly Castle' and 'The Giant who ate up Little Girls': drawings for a story for children	433
120.	How to draw horses: sketches	434
121.	Equine hexagon, formed of six horses	434
122 and 123.	Doodles: devised on journeys from the letter headings of shipping lines	435–6
124.	Queen Mary's Dolls' House	445
125.	Queen Mary's Dolls' House: the centre of the front raised	445
126.	The Queen's Dolls' House: the queen's bedroom	446
127.	The dining room in the Queen's Dolls' House	446
128.	The Queen's Dolls' House: the grand staircase	447

LIST OF PLATES

129. The Library, stocked with miniature books	447
130 and 131. Sides of the Queen's Dolls' House	448
132. Clifford Manor, Stratford-on-Avon	465
133. The Midland Bank, Piccadilly branch (*Photo: Midland Bank*)	465
134. Britannic House, Finsbury Circus (*Photo: Anglo Iranian Oil Co.*)	466
135. The Midland Bank, Poultry (*Photo: Midland Bank*)	467
136. Gledstone Hall, Yorkshire: approach and entrance front	468
137. Gledstone Hall: the staircase	468
138. Gledstone Hall: the south front and sunk garden	468
139. Tyringham Park, Buckinghamshire	477
140. Tyringham: the bathing pavilion	477
141. Tyringham: interior of the Temple of Music	477
142. Etaples: Imperial War Graves Cemetery	478
143. Dublin War Memorial	478
144. Thiepval: the Memorial to the Missing	479
145. An early conception for the design before its rationalisation	479
146. Westminster Housing Scheme, 1928	480
147. Staircase, 42 Cheyne Walk, Chelsea	480
148. Washington. The British Embassy: entrance front (*Photo: F. B. Johnston*)	489
149. Garden front of the British Embassy (*Photo: Orville K. Blake*)	489
150. Plumpton Place, Sussex	490
151. The Grange, Rottingdean: main sitting room	490
152. Viceroy's House: nursery landing and three electroliers of painted wood	499
153. New Delhi: the round walled garden	500
154. One of the two big fountains near the house	500
155. South retaining wall of the Viceroy's garden	501
156. Part of the garden front of Viceroy's House	501
157. Air View of New Delhi from the west (*Photo: Crown Copyright*)	502
158. New Delhi: Viceroy's House and Viceroy's Court as completed	511
159. Viceroy's House: under the main portico	512
160. The vestibule	512
161. The south main corridor	513
162. The south main staircase	513
163. The state drawing room	514
164. The state dining room	514
165. The garden loggia	515
166. The state library	515
167. The Viceroy's staircase	516
168. The Durbar Hall	517
169. New Delhi completed: portrait group by Mrs. A. G. Shoosmith	518
170. Metropolitan Cathedral of Christ the King, Liverpool: the model	535
171. Halnaker House, Sussex	536
172. Campion Hall, Oxford: the entrance	536
173. Middleton Park, Oxfordshire: entrance front	536
174–7. 'The Flower Hunt': drawings in pen and chalk	561–4
178. Death mask of Sir Edwin Lutyens (*Photo: Sydney W. Newbery*)	581

PREFACE TO
THE SPECIAL EDITION

THE appreciation accorded to *The Lutyens Memorial* volumes was combined with the widely expressed desire that *The Life of Sir Edwin Lutyens* might be made available separately for the general reader. In response to this demand the publishers are issuing this special edition. No alteration to the text has been made.

The four Memorial volumes were designed to compose a unity, in which the *Life* should be complementary to the three volumes on *The Architecture of Sir Edwin Lutyens* by Mr. A. S. G. Butler. But the possibility that the biography might in due course go forth alone, unaccompanied by its three large quarto brethren, was recognized at an early stage. This book is, consequently, complete in itself, and contains not only non-technical descriptions and appreciations of all Sir Edwin's principal buildings, but also his verbal contributions to the theory and practice of architecture. Moreover the last chapter, 'Lutyens and the Architecture of the Future', which presents the conclusions which it is suggested can be drawn from the matter of all four volumes, was written in collaboration with Mr. Butler.

Nevertheless, it remains largely true, as remarked in the Introduction, that 'unless the reader has digested the *Architecture* first, the biography must demand of him an initial act of faith in the great qualities of its subject, which were demonstrated almost entirely in building'. This qualification, applicable to biographies of all skilful architects, applies so particularly in the case of Lutyens, for reasons succinctly given on pages xviii and xix, that no doubt the effect of thus republishing the *Life* will be to reverse the process as originally envisaged and to send many readers to the perusal of the *Architecture*.

The problem of how to maintain in presentation the unity of Lutyens's life and Lutyens's work was indicated by Sir Jasper Ridley in his Preface to the Memorial Edition when recounting the origin and purpose of the volumes. He described how the responsibility for the vast mass of drawings at 13 Mansfield Street fell, after the death of Sir Edwin, upon his son Mr. Robert Lutyens, then serving in the R.A.F., and with it that of deciding, in consultation with the executors, on the appropriate Memorial to an artist of supreme eminence. It was felt that the various physical monuments erected to his memory were, by their unconstructive nature, incommensurate with the achievements of an architect who had exerted such an influence on his times, and indeed with the life of one described by Mr. Winston Churchill as a great Englishman. The fact that his office was still (1944) in being, and confidential assistants in his service for thirty years were available for consultation, suggested the idea of the Memorial taking the form of a comprehensive architectural record, which should contain relevant biographical material. Any proceeds from the publication of the volumes were to accrue to the endowment of the Royal Academy School of Architecture, the development of which was a project close to Sir Edwin's heart. A distinguished representative Committee was formed, of which Sir Jasper Ridley was Chairman, to raise funds for and to administer the project; the authors were approached; and the proprietors of *Country Life*, possessing an approximately complete photographic record of Sir Edwin's work, agreed to undertake publication.

But as the undertaking took shape its conception required to be modified. As initially envisaged, each of the three volumes in large quarto would have contained biographical material and so have maintained the essential unity of Lutyens's life and work. In view, however, of the great quantity of intimate correspondence generously made available to the biographer by Lady Emily Lutyens and by those acknowledged in the Introduction, it became clear that the limited biographical sections contemplated were too confined, and that such a biography as was thus rendered possible would make uneasy reading in so large a format. Consequently it was decided to expand the original project to comprise a full-length *Life* in a separate volume of suitable size whilst maintaining the unity of the *Life* and the *Architecture* by issuing the four volumes simultaneously as a single Memorial.

This is the place to acknowledge, on behalf of all connected with the production of the Memorial volumes, the debt owed to Sir Jasper Ridley. His death, so soon after their publication, was felt as a personal loss by many in diverse walks of life, not least by those who had vivid recent memories of his capable guidance of the project for commemorating his own friend. The combination in his personality of acumen, tact, and genial humanity, with informed percipience in everything connected with the arts, suited him ideally to this as to so many other cheerfully accepted tasks.

Since the publication of the Memorial edition, Mr. Robert Lutyens has presented all his father's drawings to the Royal Institute of British Architects, and their removal from the basement of 13 Mansfield Street has for the first time enabled them to be fully examined. This operation, undertaken on behalf of the Royal Institute by Mr. Butler, was rendered possible by Professor W. G. Holford allocating to it a large empty room at the London University Department of Town Planning, and it has required considerable physical labour on Mr. Butler's part for many hours every week for eight months.

A great deal of important material has come to light, the existence of which was unknown even to Sir Edwin's close associates. The access of available time and of unencumbered space for unpacking and spreading out the contents of scores of heavy bundles, containing in all some 80,000 drawings, has yielded a total of 2,742 pencil plans, elevations and sketch perspectives by Lutyens himself. About 70 per cent relate to projects which failed to mature, for example, the Edward VII Memorial, London University, the War Shrine in Hyde Park, Delhi Cathedral and residences for Maharajahs in Delhi; also studies for a superb memorial arch at Arras, even more impressive than that at Thiepval. There are 63 sheets of preliminary studies for the Viceroy's House, 94 large sheets of interior elevations of its rooms, drawn by an assistant, with all furniture, etc., drawn in by Lutyens; and all the preliminary drawings for the Spanish projects. There are, besides, numbers of his sketch-designs for country houses, beginning with the earliest. The collection must add greatly to Lutyens's reputation as an architectural draughtsman. Throughout, the drawings show a characteristic touch and line which suggest that he was thinking all the time in terms of *building*, and thus confirm the claim made in the Memorial volumes for his greatness above all as an artist in building.

The circumstances prevailing at Mansfield Street after Sir Edwin's death, and the scope envisaged for the Memorial, account for the little use made of these drawings in the published volumes. Mr. Butler, with Mr. George Stewart, Sir Edwin's senior assistant, aimed at presenting Lutyens's architecture objectively; that is, his buildings as erected. It was not intended to show him as an artist with the pencil. Nor was there the space or requisite time to go through all the rolls closely stacked in the basement of Mansfield Street, besides unearthing the drawings relating to work actually carried out, the existence of which was known to Mr. Stewart. Some samples of similar sketches and drawings are included in the *Life*.

The drawings will shortly be available for study at the Royal Institute of British Architects, and it is to be hoped that a selection from them will be edited and published.

C. H.

ADDITIONS AND CORRECTIONS

p. 17, l. 32, *read:* the village shop at Thursley (1887).

p. 122, l. 31, *read:* this must tell in the long run.

p. 461, *in Chapter XVI and elsewhere, for* 17 Queen Anne's Gate, *read* 15 Queen Anne's Gate.

p. 486, l. 5, *for* Garrett *read* Barrett.

p. 550, l. 25, *insert:* In addition, he designed the garden in Knebworth churchyard containing the grave of Antony, Viscount Knebworth, and the memorial in the church of his brother John, Viscount Knebworth, killed at Alamein.

p. 560, l. 25, *and other references to Sir Walter Lamb: for* Keeper and Secretary *read* Secretary.

p. 591, Australian National War Memorial: *for* 456 *read* 474. Beatty, Admiral Earl: *add* 565.

p. 596, Jellico and Beatty Memorial: *add* 565.

p. 602, War Memorials: *add* 369, 462, 473–476, 566.

AUTHOR'S PREFACE

THIS biography could not have been undertaken but for Lady Emily Lutyens entrusting me with all relevant letters of Sir Edwin to her. A formal acknowledgment of her courtesy as sole executor might alone have been required from the biographer, had 'relevant'—the operative word—been narrowly construed by her. I wish, on the contrary, to take this earliest opportunity of expressing my gratitude to her for the generous interpretation that she came to place upon it as the nature and scope of this book developed; for the confidence that she has been so good as to place in me regarding matters sometimes of an intimate nature; and for her constant help and patience. The extent of my indebtedness is explicit on almost every page that follows, where all quoted passages unless otherwise noted are from Sir Edwin's letters to his wife. My implicit debt to her can best be expressed, perhaps, by recording that at no moment was the biographer, as under the circumstances might at times have been the case, conscious of an embarrassed or strained situation. The thanks due from me to Viscountess Ridley for understanding help, with permission to quote from and reproduce letters from her Father, are of the same order.

The generosity of the late Sir Herbert Baker, K.C.I.E., R.A., in allowing me to use all Sir Edwin's letters written to him over forty years, and other papers relating to their collaboration in India, puts me under a peculiar debt. The nature of it will become evident, as will also, I hope, that I have tried to repay the trust expressed by him in the following extract from a letter to me written not long before his death:

> I feel so relieved that you have the papers about Delhi, as I know you will, in my simile, 'reject all bad stones in the monument of national character': 'All evil shed away, a pulse in the eternal mind', as Brooke sings.

But the relationship of Sir Edwin Lutyens and Sir Herbert Baker—long of close friendship, then strained to breaking point, but at last repaired if not wholly restored —is of a pathos that has needed to be allowed to tell itself, leaving the reader free to engage his sympathies where they are due. Thus only, I became convinced, could I discharge my responsibilities to both men and to 'the eternal mind'.

I am beholden to the Hon. Mrs. Harold Nicolson, C.H. (V. Sackville West), for permission to quote extracts from *Pepita*, to reproduce the sketch of the Cenotaph (p. 384), and for much helpful conversation; to Sir Osbert Sitwell, Bt., for permission to quote passages and some anecdotes from *Great Morning*; to Messrs. Longmans, Green in respect of extracts from *House and Garden*, by Gertrude Jekyll; to the Executors of the late E. V. Lucas for leave to quote from previously unpublished verses: to the Hon. Harold Nicolson, C.M.G. and the Editor of *The Spectator*, regarding quotation from an article by him.

To H.M. Queen Mary I gratefully acknowledge her gracious permission to quote a personal letter to Sir Edwin. I acknowledge also the kindness of the Earl of Halifax, K.G., O.M., in lending for reproduction Mrs. Shoosmith's painting (p. 518), and permitting me to quote from a conversation and a personal letter to Sir Edwin. To Lord Hardinge of Penshurst, G.C.V.O., I am grateful for his concurrence in the publication of matter contained in personal correspondence of his father with Sir Edwin; to Lord Hailey, G.C.S.I., G.C.M.G., for permission to quote letters.

I wish to thank all those who have contributed reminiscences and material which, with or without acknowledgment in the text, I have been enabled by their kindness to incorporate in this narrative. In particular I am grateful to Mr. S. H. Evans, Mr. Norman Evill, Mr. Nicolas Hannen, Mr. Oswald Milne, and the Hon. Paul Phipps, for background material relating to the Bloomsbury Square office; to Mr. A. G. Shoosmith, O.B.E. and Mr. J. L. Sale, M.Inst.C.E., for invaluable information and discussions on Delhi; to Lady Railing, Mr. W. A. S. Lloyd, and Mr. H. A. N. Medd for facts and reminiscences of later office practice in London and Delhi. I thank Lady St. Levan, Lady Colefax, Mrs. C. P. Hawkes, Sir Walter Lamb, K.C.V.O., Sir Herbert Morgan, K.B.E., the Rev. Father D'Arcy, S.J., Mr. Clough William Ellis, and Mr. H. Austen Hall for recollections, clues, and other valuable help.

My colleagues on the Lutyens Memorial Committee, notably Miss E. Webb and Mr. George Stewart, have given me frequent help for which I am no less grateful for its having been *ex officio*. To this category may properly belong the initial encouragement, constantly renewed and salted with helpful criticism, of my friend Robert Lutyens. The conception of a Memorial to his father in this form was largely his but, with exemplary reserve, he has accorded me full freedom in the execution of my part of it. To Andrew Butler I pay my tributes as colleague and fellow-author in the *Introduction* and elsewhere, but here acknowledge with gratitude the many suggestions, forbearances, rescues, and other virtuous acts of co-operation which have made our collaboration real.

INTRODUCTION

There is no excellent beauty that hath not some strangeness in the proportion.
BACON

THE genius of Lutyens was a legend that dawned on the early Edwardians, had become a portent before the first World War, and remained a fixed star in the architectural firmament, despite the rising of the constellation of Corbusier, till his death on New Year's Day 1944. It was a *cliché* for journalists—

*How sweet the name of genius sounds
In the reporter's ear,*

he irreverently and typically twitted them—an article of faith to contemporary architects, and an enchantment to everybody who had met him. In his lifetime he was widely held to be our greatest architect since Wren if not, as many maintained, his superior.

The legend was sustained on three foundations. Its principal emplacement was naturally his buildings, exceeding in quantity any noted designer's in these or other days and by their variety and distinction almost defying classification. But the reverential awe they inspired invariably received a shock on encountering their creator. The acquaintance or intending client could with difficulty connect the genial, whimsical, disconcertingly irreverent and facetious social figure, seemingly so irresponsible and almost inarticulate, with the prolific, fastidious, meticulously learned author of national monuments—except in so far as neither were ever dull or, for that matter, predictable.

That was the legend's second leg. It was enhanced by the paradox of his personal traits. He had a peculiar, irrepressible brand of humour which, habitually schoolboyish and often impish, as frequently struck a brilliant spark. There was the handful of little pipes successively lit and laid aside as a new idea was started. And his invariable familiar, the pocket pad known as a virgin, on which might be sketched in a few quick lines the geometry of a moulding, the plan of a palace, or an epicene caricature—one never knew which was coming.

Then the paradox would be momentarily resolved, this play be accounted for to the thoughtful, by a sudden comment piercing the smoke-screen like lightning. But these flashes were apt to be one of two kinds. At times they revealed an extraordinary intuitive understanding of the person or topic under discussion. At others they evidenced the existence, behind the laughable, lovable façade, beyond the abounding inventiveness, of something marmoreal, austere, as icy as Euclid.

A sense of the existence of this ulterior personality was the third source of the legend. Rarely, and never wholly, manifested outside his art, this was the genius within the man. At the outset these attributes of it seem contradictory—intense sympathy and almost inhuman abstraction. That contradiction did, it appears, exist at the very centre of his paradoxical personality. He had his amazing capacity to project his imagination into every space of whatever he was building, so that he lived the life of the people who would ultimately inhabit it, more vividly perhaps than they ever would themselves, and in a sense *became* the building. Yet his ultimate allegiance was not to their human needs but to certain abstract and, he was convinced, eternal values transcending mortal considerations. It was this allegiance, which became progressively stronger in him, that forced one observer to the conclusion that he completely lacked social conscience. His son defined it as the fundamental integrity of the artist, unmoved in the last resort by sympathy or charity, dispassionate and authoritarian. The development and harmonising of these two sides of Lutyens's genius may be said to be the underlying theme of this study. In the earlier chapters his power of sympathy and self-adaptation hold the lead. But during the conflicts centring round Delhi he was forced to draw increasingly on his profounder virtue of integrity, which subsequently, by whatever epithets it is qualified or paraphrased, became the atomic force within him and constituted Lutyens a phenomenon in the annals of architecture.

It is, of course, in architecture that this process was of the greatest significance. These memorial volumes have been undertaken to substantiate the conviction that, above the beauty, invention, and brilliance of his buildings, this integrity of Lutyens as an artist entitles his work to high and permanent place in the achievements of the human mind.

The author of *The Architecture of Sir Edwin Lutyens* pronounces him to have been *the greatest artist in building* that this country has produced. I concur with that high claim, but the burden of proving it falls upon my colleague. It is a formidable undertaking, involving not merely the appraisal of superficial visual and structural qualities. For the essence of Lutyens's greatness lay ultimately in the integrity of conception and handling of each of his scores of works *throughout*. Therefore the argument can only be rendered fully intelligible by close, lucid analysis of them. Moreover, the judgment required for these processes must be informed by extensive knowledge of the theory and tradition of Western architecture and no less of its current practice. In those stately volumes devoted to *The Architecture*, Mr. Butler does perform this essential and most appropriate part of our task, with the help of Mr. George Stewart's superb renderings of Lutyens's original drawings, and very little, I fear, from the other collaborator who is honoured by the inclusion of his name on the title page.

Yet the quality of an artist even as artist cannot be gauged solely from his works. His art is the expression of emotion generated by experience, and is therefore not to be fully appreciated apart from the circumstances of the artist's life. Unless the reader has digested the *Architecture* first, the biography must accordingly demand of him an initial act of faith in the great qualities of its subject, which were demonstrated almost entirely in building.

Not that it is here attempted to narrate the story of Lutyens's life leaving out his work. That would indeed be to play *Hamlet* without the Prince. Buildings naturally bulk large in the biography of a man whose life was dedicated to their creation. But here they are taken in their chronological sequence and quoted primarily as illustrating the development of his personality, whereas the student of their intrinsic qualities must refer to *The Architecture*. Yet it is hoped that the more important examples will be found in this book sufficiently described and illustrated to provide the general reader with a superficially complete survey.

It can be claimed, too, that this narrative is of value in its own right. Not only is it a study of one of the most extraordinary men in a vivid period that has suddenly receded into history; it is also unusual as the biography of an architect, a class of artist whom writers contemporary with them have unaccountably ignored; of the architect, moreover, who was called upon to embody in substance the late flower of English civilisation in circumstances which will never recur.

But its immediate purpose is to elucidate the enigma that Lutyens presented to his contemporaries: the contrast of the *enfant terrible* of the dinner table with the supreme artist in building, and to trace the relationships of both these aspects of him to that sometimes-sensed, occult, remote but insistent spirit whose discipline integrated all his actions as an artist. Such a project must be to some extent speculative, compared with the factual method which Mr. Butler employs to the same end in *The Architecture*. In compensation the biographer has been permitted to draw upon a rich mine of authentic material the very existence of which was scarcely suspected, enabling a study from within of that which architectural exposition is confined to examining from without.

The mine is Lutyens's correspondence with his wife, covering half a century's devotion, and it makes possible the effigy which it is now attempted, not to outline vaguely, but to model, colour, and animate—largely with the original's own words. This correspondence together with many letters to his children and a notable series covering many years, which Sir Herbert Baker generously put at my disposal before his own death, may be found not only to compensate for Lutyens's public inarticulacy but, with unexpected fluency and intensity, to substantiate the nature of the third element in his legend: the spirit within. Whether or not the rather embarrassing term genius is used to describe this aspect of him, we have to recognise that Lutyens does appear to have possessed at times an intensity of vision, a strange power of faith, which impressed itself not only on people but, as they curiously bore witness, on events. He willed himself to be an architect, a great architect, and he believed insistently that he would be called upon to execute great designs. He even pledged this faith, as a young man, upon the token given to his future wife, on which he inscribed the words:

As Faith wills, so Fate fulfils.

The two phrases of this prophetic sentence have therefore been adopted for the opening and closing parts of this narrative.

This underlying spiritual quality in him was recognised by one of the most perceptive of those for whom he worked, the Earl of Halifax when Viceroy of India, in a description of him as 'part schoolboy, part great artist, part mystic'. It is to elucidating the nature of this mysticism that the third part of this book is more particularly devoted, covering the period when Lutyens himself was seeking to define and embody its nature in his profoundest works. The ideal of integrity, always present in his mind, then took the direction of achieving absolute, mathematical, perfection of form which, as an artist, he held to constitute an attribute of divinity. That this ideal was a cold abstraction, compared to the aesthetic opportunism demanded by a social conscience, is not denied. That it postulated intense purity of discipline, and an intellectual authoritarianism the reverse of sympathetic, is obvious. But was the Parthenon, as he often asked in so many words, produced by a warm social conscience? Lutyens came to the conclusion that all great architecture is the product only of the fusion of science, aesthetics, and practical human ends, the greatest of which would be science *interpreted with an artist's sympathy*. In his later years he applied his remaining powers and great prestige to the object of bringing about through modern architecture such a union of scientific, aesthetic, and practical humanism. To him it became his religion, as indeed in less finite form, it had always been. It is significant that modern Christianity is striving, by a parallel route, towards the same fusion, which renders the more unfortunate the indefinite delay in the construction of Lutyens's own exposition of it: that immense Cathedral in the designs for which he embodied to some extent his vision of this union.

Schoolboy, Artist, Mystic: these summary attributes might be applied to the three parts into which the narrative of his life divides itself, and in which each in turn tended to predominate over the others. It has been a problem to the author to marshal within manageable space the teeming evidences of this trinity. In Part I we encounter the adaptable, sympathetic Romantic, and a lover whose courting was of such intrinsic charm and originality that the story of it has to be told in some fullness or not at all. For Part II, researches into the history of the planning and initiation of New Delhi resulted in the piecing together of the story of Britain's most ambitious architectural enterprise. For the telling of that epic elsewhere neither the time, nor the historian, may ever now be forthcoming. It was felt, therefore, that the leading part taken in it by Lutyens should not exclude some account of the accompanying circumstances, so that a considerable amount of important material, not strictly biographical, is included. In Part III there developed, during the most prolific period of his practice, the partial fulfilment of his genius's faith in the architectural creed and mode which we term Elemental. Unavoidably, therefore, this book has grown to proportions unforeseen at its beginning but which it is hoped, will be found to be justified by 'some strangeness'.

The personality emerging from it is, admittedly, the reverse of the popular notion of the facetious mischievous wit. Instead we discover one arrayed in the mantle of a prophet. Yet the reader who, although mistakenly, has expected sustained comedy in the biography of so famed a humorist, will not be wholly disappointed. As many of Lutyens's *scintillae* as I have been able to collect, and that still sparkle in black and white, are included in their appropriate places. Yet so many depended upon context and occasion that, like other *ephemeridae*, they cease to tickle when transfixed with a pen on a page. Another aspect of his wit, his brilliance as a comic draughtsman, is plentifully represented. And his constant sense of the comic, always on the surface, permeates his letters when they are not giving us their unexpectedly deep insight below it.

But it is owing to more profound considerations than those already set down that the life and work of Sir Edwin Lutyens have been made the subject of such minute study in these volumes. It is because of the conviction that they not only marked an end but foreshadow a beginning anew of fine architecture.

During the years since his death nothing has occurred to modify the conviction that he was the last great exponent of the European tradition, built up by classic, medieval, and renaissance masters, of architecture as fine art; that he was the last great architect of the age of humanism. The kind of mind that perfected the fine art of humane architecture is at present in abeyance. The class of person for whom Lutyens designed is being followed into the shades, it might seem, by the very conceptions of freedom within law, variety within rule, of an Empire founded on that vision to which he devoted the most fruitful years of his genius's bearing. We dare scarcely say of him, with the confidence of Wren's epigraphist, *si monumentum requiris circumspice*. To limited vision the end of an age is at hand. The moral supersession if not the physical destruction of European civilisation appears at least a possibility. Assuming its and our survival, it is none the less difficult to visualise such conditions of society, prosperity, and skill of hand being combined again so as to make capable of accomplishment buildings of the quality that Lutyens erected.

But the course of history is unpredictable. So might a Greek of the last age of Athens, or a Roman confronted with the hordes of Alaric, have contemplated the horizon, ignorant that in centuries to come a rising sun would warm the Parthenon to golden life again and engender a renaissance of that free orderliness, the origins of which are deep-rooted in the human spirit.

The humanist ideal, we may still believe as he did, will some day be integrated with the scientific ideal and overcome the present spiritual and material impediments to its expression. When men are free again to work for the glory of the spirit, then Lutyens's example and precept will help to inspire the rebirth, to shape the form, of a new and reinvigorated humanism.

The authors of these volumes therefore draw the attention of the reader to the *Conclusion* of this book. Therein they make, and seek to substantiate, the claim that Lutyens's last, Elemental mode of design, taken in conjunction with his elucidations of his theory of architecture now for the first time brought together, constitute a vital legacy for the future. It is their hope that these volumes will go a considerable distance towards meeting the demand for a record and an illumination of the great artist and inimitable man. It is their firm belief that their labours will be justified in so far as they reveal for future generations the creed of a prophet whose words were architecture.

PART I

'AS FAITH WILLS'

The Purpose of the Universe is Play. The artists know that. They know that Play and Art and Creation are different names for the same thing—a thing that is sweat and agonies and ecstasies.
　　　　　　　DON MARQUIS: The Almost Perfect State

CHAPTER I

SOURCES

LUTYENS is a Danish name with the sense of 'Little John' or 'little fellow' and was introduced to England by a certain Barthold Lutyens of the free city of Hamburg, born in the Danish province of Schleswig-Holstein. He acquired British nationality in 1745 leaving one son—whose name is given in the family bible as Nathaniel but as Nicholas on a tablet in Broxbourne Church, Hertfordshire—a West India merchant, friend of Wilberforce, and resident in that parish where he was a well-known rider to hounds. He died 1795 aged 53, having had by his wife Mary, daughter of Daniel Messman of Palmers Green, eleven children. Of the sons, two became bill-brokers, one a wine-merchant, four joined the army, and one was a chaplain to the forces. The military Lutyenses are the more vivid in retrospect: Englebert was orderly officer to Napoleon on St. Helena; Benjamin was taken prisoner at Corunna when A.D.C. to Sir John Moore and during his twelve years captivity in France started the Pau Hunt with foxhounds procured from England; and Charles was grandfather of Sir Edwin.

General Charles Lutyens, the most picturesque figure in this family picture gallery, married the daughter of a Hanoverian General de Vongenheim. This marriage, though childless, was instrumental in his making a modest fortune that conditioned the careers of his descendants. It came about by General Lutyens being entrusted to convey to Denmark the indemnity for the destruction of the Danish fleet by the British expedition of 1806. His reception at Copenhagen, however, was so hostile that he proceeded to Sweden in order to hand over the money through diplomatic channels. There the King of Sweden discovered that the envoy was married to the daughter of General de Vongenheim who, it appeared, had saved his, Bernadotte's, life on some occasion. The royal gratitude, though vicarious, took very substantial form and enabled General Lutyens to purchase Southcote Lodge, an ample moated grange near Reading where he dispensed ripe Georgian hospitality for many years.

By a second marriage he had two sons who were killed in action, one when fighting with Byron for Greek independence. He married thirdly a Miss Fludyer

Hopkins, to whom seems traceable the first introduction of a more sensitive strain into the robust but hitherto not notably imaginative Lutyens stock. These progenitors concern us only in establishing the basic Lutyens stock as muscular and conscientious; they were professional men with a respect for success, whether in the city, the Services, or the hunting field. What little more is known of them is recorded in Robert Lutyens's *Sir Edwin Lutyens: An Appreciation in Perspective*, (1943).

Charles Henry Augustus, born 1829, one of the General's four children by Miss Fludyer Hopkins, turned out to be a man of marked and original talent. Tall, and in his old age patriarchal, he must have been extremely handsome when he was commissioned in the XXth Foot (Lancashire Fusiliers), then stationed in Canada. As a subaltern he emulated his captive uncle by being one of the founders of the Montreal Hunt. But he also employed his leisure on the hitherto ungeneric exercise of painting (many of his drawings still decorate the walls of the Montreal Hunt Club), and gave further proof of originality, this time in the technical field of applied geometry, by inventing a range-finder, the Stedeometer. Instead of going with his regiment to the Crimean War, he was posted to Hythe as a musketry instructor to teach its use, and there he was also called on to examine and report on an American invention, a breech loading rifle. The weapon with which Germany conquered Europe in the next decade was rejected by the British military authorities, but Charles Lutyens is said not only to have recognised its revolutionary importance but to have improved upon it himself, although the man who had made his range-finder for him subsequently obtained the credit, and the reward, for the new rifle.

After the War, Captain Lutyens resigned his commission and resolved to devote his life to painting and hunting. In Canada he had married Mary Gallway, a beautiful Irish girl, sister of a brother officer, and now, to house a growing menage of children and horses, bought an old, rambling, and quite large house known as The Cottage in the Surrey village of Thursley. He studied under Sir Edwin Landseer, whose favourite pupil and intimate friend he became, sharing his studio. Horses and hounds were his stock subjects in what soon became a lucrative connection among the sporting Victorian nobility. As a successor to Herring and Ferneley, Charles Lutyens deserves a higher reputation than he yet enjoys. But he also painted the Surrey landscape, portraits, and some strange historical pieces. He studied technique with the originality he had previously evinced in ballistics, experimented in mediums and effects of lighting, and finally claimed to have rediscovered what he termed 'the Venetian Secret'. This mystery, which he said that he had discovered from reading Pliny, seems to have concerned a system of tonal perspective obtained by means of underpaintings. His offer to impart the secret, under certain conditions, to the Royal Academy not being accepted, he developed in his later years something of a persecution complex against that institution, members of which he accused of suppressing his discovery. Its nature is not rendered any clearer by a novel that he wrote with the same title. He kept on painting till his death in 1917, at the age of 88, despite failing eyesight and, latterly, entire failure to interest anybody in his work. By then he had become a rather pathetic, but still immensely dignified old man. He is described in age as fulfilling one's notion of the patriarch Moses. 'He used to stalk into Thursley Church with his family, and while they knelt in prayer he stood erect and "smelt" his tall hat—he was very Protestant. When a visiting parson once said something he disliked, he marched down the aisle and banged the church door behind him. In his prosperous days he used to be much away at big country houses, painting favourite horses. He himself had an old white pony on which he rode about, sometimes to Meets, though he had to ride very short to keep his feet off the ground.'[1] The impression we form of him is of a combination of artist and scientist not wholly resolved, a disciplinarian and dreamer, with rigid puritanical virtue. But in his prime he is said to have been a hospitable if somewhat Bohemian host to fellow artists and clients, both at Thursley and his London house, 16 Onslow Square.

Mary Lutyens can have had little time for other interests left over from the launching of fourteen children into the world. She lived in her children, to whom she was the motherly ideal of gentleness, goodness, and beauty. Her grandson has written: 'She was born a Catholic, turned Protestant: a devout, ingenuous and patient creature. Father always dwells lovingly in recollection of her small wrists and hands, and treasures the gold marriage ring of the Cladah Tribe which was given her in her youth by Tom Moore. I have no doubt that her gentle piety was in no little part responsible for my father's incorruptible nature.'[2] Her sweet serenity implanted a personal, private, ideal in her children.

There were eleven sons and three daughters, their births spread over twenty years, so that a daughter of the eldest was brought up with uncles and aunts of almost the same age. They were all original in varied ways. Charles Benjamin, the eldest son, planted tea in Ceylon but was musical; John Galway, the next, became a soldier and left in India a reputation for genial wildness which was still remembered when his young brother crossed his tracks. Of the succeeding children who grew up, Fred became a painter and, six years older than Edwin, sometimes acted as his tutor; there were Frank, Lionel, and Arthur; then Mary, the beauty of the family and later Mrs. Wemyss, in whose delightful books *All About All of Us* and *Things We Thought Of*, something of the happy country life of this populous household is recorded. Another family publication, *Mr. Spinks's Hounds*, by Fred (1890), is illustrated with drawings by his father somewhat in the style of the family's friend and neighbour Randolph Caldecott. The eleventh child was Edwin, born in 1869, then came Aileen, Marjorie, very musical, and finally Bill—Canon William, to whom the ancestral thews were

[1] Information supplied by Mrs. C. P. Hawkes.
[2] Robert Lutyens *op. cit.*

notably transmitted, since he held for twenty years the world record for sprinting the hundred yards.

When the eleventh child was born on March 29th, 1869, Sir Edwin Landseer asked to adopt the boy. Mrs. Lutyens, however, would not even allow him to be godfather, since, she told him, he had never been a man of God. But it was agreed that the baby should be christened Edwin Landseer in distinction to all his conventionally named brothers and sisters, and thus apparently be dedicated in name at least to the arts. Edwin Landseer Lutyens was never reconciled to his Christian name, preferring to be known as Ned, but this connection was to be of great service to him at a crucial juncture.

Ned inherited much from his mother; his dark curly hair and big blue eyes, the Irish gift for fantasy and laughter, but from the Lutyenses a dogged conscience and adventurous, pragmatic mind. In childhood he had a severe illness, probably rheumatic fever, which had a far-reaching effect on him in that it left him too delicate to be sent to school. Thus he had an irregular, scrappy, education derived from his brother Fred, the future artist, during the latter's holidays and, it may be supposed, that which his sisters were receiving at home. Yet his brothers and sisters, except Fred, Mary and Aileen, seem to have meant little to him, or he to them. Nor did his father, aloof in his studio, do much about the lad whose future wife, indeed, was for some time under the impression that he was the only son of a widowed mother. He idolised her as all that was gentle and good, and indeed she transmitted to Ned, besides the Irish capacity to charm, her ideals of honesty, sweetness and simple virtue. She brought up her large family in the strict Protestantism that moulded her son's character and that, in spite of vestigial sympathies for a warmer Catholicism, was to show itself unexpectedly in after life whenever the veneer of the man of the world was scratched.

This ideal mother and son relationship had lasting effects. He knew how to appeal to, and benefit from, older or more experienced women. In the common acceptance of the term, women had very little place in his thoughts. But, deprived of the normal hardening contacts at school with boys of his own age, he never entirely accustomed himself to male society, and long retained his adolescent instinct to seek the company, and it might be the help, of women older or wiser than himself, to supplement some fancied weakness of which as a child he was conscious. As a young man it is clear that he was more at ease with them than with men and girls of his own age, and he certainly made use all his life of the little boy's art of amusing, cajoling and winning their affections.

The women who most influenced his early life, in addition to his mother, were Mrs. 'Bob' Webb, Miss Gertrude Jekyll, and his wife. Mrs. Webb provided the earliest, most crucial, links in his progress, introduced him to his first client, which led to his meeting Miss Jekyll, and soon afterwards to his future wife, who transformed the whole pattern of his life.

Barbara Webb was a sister of Sir Alfred Lyall.[1] She is described as having been beautiful in an ugly way, with great charm and a sense of humour that bubbled up in an infectious and delicious laugh. Her brother had been on the Earl of Lytton's Viceregal staff in India, 1876–80, where his sister, having accompanied him, became the friend of the Lytton family. Somewhat to the surprise of those familiar with her attractive qualities, she married Mr. Robert Webb, the typical English squire of Milford House near Godalming, Surrey, that beautiful brick Georgian house now seen from the road at the south end of the Guildford by-pass. Mrs. Webb moved in 'county' circles in Surrey and, with her Indian connections and intellectual interests, enjoyed a wide London acquaintance. She knew the Lutyenses living at Thursley and, without children of her own, was particulary fond of the boy Ned. In his adolescence she gave him the sympathy and encouragement that the artist in him needed, and was perhaps the first to detect a streak of genius in him. Her warmth overcame his shyness, enjoyed his jokes and encouraged his artistry, whilst she contrived also to quiet and direct his boyish exuberance. She gave his manners a touch of polish that might not have been forthcoming in the crowded rusticity of Thursley. For his part, he made his first acquaintance at Milford with a country gentleman's home and with a style both of living and building—the Georgian tradition, though as yet undefined as such—which was strange to him. To her personally he gave the adoration of youth concentrated hitherto upon his mother. He called her his Blessed Barbara, his Baa Lamb, picturing her in his letters by a hieroglyph of a woolly lamb with a halo. Her death a few weeks before his marriage was his first experience of personal tragedy.

He must have been a queer, rather pathetic, youngster—slight, curly-headed, long-legged, with a pointed nose, sensitive mouth, and big sharp blue eyes—a hobbledehoy as often as not, clothed in ill-fitting garments handed down from elder brothers. Thrown much on his own resources he would tell himself long stories, composed of images from river and field, story books, and his mother's religious teaching. One of these has been preserved and gives an insight to the sweetness and tenderness of his nature. Probably it was this quality in him that had captivated Barbara Webb. Just after her death he wrote to his bride:

> I used to tell the Blessed Barbara[2] long stories, how she would come to a valley full of daisies, framing a merry rippling river, rolling in happiness to the sea, and the Baa-Lamb would be so happy and all should be sunny, and beautiful trees would throw soft shadows over her, as blessings, when she paused her gambols midst the daisied meadows! Then when she was ill I drew pictures of

---

[1] K.C.B., G.C.I.E., P.C., b. 1835. Lt. Governor North West Provinces, 1882–7. Member of Council of Secretary of State for India, 1888–1902. Ford's Lecturer in English History, Oxford. Author of biographies of Warren Hastings and Tennyson, and of *Verses written in India*. d. 1911.

[2] The lamb hieroglyph is used (see p. 10). Letter dated July 14, 1897.

Baa Lamb in amidst daisies, and over was the hand of God to bless and His wing to give protection. Now it all seems to have come true somehow.

'Don't think me cracked,' he continued, and characteristically: 'it is so much easier to write as a child as I used to write to Mrs. Webb, than as something of this world 28 years old! and she said she loved it. To write as a man requires more words than English gives, so by lowering . . . well I don't know—lowering the key to fit my weakly voice. . . .' He could not finish the sentence.

This inarticulacy, though temperamental, was no doubt due partly to his lack of schooling—the reverse side of his immunity from the repressions of conventional education. On balance, the freedom was an immense advantage to him, responsible for his precocious individuality. In after life he both regretted and rejoiced in it. 'I do wish that I knew more,' he confessed to his wife, 'had been better educated, had a wider range giving greater power of sympathy, yet keeping my appreciation for character and things of *faire valoire*'[1]—his intuition. But to Sir Osbert Sitwell, who once asked him whether any other member of his family shared his genius or had found a similar direction for their gifts, he said 'No. . . . Any talent I may have was due to a long illness as a boy, which afforded me time to think: and to subsequent ill-health, because I was not allowed to play games and so had to teach myself, for my enjoyment, to use my eyes instead of my feet. My brothers had not the same advantage'.[2]

The way he set himself to compensate his deficiencies by light of nature is the earliest solid evidence of his innate capacities. If his self-tuition accounted for much of the child having survived into the man, equally the artist in the child was able to grow uninhibited—and no complete artist but has much childhood in his manhood. An innate spirit of emulation provided his original and continuing stimulus. Beginning as he did with certain disadvantages, it took the form of determining to prove himself in no way inferior, physically or intellectually, to his brothers and sisters, and if possible to go one better than they or, in work or wit, anybody else. Yet all his life he had a secret respect for big strong men, for scholarship, for achieved success, though he mistrusted those who expressed themselves too glibly. Expressing his own convictions with difficulty, he suspected talkers of loose thinking. He himself, instead of talking, looked and drew, acquiring knowledge through watching, and judgment through seeing. It is not, of course, surprising that, in a home centred on a studio, he should have developed his visual faculties. Throughout his life rapid almost hieroglyphic sketches, executed with a fine assured line, were his readiest means of expression. What is remarkable is how quickly he seems to have apprehended, from chance remarks of his elders, how best to apply those faculties.

One of these mentors was Randolph Caldecott, who at that time was delighting

[1] Ap. 29, 1908. [2] *The Scarlet Tree*, p. 224.

people with his illustrations of Washington Irving and nursery rhymes. His bent was horses but his simplified landscape backgrounds were filled with an enchanting assortment of gabled cottages, picturesque farm houses and Georgian mansions—actually the buildings of his native Cheshire, but like enough to the Surrey scene, all reduced to their elements in a few suggestive lines. He often came over to Thursley and Lutyens used to say that Caldecott's drawings first turned his eyes to architecture. Another family friend was 'Dicky' Doyle of *Punch*. Having heard him say that he drew something every day, the boy resolved to design something every day, but his nurse apparently threw away all these primitive essays, the date of which is suggested by Doyle having died in 1883 and Caldecott in 1886.

Architecture, in those days, and in the West Surrey countryside more especially, meant picturesque buildings in the peculiarly rich vernacular of that favoured and (in the 'eighties) still wholly rural area. The borders of Surrey, Sussex, and Hampshire were then the painting field of Birket Foster and Mrs. Allingham, admired of Ruskin, abounding in delicious uses of all the old English building materials: timber-framing filled with colour-washed wattle-and-daub, mellow brick nogging, sweeping roofs of thatch or tiles, or thick, moss-grown Horsham slabs. Yards and paths of the gay cottage gardens were paved with those stones too, or pitched with thin layers of local ironstone set on edge, whilst there were walls of cob (with little thatched roofs of their own), clunch, the brown Bargate stone with garretted joints, or gauged vermilion brickwork recalling the time when Farnham was the greatest corn and hop market in England, and Cobbett, whose home it was, championed the agriculture later to be overlaid by suburbanism. There was certainly no lack of building techniques for a romantic young artist to study, and for years the traditional buildings of West Surrey provided him with all the examples he needed.

His method of studying them was individual. He would memorise their colour, texture and materials in his rambles alone on foot or bicycle. What fascinated him was their form, the composition of their planes from different points of view in relation to their setting—the aspect Caldecott emphasised. He soon decided, characteristically, that sketching them was unnecessarily laborious, besides involving the inclusion of irrelevancies, so he invented a transparent sketch book. In a saffron bag he carried a small framed sheet of glass which he held up to the view and on it traced the lines he wanted with slices of soap cut to a fine edge. By this means he mastered the peculiarities of perspective, developed quick and accurate vision, and co-ordinated eye and hand. Soon, by this device, he was able to memorise all the essentials he wanted of a building and so to dispense with the need for a sketch book—a fact that later was to cause surprise to his fellow students and has resulted in there being few extant sketches by Lutyens. But though he so rarely made sketches or notes of constructional details, it is obvious from his work how minutely he had observed and memorised the principles as distinct from trying to imitate what he saw.

He varied these explorations with long sessions in the Thursley carpenter's shop and Tickner the local builder's yard at Godalming, or on jobs where they were working. He used to say he had learnt all he knew about building from old Tickner. It is probable that it was a case of the pane of glass over again, and that he handled neither tools nor materials himself. But 'I am most awfully inquisitive', he confessed, and by questioning, watching, comparing processes with results already noted, he acquired insight and varied skills in traditional building technique. With an inherited aptitude for figures, too, he soon assimilated the import of builders' tallies and bills of quantity. He learnt from the working end the essential requirements of a drawing: 'merely a letter to a builder telling him precisely what is required of him, not a picture wherewith to charm an idiotic client.'

His only recreation, other than exploring, was fishing, and his delicate hands early made him skilful at catching trout—fairly numerous then in the upper Wey. He loved rivers, and water in movement always fascinated him. As the little river eddied by under the willows, with now and then a splash when a trout rose, and a glorious swirl if he hooked it, he sometimes thought of his own life as a river and himself as a fisher of men—enticing them gently to invite him to build houses. He often used the simile for his early fortunes.

CHAPTER II

SURREY PICTURESQUE

§1. PUPILAGE

HE was certainly original in an odd way, if one succeeded in singling out the shy boy from among the sturdier personalities of his brothers and sisters. Barbara Webb did so, and discovered a spirit that might become poet, priest, or artist if it could survive adolescence unspoilt and unsuppressed. He was still a child in many ways, with his dream-stories and visual world of his own. But behind that, and his waywardness and high spirits, there was a will of fine steel wire supple but tough. And in other ways he was extraordinarily precocious for his age, intensely keen to know and to know right.

So may his parents have discussed the boy when he was about 15, wondering what to do about him. Looking back on his life we can see how important it was for him to discover *himself*, to gain confidence in that self, and establish his personality uninhibited. It is a difficult thing for a boy to do, the more so if he is sensitive of being in the wrong. He has to stake his all against the immense odds represented by the grown-up world. There were, it would seem, three crucial occasions during his early years when Ned Lutyens staked everything on his being right. The second time was when he set up on his own as an architect aged barely twenty. The third time was when he married, adventurously, without any capital but the conviction of his rightness—in love and lore. But he would probably never have had the courage to take these two risks if he had not won the first. It came about like this.

In 1885, at the age of 16, he was sent to what is now the Royal College of Art, South Kensington, to study architecture. A letter of this period to his mother, the earliest to have survived, is so illuminating that I quote it in full. Besides the light it throws on the boy's appreciation and perception of a great building, it records the actual occasion when he resolved never henceforth to defer his judgment on a matter of architecture to the opinions of others. In this case the protagonist was his father, and incidentally the letter reveals the respectful attitude of the son to the Victorian parent, to contradict whom involved some courage, and hints at the extent of the father's interest in the lad's studies of architecture. The letter is also remarkable as containing a solemn self-dedication to architecture from which thereafter he never relented: 'to concentrate my whole attention, energy and time on possessing that confidence (in myself), also to obtain that great amount of knowledge required to help make a "successful architect".' The Mr. Peploe referred to was the vicar of the parish containing Onslow Square. The original spelling and punctuation are followed.

16, Onslow Square,
Tuesday morn.

My darling Mother,

You are going to get a letter at last.

On Sunday I went to Great St. Bartholomew's, Smithfield. a most beautiful old church full of interest (it is the oldest church in London)

It is completely built in so that when you are within a stone's throw of it you cant see it. You enter through a ruined gateway (Early English) under an old house, which has been built over it, into a small churchyard with tombstones at every angle but the right one it is completely surrounded by houses of plaister and brick the ground floors of which are below the level of the churchyard, at the end is, the Church, and is an exceeding uninteresting one on the exterior, a brick front with one large square window and a brick tower by which you enter into the church. This brick front is of course a late addition, in fact a mere screen.

The interior is beautiful!!

Norman with a norman apse (has lately been very well restored by Aston Webb) there is also a remainder of a Norman Arcade down the church 3 or 4 piers still remaining with their semicircular arch and norman triforium the clerestory is of Later work there is also some traces of Early English evidently built at the same time as the gateway additions in perpendicular also of course.

It is full of old monuments etc.

Take away the gas and you can imagine yourself in a country church, the congregation is quite small and you and it face one another, no one knows where to find it I suppose The choir and morning service is carried on down in the West End where the organ is (the organ completely hides the large square window spoken of before) and the clergy walk up to the east end to the communion table in the apse.

There is a Lady's chapel and other small ones of which I had not time to go into as it was I did not get back to Lunch till 2. I walked back, and I looked into St. Pauls Cathedral on my way the congregation was composed chiefly of bobbies.

Father would admire St. Bartholomew's very much I mean to take him there it is no distance from Blackfriars Station. I am going to sketch there as soon as I get my competition drawings done, over which I have had a run of bad luck and so will not be able to make so good a show which is very disappointing.

Read the following extract to father it is from the Surrey Archaeological Society's paper.

Speaking of Sutton Place, Guildford, 'The whole house is built of brick and terra cotta no stone whatever being used in its construction or ornamentation.'

When I came home from my first excursion to Sutton I told father that it was built of terra cotta and brick which he flatly contradicted and said that it was impossible terra-cotta being used for building purposes then, and that it was a fine sandstone.

Not that I bring any accusation against father but only to show him, what a small amount of confidence I have, in the little that I know, to allow myself to be convicted of a thing which I knew was wrong and that it only shows how necessary it is for me to concentrate my whole attention, energy and time on possessing that confidence and also to obtain that great amount of knowledge required to help make a 'successful architect'. and an architect without that success (not financial necessarily) is, well I can't describe it.

I hope to be down at Easter and hope to go on with sketching excursions harder than ever, and I hope to benefit by the experience obtained last summer.

I doubt very much indeed if my competition things will win anything So be ready for a blow when my failure is announced.

I heard to-day that a fellow called Mayhew who has been working at S.K. Museum has gone violently mad it took 6 men to take him to an asylum he was 19 years they say it was from overwork but thats all bosh, I expect he had something else the matter with him some home troubles or something and then perhaps worked hard to drown them. But he was a curious sort of chap, used to come in and argue for hours on something he overheard he was supposed to be very clever I never saw it never seeing the point of his arguments perhaps that was my stupidity and perhaps I did not listen.

Met Hugh Lathom on Sunday and on the same day met Mr. Peploe he asked me where I had been to church. I told him where I had been to, but could not answer any of his questions as to who was the vicar etc. and when I told that I went for the sake of the architecture he looked shocked and asked me whether I brought back a good word. I said O yes!! Did he mean an architectural tip? Next Sunday he will bring in his sermon My-de-ar brethren—last —Sunday—I met—a lad who went to the house of God (here looks round his crooked eye fixed on me) for architecture etc etc.

Now I feel much better disposed to man and beast and feel [holier?] when in a beautiful church with good music, and after all you get the lessons prayers etc wherever you go and that the sermon is at the best a bad translation of the bible even if it mentions anything of the bible at all

I hope you wont think me a heretic I admire Mr. Peploe as much as ever I did.

Give my best love to all

Does Arthur come up next Sunday we will have to share our top hat again. I have not one I use Arthurs ask him if he remembers when we changed hats in the street much to the amusement of the cabby.

My billy-cock, handed down from Frank has a hole in the top it was there when I had it

So with much love and hope you've got a letter this time I remain

Your very loving son
E. L. Lutyens

P.S. I hope Father's big picture is getting on all right. Frank says it is beautiful. It sounds good. When does the family arrive? up here.

In great haste

12 p.m. I will get thru' another hours work yet goodnight

I am still charged with the old complaint of singing in the early hours of the morning at hours when I can prove that I was in bed (asleep). Perhaps I dream of Palaces etc and trumpet in my joy or rather sleep. A dreamless sleep is a joy.

It was probably at South Kensington that he met as a fellow student his contemporary Detmar Blow, radiant from intercourse with the Light. Ruskin had come across young Blow drawing the church at Abbeville and had befriended him, packed him into his carriage and taken him with him on a tour of French churches. In the evenings Blow was invited to read aloud from Gibbon, and subsequently Ruskin introduced him to Morris and Burne Jones. Though destined to become competitors in the field of domestic architecture, Lutyens and Blow were on very friendly terms in their early years. They shared an admiration for the ideals of William Morris and the architecture of Philip Webb. Between us, they used to say as young men do, we could transform the world. To Webb, in after years, Lutyens attributed the inspiration of much of his early work, in which it is at least more evident than that of his actual master, Ernest George. The moral virtue of right craftsmanship and the beauty of simplicity were the modern ideals of young men at art schools in the 'eighties and accorded well with the vague but romantic piety of this letter. It was the time, too, of Morris's 'anti-scrape' campaign against excessive restoration of churches, which led to the foundation of the Society for the Protection of Ancient Buildings. Significantly, in 1886, whilst still at South Kensington, Ned Lutyens made a set of drawings for the restoration of Thursley Church, though his scheme was not executed.

1. CHINTHURST HILL, SURREY (1894). These sketches and those in Pl. 2 and 3, reproduced to their actual size, are among the few surviving free-hand sketches of his buildings by Lutyens. He made them for Herbert Baker

2. THE HUT, MUNSTEAD WOOD. For Miss Jekyll, and a house at Effingham (not executed)

3. RUCKMANS, OAKWOOD PARK, SURREY (1894)

How he fared in the Art School Examinations is not recorded. But there exists a copy of Richard and Gilbert Redgrave's *Manual of Design* (South Kensington Museum Art Handbook No. 6) inscribed 'Queens Prize, South Kensington School of Art, presented to Edwin L. Lutyens, 1887'. It is a depressing little book not only for its wood-cuts of encaustic tiles, but for the fact that almost all its sentiments read just as well to-day as in its year of publication, 1876. 'Once properly instructed, there is little doubt that the plain good sense, the energy of will, and the dislike of mere display of our countrymen will result in works of much higher excellence. . . .' There is no sign that Ned Lutyens ever read the volume, which does not look like a very high prize. In any case he was not destined to take the full course, for, later in the year, 1887, he was placed as a pupil in the busy office of Ernest George and Peto, where among his fellows were Guy Dawber, Herbert Reid, and G. Weir Schultz.

The senior assistant was a tall, idealistic, public-school man named Herbert Baker. He was a little older than the new pupil, had been Captain of cricket and football at Tonbridge, and liked to spend his holidays tramping the Fells with Wordsworth in his pocket. He observed that young Lutyens did little work himself, though, watching and criticising other people's and seeming to joke his way through his pupilage, he quickly absorbed all that was worth learning. 'He puzzled us at first, but we soon found that he seemed to know by intuition some great truths of our art which were not to be learnt there.'[1] Among them was the futility of sketch books, to which their employer was notoriously addicted. In after years Lutyens used to remember with amused contempt 'a distinguished architect who took each year, a three weeks' holiday abroad and returned with overflowing sketch books. When called on for a project he would look through these and choose some picturesque turret or gable from Holland, France, or Spain, and round it weave his new design. Location mattered little, and no provincial formation influenced him, for at that time terra cotta was the last word in building. All honour to Philip Webb and Norman Shaw (in his later period) for their gallant attempt to bring England back to craftsmanship and tradition'. With their examples in his mind, not his master's charming sketches, he undertook his first commission whilst yet in the office— alteration of the village shop at Thursley (188-).

The two young men became friends, tasted together the rare treat of discussions in the Bohemian atmosphere of the Art Workers' Guild, and in the autumn of 1888, set off on a walking tour of the Welsh Marches. Baker 'greatly enjoyed' the company of his young friend, 'his insight into some of the arcana of our art, his wit and good stories,'[2] for his part drawing on his fine memory for poetry. They climbed the Wrekin, followed a grass-grown Roman road, and stayed their hunger

---

[1] Sir Herbert Baker, *Architecture and Personalities*, p. 15.
[2] *Ibid.*

with blackberries till Ned was sick and exclaimed that the red fluid was his blood. The tour was notable for three buildings visited which had a lasting influence on the younger's work: Wenlock Abbey; Stokesay Castle—of which Lutyens said that its timber-framing inspired the best of his subsequent designs for carpenters' work (its lessons can doubtless be seen in the gallery at Munstead Wood); and the little Welsh church of Rug—'painted by some Jacobean—red and blue—even the timbers of the roof painted with blue, white, and red roses' as Sir Edwin recalled in a letter to Sir Herbert fifty-six years later.[1] There was also 'a delicious old chandelier, all made of wood painted green', and remembered when designing similar fittings for Viceroy's House at Delhi. But he would make no sketches, only stand and look at these things, committing their essentials to memory. Then, at the beginning of 1889, when he was barely twenty, he was commissioned to build a small country house, on a site at Crooksbury, near Farnham. His client, Mr. (later Sir) Arthur Chapman, was a friend of Mrs. Webb, and had kept a benevolent eye on the young architect during his pupilage. In a letter of 1886 to his sister, Ned had written: 'Chapmans want you to stay with them these holidays. They have a jolly house in Hereford Square, awfully kind, drive there every Saturday.' On receiving the commission, he left George's office and opened one of his own at 6 Grays Inn Square.

§2. 6 GRAYS INN SQUARE

For a young man, barely twenty, with only six month's technical training and no professional experience, to set up in practice on his own, must have needed self confidence—it might have been called cheek—even in those days when architectural education, as now provided, was unknown. For a youth temperamentally shy and unworldly, it cannot have been but an act of faith. But faith in that something within him, in his rightness of intuition, was already his lode-star. And he was impelled to it. He saw that he was learning nothing, wasting his time and his father's limited means, by staying with Ernest George. His elder brothers Charles and John had 'had what money they wanted', but as their father grew older, and the taste of the time turned away from his realistic paintings, his income from equestrian portraits dried up. He had invested part of his capital, too, in the interests of Charles's tea plantation in Ceylon which not only paid no dividends for many years but showed all symptoms of being a total loss. Consequently the strain on the family exchequer of launching the younger children was becoming severe.

Relative indigence was having another effect. The Thursley cottage and Onslow Square, besides being overcrowded for so many adults, were beginning to become squalid. The Captain was practising strange economies: newspapers were used instead of table-cloths, he would mend his own boots, clothes were worn by a

[1] January 28th, 1942.

succession of children. Then no meat was allowed in the house and cabbage became the staple fare, but it must be cooked in oil. Yet, chatting to a friend after church, the old man would absent-mindedly abandon his family, walk home with his friend, accept the eventual invitation to lunch, and, still absent-mindedly, consume more beef than anybody else. Mrs. Lutyens, faced by these recurrent crises, would pray, with her Irish serenity, for guidance and means to be vouchsafed, but was not a practical housewife. Indeed, the home was kept together by the children's old Nanny, Priscilla, who mothered them all till her death.

Ned, though he never ceased to adore his mother and honour his father, found it impossible to work in this atmosphere, though the dining-room was put at his disposal when not required for meals. He continued to sleep at Onslow Square till he married, but the atavistic Lutyens strain in him was pained by the evident lack of present success; and his aesthetic sense was outraged by the happy-go-lucky makeshift and congestion of the household. This background of chaos begot by reaction a passion for neatness and order which became characteristic of his work, and shaped his vision of the imaginary homes which he drew for his future wife. For years he could not bear a sofa in a room, and had none in his home, because that piece of furniture was associated in his mind with shabby chintz under the flounces of which the oddments of an untidy room were hurriedly thrust when a visitor was expected.

But it was no less psychologically necessary for him to work out his salvation on his own, by himself. As he had written to his mother when still at South Kensington, he was consumed by the necessity 'to concentrate my whole attention, energy, and time on possessing confidence' in himself and 'to obtain that knowledge required to make a successful architect'. He was always an individualist, from his solitary childhood to the height of his success, when repeated suggestions by friends that he should take a partner to ease his burdens were set aside on one pretext or another. People distracted him.

A legacy of £100 from Miss Landseer, his namesake's sister, made it materially possible for him to set up on his own. 'It was that £100 (which made me get into debt at once!) was the first cause of my getting on rather better than my brothers', he wrote long afterwards. The reference to his getting into debt, though understandable under the circumstances, cannot be further expanded. It does not seem to have been serious but it does seem to have contributed to the dread of insolvency that haunted his early married life and which he never quite got over as long as he lived.

So, as soon as the contract for Crooksbury was signed, a plate inscribed 'Mr. E. L. Lutyens, Architect' went up on that door in Grays Inn Square. The old white-panelled rooms looked over the garden. Rooks built in the trees and it was as quiet as in the country.

Crooksbury is an important document in the study of his progress, for, in addition to its being his first house, he was engaged there twice subsequently on additions—in 1898–1902, and 1914. In later life he would excuse himself from revisiting the place; he said it had too many ghosts. The house stands on a high heathery site below that prominent pine-capped hill near Farnham, on the Surrey-Hampshire border. The 1889 building gives one a slight shock: not very good Norman Shaw Early Tudor, timber-framed with brick nogging and ornamental brick chimneys, on an L-shaped plan. The design (p. 22) was exhibited at the Royal Academy of 1890 and was published in *The Builder* (Oct. 18, 1890) with this description, no doubt supplied by the architect:

> This house is now being erected from designs of Mr. E. L. Lutyens. It is intended as a summer residence and is built of red brick with old tiles on the roof and for the tile hanging. The house is planned following the natural levels of the site. There are 9 bed rooms and bathroom on the first floor. There is an entrance hall and living room of wood blocks with red brick margins. Builder, Mitchell Bros., Shalford.

It is almost entirely derivative from Norman Shaw's nearby Pierrepoint and the Caldecott farm-houses and cottages that he had been sketching in the neighbourhood. What surprises one now about it is the use, whether for economy or lack of supplies, of the wrong materials—stock bricks of indifferent quality, deal where oak should be used, and white painted bargeboards. The interior has been much altered, but the living-room occupying most of the ground-floor has a capacious ingle in the base of the massive chimney stack at the side of the front. A decade later, when called on to enlarge the house, he added his first essay in renaissance design, and a little later an entirely Wrennish stable block and forecourt, so that Crooksbury was also the scene of his second beginning. The 1899 addition no longer exists in its entirety, since a later owner made him remodel it, as a reversion to the cottagey style, in 1914.

If Lutyens, at this stage, was critical of his elders, he was doubly so of himself and so nervous about this first job that, when possible, he inspected its progress after the workmen had left in the evening, by which time it was sometimes dark.

There followed a number of smaller local commissions, in the building of which he made use of the soft local Bargate stone and a picturesque version of the traditional style of West Surrey. A pair of new lodges at Park Hatch, Hascombe, for Mr. Joseph Goodman are described in *The Builder* (Nov. 15, 1890) as 'To flank the principal entrance to the Park between old yew hedges'. The perspective (drawn by Herbert Baker) shows an elaborate Ernest Georgian conception but enriched enthusiastically with local materials—Bargate stone, Horsham slates, oak timber work in gables, the carriage-way pitched with ironstone as in the Farnham streets, and covered ways to the lodges paved with red brick.

He continued to see a good deal of Herbert Baker, then beginning to acquire a little practice of his own in restoring timber houses in Kent, and he drew for Lutyens some of the perspectives of his earliest jobs.

Unfortunately none now exist prior to 1902, when Baker began to preserve Lutyens's, except for three invaluable sheets of sketches that must be of 1892–3 (pp. 15 and 16). These represent the spirit of their designer in his twenties better perhaps than the buildings themselves, which have aged in half a century in a way that, whilst testifying to their soundness of traditional workmanship, has blurred the freshness that was their outstanding quality at the time.

His first assistant at Grays Inn Square was an extraordinary character whom he described fifty years on as

> Dear old Barlow. The head of the South Kensington School of Art, John Sparkes, put him on to me. Sparkes, on retirement, designed himself a house to be built at Ewhurst, and Barlow was employed to build it, as Clerk of the Works. They had no sooner started than they ran into running sand. Engineers were called in, and they bored great iron tubes through the sand to a rock bottom, to carry a concrete slab on which to build the house. Sparkes wrote to Barlow to say that all was now well, and to get on. Barlow wrote back to say that Mr. Sparkes had had so much trouble that Our Lord could not possibly intend him to build, and he dared not have anything to do with it. This very pious man was my first assistant.[1]

The five or six years while he was establishing his little practice in Surrey are almost recordless. 'I went to no parties, I knew no one and worked till 12–2 in the morning. I bicycled a lot and walked a good bit, but no sport and no relaxation; just work.'[2] But probably to this time belongs an episode which he described as 'a great personal adventure' and as having taught him a lesson never forgotten:[3]

> Staying at a house I met my hostess's father who, as a Sapper in India, was told off to build barracks. His design, probably like those pre-Mutiny buildings of which we should be proud, had been turned down, and a typed set of plans of bungalow style sent to him to erect. These he had criticised as being ungentlemanlike, refused to build them, and resigned.
>
> When I met him he was 80 years old and blind. At dinner he told me that since he had been blind he had designed two buildings, a Cathedral and an Opera House. I asked him what they were like. He said he could not see to

[1] Story told by Sir Edwin at the dinner given him by former pupils and assistants on his election as President of the Royal Academy, February 24, 1939.
[2] In a letter, January 26, 1928.
[3] Address to Cambridge Architectural Society, November 8, 1932.

draw and had found no one who would draw them out for him. I volunteered my services.

His lady wife, overhearing our conversation, shook her head, tapping her forehead with her forefinger. I said, 'May I draw?' and directly after dinner the table was cleared and, with plenty of squared paper, we began. He warned me that the Opera House was ellyptical and the Cathedral rectangular. I have always regretted that I chose the rectangular building as being the easier to draw. I began to his dictation. He dictated rather quicker than I could draw. I made some mistakes, but my dictator being blind seemed to make my errors of small account, and on I went.

It was nearer two than one o'clock when his old wife came down in her dressing gown, to scold us as naughty children who ought to be in bed. Looking over my shoulder at my rough plan, section and elevation, she said 'Oh! but it is *beautiful*! and the old man's blind face lit up as though all sorrows were of the past.

The blind man's feat of memorisation was of course, phenomenal; but the younger's having been able to draw things from dictation shows the technical level of his ability. The lesson he gained from it, and recommended to young architects in after years, was that students should try dictating a design in figures from memory: 'it entails much thought and accurate statement of fact and there is no danger of being run away with cross-country by a soft-nosed pencil. The draughtsman will be no mean critic, but he will not have to be over-critical, for it will be his turn next to dictate his design.'

CROOKSBURY, PERSPECTIVE DESIGN. (From *The Builder*, Oct. 18, 1890)

§3. GERTRUDE JEKYLL AND PHILIP WEBB

It was when working on Crooksbury from Thursley that he met his fairy godmother. That is not quite the right description of Gertrude Jekyll, earthy and practical and determined. Yet fairy godmothers before now have issued from woods in no more glamorous guise; and her influence on his character, development, and career during this first decisive decade of his practice was magical. Just as Mrs. Webb had watched over the boy, encouraging and restraining, so Miss Jekyll disciplined him through his twenties. Only a great artist, whom he respected as such, and a most determined character, capable of asserting her will over his, could have done that, and only, in the last resort, through a relationship of deep mutual affection. His godmother she certainly became, and not all fairies are ballerinas.

Perhaps the greatest *artist* in horticulture and garden-planting that England has produced—whose influence on garden design has been as widespread as Capability Brown's in the eighteenth century—was then nearing fifty. She lived with her mother at Munstead House near Godalming, and was short, stout, myopic, downright. William Nicholson's portrait in the National Portrait Gallery (p. 350) and his picture of her working-boots painted for Lutyens, have recorded her appearance in old age, which Logan Pearsall Smith has described as 'of some ancient, incredibly aristocratic denizen of a river jungle, gazing gravely out from the tangled reeds'. She was just such a frightening but kind, wise, old lady when I used to have occasion to visit her in connection with the revision of one of her books and, I remember, she impressed on me amongst other things that *claire-voie*, not 'clairvoyée', was the proper term for the wrought iron screen at the end of a garden alley.

Before Lutyens was born, the artist George Leslie had described her as 'a young lady of singular and remarkable accomplishments—carving, modelling, house-painting, carpentry, smith's work, repoussé work, gilding, wood-inlaying, embroidery, gardening, and all manner of herb and flower knowledge and culture.'[1] To which may be added the shoeing of horses and the making of shell-work pictures of much beauty. She wrote, in a small neat hand, English as direct, simple, and discriminating as her nonsense-hating self. By now her eyesight was already causing her anxiety, so that in 1891 she had been ordered to give up painting. But already she was becoming known to a widening circle of horticulturists for her revolutionary views on gardening, developed simultaneously with William Robinson's in essays contributed to his paper *The Garden*. In a wood across the road from her widowed mother's house she had begun, in 1880, to put her principles into practice, applying to the design and planting of a garden the sensitive artistry and skill of hand hitherto devoted to her painting and handcrafts. She shared her master Ruskin's reverence

---

[1] *Our River* by G. B. Leslie, quoted by Francis Jekyll, *Gertude Jekyll: A Memoir.* (1934).

for nature and contempt for the slapdash and pretentious. Her conviction—and the nature of her influence on Lutyens—is summed up in a sentence from her first book of collected papers:

> No artificial planting can ever equal that of Nature, but one may learn from it (i.e. Nature) the great lesson of the importance of moderation and reserve, of simplicity of intention, of directness of purpose, and the inestimable value of the quality called 'breadth' in painting. For planting ground is painting a landscape with living things.[1]

They were brought together by a mutual friend and neighbour, Mr. Harry Mangles of Littleworth, one of the pioneers of rhododendron growing, for whom the young architect was building a cottage at Tongham in 1890–1. Lutyens, de-describing this beginning 'of a friendship that lasted some forty-four years'[2] told of a tea-party at which she was 'a bunch of cloaked propriety, quiet and demure, of few words, and those deliberately uttered in a quiet mellow voice—with keen, bright eyes that missed little in their persistent deliberation. She spoke no word to me' (it must have been a trying occasion for the shy young man) 'but on leaving, with one foot on the step of her pony carriage and reins in hand, she invited me to Munstead on the very next Saturday'.

A somewhat different Miss Jekyll then received him, 'genial and communicative, in short blue skirt and the boots made famous by W. Nicholson', the 'Aunt Bumps, Mother of all Bulbs' as he christened her, Mab for short. This first visit led to many more, also to knowledge of her brother, Colonel, later Sir Herbert Jekyll, destined to be his wise counsellor and invaluable supporter on many important occasions. Lutyens has recorded:

> The week-end at Munstead became a custom and gave opportunity for many a voyage of discovery throughout Surrey and Sussex, within a range possible to Bessie and the pony cart she drew. Old houses, farms and cottages were searched for, their modest methods of construction discussed, their inmates and the industries that supported them.[3]

In these expeditions, useful to the architect in widening his intellectual and spiritual background as well as his topographical range of knowledge, it was clearly he who contributed most to discussions on the 'modest methods of construction' encountered, since Miss Jekyll's references to buildings,[4] for all their copious observation of traditional customs and materials, give no evidence of technical knowledge of architecture. Indeed she laid no claim to that, which was the principal reason why she adopted Ned Lutyens. She was not a woman to have patience with the second-

---

[1] *Wood and Garden*, 1897.   [2] In the Foreword to *Gertrude Jekyll: A Memoir*.
[3] *ibid*.   [4] e.g. in *Old West Surrey*, 1904.

rate in persons or views, and evidently she had quickly divined that in this young architect she could find the technical insight and possible collaborator that she realised she needed. Yet it is difficult not to see also in their relationship a repetition of that already noted in the case of Mrs. Webb: an elder woman delightedly yielding to the Lutyens combination of ingenuousness, fancy, skill and spontaneous affection. An immediate result was her offering, almost at their first meeting, tentative suggestions for the garden at Crooksbury. This was quickly followed by her introducing him to deal with the architectural adjuncts of gardens on which she was consulted.[1] She discussed with him the building, on which she was embarking, of 'The Hut' as she called her first cottage in the garden (1894). This collaboration resulted in her entrusting him with the realisation of her long contemplated dream for her house, Munstead Wood, in 1896. The reputation that he gained as its architect led in turn to other commissions for buildings of similar nature, whilst through the Jekyll family and their circle he was brought into touch with people prominent in the intellectual and artistic life of the time. Among them were H.R.H. Princess Louise, Duchess of Argyll, and Edward Hudson, proprietor of the recently established journal *Country Life* to which Miss Jekyll contributed garden notes.

The Jekylls, too, with their fastidious learning, probably encouraged his appreciation of the classical ideal and its searching standard of values. A few years later we shall find Lutyens taking William Nicholson to admire old Newgate Gaol; but at least a year previously Miss Jekyll had exclaimed in one of her garden essays 'how well that fine old architect George Dance understood this (i.e. a building's need to express its purpose in its design) when he designed the prison of Newgate!' Who had pointed it out first to whom? No doubt Lutyens had found it on a similar walk to that which took him to St. Bartholomew's, but I think that Miss Jekyll helped him to see it, and that, as they ambled around Surrey in the pony cart, they discovered that Georgian architecture is part of country tradition. A clear instance of how the Jekyll's classical lore worked on his impressionable mind is given by his choice of the word Cenotaph, and to some extent the conception for the Whitehall memorial. Twenty years before, he had designed a massive timber seat for Miss Jekyll, which had been christened 'the cenotaph of Sigismunda', and it was then that he had first learnt the significance of the word. Herbert Baker, who used to join them sometimes at Munstead at this time, recognised that 'Miss Jekyll's outstanding possession was the power to see, as a poet, the art and creation of home-making as a whole in relation to Life; the best simple country life of her day, frugal, yet rich in beauty and comfort, its garden uniting the house with surrounding nature. This intimate friendship was, I think, the most valuable influence in Lutyens's early career'.[2]

She designed the gardens for the majority of the houses built or enlarged by

---

[1] A list of these is given by Francis Jekyll *op. cit.*, and number fourteen between 1891 and 1897.
[2] *Architecture and Personalities*, 1944.

Lutyens in the 'nineties (as she continued to do for thirty years). An immediate instance of her recommendation of him as architect may have been Munstead Corner, Godalming, for Mr. C. D. Heatley, exhibited at the Academy in 1891 and nearing completion in January 1892 when the perspective was published in *The Builder*. It is a small house with Bargate stone walls, the upper part and gables half timbered, and red tiled roofs. Stables at Little Tangley, Hoe Farm at Hascombe, and a gardener's cottage at Crooksbury filled his first two years of practice.

It was in 1891 that he began to be influenced by the work of Philip Webb. The quality in it which first impressed him, he has recorded,[1] was that of surprise.

> 'That's good,' I remember exclaiming, 'I wonder who the young man is.' The freshness and originality which Webb maintained in all his work, I, in my ignorance, attributed to youth. I did not recognise it then to be the internal youth of genius, though it was conjoined with another attribute of genius—thoroughness!

The closer he looked, the more he was impressed by the integrity of Webb's buildings. They were unsensational, unsentimental, conceived in materials, not of words, with nothing about them 'that was not an integral part of the fabric'. Though he considered that Webb had no great architectural sense, he admired his logic, his knowledge of proportion, his mastery of materials, and fertile invention. 'Had Webb started his career under the influence of Alfred Stevens rather than of Edmund Street, had he come into touch with those who could have bent his constructive genius to the grand manner of architecture, there would have been produced a man of astounding mark in the authentic line of Western architecture.' That tribute, made by Lutyens in 1905, which forestalls almost word for word what Lutyens himself is recognised to have achieved, clearly shows how he set himself to emulate Webb.

The immediate effect on him is perhaps traceable in Chinthurst Hill, a large country house built 1893–5 for Miss Aemilia Margaret Guthrie, later Mrs. Elliott. The site is dramatic, the top of a steep hill, up which the drive zigzags through open birch and oak coppice, overlooking the Wey gap between Wonersh and Bramley. The house is of dressed and pointed rubble (not, however, laid in the native way as in his subsequent, better known, vernacular work), with tile-hung gables and bold brick chimneys. It is more ambitiously stylised than any that he had attempted hitherto, suggesting a medieval manor house altered in Elizabethan times, and has several points of contact with the later work of Philip Webb. The irregular plan is designed to give the living-rooms continuous sunlight and to make the most pictorial effect of the steeply sloping site. Entering from the back you pass through

---

[1] In an article in *Country Life*, May 8, 1915, at the time of Webb's death. Webb's buildings most likely to have been seen by Lutyens in 1891–2 were his London houses, Joldwynds near Dorking, and Coneyhurst at Ewhurst, both in Surrey. Clouds, his most important house, is in Wiltshire.

into a hall facing south at first-floor level and overlooking the terrace and tree tops below. This hall is singular in being simplified domestic gothic, with two bays of oak arched-brace roof and deeply embrasured windows with flamboyant gothic tracery. These windows, recessed beneath arched buttresses and above a kind of cloister, are the chief feature of the exterior (p. 15). From the hall opens a dining-room with deeply embrasured windows, and an oak staircase hall with studded walls and open roof (see sketch below). The impression given, both by the reality and by the sketches, is that, at this stage, the young Lutyens was experimenting in materials and techniques at the cost of coherent design, in which the whole is somewhat lacking.

His first work outside Surrey was done in 1893 for Adeline, widow of the 10th Duke of Bedford who had died in March of that year; the garden layout at Woodside, Chenies. Ruckmans, Oakwood Park, Surrey, for Miss Lyell (1894) was the first of several sympathetic alterations of old cottages, in this case a brick farmhouse with Horsham tile roof. The effect intended is seen in the free-hand sketch (p. 16) which emphasises the Caldecott conception. The reality has the oddity of vernacular building but gives evidence of a growing feeling for form and materials. With the earliest portion of Sullingstead, Hascombe, for Mr. C. A. Cook (1896) we feel that intention and result have coincided. The site is a romantic one, on the side of a wooded hill, down which the timber-framed entrance front is approached. The quality of the carpentry (p. 34) and the sweep of the tiling on the garden front suggest that in these two techniques he had by now nothing more to learn.

CHINTHURST HILL. SKETCH OF STAIRCASE, 1893.

§4. IN MUNSTEAD WOOD

Meanwhile, Miss Jekyll's Hut was the background of much of his working life and, since it became the scene of one of its turning points, we must be able to visualise the little house in the wood. The approach to it was through the trees by a brick-paved path which, for the last few yards before the door, ran through a tunnel of yew—above which peeped its tiled roof and single stone chimney. Indoors there was one large room 'good to paint or work in' wrote Miss Jekyll, with a handsome inglenook, a brick floor, unplastered brick walls whitewashed, and oak-beamed roof. Her bedroom, sitting-room, and a kitchen were also on the ground floor, and a couple of small bedrooms upstairs. 'Though the simple ways of living in the Hut may sound as if bordering on the ascetic, yet there was no feeling of hardship', she assured her friends. 'When on winter evenings there is a great log-fire blazing, and hot elderberry wine is ready for drinking and nuts waiting to be cracked, and good comrades are sitting, some on the inner fixed benches and some facing the fire's wide front, singing "*Craignez de tomber*" or "*Lets have a peal*" or other familiar rounds and catches, it is a very cosy and cheerful place.'[1]

But she realised that she must have a settled home for life and for her accumulating possessions, so set about its planning with her young friend. As early as 1884 Miss Jekyll had been discussing the idea of her house with Ruskin, whose reply to an inquiry of hers on the suitability of English marbles contains a phrase that she evidently remembered. 'Good whitewashed timber, and tapestry', the oracle had said, 'are the proper walls of rooms in cold climates.' 'How the House was Built' is the title of the opening chapter in the second of those notable books[2] in which Miss Jekyll wove from the materials of Munstead Wood—its trees and walks, its artfully contrived marriages of flowers and verdures, and the incidents of her industrious life—a spell that not only captivated, indeed created, a generation of woodland gardeners but did much to establish the Edwardian cult of the picturesque country cottage. Soon she became the cult's high priestess, the wood its sacred grove, and her 'good architect' its acolyte. The ideal realised by the Jekyll-Lutyens collaboration at Munstead was, in effect, a humanised and technically matured restatement of the William Morris-Philip Webb conception of an aesthetic based on folk tradition and moral rightness. The earlier partnership had established the basic values of simple materials and sound craftsmanship; to these were added at Munstead visual and sensuous elements—the notions of harmony with landscape and of colour—and the fact that the architect-partner in this case was Lutyens, not Webb.

The Munstead collaboration had such enduring results, not only on Lutyens's future but on the English country life ideal, that we must turn to Miss Jekyll's own

[1] Gertrude Jekyll, *House and Garden*, 1900. [2] *ibid.*

description of how it worked. From that it will be seen how much he had learnt, was learning, from her, and the extent to which at twenty-seven, he was master of his craft. And incidentally what a propagandist he found in her. In *House and Garden* she wrote of the new house (among themselves they called it 'Plazzoh'):

> In some ways it is not exactly a new house, although no building ever before stood upon its site. But I had been thinking about it for so many years, and the main block of it and the whole sentiment of it were so familiar to my mind's eye, that when it came to be a reality I felt as if I had already been living in it a good long time. And then, from the way it is built it does not stare with newness; it is not new in any way that is disquieting to the eye; it is neither raw nor callow. On the contrary, it almost gives the impression of a comfortable maturity of something like a couple of hundred years. And yet there is nothing sham-old about it; it is not trumped-up with any specious or fashionable devices of spurious antiquity; there is no pretending to be anything that it is not—no affectation whatever.
>
> But it is designed and built in the thorough and honest spirit of the good work of old days, and the body of it, so fashioned and reared, has, as it were, taken to itself the soul of a more ancient dwelling-place. The house is not in any way a copy of any old building, though it embodies the general characteristics of the older structures of its own district.
>
> Everything about it is strong and serviceable, and looks and feels as if it would wear and endure for ever.

Miss Jekyll emphasised that, in the fittings and the parts, there were 'no random choosings, no meretricious ornament, no moral slothfulness', and contrasted the methods of commercial contract builders and their mechanical accuracy with those of the old country builder who goes into the woods and buys his timber standing, to season slowly, and yield in time the very log required by the architect's drawing for the cambered beam or curved brace. A perfect understanding existed between architect, builder, and proprietor, so that there was no need for a contract or for a clerk of the works: all three were 'reasonable and honest folk, at one in their desire of doing a piece of good work, like an interesting game of serious and absorbing interest.'

A fundamental point in the Munstead ideal was the right use of local materials and harmony with the landscape setting:

> The architect has a thorough knowledge of the local ways of using the sandstone that grows in our hills, and that for many centuries has been the building material of the district, and of all the lesser incidental methods of adapting means to ends that mark the well-defined way of building of the

country, so that what he builds seems to grow naturally out of the ground. I always think it a pity to use in any one place the distinctive methods of another. Every part of the country has its own traditional ways, and if these have in the course of many centuries become 'crystallised' into any particular form we may be sure that there is some good reason for it, and it follows that the attempt to use the ways and methods of some distant place is sure to give an impression as of something uncomfortably exotic, of geographical confusion, of the perhaps right thing in the wrong place.

For I hold as a convincing canon in architecture that every building should look like what it is.

Skilled and versatile craftsman as Miss Jekyll was, and clearly as she knew what she wanted, she recognised all the more that architecture was not for the amateur:

> I agreed with the architect how and where the house should stand, and more or less how the rooms should lie together. And I said I wanted a small house with plenty of room in it, and I disliked small narrow passages and would have nothing poky or screwy or ill-lighted. Indeed one of the wishes I expressed was that I should like a little of the feeling of a convent,

—or as an antiquarian friend paraphrased it 'of a work-house in the time of the Heptarchy'.

> So he drew the plan and we soon came to an understanding. Every portion was carefully talked over, and I feel bound to confess that in most cases out of the few in which I put pressure on him to waive his judgement in favour of my wishes, I should have done better to have left matters alone.

There was the battle of the casements, for instance. The lights are set in long rows, oak framed, and in each he had marked, as a casement to open, not the end lights but the ones next to them. She thought the end lights would be more easily accessible, so the casements were placed accordingly, with the result that rain wetted the curtains and the thin sun-curtains would wave out in the wind like flags.

Logan Pearsall Smith has remarked that Miss Jekyll, with all her kindness, was a formidable person and had no exaggerated disinclination for a scrimmage. She had also a craftsman's fastidious choice of words, short, serviceable, and Saxon for daily use but including a selection of curious, highly wrought, collectors' pieces for appropriate occasions. Pearsall Smith has described[1] their discussion of the exact meanings of '*epergne*' and 'armigerous', the latter meaning a person 'entitled to bear arms' and to put Esquire after his name. 'That's my class, the class I belong to', she mentioned, and went on to adduce a number of words and things that an armigerous person

[1] Logan Pearsall Smith, *Reperusals and Recollections*.

would or would not use or do. These characteristics appear in her account of the one occasion that she could remember 'when one might say that any fur flew' between architect and client at Munstead:

> I do not now remember the details of the point in question, only that it was about something that would have added a good bit to the expense for the sake of external appearance; and I wound up my objections by saying with some warmth: 'My house is to be built for me to live in and love; it is not to be built as an exposition of architectonic inutility.' I am not in the habit of using long words, and as these poured forth like a rushing torrent under the pressure of fear of overdoing the cost, I learnt, from the architect's crushed and somewhat frightened demeanour, that long words certainly have their use, if only as engines of war-fare.

'Bumps rampant', as her Ned would say, 'is an awful sight.'

The house had to be designed so as to fit in with the already formed garden, with grass walks cut and planted among birch and chestnut coppice (p. 33). It is built of the golden-brown sandstone, with tiled roofs, tall brick chimneys, and oak-framed casements in the regional tradition. At the back—the way to the garden proper, northwards—is a little court recessed between wings, spanned at its inner end by a timber-framed hanging gallery, forming a shady sitting place for summer.

The rooms were purposely designed to be rather dark, since Miss Jekyll's eyes could not bear strong light. She was particularly fond of her stairs (p. 34), they 'feel firm and solid, the steps low and broad', and of the great shaped newels bedded on masonry beneath. It is indeed a grand piece of carpentry, of a type that was to reappear with variations in many of Lutyens's houses for a decade. That *feeling*—of strength and firmness on which she commented—was also to become a characteristic of his work not shown by drawing or photograph, and proceeding from his insistence on consummate workmanship. The superficial eye sees nothing to justify the extra cost it involved, and so Lutyens was often said to be an 'expensive' architect. Nor does anything show in that high quality of material and workmanship of which, years later, one of the Baring children gave proof when she said, of waking up in another Lutyens house, that she thought she was at home on Lambay 'because it smelt the same'.

At Munstead this pride of workmanship is seen above all in the oak gallery to which the stairs lead (p. 33). 'One feels some hesitation in praising one's own possessions' Miss Jekyll modestly said:

> but it is a part of the house that gives me so much pleasure, and it meets with so much approval from those whose knowledge and taste I most respect, that I venture to describe it in terms of admiration. Thanks to my good architect,

who conceived the place in exactly such a form as I had desired, but could not have described, and to the fine old carpenter who worked to his drawings in an entirely sympathetic manner, I may say that it is a good example of how English oak should be used in an honest building.... And because the work has been planned and executed in this spirit, this gallery, and indeed the whole house, has that quality—the most valuable to my thinking that a house or any part of it can possess—of conducing to repose and serenity of mind. In some mysterious way it is imbued with an expression of cheerful, kindly welcome, of restfulness to mind and body, of abounding satisfaction to eye and brain.

This gallery was to be the most coveted, and repeated, feature of Munstead. Miss Jekyll chose as her bedroom one at its further end especially for the pleasure of walking through it the oftener. It is framed on a series of oak posts and tie-beams with braces, lit by a continuous range of windows along its north side, whilst the other side is lined with oak glass-fronted cupboards, much needed by a person, as she put it, 'of an accumulative proclivity.' Seemingly so simple, it is an early and typical instance of Lutyens's cleverness in overcoming a difficulty and producing an effect, with all appearance of inevitability, by the same stroke. The trick here was to find the breadth where the plan left space only for one of the narrow passages Miss Jekyll had stipulated that she would not have. It is done by overhanging the outer half of the gallery, forming at the same time the sitting-out place in the court below; while the solid ends of the gallery where it passes into the wings are lost in mysterious darkness exaggerating its diminutive length.

With its massive yet elfin simplicity, its lovely setting and covert cleverness, the house surpassed anything that Lutyens had yet built. It is a question whether, for some time, he equalled its quality in the more elaborate romantic designs that followed for the many admirers of Munstead Wood. They were apt to lack the restraint and dignity, the seasoned calm that are so notable here and absent also from his work before. In fact it is clear that these qualities were due to Miss Jekyll, who, as has been shown, added to the claims of a client the influence of a collaborator.

This full partnership was repeated once—in her speculation in real estate by building Millmead, Bramley—and in looser form continued in the gardens for the design and planting of which they were to collaborate till her death in 1932. In some of these, notably Deanery Garden, Hestercombe, and Lambay, the particular quality that distinguishes Munstead Wood—that visible evidence of the marriage of two disparate but complementary minds, of 'breadth' with brilliance—seems to me to have been recaptured. But this particular concert was struck only when he restricted himself to playing on Miss Jekyll's own instrument, her sweet, clear, but limited clavichord. Yet if he himself did not always succeed so well, in fuller orchestrations of similar themes, as in the Munstead duet, how much less did most of its hundreds of

4. MUNSTEAD WOOD (1896) seen from the south, through Miss Jekyll's woodland garden

5. MUNSTEAD WOOD. The gallery on the north side

6. MUNSTEAD WOOD. The sitting-hall and staircase

7. SULLINGSTEAD, HASCOMBE, SURREY. Detail of the entrance side, 1896

imitators! 'Preoccupation with beauty and colour' it has been said,[1] 'has lately come nigh to stifling all truly architectural qualities in our building tradition and there can be no doubt that the example of Lutyens has many caricatures to answer for in the way of spotty roofs, scrubby brickwork, and wire-brushed oak. Used as he used them, however, the old processes of which Miss Jekyll could tell, and the new fake processes he evolved to supplement them, produced exactly what was required in the picture preconceived, and that picture was often a masterpiece of its kind.'

Miss Jekyll put a roomy workshop at his disposal for jobs in the neighbourhood and their joint undertakings. Munstead Wood with its conventual atmosphere became for many years his second home, where she enjoyed seeing him 'use up yards of tracing paper. It is very nice for me', she said,[2] 'as I have a passion, though an ignorant one, for matters concerning domestic architecture that almost equals my interest in plants and trees.' And, when still under the spell of her magic groves, he met his future wife. If he saw in her his princess, and himself as a chivalrous knight setting out on deeds of daring in her honour, the fantasy surely owed something to Munstead's background of tapestry romance. The fairy tale of his marriage took shape in the inglenook beneath god-mother's high-roofed Hut and her approving if appraising eye.

MISS JEKYLL, *c.* 1896.

---

[1] H. Goodhart Rendel, *Journal of R.I.B.A.*, March, 1945.
[2] In a letter to Herbert Baker, quoted in Baker, *op. cit.*, p. 16.

CHAPTER III

THE CASKET

WE are in London, at the beginning of the season of 1896. At the Grays Inn office the Munstead Wood designs are in their early stages, but to-night they and the plans for Sullingstead, for Lord Battersea's house at Cromer, and the other jobs in progress are rolled up. The scene is a musical soirée in South Kensington to which Ned Lutyens has been taken by Mrs. Webb. He is not exactly in his element at social gatherings, least of all at solemn musics, although, as an enthusiastic if unconventional dancer, he receives his share of ball invitations; and Mrs. Webb, who moves in circles wider than that of the Lutyenses—circles frequented by the more cultivated elements of Society—sometimes takes him with her. On this occasion it is one of the weekly musical evenings given by M. and Mme. Jacques Blumenthal at 43 Hyde Park Gate. Their host is himself well-known as a pianist and composer of songs, with a chalet at Les Avants where the Jekylls, Hercules Brabazon, and their artistic and musical friends often stay. Gertrude Jekyll has decorated one of the rooms in this Hyde Park Gate house where, amongst the guests, might sometimes be met Princess Louise (Duchess of Argyle), the Duke of Westminster, Lady Westmorland, Lady Shrewsbury, and Lady Betty Balfour.

In this particular and, as we should call it now, somewhat highbrow gathering, Mr. Lutyens notices across the room a young lady looking cross. Probably his eye is first caught by her fairness. Her hair is a pale gold and, if their eyes met across the room, hers are light blue, serious and habitually questioning, and at the moment unhappy. Then at something said—an allusion to someone dear or that tickled her rich sense of humour—her fine-cut 'aristocratic' features light up with a peculiar magnetism and she chuckles delightfully. No doubt he also took in that she is above medium height, naturally graceful, though rather quietly dressed.

He was not sure afterwards whether he fell in love with her at this first sight, but he remembered an impulsive desire to make her laugh again. Mrs. Webb said that she was with Lady Betty Balfour, her elder sister, whom she had known since Indian times, and, on his insistence, introduced her: Lady Emily Lytton. Presumably the introduction had the desired effect on Lady Emily, though all she remembered of the ensuing conversation with the nice looking and refreshingly unconventional young man with twinkling blue eyes and dark curly hair was that, on her remarking that she was going on to a ball, he asked, 'And do you dance till you are dishevelled? I do.' During the course of that summer she found that that was the case, for they met often at dances and he danced with her as much as he could. He proved to be a high-spirited partner, whose eccentric movements it was not always easy to follow. Doing a barn dance one night he told her to dance as if he were the only crowned head in Europe and she the only queen; they made little bows to each other, and she thought him quite mad, but nice. He talked much of his mother who, he said, was a saint, and very beautiful; she gathered that she was a widow and he an only son, since he never mentioned other members of the family. He would never stay late at balls, saying he had to be at his office punctually in the morning, so she imagined he must be a clerk of some kind and thought how he must fidget on an office stool. For a time she never quite caught his name: something peculiar like 'Luncheon' or 'Luggage'.

For his part, he had fallen in love, for the first time so far as is known, entirely, and, it seemed to him, hopelessly. For, so long as Queen Victoria lived, social distinctions were very real, particularly with families connected with the Court—and the Countess of Lytton was a lady-in-waiting, whilst he was an obscure young architect, although with a fairy god-mother. Lady Emily's father, too, though he had been startlingly unconventional, to the extent of being a dual personality with two identities, had been Disraeli's first Viceroy of India and, at his death five years before, Ambassador to France.

Mr. Lutyens had not met the Countess of Lytton; indeed, as she had occasion to point out to him subsequently, was quite unknown to her, and it is doubtful whether he had much fuller acquaintance, at this time, with the late Earl's claims to fame. On this point, however, we must briefly acquaint ourselves, not only in order to visualise the formidable situation into which Mr. Lutyens's passion was leading him, but because the short, if romantic, shade of Robert Ist Earl of Lytton will be distinctly visible in the background of the events we are about to trace. We shall, too, detect queer echoes of the statesman-poet's dilemma in later pages of this chronicle. The Fates began weaving one of their inscrutable but repetitive patterns when, in that Kensington drawing-room, the threads of Ned Lutyens's and Emily Lytton's lives first crossed. The design had originated long ago when young Mr. Disraeli had had the whim to visit his unhappy friends Bulwer and Rosina Lytton's boy at his preparatory school and won the lad Robert's lifelong devotion by giving him half a sovereign—his first tip. 'And now', Lord Beaconsfield had told Lady Bradford in 1875, 'I have tipped him again and put a crown on his head,' referring to his choice of Robert Lytton as first Viceroy of the newly-to-be-proclaimed Indian Empire. Thus the Fates suddenly transported Lytton, from contentedly fulfilling a diplomatic career at Lisbon, to hail the Empress Victoria, and find misery for himself, on the plains of Delhi where a generation later his son-in-law was as suddenly translated to raise a palace for his successors in Disraeli's imperial pageant, until that too should pass.

Bulwer, apprehensive of there being two writers of the name of Lytton, had forced his poet son (who called himself, on his title-pages, 'Owen Meredith' and sat at Mrs. Browning's feet in Florence) into the mould of public service, not unsuccessfully. The Earl of Lytton, proconsul, earned more laurels than the voluminous and pedestrian poet, modified as his success was in India by sanctioning the Second Afghan War. Yet, till his premature death at his post as Ambassador in Paris, he believed that he was fundamentally a poet. Whether or no he was deceived in this, two lines of his interminable poetic novel *Glenaveril* sum up the dichotomy of his life:

Duty's whole lesson thou hast learnt at last
Which in self-sacrifice begins and ends.

Revolutionary romanticist by instinct, conservative statesman by career; at heart a writer, by birth country gentleman—the Lytton dualism was transmitted to his children and seems to have equipped his youngest daughter with instinctive understanding of her lover's nature.

His widow, who was sometimes alluded to as one of 'England's most famous twins', need not be introduced until Mr. Lutyens encounters her, beyond at this point remarking that, with Lady Loch, she was twin daughter of the Hon. Edward Villiers, brother of the then Earl of Clarendon. She had not been left well-off and, in order to educate her two boys, undertook the Court appointment, in which she continued with Queen Alexandra. Knebworth and the family estates had passed to the elder son, Victor, 2nd Earl of Lytton; Neville, the younger, was going from Eton to study art in Paris. The elder daughter, Lady Betty, her father's biographer, was married to Mr. Gerald Balfour who eventually succeeded his elder brother Arthur, the Conservative statesman, as 2nd Earl Balfour. The second daughter, Lady Constance Lytton, never married and, although of delicate constitution, became a leading figure in the Women's Suffrage movement, in which cause she eventually went to prison where she suffered grave injury to her health.

Lady Emily, the youngest, was four years her admirer's junior, but in many ways his elder. She inherited the Lytton itch of writing, also the gothick temperament of the family alternating between wit and melancholy; and, surprisingly in a young woman, her father's close friendship with the Rev. Whitwell Elwin, editor of the *Quarterly Review*. His influence encouraged the studious, idealistic, and religious earnestness underlying her shrewd sense of humour. Of architecture she was entirely ignorant, having an intellectual not a visual mind. Yet these very differences, and her sane seriousness, supplied something that Ned needed, that spiritual keel with which first his mother, then Mrs. Webb, and latterly Miss Jekyll had balanced his head of sail. The socially inexperienced young man, uncomfortably conscious of all the unmentioned members of his family circle and with his determination to become a successful architect as his only capital, beheld this fair being as an apparition from another world, infinitely desirable but almost unattainable.

A theatre party in July at which both were present but at which, by chance, he was separated from her the whole evening, seems to have typified to him so poignantly their nearness yet remoteness, that in desperation he confided his feelings to Mrs. Webb who undertook to bring them together at Milford House. This was arranged for September, 1896, when Mrs. Webb was already suffering from the incurable illness of which she died in the following year. We have detailed accounts of the occasion, both in Lady Emily's letters to her mother and in the first of the wonderful series of love-letters that, beginning at this time, Ned wrote to her throughout his life whenever they were separated for a short time. From these sources every episode can be reconstructed in the ensuing courtship. It is a most touching and indeed astonishing romance, not only charming to the connoisseur of period sentiment—with its background of old West Surrey when bicycling was the fashionable vogue—but very revealing of the personalities of the participants. To me, it reads as though J. M. Barrie and Charlotte Yonge had collaborated to invent it after reading William Morris, then got Randolph Caldecott to draw the pictures—except that Lutyens plentifully illustrated each chapter himself.

Lady Emily's invitation to Milford seems to have been, in the leisurely custom of those days, for a week or more. At the beginning of it she had arranged a day's outing with another young man, Gerald Duckworth (who later founded the publishing house of that name). So he bicycled over to bring her to his stepfather Leslie Stephen's house at Hindhead. His beautiful sister Stella was still alive, and there were his step-sisters Virginia (later Mrs. Woolf, the novelist) and Vanessa (later Mrs. Clive Bell). If Mr. Duckworth had taken full advantage of that September day, this book might have had an entirely different story to tell, for he evidently admired Lady Emily, and she thought him 'very nice'. But he did not; the time was spent racing the bicycles down the steep grassy slopes of the Stephens' garden, during which Vanessa 'came a tremendous cropper', and Emily peddalled back to Milford a little disappointed perhaps, and certainly tired physically; to find Mr. Lutyens had arrived from London for the week-end.

The tempo of events changed immediately. As it was a fine moonlit night, he proposed that she and he should cycle over after dinner to Warren Lodge, a house that he was building for Mr. Webb on Thursley Common. In spite of her tiring day, she thought it would be great fun, and Mrs. Webb, who of course was in the know, raised no objection, though another lady guest thought such goings-on quite shocking. So they jumped on their bicycles again (Mr. Lutyens's machine was named Angelina) and set off in the moonlight. The house, of course, was shut up but he forced a window and they wriggled in. It was at Warren Lodge that, next year, they spent the first days of their honeymoon. The only result of this preliminary visit, however, was that the architect got a scolding, when they at length returned, for keeping a young lady out so late.

The next evening he planned a surprise supper party with Miss Jekyll in the Hut, taking contributions to the repast with them. Lady Emily, writing next day to her mother, described Miss Jekyll as

> the most enchanting person in the loveliest little cottage, about 4 miles from here. Mr. Lutyens calls her Bumps and the name suits her admirably. We spent the afternoon buying mutton chops, eggs, sponge cake, macaroons, cream, almonds and bulls eyes, and turned up about 6. [In her agitation when being introduced, Lady Emily dropped the eggs.] We helped cook the chops and made tipsy cake, and had a most luxurious meal. Bumps has about 6 cats, three quite kittens and they romped about the room. After dinner we sat in the chimney corner. A real old chimney with a huge wood fire, and there we sat and eat almonds and drank hot elderberry wine until we were quite tipsy and came home.
>
> Mr. Lutyens has gone this morning but returns Thursday.

The same day, September 22, Mr. Lutyens also wrote, from Grays Inn Square, heading the paper with a picture of their ride home by moonlight:

My dear Lady Emily,

About plots—since I left my Angelina at Milford I will have to fetch her first thing Thursday morning, and then go to Puttenham. Would this amuse you? I am awfully low and *desœuvré* after yesterdays gorgee at Bumpstead.... Col. Spencer will keep me an hour or so. What will you do then? It is too cold for a book which I would love to carry for you, however large. We could then go to Crooksbury but I'll think of something better. Friday Miss Lawless has collared me, but I am writing now to say it is impossible.... Whatever happens you must not be bored. I feel awfully guilty at playing truant to work. I have never done it before—so do be kind to me and make me feel it to be all right. The cartoon for the week is doubtless the stern spirit of Architecture swearing at me for going—whither I would follow.

We will go housebreaking Thursday night somewhere, Friday and Saturday we will dine all 3 with Bumps. Sunday to the Tennysons, and housebreaking again at night to Warren Lodge, and then Monday (for me) it will be heartbreaking.

Yrs. v. sincerely
Ned Lutyens

Lord Tennyson (the poet's son) lived at Aldworth, on the top of Blackdown, eight miles from Milford. In the course of one of the expeditions, during this second week-end, designed by the architect to be decisive, it came on to rain and the green dye of Lady Emily's hat—the straw boater of the period—ran in streaks down her face. The effect, grotesque enough no doubt, appears to have moved him in the same way as her unhappy eyes at the Blumenthals' musical party. Green-faced and cross, she made him feel less at a disadvantage; they had their discomforts in common; he could cheer her up and feel manly. So when, in Guildford, they looked into Williamson's antique shop, he went so far as to remark that a red lacquer cabinet and various other pieces of furniture would look nice in 'our' house.

It must, I think, have been during the second session in the inglenook at Munstead that he developed the idea of The Casket. The Casket became the mystical symbol of all that in these fantastic bicycling exertions he had so far failed to say: that he worshipped his divine companion, in her gray skirt, red jersey, and green hat; dedicated his soul, his life, his art, to her service; would conquer the world for her and crown her with honour; if only she would—no, he could not dare ask her to marry anyone so insignificant—but, by accepting his love, make him feel a Man with a high, a great, Purpose.

Later on he said all that and much more; and in due time he performed it. But at present he was quite unable to, at least coherently, and at some juncture during this week-end (the context gives a definite reference to Miss Jekyll's elderberry wine) he evidently promised to design for Lady Emily and give her a Casket containing various objects—to him symbolic—of his inexpressible devotion and domestic ideals. It was, in due course, made but, as will appear, could not be presented when and as intended, though it stands to-day in its destined place. These anticipations will help to clarify his letter, written on the following Monday (the 29th). At the head of the paper is a drawing of a Bible reposing on a cushion.

My dear Lady Emily,

The little ewee bible found me this morning, hard at work. I send it you, tho' it seems so small a thing to give where I would give so much . . . . . . [the dots are his]

The casket is rapidly gaining shape in my mind and on paper and will soon be put on the stocks. I hope it will be ready to go to its owner by 26.XII.96. [Here occurs the drawing, p. 52.] This is a very rough sketch and the color has made the ink run—anyhow it gives a suggestion as to how it will come—outside. The upper part of green leather with a polished surface tooled with gold in many quaint and cunning devices, with gilt handles, hinges, and lock plates etc. Standing on and secretly attached to a stand of hard wood painted in divers colors on a white ground, with birds and flowers—and emblems galore.

Inside will be divided into spaces 4. viz to the right will be Lodging for Marcus [a little brass pipe-stopper with a human head, symbol of fire-side pipes] —next to a division for the Bible—in the centre there will be space for 2 trays giving three compartments. The top shelf will contain an anchor [symbol of Hope] the 2nd a heart, and the bottom, under the trays, will contain a book bound in white vellum about 2 inches square and strapped with vellum and sealed and this book is not to be opened nor the seal broken—(not even Röntgen Rayed) nor the contents ascertained until I am man sufficient for the revelation. [It contains a long poem by him, in writing too small to read.]

The Book shall have on it a ✠ tooled by Roger de Coverley who does my book binding, the third emblem—and the contents illuminated. Will you keep this Faith?

The fourth space will receive a roll of plans for a house such as we talked of and like to where we sat, drinking the elder vintage.

You nearly lost your casket to-day! I got pitched softly out of a cab and rolled amongst the busses. Glad I was there was no mud.

The Batterseas have put me off for a week. So I will be able to make up time and regain the good graces of Bumps at least I hope.

I saw in to-days paper an epitaph which amused me, listen—

Beneath these monumental stones
Lies the body of Mary Jones

NB

Her name was Smith, it wasn't Jones
But Jones was put to rhyme with stones.

Yrs truly Ned Lutyens.

The bathos of the ending, its flight from the sublime to the ridiculous, with allusion in passing to what might have been tragedy, are as characteristic as the poetry in every detail in the Casket's design. He was nearly incapable of saying, even writing, what he felt so deeply and he could only express his emotion in the medium of design, but that naturally and almost instantly. The complicated, highly wrought, box with its symbolic contents was his version of a lover's sonnets. The 'roll of plans for a house' is the miniature coloured design, four inches square, for a white-walled, tile-roofed house set in a formal garden (p. 52). The ground plan of the house, like that of the Elizabethan John Thorpe, forms their initials, E.L.

The lovers had another meeting at Milford in early October of which we know nothing but that, on the morning when Mr. Lutyens took his leave, Lady Emily accompanied him to the railway station, both still on their bicycles. He had been unable to come to the point of this three weeks' idyll and was evidently in suppressed agony, when Lady Emily mentioned, on their way, that she had that morning received a letter from her mother saying that she had some news to give her on her return, and adding, a little mischievously, that perhaps Lady Lytton had found her a husband. This idea was so agitating to him that he ran Angelina into a wall and fell off, cutting his hand.

It seemed that his worst fears were confirmed. The idyll was at an end. He was even then prepared to miss the train at the least sign of encouragement, but he could only note a 'polite, dont bother, sort of way' about his cool and unattainable companion. With a bleeding hand and broken heart the train carried him away. He had a great mind to join Herbert Baker at the Cape, or go anywhere to forget. However, returning from Frome that evening, he was sitting in a coupé at the end of the train—one of those delightful inspection compartments which have disappeared from railways. 'The receding landscape through the windows draws, with quick perspective, my very hope,' he wrote, and with an unsteady hand haltingly committed himself:

> It is with your little pencil that I write.
> I felt wretched in the train, leaving you this morning and now how I regret —Bumps or no Bumps—that I did not have the courage to play truant to my work and stay by you—but then I should have broken away and you might have hated me.
> I would have told you how I loved you.
> Would you have laughed? Except my love, I have nothing to offer you. I am poor—unknown—and little altogether.
> My life's work would be your's and I shall now work the more earnestly so that I may, in time, become more worthy of your dear self. All that I have is at your feet—I love you ever so. I dare not ask anything of you. The little hope I have in me is so large a stake to lose, that the very thought of it makes me feel ill and sick.
> One word from you would turn my world, to one great sphere of happiness and I would become a man. Give me some chance to prove it.
> Before I realised your name I loved you and being with you at Milford House has only made it grow the more, so that my whole horizon is filled with and by you. . . .
> Everyone must love you so that I can only be one amongst many others. I could write miles to you but I dare not persecute you and after all I cannot say more than that I love you—I love you—
> Yours
Ned Lutyens

Lady Emily's reply is dated Oct. 19, from Milford House and it appears from it that Miss Jekyll, though noncommittal, approved of the romance.

> Dear Mr. Lutyens,
> Yr. letter has touched me very much. Why did you think I shd. laugh? At present I can only say thank you for what you say to me. My mind is too

uncertain for me to say more one way or another, and I can only ask you to wait and give me time to think it over. But whatever I settle I hope you will believe that my interest in you and yr. work is very real and deep. Bumps is quite right in what she says. I do not want to be a frivolous influence in yr. life, but the reverse, and yr. work is what will always interest me most. No one will be more pleased than I am to hear that you are getting on and making a name for yourself, as I am quite sure you will in time.

Does my letter sound horrid? I hope not, but it wd. not be fair if I said more, when I know so little at present what I feel.

We saw Bumps yesterday who was charming to me. I do love her.

When we come back from Paris perhaps you will come to the Danes for a day or two and we will talk about it.

Yrs. very sincerely,
Emily Lytton.

P.S. Thank you for the little pack
of cards. Strange that Judith shd. have
sent me a pack of cards by the same post.
A wicked post for Sunday morning.

He received this the same evening at Grays Inn Square with mixed feelings, and immediately reassured her that her influence on him was indeed great and good. 'If I frivol when with you, it is with the happiness of being with and near you.' A band outside was playing the 'Washington Post' and made him ache with memories. Her noncommittal reception of his declaration was as kind as he could expect, seeing that he had so little to give her, merely the prospect of 'a small white house and my poor life. I always', he added, 'see you in that wee white house, with a red cabinet, It is not size that helps in life.' Her words 'one way or another' gave him a gleam of hope, 'May I hold to this? It is enough for me to work for.' He would wait, 'only don't let it be long.' He dared not press her further—it seemed so selfish, even the fact that he wanted her because she brought out the best in him. He agreed that Bumps was lovable, 'only don't let her abuse me. She knows nothing of how much you are to me, and if she did, even Bumps would see that you could make me a man! and give my work the serious touch it wants.' He would have pleasure in coming to see Lady Lytton at the Danes, though there was so little he could say. 'Here I shudder, knowing how small a manner of thing I am.' After describing a plot he was hatching to entertain Mrs. Webb in her mortal sickness by persuading Princess Louise (of whom more later) to call on her, he pictured the progress of his pilgrimage:

I stand as on some drear hill alone, a desert round me.
The lovely valley seems to rise and give me warmth—and you. Then I wax strong and great and worthy of you. Nothing there is between us, and all seems

beautiful. Then I realise to wake and I turn cold and bleak and tho the valley is still beautiful it is far distant and I alone.

That was already, we may observe, as it was to be throughout his life, the moral and psychological issue in their relationship. As then, so always with her, his desire was of the spirit and the realisation of an imaginative rather than a physical passion. He wanted reassuring, stimulating, stabilising and directing by a personality who would sustain the rôle hitherto taken successively by his mother, Barbara Webb, and Miss Jekyll, but one irradiated by youth. He wanted a wife round whom to build a home: he longed to realise the ideal of marriage—and thereby reassure himself that he was no longer the weakling of his family but 'the successful architect'. But, above all, that other self within him, his genius, demanded a mother—a self-effacing embodiment of goodness, a gentle comforter, a wise and patient prompter, to be present at need but undemanding on his time and nervous energy. He felt, intuitively, that he had found this ideal in Lady Emily—and, so far as any woman could, she was to fulfil it, and more besides. But in rare moments of introspection, as now when he surveyed the bleakness of life without her, he seems to have known that the relationship must be one sided; that he could not give back, in kind, all the tenderness and solicitude and stimulus that he craved, because his art must always have first call on his vital forces. Hence the harping on his deficiencies, though he disguised them to himself as lack of worldly goods; and vows to win her fame in compensation—though they too are understandable in terms of financial necessity.

This interpretation of these most intimate letters is offered with no intention of questioning the reality of his love. It possessed and transfigured him as wholly as he was capable of so being. But because it remained the secret strength and background of his life, it is necessary to apprehend its peculiar nature. This attempted analysis may help, too, to explain how two so apparently disparate young people, with singularly little in common, one would have said, not only fell in love but addressed one another as lovers for nigh fifty years. It cannot always have been easy for the wife.

At this point in his courting, however, it was he who was to suffer. When Emily at length returned home and confessed to her mother what had been going on, Lady Lytton was adamant. The whole thing was out of the question. Emily must tell the young man that it was hopeless to consider the matter and that her mother would rather they did not meet, or write, or see each other again. Obediently and very nicely, she did so, on October 23. 'We have had some happy times together,' she told him, 'which we shall both like to remember.'

But then she affirmed, with wonderful penetration and simplicity, her belief in him.

> I want, [she added] to say something to you for the future, if only I knew how. You said I could have made you a man, and give your work the serious

THE CASKET

touch it wants. I may not help you in the way you want, but I should like to tell you how much I believe and trust in your power to become a distinguished man some day. I feel sure you will if only you put your whole life into your work. You have it in you to do great things. I am sure of it, if only you believe in yourself as I believe in you. I will pray God to bless you and give you strength to prove before all the world that I was right, and put my faith in you.

He must know, she went on, that she wrote as she did only against her will and with much distress. Then,

> Will you send the Casket still? I should like to have it. Only perhaps it would be better not. I should like to hear from you just once again, to know that you understand what I have said so badly and that you will take comfort and courage, and go forth like a knight of old (as you said) and conquer a name and fortune for yourself. . . . Goodbye, and may God always bless you.

To that admirable letter, which reveals much of the character that bound Ned so helplessly to his Emily, Lady Lytton added one of her own, kind but firm. She pointed out that Mr. Lutyens was entirely unknown to her; also that 'Emily has nothing but a very small allowance which I give her and even at my death will only have a small sum of settled capital which her father left her'. She must beg him therefore not further to seek Emily in any way, and try to overcome his kindly feelings for her. She apologised for the business character of this letter, but thought it would be less painful to both of them than a personal interview.

To Lady Lytton's he replied on October 25, thanking her for its kindness and consideration. He did not see how else she could have written, but he could not alter his love for Lady Emily. 'I should have remembered that I have practically nothing to offer beyond the income I make of some £1000 and the possibility of a life insurance.' If only he could have some gleam of hope, he ended.

To Lady Emily he wrote somewhat more, with more evident anguish. He would try to obey Lady Lytton's behests, but it would be hard. 'If only like that knight of old, I could have some hope—some "Grail". How I would fight!' As regards the Casket, 'I cannot keep it even if I would nor could I destroy it. It belongs to the past and is no longer mine. I would take it as another kindness from your hands to accept it. . . . May you never have the sorrow that is mine. You must not suffer for me: I cannot bear that thought. There are things which are inevitable and by them man may prove himself man. I will trust in the God you pray to.' He was hers ever Ned Lutyens. But, in a postscript, if she would be kind enough to accept that casket, 'you must let me know somehow what inscription you would have on it. I dare not trust myself. God bless you and help me.'

But for the Casket, all now seemed over. His reasonable inquiry, however, about a suitable inscription gave Lady Emily a reasonable excuse for just one more letter, October 28. And, since it would of course be the last, she resolved also to give him the gleam of hope he craved.

> Would it comfort and help you [she began] to know I could have loved you, oh so well! which means, I suppose, that I love you now. If it is wrong to have told you, God must forgive me . . . I thought it might make you happy to know. I had not the strength to resist the happiness of making you happy.

She dared not, she continued, tie herself or him. They might wish to change. She would be the first to rejoice if he found somebody who could bring him more than she.

> But should all be as it is now, come to me when you feel you are man sufficient and that like that knight of old you have proved your knighthood. No one must ever guess (this).
>
> I should so love that casket. If you would send it, I will explain to Mother that it was promised in the past. Whatever the future I shall always love and treasure the casket for your sake, in memory of what has been. I should like a little Crucifix if there is room besides the other things, and you will not forget the plans for the little white house, because I love it.
>
> For the inscription I do not know. I read these lines in a poem of my Father's
>
> > *Man cannot make, but may ennoble, Fate*
> > *By nobly bearing it.*

The revelation was dazzling. Its light put all the darkness to flight. On receiving this communication the same evening, at Onslow Square, he dropped for the first time the formal address to 'dear Lady Emily':

My darling—Your letter brings me hope and great joy . . .
I have seen the *Holiest* Grail and I can now go forth with great comfort. Pray that I may hold it.
The casket shall come and it shall be as you ask.
Below the lowest tray, there will yet be a space—look for it . . .
Do you remember that we thought the world a flat place? Now I find it is round, quite round, and full of hope and blessings with more yet to come . . .

And so they were parted.
But in the winter darkness that descended on the lovers, warmed only by the gleams in their hearts, a flash of lightning gives us an occasional glimpse of their vale of woe. Ned confided his troubles to Miss Jekyll. But fairy godmother was at her

most sardonic. 'She laughed,' he wrote afterwards, 'because you had a handle to your name. That quite broke me, and I just cried like a little boy.' It adds a sublime quality to this picture of distracted lovers to know that their plight was brought to the notice of a yet more august personage. Lady Lytton confided her daughter's misfortune to her royal mistress. The Queen quite agreed with her; Lady Emily would be poor; she was very sorry. These majestic if compassionate rumblings from Buckingham Palace were no less ominous than that clap of sinister laughter at Munstead.

What, we cannot but ask nowadays, was all this fantastic drama about, menacing two particulary worthy young people with tragedy and casting an exceptionally sweet and gentle mother for the rôle of Hard-Hearted Parent? It was not only the Class System, that theory of Breeding which, abused as it is, had a great deal in its favour. Admittedly the Lutyenses had been middle-class merchants of foreign extraction, yet the Lyttons had been Norfolk squires a generation back—and Bulwer had not been over-particular in his marital choice; better perhaps if he had been. Convention was a factor; mother and suitor, and still less his parents, had not been formally introduced, so that the ritual of 'approval' could not be enacted, however summarily. It can be ascribed chiefly to the Capitalist System, one of the rules of which—inherited from agrarian tradition—was that the husband in the marriage contract must be able to endow the wife with either the substance or the value of a home. Lutyens had no Capital—no background of paternal acres that, even if unproductive, represented something solid. He was not even in one of the Services, with the prospect of a pension, nor in Business that, however undefined and rackety, was at least actuarially assessable. He was an artist, an outcast.

Therefore, a betrothal appeared at this stage to comply with none of the Victorian principles of matrimony—money, breeding, manners or background—though everybody recognised that the couple were in love.

The first move to end the deadlock came from the sister who, since her fleeting but accessory appearance as Lady Emily's chaperone at the Blumenthals', has dropped out of the tale. Lady Betty Balfour brought her keen, practical intelligence to bear on the problem objectively, and, in a letter to Lady Lytton from Adare Manor, Ireland, summed up the situation point by point. The exposition and the reasoning—and the singularly perceptive estimate of Lutyens's position and character—merit quotation:

Nov. 26. 96.

... And now darling as it may be long before we meet I think it best to keep silent no longer on this new crisis in Emmy's life. Whatever may be the outcome of it all I think it is no use ignoring it. Let us face the fact. Lutyens has proposed to her, is—from his letters—clearly in love with her, and she believes herself to be whole heartedly in love with him.

He is a gentleman, he is four years older than she is, and he has made a remarkable start in a profession wh: calls forth some of the noblest faculties of a man's mind and is eminently a profession which a gentleman of ability may be proud to follow. That he has an exceptional gift is evidenced by the fact that at 26 with no social advantages at the outset he is already making £1000 a year at his profession. As to his means—he has no capital. No more have half the professional men of the world, no more has Neville, yet I hope he will not die a bachelor. This means however that any provision for children must be put by out of income and this of course is a risk. But between *risk* and imprudence I think there is a distinction to be drawn. I have talked it all over with Gerald and he said if you ever wished to have his opinion he would tell you that the minimum he would advise you to ask, before marriage was contemplated would be an insurance out of income for the amount of £10,000. But if this could be undertaken he would not himself advise you to forbid the marriage on such terms.

Now as to character. Barbara (who of course never in her dreams contemplated such an event—but who has long hoped he would marry a woman worthy of him, and who has talked to me freely about him) Barbara has convinced me that he is exceptionally pure minded, and honourable. I have seen enough of him to believe this from my own observation and I think him attractive and loveable. So far I think his defect in my judgment has been a sort of frivolousness of talk which attractive in its way seemed to indicate a certain absence of seriousness. But this may have been purely superficial, and a great genuine love wld. bring out all that is deep and determined in his nature. Finally there is the great and far the most important question—is their love of the highest and most lasting kind? Now I think you could put this to the test. If I were you I would send for him or write to him, let him feel he has incurred a grave responsibility in telling yr. daughter of his love. Tell him straight out what are the money conditions you require before you would consider marriage anything but wild imprudence and tell him that till those conditions are fulfilled you will trust to his honour not to speak or write of love to Emmy, or to seek her except in so far as you suggest or as the society of wh: they are both members naturally throws them together. Personally I shld. be agst. forbidding them to meet altogether for this encourages the cherishing of an ideal and if you are to test the truth of their love they had better get to know each other better. To such conditions I believe they wld. willingly submit, and be grateful for the test it wld. impose upon them. They are both very young and waiting could do them no harm. Especially as I believe he might be able in two years at longest to fulfil the conditions. That the whole affair shd. be a distress and disappt. to you I understand well. I don't pretend to think that Father wld. be delighted about it. But after all grandfather did not sympathise in *his* engagement but he

8. THE CASKET. Designed by Lutyens for Lady Emily Lytton, 1896, with some of its contents. Total height 9⅝ in. The casket itself is covered in green leather with gold tooling and lined with silk; the walnut stand faced with vellum decorated in water-colour

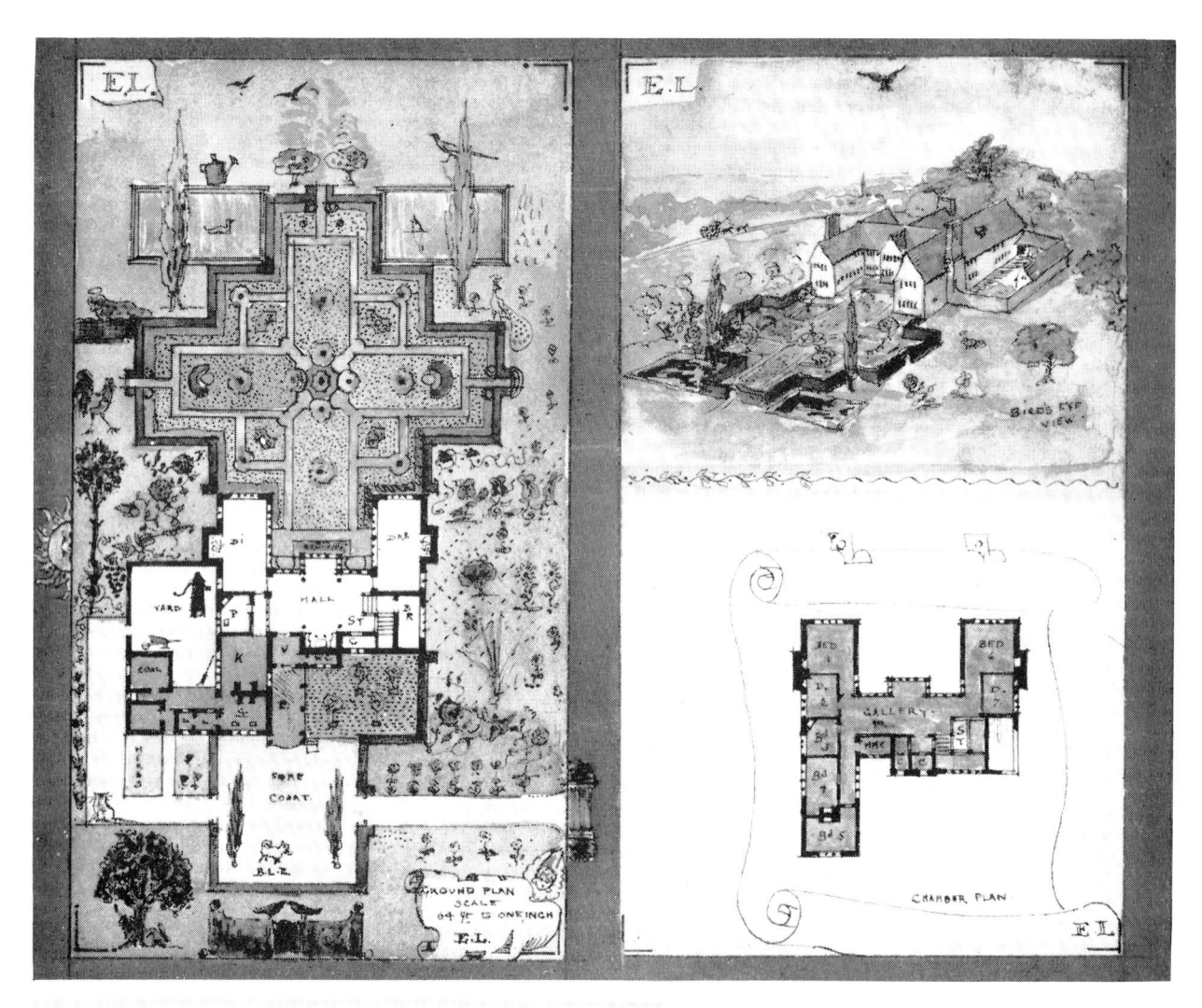

9. Designs (actual size) of 'The Little White House'. They are among the Casket's contents. The plan of the house embodies the linked initials E. L.

10. Sketch of The Casket (September 29, 1896)

THE CASKET

lived to bless it. After all a girl who leaves her family when she marries can do little for it if she married a millionaire. To marry a gentleman in heart as well as birth, to love him passionately and faithfully and to give up all things to follow him thro' life—that seems to me an ideal wh: can only bring honour to any family that holds to it.

The allusion to Bulwer Lytton refers to his having refused to approve of his son's marrying Miss Edith Villiers owing to her family's Liberal politics.

Evidently Barbara Webb, dying as she was, was exerting herself on Ned's behalf. It seems that Lady Betty had suggested to her that Lutyens might re-open negotiations on the basis of his obtaining a life insurance policy to take the place of a capital settlement. He had himself mentioned the possibility to Lady Emily in a recent letter, but it is unlikely that the notion had originated with him. Not only was it not the kind of financial transaction which would have occurred to his uncommercial mind, but for the rest of his life he harboured something of a grudge against having had to mortgage his future, as it seemed to him—implying that the step had been forced on him. From these allusions it appears that the suggestion of life insurance made to him through Mrs. Webb originated with Mr. Gerald Balfour.

Consequently, at the beginning of December a letter from Mr. Lutyens requesting an interview was received by Lord Loch, Lady Lytton's brother-in-law, and retired Colonial Governor, whom since her husband's death Lady Lytton consulted on all family affairs, and to whom Lady Emily had confessed her problem. At first Lord Loch supposed that 'it might be in connection with his profession, to further his efforts for employment with the Duke of Westminster' (a quest that he was to pursue tenaciously, but with slight success, for thirty years) 'or others with whom he may have known I was intimate. I was therefore', Lord Loch told Lady Lytton, 'somewhat surprised at finding . . . it was about dear Emily.' In short, he said he had been advised by Mrs. Webb to place a statement of his affairs in Lord Loch's hands, which the latter could examine and report upon to Lady Lytton. This balance sheet, obtruded thus into the story of the Casket, is of almost as much interest to us as to its original recipients, as summarising the economics of his practice since the undertaking of Chinthurst Hill in 1894.

1894–95

	£	s.	d.		£	s.	d.
Office expenses	300	0	0	Fees received	1000	0	0
Balance	700	0	0				
	£1000	0	0		£1000	0	0
					£	s.	d.
				To Balance	700	0	0

E

1895–96

	£	s.	d.
Rent	55	0	0
Clerks	312	0	0
Caretaker	20	0	0
Taxes	13	0	0
Stationery	20	0	0
Balance	945	10	0
	£1365	10	0

	£	s.	d.
Fees received	826	15	0
Sundry debtors[1]	538	15	0
	£1365	10	0
To Balance £945	10	0

[1] ['Does this mean money *owed* for work done?' 'Yes.' (note in the original document)]

Estimate for 1896–7

	£	s.	d.
Office expenses (maximum)	500	0	0
	1303	0	0
	£1803	0	0

	£	s.	d.
Fees on work already ordered	1803	0	0
	£1803	0	0
To Balance £1803	0	0

[Note against total of £1803 0 0: 'does this mean fees for work ordered but not executed?' 'Yes']

Private Account. 27 Nov. 96

	£	s.	d.
Sundry debts	60	0	0
Balance	678	0	0
	£738	0	0

	£	s.	d.
Cash in hand	200	0	0
Sundry debtors	538	0	0
	£738	0	0
To Balance £638	0	0

'From this you will observe that his income has been steadily increasing,' Lord Loch remarked, '—a clear net £1300 a year with some £650 in the Bank. With respect to making any settlements, he thought he could have £1000 from his father which, if paid to an Insurance office, would secure £3000 at his death, and he could further insure his life.' Lord Loch pointed out to him the need for the payment of the life insurance premiums to be guaranteed, and that the guarantors would probably require a lien on the policy for their own protection. If, he continued for the sake of illustration, Mr. Lutyens added to the £3000 accruing from his father's contribution a life insurance policy for £12,000, the annual premiums would be about £240 which would leave, according to his statement, a clear income of £1000 a year, and produce a certain settlement of £13,000 or, if his guarantors were never called on to pay the premiums, £15,000. 'I did not encourage Mr. Lutyens with any hope your consent would be obtained' by such an arrangement, Lord Loch continued, but 'it seems to me the pecuniary objections are not insurmountable'. He suggested that Lady Lytton should see Lutyens, hear what he had to say, and propose that the matter should be reviewed in a year's time, during which the parties, so far from any engagement, should not communicate with one another. In this way his professional prospects and the permanence of the feelings of both would be tested.

A week after this interview, the emotional effect of which upon the young man has to be imagined, Lord Loch communicated Lady Lytton's reply, which was along the lines that he had recommended to her. Evidently she also made Lady Emily, then staying at the Chief Secretary's Lodge, Phoenix Park, acquainted with the decision thus come to, for on December 14 the latter wrote:

> My own Beloved Mother
>
> How sad that you are becolded and miserable. I feel it is high time I returned to take care of you. I am sure you do rash things and must be looked after. It will be nice to hug you again. It seems so long since I saw thy darling face.
>
> In answer to your letter, I do not think you will feel so unhappy about my poverty if I married. We should have about £1100 a year to begin with, and that is nearly as much as Betty had, and you know I have not luxurious tastes. It wd. not be necessary for his profession that we shd. go into society, and a simple life is the happiest when there is love to make it so. I know you have not been happiest in your greatest positions. Besides it gets easier every year to live cheaply, and I think it is a good thing to begin poor. By the time we have sons to educate we may be quite rich, besides which they need not go to Eton. I wish you had seen him, but you thought better not. I will try to prove to you that I am serious, and I mean to be wise and patient. . . . He can prove himself by his work, and I by my patience, and we both trust to your kindness for the rest. God help us all.
>
> We went to such an awful place yesterday morning. There is a church in Dublin where the vaults have some properties which preserve the corpses in a mummified condition . . . horrible vaults where a kind of mildewy damp poured off . . . strong smell of old cheese. . . . Sir R. Vicars, odious man, poked all the bodies with his umbrella and said cheerily 'Just like leather, you see. . . .'

I have quoted the three paragraphs of this letter almost verbatim because (in addition to their macabre contrast) they seem to me to present so vividly to us the personality of the woman who will be in the background, generally behind the scenes, for the rest of this book. Considering the import to her whole life, and to the ensuing twelve months particularly, of the letter that she was answering, it is impossible not to marvel at the tone of her reply. (Especially revealing is the use of the almost obsolete, intimate 'thy'.) It expresses, in sequence, dutiful love, protective solicitude, physical warmth, then coming to her own affair, complete absence of emotionalism but, instead, evidence of decision coolly but irrevocably made, with practical, maternal, comprehension of its implications, summed up in that phrase prophetic not merely of twelve months but of fifty years: 'he can prove himself by his work and I by my patience.' And finally the dryly humorous and economically worded picture of the revolting old man in the catacombs. Read in this light, it goes a long way to explain the origin and purpose of the Casket.

This gift had been intended for Christmas. But the only seasonable communication that passed seems to have been one from Lady Lytton to which Lutyens replied on December 30:

My dear Lady Lytton,

I know not what I may say to you, but I must thank you for your letter and for your very great kindness in writing to me. I look forward to seeing you, and I cannot help hoping, that by some good fortune it may be before March. Time seems to go so slowly now. I have asked so great a thing of you already, that I hardly dare ask more, or trespass on your kindness: but I have designed a small leathern casket etc. It was arranged, before anything was said, and I now ask, if I may send it, through you? To give or not, as you may decide. I should so like it to be given. I should not consider the little gift, to alter my position in the matter at all.... I *want* to comply with your every wish, so that I may always have your confidence.... I will date my new year from the time I may be allowed to see Lady Emily....

The rough draft of Lady Lytton's answer survives. It was not favourable.

Excuse the delay in my thanking you for yr. note and kind offer to send the lovely casket, but I had to think over my decision. I fear you will be disappointed in my asking you not to send it for the present but I dont feel I can decide otherwise.

Her letter may have been slightly less uncompromising, since his acknowledgment, dated Jan. 15, 1897, from Roseneath, Argyllshire, though taking up the very words of her draft, put an ingeniously different construction on them. He said he *was* disappointed: feared that Lady Lytton would find it little more than a toy and hardly lovely—though he owned he would wish it beautiful. The only satisfaction

THE CASKET

he had in her decision was that he could do something she asked of him, and for that he was glad. 'Only I hope the Present will not reach too far into the future! Please? You will not mind my pleading to you? All my happiness lies in your hands. I am up here alone on some work, but will be better nerved when I get back to town this week.'

He had not made one of his puns—playing on the two senses of 'present'—to Lady Lytton before. But it was not this technique, so often to melt icy clients, that ended the freeze-up. Nor that pleading note. Did Lady Emily stage a well-timed distress scene? Or was the effective word 'Roseneath' with its royal and ducal connections? A little of each perhaps, and many tears on her daughter's part. For within a fortnight Lady Lytton surrendered. On getting home at midnight on January 28 Ned found a letter from her apparently telling him that, on the following Saturday, he might come to The Danes, Hertford, and give Emily the Casket—with all that it contained and symbolised. He dashed eight pages off to catch the 3 a.m. post:

16 Onslow Square.

My darling E.

God bless and keep my own darling Em.

To think that I may after all these months, write and tell you how well I love you seems too wonderful! ...

I have been thinking of you darling day and night—longing to send word to you but did not dare—and now your best and kindest of mothers has asked me to write to you! and now I wonder why I did not before. but I have been almost paralysed lest I should postpone seeing you for one hour by some chance mistake!

God bless my darling Emmy. You will be wife to me? It is too much for me to dare ask I feel so unworthy of you and so small beside you. Emmy you will say yes wont you? and make me the proudest man in the world? ... You will make me ... a man good and great. ...

Of course I bring that casket. Do you remember when I offered it to you— I was so feared lest you should say no—or guess what I meant and then say no.

The casket is a funny little thing not one quarter worthy of you—but you will like it for my sake wont you—and we can put in little treasures as the years go by. Dont expect too much. I would hate to disappoint you in any way. ...

Do meet me at the Station, please! I dont believe I will be able to exist through tomorrow. ...

My darling *I am your*   ever loving
                                              Ned

  Your
    Ned   ☞   Thats me! that writes
                 I can hardly believe my fortune
                 is so great!!

He wrote again next morning before leaving home, wishing he could rush to her at once; but 'I must see these people—Cook—Verity—Grove—you will know them all by name!' And again from the office, between callers, a letter ecstatically embellished with a monogram of linked E.L.s and hearts and a drawing of a little architect worshipping the Queen of Beauty.

I have no great City to offer you to reign over - but with such little as I have I worship you + pay homage to my Queen. God save her!

There is also in it a sketch of Sullingstead, the house he was designing for Mr. Cook, and he told her:

I have done such a lot of work to-day, more than I have done for days past—this is all your doing and it is gorgeous. Cook is building a house at Hascombe and Archibald Grove at Overton in Hants [Berry Down]. This is Cook's. I can't draw you a little picture now—but I will make for yourself, if you like, little pics of all I am doing. Sixteen or seventeen more hours, and then ... I can think of nothing else... I try so hard to be modest and not conceited!

This is Cool's →

That you of all people in the world should care for me—you wrote and told me so. Bless you for it. I have no great City to offer you to reign over—but with such little as I have I worship you and pay homage to my Queen. God save her!... Here is Grove.

When he arrived at Cole Green station it had been snowing. There was no Lady Emily and no vehicle to meet him, so, regardless of his elegant pair of patent-leather boots donned for the occasion, he set out for The Danes on foot. Lady Lytton, more suitably shod, was herself walking to meet him, whilst Lady Emily stayed indoors, in an agony of apprehension at the impression he would make on her mother.

For, of course, she had never yet met him. Nor have we, so far, been introduced to Lady Lytton who all this time has been sustaining the rôle of ferocious dragon. In reality she was not that at all. When Robert Lytton had married Edith Villiers, despite Bulwer's antagonism, because the Clarendons were Liberals and her parents badly off, she was described as beautiful—tall and fair and soft of voice—and proud of her descent from Oliver Cromwell. As Ambassador's wife and Vicereine there are many testimonies to the gentle dignity of her splendid physique (Lord Lytton, notwithstanding his imposing beard, had been an unusually short man) and her social capacity. She delighted, also, in the unconventional. There is a story of her exclaiming, in her joy of getting back to England from India, 'Oh the dear drunken people in the streets, how I love them!' Now, striding through the snow, this great Victorian lady was only fifty-six, still very handsome, and, it seems, was suddenly warmed by the grotesque circumstances of this long delayed, much feared encounter. Her daughter's depression had made the main breach in her defences, but the woebegone figure's sopping patent-leathers—and the way he had with him—seem finally to have won her over. As they tramped back, to make conversation she perhaps talked vaguely of getting him to build a house for her some day, and renewed her regrets about the boots. For, recalling the day afterwards, Ned wrote to Emily:

> If I had only known that your best Mother liked my boots I should have been bolder, but I just made belief she wanted me to build a house and listened vaguely and dared not say anything lest it should be wrong, and then [having reached the house] she questioned me and I was terrified, and in every question and answer I thought I was undone, and all Emmy did was to wink.

He and she had not met since those days at Milford. Now he returned as her accepted lover. Both were shy. His greeting, at this supreme moment, was 'Dear old thing'. But at the same time he gave her the parcel containing the Casket, and when she examined it she found that, to the inscription she had proposed:

> *Man cannot make, but may enoble, Fate*
> *By nobly bearing it,*

he had added this device of his own, destined to be his guiding precept in life and art:

> *Yet as Faith wills*
> *So Fate fulfils.*

CHAPTER IV

BETROTHAL

WORK, though it had to go on, had inevitably been overshadowed by the glooms interspersed with dazzling gleams of the past months' emotional storms. The ban on correspondence between the lovers incidentally deprives us of the chief source of information on the architect's fortunes during the latter part of 1896. But Berrydown and Hascombe, on which he was working when the clouds at last cleared, were new jobs since the summer; and a letter from Milford of February 8—the week-end following the reunion at The Danes—refers to professional visits to Crooksbury, Warren Lodge ('which Ayling the builder thinks a most pictuous—good word, pictuous—place'), the Streatfields, 'a small housekin at Camberley' for a Major Crawford, and 'a small new job from Mr. Webb for Mr. Whitaker Washington Wright, that means £20 for E. E.'. This last was Lutyens's only known contact with the eccentric millionaire of Witley Park, much the richest man in the Lutyens country. For the Streatfields he was to build Fulbrook, an important house near Farnham, and this seems to have been his first conference on the project.

But the most important event of the week had been a second interview with Lord Loch, at which Mr. Gerald Balfour was also present, upon the thorny matter of a marriage settlement. Upon its outcome depended the announcement of the two E.L.s' engagement.

In the same letter of February 8, announcing its satisfactory conclusion, Ned sketched his ordeal: 'This is what I saw and would go through 1,000,000 times.' Writing to the Elwins, Lady Emily also sketched a word-portrait of Ned. 'He is just my height, or a little bit taller, has very dark hair which begins the day all smooth and sleek, towards evening gets beautifully rough and curly, very blue eyes, a pointed nose, a little curly fair moustache, and next to no chin.' She went on to describe her first meeting with the Lutyens family during a visit to Onslow Square. The experience produced mixed feelings. She became devoted to beautiful, vague, serene Mrs. Lutyens, and was evidently touched with awe and compassion for the Quixotic Captain. 'He is a splendid looking old man, very tall, with splendid white hair; absolutely regardless of appearance or conventions, but perfectly pure and childlike in mind. He weeps at every pathetic touch. He talks of his children as absolute perfection.' But then he led her to his untidy studio and showed pictures some of which struck her dumb. One was particularly curious, of his daughter Aileen—whom she had immediately taken to—as a Black Venus seated in a Surrey field. All the time he was explaining his discovery of the Venetian Secret and how scandalously the Academy had treated him. The penurious atmosphere, and Charles Lutyens's domestic eccentricities—at meals insisting on using a single plate with the pudding mixed with congealing gravy—came as rather a shock, if only for its contrast to anything she was accustomed to.

The more she saw of the disorder here and at Thursley Cottage, the better she understood Ned's craving for orderliness, and the sooner, she realised, they must find a home of their own, however austere. The search began as soon as the engagement was published. The house they, or rather he, eventually chose can be seen in retrospect to have played an important part in his subsequent meteoric success, but it was certainly not selected according to plan. From letters written during the first half of 1897, while the quest was still on, we obtain a composite impression of quite a different kind of house to the stately Georgian mansion in which it ended. They also depict Lutyens's ideal of internal decoration and furnishing at this date. 'Ideal' is the word, for these schemes were all conceived before the reality was found. In designing it, he may have been to some extent playing for time, and for their mutual pleasure. But the picture presented is none the less revealing of his notions. In contrast to his family's higgledy-piggledy, he envisaged a home of exquisite simplicity with plentiful simple fare—although Lady Emily was no cook and became a vegetarian. The combination displayed, of hearty appetite with aesthetic discrimination, adds a succulent Chardin note to the serene Vermeer interiors. These imaginary rooms rather suggest a country house, of the kind depicted in the drawing deposited in the Casket, than any of the eligible London premises.

They would have liked to live in Gray's Inn, at or near his office, but that was ruled out by married couples not being admitted. He wondered 'if a house is to let belonging to St. Paul's Cathedral—there are some delightful houses there and the very shadow of St. Paul's would be lovely'; an idea that he may have recalled in 1942 when plotting the Royal Academy plan for the devastated precincts. Addison Road, where the Balfours were established, was considered but dismissed. 'Uncle Loch', on the other hand, 'thinks Bloomsbury by far the wisest plan,' and as usual he proved right in the end.

At various times and places, in the intervals of his work, Lutyens outlined and filled in the picture:

> Small and very simple must our little home be. I don't care for comfort. I see a white bedroom with gay flowery curtains to windows and bed. The bed of wood and rather Italian in feeling—high head and no foot, a *cassone* at the foot. Look ye here. There are all sorts of impossible points about the above bed wh. must be worked out. Red-gold posts. Blue curtains, red ceiling. Shelf for candles and the Casket. It would be jolly to keep all washing apparatus in a separate room, and make the Bed Room itself jolly without cluttering it up with paraphernalia! You *shall* have the dearest little glass in the world and a three sided one too. The pictures we shall have if any will be small, Italian in feeling, gorgeous in colour, and in exquisite frames— Madonnas and St. Georges to inspire our respective selves. Flowers. Yes, but

few and then arranged very simply—Japanese methods I love but they must not rush at one shouting *vive japonaise*! Remember Holland! de Hooghe's interiors.

But one really wants the house first. . . .

(2.III.97)

Shall I design a Dining Table? no not green—do you think?—it would be too ARTY, and then the plain wood would look so nice peering up through the blue table cloth—for I vote if E. approves to have one little blue cloth for each person and not a great sheet of superfine damask! We shall have say 2 dozen of them and kept in a press in the Dining Room and if anyone unexpected comes

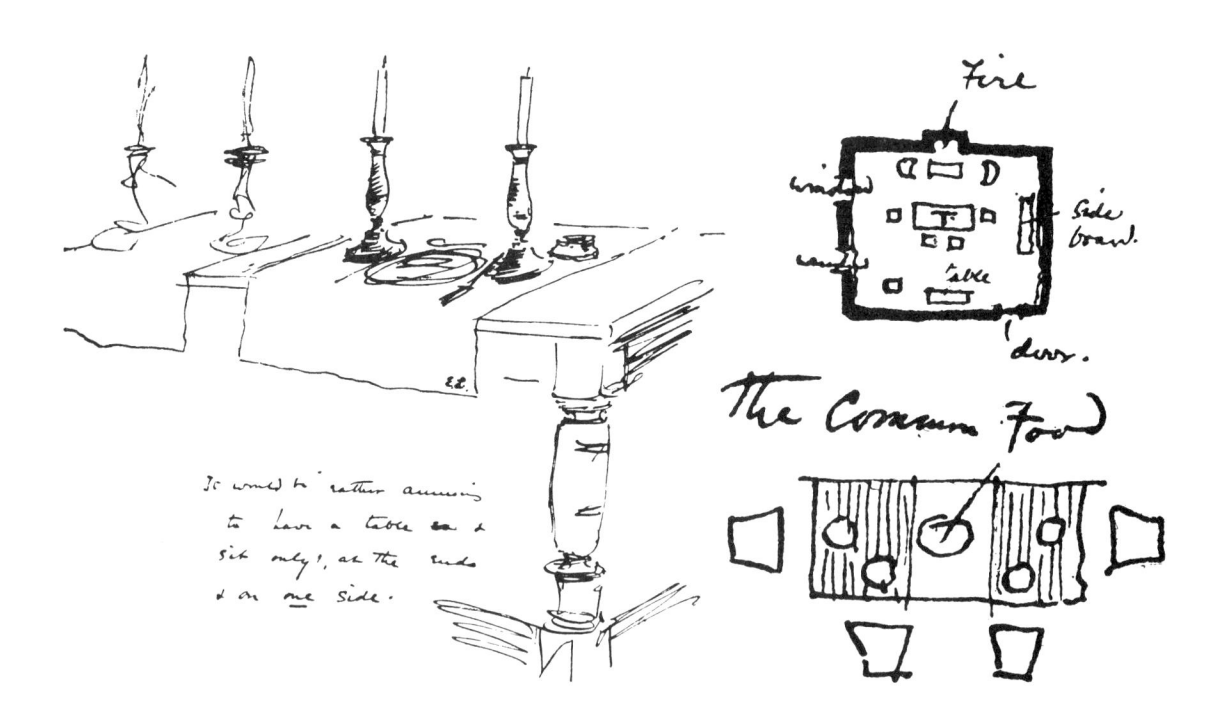

in to feed wi' us then Josef will go to de pressa and get himself anoder liddle cloth—salt cellar, knife (green handled), spoon and fork etc. tout complet! Salt Cellars in some nice delft ware, coloured, and a brass pair of candles to each body. I have no time to draw a picture—but you imagine! It would be rather amusing to have a table and sit only at the ends and on *one* side. Blue cloths, oak table, white china, and brass candles, coloured delft ware and green handled knives would make a most pretty and dear effect. Then will we put coloured gourdes and heaps of color fruits for deserts on occasions of state. That is when another couple are tolerated by we.

(12.XI.97)

We must have in our dining room a press for linen. A press where you squeeze the cloths between meals. They are never used now, I wonder why? The cloths are so big?

(11.IV.97)

The drawing room, more rather the Parlor, is what puzzles me. A good fireplace is essential in all rooms. Armchairs and sofas etc. covered with jolly stuffs. Then your cabinet (which is now in my office) and good writing table for my darling and a long range of low bookcases. What about a piano? This I shall design when the time comes—small, square, and refined, and the colour inside gorgeous. I shall try to get Guthrie of the Glasgow School to paint whispers—I almost prefer his painting in this sort of decoration to E. Burne Jones.

(2.III.1897, from The Inn, Roseneath)

The duties of the day shall be heralded by the striking hour, and we shall rise—but how difficult! Breakfast—simply and prettily placed upon an oak table. Breads and fruits and flowers, one or two—crisp curling bacon in its casserole, on occasions of great state a sauseage! hams, and eggs to boil at our own pleasure, and tempting toast upon a bright iron grid before the fire—of wood! The smell of papery pot-pourri by Bumps and the blue cloth with Lavendar's fresh presence there. So we shall eat and read the other's letters each to the other.

Then to my work I shall have to go. The cloths shall to their press retire and the table left bare with the one small glass or plate of flowers and all be left in neat rectangular arrangement.

Emy to her accounts shall go and write in her nut brown bound ledgers the monies of the day—Peerless mistress, with apron and a bunch of keys that chime of house and honey in the store—and to the kitchen, where the pots and range glisten in the light, where the cheery cook turns mountains into mole-hills and frugal fare into a feast.

The breadpan with his father oven open and shut in busy intercourse, the larder restocked from Smithfield Mart, and the washed-wood bins are filled with clean fresh vegetables from Covent Garden.

Lunch—a simple meal to which I shall return—perhaps a friend—cold meats, a salad, quaintly dressed in colored bowl, and refreshing coffee brewed by host and hostess—Mocca fresh ground, cream and golden candy—placed upon its own green linen cloth. Exchange of news—and then away I go to work and Emy to her duties social.

The evening shall draw in, bringing with it the dinner hour. Tea in or out, not in the Drawing Room but in the Dining Room—a kettle on the hob, crumpets and buttered cakes and frothy cream on gala days.

But dinner—four softly burning candles—two more for each guest. Food matters not! except how it is served, with quiet grace with all hospitable intent. Then, darling, the long quiet evening that shall ever draw our hearts the closer.

The white fire-lit room—the bared table except for what we have in use—two chairs quite close.

We shall have spent the day so that before we sleep we can thank God for all our happiness and pray for more to come. . . . It wont all be feeding as this note on a happy day seems but to tell. . . .

(9.IV.97)

Our house affairs are described in *Anthony & Cleopatra*:

To business that we love, we rise betimes
And go to't with delight.

wont we, love ?

(14.V.97)

I am most exercised about Towels. I wonder if nice ones are to be had in Italy or Southern France, where by cunning work red and blue threads sing their joyous chorus in a border of thanks and praise for the honour of touching my sweet Emy's face.

(2.III.97)

Don't let's get linen that wears out soon. If we get rich we can always buy good and oh so fine day by day, if we get poor then it may be difficult to replace and I should hate holes in our sheets! [Then follows a list for the linen cupboard.]

The picture is a period piece, hesitating between the arts and crafts of Munstead and what was to become the characteristic Lutyens taste. It is, perhaps, most significant as a detailed example of the way he projected his imagination into the life to be led in his designs, a life more intense than might ever in fact be lived in them. Yet one cannot help feeling that it is more of a still life than a conversation piece. As a 'plan for marriage', it is a one-sided design, making no more allowance for his bride's possible idiosyncrasies than for the actual houses they were then considering. The whole elaborate conception was a vision, a picturesque design for 'a young married architect at home'. His bride, like some of the clients for whom he projected similar ideal homes, is an incident in an early Lutyens interior. Some brides might have justifiably asked 'Where do I come into this?' But Lady Emily apparently thought it all beautiful, if not very likely to take shape.

Within a few weeks, however,—on July 14 to be precise—this ideal was displaced by an actuality of entirely different character and evoking his other, practical and precise, side. He found he could get the remainder lease of 29 Bloomsbury

Square, formerly Norman Shaw's office, from A. Heaton, Shaw's interior decorator who had already been helping in the house-hunt. Its spacious Georgian plan and perfection—no less than its distinguished associations—instantly captivated him, although in size, shortness of lease (sixteen years) and classical character it cut clean across their preconceptions. The house has now been pulled down.

The excitement of discovery was almost overshadowed, but not quite, by tidings of Barbara Webb's death and the need to make arrangements for attending the funeral. They would go to Milford together where 'I shall love but oh so sadly to pay the last little tribute to that darling [lamb symbol] who has been so brilliant a light in my life—our lives'.

> Now if I were a Duke I should love to take my Emy to live in 29 Bloomsbury Square. The house is beautiful, large airey rooms, beautiful mantlepieces and staircase. You enter a square hall and a beautiful staircase on beyond. Three rooms which the great Norman Shaw used as his offices!! during his busiest period!! Such lovely doorways and cornices everywhere. Kitchens splendid, all in good working order and simple.... Such a beautiful staircase, with a delicious wooden gallery upstairs overlooking it. It is like a country house.

Later, the same evening,

> So absurd to write to you again but I have just had dinner and . . . I am full of 29 B.S. The house is so delicious. It does for an office so well. First because the first architect of our day used it, and then the charm of the house is in its plan. Although it looks grim and square outside, inside it is a paradise. The outer hall gives access to the offices—all with their own w.c.s etc, and then from this dear square hall you go into the bigger hall with the big staircase, and there is hardly a dark corner anywhere and all is fair, square, and spacious, with any amount of cupboards and housewife's delights. Aspect east and west, good. Garden at back. If you think we can afford £200, I think we have found a house and we are lucky.

Confronted with the classic lines of a real house, his Morrissy ideals (though he would have repudiated the epithet) seem to have been forgotten, and he was at once immersed in the practical and financial facts. He estimated the combined budget of home and office as:

> House, including ground rent, £200; taxes £60; Assurance £190; Living £500; Clerks £400; odds and ends £100; Total £1450.
> This means £29,000 of work in a year, which I ought to get.

The same letter contains one of the devastating verbal or linear impressions of a personality, usually a new client, which he often formed simultaneously with his *aperçu* of a fresh commission, in this case of the intending lessors:

> Mr. Heaton is an old man—made a fortune decorating for Norman Shaw principally. He has had a stroke and has one arm bound up. He discourses on art and truth of beauty whilst his upper teeth insecurely fixed clap applause, most bewitching and engrossing to observe. Mrs. Heaton with gout in her knee is fat, iron gray, and oh so motherly. God made her—not a 'soul'—very frightened of your coming. That is the family to which we may succeed.

A satisfactory arrangement was reached: Mr. Heaton was evidently pleased by his successor and eventually agreed on a rent of £190 per annum for the first five years and £240 for the remainder of the term, giving occupation early in November. Moreover his son-in-law Mr. Ledward agreed to take over Lutyens's rooms in Gray's Inn. So originated the occupation of 29 Bloomsbury Square, home and office till the lease expired in 1914.

Even before they had settled on Bloomsbury Square, the imaginary home had begun to take concrete shape. One or two pieces of furniture were actually being made, including the bed and a dining table, others were found in antique shops. Wedding presents began to arrive. Their more intimate friends consulted their requirements—Princess Louise gave a lacquer cabinet on stand, Lord Battersea the set of pewter plates always intended for meals. But some of the others did not fit in at all. A silver and glass inkstand, the stand made of an old wine coaster, prompted the agonized exclamation, 'Why do people always turn something into something else then stroke their tummies and call themselves of good taste!' One day Ned opened a parcel addressed to Emily containing a toast rack that evoked even more pungent criticism, to which she replied with some heat that it was from her Nanny and why should he have opened her parcel anyway. An awkward moment. He apologised most humbly, but was firm: 'We shall have a cupboard where we will put these dear thoughts and not necessarily use them as things. I am most awfully inquisitive—a fault you must teach me to be rid of.' He was, of course, very inquisitive; that was how he taught himself most of what he knew, but he seems to have learnt from the incident the primary lesson in the etiquette of married life.

Relations and close friends for the most part gave presents of cheques. They were very much welcomed, but a slight difficulty arose when it emerged that Lady

11. THE INN, ROSENEATH, DUNBARTONSHIRE (1896-7)

12. CROOKSBURY, FARNHAM, SURREY. The east front, added 1899

13. CROOKSBURY, THE FIG COURT. Showing the junction of the 1889 building (left) with the 1898 addition

14. Deanery Garden, Sonning (1899)

15. Le Bois des Moutiers, Varengeville (1897–8)

16. Deanery Garden. The Court

Emily had no banking account. Ned urged her to see about opening one at once—he believed bankers got into muddles unless cheques were banked quickly; but owned he did not know what happened to an account when one changed one's name. Such subventions, however, were a considerable help. In May the financial situation was:

We have spent on the house, so far,	£53		
China	£60		
I have in the bank of my own	£561	8	9
In presents	£110	10	0
making	£671	18	9
With presents to come: total	£712	8	9

So you see the Budget is working out right so far.

But this was only a supplementary budget to the main problem of living costs, to be met with fees from work in hand or in prospect. A few friends and relations made contributions in the form of commissions, Lord Battersea coupled the pewter plates with one for a non-conformist chapel at Overstrand but, Lutyens complained, would not pay enough for it. Besides, the reputation of Munstead Wood was beginning to attract further business. Against the cost of 29 Bloomsbury Square and living expenses generally, estimated at £1450 for the ensuing twelve months, he could list twenty-five jobs, either finished, in progress, or contemplated, which might be expected to bring in £1720. In the following catalogue, dating from midsummer, 1897, place names and brief specifications have been added to the personal name which alone is given in the original; those not so qualified either are not identified or were garden designs handled through Miss Jekyll. The figures in brackets are the expected commissions.

Col. Jekyll. Alterations at Munstead House (50). H.R.H. Princess Louise, additions to The Inn, Roseneath (150). Capt. Ernest Rhodes, Binfield Lodge, Newbury (100). R. A. Wickham, Tower House, Mayfield (40). Lever Bros. (30). Busbridge [Church] (30). Mr. Gerald Streatfield, Fulbrook (250). Sir William Chance Bt., Orchards (250). Ree (75). Miller (25). Farnborough (30). Peterborough, alterations to the Palace for the Bishop of, (100). Lord Loch, additions to Stoke College, Stoke by Clare (150). Northbrook (30). Major Crawford, House at Sunningdale (25). Lord Myddleton, work on Peperharrow estate (30). C. A. Cook, Sullingstead (balance 50). Mr. Longman, cottage and wheelwright's shop, Apsley End, Hemel Hemstead (50). Hon. Emily Lawless, Burrows Cross, Shere (50). Mr. C. Guthrie, East Haddon Hall, Northants (garden) (20). Mr. Archibald Grove, Berry Down, Whitchurch (75).

Miss Hale (?) (75). Bumps (Miss Jekyll, Munstead Wood, no commission). Total £1720.

A slightly earlier letter, May 28, contains a similar list without figures but including the names of Lord Battersea (The Pleasaunce, Cromer), Mrs. Irving (alterations to 94 Eaton Place, London, and to Rake House, Milford), W. Cattley (Holmwood, Dorking), Rev. W. H. Evans (House at Charterhouse, Godalming), Lord Northbrook, Mrs. Hall, Mr. Wethered, and the Duke of Westminster (work at Eaton Hall, Cheshire, where Miss Jekyll had previously contributed decorative work). This provides the earliest full list that we have of his practice at any one time. Some of the subjects have been already referred to; of some nothing seems to be known. Lord Loch, it will be noticed, had turned up trumps and employed his prospective nephew to enlarge his picturesque old house in Clare village—the addition consisted in a brick and tile-hung wing which his successors wish had never been built—but the intention was kindly. Among the others, half a dozen are of sufficient importance to require the following notes, either as architecture or as shaping the framework of his life at this juncture.

Fulbrook. On a wooded hill at Elstead between Crooksbury and Farnham, for Mr. Gerald Streatfield. First visit to site is noted February 5, 1897. The design, an exuberant outcome of Munstead undertaken in the first flush of his excitement following his betrothal, is the worst he ever made. All his current techniques are employed at once, rubble and stone walls, large brick chimneys, tile hanging, timberwork and weatherboarding. Also the interior contains his earliest and least happy essay in handling classical forms.

Berry Down, Whitchurch, Hants. The visit of the client, Mr. Archibald Grove, is mentioned in letter of January 29, 1897. The long line of its rough-cast stable buildings backs on to the Basingstoke-Andover road, and is reminiscent of a Caldecott farm. The undistinguished medium-sized gabled stone house is seen from the road through a covered gateway in the line of stable buildings.

The Inn, Roseneath, Dunbartonshire. In 1895 H.R.H. Princess Louise, daughter of Queen Victoria and wife of the Marquess of Lorne, later 9th Duke of Argyll, consulted Lutyens on alterations (not executed) to Kilkatrine House, Inveraray. In the following year she commissioned additions to the Ferry Inn at Roseneath on the shores of Gareloch. Roseneath itself, a property of the Dukes of Argyll, is a great classical mansion. It was required to add a wing, containing reception rooms and bar with bedrooms above, to the Inn, a commonplace building in the local gray stone. A perspective dated March, 1896, is, like that for Kilkatrine, interesting as drawn by his own hand and being still in the Caldecott manner. Neither are very distinguished in design, being half-hearted adaptations of Surrey picturesque to

Scottish baronial in the local material. That for the Inn was eventually rejected in favour of a development from Sullingstead with tall Elizabethan chimneys, white harled upper storey above a ground floor of rubble masonry, and small mullioned windows set tight beneath broad expanses of a hipped roof of stone slates. The executed design (p. 69) is a great improvement on the earlier one. It has been said of it that here 'we first feel there is magic in the air'.[1]

The commission, from so august a source and so far outside Lutyens's field hitherto, came through Miss Jekyll. The Princess owned a house in Surrey and was well acquainted with her, being a talented handicraftswoman and a sculptor of distinction, besides a member of the Blumenthal circle. Among her works is the statue of Queen Victoria outside Kensington Palace. Lady Emily was also a connection of the Marquess whose sister, Lady Frances Balfour, was sister-in-law of Gerald Balfour. Witty and downright in conversation, Princess Louise evidently took up the young architect, who was not unnaturally flattered by frequent summonses to Kensington Palace, and employed him on sundry occupations not strictly connected with his profession. During their engagement Lady Emily had to complain of his being unduly assiduous to *Hoheit* (as she was known in the Jekyll circle). Lutyens admitted that he found her august commands difficult to resist; 'one makes believe and has jokes innumerable'; and pointed out the prestige value of the connection. The gossip reached Miss Jekyll's ears. 'Bumps rose in her thousands and gave her (the Princess) such a lecture about wasting my time.'[2]

The Campbell connection led also to his employment for alterations to the *Bishop's Palace, Peterborough*, for Bishop Glyn (son of 1st Baron Wolverton, married Lady Mary Campbell). Princess Louise, he wrote (April 12, 1897), had warned him to be careful: 'They say I can only build cottagey things and I am not to make Peterborough look cottagey. How can I make a few servants' bedrooms and coalhole look like a Palace?' On a later visit to Peterborough he sent Lady Emily an account of a fantastic experience that, he said, had befallen him when taking a midnight stroll in the precincts of the Cathedral.

> As I walked the ruined site of the ancient cloister beneath a fitful moon, I heard a sound as of an organ chord sweeping the world to reach God's heaven. Startled I looked and lo! the cloister grew restored, the doors opened and there came through with mournful paces a throng of holy white-robed monks, chanting. The Cross and Rood were carried aloft, the bell tolled and it was so solemn, for a coffin was carried by. A shrouded figure grim to look on bade me look within the coffin ... I saw my Bachelordom carried to decent funeral!

Repeated visits inspecting progress at Roseneath were the occasions of some of

---

[1] H. Goodhart Rendel. 'The Work of Sir Edwin Lutyens.' Lecture to the R.I.B.A. February 13, 1945.
[2] Sir E. L. to Lady E. L. May 5, 1897.

the letters written at this time which have been quoted in connection with his search for a home and conception of its ideal character. In one of them he puzzled over *art nouveau* and the aesthetic fashions of the 'nineties, *à propos* a room in Glasgow where he had to break his journey:

> Surroundings prompted by the New Art Glasgow School—greens, golds, blues. White rooms with black furniture, black rooms with white furniture. Where Whistler is worshipped, Degas tolerated, Rodin extolled for his impertinence and admired for his love of oddity sometimes called originality.

These two quoted passages lightly reflect a trait never far beneath the surface of his mind, an instinctive yet imaginative conservatism, which religious tradition evoked and modern art was apt to repel—though characteristically he soon adopted black walls for the drawing-room at Bloomsbury Square which became famous. At this stage, however, he was still openly romantic in outlook, though increasingly beset by practical exigencies. There are unexpectedly few allusions in these letters indicating an interest in old buildings and those there are, oblique: of Hatfield House, lately seen: 'a scent rather than a reality, mixed with an undercurrent of Arras and Abbeville (which last I can but imagine never having seen)'; and, 'I have only seen photos of Blickling. O to do and have the chance of doing big work. Those grand old houses bear on their dear faces the stamp of quiet, repose, impossible now with all this rush of competition. . . .'

Yet how often was he not to achieve those very qualities, which Miss Jekyll acknowledged, in his work! He was still dreaming cheerfully of 'big work' when, in May, she summoned him mysteriously and urgently. He speculated wildly to Lady Emily on the possible reason—an appointment from the Duke of Westminster, Princess Louise proposing to give his name to her Mama to rebuild Windsor, the commission to build Capetown Cathedral (for which Herbert Baker had hopes), a big church in England, or a means of advancing their marriage to June or July. When Miss Jekyll met him in Godalming she still refused to vouchsafe the secret till 'we sat cheek by jowl on the Cenotaph of Sigismunda. She then recounted several visits by Mr. and Mrs. Chance. The latter has described[1] the first of these: 'Passing through a sandy lane we saw a house nearing completion, and on the top of a ladder a portly figure giving directions to some workmen. The house was a revelation of unimagined beauty and charm, we stood entranced and gazing, until the figure descended and we found ourselves, after due explanation, being welcomed as future neighbours.' Munstead Wood deeply impressed, but depressed them too, since they were committed for an intended building to Halsey Ricardo, an old friend. Ned takes up the tale (May 27, 1897):

[1] Quoted in Francis Jekyll *op. cit.*

> What could they do? Woozle said they could not possibly chuck Ricardo; Nedi would not oust him on any account. O Bumps had such a long story to tell, played so nicely with the Chances, and eventually undertook to overcome my scruples.... To make it short, the Chances have chucked Ricardo and I am to do their work! and I am to meet them on Wednesday on the site. Chance won't hasten our wedding, but I know I shall always be talking of good chances to Mrs. Chance. So another rippling ring will be made by my 'splash' in the surface of the world.

Orchards, Godalming, of which this was the origin, will be referred to more fully in the next chapter. But not all the contacts for which, directly or indirectly, Miss Jekyll was responsible were so fruitful. In the previous April, William Robinson, probably encouraged by the successful collaboration of his old gardening ally with the young Surrey portent, proposed some kind of collaboration between Lutyens and himself. Its nature is obscure, but involved discussions of alterations to Gravetye. It was not a success.

> Been for a long walk with W. R. I left him—he bores so. He starts for a walk, never says where he is going and then stops here and there and goes off at tangents—his conversation wayward and contradicts himself every two minutes—until one feels inclined to explode... Robinson picks one's brains—takes me to an old building and asks questions then gives them as his own to his builder who carries out my ideas all wrong... He is like a jibbing horse and it does tire me getting him along.

The jibe about being only a cottage architect cropped up again in connection with Burrows Cross, Shere, for the Hon. Emily Lawless:

> A just criticism is ever welcome and right to listen to humbly, but an unjust one (like the Lawless w.c.) is so impossible to meet or alter, and the idle repetition goes its way—
>
> 'Mr. Lutyens can only build a cottage and he never allows more than 1 w.c.'—you know the sort of thing, and then somebody gives his palace to someone else. Lawless has 2 and can have 3 for another £5 or so! The Streatfields have 7! Lord Battersea 10 or eleven!

The work for Lord Battersea[1] referred to is *The Pleasaunce, Overstrand*, in Norfolk. This involved the combination of two villas into a single residence and the laying out of a large seaside garden in collaboration with Miss Jekyll. At the same time the chapel already referred to was building: important only because in it he used pantiles for the first time.

[1] Cyril Flower, 1843–1907. M.P. (Liberal), cr. Baron Battersea of Battersea and Overstrand, 1882; m. Constance 1st d. and coh. of Sir Anthony Rothschild.

With July ended these six months so fortunate for Lutyens that they have been depicted in some detail. The month brought forth the sketch designs for one of his most characteristic Surrey houses—Orchards, the decision to lease 29 Bloomsbury Square and the financial fears attached, the signature of the marriage settlement based on the life insurance policy that caused such heart-searchings, a mounting list of wedding presents, and the death of the beloved Barbara Webb within three weeks of the marriage for which, directly and indirectly, she was responsible. A less emotional character than Ned's might be expected to have been unsettled by such varieties of stress, and as August 4, the wedding day approached, his letters witness to quick alternations of mood in which, however, intense zest for his work and passionate attachment to the ideal of matrimony form the constant theme. Yet nervous reaction is traceable in the repeated, tenuously balanced, budgets; in the explicit confession on at least one occasion of fear and faith, 'lest I am unable to make enough money to keep our bodies and souls together—I know really God will give me power to work and work to do;' in unwonted introspection and hypersensitiveness to criticism. It was Barbara Webb's death that wrung from him yearning for speech—'if I had but words at my command I should never be thought flippant and shallow', and that tenderly beautiful recollection of his tales to Baa Lamb in childhood, ending with a prophetic phrase: 'when the time comes for us to part—silence —just silence will be my medium of expression.' Yet the same letter contains the farcical caricature of old Mr. and Mrs. Heaton's false teeth and gouty knees, and the appreciation of No. 29's Georgian plan. In the narrating, these themes have been separately treated, but, in envisioning the personality of Lutyens, they must be conceived as simultaneous trends of thought, rapidly succeeding images, scarcely related but each vivid and complete, reflected by the bright facets of his continually revolving brain. Yet in intercourse these *scintillae* were often obscured, 'scrambled,' to use a modern technicality, by his verbal inhibition which it is to be doubted whether even the warmth and intimacy of courtship, and still less of domestic life, entirely overcame.

They were married at Knebworth on August 4, 1897 and spent the first days of their honeymoon at Warren Lodge, returning to Knebworth for a day to attend the Earl of Lytton's coming of age. Thence they went for a fortnight to Holland. It there became evident that Lady Emily's idea of enjoyment was not sightseeing nor museums nor hunting for Delftware in old shops, but that she loved looking at the sea. Whereas Ned, who could and did look at everything else, hated the sea, particularly looking at it from a beach. He called it 'that half apple of the world'. There came a morning when at last they went to the seaside at Scheveningen and sat side by side in two chairs—hers looking seaward, and his landward. They were perfectly happy, though they said very little, close together but looking in opposite directions.

CHAPTER V

ROMANTIC ARCHITECT

§1. IN SEARCH OF THE PICTURESQUE

DURING the decade 1898–1908 the naïve, surprising young man made himself the leading architect of country houses by a brilliant sequence of homes for rich and fastidious Edwardians. He was still very romantic; the vision of himself, conceived in his courting days, of a Galahad in shining array bent on winning substantial laurels for his Emily, was still bright, and he cheerfully caricatured it, as in the drawing reproduced on page 60. At this time he did seem to trail almost perceptible clouds of freshness and enchantment, emanating partly from his spiritual home in the Munstead woodlands but mostly from his genius and ardent and inventive happiness.

Yet, quite early, signs of a change are perceptible, in the character of his work and the nature of his ideals. It was not only that he was maturing, as man and architect. He was becoming convinced that the heights of architecture as an art were attainable only through classic finitude, and therefore determined that in that realm his future must lie. As he became more conscious of his powers he discovered delightedly the logic, force, and subtlety of the Orders, and impatience began to consume him for opportunities wider than the largest of country houses could afford for exercising his and their capacities.

The extent of the change in his architectural allegiance during these ten or twelve years is illustrated by comparing Orchards, at Godalming, the romantic house that he was commissioned to build on the eve of his marriage, and that great classic villa, Heathcote, Ilkley, undertaken in 1906. The decade is further defined by his appointment to, and method of handling, two International Exhibition buildings —Paris 1900 and Rome 1911 (later to become the British School at Rome)—on each of which he was engaged for two years previously. Both loomed large in his practice at the time and both had far-reaching results on him.

The process and manner of his transition between these two poles is interesting. In the course of it he contrived to assimilate the spirit, besides the grammar, of humanist architecture. This formative decade was of such importance to himself and his art that it must form the subject of two chapters. In this one will be traced the development of the romantic young architect of the Surrey countryside; in the next, his discovery of and growing proficiency in the classical ideal. In fact, however, the two processes were taking place simultaneously: his earliest experiments in renaissance design date from the very beginning of the decade; and his work at Lambay—the climax of his romanticism—comes after he had crossed the Rubicon. Indeed he returned again and again to the romantic mode in later years; for notwithstanding his absorption of and in the classics, the significant point is that his imagination was and remained fundamentally romantic, even when he harnessed it with abstract mathematics. In André Gide's phrase, his 'classical work is beautiful by virtue of its subjugated romanticism.' It was this dualism that gives his architecture its peculiar vitality and made him so attractive as a man, absorbing though at times puzzling as a subject for study. His two simultaneous lines of development did have repercussions in the curiously divided household at Bloomsbury Square, which will be described in Chapter VII.

At this point the term romantic or picturesque, as used in these chapters, must be defined. The whole approach of the young Lutyens to architecture, through his study of the landscape, traditions, and vernacular techniques of his home county, was in the romantic tradition that regards buildings as properly the product of their soil and of the country craftsman's lore; and their planning as properly ordered by the circumstances of the site and the needs of their inhabitants. At the beginning and again at the end of the nineteenth century these principles were habitually qualified by another, that the resulting building should possess the qualities of picturesqueness, that is, 'compose' picturesquely both as a design and in its setting. This qualification presupposed that everybody was potentially an artist searching for subjects of a particular kind of picture. It derived from the great epoch of landscape architecture, when landowners felt responsible for the beauty of their estates and when the subsequently typical landscape of rural England was thereby formed. The theory and practice of 'the Picturesque' were finally established in the last decade of the eighteenth century by Sir Uvedale Price's widely read *Essays on the Picturesque*, and the work of many subsequent disciples, both authors and architects, professional and amateur. The Picturesque became the accepted aesthetic of most cultivated people throughout the nineteenth century notwithstanding the doctrinaire and in its time 'modernist' creed of the gothic revivalists and Ruskin, who himself sublimated Picturesque theory to his own ideals. So generally accepted was the conviction that a country scene should possess the qualities of a picture by Claude or Ruysdael or Constable, a country building the texture and irregular outline which made it suitable for inclusion in a painting of one or other of those kinds, and so universal was the pleasing custom of sketching more or less in the manner of De Windt or David Cox, that by the end of the nineteenth century the very name of Price and the very fact that this scale of values was artificial, had been forgotten. This can be illustrated by my

17. ORCHARDS, GODALMING, SURREY (1898-9). The entrance

18. ORCHARDS, from the garden

19. GODDARDS, ABINGER, SURREY (1898)

20. Grey Walls, Gullane, E. Lothian (1900–01)

21. Tigbourne Court, Witley, Surrey (1899)

22. Marsh Court, Stockbridge, Hampshire (1901). Entrance (east) front

23. Marsh Court. Sunk garden and north-west corner

24. The Hall at Marsh Court

25. LITTLE THAKEHAM, SUSSEX (1902). The garden front

26. LITTLE THAKEHAM. The entrance side

mentioning that, having some twenty years ago published a book called *The Picturesque*, the *doyen* of 'the wild garden', William Robinson, summoned me to Gravetye to account for a remark contained in it to the effect that his conceptions restated (much more practically and authoritatively) the ideas of Uvedale Price. 'Who was Price?' he demanded; 'I've never heard of him.' Similarly the young Lutyens, in the early years of his practice, was probably unconscious that he was following romantic, picturesque, principles in the design and texturing of his buildings; but, on the contrary, was satisfied that he was building according to William Morris's and Philip Webb's modern precepts and the promptings of his own eyes. Nevertheless the effects that he aimed to produce, and did for years succeed in producing with unmatched artistry—the asymetrical plans following the contours of their sites, the irregular silhouettes building up into a series of effective compositions, the lovely textures secured by using varied local materials—were in fact those that had been envisaged and recommended a century earlier by the apostles of picturesque theory.

The romantic sanctions of architecture are beginning to be recognised afresh. In recent years some writers on town planning have put forward the view that the values attached by picturesque theory to irregularity, composition by contrasting masses, and asymetrical layouts, are particularly relevant to modern architectural practice and the practical exigencies governing contemporary town planning. The extrovert plan of the modern city building, devised to eliminate internal light wells; the need of space between them for sunlight to reach, and noise to escape from, the street; the eccentric street plan demanded by traffic-managers;—these are among the practical modern factors militating against the classical conception of city architecture as a matter of axial symmetry and stately façades. It may well be that they postulate an aesthetic approach having much in common with the theories of the picturesque which remodelled the rural landscape in the eighteenth century and inspired unconsciously Lutyens's early houses. Texture, excluded by the more intellectual analysts from their studies of architectural form and dynamics, is also, nevertheless, one of the primary factors in the visual appeal of architecture. With a sensitive handling of texture it is possible, with little apprehension of the more profound principles of architecture, to produce a result that charms the senses if not the intellect. And where considerations of texture have been ignored, the more monumental virtues, though not impugned, yet have their effect reduced or exert less effect on the spectator than they might. Deficiencies in texture are mainly responsible for the disrepute into which Victorian gothic has fallen—despite those champions whose imagination is able to supply the lack; and the failure of much recent building to solve the problem of texture may hamper acceptance of contemporary ideals, if it does not eventually limit their application to utilitarian structures. Texture is not architecture; but architecture is not wholly successful without it. The modern student of architecture can therefore learn much from some of the works of Lutyens's romantic period: his methods of composing irregular forms, his handling and combination of materials, and in particular his selection and proportioning of those forms.

In this sense, Lutyens's abandonment of picturesque composition for the classical and symmetrical was not entirely compensated by the height and perfection to which he carried the renaissance ideal. One is tempted to speculate how he would have developed had he not accepted the classical regimen but had followed up the free empiricism—seen for instance in part of the 1898 addition to Crooksbury (p. 69)—to its fuller implications. At Deanery Garden (p. 70) he achieved well nigh perfectly that which some Continental architects arrived at fumblingly a decade or so later and on the strength of which they are hailed as fathers of modern architecture. Had he not rejected quite so decidedly the experiments of the Glasgow School, but explored with his endless inventiveness the further possibilities of his early jugglings with form-patterns at Crooksbury, would he not inevitably have been led to study the newer methods of construction and of using new materials? Had he done so there would not be that sense of finality, of his being *ultimus Romanorum*, the last consummate exponent of an ageless but, for the time being, obsolescent form of art, which accompanies one's admiration for the accomplished virtuosity of his later masterpieces. Instead, might we not have been able to say more often than conscientiously we can, 'herein and herein are examplars for the architecture of the future, not fully evolved perhaps yet handling its materials, concrete, steel, and glass, with inventive genius and the sensitiveness and artistry only attainable through mastery of classic logic?'

In later chapters an answer to that question will be made. It is asked now in order to emphasise the fact that Lutyens's romantic work is by no means to be thought of as the immature product of a sentimental period but as actually and potentially among his most important.

The autumn of 1897, after the honeymoon in Holland, was occupied by settling into 29 Bloomsbury Square. The works in progress have been enumerated in the last chapter and no new commissions seem to have been immediately received. But in May 1898 Col. Jekyll, as Commissioner for the British Section of the International Exhibition to be held in Paris in 1900, asked Lutyens if he would design the British Pavilion. It was to be, Lutyens reported,

> a house in which the Prince of Wales will entertain when in Paris. It will be a pretty house that will stand six months only, like 'Old London', and no scope for originality in design. An Elizabethan house!

A few days later (May 12) he was in Paris on the first of a succession of flying visits, meeting the Exhibition Committee (where 'I spoke English, French, German without any regard of grammar or tense, and demonstrated with sketches'). The British Committee comprised Sir A. Ellis, Col. Jekyll, Sir W. Agnew, Baron F. de Rothschild, G. Murray Scott, Prof. Aitcheson, Purdon Clarke, Thompson Lyon, with Lionel Earle—the son of Mrs. C. W. Earle ('Aunt T')—as one of the secretaries. Ned was able to foregather with his brother-in-law Neville Lytton, then studying art in Paris. On one of these visits some of the Committee devoted an evening to seeing night life. Ned's letter to Lady Emily describing his reaction to Montmartre shows his hereditary puritanism recoiling violently from a 'nauseous experience'. After dining on frogs 'for the first time', he was taken to the *Moulin Rouge*. 'I was asked what I thought of it and could only say "Well, yes, but I cannot help trying to realise my mother's face were she here".... I have eaten and seen beastly fruits.'

A few days earlier he had, when in Glasgow, criticised in the letter already quoted (Chapter IV), the modernist room deriving from Mackintosh and the Glasgow Art School. During the course of the summer he was able to combine Exhibition visits with a commission from M. Guillaume Mallet, a Protestant banker who, with his family, became a life-long friend of the Lutyenses. It was Mme. Mallet who later introduced Lady Emily to Theosophy thereby greatly affecting both their lives. In the design of *Le Bois des Moutiers* at Varengeville, whether deriving from Paris or Glasgow, occurs one of the rare instances in his work of the influence of *nouveau art* modernism. With its tall slender oriel lights, some of them used hinge-like at the angles, the Varengeville house is another instance of that hesitation in his development which, if pursued, might have transformed the course of English architecture in the Edwardian decade (p. 70).

The estimated cost of *Le Bois des Moutiers* was 93,000 frs. Language presented no insuperable obstacle to the job.

> 'Such a day of it yesterday. Seven French builders, the different trades. Oh such talking, such tremendous demonstrations and excitement from 9 a.m. till 7 p.m. Whenever excitement reached its highest we all went on our knees and drew pictures on the floor.... I made a French joke with the mason who wanted to do something in stone which belonged to a wood construction, so I said in indignation it was *pour bois* and added *mais pas pourboire*! Great fits, and I *was* pleased!'

During the summer which also saw the birth of his eldest daughter, christened Barbara, after Mrs. Webb, Overstrand Hall for Lord Hillingdon and Goddards for Sir Frederick Mirrielees, Bt., were initiated. In September, when Lady Emily with the baby were in the country, he spent the week-ends at Munstead Wood where Miss Jekyll kept the studio at his disposal, to be within walking distance of Orchards. There he worked on the Pavilion ('Ricketts brought the Paris plans down with a roll

5 ft. long taller than himself') with Col. Jekyll in convenient proximity, and from there Miss Jekyll accompanied him to the Goddards' site.

> Sept. 18. ... Went over yesterday to Mirrielees. He wants to build a little house, or rather two cottages with a common-room between them, to lend poor people, sick children etc., with a court. He don't know what he wants to spend but wishes to do it well. He is very rich and it all seems ideal as regards conditions under which work will be done. I am very happy and keen about it. Have got out a delicious scheme for Hillingdon if he will use it.

A few days later 'a nice letter from Arthur Chapman' is alluded to, 'but I guess I shall get a scold when we meet.' This most likely referred to the addition projected to Crooksbury, and the expected scolding, perhaps, to the extraordinary way Lutyens was proposing to do it. We must now look more closely at these notable works.

It was with Orchards that he was now most actively occupied. Its site is on the edge of that wooded sandstone massif east of Godalming and overlooking the Wey valley, with the prettiest part of Surrey lying below to the south-east. Munstead Wood is a mile or so nearer Godalming, by a sandy lane, Hascombe on an adjacent slope, with Park Hatch at its foot, Chinthurst across the valley. So this house, built during the happiest months of his life, and, after Munstead Wood, his most outstanding performance hitherto, may be said to lie in the heart of 'the Lutyens country'. It took three years to build—such was the leisurely careful craftsmanship with which these intensely personal early buildings of his were brought into being—and before it was finished half a dozen houses prompted by or in various ways related to it were going up.

It will be remembered that Sir William and Lady Chance (as they became), after coming upon Miss Jekyll perched on her ladder, had fallen in love with Munstead Wood and commissioned Lutyens to give them something similar. It could, however, be more spacious, with four or five servants' bedrooms besides four or five *chambres de maître*, a studio for the mistress, and stables. His design arranged these elements round a court, as it might have been the converted yard of some old farm, with a continuous warm red blanket of roof covering them all. The small-sized golden rubble stone of the district, the same as at Munstead, is the material chiefly used for walling but with tiles built into many of the archways and over the windows. These throughout are oak-framed casements, grouped in long continuous runs and, in the studio, as a big oriel. Oak frames the gable of the porch and the ways through into the court and stable yard. Thus the three materials of the building, stone, tiles, and oak, were combined throughout in continually changing harmonies, and each given solo passages in which the craftsman's virtuosity could be displayed (p. 79).

Orchards is essentially that, a symphony of local materials, conducted by an artist, for artists. It was this esoteric quality in his work that attracted his early patrons, and this that they were so enchanted and flattered to obtain. Nearly always the work of art succeeded, often brilliantly; and in most cases it worked reasonably well as a place to live in. In any case domestic service was cheap and plentiful; the servants were not wanted too near the family and guests' rooms; and labour saving was not considered in those days further than giving the staff pleasant quarters. If you were that tiresome and now almost universal type, the practical economical householder or his wife, then you should not have gone to Lutyens for your house. But if, like those who did, in those ample easy times, your romantic and artistic susceptibilities sought escape from Victorian conventions into the new century that was dawning—the century, it seemed, of sensitive and graceful living and delighted recognition of the beauty and goodness of the world—then no one could give it to you with such imaginative artistry as Lutyens! This fundamental difference in the time-spirit must be kept in mind as seriously in appreciating his early houses as in criticising the 'unworkable' plans of a Vanbrugh or Palladian mansion.

The plan is one that he often used again—for part of Overstrand Hall almost immediately, and a year or two later for Marsh Court and Little Thakeham (see p. 102): a long transverse corridor with the staircase at one end, the front door in the middle, and the pantry and servants' quarters at the other; the living-rooms opening off it southwards. The Orchards staircase is of the massive, Munstead kind and, as there, leads up to a first-floor gallery, framed of wrought oak. The garden, on descending levels, carefully patterned and worked up, is saved from fussiness by the contrast to the spreading landscape below it and the strongly accented but simple lines of the house above it which, seen from any part of the garden, come together in a succession of picturesque shapes. Orchards has not the simplicity and subtlety of Munstead Wood—is a little diffuse where Miss Jekyll's house is, like its mistress, terse and epigrammatic. But as picturesque building and gardening I think it should be regarded as Lutyens's first unaided major success.

Goddards, on Abinger Common below Leith Hill, (p. 79), was conceived, as has been mentioned, as a Home of Rest where ladies of small means might repair for holiday. After the South African war it was used for invalid soldiers, and was altered in 1910 to be a private house. Its purpose involved a Common Room, occupying the ground floor in the middle, with bedrooms above and others in wings which project obliquely to form a garden court. The walls are rough-cast and white-washed, with red brick mullioned windows and tall chimney shafts, the roof of tiles with Horsham slates on the lower slopes. The court between the wings is random-paved with Horsham slabs and brick-framed mill stones, among which Miss Jekyll naturalised grey foliage plants around clumps of roses and irises and a circular dipping well, the garden being enclosed with yew hedges. Inside, the walls are whitewashed, the raftered ceilings supported by oak posts, and the fireplaces of brick. The whole effect is exquisitely pretty—the Caldecott ideal of a traditional country building, delicious in colour and texture, and realised with every resource of craftsmanship. The flanking wings, splayed, not at right angles, to the centre, originally ended in gables. When extended in 1910, cross gables containing bow windows were added and immense chimney breasts in the same manner as the original work, without spoiling the design. To modern eyes it may seem over-precious, but how well done it all is in its vernacular *genre*! Its effect forty years ago on a young architect is described by Mr. G. Blaire Imrie who has told me how, coming upon Goddards by chance, he remembers standing spellbound by the complete accomplishment in the building 'of everything we were trying to do in those days'.

The begetter of this charming charity (later Sir Frederick Mirrielees, Bt., K.C.M.G.), was an Aberdonian who, after long residence in Russia and Persia, had settled near Dorking, and was the head of Currie and Co., merchant bankers. Lutyens observed him and his wife objectively:

> They are a good sort of small sort, but any amount of horses and a delicious country and numberless animals of all sorts. A new house (*Pasture Wood*), architect Flockhart—ornée, rather, comfortable—bad service, rather: I mean you go to dress and find your bag not unpacked, and in the morning the maid knocks timidly at one's door leaving cans and boots outside in timid propriety. Such a bore. Mrs. Mirrielees is a daughter of Sir D. Currie and will eventually come in for a million of money, so they say. So it is say I worth while to 'cultivate'. This sounds beastly and is, specially as they are wondrous kind and easy to get on with.

On another visit, July 11:

> Nine horses ill with inflammation of the lungs, two at point of death. They are being fed on beef tea, butter, and port wine!! Those that are better are having ale. I didn't know a horse would eat butter and beef tea—

which he illustrated with a picture of a horse holding up a glass of port, inscribed 'not a bad colour, too much body tho'', and with the note 'You try and make a horse sit on a chair!?'

The calculating gleam in the earlier of these two letters reflects a less attractive aspect of a rising architect on the make, yet its objectivity is the mood in which he must approach the technical factors in a new commission—and the first dispassionate estimate of the client usually warmed later into friendship, as in this case.

Overstrand Hall, Norfolk, was built for the 2nd Lord Hillingdon who had succeeded his father in the previous year. He was a partner in Glyn Mills, Currie & Co., and so associated in business with Sir Frederick Mirrielees; his wife, a Harbord, daughter of Lord Suffield. In this household, both wealthy and aristocratic, Lutyens felt himself in a more sympathetic atmosphere. 'I like Lord Hillingdon, he likes all I like and looks at things from the same point of view.' He appreciated his hostess's beautiful frocks, and was amused by her sisters' tailor-made 'county' turn-outs; also by his having to interview the chef, butler, and housekeeper about the technical requirements of their departments.

The house is more interesting than, perhaps, attractive: built round two courts of which the principal one, the Fountain Court (an elaboration in plan of Orchards) has, instead of a porch, a pleasant early renaissance loggia opposite the gateway. The plan is ingenious and dignified. But the elevations, in flint, brick, and half-timbering, with long runs of steep tiled roofs ending in tile-hung gables and plain brick chimney shafts, lack the picturesqueness of his best early works without having the classical orderliness that he was to evolve later to meet this contingency.

The Paris Exhibition opened on April 20, 1900, but the British Pavilion, in common with most of the buildings, was not finished and Paris was 'like a madwoman whose hair was full of straw and plaster'. Lutyens heartily disliked the contractors and foremen with whom he had to deal there; so unlike the English country builders he was accustomed to work with, speaking the common language of craftsmen and the countryside, and, so, spiritually akin to himself.

> These men act and do the jealous and say bitter nasty things. I should like a Bishop to be clerk of works and insist on morning prayers. It is the only way I see of getting any *esprit de corps* into these jealous gangs. One or two firms and their men are brilliant exceptions and I love them for it. Without exception the men reflect their employers' character.

By May the Pavilion was ready for opening and he had to escort thither a bust of Queen Victoria by Onslow Ford. In describing their journey he said:

> I have never travelled with the Queen before, so must remark on the auspicious occurrence. I feel quite calm and am still able to show an absolute *sang froid* in the face of the public, so necessary for the maintenance of self-dignity. If it is overdone one is liable to be mistaken for a footman. So the dignity must be just a bit self conscious. If overdone you become a snob. It is a very great art to appear natural—to be natural is surely fatal—whilst travelling with the Queen. And of the Queen—she was carefully waxed and laid on her back in a big deal square box with her crown put under her chin for safety. Being Sunday, she reverently stares skyward.
>
> It is a great day. I travel with the Queen!

It had been decreed that the Pavilion should be a reproduction of Kingston

House, Bradford-on-Avon—an unusually ornate early seventeenth-century manor house. The British exhibit had the great advantage, not shared by any other copies of national buildings in the '*Rue des Nations*', that the reproduction was on the same scale as the original, instead of a miniature replica. The interiors reproduced and combined famous period examples, the drawing-room being partly the Cartoon Gallery at Knole with a ceiling from Broughton Castle cast from moulds provided by the Victoria and Albert Museum. A bedroom was lined with Elizabethan oak panelling, and all the rooms were furnished with appropriate original furniture and important paintings of the English School. 'The Press were all very complimentary (and oh what a funny lot of people)' Lutyens recorded. Frederick Harrison reported of the Pavilion, 'it is the best and most truly artistic in the whole Street of Nations, the only one indeed that a man of taste could view without a smile or a groan.'

Two jests cheer Ned's account of the tedious ceremonies attending the Pavilion's opening. Regarding a Christmas present from his wife worn on the occasion:

> Your pin has been much admired. If asked who gave it me, I say the Queen —for singing at Windsor one evening—sounds so complete doesn't it?

And of Mrs. Eden, Gertrude Jekyll's sister and owner of a celebrated garden at Venice, whom he met at Col. Jekyll's Paris house:

> More like Bumps and the Colonel than either are to themselves: a nice tame smiling Colonel and a worldling Bumps mixed—uglier than either but more knowledge and care for clothes and everyday appearances. Her life is given up to a husband entirely selfish and self absorbed.

§2. A POET IN PRACTICE

In opening the Paris Pavilion at the end of the last Section we have anticipated events by a few months. But it will have illustrated one of the two conflicting trends most evident in Lutyens's development at the turn of the century: the growing scope and importance of his practice. The other was the perfecting of that quality in his architecture—present from the first, but now becoming predominant—which can

27. LINDISFARNE CASTLE, HOLY ISLAND, NORTHUMBERLAND

28. LINDISFARNE. The staircase to the gallery (1903–4)

29. MONKTON HOUSE, SINGLETON, SUSSEX (1902). South aspect

30. DANESHILL, BASING, HAMPSHIRE (1903). Entrance (north) front

31. NEW PLACE, SHEDFIELD, HAMPSHIRE (1905). Garden front

best be described as poetic. To define the poetry of architecture might require an essay to itself, but essentially it implies, when referring to romantic building of the early Lutyens type, such a union of visual harmonies, structural intricacies, overtones, fantasy, and technical skill, that the result stirs in the beholder a spontaneous delight akin to that produced by a good poet by similar means. As Lutyens's command of his medium extended and became more assured, he dared further, with growing success, to charge his buildings with the intensity of his feeling.

The danger was that, with his rapidly increasing practice, the poetic artist in him would be overlaid by technical and professional cares. That this never took place—that to the end of his life, despite the most intensive application to his enormous and spectacular practice, despite honours and fame, he succeeded in maintaining the spiritual elasticity of youth—was the abiding puzzle to his contemporaries and, indeed, is the most extraordinary characteristic of his life. It was undoubtedly this dualism that enabled him to achieve his singular position as an architect, in which he contrived to unite the romantic ideal, of always doing and saying exactly what he felt should be done and said, with the insistent claims of professional efficiency. In architecture, of all professions, it is the psychological difficulty of preserving, amid its pressing material considerations, the ingenuousness of the creative artist, which constitutes the greatness of the very few who have achieved it. Lutyens had the advantage, as he sometimes admitted, of never entirely growing up in the worldly sense. There is no doubt that he consciously and intentionally, preserved his innocence, sensing that that was the creative part of his being.

It was at this stage of his career that he had to evolve a practical method of self-protection consistent with extending his work. Hitherto he had had no staff to speak of at the Grays Inn office. His first assistant, before his marriage, was the pious and melancholy Barlow. In the autumn of 1898 he engaged his first secretarial assistant, named Dalton. 'Rather a good find, I think,' he wrote, '—shorthand, a gentleman, A1 accountant and wont mind opening the door; a first class character from Col. Spencer whose servant he was throughout the Berber campaign with the Camel Corps; cheap at 25/- a week.'

He now also took into a kind of partnership E. Baynes Badcock, whose qualifications for relieving him of the grind of routine work seemed equally good. He was a persuasive talker, an athlete who had jumped for Cambridge University, something of a big-game hunter, fond of fishing, and owned an interest in a firm of builders. Moreover, he had a charming wife, who was an artist, and a cottage at Rhayader where the four spent an enjoyable holiday.

What Lutyens needed was a business manager, to handle the technical and financial side of his practice. Other architects at this stage of their careers generally go into partnership. He, however, was too much of an individualist to consider sharing artistic responsibility, and, at this stage certainly, too anxious for the bank-balance to submit to its partition with anybody. To avoid these commitments, it appears that he entered into a friendly arrangement with Badcock, probably made piecemeal, whereby Badcock might take work on his own account and use identical note-paper with his own name instead of Lutyens's on it, whilst acting as technical partner. It is not clear what salary, if any, he was to receive, but some emolument was due to him on contracts above a certain value, and Lutyens undertook to introduce him to his worth-while clients.

It was a curious arrangement, which no one but a romantic idealist would expect to work for long. However, for the time being the two men got on well enough, and it enabled Lutyens to produce some of his most exciting early houses.

Ten years had now passed since the building of Crooksbury, and that week-end cottage was now required for the permanent residence of an augmented family, involving its being more than doubled in size. Lutyens the artist revolted from the notion of extending the scale of the original building, with its Norman-Shaw-Medieval design, in the same style. He felt that the addition must represent stylistically the passage of time, and the whole, including the addition, be composed anew. The addition, therefore, took the form of a brick William-and-Mary wing (p. 69) such as might have been added two centuries later to a yeoman's hall, but in this case turning its back literally on the old gables and weather-tiling of the nucleus, to which he connected it only by a long neck of passage. The transition between the two blocks he managed by juggling sensitively with chimney-breasts, balcony, jutting roofs, and a pergola for vines in front of them. The old nucleus was left unaltered and continued to provide the entrance from a forecourt redesigned in terms of Wren and overlooked by new William-and-Mary stables. The new garden front was his first experiment in a renaissance elevation, though, with its doorway off-centre, casement windows, and asymmetrical chimneys, the source of it was still homely—the houses of Surrey farmers who had prospered under the Corn Laws. This front, so interesting as a biographical document, no longer exists and has since been remodelled internally also.

This method of extending a house, with additions in an entirely different style but so designed as to compose a picturesque harmony, was used again at Ashby St. Ledgers, Folly Farm, Lambay, Clifford Chambers, and elsewhere. The pergola in the Fig Court at Crooksbury, as it is called (p. 69) corresponds to the brick cloister linking the symmetrical little house at Folly Farm to his barn-like addition. But at Crooksbury the combination of such unconventional shapes as round windows and sharp-roofed turret, the handling of the balcony on the right (with Lady Chapman looking over it), and the original effect produced by the pergola in relation to the various roof lines—although these varied elements are not wholly resolved—suggest that, had he pursued this free way of designing, it would have led him to modernity.

No wonder he expected, at the time, that Sir Arthur Chapman might be startled at first sight of the drawings.

At the beginning of 1899 he was in one of his rare moods of despondency. 'Business and letters all day—no designing and drawing—and I always feel it a day wasted.' 'Depressed. Money matters seem all right but now it is my work. It aint good enough—and I dont work hard enough or think enough. ... I do wish I could make a greater name for you and Barbara and me. Do pray I may have the gift of doing *good* work.' Yet good work, in either sense, was not begotten, he was certain, by affectation of moral rightness nor yet of pre-eminent virtue.

> Wish I had the Welwyn church to do. Schultz [a fellow student in Ernest George's office] was at Athens measuring and drawing for some Society. He draws beautifully but is himself a coarse swearing sort of chap. Burgess the great church builder used to 'damn' the Bishops to their faces!! So much for the pose of a saintly frame of mind to beget Church work!

The relevance or otherwise of high-mindedness and great literature as inspiration to good architecture was a topic on which he had often argued, and was to continue arguing for years, with Herbert Baker. Lutyens held that 'the poet can inspire another artist, but once inspired he (the artist) should go to work, not dissipate his inspiration and emotions by absorbing more poetry. ... The poet in the architect can only be expressed in his building'.[1]

Though he propounded that truth long afterwards, he demonstrated it in practice a few months later. Deanery Garden, Sonning, may be called without overstatement a perfect architectural sonnet, compounded of brick and tile and timber forms, in which his handling of the masses and spaces serve as rhythm: its theme, a romantic bachelor's idyllic afternoons beside a Thames backwater. For Deanery Garden and Marsh Court (which came soon afterwards), both poems of building, are alike emanations from rivers—the emblem to Lutyens of happiness, and beside which as a fly-fisher he found almost his only and by much his most loved recreation.

Deanery Garden was commissioned by Edward Hudson, managing director of *Country Life*, the paper that he had founded in 1897 and of which from the first the central feature was an illustrated article on an old or new country house. Lutyens had almost certainly owed his introduction to him to Miss Jekyll, who contributed garden notes to his paper. The connection of the two men, thus initiated, developed into a life-long friendship and must be numbered with Lutyens's marriage and collaboration with Miss Jekyll among the more fortunate events of his career. For Hudson, conceiving a boundless admiration for the architect, not only gave him all his subsequent commissions but proceeded to publish in *Country Life* illustrated

[1] To Herbert Baker, January 29, 1911.

accounts of his principal buildings.[1] The work of most other domestic architects was publicised in the same paper, but not quite so regularly or fully.

Hudson and Lutyens had much in common in their natures. Both were largely self-educated, with an instinctive appreciation of beauty; both were inarticulate, Hudson finding his means of expression in his publications. Through *Country Life* Hudson exerted a far-reaching influence on the domestic architecture of the early twentieth century, popularising those aspects that he admired with results comparable to Ruskin's in the nineteenth century and Lord Burlington's in the eighteenth. Lutyens in addition benefitted from Hudson's shrewd common-sense and business acumen. Whilst he addressed him as 'Huddy', the latter got no further than 'Lutyens' throughout thirty-six years. Lutyens rightly esteemed Hudson 'a brick', but after many years' experience of his always kind but sometimes clumsy good nature, added 'he had no hands'—in the horse-master's sense.

The inspiration of Deanery Garden was an old brick wall, between river and village street, enclosing what was an ancient orchard. The house, set against the northerly section of this wall, lies round three sides of a paved fountain court with a chalk-vaulted cloister leading through to the garden. House and garden are a single interpenetrating conception—parts roofed over, others open to the sun, with the garden walks leading right into and about the house, and the windows placed to catch the sparkle of a pool or complete the pattern of a terrace. Using brick and chalk instead of rubble masonry, with intensified discipline and subtlety, the conception can be seen to have grown out of Orchards, achieving completely the interpenetration of house and garden there essayed. Deanery Garden, at once formal and irregular, virtually settled that controversy, of which Sir Reginald Blomfield and William Robinson were for long the protagonists, between formal and naturalistic garden design. Miss Jekyll's naturalistic planting wedded Lutyens's geometry in a balanced union of both principles (p. 70).

Tigbourne Court was built at the same time for Mr. Edgar Horne. Its exceedingly gay gabled front and curving wings are to be seen beside the Petworth road just south of Witley. The site was determined by the existence of well matured gardens belonging to a cottage which was preserved and incorporated in the stables. The client was a warm admirer of the architect whom he half jokingly compared to a modern Inigo Jones, and evidently expected something exciting. In essence Tigbourne is an application in Bargate stone, with garretted joints, tile roofs and quoins, of the Munstead-Orchards type. But in the road elevation Lutyens gave his high spirits free rein. The triple gabled front above a recessed loggia-porch is flanked by single-storey wings (kitchen, left; drawing-room, right) which end in immense chimneys. These ends have concave angles, the outer of which sweep back in high

---

[1] Collected in 1913 as *Houses and Gardens by E. L. Lutyens*, by Lawrence Weaver. The first article published was on Crooksbury, September 1900, probably written by Miss Jekyll.

semi-circular screen walls containing arches. All these walls are contoured with tile bands which emphasise their curves. The parts are architecturally coherent and it is a remarkable exercise of his early virtuosity, corresponding, one might say, in his evolution to the geometrical fantasies of John Thorpe in that of domestic architecture (p. 80).

Overstrand Hall, Goddards, Deanery Garden, Tigbourne Court, first designs for Grey Walls, and alterations to Calcot Park near Reading for Captain Mills occupied the remainder of 1899. In September, work worth £30,000 was listed, prospectively yielding £1500 in fees, pending which, however, Ned became so apprehensive about his bank balance that in January 'a cheque from Mills for £400 relieves my Ladysmith'. Two will-o'-the-wisps beckoned short cuts to fortune during this millenial but difficult year. During its last months Lee Hill, managing director of the Savoy, invited him to make sketches for interior redecorations of the hotel, but his proposals were not adopted. Four years later Lutyens wrote, 'I hear they have spent £300,000 on the Savoy. If only I had got that job! It would have been £15,000.'

The other excitement, which petered out, was a commission in the Spring of 1901 for laying out a sea-side garden village at Rossall Beach, on the Lancashire coast near Blackpool, for Mr. Lumb. Lutyens described it as 'my new Town' and estimated that the shell of it would cost about £400,000. As he had been upset about his overdraft at the New Year, Mr. Lumb's proposal was highly encouraging. He was prepared to pay £100 for sketches, and the architect was to receive $2\frac{1}{2}$ per cent on general building except for the church, hotel and similar public buildings. Unfortunately the speculation came to nothing. The layout was partly executed but only one of Lutyens's houses was built—occupied by Mr. Lumb himself. All the other lots were eventually filled by ordinary villas.

At this juncture—March 1901—Badcock gave notice to terminate his agreement. To all his associations in life and work Lutyens brought his peculiar innocence, of which one aspect was his assumption that no legal agreement was needed to ensure that those with whom he had dealings would be actuated by impulses any less virtuous than his own. In his single-minded enthusiasm for his art, too, he was prone to assume like enthusiasm, and even more disinterestedness, in others. Another obstacle to sound professional relationships was a tendency to rely on an aesthetic scale of values in judging human character, so that when, as generally happened sooner or later, a colleague's work fell short of the Lutyens standard, then his moral and intellectual worth declined correspondingly. A bad architect must be failing in truth and therefore a bad, or at any rate a dishonest man.

The occasion of the breach was Lutyens chancing at a railway station to run into Badcock going fishing when he was supposed to be going to inspect a building. But the dissatisfaction appears to have been mutual. 'I am in very low position', wrote Lutyens, 'because he has neglected my work. He says he neglects my work because I do not introduce him. If I do introduce him he is familiar.' The works in which Badcock participated are given as: Fisher's Hill; Woolverstone (? St. Peter's Home, Ipswich, for Lord Berners); additions to Rake House; Tigbourne Court; Varengeville; house in Little College St., Westminster; Littlecroft, Guildford; cottages at Apsley End, Herts., and Old Basing—none of them among Lutyens's more notable undertakings. Paris, Sonning, Grey Walls, Rossall Beach, Overstrand, Abbotswood, and Marsh Court are specifically excepted as 'I alone'.

Lutyens sought the advice of Hudson ('a brick', 'an angel') who introduced him to his solicitor Mr. (later Lord) Riddell and assured him that he need have no anxiety in the matter. With the settling of certain disputed arrears of payments due, the incident ended in a dignified manner. But shortly afterwards Lutyens noted with chagrin that Princess Louise had transferred her patronage to Mr. Badcock for work at Cowes, and of course he was left, at an exceptionally busy period, without his chief assistant.

Then Dalton, the admirable secretary, bolted; with £400 from the cash-box and an attractive housemaid from the domestic side of 29 Bloomsbury Square. His successor for a time was Nigel Severn, son of the artist Arthur Severn; and in 1902 the position of manager was filled by A. J. Thomas who continued to be Lutyens's trusted left-hand man for thirty-three years, entirely solving the problem of the poet in practice. It was at this period that the series of pupils and assistants, many of whom were to make names for themselves in future, came together in the office: Norman Evill, Sidney Evans, Maxwell Ayrton, Horace Farquharson, J. D. Coleridge, Oswald Milne, Paul Phipps, Nicholas Hannen and the rest, some of whose impressions of their service under Lutyens will be found in the Section devoted to the Office in Chapter VII.

§3. SPIRIT AND SUBSTANCE

In all his romantic houses Lutyens observed the cardinal principle of Morrisian picturesque doctrine: that the design be conceived in terms of the local material. An early writer on Marsh Court in *Country Life* (E. March Phillipps, in 1906) expressed this conviction forcibly by saying, 'We are never very far from humbug and pretence when we lose touch of native character, native scenery, and native material,' and claiming that the main attraction in Lutyens's work was the strength and certainty in it due to the regaining of that touch. A raciness of the soil was a large element in the poetry of his early houses, particularly where he knew and loved the land, but he never lapsed into homespun. A bigger element in his successful designs was the extent to which all the contributory factors fused into a spontaneous conception. This did not happen always. In some cases the result gives a sense of labour, instead of that delicious sense of effortless ease where his genius flashed.

Neither at Grey Walls (1900) nor Marsh Court (1901), remarkable buildings as they are, do we quite get that feeling. But in two immediately subsequent designs the perfect fusing of the elements is not only felt but can be proved to have taken place.

Grey Walls, at Gullane (p. 80), on the edge of the famous Muirfield golf links, had an unusually prolonged gestation. It was built for Alfred Lyttelton—the cricketer, golfer, statesman, and valued friend to Lutyens till his death in 1913—and was already under discussion in 1896. At that time it was to be called High Walls and to have been of a lofty, fortress-like character. Mrs. Lyttelton apparently took exception to the small windows designed to emphasise by contrast the massiveness that was to be the 'poetry' of the whole; to which Lutyens rejoined, briefly, 'Mrs. Lyttleton can't have a fortress and large windows too,' illustrating that truth with

two sketches. The result is remarkable for being entirely unlike anything he had designed before; he evidently observed the lowland Scottish tradition of building; but the conception was certainly not spontaneous, as indeed appears from its curious plan and varied parts. The elliptical front, the most attractive feature of the design, was perhaps a remnant of High Walls turned inside out (the original designs, existing till quite recently, have unfortunately all been destroyed). Framed between big chimneys, it is a delicious shape with its curving horizontal planes, white casement windows and Georgian doorway. The walls are rubble of a rich cream colour, the roof grey Dutch pantiles. Sections of these are inlaid in the window lintels and by their repeating curves (garretted with dots of red tile) enliven the simple texture of the façades. A big tea-room attached to the east corner is delicious garden architecture, with its early instance of that rich texture—employed later so effectively at Lindisfarne and Lambay—which Lutyens got with tiles or slates and thick mortar. The lines of the approach, joined with the lodges added later for Mr. Willie James, equally foreshadowed in miniature his big designs in formal layout. The blend of renaissance and romantic impulses so appealing at Grey Walls is typical of this phase—it enters into each of the subsequent buildings in this section, and in none more happily.

Already the designs were in hand of Marsh Court on the River Test (p. 81), the most sensational of these early Edwardian houses, for a typical Edwardian. Herbert Johnson, 'adventurer', stockjobber, and sportsman, had noticed the photographs of Crooksbury in *Country Life* and sought its architect. 'Johnnie' and Ned, perceiving one another's greatnesses, became life-long friends.[1] Lutyens came to love his courage, vigour, and honesty which, with more than a touch of flamboyance, he worked into the building. The architect's love of rivers, too, and of chalk-streams and downland in particular, undoubtedly helped, as at Deanery Garden, to shape what has been called a *tour-de-force*, this unique and elaborate structure of hewn chalk.

'Clunch', from the hard lower beds of the chalk, had been used in the Middle Ages for vaulting, in Salisbury Cathedral, for example; commonly for the internal walling of churches; and in conjunction with flint and brick for cottages up till the seventeenth century; but had rarely been used since, until by Lutyens for vaulting at Deanery Garden. Use of it as the principal material, on such a scale, was therefore daring in the architect and betokened bold faith in him on the part of the client. There is evidence, in the sketch for his imaginary 'little white house', which Ned made for Lady Emily to put by in the Casket, and which looks like the embryo of Marsh Court, that he had long hoped for a chance to build in chalk. Besides the lure of re-establishing a common but neglected building material, it must have attracted him for its whiteness, which enabled him to realise his conception exactly, without introducing adventitious colour in stone and weathering: just white and russet-red. And he was, one feels, particularly drawn to the idea of moulding into a house the substance of the landscape that he preferred to all others.

Romantic scenery, in the common acceptance of the term, and particularly 'views', bored him. They were emotional and unsettling, just as he mistrusted the emotional appeal of colour in painting. But the clean contours, simplicity, and low tones of chalkland scenery seem to have excited his aesthetic sense without disturbing his emotions. He most enjoyed the scenery of India and South Africa when it reminded him of Hampshire downland. In a train in the middle of Bengal, he ex-

[1] Herbert Johnson was the ideal type of Lutyens client. Born 1856, the son of a clergyman, he had sought his fortune in the City, where an uncanny flair for figures and the stock-market's pulse had enabled him, by 1900, to make £500,000. He was still a bachelor, devoted to every form of open-air life and, subsequently, to every stone of the extraordinary house that Lutyens contrived to make symbolic of his adventurous traditionism. He lost a fortune and made another, married a widow who brought him step-daughters (later Lady Apsley and Lady Somers), became Master of the Hursley Hunt, and in 1929 added a ballroom to the house. In his later, solitary years fortune turned against him, his sight began to fail and by 1938 he was totally blind and partially deaf. Yet almost to ninety-three, he preserved the physical vigour of a man of fifty, conquering his blindness to the extent of being able to run down the steep slope to the river and cross it by a plank unaided. In 1940 he was obliged to let Marsh Court and at the end of the war to sell it. He died in 1949.

claimed of the country he was passing through, 'Hampshire is the mother of many scenes'.

Marsh Court is the work into which he put his feeling for this maternal chalkland, as Thakeham expresses the combination in Sussex of down and weald, Deanery Garden the Thames valley, Lindisfarne the ruggedness of the Northumbrian coast, and Lambay the soft grey mystery of that isle in the Irish Sea. At Marsh Court, the chalk walls, with here and there an embedded flint sticking out, rise like a cliff on the lower side, the parapet and chimneys silhouetted against the sky. But on the approach side the russet roofs are spread like the brown blankets of fallow fields over the chalk contours.

This external evidence of his special interest in the design is confirmed on close inspection. A casual glance at photographs might lead the modern reader to dismiss it as a 'stunt' in Tudor style. None of Lutyens's architecture can ever be so dismissed, and least of all Marsh Court. One may not 'like' it; a tenant called it 'that ghastly house'; but to see and examine it is a memorable architectural experience. It is a visual embodiment of that zestful vitality which we associate with Elizabethan England. But it was the spirit, not the style, that was revived here; the Elizabethan form, though appropriate, is incidental. The vehicle of this intense activation of spirit was Lutyens's perfected art in building. Marsh Court is a great work of building art.

From the tiered, rectangular framework of garden formed by brick paths, chalk and flint walls, and the intricacies of the surprising sunk garden under one end of the front, the white walls of the house seem to shoot up to the spiralled and fluted brick chimney shafts set on bases of brick and chalk checkerwise, which rise from the parapet diapered in bands of chalk and tiles. Brick, tiles, and in the lower courses flint, texture the chalk throughout, handled with thrilling verve and yet restraint. Notwithstanding its elaboration the effect is monumental, simplified by the uninterrupted blanket of roof which, on the entrance front and in the more distant views, is seen to dominate the composition. Herbert Johnson's enthusiasm no doubt worked on Lutyens's exuberance, enriching the first simple idea of 'the little white house'. In places, especially within, it may be felt that the care and invention were carried too far. The oak timbers and white walls delight; a billiard table of solid chalk ('to chalk your cue') as massive as an altar astonishes; but in some of the rooms our stomachs, weaker than the Edwardians', may not be able to take such rich fare. A masterpiece it is, essentially of craftsmanship. But perhaps we miss the impression of spontaneous wholeness that characterises his happiest works—some of the most successful of which he can be shown to have conceived, in all essentials, within a few hours of first visiting the site.

Abbotswood, Stow-on-the-Wold, was an adaptation of a nineteenth-century gabled house of no particular interest, for Mark Fenwick, a country gentleman with business interests, a noted amateur gardener, and fisherman. His introduction to

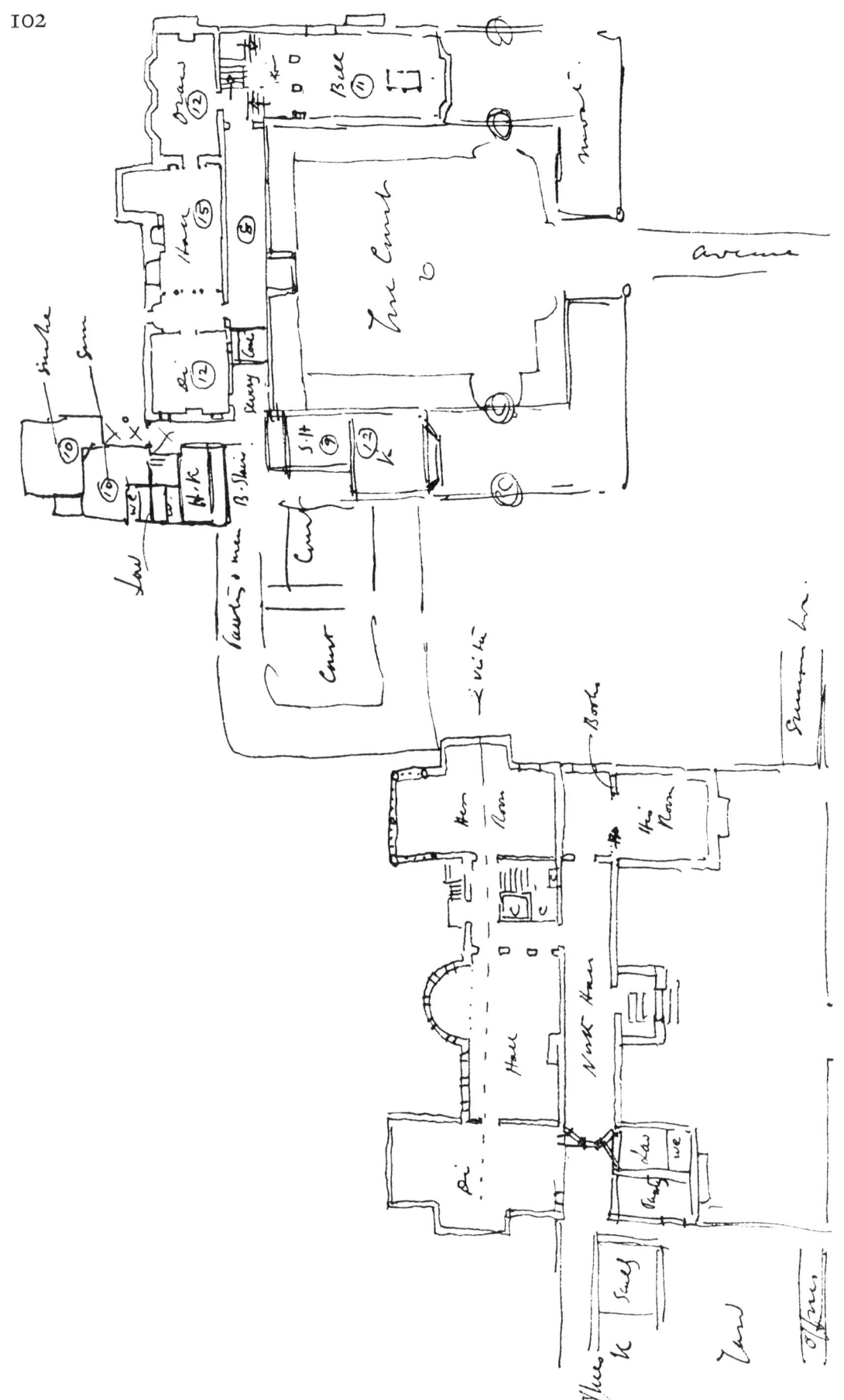

Little Thakeham (left) and Marsh Court (right). Comparative Sketch Plans, from a Letter to Herbert Baker, Feb. 15, 1903

Lutyens, who became a friend of the family, was through Miss Jekyll whom he had visited at Munstead. Mrs. Fenwick was a daughter of Nathaniel Clayton of Chesters, Northumberland, for whom Norman Shaw had designed that remarkable classical house. Abbotswood, as rebuilt, is an essay in Cotswold masonry in which Lutyens re-affirmed his conviction that additions should not follow the style of an existing nucleus. The result is not an unqualified success: a renaissance front door set in a gigantic gable, rising almost from ground level to the ridge above the second floor, is more curious than attractive. But the composition of the adjoining side, where the window of the principal room overhangs a lily pool and alcove fountain between a pair of tall sharp gables, was excitingly novel. The alcove fountain is the earliest appearance in his work of this subsequently much used feature.

In both Marsh Court and Abbotswood his increasing attention to renaissance forms is notable—the interiors of the latter are wholly Georgian, and Marsh Court has a hall of elaborate 'Wrenaissance' beauty (p. 81). At Little Thakeham, Sussex, the house which he himself thought 'the best of the bunch', and which was designed in this year, the transition of allegiance is clearly seen (p. 82). Thakeham, incidentally, was another instance (as at Orchards) of a client commissioning Lutyens when already committed to another architect; in this case to the extent of the walls already having begun to rise. Ernest Blackburn, who was an amateur gardener of exceptional skill, was dissatisfied with the designs of his architect, Hatchard Smith, and consulted Lutyens upon the possibility of his converting what had been begun as a brick house into something more in the character of Munstead Wood or Orchards. Lutyens refused to displace another architect on a building already begun and declared that, anyhow, the existing work could not be used. Blackburn then proceeded to pull down most of what had been built, when he again approached Lutyens, who accepted the commission in August, 1902. Oswald Milne, who was a pupil in the office at the time, remembers Lutyens returning from a preliminary visit to Thakeham and giving him the complete design roughed out in the train on squared paper.

The local stone used for Thakeham, of marble-like consistency but brittle, necessitated massive, simple treatment and marries happily with the russet tiles and bricks of the chimneys. The plan of the house has much in common with Marsh Court, an H entered across a walled forecourt on the north (in the middle, as there also, of a long corridor-hall). These elements come together with the sweet inevitability of a traditional manor house. They give an impression of certainty on the part of the architect but without that over-emphasis which at Marsh Court betrays some underlying uncertainty. This is the quality which distinguishes Lutyens at his best. It is the more remarkable in this case since, in the big hall which occupies the whole of the centre on the garden side, he abandoned vernacular for classical idiom entirely. The staircase filling the end of the hall, in combination with a classic rendering of a medieval hall screen, is one of the outstanding instances in his work of a complicated problem solved with that originality and skill which makes it appear simple. It is clear evidence, too, that Lutyens's accomplishment had by now attained the pitch at which the loose articulations of his romantic work hitherto were becoming too easy to stimulate his imagination. He needed to get his teeth into the more complex, more resistant medium of the Orders. Looking at the elevations of Thakeham again in this light, at the beautiful clarity of the garden plan, one realises that it is essentially classical in all but style; like some Carolean manor houses that maintained vernacular tradition although Inigo Jones had already built his Banqueting House.

The same is apparent in two small houses—Homewood at Knebworth built for his mother-in-law in 1901, and Monkton, near Singleton, for Mr. Willie James. The former, which evolved after long discussion, is in essence one of those pretty little gabled houses, with weather-tiled upper floors, to which the young aspire and the elderly withdraw, but which Lutyens here converted into a rustic trianon. Monkton, on the top of the West Sussex downs, was actually required to be a trianon, and was built as imagined on the spot (p. 92). We have his first-hand account of its conception, written a few hours afterwards (March 15, 1902):

> This morning we motored to the site, 4 miles then a mile and a half walk. Site quite lovely. Beech, heather, gorse, thorn, grass, down, with views across hills and Chichester to the Channel. They want a small house for Mrs. James and the children to go to in hot weather when West Dean becomes relaxing. They liked my ideas . . . a house about the size of Homewood, but there will be additions of cloisters etc. and a more generous layout to a gorgeous South view.

There we have, in his own words, the origin of that quality of assured conviction that makes itself so strongly felt both here and at Thakeham: Lutyens's power of spontaneous conception. It is evident that, on this first visit to the site of Monkton, he succeeded in visualising the house complete in its broad essentials. 'They liked my ideas'—evidently he made other suggestions than those mentioned. By the time he got home the sketch design was more or less complete, ready for scaling up. The result, as he said, is a larger Homewood, with a similar recessed centre to the front, but the dwarf pavilions there have here grown into blunt wings, with sleeping porches above sun-rooms beneath a portico formed by a couple of columns carrying the roof. To either flank loggias—long roofs carried on piers—enclose three sides of the tiny garden formed out of the downland. The spectacular feature is the two square columns of the portico, built up of tiles on brick bases and with a lovely entasis: a preposterous material for free-standing columns but how fitting for these, buttressed by the arches and balustrades of the porches! In its general silhouette, too, with enveloping Mansard roof and three plain chimneys, Monkton is the prototype of all the Lutyensish medium-sized houses that became standard twenty years later.

He approved the final Monkton drawings the night before the postponed Coronation of Edward VII.

A few weeks later Hudson published designs 'from the hand of Mr. E. L. Lutyens, whose work, by its structural excellence in all materials, especially in brick and timber and by its good sense and good taste, has won lasting reputation in every department of country architecture', for repairing the old bridges over the Thames at Sonning.[1] The County Council was proposing to replace this picturesque structure, partly of brick and partly of timber, with one of steel girders. Lutyens showed how most of the brick arches could be retained and proposed replacing the old wooden approaches to them by stout oak piles resting on brick piers and carrying a concrete carriage-way with oak-framed hand-rails. It was a characteristically effective application of traditional timber structure. He made use of its principles in the little rampart-bridge at Lambay (p. 111), and many years later in his timber bridge at Plumpton (p. 490) and over the Pilgrim's Way.

Another small, romantical, house dating from this *annus mirabilis*, was of greater importance to his future work than might be imagined from its design. It is true that Daneshill, at Old Basing, (p. 92), shows in its entrance front that new breadth and simplicity which underlay Lutyens's transition to the classic mode and which Thakeham typifies. But it is more notable for the beautiful craftsmanship of the brick and tile work for which Lutyens here, unlike his earlier essays in vernacular brickwork, had access to first-class material. His client, Walter Hoare, had started the Old Basing brickfields with a view to producing supplies of hand-made bricks of fine quality, hitherto only available from Holland. He succeeded in recapturing the colour and texture of Tudor brick, which the front of Daneshill was largely designed to display. Lutyens further designed for him a number of special shapes—jambs, mullions, sills, parapets and the like. A building that dates from this year (1903) and may be mentioned here, though it more properly belongs to the next chapter, was the Mount (Amesbury) School, Hindhead. Its interest is romantic in quality for it became the scene, before D-Day, of Lord Montgomery's short periods of rest when planning the invasion of France, having been his son's preparatory school. The building, added to an earlier nondescript house, is a brick range in the pure Wren manner with a central pediment and modillioned cornice recalling Morden College.

'I am *so* busy,' he reported to Lady Emily that August, 'I have £860 in the bank and £180 accounts sent out—£1040: but then I have to pay out £60 or £70 this month, which spoils my £1000 balance. But we are getting on aren't we? And I am I think working keenly and with some confidence and definiteness.'

[1] *Country Life*, October 4, 1902. (p. 421.) One of his designs is reproduced here, at the end of this chapter, p. 117.

§4. ISLANDS OF ROMANCE

The big event of this time was Edward Hudson's decision to sell Deanery Garden and plunge into mortar again by putting in hand the restoration of Lindisfarne Castle (p. 91). It had been in January 1902, when Lutyens was on a progress-visit to Grey Walls, that Hudson had telegraphed him 'have got Lindisfarne' and asked him to look in at the place on his way south. The designs were generally approved, a few days after the Coronation, during a week-end party at Deanery Garden, at which Lutyens also met Mrs. Belleville—who commissioned Papillon Hall. Lindisfarne, a St. Michael's Mount approachable at low water from the coast, was made by Aidan and Cuthbert the matrix of Northumbrian Christianity. The ruins of the abbey, that succeeded the primitive mother-church of Durham, still stand on the lower ground of the island where it was a constant prey of Danes and Scots. The massive walls crowning the crag above it were those not of a medieval castle but of the fort established after the monastery's dissolution at the time of Lord Hertford's Scottish Expedition in 1543–4, for which the island served as a base. The Border Survey of 1550 schedules 'The Fort of Beblowe' which 'lyeth very well for the defence of the haven there'. A century later, in 1639, another military expedition against the Scots occasioned a more circumstantial report:

> Wee rode over to Holy Island when the tyde was out. It is about 5 mile in compasse, a level ground with a short green swarde upon it, noe part of it tilled nor affording anything but conies... There is a pretty fort on it which upon this occasion was repaired and put into forme... The Captain at our being there was Captain Rugg, knowne commonly by his great nose.

When Hudson and Lutyens first saw it, the shell of this structure, rising out of the almost sheer crags, stood derelict. A sloping way climbs from east to west round the south end of the rock to a platform and portcullissed door. Going through this you climb a flight of steps which curves back under part of the building and comes out on the Lower Battery—an embrasured terrace commanding the southern approach. The building which forms the Battery's inner side—the front of the fort—had to be partly rebuilt by Lutyens and contains the entry hall and kitchen with bedrooms over.

The keynote of his treatment of the inside is given by burly pillars that support round arches, across the entrance hall and are seen elsewhere (p. 91). At first sight they are Norman, then we notice that the columns differ and in each case die away into the floor without bases. These piers, in effect, are Romance without period, which defines his method throughout the Castle. From the hall a passage hewn out of the rock leads to two vaulted chambers at right angles to it— the dining-room and the Ship room—which were little altered but for the insertion of big hearths and traceried windows in place of loopholes in cavernous embrasures. From the hall end of the same passage a staircase, also cut through the rock, climbs irregularly to a stout doorway opening into the open air of the Upper Battery. Near the foot of the stairs another ascent has branched off towards the pair of coupled arches illustrated, through which, up more steps, a glimpse is caught of the raftered ceiling of a long gallery stretching mysteriously away. This gallery is nearly all Lutyens and was built to serve the row of bedrooms facing north over the vaulted chambers and to connect up a detached mass known as the Guardhouse standing on the Upper Battery. The gallery, with its run of mullioned windows facing south and doorway on to the Upper Battery, was the sunniest place to sit, and an exciting one too with its wide arched hearth and vista of arches down the stairs.

The dwelling is thus not big, four reception and nine bedrooms, and really quite small in scale. Except that there was only one bathroom—a shortage common to many houses built at this date—it is comfortable and workable. But it is almost unique in the degree to which it satisfies the feeling of eerie excitement felt first whilst crossing the sands, worked up by the shrieks of swooping gulls as one climbs the rock path, and brought to the boil in staggering up tortuous steps to battery after battery. The poetry of the building derives from the effects having been got almost entirely by structural means—walls, vaults, apertures—and in the avoiding of all but the broadest suggestion of 'period'. Consequently there is no hint of faking and so of make belief: the new masonry is as generously devised as the old but its profiles are not copies, they are solutions attained by reviewing the old mason's traditions afresh: the romance is real.

Simultaneously with beginning on Lindisfarne, Lutyens made additions and gardens to Buckhurst Park, Sussex, for R. H. Benson (p. 109). This was a gabled house by J. A. Repton, recasing parts of an Elizabethan building in the romantic manner of about 1830, and the owner was to make it 'a treasure house of pictures and furniture, textiles and ceramics' besides laying out a 'balanced progression of formal and wild gardens'.[1] Lutyens's part was to extend the garden front with a big music room and other rooms; to remodel the existing ground floor as a big library in prolongation; and lay out formal gardens in front of them. The additions are interesting as the first appearance in his work of that modified, massive, Tudor idiom—with polygonal bows, tall transomed windows, and continuous coped parapets—which he developed later at Castle Drogo and Abbey House. The addition contrasts forcibly with Repton's pinnacled gables. But the transition is softened by a low, pantiled, Italianate loggia with frieze of fat sculptured swags of fruit; a concession, perhaps, to the owner's Italian tastes, as was certainly the remodelling of the library with Venetian arches of statuary and coloured marbles set in oak wainscot, to go with a collection of Primitive paintings.

[1] H. A. Tipping, in *Country Life*, May 11, 1912.

Another and bigger work of adaptation, initiated in 1903, was that of Ashby St. Ledgers, in Northamptonshire, which the late Lord Wimborne (then the Hon. Ivor Guest) had bought (p. 109). The rambling old house was originally the home of the Catesbys, implicated in the Gun Powder Plot. Lutyens was intermittently engaged there till 1939, linking up and extending the varied but predominantly Jacobean buildings and devising the gardens. The client throughout was definite on his requirements and possessed the will to obtain it. The result has much of charm and interest, but it is impossible in short space to give a coherent account of the complex operation which was rather one of those romantic games on the part of a wealthy man (of which the exaggeration of Hever and St. Donat's Castles are less justifiable instances) than a work of architecture. In the garden pond illustrated, the corner on the left is 17th century; in the rest of it, for almost the only time, Lutyens kept predominantly within the stylistic idioms prescribed by old work, though a great hall gave him the occasion for an original timber roof. Better representative of his picturesque work in this connection is the row of cottages built at the same time and place (p. 110). A letter of August 15, 1905 throws a light on the general position then prevailing:

> Ivor Guest talks of going on with the house etc. and the gardens, the house at some indefinite period, the gardens at once. He is nicely outspoken. The cottages are to go on. I have got another £300 for them and a lot of stone and other material, so the price has become possible.

There are four cottages with parlour, kitchen-scullery, and three bedrooms, but in the usage of the time, which made cottage planning easy, without bathroom and with only earth sanitation. Their pictorial quality, with stout brick chimney stacks, sweep of Norfolk reed thatch, and old masonry used in the lower courses of the walls, made considerable stir at the time. Excluding the material supplied, the estimated cost came to £1500.

The year 1904, and more particularly its end, will be shown in the next chapter to have been the decisive time of Lutyens's transition from predominantly picturesque to predominantly renaissance design. In that year Marsh Court and Little Thakeham, Monkton and Daneshill, Buckhurst and Papillon Hall were finished or nearing completion. The most important new commission, apart from the cakes and ale of Ashby St. Ledgers, was *Country Life's* office—inspired by Wren at Hampton Court. Besides Lindisfarne, there was in hand a house in France, *La Mascotte* for Mme. de Montbrison, and Miss Jekyll's speculation in building a small house at Bramley called Millmead— of which Wren was also the grandfather. There was talk with Hudson, too, leading to a survey and designs, about restoring Lympne Castle, Kent, which came to nothing and eventually brought Robert Lorimer from Scotland to do it for H. J. Tennant.

It is no wonder that Lutyens was becoming known as an extremely busy architect. This reputation began to deter some clients. Mrs. Franklyn, discussing the

32. BUCKHURST PARK, SUSSEX. Additions made in 1902–3

33. ASHBY ST. LEDGERS, NORTHANTS. The east front, 1904–5, extending the Jacobean south-east corner; and sunk garden, 1909–10

34. Cottages at Ashby St. Ledgers (1905–6)

35. Lambay, Co. Dublin, 1907–8. The old building (left) and the new, from the south-east

36. LAMBAY ISLAND, FROM THE AIR (By courtesy of the Stationery Office, Dublin)

37. LAMBAY, THE APPROACH THROUGH THE RAMPART

38. NASHDOM, TAPLOW, BUCKINGHAMSHIRE (1905)

39. PAPILLON HALL, LEICESTERSHIRE (1903). The round court

undertaking of New Place, Shedfield, in February, 1905, apparently remarked that she wanted a man young enough to take an interest in the work but old enough to be trusted. To which he replied that, whilst old enough alas to be no longer young and unable to lay claim to fame, it would do his reputation serious harm if the story which he had often heard repeated got about that he was too busy to give proper attention to buildings. The office organisation, disrupted by Badcock's defection and later by Dalton's, had by now been made good by the arrival of A. J. Thomas. But there is no doubt that the growth of the practice, with as many as a dozen houses going on simultaneously in different stages and in different parts of the country, the detailed design of which he had learnt could not be delegated, exerted a mounting strain and left little leisure.

'I get so anxious in my work, the work that has been, the work that is, and that which is to be—or not! So many little half-formed, inexpressible, almost unconscious thoughts of it surround me . . .', he confided to his wife (February 4, 1905). When he felt like that it meant he was overtired, and would begin worrying about money. Sure enough, three days later, he worked out a comparative note on income and expenses of the past two years:

	Income	Office Expenses	Net income	Spending as percentage of income
1903	3321	$22\frac{1}{2}\%$	2572	63
1904	3681	$21\frac{3}{4}\%$	2884	69

New Place (p. 92) had to be traditional, since the client wished it to contain the splendidly ornate rooms and staircase of a Bristol merchant's house—John Langton's on the Welsh Bank, built 1623–8—which had descended to Mrs. Franklyn in poor condition. The Jacobean gabled theme, whilst handled more prosaically than any of his works since the Paris Pavilion, is nevertheless characteristic in the skilfully co-ordinated variety of the four symmetrical fronts and the outstanding quality of the bricks and brickwork. This was an outcome of the preparatory work at Daneshill, the mullion and coping mouldings prepared for which were here used on a grand scale. Similarly Lutyens's prolonged early studies of brick and tile craftsmanship, and appreciation of the value of plain walling, could at last be expressed in English handmade red bricks of good proportions, well burnt.

Long before New Place was finished he was immersed in 'the great game, the high game' of classicism, at Nashdom, Hestercombe, Folly Farm, Walton Heath Dormy House, and Heathcote, the latter, initiated 1906, the culmination of the series of Renaissance country houses to be noticed in the next chapter. But as that series of works approached its peak in 1907, his designs for renewal and enlargements at Lambay, which he had first visited in 1905, were completed and began to be put into effect in 1908. This long period of gestation was due partly to material and transport difficulties on that almost uninhabited island in the Irish Sea off the coast of County Dublin. And, even when begun, work was unhurried, indeed more or less continuous for a generation, so that in 1932 a house was built for the daughters, and their families, who had been babies when Uncle Ned, as they called him, arranged for first-aid repairs to the derelict little castle. In the chronology of Lutyens's work, however, Lambay belongs to 1907, for it was then that the designs for restoring and enlarging the building, and laying out its precincts, were finalised. The time factor thus helps to account for the place Lambay holds among his works—and held in his affection; and for the classical conciseness of what is essentially a romantic conception—a realisation, one might say, of his friend Barrie's 'island that liked to be visited', with a similar but less sinister magic. But the personality of his client and the nature of the place, both exceptional, also contributed much to the ensuing work of art. Lambay can be regarded as the climax of his romantic architecture as well as foreshadowing his more abstract conceptions in the future, towards which his art must be visualised as progressing (pp. 110, 111).

The green, rocky, whalebacked island, an oval mile or so in area, rises to a windy peak northwards. From the moment you set foot on the jetty the wailing chorus of a myriad gulls and guillemots is never out of your ears. The black cliffs of the seaward side are honeycombed with caves inhabited by great grey seals. A little rough Doric temple—actually the island's chapel—stands on the sward a hundred yards away from the cluster of white-walled, grey-roofed cottages round the tiny harbour. From the jetty a mown path across the grass leads inland towards a wind-cropped grey wood of ashes and sycamores enclosed in a circular rampart and through the branches of which the crowsteps of harled gables are seen under the lea of the hill. They belong to the Castle—more accurately the castellet or fort—built in Tudor times to secure the island's lawful inhabitants. Until then Lambay had technically belonged to the Church, actually to pirates who, with 'Spaignardes, homes de ffraunce and Scottes', made it 'a receptacle of the King's enemies', according to a writer of 1467. In that year John Tiptoft, Earl of Worcester, Lord Deputy, proposed to erect a fort on it. In 1555 John Chaloner took a lease of the isle in order to work copper mines, and, as interlopers of every kind multiplied, between 1575–95 built the present 'fine little castle of freestone' as it was described in 1645.

To this scene—in 1904 derelict and forlorn, the little castle scarcely habitable—came the Hon. Cecil Baring. In 1905 he brought Lutyens for consultation on first-aid repairs. When the house had been made weatherproof with a roof of grey pantiles, Mr. Baring brought his wife whom he had married in romantic circumstances, with their two little girls. Whilst the transformation involved by the full scheme of reconstruction was going on, after 1908, the family moved into a shepherd's cottage higher up the hill, where their life, looking across the sea to the

Wicklow Mountains southwards and the Mountains of Mourne in the distant north, would have been even more Spartan than in the castle had not the disposition of the occupants rendered it, rather, Arcadian. For in the intervals of their simple if numerous household cares, Mr. Baring had taught his wife Greek sufficiently for them to read Theocritus together and of Ulysses' adventures returning to Ithaca. This pleasing trait is mentioned because a man who so improved shining hours can be conceived as evoking a like fine simplicity in the handling of the grey walls that he could watch taking shape among the sycamores each time the children went fishing or the yawl put out for the weekly marketing. Indeed it is Homeric rather than Celtic overtones that sight of Lambay arouses, and which Lutyens sensed should be the keynote of the conception, just as at Munstead Wood he caught, in the personalities of the Jekylls, and unconsciously embodied in that simpler conception, echoes of classic mythology.

As you cross the turf to the bastioned gateway in the rampart, the place looks a much more formidable fortress than it can ever have been historically. For the rampart, with a grass walk along its top protected by a breast-high parapet, is an exaggeration of a low wall that enclosed the former garden and farm, built for shelter from the salt-laden winds (and constructed with the spoil from the excavated foundations of the house). The rampart walk is carried by a timber bridge over the outer gate, through which and another beyond it, up a paved path between mulberry trees, is seen the front of the fort. The old building is square in plan with a gabled tower at each corner, the sides of the towers splayed so that their outer angles are less than a right angle. By this device each could be enfiladed from a shot-hole in the return face of its neighbour. On two sides (south and east[1]) the space between the towers had been filled in. The only original fireplace was in the hall occupying the ground floor of the centre block, and the simple accommodation seems not to have included a staircase.

The old building, like the whole island, takes its colour from the sea, bright colours washed out by ages of storm and bleaching sun, except where the cultivated grass is a vivid green. All the island porphyry of which the walls are built is of coppery green and coppery brown with purple streaks, like a stormy sea, shot with feldspar crystals. The quoins are old red sandstone and pale limestone from the mainland. The modern window dressings, owing to the refractory nature of the porphyry, are also of cool grey Milverton limestone. The walls of the old fort, being roughly constructed, had been and are covered with grey harle that softens every surface and angle. In the new work thick mortar half covers the stone—a technique Lutyens described as 'a stratification of slate with a tide of masonry; only the outer or

---

[1] The entrance front actually faces north-west, so that the towers stand to the cardinal points. In the following description, however, it will be called the north front, for clarity and brevity, the south-east side the south, and so on.

higher parts of the slate show, and they give the necessary hardness to the walling'. The roofs are of grey pantiles. Thus all the buildings are of much the same colour as the rosemary that flowers below them, and the sea on a misty day.

The works begun in 1908 involved building a squat tower, and a kitchen quadrangle unconnected above the ground floor, the castle standing alone to tell its own story. The determination to ensure that the new roofs should not conflict with the old also involved to some extent sinking the new quadrangle buildings into the hillside. The eaves of the kitchen roof are almost flush with the lawn on your right as you look from inland to the garden front (p. 110).

As at Lindisfarne, and in his additions to earlier buildings of his own, reproduction in the new building of any feature characteristic of the old was avoided. The materials are the same, but it is the pantiled roofs that predominate in them, with the dormers in them hipped, and a lovely sweep produced by their bell-cast. Roofs, too, dominate the kitchen court itself, set herringbonewise with cobbles from the shore. The rooms are simply handled, even austerely, with whitewashed walls and scrubbed oak furniture, almost the only notes of colour coming from rugs and green reflected light from the grass outside the windows.

The classical clarity of texture and colour, blended with an intricacy of plan that is truly romantic, compose the peculiar harmony struck within. Its effect is intensified by the design of the surrounding precincts, in which the same values are transposed: a plan geometrically regular but developed with utmost romance of colour and texture. The circle formed by the outer rampart is bisected by the approach path and, beyond the castle, by a long lawn—the sides of which radiate slightly outwards as they recede and rise. There is a forecourt enclosed on the approach by a clairevoie and gate of oak lattice contained in a cross-wall, with iris-channels, the paved path and mulberry avenue subdividing its lawn. Beside it are walled gardens with a pergola of sturdy, harled piers, made out of the farm buildings formerly occupying the area, and providing a sheltered enclosure of which the new and old buildings of the house make the other two sides. The rectilinear pattern—with a tennis court and other garden features elsewhere—merges in every direction into the silver stems of the enclosing and enclosed wood, which generates a feeling of sheltered secrecy. Through the trees you catch endless cross-glimpses of the grey shapes of the buildings and can appreciate the subtle play of levels created by the raising and levelling of the southward lawn in relation to the natural slopes of the ground. Then, through the wood, you come always to some segment of the rampart, clothed with cotoneaster horizontalis, escallonia, buck-thorn, great bushes of fuchsia, and other shrubs thriving in the soft Irish air, while the wind whistles overhead through the tree tops burnt with the salt spray. In one of these hidden evergreen segments against the rampart stands an austerely designed altar-tomb of the dove-grey limestone, inscribed to the memory of the man and woman much of whose natures, one feels, Lutyens reflected in the calm, firm, yet so sensitive and implicitly emotional shapes composing the visual poem that is Lambay—the most sustained expression of his poetic genius.

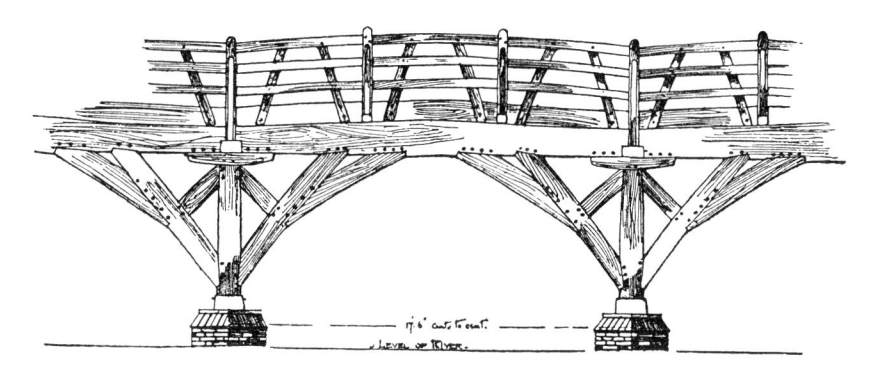

DETAIL OF THE WOODEN BRIDGES AT SONNING, 1902

CHAPTER VI

THE HIGH GAME

§1. CLASSICAL MORALITY

THE Queen's death, following the opening of the new century, was a great deal more than the convenient milestone marking the end of the Victorian Age, which it provides for us now. The coincidence of the two events with the national reaction to the South African War and the distinct personality of Edward VII constituted, to all but the most thoughtless, a portent of the changing spirit of the time. It is not easy for us, inured to a continuous state of flux and catastrophe, to recapture the sensations begotten in contemporaries not so much by the passing of Victoria as by the accession of her son. They produced a real if indefinable psychological crisis, and Lutyens experienced it acutely. Indeed the gradual but complete change in the character of his work during the ensuing years is in part traceable to the change in the national spirit which the Accession symbolised and accentuated for him. His letters at this time register the effect of the widely experienced portent upon an artist of exceptionally sensitive mind.

One of the changes to which a new reign and century drew attention was intensification of the already increased flow of wealth into the country from America and South Africa, in the form of returns from overseas investments, especially the Rand gold-fields and the Argentine, and in the persons of wealthy men without territorial connections. They materially symbolised the atmosphere of rather vulgar prosperity and confidence which was reflected in the fact of Stock Exchange prices—that barometer of the social weather—attaining in 1901–2 a peak not equalled till 1911. Both those peaks correspond closely to crucial points in Lutyens's career. At the peak of 1901, however, an ambitious young domestic architect to whom economics were a sealed book could not comprehend the causes but only note the symptoms, as he sensed them in himself, of this particular change—which to a professional man ministering to fashionable society was necessarily of great importance. Other changes ultimately to revolutionise the world were germinating in the national conscience during this Indian Summer, the fruits of which soon began to be apparent to him. A deepening sense of the necessity for 'social progress' mobilised much voluntary effort. A general awakening of all classes was taking place to the terrible consequences of environment in the slums. The scientifically guided Christian aspirations of such men as Canon Barnett and his wife; Charles Booth's statistical investigations into the ugly facts of London life; the civic patriotism of the new

London County Council; and in the political field, the Women's Suffrage movement, were beginning to transform the familar Victorian landscape. Lutyens was destined to be brought into close contact with their effects either professionally or in his home.

His immediate reaction appears to have been a vague but pervading *malaise*, a sense of disenchantment, and of the need for change in himself and in his work. In 1901 he was thirty-two and, despite having accomplished Deanery Garden, Grey Walls, Marsh Court, Abbotswood, and the Paris Pavilion, felt he was not getting on. In one respect the Queen's death affected him professionally: schemes for a great memorial were immediately put on foot and the choice of Sir Aston Webb to design it mightily depressed him. 'The Queen's Memorial is horrid as far as I have seen it,' he wrote to Herbert Baker (November 30, 1902); 'Aston Webb has got it all inside out and far too small in detail and too funny for words... The King is not building, and if he did Edis would get it or young Blomfield & Son. They stick to their people very well I believe.' Not that he had the slightest claim or expectation of being given public works to do; but the fact that such commissions were to be had in the new century seems to have made him discontented with his own considerable achievement and stirred ambitions towards the monumental possibilities of his art; possibilities which, successful designer as he was of picturesque country houses, he realised that he had not so much as essayed. In July he had written to Lady Emily:

> How awful, Aston Webb has got the Queen's Memorial. How does do he it! He doesn't really but has good people to help him, which I haven't somehow [His assistants Badcock and Dalton had just left him, and that rankled]... I am, stupidly but very, depressed about [it]. I do wish I could get on. I have done nothing yet that would give me the slightest claim to be remembered as an architect of my time... I must get, if only I can, a better class of work—not so many little things [on which] all one's ingenuity has to go in saving tuppences. All this season I have seen no one nor hardly dined out or made any new friends or influences.

That his poor opinion of Sir Aston Webb was not due to jealousy is evident from a reference in a letter to Baker of December, 1904: 'delightful man as he is, [he] is absolutely futile—worse, vulgar! and quite ignorant on his own showing of all great architectural principles.' By the time that was written Lutyens had diagnosed his own malaise of the Accession period as the first symptoms of changing allegiance from the romantic to the classic mode, and had become passionately, though as yet privately, addicted to 'the high game', as he called it, of the great Vitruvians.

The precedent of Norman Shaw's similar transition was always before him, since Lutyens lived in his former house and knew him personally. In 1901 he had had the opportunity, when staying with Mark Fenwick in Northumberland in connection with the Abbotswood plans, of seeing Shaw's classical masterpiece, Chesters, the home of Mrs. Fenwick's mother, Mrs. Clayton. 'It was lovely and loveable in great and many respects, but there are mistakes which I could not help thinking I should have avoided. An enormous house and all details left go lucky beyond a point, yet the planning of it all is a masterpiece.' Already, we see, he was fully alive to the inevitable beautiful intricacy of the classical medium. Indeed it was that, perhaps, that most attracted him to it. Looking at Gosford over the Scottish border, a year later—a huge Adam house heavily altered for the Earl of Wemyss, 1880–90, by William Young, architect of the War Office buildings in Whitehall—it was the failure of the architect to work out the implications of the style fully that irritated him. Gosford had 'great qualities but oh so many technical mistakes. In the grand classic [manner] it is like music on a grand scale. [But] if the drums beat loud and the people shout "God Save the King" all flat—[it] is a bit of a nuisance'.[1] If you attempted 'the high game', you must go through with it all the way. Once you invoked the Orders you must see that their ordinances of scale and proportion were carried right through the design and plan, or be destroyed by your own magic. Nothing could be left to chance, even less to the intelligence of workmen.

> In modern work, unlike the old, the thinking machine is separated from the labour machine, so that the modern architect has the same absolutism as we give the old men—where the thought and labour were from the same individual. This is where modern conditions must prevail, where they should tell. The thought and design, in that they are specialised, should become super-thought; and, in that they are specialised, they must be in advance of and distinctly beyond the conceptions of the architect's fellow men.[2]

This growing preoccupation made Lutyens a propagandist for the then almost wholly ignored merits of Georgian architecture, and, the night before the Coronation, he introduced a new friend—destined to become one of his oldest—to a great example then due for demolition:

> [William] Nicholson came to dinner. He was very amusing and nice. He stayed till 11.0 and then I took him to see Newgate: he had never seen it. He is going to illustrate the Oxford Colleges and I wanted him to see Newgate before it goes. It would be so splendid for his woodblock-cutting methods—the stone upon stone, its grim severity and grace withal.[3]

'Severity and grace'; the majesty of Dance's prison, its cavernous recesses and

---

[1] To Lady Emily, January 2, 1902.
[2] To H. Baker, January 29, 1911, and therefore ten years later. But it summed up another of the factors that drew him into the Vitruvian system.
[3] To Lady Emily, August 9, 1902.

white Portland rustication exaggerated by the flaring illuminations, were probably etched on his mind when, on reaching home, he finished off the Monkton drawings 'and got them off at 2 a.m.' The impression seems to have been still sharp next morning, for he watched the Coronation procession in rebellious mood. He could not 'help feeling the cheap mockery of the great spirit that moved the men of old to pageantry—and now but a husk that shelters little but shere vulgarity... A Crown the shape of which I could not read—a complex muddle of materials, and might have been feathers! There was a feeling of simple reality about the little knot of Colonials on their dowdy bay ponies among all the Household Cavalry, that all else seemed to want'.[1]

Before the month was out he received his first opportunity for a classical composition, which he was able to control by restricting it to a limited space: the circular court of Papillon Hall (p. 112). I believe that diffidence at the technical and aesthetic responsibilities involved in the style used by the great masters of architecture partly account for the queer anomaly which this house has always presented, with its rather dull traditional exterior (dull, that is, except for its extraordinary plan), and almost baroque circular classical courtyard. How great the responsibilities of him who uses the Orders, Lutyens almost alone among contemporary architects realised, and in a very remarkable passage in a letter to Herbert Baker, written the following year, he hinted at their nature.

The moving of Alfred Stevens's Wellington Monument in St. Paul's to its present (and originally intended) site, and its completion by the sculptor John Tweed, was stirring up vigorous discussion at the time. The letter (February 15, 1903) is mainly devoted to a constructive analysis of the problem involved and Lutyens's reasons for opposing Tweed's proposals, chiefly on the grounds that it was essentially a matter for an architect, not a sculptor, and that Tweed in any case professed himself a disciple of Rodin.

> You cannot follow Rodin and Stevens unless, as the Irishman said, you are like a bird and can be in two places at once. I admire Rodin and I admire Stevens, though personally I should rather follow Stevens than Rodin. Rodin is purely individual. ... Tweed's work ... is illogical and bad and has no countervailing value in the design. It may be picturesque but it is bad art.
>
> In architecture Palladio is the game!! It is so big—few appreciate it now, and it requires training to value and realise it. The way Wren handled it was marvellous. Shaw has the gift. To the average man it is dry bones, but under the hand of a Wren it glows and the stiff materials become as plastic clay.
>
> I feel sure that if Ruskin had seen that point of view he would have raved as beautifully as he raved for the Gothic, and I think he did have some insight

[1] *ibid.*

before he died: his later writings were much more gentle towards the Italian Renaissance.

> It is a game that never deceives, dodges never disguise. It means hard thought all through—if it is laboured it fails. There is no fluke that helps it—the very what one might call the machinery of it makes it impossible except in the hands of a Jones or a Wren. So it is a big game, a high game, a game that Stevens played well as an artist should—though he never touched Wren; far beyond the comprehension of a Tweed, and beyond I do not say the mind of Ruskin, for he is a big man, but quite outside his preference.
>
> Preference is a perfectly sound and honourable factor in all these questions, and one that should be more often taken count of in discussion.

The letter concludes with comparative sketch plans (p. 102) of Marsh Court and Little Thakeham, then nearly built: a significant cross reference to Lutyens's work and Lutyens's allegiance at the time.

Usually so reticent and inarticulate about his art, he never defined his approach to classical design with greater clarity and, indeed, passion than in this notable passage. He concentrates into two paragraphs of brilliant appreciation the very essence of the Classical canon, the basis of its mounting attraction for him personally, and the secret of his own later supremacy among modern exponents. Yet he ends by reminding us how tolerant he was of the other 'games', provided they were played well 'as an artist should', including the picturesque—though the evidence of the work he himself did thenceforth shows that he had come to recognise this as easy game, unless, as at Lambay, played with classical rules.

The theme of several passages, in succeeding letters to Herbert Baker, is HOW this high game, for high stakes, is to be applied to actual practice? and HOW does a quest of aesthetic perfection consort with the domestic architect's responsibility to his client?

> To make a house in which people are happy and content is a very great thing. To make a house which satisfies your own critical faculty is a very good thing and encourages to do better and go on from refinement to refinement. This must tell in long run and make people want to do better things and make them think.[1]

In other words, though he does not here come to the decision definitely, the architect's responsibility, as between client and posterity, is to posterity. To satisfy himself; to 'go on from refinement to refinement', even if he is the only man to know and appreciate fully what has been achieved, in the faith that, one day, the really great building of world-wide—or supreme aesthetic—importance will come his way, and he be ready for it.

[1] December 26, 1904.

Big work, in this Jack-in-office old country, may or may not come; far more likely not than otherwise. The only thing to do is to go on and be ready for it—and endure the bitterness of seeing little men wasting great opportunities.

On the other hand, 'I believe Norman Shaw is a really great and capable designer, one of the first water. I put him with Wren—really.'

> Our new streets, oh the vapour of it all! Look at Paris, how well they lay out there, the courage, sense, and big obvious simplicity of it all. I mean their modern work, excepting much of their detail which as an Englishman perhaps there is no need or call to admire without reserve. Our L.C.C. is appalling compared with French authority.
>
> So there it rests, and will, until some one can awake the ignorant torpidity and guinea-pig waste of national energy. This saving of ha'pence and confusion of accounts, philanthropics, and trade does waste and mislead woefully. It is a long story and is bred in the bone of the nation.[1]

Peering into the future, by virtue of our posteriority, we see how accurately Lutyens was foreseeing, in 1904, the obstructions besetting the classic idealist working in Britain under democracy. We can see his great New Delhi conception, his supreme stake in 'the high game', and realised with how much tribulation and toil, marred as regards its most essential aesthetic feature—the graded ascent of the Processional Way to the Viceroy's House—by 'political considerations'. The bitterness of that blow was immensely aggravated by his conviction that the friend and colleague to whom, indeed, he had foretold the event, could have saved the grand design had he not, in Lutyens's view, yielded to precisely the woolliness of mind here castigated: 'this saving of ha'pence and confusion of accounts, philanthropics and trade.' We can see, too, the classical Royal Academy plans for London, devised under his leadership during the second Great War, set aside in favour of methods of planning based on practical and scientific values but coloured also by the naturalism that, at this time, he was abandoning. In this Pisgah sight we may not distinguish between the merits of the causes involved, but it is clear that the artist who founds his work upon Roman ideals—the Rome whether of Nero, the Antonines, or the Medici Popes—and a Euclidian geometry, in an age of Wellsian democracy and Einsteinian Relativity, is courting trouble. It is a question of sanctions. The classical Orders, like those societies that have successfully employed them in their buildings, connote the authority of an autocrat, omniscient or benevolent or neither. In proportion as that authority is reduced or diffused, the sanctions demanded by the classic canon are weakened, until, in a society based upon the greatest good of the greatest number, they become unworkable. The architect under such circumstances is bound

[1] *ibid.*

to adopt the alternative aesthetic founded on function and practical and social relationships: a romantic empiricism for which no aesthetic canon comparable to classical logic has, so far, been evolved. Though Lutyens eventually set himself to do so.

Now, neither scientist nor sociologist, but wholly artist, he proceeded to enlist his genius in allegiance to the only complete aesthetic philosophy that civilisation has produced. He thereby dedicated himself to the service of a super-mortal abstraction, the realisation of an eternal ideal, to which the needs of humanity must take second place.

The psychological process is not dissimilar to that with which he dedicated himself to matrimony, remaining as loyal to the one as to the other ideal whilst recognising—and retaining—liberty of preference under particular circumstances.

§2. EARLY ESSAYS

Little Thakeham, Papillon Hall, and the two small houses Homewood and Monkton, all designed before the end of 1903 have been indicated as illustrating the transition to Renaissance idiom. Mount (now Amesbury) School, Hindhead (1903) was the earliest design completed in the Wren manner, which is also apparent in the music room added to his early house Sullingstead at Hascombe in this year. Some of the garden layouts, that formed a considerable part of his practice, enabled him to experiment in axial and symmetrical arrangements, a notable instance being that at Ammerdown, Somerset, for Lord Hylton (1901), where the principal feature is a great rotunda of clipped yew with radiating alleys. Then in 1904 the established success of Edward Hudson's paper demanded new editorial premises in Covent Garden and gave Lutyens the opportunity for his first London building. *Country Life* Offices present a dramatic yet highly accomplished façade of brick and Portland stone centered on a majestic portal. The fineness and multiplicity of the mouldings, and crispness of the sculpture, in frieze and knots of fruit and flowers, make the composition a continual pleasure, whether seen in elevation or, as the passer-by must see it, in sharp perspective. The fact that the front is inevitably seen at a sharp angle accounted for the prominence and elaboration given to Broadbent's key-stones of the ground floor windows, delicious Grinling Gibbons' designs of flowers and game round a scrolled cartouche bearing the cypher C. L. The attractive composition of the vaulted entrance hall has the air, unexpected in an office building, of a gentleman of the old school, rather like Hudson himself; and the accommodation, limited by the shallowness of the site, was further sacrificed for the same class distinction. The *piano nobile* with the editorial rooms has high coved ceilings and very tall sash windows, doorways of full Palladian entablature, and tall overmantels, which is no doubt extravagant but—speaking as one who has spent much of his working life in them—has paid a handsome interest by communicating to their occupants something of the founder's and designer's spirit. The blind attic, containing printing offices and raising the pantiled roof well clear of the cornice, actually balances, by weighting down, the vertical pattern of the windows. The height of the design, in particular the chimneys, seems to have worried Lutyens. 'I funk the chimneys,' he said (February 4, 1905) 'and they are going up up up and they look enormous, like two campaniles perched on my big roof and if I reduce the height *a–b* it throws the proportion *c–d* all out and wrong-looking. I am nerving myself to some decision on Monday.'

He had hopes of securing the *Morning Post* building, Aldwych, as someone from that paper called on Hudson and admired *Country Life* Offices. In the event the architects selected were Mewes & Davies who produced the exquisite result of which the contrast with the Gaiety Theatre opposite (with improvements by Norman Shaw) led contemporary architects to dub them 'beauty and the beast'.

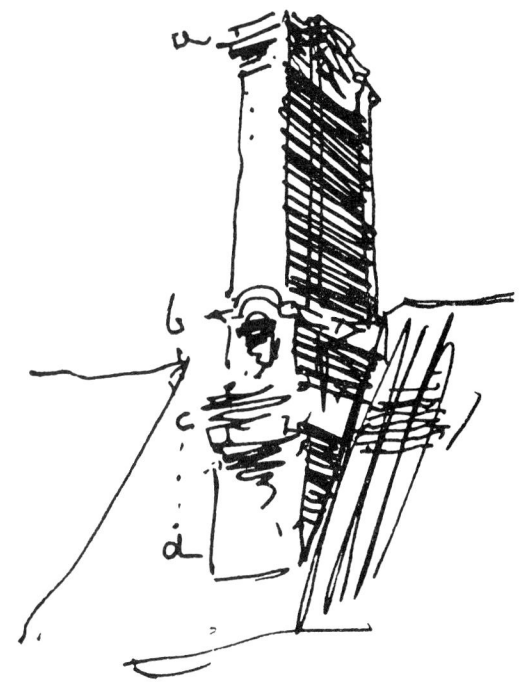

CHIMNEY, 'COUNTRY LIFE' BUILDING, 1905

In the same letter, to Lady Emily, is a note showing how eagerly he sought confirmation for his personal conviction of the virtue of English classicism:

> Herbert Jekyll is in complete agreement with me about Versailles—and indeed all French work: its immense inferiority to our English work. After the great schools of Greece and Italy (excepting the great French gothic cathedrals superb and wonderfully glorious), as a work of art Versailles cannot be compared with our Hampton Court. This for a firm belief is very comforting.

Another London building of this year, familiar to many but not generally recognised as his, is St. John's Institute, Tufton Street, Westminster, with its three Wren arches to the street and big stone-framed surfaces of brick.

The year 1905 also saw the initiation of Folly Farm for Mr. Cochrane, Nashdom at Taplow for Princess Alexis Dolgorouki, and the gardens at Hestercombe for the Hon. E. W. B. Portman, with the great orangery in which his classical ideals found full scope, parallel to the romantic and traditional developments at Holy Island, Ashby St. Ledgers, and New Place; whilst Marsh Court, Papillon Hall, and the *Country Life* building were completing.

The Hestercombe gardens (p. 129) represent the peak of the collaboration with Miss Jekyll, and his first application of her genius to classical garden design on a grand scale. The site, overlooking Taunton Dene, called for an immense parterre below the terrace in front of the house. Picturesque recesses extend to one side of it out of immediate sight. For the parterre, massed herbaceous planting is used as texture within the framework of a simple pattern formed by grass walks with paved edges intersecting in the centre, the whole bounded at the sides by iris canals, and along the far side by a massive pergola of dry-stone piers. The picturesque section, tied to the parterre-terrace layout by a masonry rotunda and flight of steps, contains an orangery, built of the golden Ham Hill stone and the most highly wrought building in the Wren manner that he had as yet designed. It makes grand use of the arch forms used less exuberantly in Covent Garden and Tufton Street. The whole conception of the Hestercombe gardens, with the brilliant handling of the varying levels to produce at once a lucid and an intricate horticultural drama, is entirely mature, indeed unsurpassed in Lutyens's garden repertory.

Sketch designs of Nashdom were approved in September, 1905. Princess Alexis Dolgorouki was formerly Miss Wilson and a great heiress, whom it was said that her Russian husband had married to pay his gambling debts. A fashionable hostess, she required something in the nature of a large Riviera villa for week-end river parties. A narrow sloping site dictated that the house should stand right on the road that bounds one side of it, and the client's views on cost that the materials should be whitewashed brick walls, tiled roofs, and green shutters. These limitations, added to the height and bulk needed for the accommodation stipulated, were used by Lutyens with singular effectiveness. Outwardly a big white many-windowed pile, it contains a simpler version of the round internal court at Papillon Hall. There are many happy secondary features about the design, in which he was trying out classic motifs. But the great terrace and steps (which must have added a good deal to the estimated cost for the house (£15,000) are the most impressive things about Nashdom after the simple brick masses of the body, plain roofs, and bold upstanding chimneys of the house (p. 112).

Folly Farm at Sulhampstead, near Newbury, contrasts in almost every respect. It is minuscule, richly coloured, precious, but like Nashdom also stands beside a road. In 1912 a big enlargement was demanded, leading to the most sensational of Lutyens's contrasts (p. 130). In the first instance, however, an existing timber-framed cottage facing but lying a little back from the road was to be extended. So he set at right angles to it, and nearer the road, a trim little H-shaped house with hipped roofs, soft blue-grey brick walls, and quoins and stringcourses of a strong red. This is wholly delightful, and entered from one end by a neat walled court with an arched gate to the road. Since the old cottage could contain the kitchen etc., the whole middle of the new building could be devoted to a two-storeyed vaulted hall, tiny in scale but stately in proportion. A window in each end of it, lighting first floor passages, was given a Chinese Chippendale balcony, painted lacquer red, which, with black walls and white members, reproduced the colour scheme of the drawing-room of 29 Bloomsbury Square (p. 130). With appropriate furniture, it is brilliantly effective; the idea, a typical Lutyens application to *architectural* use of the aesthetic colour scheme he had noticed a decade before as emanating from the Glasgow Art School. As he used it, the association is rather with the pictorial use of black by James Pryde and William Nicholson: there is a Prydish feeling in the arched ends of this hall silhouetted in black. Years later Nicholson actually decorated the dining-room with low-toned grisaille murals depicting a series of windows in which bird-cages are hanging.

It was obviously impossible to extend this neatly facetted gem. So when completely new servants' quarters, dining-room, and seven new bedrooms were wanted, an entire contrast was the only solution. As at Crooksbury he had added a symmetrical house to an irregular one, now he reversed the process. The Dutch doll's house was married to a formalised barn with great sweeps of tiled roof—a reversion in 1912 to his earliest picturesque manner. But handled with what conscious design! The two houses are linked only by a corridor in plan, the court between occupied by a square pool or 'tank', round the two new sides of which the roof of the addition is brought down to within five feet of the water to form a cloister. The roof is carried on a series of massive brick piers splaying outwards to their bases on the water side, and forming the abutments of heavy brick arches over the cloister. The other face of the new wing is a balanced irregular composition comprising a sleeping porch with hipped roof, big brick chimney stack, and a tile-hung tail. For sheer originality the Folly Farm twins are unique even in Lutyens's repertory. The clash could have been deplorable. But the art of it, as brilliant as the marriage at Lambay which the result recalls, is that each half sets off the other:

Each gives each a double charm
Like pearls upon an Ethiop's arm.

§3. FIRST CLIMAX

In 1906 Lutyens was reaching a climax in the extent and quality of his work. Besides New Place, Lindisfarne and the buildings just described, in course of design or progress, and a dozen others I have not mentioned, there was Lambay in gestation. In that spring, through Hudson's interest, the Dormy House, Walton Heath, was designed; the picturesque whitewashed and tiled house, Barton St. Mary at East Grinstead came off the drawing boards as a charming but, to me, somewhat mannered reversion to the Caldecott manner of Goddards; and a rich Yorkshireman 'who could not spend his money—until he met me' (the jocular phrase occurs in a letter to Herbert Baker years afterwards) commissioned the classical villa near Ilkley called

Heathcote. There was a day in May when, in the train to Taunton (for Hestercombe), Lutyens wrote to Lady Emily: 'Hemingway has signed contract for £17,500 [that is for Heathcote], Dolgorouki accepts £15,000, Birds £7800 [Barton St. Mary], Mrs. Franklin £9300 [New Place]. So this week, signed and sealed, £34,600... I am happy at all these jobs coming out right this week as regards prices. But it is only when they come out right, and the work is to begin, that I wake to a horror that I have yet to work it all out—and they loom practical and into the realm of the real to bes.'

The kinship of the Dormy House to Mr. James's trianon at Monkton and to Folly Farm is apparent; a whitewashed and brick-quoined oblong with green shutters, steep pantiled roof, and three lovely plain chimneys. But the design, simple and compact in appearance, has something more: a bigness of conception that recalls Nashdom; and a discipline for the full martialling of which we must look forward to Heathcote—'Sanmichele' as Lutyens called it to himself. The something more about the Dormy House is the implicit geometry in it based on the proportion of the Orders, giving a distinctive 'zip' over and above the sensitive ingenuity. How inevitable, yet fresh, is the pattern formed by the entrance side—the roof just that much lifted above the cornice so that the lines of both tell, and the symmetry just that little relieved by the odd window! Incidentally metal-framed casements are used instead of the Queen Anne sashes that one would expect (p. 131).

The full classical orchestra of a Doric Order—bases, columns, friezes, cornices, with their correct mathematical ratios—implied in the Dormy House and earlier Renaissance designs—is martialled in Heathcote. The commission was the opportunity for which Lutyens had been waiting and perfecting himself for five years; the occasion for mounting the conductor's rostrum before such a band as he had noted playing out of key at Gosford, but now awaiting his beat and rendering his own score. His Heathcote concerto, though using the same instruments as the hundreds of so-called Palladian compositions produced in eighteenth-century England, differs radically from them because, to continue the metaphor, whereas they are more or less clear echoes of one Italian composer's, Andrea Palladio's, variations on Vitruvian airs, Lutyens here goes straight, for his basic theme, to the Doric Order itself as used by Sanmichele, working out his harmonies and intervals from the proportions inherent in that Order, and weaving them into the orchestration of his melody—namely a country house for a particular man, with particular requirements, on a particular site (p. 132).

But we have the whole process of the design's conception and working out sketched by Lutyens himself in a letter to Baker (January 29, 1911). It is an unique instance of his describing, with the technical details that a fellow architect would appreciate, his mode of approaching and evoking a Classical composition, and it is fortunate indeed that he should have selected for analysis his most elaborately articu-

40. GARDENS AT HESTERCOMBE, SOMERSET (1905)

41. HESTERCOMBE. The Orangery

42. FOLLY FARM, SULHAMPSTEAD, BERKSHIRE (1905–6 and 1912)

43. A Corner of the 1912 Addition

44. The Hall (1905–6)

45. MIDDLEFIELD, SHELFORD, CAMBRIDGESHIRE (1908)

46. DORMY HOUSE, WALTON HEATH, SURREY (1906). The end containing the entrance

47. HEATHCOTE, ILKLEY, YORKSHIRE (1906)

48. The Doric Order as handled at Heathcote

lated work hitherto. The site he was given for 'Sanmichele' was four acres on the outskirts of Ilkley:

> in an ultra suburban locality over which villas of dreadful kind and many colours wantonly distribute themselves. The ground was four square and compact, standing high with large pieces of moor-clad mountain claps about the horizon. The material was York stone—a stone without a soul to call its own, as sober as a teetotaller.
>
> He, the man, wanted cupboards galor, in all rooms, right and left of windows. I wanted something persisting and dominating, with horizontal lines, to stratify the diarhetic conditions produced by the promiscuous villadom: in fact an architectural bismuth! To get domination I had to get a scale greater than the height of my rooms allowed, so unconsciously the San Michele invention repeated itself. That time-worn doric order—a lovely thing—I have the cheek to adopt. You can't copy it. To be right you have to take it and design it.
>
> You, as an exercise, take the order out of a book, as it stands, and couple the columns (But why couple them, you say: I say, but I didn't—I take them as an instance. I adopt a pattern with a great tradition. Period is not the easy method of any copyist). See what happens? Your bases interlock! Inigo Jones solved the difficulty in one way and very good. Vanburgh failed lamentably and clumsily. Wren avoided the problem. The problem is to get the two posts, with their triglyphs and metopes complete, proper in all parts, and not let the bases interlock, and without distortion of their bases, and then the soffits of the stones and their digested completeness. You cannot copy: you find if you do you are caught, a mess remains.
>
> It means hard labour, hard thinking, over every line in all three dimensions and in every joint; and no stone can be allowed to slide. If you tackle it in this way, the Order belongs to you, and every stroke, being mentally handled, must become endowed with such poetry and artistry as God has given you. You alter one feature (which you have to, always), then every other feature has to sympathise and undergo some care and invention. Therefore it is no mean (game), nor is it a game you can play lightheartedly.

Glancing ahead of our chronological progress, but backwards when he wrote the letter, the house he is about to refer to is his final type of the Monkton-Folly Farm-Dormy House series; the perfected Wren-Lutyens model of a house (p. 131):

> A Middlefield would have lost all character and point [i.e. on the Heath-

> cote site] and would only have become part of the dysentric chaos prevailing and made no protest against the disease...
>
> I have been scolded for not being Yorkshire in Yorkshire. The other villas have a window from this, a door from that etc—a pot-pourri of Yorkeological details.
>
> The result is futile, and absolutely unconvincing!
>
> My house does stand there—plumb,—and I dont think it could be built anywhere else!!

In the ensuing paragraphs he states his conviction—perhaps carrying on an argument begun with Baker in South Africa whence, at the time of writing, he had just returned—of the universal relevance of the classic ideal. Though it leaves Heathcote behind, his statement expresses vividly the convictions that he took to Delhi and to discussions of the style appropriate to the new administrative capital—on which the principles employed at Heathcote had immediate bearing.

> Would Wren (had he gone to Australia!) have burnt his knowledge and experience to produce a marsupial style—thought to reflect the character of her aborigines?
>
> He would surely have done his best. He might have had a greater grievance than he did even in London with his Deans and Queens and Chapters. Would the builders of Westminster Abbey have sacrificed their attainments to a theory that Britons dressed in woad, and made their architecture brutal—for no man's life was safe, safe as we understand it? Hadrian displayed acres of plaster domes, ceilings, and walls. Did he muddy his conception because he worked in plaster? and will the Round Table confederates mis-spell their articles and misquote because a Gladstone is with them?

This is a dig at Lord Gladstone, then Governor-General of South Africa, of whom Lutyens had a poor opinion, and refers of course to the well-known magazine on Imperial politics to which Milner's Young Men in South Africa were the principal contributors. Then follows the claim which I have introduced earlier in this chapter, that the modern architect must use a finite system of design owing to the absence of artist-craftsmen to interpret the implications of a free system of building such as regional or traditional styles. Therefore the architect's thought and design must be 'super thought', fool-proof. The development of this argument, in this remarkable letter, applying to South African building methods, will be found quoted in Chapter VIII where Lutyens's visit to the Cape is narrated. But in an added postscript he sums up with profound clarity the quintessence of the classical humanist's creed. The passage is a memorable one:

> You cannot play originality with the Orders. They have to be so well

digested that there is nothing but essence left. When right they are curiously lovely—unalterable as plant forms...

The perfection of the Order is far nearer nature than anything produced on impulse or accident-wise.

Nothing in nature is done by accident—even sports are produced by the great natural forces being unbalanced.

These clipped sentences give us a sight of the 'super thought', the power of which drew him from the looser naturalism of romantic craftsmanship. He never stated more explicitly than here the conviction that was to inspire his work henceforth, until the time when he learnt how to dissolve and reconstitute the Orders into 'a new Elemental Architecture'. Here he stated the ideal to which, at his best, his classical work attained. The analogy between the Orders and nature expresses elliptically the truth common to religion, art, and science: that the infinite variety of spiritual, natural, and artificial beauty evolves alike not by accident or impulse but by following their kingdoms' laws, which kingdoms are ultimately one. Inflexible as are these laws, Christian religion and classical aesthetics drew the familiar parallel conclusions: in their service is perfect freedom; *ars est celare artem*. Which Lutyens paraphrases in his words: 'they have to be so digested that nothing but essence is left.'

Heathcote, which prompted this reflection, needs a more technical appreciation than is appropriate to this book; for that the reader is referred to Mr. Butler's analysis of the design in the first volume of the *Architecture*. And we have to look to the houses designed immediately afterwards for the *essence* as contrasted to the full expression of Lutyens's classical ideal. There are brilliant reticences in the extraordinarily ingenious conversion of four adjoining houses along a Northumbrian village street, known as Whalton Manor, for Mrs. Eustace Smith (1908). In the group of brick country houses designed in 1908–9, the process that he had described as 'going on from refinement to refinement', in the sense of elimination to elimation, till only the essence is left, was worked out and crystallised in the characteristic style associated with his name. There were the large alterations and additions to Temple Dinsley, Hertfordshire; the smaller houses Middlefield, Cambs., and Chussex, Walton-on-the-Hill; Knebworth Golf Club; Great Maytham, Kent; and The Salutation, Sandwich.

Temple Dinsley (1908), the home of Mr. H. G. Fenwick, a cousin of Lutyens's early client at Abbotswood, involved the adding to a Queen Anne nucleus of wings occupying three or four times its area. This nucleus, though presenting a delightful front with flat arched key-stoned windows flanked by curious little gabled extensions, was not so finite an entity as to necessitate the additions being set apart from it as with Crooksbury and Folly Farm. On the contrary these took the form of framing wings with extensive office and stable quarters adjoining one of them, assimilated to the nucleus in style but digesting and restating its elements. These elements were brick walls, chimneys, sash windows, and hipped roofs of tile. The old fronts have the charm, without particular distinction, of some mason-builder of Queen Anne's reign. The additions use the same elements with extreme but reticent distinction, developing each as a theme in a balanced symphony (p. 149). The brickwork theme has a solo passage in the projecting flanks of the wings on either side of the old fronts, with the chimney motif elaborated as a grand rectilinear descent. The roof element—rather indistinct in the old tune—is clarified and emphasised, dominating the views of the new wings from the sides; and the fenestration pattern, subdued where it would clash with the old, is rendered fortissimo in the kitchen wing. The musical metaphor of a variation on an old air is apt in so far that the variations constitute a major work out of simple motifs—Temple Dinsley is a whole much finer than the original part—yet preserves that part essentially intact. The long-term importance of the work is that it illustrates the actual distillation, from the Wren tradition, of the Lutyens essence.

This is seen in its purity at Middlefield in the view (p. 131) of the entrance front taken soon after it was built and before the trees and gardens, now grown up, have softened its original austerity. The same elements, handled as harmonising accompaniment at Temple Dinsley, have here become the only elements in an original composition of force and beauty. Roof, a rich ingredient in all Lutyens's romantic work, is here at once developed and disciplined into one of the loveliest, surely, ever raised, set continuous over every part, its valleys trimly swept, its junctions with the brickwork of walls and chimneys effected so that the lead flashing is invisible. And what chimneys!—each a campanile of finely proportioned parts, at first sight identical. But in the middle one the centre is recessed, whilst in the lateral two the centre projects, giving just that variation required to avoid unresolved trinity. Chussex, smaller, more compact, with only two great flues; and Knebworth Golf Club, low, with steep pantiled roof, were less exciting developments of the same mode. But the four buildings together, following on the Dormy House and Folly Farm, established the mode, almost by their own influence, of English domestic architecture for a generation. Their children have been as the sands of the sea—Council cottages after the 1918 Peace, rich men's mansions, by-pass semi-detached, petrol stations and road-houses. Lutyens did not originate the mode, nor by any means was he the only architect purveying it—it goes back to Norman Shaw and Marlow at Bedford Park. Sir Ernest Newton, Detmar Blow, Sir Reginald Blomfield, Sir Guy Dawber, their contemporaries and successors, each produced many versions of it. But none handled 'Wrennaissance' with such consummate artistry as Lutyens, from whom the style, like the joke, cannot be dissociated.

His most extensive use of it was for Mr. H. J. Tennant at Great Maytham in 1909 (p. 149), a house incorporating an older one with many good qualities, among them economy of cost. 'Hudson thought Maytham most extraordinarily cheap. . . .'; 'Mrs. Tennant is pleased with the admiration the house is receiving. I think listens to me more, but she do argue, talks one dry, dry to parch, but has charm in that she is always ready for a laugh or a diversion, though it is seldom one can switch her off altogether from any point', (March 29, 1911). Incidentally, Miss Hodgson-Burnett's delightful children's story *The Secret Garden* was written about that of Great Maytham. Lutyens never used multi-coloured brick to better effect than in this bluegrey and purple house with crimson quoins. But for all its dignity and noble chimneys I find the result a little dull. That is the last criticism, however, that can be made of The Salutation, Sandwich, for Mr. Gaspard Farrer (1911), where a plan as ingeniously compact as that of Heathcote and grouped round a staircase as monumental but smaller, matches three fronts and a garden layout as concise as they are accomplished (p. 150).

§4. FAILURE AT COUNTY HALL

In the first flush of exhilaration after composing Heathcote, Lutyens was given the opportunity, afforded by the competition for the London County Council's new headquarters, to make a bid for a great metropolitan building. It offered a chance for that 'big work' on the coming or not coming of which he had speculated to Herbert Baker when preparing to lay his stakes in the High Game. It is evident that he devoted most of the latter part of 1907 to the County Hall drawings in the intervals of work on Lambay, alterations to Wittersham for Mr. Alfred Lyttelton, and to Grey Walls for its new owner Mr. Willie James. His letters first refer to work on the designs in April. Later, 'I wish I didn't keep on wanting to win the L.C.C.,' he wrote to his wife. He had no other large commission on hand and confessed that 'my chief feeling is a wish to get back the excitement of big work'.

Lutyens was one of eight leading architects invited by the Council to submit designs for the final competition, following the original open competition in which ninety-nine designs were received. The other seven in this class were Messrs. Belcher, Flockhart, Ernest George, Hare, T. G. Jackson, Mountford, and Charles Nicholson and Corlette—some other distinguished architects having declined owing to pressure of work. The assessors were Norman Shaw, Sir Aston Webb, and W. E. Riley the L.C.C. Architect. The conditions of the competition were established by the replies given to competitors' questions by the assessors, which were then circulated to competitors. Of these the crucial one, since the result was quite improperly to be decided on it, was whether corridors might have rooms on both sides, with borrowed light; to which the assessors' reply was 'No'.

The submitted designs published in *The Builder* fall roughly into three groups; those of an early Renaissance character (T. G. Jackson, A. Gilbert Scott); Beaux-

Arts Baroque (Lanchester and Rickards, S. B. Russell and Edwin Cooper—both of which firms subsequently adapted their designs for Westminster Central Hall and the Port of London Authority Building respectively); and nondescript classicism. The plans were in almost all cases symmetrical and, whilst showing wide variations in disposition, displayed surprisingly little originality. Compared to Ostberg's not long subsequent design for the analogous Town Hall at Stockholm, none showed imaginative recognition of the river's presence—which John Burns once termed 'liquid history'. One feels that, whichever of the majority had been erected, the general effect would have been much what it is, and in several cases better. The chief distinction in general treatment was between those designs that emphasised the centre of the river front, and those that stressed the lateral sections, leaving some kind of court in the centre of it. Many of the rejected designs were disqualified primarily on their cost, to which their non-functional domes or towers greatly contributed. The cost to the ratepayers and the amount of office accommodation provided were the deciding factors with the assessors. Indeed their choice, which was violently attacked in the Press, was open to the grave objection that it ignored the issued conditions and, although the winning design was fundamentally altered after adjudication, it remains hard to justify. The assessors, having stipulated that corridors should have rooms on one side only, proceeded to select the one plan that placed rooms on both sides of corridors. The late Ralph Knott, at the time an unknown young architect, won the competition with a design having a great portico in the centre of the river front where the semi-circular court is now; whilst that feature occurred in his original design on the axis of his Belvedere Road front where it contained a detached circular public hall. After the competition the portico was eliminated and the semi-circular court brought round to take its place, without the hall it was shaped to contain.

A correspondent to *The Builder* in the summer of 1907 had expressed the hope that the County Hall design might reflect those of Inigo Jones, never executed, for the Palace of Westminster, intended to occupy a site of almost the same size on the opposite bank. Lutyens's design, though it did not do that, was the only one (of those subsequently published) which made acknowledgement to Jones and Wren as exemplars for the general design. He had closely observed the work of both; and in his competition design the twin cupolas clearly derive from Greenwich and internally echo St. Paul's.

In his symmetrical plan (p. 150) the centre of the river front was recessed between lateral blocks rising sheer from the water. The Belvedere Road front had a wide, slightly projecting centre containing the main entrance, and the public hall projecting eastwards as a semi-circular bow at the north end. From the main entrance double staircases led to an oblong Council Chamber on the centre axis of the upper ground floor, beyond which was a large lobby giving into a loggia overlooking the river. The staff entrance was in Westminster Bridge Road where a broad staircase led to the upper ground floor, at its head an octagonal hall with eight piers and arches supporting a dome, and served by cross corridors. Thence the main vaulted corridor ran parallel to the river, passing through the lobby of the council chamber to another octagonal hall. There were pairs of courts inside the lateral blocks, and two more courts flanked the Council Hall and its ancillary offices between the east and west fronts. The corridors were for the most part lit from these courts, having rooms on one side only in accordance with the assessors' advice. On the river front an arcaded walk under the lateral blocks gave access to a riverside public terrace between them. Above the two octagonal halls were domed cupolas marking these main junctions of the plan, set back from the meeting of the lateral blocks with the central mass.

The general external treatment was very simple: plain rusticated walling was carried up to more than half the height of the fronts, forming an immense base above which a comparatively small order of columns was introduced at the emphasised points of the design, the remainder being plain wall-face with pedimented windows on the principal upper storey. There were six storeys with an attic storey in the roof, four of them in the nature of mezzanines (as in the *Country Life* Offices). In the ground storey of the lateral blocks five arches lit the public arcades, and below the public terrace were three vast arched openings to water-gates communicating with the storage rooms and cellars.

The three main blocks each had a mansard roof crowned with chimneys of the Middlefield type, but of course in stone. At the junction of the lateral and central blocks the re-entrant wall was canted, beyond and above which the square base (with canted angles) of the adjacent cupola would have been visible between the mansards in a diagonal view. Alone among those competing, Lutyens's design shows a real sense of scale. Baker thought 'your Council Hall the only one with any poetry in it, and which grew out of Father Thames'. The three related blocks, their upper surfaces of gleaming white, their lower shaded black in the rustication channels, and held together by the cupola towers at their junctions, would have formed superb architecture, seen across the river, and have combined into a succession of grand patterns in sharpening perspective. The effects within, with the long perspectives of arched corridors and domed halls, would have been of great architectural magnificence—indeed too great. As with most of the other designs submitted, it would have been costly; and, judged in the light of Lutyens's later work, the designs are surprisingly derivative though no doubt, as at Delhi, they would have been worked up 'from refinement to refinement'. Their most characteristic qualities were the big simplicity of general treatment, their grasp of scale, and the very English value accorded to roofs and chimneys. In that, the designs represent the expression, on a monumental scale, of his current domestic idiom as displayed in Heathcote and Temple Dinsley.

With his faculties keyed up and perhaps tired by this sustained effort, one evening in September he wrote to Lady Emily an affirmation of his belief in the subconscious or supernatural inspiration of great creative artists. Its transcendentalism is in sharp contrast to the logic of his Sanmichele letter to Herbert Baker, quoted earlier in this chapter (but written three years later); for here it is the romantic artist in him speaking, whereas the intellectual positivism of the Sanmichele letter was the creed of his classical *alter ego*. This evidence of his dualism is remarkable, coming when he was in the middle of executing a big classical design. It may imply a difficulty at this time in resolving his emotional and intellectual impulses, and should perhaps be regarded as a temporary reaction *from* the logical concentration involved in producing the County Hall designs. In any case it suggests the extent to which he had been thinking about Inigo Jones and Wren. But I regard it as more than that. Though words eluded him, I believe he was groping to express the experience of the creative artist, to define the very springs of his inventive genius before its flow was subjected to the canalising and disciplining process of his intellect:

> There is that in art which transcends all rules—it is the divine (I use poor words). It is the same in the best of all man's work (G.B.S. shows it amusingly, though he makes it ludicrous, in *Cashel Byron's Profession*, applying the language of a 'painter' to the mouth of a boxer on boxing). With inspiration rules are forgotten and some great immeasurable cycle of law is followed, unconsciously, by some accounted impulse in my own kind of work and with the moderns. There is Inigo Jones breaking through all rules when it suits him: he does it softly and it is hard to find out. Wren flagrantly defied them and he applies his ingenious intellect—he had more an intellectual than an artistic gift—yet with rules broken there was the great result—as you say—as there is with Carlyle in his work.[1] There is the same effect produced on all, and in all, work by a master mind. To short sight it's a miracle. To those of a little longer sight it is Godhead. If we could see yet better, these great facts may be revealed, before which the very God as we can conceive him will fade dim. It is that which should bring all arts—Architecture, Sculpture, Painting, Literature, Music etc., into sympathy. There is no ploy which cannot be lifted to the Divine level by its elevation as an Art, and oh Wren, Jones, are small beside Michael Angelo and men like Leonardo da Vinci. They had this touch! and were able to apply it to every work and kind of work they touched—war, architecture, painting, sculpting.
>
> I do hope my sermon on beauty wont bore you. But oh! Emy's loveliness is akin indeed to heaven and the thought of it to God.
>
> If only the nations of the world would go for beauty with their whole

---

[1] He was, at the time, reading *Heroes and Hero Worship* (but could not get on with it).

resource and energies, it would solve all the difficulties and I do believe *all* sorrow, and the millenium would be ours!!

Apart from the recognition of Wren's mathematical rather than aesthetic mind, the most notable passage is the testimony to his belief in the possibility of ultimate revelation, relating the very nature of God to aesthetic ideals and achievements. The notion is as near as he ever came to stating, in words, the belief which became his religion that perfect shapes and relationships—architectural facts arrived at empirically and by 'refinement after refinement'—have in them a supra-natural, an eternal, relevance; are indeed, reflections of divinity. It was this conviction that he at last sought to embody in his elemental designs.

In January of 1908 he heard unofficially that, although he had been a strong favourite for County Hall, 'the result was a great surprise' and that somebody else— Ralph Knott, whom no one had heard of—had won it. 'All my nine months' work is lost,' he wrote to his wife. 'You will be kind and not ask too much this year. Our dear little country house must wait a bit. All my little bits of work seem dull— But I shall soon pick up and be happy in it again.' In a letter to Herbert Baker (May 10, 1908) he said:

> The L.C.C. I feel sick of—bruised with. One was so in the dark as to what was wanted. The site so lovely, the conditions so difficult. You will see the drawings and I know I lost much by working on so carefully without a chance of amending the conditions. What they chose was a corridor 700 ft. long, 8 ft. wide, shocking detail, without any architectural quality. I feel mine was all quality! only to be appreciated in a building *built*.

This was largely true. His County Hall was a work of very fine quality—much finer than the authorities, in the event, required. Knott's plan, as he contemptuously notes, was precisely a series of very long office corridors with rooms on each side, the Council Hall in the middle, and four similar oblong internal courts. It recommended itself presumably as attaining an effect with the minimum of expense, and notably not proposing as top dressing anything more than a lantern on the roof— even its front portico was omitted. But even so, and in disregard of their own condition as regards corridors, the assessors' award was capricious to say the least.

It is an interesting speculation what would have been the effect on Lutyens's career had he won the County Hall competition. Would he, like the architect who obtained the commission, have been so engulfed in it that it became his grave as well as his memorial? His failure, deeply as he felt it at the time, proved in the event fortunate. 'What I want is a nice big house to do and the heart to do it well,' he told Lady Emily in January, 1908. Again, writing from Lindisfarne in July whither Hudson had summoned him to assist in receiving the Prince and Princess of Wales,

'I have not yet arrived at a church, which is depressing.' Before the end of the year he was commissioned to design two churches—at Hampstead—and two 'nice big' country houses were not far off—Temple Dinsley and Great Maytham, which have already been described.

He had lost his first big stakes in the High Game. But in the process he had established himself as the most distinguished architect of his generation. He was not yet quite forty; discerning critics had recognised the outstanding quality of his County Hall designs; in the event the High Game for him was only about to begin.

HOW TO TELESCOPE AN ENTABLATURE (*see* p. 181)

CHAPTER VII

29 BLOOMSBURY SQUARE

THE speed of Lutyens's success in the first decade of the century aroused noticeable jealousy in certain senior competitors such as Aston Webb and Reginald Blomfield, and at least made other colleagues wonder how he got such a phenomenal sequence of commissions. The quality of his work was not questioned. But its quantity and his apparent aloofness, tended to surround him with an aura of mystery that, to unfriendly eyes, seemed equivocal. 'He has had advantages we have not had,' was a comment, accompanied by a meaning look, sometimes to be heard in architectural circles. The way, too, in which several well-known architects had found themselves supplanted by him was remembered, though the circumstances, narrated in Chapter V, were either not known or distorted. Few colleagues were invited into his home or had met his wife who, giving her 'handle' to his name, was suspected by many of manipulating social wires to further his interests from the privacy of 29 Bloomsbury Square. The fact that home and office were under the same roof heightened rather than allayed this suspicion. Occasional fleeting encounters with a lady in the hall, or nursery sounds from up the stately staircase, emphasised the existence of an invisible wall, which few other architects penetrated and which, some thought, screened the mysterious Lady Emily's occult designs.

There were elements of truth in this notion, but, as is often the case, wrong conclusions were drawn from the facts. There certainly was feminine influence behind Lutyens's architectural beginnings, but less that of petticoats than of hobnail boots. For every one commission due to his wife's connections, quite ten can be traced directly or indirectly to Miss Jekyll's recommendation. Soon after 1900, however, the reputation of his own work, with Edward Hudson's publicising of it in *Country Life* and his own peculiar technique in cultivating social contacts, began to yield their cumulative results. The propaganda department at 29 Bloomsbury Square was situated downstairs not upstairs, and for most of his life he was 'working to get work'. The Lutyens publicity service was quite ingenuous, but no less ingenious and effective.

§1. WALLS AND OPENINGS

That there was a rigid if invisible partition between office and home was due primarily to Lady Emily. But it betokened no sense of *social* cleavage. Indeed it was inevitable, as in any house divided between professional and domestic life.

It had originated as soon as the young couple had decided to make home and office under a single roof. Then Mr. Bob Webb of Milford had read Emmy a lecture on her regarding Ned's office as entirely sacred to his work, into which she must never intrude unless after office hours or at week-ends. That became a fixed principle, and applied equally to the children. Nor did the office staff, any more than their visitors to the office, penetrate upstairs except by invitation. The need for this rigid separation was vividly illustrated by the elopement of Dalton with the pretty housemaid.

But it was to have much more far-reaching results on husband and wife. Its very artificiality tended, as time went on, to emphasise the separateness of their interests. And the partition was strengthened by the comparative failure to develop a joint social life that would have merged, at least occasionally, the professional and domestic sides. It was this absence of promiscuous hospitality that was often misinterpreted into exclusiveness. The truth was the reverse. Both were innately shy, neither really had social aptitude, and Lutyens, with the most worthy intentions, was the reverse of open-handed. The causes of his carefulness with money, and many instances of the way he worried about it, have already been noticed. Its bearing upon the partition between his professional and family life is curiously illustrated by Robert Lutyens's recollection that, on the occasions when the family travelled *en masse*, father went first class and the rest third. This distinction was, in the main, simply an admission of the partition of the house: travelling time for Lutyens was office time, its cost coming under 'expenses'. But usually the family's came from the domestic budget, which he considered that his wife, though she herself always lived with utmost simplicity, was inclined to overtax by her solicitude for the children's welfare. They were darlings, but he was a poor man and they must learn to travel 'hard'.

The move to Bloomsbury, in the winter of 1897, had been prophetic, in several ways, of how things were to work out. After the honeymoon, the Balfours had lent the Lutyenses 24 Addison Road. Just before the move was arranged, Ned got influenza. He was so anxious to open the new office that, as soon as he was well enough to go out, it was decided to hire a Coupé[1]—in those days a considerable extravagance to them—and set up house in Bloomsbury Square. On arrival, he became immersed in the office, and Lady Emily went upstairs to find that there was of course not a stick of furniture or carpet anywhere. Appealed to by telephone, kind Mr. Heaton the decorator and previous resident, whose place of business was in Bloomsbury Street, sent round a bed, a chair, a table, and some matting for the bedroom floor.

---

[1] A smartly turned-out brougham with rubber-tired wheels. About 1890 a company for the hiring-out of these conveyances—the only alternative to the 'four-wheeler'—was formed by Mr. Courtauld Thomson then recently graduated from Oxford and now Lord Courtauld Thomson. Within a few years the Coupé Company owned mewses for its vehicles all over London. The founder disposed of his interest in the concern immediately following the appearance of the first internal combustion machine in London.

That was the only living-room habitable for months, and the smell of the matting made Lady Emily, in the early stages of pregnancy, feel sick. In the evenings she would sit in the office, where the smoke of Ned's pipes had the same effect.

In the ideal home they had been supposed to sit thus of an evening discussing jobs and schemes, and the young wife was indeed passionately interested in every one of them. When left by herself she decided to be helpful by collecting all his loose photographs and postcards of buildings and sticking them in an album, which would be convenient for him to show clients as examples of his work. When complete 'The Works of Edwin Landseer Lutyens' was presented to him. Unfortunately the pictures were not of his work at all, but odds and ends, advertisements and 'awful warnings'. They were both rather hurt by the episode. It sadly confirmed her in the realisation, which she had always suspected, that she had not the kind of mind to be a technical helpmate, though she hoped in time to learn to read a plan and make some sense of the walls and openings representing a building in course of construction. Meanwhile he filled and lit and half-smoked and relit his innumerable little pipes. Under protest he could get on without her but never without tobacco. Unless smoking was a sedative or a catalyst to him, she concluded that it must be a defence, literally a smoke screen, against a critical world, in the same way that he presented himself to people as a punning and slightly ribald jester.

So for some time Bloomsbury Square was in no condition to receive visitors. Then its châtelaine did not want people with whom he dined or stayed in the course of business (or possible business)—people whom they could not afford to entertain in return—to feel it necessary to include her in the invitation. He, on the other hand, was naturally sociable, up to the point when his own shyness would suddenly get the better of him, and so it came about that he went out, and she generally remained at home.

In these social and professional contacts, his enthusiastic naïvety constituted a great part of his charm; and whilst he would lament his lack of an impressive manner, and reiterate to his wife his very real need of her sensible seriousness, he was aware of naivety's value to him as a social technique. It distinguished him from other architects, could be used to delight and divert clients at awkward moments or whilst he was thinking. Indeed the *enfant terrible* touch was to become his outward habit. In later life the more serious-minded often took exception to what they regarded as a tiresome pose or genuine irresponsibility. Yet it was that true ingenuousness, God-given to a few great minds. Now, in his late twenties, slim, with dark hair curling back from a high semi-dome of brow, blue eyes like wide-open gimlets and delicate hands rarely still, his boyishness was still entirely natural, since, having never been subjected to the process of 'all that being knocked out of him' at school, and growing up in the protected feminine world of Milford and Munstead, he had developed no inhibitions. Yet extreme delicacy and sensitiveness of feeling, his innate gentleness, and observant curiosity of others' methods and manners, saved him from the uncouthness that sometimes accompanies and often simulates natural genius. But his seeming ingenuousness was not simply to be excused by his precocious ability as an artist; it was largely caused by and needful to his absorption in his art. To the entire artist all knowledge, conventions, techniques, not directly necessary for the fulfilment of his art, are encumbrances; subconsciously he avoids them as potentially repressive of his art's, his ego's, fulfilment. It is not only because Lutyens was that rare and socially precious being, an artist entire and unrepressed, but because with all his tiresomeness he was so lovable, that the study of his peculiarities, and of the psychology of his marriage, is so engrossing. In one of his letters at this time he accurately summed up his preoccupations by the injunction to his wife: 'pray that I may work well for Art and Emmy, Emmy and Art.' The essential significance, and success, of his marriage lay in the integrity and unselfishness with which his wife filled the third corner of this triangle.

During those first months he was busy on Orchards, the Roseneath hotel, Fulbrook, Lord Battersea's house at Cromer, finishing off Berry Down, and the trips to Paris connected with the Exhibition Pavilion. And Lady Emily, increasingly a mother-to-be, had her hands full trying to get the house in some order. Like other young ladies of the period, she had no experience of household management, whilst he was sure, from what people like Miss Jekyll and Mrs. Earle (Lady Emily's aunt) always said, that good cooking was really quite simple. He was also insistent that he should have all the household books fully made up weekly for inspection and settlement from his own bank account. An admirable precept had he given the time to look at them.

Being herself inexpert in cooking, indeed until marriage a vegetarian on the precept of Mrs. Earle, the mistress was not able to teach a succession of very plain cooks to be anything else, so that entertainment at Bloomsbury Square was further discouraged. One of their first guests was a hospitable hostess who had often entertained Ned as a bachelor at an admirably appointed table. Lady Emily long remembered the agonies of dismay that she felt for him—and the guest—at a high sounding soup which proved to be gravy, followed by 'salmi of duck' consisting of a few bones and more gravy. On the other hand, whilst insistent theoretically on economy, his ideas of hospitality were generous. A typically marital *billet doux* from the housewife may be given here whilst we are on the subject, though a little later in date:

June 2nd 1902.

About Heatleys bill, I think there must be a mistake, but you are so extravagant over the champagne and never think it must be paid for, and it is too silly for a man in your position to give champagne as you do.

Some similar reproof drew from him a characteristic soft answer: 'Your scold falls on such nice moist growing ground.'

In the redecoration of the house 'Bareness and Whiteness' was the key-note. Repainting the walls white, instead of the 'art shades' currently affected, showed up the fine Georgian proportions and details and produced the effect outlined in the 'ideal' home, where touches of pure colour in a lacquer cabinet, table linen, or woodwork were contrasted to prevailing lightness. As a decorator Lutyens was always austere, averse from rich colouring because *form* was his dominating interest and he mistrusted the sensuousness of colour effects. Colour, when used, must be strong and even, part of the architectural design and not overlaid and incidental. In the drawing-room at Bloomsbury Square, which had a very fine marble chimney piece and modillion cornice, he produced a characteristically 'daring' effect with black walls, white woodwork, the floor painted green on white, yellow curtains, the red lacquer cabinet and a magnificent black lacquer screen which had cost him more than he could afford. The effect of the walls was not black of course, but of reflections from the strong colours and light surfaces. There were a few distinguished-looking chairs, with cushions bought on the honeymoon, a specially designed bookcase in natural wood, and no comfort, since a sofa was taboo. The desired bareness was produced, in any case, by absence of many possessions. In the dining-room, red walls, a geeen painted floor with a few old rugs, and the bare oak table that he had designed, laid with red or blue napkins and pewter plates, produced a greater semblance of cheer, but was comfortless enough—though undeniably striking, especially to the knees of guests encountering the framework of the table. In the bedroom, the Casket held pride of place, but there was also the massive oak four-poster bedstead designed for the 'ideal' home. This had slender baluster-shaped posts of wrought iron and is extremely heavy. A handsome object, of the kind sometimes depicted by Italian masters in such solemn scenes as the Annunciation, its beautifully sharp mouldings proved in practice a source of considerable pain to a succession of children.

Their first child was born in August, 1898, when Lutyens was dividing the time between Paris, Varengeville, Surrey, and London. As soon as she could travel Lady Emily set off with the baby on the first of the yearly migrations to the east coast, staying on the way with her learned old friend Whitwell Elwin at Booton, where the baby was christened. They then went to the Locker Lampsons at Cromer where father, since he was building Overstrand Hall and Lord Battersea's pleasaunce, could be with them for week-ends but, in between, had his first experience of going upstairs in the evenings to an empty home. 'How I miss you,' he wrote in September, 'the house is so silent and blank and growls at me because you are far from it. My sole companion is the empty pram.' From Munstead he sent 'a page of drawings for Barbara.' Barbara, and Emily's motherhood, was enchanting to him and inspired some of his most delightful sidelines—the exquisite mother and child group on p. 154, sketched on the way to Paris in January '99, and 'an epic written in one half minute' with a picture of Barbara on top of the world.

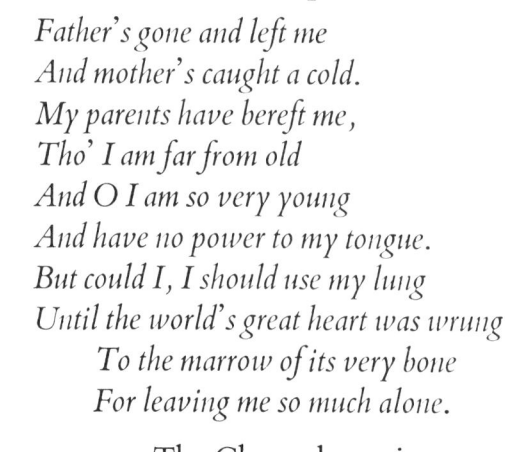

Father's gone and left me
And mother's caught a cold.
My parents have bereft me,
Tho' I am far from old
And O I am so very young
And have no power to my tongue.
But could I, I should use my lung
Until the world's great heart was wrung
  To the marrow of its very bone
  For leaving me so much alone.

  The Channel crossing was a bad one, but we see him 'very brave and stalwart', facing the elements, and then he drew a series of Barbaras in various guises, on the theme of 'Wouldn't Barbara make a darling angel Pope... or at the least a Bishop.... Whether she is Pope, Bishop, or Queen... she holds my heart in complete subjection and I long for her Presence, which means you [with a tail of underlinings] too'.

49. GREAT MAYTHAM, ROLVENDEN, SUSSEX (1909)

50. TEMPLE DINSLEY, HERTFORDSHIRE. The new wing, 1908

51. COMPETITION DESIGN FOR LONDON COUNTY HALL (1907)

52. THE SALUTATION, SANDWICH, KENT (1911)

These Barbara sketches may give some idea of a series of mural drawings of her with which he decorated the whitewashed walls of a room at Berrydown for Archibald Grove. It will be recalled that he was working on this Hampshire house at the time of his betrothal, and consequently, perhaps, Mr. and Mrs. Grove took a lively interest in their architect's marriage. The Groves figure prominently in these early Bloomsbury Square annals, for they were among the very few clients who became friends of both, often having the whole Lutyens ménage to stay. Archibald Grove, with Arthur Chapman of Crooksbury, was one of those business men liable to mysterious fluctuations of fortune. He is said to have been a very small enthusiastic man, with very tall wife and stepdaughter, whom it was diverting to see him energetically chivying around, and he had a passionate admiration for artists. Not only for Lutyens, who consequently expanded in his company, but for J. M. Barrie and his wife, whom the Lutyenses first met at his house.

This was the beginning of a life-long friendship. Barrie and Lutyens had traits in common, intensely fastidious and sensitive, liable to go shy to the point of inarticulacy, yet with the spirits of schoolboys and the same nonsense. As artists both possessed the peculiar gift of giving shape to that which often lies perilously between intuition and knowledge, of expressing the inexpressible. At this juncture Barrie, according to Mr. Mackail, was germinating simultaneously ideas for *The Little White Bird, The Admirable Crichton, Quality Street,* and *Peter Pan*. He was already famous and rich, and 'without knowing it becoming just a little spoilt. The money was doing that. It made his friends look at him differently and him more difficult to contradict. But with it he was so often doubly in a world apart'—from those friends and from his secretly disappointed wife. After dinner at the Groves', on this or a subsequent occasion, there was a game of dressing up, and Lady Emily, by rearranging her hair and putting on a shawl, transformed herself so completely that, Barrie said afterwards, she gave him one of the central ideas in *Quality Street*. This must have been the origin of Phoebe Throssal who, in the play, has so many tricks played with her real and apparent age. When *Quality Street* opened in London, in the summer of 1902 (it was first given in the United States in the previous autumn), Lutyens was engaged to design the scenery. It was just about the time when we have seen him beginning to interest himself critically in the neo-Georgian work at Chesters and Gosford, and when Monkton took shape. Seen against the pattern of his private life, that transition away from romanticism towards the human and rational values of classicism may well have been initiated, or speeded, by the new contentment that he was finding in the realisation of his marriage ideal.

After the first night of *Quality Street*, both the Lutyenses wrote to the author—with a little trepidation, perhaps, since they both made first copies which have survived. Lady Emily said how proud she felt to think that she had been 'the unconscious inspirer of such a real work of genius' but ventured a few criticisms, as that

'Mr. Hicks I thought was good but still rather too noisy'. 'Miss [Ellaline] Terriss did the part most delicately, but I am afraid I thought Miss Terry [in her own part of Phoebe] very bad—not really old enough or precise enough, or dignified enough—and there was *no* change in her appearance during the years.' Lutyens's letter is interesting for his opinion of stage realism, and shows, incidentally, that he still addressed the great J. M. B. with a touch of awed deference.

September 18. 02.

My dear Barrie

I *do*^{oo} congratulate you on the success of 'Quality Street'. There it is—and it is good!

I hope you wont think it cheek my thinking so . . . and saying it!

I have been wondering whether an animate, or an inanimate, vehicle is the more difficult for an artist to paint his picture with. The animate is apt to turn round and paint the painter—which you must allow is awkward.

My youth, save the mark . . . (of time?) convinces me that the more real a scene is the better it must be in effect and that scenic conventions are a fraud: at all events the real thing might want in force, but it would not come forcibly wrong—and if slight it might form the better background and less disturbing to a play—necessary emphasis can be procured by light—?

It was very pleasant to see Francoeur relaxed and happy.

If you care for my esteem and will allow me to put aside youth and talk as a Father—do you relax and rest—at that ½ apple of a world the seaside.

Yrs. ever sincerely,

E. L. Lutyens

and remember that [there] is always a bed here for you and a black room to be seen at night.

Another house where they were both, of course, always welcome was Munstead Wood. There is an enormous letter—written on sheets 12″ × 21″ because Lady Emily had complained of his not writing enough, which contains a portrait of Bumps that Miss Jekyll considered rather ill-natured (see opposite page). And among other matters records with pride that:

Yesterday I went to Thursley! and honoured my Father and my Mother that our days may be long in the land we have not yet got. Father looking magnificent.

At Munstead House Col. Jekyll had as guests Leonard Borwick, the pianist (over from his enchanted stone manor house at West Burton under the Sussex downs), the Mure Mackenzies (sister and brother-in-law of the Jekylls), and old 'Braby'-Brabazon—a Sussex squire, looks like a very thin Prussian Colonel and paints delicious impressionist watercolours in Venice—loves young men and fathers them and I believe does them all sorts of good and kindness. I think I shall like Borwick, he raves of Plazzoh. Mrs. Irving [of Rake Manor which he altered for her] said what she did admire us for was not minding parting from one another. O, I said, but I *did*. I minded very much—

Dictatorial Bumps says I am to tell you 'that Nedi is a great dear (something awful coming) but that I am kept occupied the whole time he is here in shutting the doors that he leaves open'. She also says—tell Mrs. Grove—that all the best she has written about flower borders is in the chapter called Flower Garden and Pergola in *Wood & Garden*. Tell Mrs. Grove, too, that I have made Mr. Robinson promise to come down in September.

In a postscript he refers to Miss Jekyll having suggested lending them Plazzoh for ten days, in September '99: 'and we shall have a honeymoon. It will be a *joy*, we *must* come'; and there is another picture of Bumps, this time angelic, and he says how he longs for another fishing day with his wife.

Fishing was his only pastime, besides playing patience. They had just spent a fishing holiday with E. Baynes Badcock, whose short-lived association with Lutyens in the Bloomsbury Square office has been described (Chapter V), and his wife in their cottage at Rhayader. At that time they had all been happy together, and Mrs. Badcock, who was a talented artist, did drawings of the Lutyenses.[1]

§2. OTHER PEOPLE'S HOUSES

Robert was born in June 1901. A few weeks later, writing of his depression about the Queen Victoria Memorial, Lutyens said that he had noticed in a paper the name of a horse, 'Heartache by Adieu out of Lady Emily; shall we call Robert Heartache?' In the next sentence he rather wished he had a motor car, and listed the jobs that one of those remarkable new vehicles would enable him to visit conveniently. But he never got one, till twenty years later he was given a Rolls Royce by Lady Sackville.

Now that there were two babies, he was all the more the diner-out and goer-away, while Lady Emily stayed in the nursery, wherever it was at the time. So we get the word-pictures of house parties and odd week-ends some of which have already been quoted. There was the 'jolly place but parson-ridden and ostentatious a bit', the homely middle-class one, with 'a bullfinch just outside this room which sings the same song as Mrs. Webb's bully used to pipe, and stops on the same bar, to

[1] Reproduced in Robert Lutyens, *Sir Edwin Lutyens: An Appreciation in Perspective.*

repeat the opening again and again'. The smart parties: 'the Curzons were with the Batterseas, but I wasn't introduced;' Lady Windsor invited them to Hewell, 'would you care to go? I should like to see the house, but don't shoot;' and a week-end at Warwick Castle where,

> the party is Mrs. Randolph Churchill West and her George,[1] Lady Delawarr and daughter, Mr. and Mrs. Archibald Flower, brewer at Stratford on Avon and Mayor, Mr. Frewen, married Mrs. West's sister, Lord Kenyon, Lady Margaret Orr-Ewing, Mr. Whittle who is lame, Sir Vincent somebody and Lord Cairns, a keen fisherman for salmon. I always feel a third in every party and out of it. My cold *awful*.

It was the high summer of the great country houses, when the stately and skilful Edwardian hostesses gathered the more with the less effective members of the ruling caste, the political peer and sporting magnate, the celebrated beauty and poor relation, the professional guest and fashionable artist, with their maids and valets and, in the case of the more venturesome, their chauffeur, into Saturday to Monday communities that peopled the flower-filled salons and great elm-shaded lawns with guests at least half of whom were well worth knowing to a coming architect. Among them might be a fellow guest with a similar mansion of his own that needed bringing up to the required standard of comfort—though even then more than one visitor's bathroom was something exceptional; it was quite normal to bathe in one's bedroom. Or a house that was too small and needed a wing for such gatherings; or, better still, could be persuaded to come to a decision over building a new house altogether. A party such as that at Warwick was calculated, as not infrequently happened with Lutyens, 'to bring all my shy side uppermost.' But regular exercise in changes of environment, and a naturally sociable temperament, soon enabled him to evolve a party technique. His pencil came to the relief of his tongue, and on the pad, known as a 'virgin', that he always carried in his pocket there would be drawn some at first puzzling lines that with the last touch or when turned upside down or held up to the light (these were called 'transparencies') resolved themselves into ludicrous, sometimes rather 'naughty', pictures, at which only the thickest ice would fail to crack. If there were children in the house they would cluster delightedly round 'the funny man' as he drew, sometimes with their own chalks, the most absurd stories, in which, say, a tall guardsman would be seen riding a little horse then, with a twist of the paper, be left standing while the horse galloped away from beneath him: or there was a calm blue sea, with

---
[1] Widow of Lord Randolph, and mother of Mr. Winston Churchill; married in 1895, Capt. G. F. M. Cornwallis West.

boats on it and reflections, and a big red sunset which somehow turned into a bather with an enormous tummy floating on his back. Or he would tell them a picture story like those that he drew for his own children, such as the tale of the bear and the goat who went a-wooing. But if it was a hesitating yet potential builder who was looking on, a seductive house might take shape before his eyes, with the particular features that he wanted ingeniously provided or deftly sketched in blank spaces of the broad design. Scores of country house and garden schemes must have burgeoned thus in after-dinner games, not a few of which were realised.

The process—a mild but effective form of publicity—was called 'keeping people up to the mark'. Just before the Coronation (August 1902) Mr. Debenham 'told me he had received £30,000 from Carnegie for public libraries in Marylebone and that he had written to Greenwood about an architect, so I scolded him. He owned he quite forgot me—though he was that very day coming to see me. It shows how important it is to keep people up to the mark!!'

Writing from Buckhurst Park, he described how he had watched the Coronation procession from Mrs. Beaumont's, 142 Piccadilly.

> She had been staying at Munstead and had evidently had a dose of me! and realises for the first time that I am an architect. Very keen that I should induce Mr. B. to let her build with me a house; rather nice of her... I met, to speak to ... Lady M. and her Sir John—she as vulgar and as assertive as ever, he a regular idiot soldier of distinction in full war paint—but nice, stroking her hand on every occasion and even getting the point of his cocked hat into her eye... and Augustus Hare with whom I made much agreeable conversation on matters of artistic citizenship. He has bought the Q Anne statue that stood before St. Pauls and erected the fat lady and her four attendants in his apparently small garden. When you realise she would not go under any tunnel, and had to go on three trucks lying on her tummy you can imagine what it means.

His critical view of the Crown and the Coronation generally has been mentioned already; it was quite unkind, referring to 'dissolute majesty dissolving in age', but he enjoyed 'the real fairy story gilt coach, absurdly large and gingerbready', and was fascinated by the way the peers' and peeresses' coronets sat on their heads—'full round and squarely like a straw hat, not small things perched all on top as I imagined'. King Edward's coronation, it must be remembered, aroused mixed feelings. Hardly anybody living had witnessed the coronation of a British sovereign, so that there was immense curiosity. But the South African War had added disillusionment to the sense of loss for the old Queen. And the new King's reputation raised little more enthusiasm in the puritanical middle class than in the critical Lutyens.

Nevertheless, when he was summoned to West Dean Park, Sussex, where Mr. and Mrs. Willie James had so often entertained the King when Prince of Wales, he was agog with curiosity. It may be imagined that a certain mysterious glamour attached to this celebrated and exclusive establishment, and to its chatelaine (a daughter of Sir John Forbes of Newe) whom, in particular, the Prince honoured with his favour. So Ned sent home a most particular account of the experience. The building that ensued was Monkton, described in Chapter V.

March 15. 1902.

I arrived yesterday. Met at station by neat brougham.

The house, West Dean Park fairly close by. The house is a church-warden pseudo Gothic erection—big: all built of knapped flints—and curiously worked: added to by E. George so bad: I think: and added again by Mr. James and the estate. Practical but worse, well as bad.

Very smart and luxurious and lots of beautiful things and a ping pong table etc etc. No untoward evidence of Royal favors by way of photos.

I arrived at 7. Shewn into her sitting room—of course I saw Mr. James first and was astounded to find him so much younger than I expected and so much more gentlemanlike. Then there were 3 ladies, which was Mrs. James? Miss Rorke shaded by a lamp was invisible. How long my moments of absent inaction were I cant imagine . . . before I discovered Miss Rorke.

Mrs. James is expecting and lay on a sofa, and then there was a Miss Maxwell whose sister lives at Tyttenhanger near Hatfield and who has stayed with Madame Grunelius. Tell me who Miss Maxwell is. Her position in the *house* seemed rather one of companion. Miss Rorke very bossful and all there, but kind and feeling responsible for me backed me up and spoke of things I had built [which] I had much rather had not been mentioned.

Mr. James very neat, small: thin: young, turning towards, but gently, to middle age. Very quiet, reserved collected: an occasional spark of human feeling shewn by a twinkle: Improving on acquaintance and for a very rich man —sitting on Hoheit's lap—delightful.

Mrs. James. 1st Impression
Roundabout bar maid
quizzy cynical and conceited

2nd Impression
VERY short sighted, strong pince nezs. hair done in *horrid* Batten way. not suited to a round cherubby face. Nose tipped and very tilted. lovely hands. Gay, thoughtless extravagant as she has rights to be: beautifully dressed lovely rings. Makes all the noises squeaks that only a little woman may or dare make.

doing, and sketch amendments on that, ringing the chosen variant. Since there was no Chief Assistant as in most other offices, each man took his finished work to Lutyens himself. The master was often severely critical of it, and of the draughtsman; but if he thought that he had hurt a man's feelings he would go out of his way to console him before the end of the day. Often the assistant would come to his board of a morning to find it had been corrected during the night. These young men learnt, if they had the wits to profit by their unique opportunity, from what they saw, by watching the master drawing, experimenting, selecting. Lutyens would never expound or explain what he was doing, though he talked disjointedly and more or less unintelligibly as he drew.

His manner with clients was much the same. They would watch fascinated, with a sense of seeing their house take shape before their eyes. On the other hand they were almost powerless to control or amend a design once conceived. If they had come to the office prepared to make a row, within a couple of minutes his charm had mollified them, with sketched ideas for this or that and probably a dig in the ribs and 'nonsense, that won't ruin you! but don't tell your wife!' Not the least remarkable aspect of Lutyens's personality was the way that, in almost every case, he not only persuaded his clients to have what he wanted to give them, but genuinely convinced himself that that to which he had persuaded them was what they had actually specified. Probably Heathcote is the outstanding example of a client thus getting the exact opposite of what he originally wanted, down to the smallest detail, and becoming immensely proud of it. In his description of the design to Baker, it will be remembered that Lutyens stressed that the client had 'wanted cupboards galore, in all rooms, right and left of the windows'. Milne, however, distinctly recalls Mr. Hemingway, a simple Yorkshire manufacturer without an *h* to his name, telling him that he and his wife were always content to hang their clothes over a chair at night!

The client's notion of seeing his house take shape before his eyes was something of an illusion too. In most cases it had, of course, already taken shape, in Lutyens's mind on the site. The genesis of Mr. and Mrs. James's Monkton on the Sussex Downs has already been instanced. Plan and elevation will have been pencilled on squared paper on the way home. In the same way Lutyens came back to the office one evening and gave Milne some sheets of squared paper to work from containing the complete rough designs for Little Thakeham.

These small pencil sketches, sometimes even on scraps of paper, would have indications of proportions noted in figures. A moulding would be outlined, but its angle would be applied to it by the assistant according to the office system. That system, which gave the distinctive Lutyens character to all his work, consisted at this time in a few fairly simple rules based on his ways of handling materials, which he had arrived at by trial and error in the course of his practice. In later years, as he developed his classical idiom, some were modified and others added. One of the cardinal rules established was that the angle of all inclined planes should be 54·45°—the angle of visual projection formed by the intersection of two planes, e.g. two roofs, inclined at an angle of 45°. All roofs and cornices were reduced to 54·45°. The same angle is also produced by the 'diagonal of a square' ratio for window panes, which in most cases also gave the proportions of the whole window. It is a coincidence; but the coincidence conferred a peculiar significance, a sense of mathematical inevitability, on this particular angle, confirming its visual rightness. One of his very few precepts, 'Everything should have an air of inevitability,' emphasises how Lutyens studied to arrive at such simple mathematical ratios; though it might seem, superficially, to clash with another of his *dicta*, 'One of the elements of beauty is Surprise.' In practice the two ideals conflict no more than when an epigram expresses truth with a surprising but inevitable word. Indeed 'Architecture is building with wit' was another of Lutyens's. And to him the soul of wit was simplicity.

The existence of these office ratios, and their continual use in his later work, has given rise to the belief (elaborated by Robert Lutyens in his Memoir) that the master worked to an elaborate preconceived system of ratios. All the first-hand evidence on this matter is to the contrary. There is no doubt that in many of his designs, particularly the later ones, their dimensions and angles do embody mathematical ratios of considerable subtlety. And, once evolved, they were used again and again, especially those governing mouldings. But these ratios were not conceived in the abstract. In the first instance they were evolved by trial and error to justify visual preference, and were converted into a mathematical formula secondly. They were arrived at mainly by juggling with his sketch design, in which he conceived the rough proportion required. If the stock ratio, as given in the text-book or by previous usage, did not meet the case, the design was delicately adjusted until the required mathematically inevitable ratio emerged.[1]

Since his spontaneous conceptions were in small and ostensibly rough drawings, which the assistant had to scale and draw up with all these niceties that contribute so much to the individuality of a Lutyens building, each of these young men came to be convinced that he himself shared direct responsibility in evolving them. He felt that he was helping to create architectural forms that would be studied and measured by future generations. As the master bent over his shoulder, muttering and wuffling, and amending what the assistant had drawn out and would now have to draw out again, the latter had the inspiring sense that that part of the design was in a real sense his own. Lutyens thought nothing of scrapping an entire set of drawings several times; there was rarely a change of design, but often of ratios or proportions which meant recasting throughout. But since he drove himself unsparingly, the loyalty and toil that he expected of his assistants were given unquestioningly. Convinced of

---

[1] For Lutyens's system of angles, see *The Architecture*, vol. I. ch. 5; III. ch. 2.

their individual responsibility, they had caught his enthusiasm and, like him, set their work before everything else. No doubt he expected it; he expressed no particular gratitude even for night work. On the other hand he left his young men alone, without complaint if their high spirits found vent in song, laughter or mild ragging.

Hannen, for instance, had a fine voice, and with Phipps and Milne, constituted a regular glee choir that would burst into harmony at the least excuse. And Phipps, besides being a clever caricaturist, possessed a full-bodied infectious laugh. I. P. Huddart came in for a good deal of cheerful teasing, and Phipps had a standing altercation, heated but always good-natured, with the little American Wallich, on the relative superiority of British and American institutions—which always culminated in a pacification formula, chanted in chorus, of 'Hands Across the Sea'. The only occasion recalled by Hannen of this uninhibited crew receiving reproof was when he threw a pat of butter (for office tea) at Evans's head which, missing its mark, smacked against Lutyens's door. Then the master's head appeared, said 'Steady', and withdrew.

To the assistants at Bloomsbury Square in the early years of the century the office evidently had exactly the atmosphere of the studio in *Trilby*, its comradeship among the assistants, its atmosphere of spontaneous happiness and of devotion to the essentials of art. This atmosphere, permeating the office and colouring the whole attitude to life and work of this particular group of men, emanated from that exquisite honesty which Lutyens brought to life and work alike and instilled into his followers as 'the true spirit'. In relation to persons the true spirit took the form of entire trust, unquestioning belief in the best side of those with whom he associated; an assumption that no one concerned with architecture would be actuated by other than virtuous motives. His distress at the ca'canny and profanity of some of the workmen at the Paris Exhibition, and his distaste for some of the types with whom he had to consort, have illustrated it. In his art the true spirit had necessarily to be correlated with aesthetic and technical factors, but constituted his ideal and permeates all Lutyens's work. An apparently simple realisation of his ideal aesthetic and mathematical truthfulness is provided by the serene roof of Middlefield, with its complete yet subtle straightforwardness. It was the great truthfulness and simplicity of Wren that held his devotion; the rhetoric in baroque that repelled him. In architecture he scorned effects not inherent in the handling of the materials or the plan. He hinted this conviction in that letter to J. M. Barrie after seeing *Quality Street*: 'the more real a scene is, the better it must be in effect; scenic conventions are a fraud.' Nicolas Hannen, who became an actor-manager, has illumined this facet of Lutyens by remarking: 'In stage production you can build up dramatic effect by dramatic, i.e. artificial, means; or—and now I see that, schooled by Lutyens's "true spirit", I have tried to realise it—you can aim at the utmost truth in the stage's reflection of life.'

Similarly the nature of Lutyens's aesthetic honesty can perhaps be crystallised by saying that he aimed at the utmost truth in *architecture's* reflection of life. Architecture's reflection of *life*, be it observed; not of abstract values, nor of structural means, nor of a building's functional purpose, but of the humanity that men of the renaissance age were accustomed to transfer to the forms and proportions of architecture. This is the essence of Geoffrey Scott's thesis in *The Architecture of Humanism*, that renaissance architecture was, consciously or unconsciously, conceived to reflect through the medium of art the physical proportions, civilised needs, and mental processes of human beings. The operative words in the thesis are 'through the medium of art'. It was the honesty, the transparent clarity, of the Lutyens art-medium, added to his inexhaustible invention, which made E. V. Lucas and some other perceptive contemporaries set him upon the Shakespearean plane of genius.

In the office this moral and aesthetic idealisation of Truth radiated as an atmosphere of happiness and creative enthusiasm, but was directly manifested only through the daily processes of work, or in an occasional phrase. Outside the office, however, there was now and then an episode when one of the young men encountered it face to face. From their accounts it must have been strangely akin to a spiritual experience yet wholly, disarmingly, natural; intensely human. Hannen has given me an example in his recollection of a visit to Lindisfarne, when work there was just finished. Lutyens had taken the younger man with him, both travelling with Hudson as his guests in the utmost style. They arrived late on the island where the two architects were sharing a room in the Castle. As they prepared for bed, the pupil, in his own words, found that the master had established a relationship of complete spiritual intimacy with him. Not only had the constraint between master and pupil disappeared, but the younger man found himself pouring out his personal problems to one who seemed to understand wholly and, listening sympathetically, to advise him as a well-known brother. 'His suggestions were no doubt idealistically impractical,' Hannen says, 'such as to emulate my family's most distinguished members. Yet the very simplicity of the advice, and the way Lut-lut overlooked every obstacle, had the effect of inspiring me with new faith in myself and the future.'

Faith in self, in one's inmost genius, one's grain of God capable of all things; that was the secret of his simplicity, underlying the work and the atmosphere of the office no less than Lutyens's art and personal life. Had he not inscribed upon the Casket *As Faith wills, so Fate fulfils*?

§4. UPSTAIRS

In the two previous chapters an account has been given of the principal houses Lutyens was building during the first decade of the century. But it is not easy to convey, in narrative form, the way they each overlapped one another and the two halves of 29 Bloomsbury Square interacted, the professional and the social, the creative and the intimate. Their simultaneity is vividly apparent when reading the letters to his wife from which so much of this chapter is inevitably drawn. As written, however, most of them are disjointed and discursive, dashed off in trains or to catch the last post, referring to perhaps half a dozen jobs in different places and stages, with impressions of people and doings of the day, personal and domestic details, expressions of financial anxiety or relief, occasionally references to the babies, and invariably some affectionate caress for her eyes alone. Throughout, the suggestive analogy of his mind, which I have used already, is a revolving sharply-facetted sphere reflecting a succession of images but each one of them tending to be distinct from the rest as it comes into focus. Or one can compare it to a compartmented cabinet in the pigeonholes of which each bundle of facts and feelings was neatly filed, accessible in a moment but, when its drawers were closed, leaving him cheerfully serene, apparently empty-minded, happily playing patience or making ridiculous jokes.

But there is a long letter, written during a tour of Somerset and the Cotswolds in 1906 when the family were staying at Holy Island, which I give almost in its entirety, since it presents such a complete picture of him, and of the interaction of his professional and personal preoccupations during three busy days. It was written at that exciting juncture in his affairs, described in Chapter VI, when four clients on one day accepted contracts for four important houses—Heathcote, Nashdom, Eartham, and New Place. He began it,

In the train to Hestercombe. May 4. 06.

Oh dear, have had such a busy time and so rushed that it is a comfort to be able to sit quiet, even in a train. First of all—

[Then follow the detailed figures of the four contracts given on p. 128.]

I went to Steinhardt and made Hudson buy 15 rugs for £130. One was a beautiful carpet and it is at B. Square at present until he gets or builds a house. He doesn't like buying so much but said he was awfully obliged to me; I said he wasn't really at all and he saw the joke and laughed.

I got back and there was an endless stream of people to see, scold, and arrange with, then at 1.15 I went to lunch with the Dolgoroukis. He was there. I had not seen him before: a tall thin man with a big plain and rather coarse head, very proud of having walked from Portland Street to Chancery Lane, mild, simple, very greedy, paints, and oh how badly... She chatty, sparklette (new word!), vague and definite on only one point and that is £15,000—well that is a distinct advance on the original £6,000! We lunched and lunched and then we talked and talked and he drove me down to Glasier's office in St. James's St; I was ½ an hour before my time so I walked up to Beale and Inman and ordered 12 pretty shirts, collars, gloves, and some lovely handkerchiefs. I shall now go to

Hawkes and get some suits, sort out my under linen and then lie low again...
Mr. Glasier is the surveyor of the Westminster syndicate. Jewish origin...
We drafted a letter [regarding a proposed transaction with the L.C.C.] Glasier gave me an enormous cigar wrapped in gold paper—I told him it was a real gaud, which tickled him—but oh what odd folk I have to truckle with. I went back to B. Square, saw someone, and then dictated letters as I dressed. I was barely late for dinner with Mr. and Mrs. Bird in Cadogan Place. They are dears and do, especially he, appreciate my jokes! He is a solicitor and goes big game shooting... I got back to B. Square about ¼ to 12 when Nobbs came with estimate and I didn't get to bed till past 1.0'c, and then and only then was I able to read and enjoy your darling letter.

I slept well—but too soon Florence [parlour-maid] brought me up my letters and awful Hemingway estimates [for Heathcote]. 17,500 odd the lowest! and then but little time to nerve myself to meet him. At 9.0 Muntzer came, 9.30 Hedges the Dormy House clerk of works and Steinhardt the carpet man. Hemingway came at 10 and left at 2.30. He went carefully through the whole house—and then quite mildly accepted the estimates. He told me he was better off than he led me to believe. He had made 20,000 in the last 5 years and spends about 3,000 a year. I got him to sign the contract and as luck would have it the builders came in and so I made them sign too.

Florence improves on acquaintance. She even put her head into the room to talk to me whilst I was in my bath, a thing even dear Nanny hardly dare do! and it is such a comfort and helps make things easy!!

I shall be away all Monday, Eartham. Tuesday, Reading for Cochrane [Folly Farm], easy journey. Wednesday, Dormy House, Walton, easy journey. Thursday Botley, a long day, Mrs. Franklyn. Friday, Holy Island, but it will be a joy to see my love. I left your letter in my drawer so cannot answer it categorically as I generally do, after giving my news. What train do you come up by? You must make yourself really comfy and not over-do and tire my darling. Tomorrow I go from Hestercombe to Stow and Sunday night back to London. So I have a fearful amount of journeying to do. It is a great blow the Barries can't come.

My letters seem so dreadfully egotistical—but my work is all I have to write about... Your mother said it was a pity that we had not our work in common; she and your father had and did everything together. But you can't mix up with my builders and men like Glasier. Political life is so different and as regards what I design and how I do it—I don't know. It just comes because I want it to—and if it don't I have to grip inside and make or force it, and there is no speech that can ever describe it. My only words are foolish—quipps and jibes—but you are there in all my works and whether you will or not are a part of it and in it. And then it is so technical. The political life and those other professions are all based on literature of sorts so that all training grounds for it. My work cannot be approached by Literature which, at the best, produces a Pater or a Ruskin—in the arts. I don't want you to be either of these.

Resuming the letter later, after a day's motoring with Mark Fenwick, he reverted to his happiness at 'all these jobs coming out right as regards price'.

It is only when they do, and the work is to begin that I wake to a horror that I have yet to work it all out and they loom practical and into the realm of the real to bes.

The first place we stopped at this morning was Chipping Campden, a dear old town, the headquarters of that most—to me—distasteful Ashbee, artist and furniture freakist. There is the ruin of an old house belonging to Lord Gainsborough—an Elizabeth or James house destroyed by fire and never rebuilt—standing near the church, a fine example of a late period.

'How dull it all must seem to you,' he interjected at this point. Then continuing the description of Campden House:

It was all of that delicious mad bad, ignorant sort of architecture called Elizabethan where the bad and curious attract more vividly than what is really good. The colour of the stonework was lovely—yet through all the colour one could see why some was better than the other—the difference between the day-work mason and the artist. There are elaborate gateways, an ornée cottage, 2 ample gazebos, and a bit of the main house left. Yet what charmed me most was the building of a ventilator in the big barn: stones arranged quite simply, so, but every stone is most charmingly placed. The invention, simplicity, and ingenuity charmed me altogether. Later in the day I saw others evidently copied but not as carefully thought out and proportioned as these were. You see the simple arrangement of 3 stones to make a charming pattern and satisfactory finish to a window or ventilator of absolutely no architectural (so called) importance—yet the function was so perfectly and so aptly fulfilled.

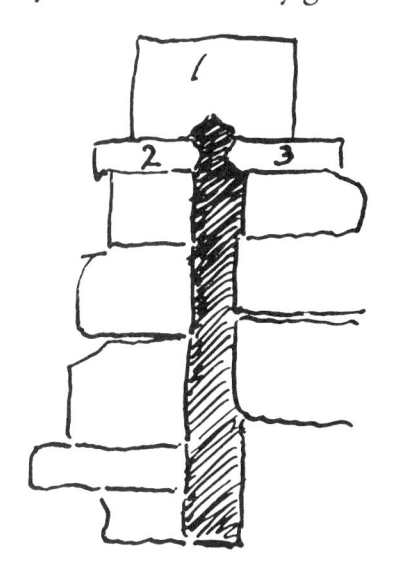

The general scheme [of Campden House] was evident from the occurring buildings and the roll and furrow of the ground. A great long house facing south cuts a great wide terrace terminated east and west by gazebos of some considerable importance, having painted ceilings, panelled walls and open loggias... The gateway itself is dreadfully bad and inconsequent—gables of many curves even now destroy to a great extent the dignified plan.

The church itself is admirable but does not bear close inspection, the intermediate buttresses divide at the top into arches and join again as pinnacles, and towards the bottom split to pass right and left over the west door—an arrangement most disquieting and unhappy. Yet the general size and proportion and fenestration of the tower is fine and from a distance very good. Dear old almshouses, but too many gables all of a row, and too monotonous to be reprieved by the Gainsborough coat of arms and sundial (that was charming). The church tower was a great conception marred by detail, and the almshouses a poor conception marring the detail—and it was all probably done by one man long syne dead and known no more.

Broadway is a village with charming houses but I was frankly disappointed. It was self conscious and everything done was done just wrong. It was clean without being tidy—every house had its sanitary necessities in glorious evidence —bad ugly curtains and other vulgarities grinned through old casements. The name boards on the houses—one was called Privet Lodge—is hardly fair criticism, for no new names can fit an old place. There was a new house near that made me start—and oh how naughty—a fearless copy of some of my work, yet dreadful and oh so foreign to the county and its materials.

Almost all his facets catch the light in this document: the effective man of business, his trepidation at the cost of a major work, his capacity for carrying on a number of operations simultaneously, and his shrewd summing-up of people. There is the unselfconscious bathroom episode, then that apology for the processes of his genius. The appreciation of Chipping Campden is characteristically penetrating, yet it was apparently made during quite a brief inspection. The acute criticisms are as typical as his dwelling on a single exquisitely simple detail—the *œiellet* in the barn. The disapproval of 'mad bad' Jacobean design—of which he was less critical in Paris Pavilion days—is significant of his new allegiance.

But clearly he was worried by Lady Lytton's anxiety over the way that the Bloomsbury Square ménage was working out, with husband and wife each absorbed, very successfully but it seemed ever more exclusively, in their different creative occupations, he with buildings, she with babies, which, for different reasons, involved prolonged separation. That interjection, 'how dull it must seem to you,' the rueful admission of his essential egoism, and analysis of the process of creative gestation, show that the partition between the two halves of the house in Bloomsbury Square had begun to be a spiritual as well as a practical reality. The shared life in the ideal home that both had envisaged had not quite materialised.

Ten years' married life had fulfilled the symbolism of their relationship presented by that day on the sands of Scheveningen during their honeymoon, when they had sat side by side but looking in opposite directions. The decade had been brilliantly successful, outwardly. And on paper, too—if one were to accept the affectionate, revealing, assiduous tone of his letters,—he was a model husband and father. There is no doubt at all that that was his determination and desire. But as his professional success increased, absorbing ever more of his time and vitality, so the partition in 29 Bloomsbury Square encroached progressively, as it were, further and further upstairs, and the Ned of the Casket became smaller and less explicit as Lutyens the famous architect loomed larger in the world. Inevitably the artist's absorption in his works—their intense reality to him and the complexity of the problems involved by their realisations—must make the everyday claims of flesh and blood often seem insubstantial by comparison.

This process was at work in the Bloomsbury household. The children—the birth of Ursula in 1904, of Elizabeth in 1906 and of Mary in 1908 brought their number to five—as yet made little practical claim upon his paternal responsibility. He delighted in them when he wanted to play, yet it was as playthings rather than as adolescent human beings. In any case they were never allowed in the office, though, as they grew up, 'the mens' downstairs became objects of almost uncontrollable curiosity. The only exceptions to this rule were Ursula who was sometimes allowed into the sanctum; and at Christmas when the nursery gave an annual tea party to the office staff, who brought gifts. This had originated as early as 1900, when father had noted 'a lovely box of Japanese toys and silky animals.... Barbie must give the office a surprise tea party one day'.

Necessarily Lady Emily, in these ten years, had become more and more the mother and less the wife. She had naturally maternal instincts and was indeed a most admirable and beloved mother. But filling the nursery may have served to some extent as compensation for a growing sense of emptiness where Ned used to be. For all his devoted assiduity as a letter writer, he was increasingly absent, mentally as well as physically, apt to sit tongue-tied and absorbed, and in spite of his efforts to the contrary, to be forgetful of the little things that mean much to a woman. She was very much a Lytton, too, with her moods and restless energy, and questioning, proselytising seriousness. The difficulty was that her acute intelligence was intellectual whilst his was visual and abstract, mistrustful of the politics and literature that attracted her. He skimmed the better books, though more to please her than himself perhaps, and always desultorily. But she was quite incapable of understanding the first thing about architecture, immensely proud as she was of his buildings and believing entirely in his genius.

Towards the end of this decade, then, her energy began to seek an outlet. Life with Lutyens had made something of a feminist of her and confirmed an innate conviction that, in many ways, women were fully as competent as men. She had long been a vegetarian, inspired by her Aunt T (Mrs. C. W. Earle), and though giving it up on marriage, reverted to the regime when converted to Theosophy and applied it in bringing up the children. Later she interested herself in the Women's Suffrage movement. She interested her sister Lady Constance in it too, who being unmarried and of even more enthusiastic temperament, eventually got herself committed to Holloway Gaol. It is outside the scope of this narrative to follow the gleam of that ardent spirit, but Constance Lytton's earnest sufferings, which made a considerable stir around 1910, must be visualised as a flame warmly reflected in Bloomsbury Square.

Then, in 1908, the Lutyenses went to stay with M. and Mme. Mallet at Varengeville, and there Lady Emily discovered not only that her hostess was a convert to the then new and suspect cult of Theosophy, but also the writings of its evangelist Mrs. Annie Besant. These made a profound impression on her, and to some extent accorded with Lutyens's aesthetic pantheism. Before long Mrs. Besant was a revered visitor at Bloomsbury Square. By 1911 Lutyens was writing to Baker:

> the difficulty this year is that Emmie had been absorbed by Mrs. Besant who is here from India. I wonder what you think of her. What you would like is her ultra Imperialist ideal: the Divine Right of King and Empire—George V, King of the Old Country she puts first. And she got 3000 radicals together the other night and talked Divine Right and Empire till they were nearly all sick!!
>
> She has courage—her Astral reincarnation theory frightens me—but, to the point, she has absorbed this summer all my wife's energies in her propaganda. All I can say is that it is better than Suffragettes!! but it is difficult to arrange anything here when Mrs. B. don't take part.
>
> One most amusing party we had was Arthur and Gerald Balfour, Oliver Lodge, Mrs. Besant, Lady Crichton (who left her husband because she saw his astral body)!! Gerald and Lodge got nettled at Mrs. B. Arthur Balfour was rather intrigued.

§5. GARDEN PATH

But in pursuing this later development of the division in the Bloomsbury Square household, we have anticipated events. The cleavage might not have gone so far as it did if the plans still reposing in the Casket for a 'little white house' had ever materialised. Ned used to tell Emily that he always visualised her in it, and she was, indeed, a countrywoman by upbringing, fond of flowers and gardens and accustomed to the duties of a country life. A country house would have solved many of the problems created by the family's annual migration to the seaside, and possibly her political and theosophical interests would not have loomed so large with that outlet and background. In the early days it had not mattered, and in any case the expense of the London house put it out of the question. He enjoyed toying with the idea but was always putting it off on the score of cost and business. He did not really want a country house, and though he designed exquisite gardens, would have sat, if he had had one of his own, indoors with his back to the window playing patience or imagining other people's. 'Barby takes after me,' he exclaimed once, 'in being bored at flower-picking.' His only country interest, other than buildings, was fishing.

Nevertheless a visit to Thakeham on a lovely July evening in 1904—'the great Downs bathed in reflected light and the garden wonderfully good'—reawakened the old dream.

> Blackburn is very slow, apparently, but is really an artist and he does little at a time but what he does is singularly good I think. He has made the pergola delightful in a way quite his own—with holly-hocks—and to enjoy the effect he postpones planting the more permanent things. His attitude is so unlike the general run of people: like leaving a picture unfinished to enjoy the initial stages ... I do wish we could have a garden and country house. If only we could do that combined with sea and river it would be perfect. We could entertain the whole families too.

Again next year:

> A country house of our own would be delicious, but I want so much. 1st, the best I know. 2nd, high ground for you. 3rd, a river for me. This means £.s.d. 2 and 3 mean a large parcel of ground, total, £.s.d; and that is the most difficult of all worldly things—the only worldly gift we haven't got —and there is so so so much that we have.

The sketch of the Never Never House, 1905 model, shows a madonna with children enthroned in an apparently classical mansion perched on a cliff whence gushes a river teeming with large fish to be caught by a small figure below, whilst in the sky is a black blob with the legend 'the sun ever to be glorious but quite black beside my Emmie—a veritable blot!'

The idea was still under discussion in 1908, when, announcing to his wife his failure to win the County Hall competition, he added 'our dear little country home must wait a bit'. After that, it was too late. The mounting pressure of his practice left him no time to think of it, still less to enjoy a country home, then came the long absences in Delhi, and the War.

It was a strange and rather tragic circumstance that the architect of so many entrancing gardens never had one of his own. But he was neither a garden lounger nor a garden grower by temperament. For him a garden was an occasion for a work of art that, once designed, he had no wish to see again until its components had reached maturity. There survives an illuminating *exposée* of his theory of garden design—one of the rare instances of his formulating his theories into words—delivered on one of the few occasions of his addressing a professional gathering. He was engaged to propose the vote of thanks after a paper on Garden Design by T. H. Mawson at the Architectural Association on April 8, 1908. The somewhat disjointed notes for his remarks, which he said that he delivered in a state of much trepidation, suggest that his thanks were not deeply heartfelt. We can see how closely his views on the practice of garden-making accorded with Miss Jekyll's when he expressed the wish that the lecturer 'had dealt with the more practical problems of garden architecture and design', and stressed that,

> the true adornment of a garden lies surely in its flowers and plants. No artist has so wide a pallette as the garden designer, and no artist greater need of discretion and reserve. When a design begins to appear as merely a collection of features, then I think it is time to look in which direction our india-rubber has bounced. Directly work becomes conscious you will find it is uncomfortable.

That, elliptically put, is the essence of Lutyensism. He did not want to discourage originality, he continued. But originality,

> like a freehand curve, can only have merit by reason of those great forces that give life to and control all good things. It is not enough to allow a facile pencil to follow the dictation of the hand and eye. There must be reasoned conviction and will behind it.

He suggested that some of the great qualities of Wren's work might be traced to his friendship and close association with Newton—and Newton and Michelangelo might have been the same man but for their different mediums of expression. His identification of architecture with science, or geometry, was pushed much closer in his final, Elemental, conceptions of design.

He defined his guiding principle in the design of gardens, so far as it is definable in this sentence:

> A garden scheme should have a backbone, a central idea beautifully phrased. Every wall, path, stone, and flower should have its relationship to the central idea.

This principle, it can be seen, he did in fact follow in all his garden designs. It accounts for their variety and also the consistency of character which is their peculiarity. In all his gardens the design, planting, and masonry are in each case related with imagination to a vivid, a 'beautifully phrased', central idea. His point in this discourse was that everything in and about a garden must be *designed*, whether the pattern were formal or 'natural'. In fact, as he went on to say with a reference to the long controversy between William Robinson the apostle of natural gardening and Reginald Blomfield the evangelist of formal design, each inevitably complements the other in a satisfying garden.

> We all remember the fierce controversy of a few years back which might have gone on for ever on paper between the exponents of the formal and the free methods of garden design. It is a significant fact that when each of the combatants became possessed of a country home of their own they were influenced by the needs of the place rather than by their conclusions, and each adopted the other's method, the formalist making a delightfully free garden with no straight line in it and the free man a charming parterre entirely rectangular in design.

I am not sure which is the garden referred to first, but the second is a paved garden laid out by Robinson at Gravetye, immediately adjoining the house, to give himself convenient access to his favourite plants.

On this very important question of relationship of garden to house, Lutyens put forward several individual points. The views of the garden 'as seen from the various parts of the house are as important as are the views of the house from the garden'. For example, 'the position of the staircase window may materially affect the garden plan; so may the manner in which the vertical face of the house is attached by the design to the garden: it is not always the best solution for the house to spring out of a briar bush!'

One result of the talk which pleased him was that 'a man has written asking if he might come into my office—he always wanted to and now after hearing my remarks, more than ever'. Another was that Sir George Sitwell invited him to Renishaw in the following September (1908). 'They want me to do the garden, ball room, billiard room, great drawing room, dining room etc. Sir George wants to build a little water palace (one room) on the lake, which would be a delightful thing to do, and to build a house in Sicily which would be fun. He is going to take me to Italy!!!'

So Lutyens reported after an evening spent in the stimulating company of that enthusiastic if erratic baronet, from whom no doubt he heard, if he could not discuss with him, the whole theory and practice of formal garden design. After being in the house only a few hours, he wrote:

> Sir George is a young and old-fashioned man like a character from a Disraeli novel. Lady Ida still of great beauty of the Lady Pembroke type. A tall and graceful daughter more like her father than he is to himself. A son [Sacheverell] evidently with character as he cannot sleep without everyone in the house including maids and guests attending his bedside. The eldest son has just gone to Eton.

In *Great Morning* this elder son has related amusing recollections of Lutyens's many subsequent professional visits to his father to whom, 'his irreverence and hatred of the pompous made him a perfect foil.' Sir Osbert also comments on his kindness and insight—of which the *aperçu* just quoted is an instance: 'he understood at once the psychological forces at work but not always the manner in which to solve them. The very sight of unhappiness made him long to put things right and then there was no knowing what he would say.'

The situation was as complicated as usual on the occasion of this first visit. Sir George's architectural projects hinged (according to Lady Ida) on his being persuaded not to change his political allegiance and stand for Parliament—an argument in which a large house-party joined and Lutyens proceeded to take his share. 'So there is a lot of fishing for work besides the actual work on the tapis,' he wrote. 'This morning I spent in the house, looking and thinking and pondering.'

This was the time when his spirits and practice were at a low ebb after his failure in the County Hall competition, and the successive eddies and pools in the stream of events at Renishaw seemed to hold large fish worth angling for. But, he added, 'this fighting with the wolf for work, and working for the work's best sake does tire.' Nevertheless, when the party went over to Hardwick, where the Duchess of Devonshire took them all round the great house which she was then doing up, 'chivying inept plumbers', and Sir George remarked that he had never seen anybody pick a man's brains as she had Lutyens's, he replied, 'But I like being picked by a Duchess of Devonshire.' 'I do wish you had been with me, and Ursula too,' he told Lady Emily, 'to see all the great fairies that live in and about the place. To do service to it, in any way, however humbly, is and must be merit making. But I do wish they would hand the place over to me,' he added wistfully.

A few weeks before he had combined some useful architectural angling with a visit to Holy Island whither Edward Hudson had urgently summoned him to help conduct the Prince and Princess of Wales over the Castle, and as a kindness to Lutyens, no doubt, to introduce him to their Royal Highnesses. The occasion is indeed significant for his presentation to—or rather accosting of—the future King and Queen with whom, in his notable further relations, he generally maintained the jesting note struck at this first encounter. It affords the first instance of his characteristic technique with royalty since the early fun and games with Princess Louise a decade before. The letter, the only one at all descriptive of Lindisfarne, also brings into focus other trends in his life during this somewhat crucial and transitional year: a picture of him together with his eldest daughter, then aged ten, a note on how he sought out potentially useful contacts, and the prophetic longing for a church to build.

> Holy Island. July 3. 1908.
> Barbie seems very happy but quiet and to have little initiative, so I try and instil selfishness into her!! She is very affectionate and a darling altogether.
> I must just tell you about the Pſs etc. From the Battlements we saw a procession of 8 carriages come across the sands... They walked up the drive and I sent Hudson down to the bottom of the hill to receive them. With Barbie I waited at the portcullis.
> Bigge¹ was walking with the Prince and I heard him say—You know Sir this place has been rebuilt by E. Lutyens. So I hollared out Hi Stop. I'm here. The Prince nearly had a fit of laughter. He said—how verry goode—ha ha, and told everybody... He was terribly alarmed at the gangway up and wanted a wall built. I told him we had pulled one down and that if he really thought it unsafe we would put nets out. He thought that very funny. He was awfully anxious to get away when he found the tide was rising; for a sailor I thought him over-nervous.
>
> The Princess couldn't bear the cobbles; they hurt her feet. I told her we were very proud of them! Hudson said he was dreadfully nervous and I think they made each other stiff. Lord Crighton and Howick were the only appreciative people. Mr. Chaplin was only conscious of his bulk. Northumberland very demure and quiet and a good deal bored. The Ladies Percy took snapshots—Hudson with Pſs, me with Prince—and picked wild flowers in spite of notices. We walked down with the party to the gate and off they went.

He then turned to the serious business of cultivating—in the most charming manner—the notables of the mainland. The following passage, though complicated, is worth unravelling as suggesting how one thing led (or might lead) to another if properly handled.

> Young Eustace Smith met me at Morpeth Station with Mrs. Robert Harrison—Lady Ottoline Morrell's friend—of Shiplake, sister of Mrs. Eustace Smith's

---

[1] Sir Arthur Selby Bigge (later Lord Stamfordham).

husband. Mrs. E. Smith [for whom he shortly undertook the reconstruction of Whalton Manor] is a widow, very rich and all monies left to her entirely. I did not have time to go to the Strakers [he designed the gardens at Angerton for them], but they, Mrs. Smith and Mrs. Harrison come over tomorrow. Col. and Mrs. Cookson, the owners of Meldon Park, come to lunch to meet me. They have come in for a fortune and want me to build them new gates and lodges, which is good. Mrs. Cookson seems a nice woman; her son married Harold Brassey's sister [by whom Copse Hill and Lowesby Hall were commissioned], so it all hangs together. Mrs. Harrison is very kind about me; she and Mrs. Smith jumped to my suggestions at once... The Bertie Fenwick job [Mr. H. G. Fenwick of Temple Dinsley] has come on: Chapman spoke to them about me.

I cannot—at least have not yet—arrived at a church, which is depressing.

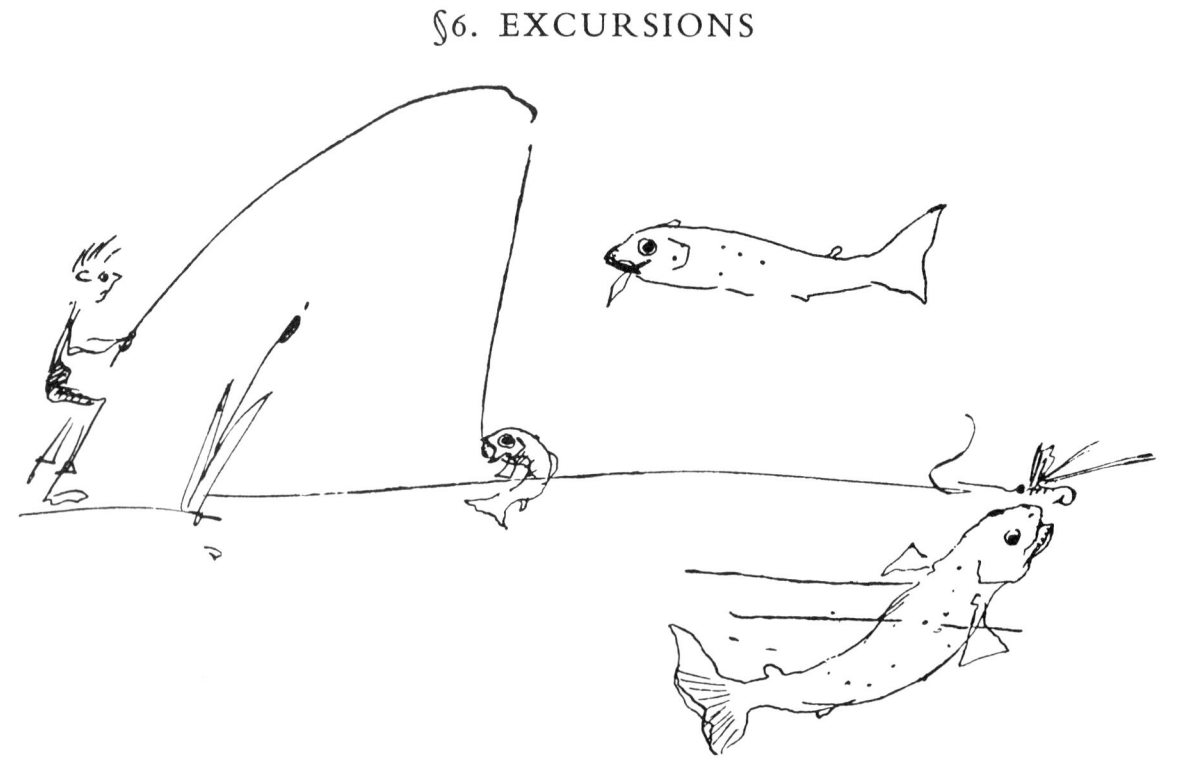

§6. EXCURSIONS

'Oh these beloved fish!' he had exclaimed on another of these expeditions that for most of his life stood him instead of a holiday catching real fish—his only form of escape. Sometimes they extended to hurried trips abroad. In the autumn of 1905, for example, a summons came to report on possible alterations to the castle of Bodrog Olaszi in Hungary. The whole expedition, with glimpses of Vienna and Buda-Pesth, took inside a week and resulted in nothing but rather horrified impressions of the Castle and of the squalor of his host's peasantry, and a description of how 'I walked round the Castle seven times blowing my own trumpet in the hopes that the walls would fall'.

Incessant travelling left him apparently as fresh and unruffled as ever, but his continual absorption in work began to cause anxiety to those nearest to him. His wife and Sir Herbert (formerly Col.) Jekyll conspired in 1906 to get him away for once on a real holiday. Sir Herbert and Lady Jekyll had been invited by a rich American Theosophist, Miss Mary Dodge, to organise a yachting party to the Baltic. They were to arrange everything, including the assembly of guests. Lutyens, during the summer, had got Nashdom, Heathcote, and New Place put in hand, and the design of William Robinson's offices for *The Garden* in Kingsway was at length settled with that cantankerous old friend, and on September 1, off they all went on the steam yacht *Miranda*. The party included, besides Miss Dodge, the Jekylls and their children, two young bachelors—Lord Gerald Wellesley and Mr. Oswald Dickenson. It was 'a very frivolous party', the days hot and the sea (for the most part) so calm 'that it all seems like fairyland. The meals bounteous and frequent'. Ned relaxed luxuriously, did some very mild and disapproving sight seeing ('Lubeck; nothing really beautiful,' though it yielded 'the most heavenly little painted wooden house— blocks of wood models of one of the principal buildings; they can be played with all day long' of which he bought a set for Ursula's birthday); he joined in games with the Jekyll children—'I dressed up last night as the German Emperor with great success' and, after five days of it, began to feel he was wasting time. 'I have not done a stroke of work yet, which is pricking my conscience a little wee bit.' However, he began to forget the dates: they found 'a delicious primitive church', at a place called Rovic, and tasted continental gaiety at Copenhagen, where the English and Russian royal yachts were on a visit; explored Wisby, then steamed into Stockholm where, after a fortnight afloat, Lutyens left the party to catch a boat for Newcastle to join Lady Emily and the children and Hudson at Lindisfarne. On getting back to the office he found 'two more pupils just come, Hughes and Watney, very shy-making'. (Did he, by any chance, originate that phrase, and the characteristic use of 'fun', which became vogue words of the bright young 'twenties?) And found, of course, that, in his absence, things had been going wrong.

Sir Herbert Jekyll was one of those who urged him to find a partner, if only in order to prevent that kind of thing happening in his absences. He suggested that Herbert Baker, who was getting discouraged in South Africa since Rhodes's death and thinking of returning to London practice, was the very man. Baker wrote asking Lutyens's view. His letter in reply is notable—for his melancholy estimate of his position just after the County Hall set-back, the astonishing picture of the rivalry among domestic architects at the end of the Edwardian decade, and not least for the extreme reluctance it displays to an idea for which, later on, he began to feel differently.

May 10, 1908. In a train.

It is absurd for a man of your calibre to stay out [in S. Africa] and put up tin buildings or at the best stone apses to tin naves [in allusion to Cape Town Cathedral]. Human nature prompts me to hope you won't come! and this remark is probably the instinct of self preservation which prompts me to pray you will stay out in Africa and at the same time prompts you to come home!! Things are quiet here—yet London is being rebuilt! You'd have a splendid chance; you have reputation and would start, with all your experience, on a clean slate. Your danger might be to be too conscious of texture.

The struggle here is horrid. I hear Blow (Ernest George told me) had to be kicked out of the house of some people who were about to build a large new house! It was one I had some hopes of getting, but the man said I was too artistic!! So they went to George and there was a regular scramble amongst the architects!! I try and pretend my position (and I am very doubtful of having any position at all) is beyond it. I cannot play that game but it has to be played and the man who plays it well wins—at least a lot...

For yourself I should dearly love to have you home in England. My position is not so good as to enable me to say I would not be jealous—but you would like that? and I shouldn't like you less!!...

I should gladly lift *you* to my 'well fortified heights' in a partnership. But I dont think, when behind my works, they look either high or well fortified—I should never say this to any other man.... But I cannot justly judge what is the true state of affairs in Africa and what you stand to lose... If I had work enough for two I should make you an offer at once, on an equal basis. But I haven't, and I don't know, even if you are willing, how a partnership could be effected. I should dearly love working with you and having the endless fun and discussion—a process I have long felt the want of.

Later that year Lutyens suggested their each putting £6000 or £8000 into a joint capital fund. Baker replied that 'if you really want help,—if beautiful Amelia really wants to marry Captain Dobbin', he might be able to contribute half that amount, assuming that his colleague Fleming continued as resident partner in South Africa. But everything turned on the outcome of the Union Convention at that time deliberating the future of South Africa. In the following February (1909) Baker could write, 'Dear dear Lutyens, the facts are intervening': he was being commissioned to build Pretoria railway station; the Convention had raised the ideals of the Government and they were more inclined to trust Englishmen; and Wernher had persuaded his partner Phillips to remain in Africa and make his home at Johannesburg (the large country house called Arcadia subsequently built by Baker). Besides, he continued, coming to self-analysis, 'though working with you where are summer and winter, flowers, spring, birds, and the prospect of being buried under a yew tree, all pull,' yet the fear of a bump between two stools, and the folly of throwing up good connections, and the feeling that he filled a gap in the Imperial wall, joined in inducing him to remain at his post. He didn't want to desert, couldn't face Kipling if he did, and realised Rhodes's scorn of colonists 'who desert to useless swamped lives at home'. By the following June the Union Building at Pretoria was taking shape and he had never been so busy, but would consult Lutyens on the design as a kind of 'consulting centre-of-the-Empire partner'.

Thus these overtures, although they came to nothing at the time, paved the way for Lutyens's venture into South African practice which led to his eventually associating Baker with himself at Delhi. In view of their long-standing friendship and growing mutual regard, this is the point at which to consider the disparities that attracted but at length antagonised the two men.

They were certainly drawn to one another by the qualities each felt himself to lack. To Lutyens, Baker was one of the 'big men'—tall, manly, athletic, outwardly calm—that seem to have attracted him. He was to look forward to his joining him in India because he was 'so gentle and wise'; he respected his 'right-mindedness' and patience, his ability to handle committees and philistines. The glamour of his friendship with Rhodes and with the progressive young generation of administrators at the Cape, combined with his aloofness from professional competition in England to invest Herbert Baker's name with a high, slightly mysterious, prestige.

From their earliest association Baker perceived and was deeply impressed by the quality of Lutyens as an architect. He continued to consult his judgment for twenty years and, always modest, even submitted the designs for the Union Building, his *magnum opus*, to Lutyens's criticisms, most of which he adopted. These reveal appreciation of Baker's imagination while contributing ideas of organisation and coherence peculiarly characteristic of the critic. For instance, discussing the cornice for the Union Building, Lutyens wrote (Feb. 1, 1910) 'I am rather fond of an entablature with the frieze omitted and the top member of the architrave becoming the lower member of the cornice', which he illustrated with the diagram reproduced on p. 142. The correspondence shows that Lutyens was always aware of a tendency to looseness and sentimentality in his friend's work.

As he came to know him better, he found Baker, beneath his reserved and serious manner, prone to be moody and introspective, and possessing little sense of humour. He would tell him, 'directly you introspect you may be sure you are wrong, —morally'. Again, 'if want of faith is shown,—convinced faith in the eventual success of the attempt, then a battle may be counted half lost, as you begin by running away. This is not meant to be ungracious or in any way critical of your really wonderful broadminded and gentle character which I appreciate so very greatly. Only just a talk-a-to, like sharpening a pencil whilst thinking or lighting a pipe already lit with a seventh match.' But, 'I never know which are your grumpy letters and which are not! Your language is never bleached with passion!'

Baker entertained reservations too, for Lutyens's character. Serious and idealistic, he was amused but often rather shocked by his levity, though he might, on reflection, be disposed to agree with its aptness. A thoughtful reader, he had a memory as retentive for inspiring passages of literature as the other had for those of architecture. Lutyens mistrusted the trait, as confusing an architectural issue, no less instinctively than Baker mistrusted facetiousness as refusal to face a moral issue. Lutyens had the morality of an artist, which subordinates human to aesthetic values, and Baker the art of a moralist for whom the arts serve and illustrate the virtues.

Therein lay the excellences of each—and the limitations. And in Lutyens's case, the cause, also, for 29 Bloomsbury Square being as it was.

The domestic partition was not removed, rather widened, when in the autumn of 1910 he moved his office to 17 Queen Anne's Gate. As the children grew to school-room age and the office work increased, both halves of 29 Bloomsbury Square needed to expand. Hudson, at No. 13 Queen Anne's Gate, was able to assist in obtaining the lease and thenceforward lunch or dinner at the next house but one became a standing invitation as an alternative to the Athenaeum. Yet despite the distance between Westminster and Bloomsbury, actually as well as metaphorically, the idyll of the linked E.L.s continued only a little dimmed, a little strained, compared to the brightness with which it shone twelve years earlier. And the atmosphere of the office persisted unchanged.

'ON HIS HIGH HORSE' (1896–7)

53. 'Mr E. L. Lutyens exhorting his Young Men'. Caricature by the Hon. Paul Phipps, 1906. *Left to right:* E. L., S. H. Evans, O. P. Milne, P. Phipps, Wallich, A. J. Thomas, 'I. P.' Huddart, G. Alwyn

54. 'Lut' in 1906. A caricature by Paul Phipps

55. E. L. Lutyens. About 1897

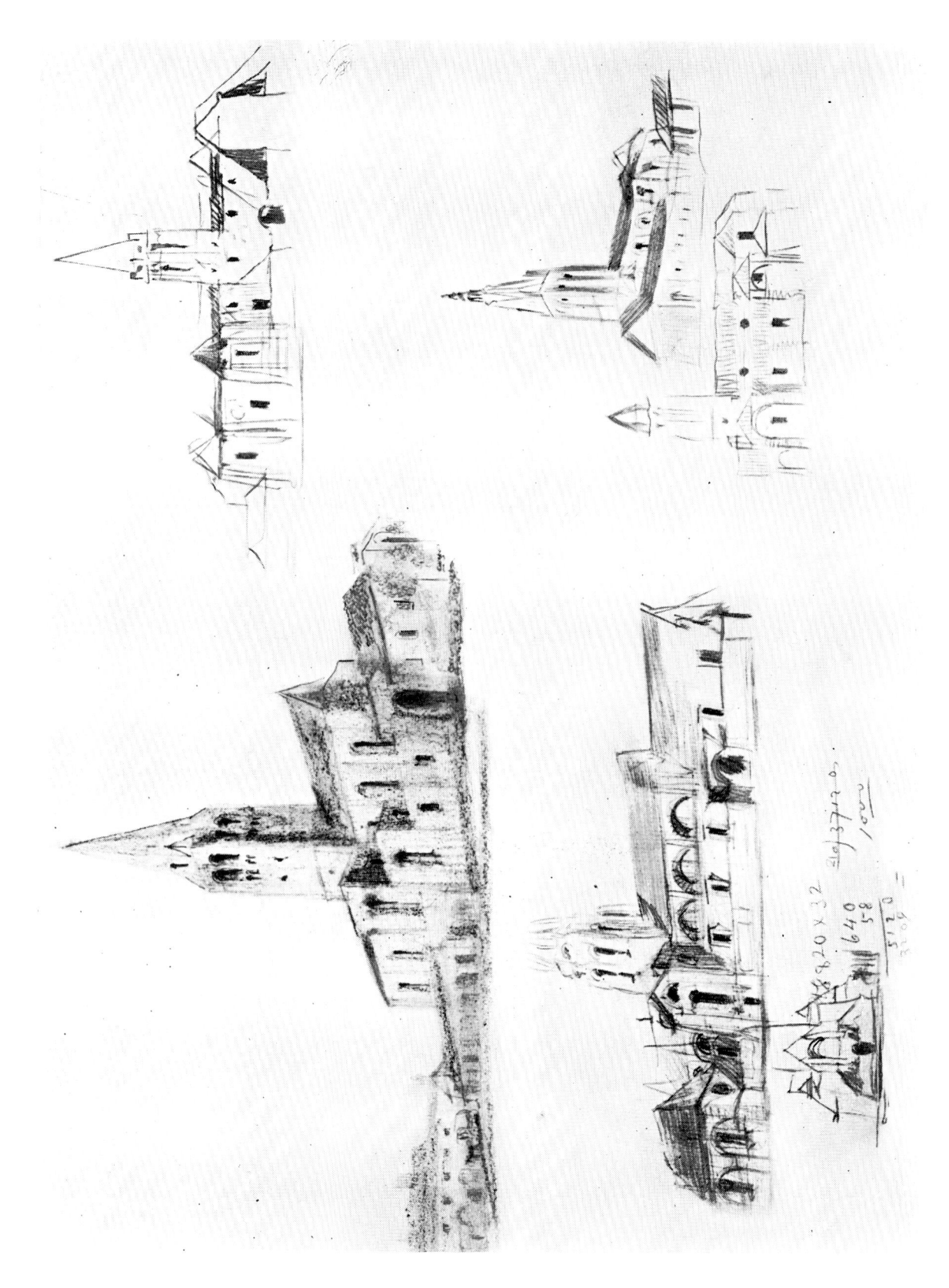

56. Stages in the Evolution of St Jude's Church, Hampstead (1909–10). Four separate sketches combined thus for reproduction

CHAPTER VIII

FLOOD TIDE

IN 1909 he was forty, and Lloyd George's Budget, with its increased Income Tax, Death Duties, and abortive Land Tax, gave a severe jolt to the class comprising most of his clients hitherto. The Chancellor's demagogy, the Lords' rejection of his Budget, followed by King Edward's death and the constitutional crisis of 1911, created an atmosphere of insecurity which gradually intensified till the outbreak of war with Germany. The gathering clouds accurately presaged the end of the Indian Summer of prosperous individualism during which Lutyens had built up his reputation as the leading architect of country houses on the old ample scale. As such, his position was particularly vulnerable. He had largely identified himself with the Edwardian oligarchy, whose excellent if conservative tastes appreciated his virtuosity. And he had reached that stage of a successful architect's reputation when clients with less than a clear £10,000 a year thought twice before consulting so 'big' a man.

In the days, a dozen years before, when he was pedalling about Surrey on Angelina, he liked to compare his life to the course of a river. We have followed its upper reaches cascading blithely through late-Victorian foothills, and where it flowed with gathering serenity across the sunlit plain of King Edward's reign, its banks lined with a succession of country mansions in elaborate gardens. Now his river has entered a suburban region and is nearing the heart of metropolis. Soon it will reach the sea. Already in 1909 we have the impression that its confining but protective banks are falling back, their landmarks almost out of sight, and that, for better or worse, he is launching out into deeper waters, subject to tidal currents and exposed to the gales of the high seas. In the event, they carried him to Eldorado. Circuitously, under full sail to Rome, then with little profit to the Cape and Johannesburg, back to London River, off again to Rome and touching at Dublin, to the Indies at length.

At first, too, the sensation of being at sea must have been very real to him. Commissions for country houses declined rather steeply in number after 1908, and there can be detected in his mind, together with some uncertainty, a restless quest for work to take their place; that 'big work' which he had envisaged as Stage Two of the High Game. From 1909, the type of client to be tackled begins to change too. We notice Liberal politicians (with a professional faith in the future), and a higher proportion of commercial fortunes. His earlier type of client, in contrast, seemed to require relatively modest alterations to London houses—Edward Hudson's (1911) to the house in Queen Anne's Gate which has her statue attached to it is an example. Yet in 1911, year of the Coronation of George V and the Delhi Durbar, to all appearances Britain and Empire basked in glory and Stock Exchange prices reached their highest level since 1901. By rights the fashionable architect should have been overwhelmed with work. There was still plenty of money about but it was passing into other hands. And not very many of them were prepared to spend it on new country houses. Therefore the architect anxious to transform it into buildings must search for opportunities, create them if need be, in unfamiliar places

But if private commissions were hanging fire, there was an altogether new spirit of public enterprise in the air. For Lutyens it meant frequenting the marketplaces more than had been his wont, convincing committees, dealing with politicians and administrators, cajoling millionaires. He did not like it; his manner was apt to belie his extreme ability; he became nervous, and concealed it with facetiousness. 'A meeting of this sort always makes me uncomfortable. I imagine all sorts and kinds of horrible ignorant and unsympathetic men, though they very seldom are—yet I don't have the confidence that they will agree with my rights and wrongs.' (To Lady Emily, February 1909.)

From now onward, however, he had increasingly to adjust his individualism to co-operating under such conditions. In the winter of 1908–9 he was appointed architect, with Raymond Unwin as town-planner, for Hampstead Garden Suburb; in 1909 he was attached as consulting architect to the Royal Commission for the International Exhibition at Turin and Rome; King Edward's death in 1910 involved him in the toils of memorial projects; in 1911 commissions for the Rand Regiments' Memorial and the Johannesburg Art Gallery plunged him into the national and local politics of South Africa; and in 1912 his association with Sir Hugh Lane implicated him in the exasperating politics of Dublin in connection with the municipal Gallery to receive Lane's famous collection of pictures. All this was playing 'the high game' in earnest, and was destined to culminate in his winning the most glittering commission given to any English architect since Wren.

But at the beginning of 1909 the transition from private practitioner to public figure is in its first uncertain phase. This chapter traces the passage, from inland waters into the high sea. The estuary abounded in shoals and cross currents, the winds veered and backed. But he carried too expensive a cargo—in the shape of an adolescent family and big office organisation—to afford missing the flood tide to fortune.

§1. HAMPSTEAD GARDEN SUBURB

'There is a boom coming for Garden Cities,' he told Baker in 1909. 'I am in the train for Tavistock to lay out a building estate for the Duke of Bedford. I have an estate to lay out at Romford collaborating with Ward, who would have had the job had he been a bigger man, and then there is the Central Square at Hampstead—two churches, 80 to 100 houses, and a big Institute yet to be decided.' The Romford project was Gidea Park, eventually the subject of a competition, nor did the Tavistock scheme get very far. The Duke was also thinking of rebuilding Endsleigh village, as that of Woburn had been, but Lutyens felt 'it wants industries and *raison d'être*'. Endsleigh House itself, with its 'twenty miles of drive, pinetum, butterfly garden, bird-oasis, and fish hatchery' he termed 'a conglomeration in the style Mary Anne'. So far as he was concerned, both these projects reduced themselves, much as had the earlier one for Rossall Beach, to the building of a few houses and cottages, the chief one being Little Court, Tavistock.

At Hampstead the opportunity was much bigger, the intention and conditions already clearly defined, and the scheme did not peter out, though Lutyens's relations with the dynamic personality of its alma mater fulfilled his worst apprehensions about conflicting scales of values.

In the decade before the First World War, the idea of planned development was taking shape, under the impetus of Ebenezer Howard's *Tomorrow* (published as early as 1898) and exemplified in his Letchworth Garden City. During the latter half of the nineteenth century a succession of practical idealists, following Titus Salt's Saltaire, developed the conception of the industrial village adumbrated by Disraeli in *Coningsby*, of which Port Sunlight and Bourneville are the best known. A true garden suburb was created on the edge of London at Bedford Park by Jonathan Carr about 1876-7, for whom Norman Shaw designed many of the buildings. Rosetti lived there for a time, and Morris approved the architecture—among the first essays in renaissance vernacular—as 'quaint and pretty'. But till the realisation of Hampstead Garden Suburb, initiated in 1908, the full architectural possibilities of this essentially English conception of planned development had scarcely been explored. That they were not only explored at Hampstead but demonstrated in a remarkable way is due largely to Lutyens, though he was responsible for neither the conception nor the layout of the famous undertaking.

The idea and its realisation was due to Dame Henrietta, then Mrs. Barnett, whose husband Canon S. A. Barnett was part founder, in 1884, and first Warden of Toynbee Hall and of the Whitechapel Art Gallery. In her autobiographical pamphlet *The Story of Hampstead Garden Suburb*, Dame Henrietta described how thirty years' ministry in the slums of Victorian London had convinced the Barnetts that any community must be based on neighbourliness, the contact of class with class. The Barnetts came to visualise *en l'air* the forming of an ideal community developing the traditional relationships of a country town or village. Then, in the 'nineties, she learnt of the plans for extending the Tube to Golders Green, near to where the Barnetts then had a cottage overlooking the Heath. That localised a possible site for realising their dream. In 1905 Mrs. Barnett became the leading spirit of a committee formed to enlarge the Heath by the purchase of eighty acres lying on the Golders Green side. It was obvious that the open land north and west along the Finchley Road would soon be built over, so she decided that there and then was the call for putting their long-cherished plan into practice. The Garden Suburb Trust was formed in 1906, followed by Co-partnership Tenants Ltd. of which she became a Director, Honorary Manager, and Vice-chairman. Its objects were defined as primarily the making of a social experiment, the shares were entitled to a cumulative dividend not exceeding 5 per cent per annum, and the first 240 acres of land were acquired. Mrs. Barnett cut the first sod on the estate in May 1907.

The principles on which the Suburb was planned were derived from a pamphlet by Mr. (later Sir) Raymond Unwin, which Mrs. Barnett had chanced to read, and which Unwin was invited to elaborate as architect to the Trust. He had already established the claim, now fully recognised, to be regarded as the father of modern town-planning in this country, by laying out Letchworth. Here he could translate Mrs. Barnett's and his own ideals into practical planning with a completeness denied him even when he later became Chief Town Planning Officer to the Ministry of Health. The broad lines of the scheme limited density to an average of eight houses to the acre, a distance of sixty feet from opposite houses across a road, and so placed houses that none could spoil the outlook of another; roads were to be forty feet wide and lined with trees; plots should be divided not by walls but hedges or trellis; and ground rents graded to enable weekly wage-earners to live on the estate besides professional and well-to-do residents. An important point was that old trees were retained in the plan, and the whole of two woods—Big Wood and Little Wood, on the north slopes of the central hill.

Some of these principles passed into the Town Planning Acts and have shaped the course of housing since the First World War, with far-reaching social and topographical results. But at the time many features of the plan, more especially relating to roads, ran counter to current practice so that an Act of Parliament was required before this experiment in enlightened planning could proceed.

Control over building was to be (and is) exercised primarily by the Trust's retaining the freehold, except of the sites of the public buildings, and exercising a censorship of all designs. The latter function was doubly important in that the Trust was to do no building on its own account; the chief tenant concern, apart from private tenants, being the Co-partnership Tenants Ltd.

In the earliest stages of planning the suburb—actually in the autumn of 1908—the Board, of which Alfred Lyttleton was Chairman, appointed Lutyens Consulting Architect and he was asked to prepare designs for the buildings in Central Square. The Square occupies the top of the hill that dominates the southern half of the area, forming the hub of the layout and of the community's life. In it were required two churches (Anglican and Free), the Vicarage, Manse, and the Institute—the latter the most integral feature of the Barnetts' conception of the Suburb as serving the functions of what is now generally called a Community Centre. The design of these buildings, the houses on the west side of the northern approach (Erskine Hill) and of North Square were assigned to Lutyens, subject of course to the Board.

His selection was no doubt helped by Alfred Lyttleton for whom he had designed Grey Walls a decade ago and was at that time transforming Wittersham, a country house near Rye. The opportunity must have seemed like a direct answer to prayer: only in the previous June he had been lamenting from Lindisfarne 'I cannot —at least have not yet—arrived at a church, which is depressing', and now came the demand for two, on a magnificent site of which he had almost complete control.

What were his sources of inspiration for these churches that must be set high among his works, and in the evolution of the modern English tradition of building? The site clearly called for the central feature of each church to stand on the axis of the two approaches to the plateau from north and south. That necessitated, if for no other reasons, their separation by a wide extent of ground. The two churches, whilst they must be distinct in character, must nevertheless be homogeneous in design and be further related by the siting and design of the Institute. The latter, set on the east side of the Square on the axis of the space between the churches, must be sufficiently commanding not to be dwarfed by the churches. All this in neat rectangular arrangement—the phrase he had used a dozen years ago of things in that ideal home that he had imagined for his wife just before their wedding. Much of that conception went, too, into the trim little houses in North Square and Erskine Hill. It is the homogeneity of all his buildings here that strikes one most. They, and the large number for which he was not responsible but which were more or less inspired by his example, constitute a little town as typical of Edwardian England at its best as, Mr. Butler suggests, Lecce or Würzburg are of the baroque. This effect is partly due to the materials—small silver-grey bricks with red dressings,—the predominance of the roofs, and the studied punctuation with white woodwork in sash windows and balustrades. Broadly, these elements derive from Wren tradition, but Lutyens's handling of them has that pictorial quality which we have traced to his early enjoyment of Caldecott's pictures of little houses. But Lutyens's style, so completely developed here, although as Butler points out, 'rooted in tradition and founded on the sympathetic handling of plain materials,' can be seen to 'rest ultimately on the fine adjustment of large masses or spaces in proportion and under the drastic rule of symmetry. It was the complete working out of this style which gives the Garden Suburb its special character. For we have rarely achieved in this country such a harmony in a group of buildings'.[1]

But besides these general influences and resources, he had within him something

---

[1] *The Architecture of Sir Edwin Lutyens*, vol. II.

for which he was impatient to find architectural expression and that could only be expressed in a church—that sublimated religious and sacramental passion of which we have had unexpected glimpses from time to time and for which he had no other outlet but in the building of a church. In a letter to Baker of a year or two later he transcribed—a thing he did rarely—a passage from a book, descriptive of Perigord, that I have not identified but which has the trumpet tones of Ruskin. It applies so aptly to his St. Jude's Church at Hampstead that I cannot help thinking that he took it as the text for the Hampstead church—the nave of which has in it elements of St. Frond.

> Let our church be 'a gathering up of all that men can do. It has fifty roofs, it has a gigantic signal tower, it has blank walls like precipices, and round arch after round arch, and architrave after architrave. It is like a good and settled epic, or better still it is like the life of a healthy and adventurous man who, having accomplished all his journeys and taken the fleece of gold, comes home to tell his stories at evening and to pass among his own people the years that are left to him of his age. It has the experience, growth, and intensity of knowledge, all caught up with one unity. It conquers the site upon which it stands'.
>
> You may laugh at me a bit, but *au fond* somewhere, I am horribly religious, but cannot speak it and this saves my work.[1]

The rhetoric of this passage has closer analogies with Bentley's Westminster Cathedral (which certainly influenced Lutyens here) than with the Hampstead churches, and thirty years later might have been written of his conception of Liverpool Roman Catholic Cathedral. Yet his transcribing the words so soon after designing St. Jude's does suggest that he had these sentiments in mind. His first sketch designs (p. 184) illustrate the words much more closely than the final result. What he did achieve in these churches, with great success, was to translate his domestic style into ecclesiastical forms applied to gothic plans—a feat that Wren might have undertaken, but avoided by regarding his city churches as essentially meeting halls. These Hampstead churches are forerunners of the many and often very effective brick-built churches of the 1920's and 'thirties.

In obtaining the agreement of the Board to his designs he soon came up against some opposition from Mrs. Barnett who, great-hearted and earnest philanthropist that she was, and taking her visual ideals very much, one imagines, from William Morris and cottagey things, saw her homely village-suburb being apparently magnified into a conception beyond her aspirations. 'A nice woman,' Lutyens described her tartly,[2] 'but proud of being a philistine—has no idea much beyond a window box full of geraniums, calceolarias and lobelias, over which you can see a goose on a green. The Central Board with Alfred Lyttleton as president is very well intentioned.'

[1] December 28, 1910.   [2] To Herbert Baker, July 15, 1909.

The earliest dispute took place in April 1909, and we may infer concerned the proportions of the churches. A majority of the Board supported his scheme but,

> Mrs. Barnett was awfully upset about it. I want a certain height of building in a certain place for general effect. Mrs. B. dead against this certain height on the ground of other houses being overshadowed. They would naturally like not to disappoint Mrs. B, the pioneer of the movement and Mother of Hampstead. I feel this, but the Board refers it back to *me*. Unwin warns me it will make things difficult. Alfred Lyttelton in agreement and enthusiastic.[1]

A few days later he reported: 'Mrs. Barnett vanquished. Church, reduced, agreed to, but O I do want more money for my church. The Ecclesiastical Commissioners congratulated me on my design.' The design for St. Jude's was formally accepted in May 1909.

Mrs. Barnett so far prevailed as to obtain a resolution regarding the houses to be built by Co-partnership to the effect that if Lutyens's designs were not suitable, another architect should be employed. Co-partnership Tenants Ltd. later took exception to the planning of some of the houses, and had the power to change it. In March 1911, writing from the buffet at the Gare de Lyons on his way to Rome, and whilst the controversy over the Edward VII Memorial was at its height, Lutyens complained that his eight houses at Hampstead so far built had been 'so pulled about inside by the Co-partners that they are found to be, as I said they would be, unliveable in'. But King George and Queen Mary made a visit of inspection to the suburb and in the following month St. Jude's was consecrated—that is, but for the western bay of the nave, not completed till twenty years later—and 'I hear it is splendid for sound. They tried the choir. Canon Barnett was there exclaiming "how beautiful"'.

The sheets of preliminary sketches for St. Jude's reproduced on p. 184 have scarcely a feature in common with the final design except the general piling up of their masses to a central spire. The first notion (top left) is noticeably gothic, with tall lancet windows. Then we see the idea of a tower consisting of superimposed arches developing (top right). The third trial (bottom left) has in it the germ of the great roof and big dormers, but the nave and chancel arches still interrupt its sweep as clerestory windows—a contrivance actually retained for the sidelighting of the east end. The fourth design (bottom right), with a west tower and portico, may either be the earliest of the series or an experiment for the Free Church.

The sketches are of great interest as showing how the apparent simplicity of the final result was reached, in this case by a process of consolidation and reduction. They show, too, how the brick arched structure, the form which the conception is seen to have assumed at an early stage and which the interior retained, was enveloped by the roof at a late stage—partly, perhaps, with the view of thereby assimi-

[1] To Lady Emily, April 7, 1909.

lating the church to the character of the surrounding houses. Only in the tower, transmuted as it rises from a square, through an octagon, to the sixteen-sided spire, does the brick arch theme obtain full external expression. Thus considered, the big round-headed windows lighting the ends seem sponsored by external considerations rather than related to the internal structure. Consequently they look more at home in the Free Church, with its renaissance dome, than beneath the romanesque arcading of St. Jude's tower.

The two churches were intended to be of the same length. The Free Church nave had immediately to be restricted to two bays, and the fourth bay and west end of St. Jude's was only completed in 1933 (as a memorial to the Rev. B. G. Bourchier, the first Vicar). The manner of its finishing, with the long drooping roof, as Butler puts it, folded round over low projections sheltering the main entrance, is particularly satisfactory. The east ends of both churches, with their low appendages, show no less happy applications of the same device, which, with the low walls, ties the scale of the churches to that of the surrounding houses, and emphasises the upward sweep of the churches' roofs.

The interior painted decoration of St. Jude's was executed by Mr. Walter Starmer, A.R.S.A., between 1921–9. The artist consulted Lutyens who, however, would have preferred that the church should not have been decorated in this way.

Whilst the Hampstead designs were in their early, controversial, stages and Middlefield was going up, in the spring of 1909, Lutyens received the commission from H. J. Tennant for Great Maytham, the big country house in Kent described in Chapter VI. Other jobs during this year included the gardens and alteration of that lovely Tudor fragment, Mells Manor, for Sir John and Lady Horner—connections of Miss Jekyll's and friends of long standing; alterations for Lord Lytton at Knebworth; at his early houses Orchards, Goddards, and Warren Lodge (which he and Lady Emily had broken into during their courting days); and the various schemes for Sir George Sitwell at Renishaw.

In the period which this chapter covers (1910–11) he also had a score of commissions in hand besides those already mentioned or dealt with more fully later. The more notable can conveniently be summarised now.

Lambay was, of course, going on all the time, and on one of his visits he was marooned on the island for two days by rough seas—thereby upsetting appointments with Gaspard Farrer in connection with The Salutation, Sandwich, and 7 St. James's Square. Opposite Lambay on the mainland he began in 1910 to alter Howth Castle for Mr. Gaisford St. Lawrence—a romantic harled house with a courtyard, where a family curse decrees that an extra place be always laid at table for the Unexpected Guest. It involved the building of a new tower, in which he neatly adapted the Irish Tudor precedent set in the older part, a chapel, the redesigning of the principal rooms, and a small formal garden (p. 202).

Great Dixter, near Northiam, restored and enlarged for Mr. Nathaniel Lloyd, is the earliest and largest timber-framed manor house in Sussex—built between 1440 and 1454 by Richard Wakehurst who had married its heiress Elizabeth Echingham. When later floors and other accretions were removed, a superb great hall with hammer-beam roof, forty feet long, was revealed, with its original porch and solar wing almost complete. The kitchen wing no longer existed, and the removal of the floors from the hall further reduced the living space. To provide this there was fortunately available the framework of another, almost contemporary, hall-house at Benenden known as the Old House at Home. Mr. Lloyd bought it, the timbers were numbered, photographed, and taken down, then re-erected adjoining the truncated corner of the Dixter hall, projecting towards the garden side. A new tile-hung office wing was then built adjoining the two old buildings and welding them together in plan. Only the most conservative replacements were made to the latter, and the new portions, unobtrusively but meticulously traditional in brick and tiling, contain some of Lutyens's loveliest craftsmanship. He worked another transformation at the same time. Fascinated admiration of his thoroughness and ingenuity turned his client, a master printer by profession, into an architect and antiquary. Mr. Lloyd's publication twenty years later of his *History of English Brickwork* and *History of the English House* have their origin in the enthusiasm and habits of observation kindled by Lutyens, who contributed a Foreword to the former volume. Lutyens's return in Great Dixter to medieval timber and brick forms also links up with his work on the 'Shakespeare's England Exhibition' at Earl's Court, opened in 1912. His connection with it seems to have originated through friendship with Lady Randolph Churchill, a leading member of the committee.

Additions made to Hanover Lodge, Regent's Park, are chiefly notable as having been for a then rising young Admiral, David Beatty. Lowesby Hall, Leicestershire, was a straightforward restoration and enlargement of a Queen Anne house for Capt. Harold Brassey for whom he had built Copse Hill in the Cotswolds six years before; his work at Little Court, Tavistock, for Major Gallie, had similar scope. But the additions, already described, to the Queen Anne house Temple Dinsley, Hertfordshire, for Mr. H. C. Fenwick (a cousin of his early client and friend Mark, of Abbotswood) was a major work, perhaps his best country house after The Salutation in the Middlefield-Maytham-Hampstead style.

The amount of restoration and adaptation he was doing was symptomatic of the period's increasingly retrospective temper. Restoring the Parliament Chamber of Inner Temple Hall needed much more time than he could afford at this busy period and he grumbled at the research and writing of learned reports for the Benchers which it involved. But at least it was a lasting service to a venerable society, whereas his large part in the set up of the 'Shakespeare's England' Exhibition was even more laborious but transient. It involved the creation of a synthetic

Elizabethan town, grouping into streets and courts reproductions, on a reduced scale, of famous buildings of the period with others of his own design. The former included some houses on the originals of which he was actually working—Ashby St. Ledgers and Great Dixter; and afforded rather amusing opportunities of picturesque juxtaposition, such as Exeter Guildhall with the garden front of St. John's College, Oxford. One of the most effective corners was a town gate and harbour containing a replica of Sir Richard Grenville's *Revenge*, in the design of which he had the collaboration of Seymour Lucas, R.A. The whole thing was a brilliantly executed 'stunt', remarkable for its conscientiousness: the reproductions, though reduced, were reduced in the same proportion. He was already in India when the Exhibition opened. 'Was it in any way convincing?' he asked Lady Emily; 'I'm afraid it was full of holes for criticism.' If so, few people took advantage of them, though some must have wondered how the architect engaged apparently simultaneously in Hampstead, Rome, Johannesburg, Dublin and Delhi could find time to do a jig-saw puzzle with bits of ancient monuments. Indeed, it remains a question, to be answered only by reflecting on the efficiency of his office management. But every drawing that went out of the office had been conned and checked by him.

§2. ROME

At the Royal Academy Banquet in May 1909, the Prince of Wales, soon to be King George V, referred to Britain's part in three forthcoming International Exhibitions—Brussels (1910), Turin and Rome (1911). A Royal Commission was set up specifically to handle Britain's representation, with the Earl of Lytton as Chairman and Lutyens as Consulting Architect to the Commission—a post for which his experience at the Paris Exhibition a decade earlier recommended him. The two Italian exhibitions were being held to commemorate the fiftieth anniversary of the Union of Italy, that at Turin being wholly industrial in scope and the buildings to be the responsibility of the Italian Government. The Rome Exhibition was to present an international survey of fine arts, retrospective and contemporary, the various pavilions to be erected by their respective nations. Lord Lytton, with U. F. Wintour, the Commissioner General, proceeded that summer to Italy to arrange for the site of the British Pavilion at Rome and attend the preliminary meetings regarding Turin.

The Rome Exhibition was to be held in the Valle Giulia adjoining the Borghese Gardens. Britain secured a fine site close to the Museo Papa Giulio on high ground dominating the whole enclosure. It was early decided that 'the usual showy style of modern exhibition architecture would be out of place'.[1]

In October Lord Lytton asked his brother-in-law to join him in Italy. The official purpose was to report to the Commission on the suitability and safety of the

[1] Report of the Royal Commission for International Exhibitions, 1913.

buildings being erected by the Italian Government at Turin, but it was also desirable for the Consulting Architect to have cognisance of the Rome site and, although his appointment did not include designing the British pavilion, to be thereby enabled to report to the Commission on the detailed handling of the design already selected by the Board of Trade. This, it was ordained, should be a reproduction of the upper storey of the west façade of St. Paul's Cathedral. Thus Lutyens was given the opportunity to make that pilgrimage to the mould and pattern of European architecture which, for good or ill, has never failed to have a profound effect on artists.

The visit came at a significant stage of his life. He was conscious of his need for wider scope—those public buildings and monuments by which the ambitious architect must make his reputation with posterity. He may well have felt that the possibilities of his 'Wrennaissance' vernacular manner had been pushed to their limit. Thus the opportunity to make the Grand Tour, however hurriedly, at this particular juncture was exceedingly fortunate. That he had been able to achieve what he had, without intensive study at the capital of renaissance civilisation—indeed without regular training of any kind—is only accountable by accepting his natural genius and astonishing capacity for absorbing the essence of whatever he learnt or saw. But the transition that he was about to make in his art, from vernacular to monumental classicism, would be facilitated by, if it did not necessarily require, some big external stimulus. Visual experience of Italy has always been, and must be, one of the supreme stimulants to the architect. Now that the design, down to the smallest details, of every important building has been published for the student, there is no need for him to spend months, like the early fathers, measuring and drawing. But no study of drawings can adequately convey the quality of the lights and shadows under which the classic forms of building were evolved, the character of the vegetation and the colouring that have been their concomitants and which, with the intellectual and social vicissitudes of the inhabitants, account for the variations those forms have undergone between their primitive crudity and ebullient blossoming in baroque. As enlightening to the architect is actual sight of the materials used, their texture and handling, the sizes of the bricks and blocks of stone, the generosity of the deep tiled roofs, as he takes the immemorial road of his predecessors to Rome. The very coming for the first time into Italy cannot but be an exciting experience to the architect. He sees around him not only the great originals, the arch-types, of his art, but the profusion of lesser buildings that reflect from a thousand unexpected facets the glow of architecture's hearth; those cottages and farm buildings, those villages clustered around church or castle with unfailing architectural sense, whose nameless authors seem to have been unable to put a foot wrong. He experiences the truth, as Lutyens phrased it, that 'there is no ploy which cannot be lifted to the Divine level by its elevation as an art. To short sight it's a miracle. To those of a little longer sight it is Godhead'.

He had written that two years ago as an article of his Humanist creed, and now he is on the point of testing his convictions in the city of Humanism. We are fortunate in having his day to day account of the effect upon him of the experience. From Genoa to Pisa (where it got dark) he kept up a running commentary, on what interested him, in a long letter to his wife which, with its successors, affords us notes of a great architect's first impressions of Italy comparable in their laconic suggestiveness to Inigo Jones's in his copy of Palladio. Together with his letters from Rome, this subjective memorandum is, to us, the most important product of the journey. By its very omissions, of most of Baedeker's starred sights in Rome, it is illuminating —though we must remember that it was written to his wife whom he tried not to 'bore' with too much architecture. Yet there was so much that he knew by heart already. In no way is Lutyens's wide classical *knowledge*, accumulated by reading not books but engraved designs and photographs, more vividly revealed than in his description of how he found himself recognising buildings which he had never seen from their backs. These letters from Italy have the further interest of enabling us to see how his architectural puritanism, founded upon faith in Wren, Palladio and Inigo Jones, reacted to the grand manner of the High Renaissance and the rhetoric of the Counter-Reformation. Inevitably his mind was full of Wren, if only because he knew that the Rome Pavilion was to be a bit of St. Paul's. He had satisfied himself long ago that Hampton Court was superior to Versailles, but all he saw in Italy challenged his insular loyalties. 'I do wish I could have come with Wren,' he exclaimed, and, 'I must keep my head.' To be among so many familiar buildings was like a picnic in the Elysian Fields, though disconcerting when he found tricks that he believed he had invented forestalled in the *cinquecento*. As he became acclimatised he tended to grow more tolerant. But generally his attitude is critical and analytical, as in the effort to discriminate between good and bad workmanship, genuine excellences and happy vulgarities, in parts of a complicated whole such as the Villa d'Este gardens. That, and the constant refusal to allow glamour of contour and colour to blur his perception of true values, was characteristic.

On the journey out, he was to have met Lord Lytton at Turin but they missed each other and Lutyens therefore had a few hours to spend in Genoa. On resuming the journey he began his notes.

    Monday (Oct. 19th)   In train Genoa-Rome.
  I rushed through Genoa to find what I knew, and with little time I found but little I didn't know. One palace I didn't know and dont know now by name, with a duplicated cornice to its doric order which was very happy.
  A real shade-compelling bright day.
  The architecture—very little I have seen—cries aloud for sculpture—and good house-maiding. The Rococo muck in churches (the three I have seen) is

dreadful—the lavish use of marble as stone. The splendid waste of space in the buildings and the economy of it in roadways makes the place the very reverse of what we lay down as right in England. The lavish space given away in staircases makes me sick with envy—but the streets are too narrow for the palaces that stand upon them from any point of view. The effect is not really great or happy.

I dont refer to the gaps between them with long up-climbing stair roads. This is fine and in a way beyond my criticism, in that they were not *designed*. I want badly to keep my head here.

Another thing that astonishes me is the fact of the small amount of window area required to light a room brilliantly well.

The architecture, a good deal of it, is very badly finished off—thoughtless—which would make me wild if it was mine.

The great buildings on the hilltops I see excite me fearfully. High, high up against the sky, and how the devil do they get to them, still more *at* them to build them?

Two years later he may have remembered the excitement of the hill-top towns and castles of Liguria when designing Castle Drogo on its feudal altitude. As the train rushed on, the great aloes on the railway cuttings gave him the feeling of 'seeing something unreal and not seen before'. He was not sure whether he liked them, or would ever like a palm tree. Then, reverting to Genoa: 'some painting in the palaces was jolly but most of it bad—almost as bad as Fontainebleau. One ceiling was ingenious and good,' and he sketched[1]:

A moment later he decided: 'I dont like the aloes. My insularity *shall* stick to me.' Then—one can see him debating whether his resistance to novelties, not aloes alone,

---

[1] In the following year he applied many of the mental notes made on this journey to criticisms of the Union Building, Pretoria, solicited by Herbert Baker. In this particular case: 'See Genoa Palaces, especially for courts and stairways,' giving sketches of vaulting with an octagonal centre set diagonally, and of double capitals of circular columns employed to give a square spring for vaulting, reproduced here.

was due to insularity or sound principles—'I do wish I could have come with Wren.' But the sensuous rightness of Italian farm and village building—scarcely architecture but always inspired building—began to sap this resistance:

> The Italians have fine ideas in scale. Stones thus ☐ instead of ☐ to build with. Then their great thick rolls of little bricks, and roofs as thick as the furrows of a plough, *blazed* with light and great shadows from it.
>
> Pisa, a glimpse of white marble buildings with *lovely* red roofs against great blue hills lit by the setting sun.

After the first day in Rome the sense of familiarity overcame the first shock of wonder.

> Dined [October 21] with Count San Maritimo, head of the Exhibition.
>
> All very wonderful and to see things one knows from illustrations—down a little street and then a corner and lo and behold stands some old loved friend in form of a doorway, staircase, a palace. I recognize some by their backs, backs which I have never seen...
>
> I have seen St. Peters, various churches, the Capitol, Medici and other palaces, Forum, and as I was looking over the Forum what should sail over but a dirigible balloon, fish shaped and bright aluminium—such a contrast to see both the first time at once.
>
> There is so much here in little ways of things I thought I had invented!! no wonder people think I must have been in Italy. Perhaps I have, but it was not Rome. I have no internal ronge[1] and nothing comes in the least where I expect it. My old friends stand in the most unexpected places and in the oddest relation to each other.

Next day they took a jaunt across the Campagna to Tivoli, seeing Hadrian's Villa and the Falls:

> Everything is gray here—black and then the crown of blue sky, all gray and velvet black, just what I like, and no bright offensive colour, except in the modern man work. Then to the Villa d'Este—lovely, gray again and wondrous cypresses and those great silver distances. Some of the work—the terrace balustrades—lovely; but more was horrible and ugly. It wants to be seen with great discrimination. Yet there is a real God-given loveliness, and oh if I could have the chances. But you can see in the work where vulgarity prevailed over good taste and sense. The same then as now—if only people would see. Inside the palace the decoration was horrible, and outside a river is taken through the garden and played with *ad nauseam*. Over it all is the great cloak of decay. There were

[1] A French word that he often used, meaning 'a memory that plucks at the heart-strings'.

great masters and bad ones, and the patrons could have had little real appreciation of what was right and what was vulgar. Then home across the Campagna facing the setting sun—and how disappointing a pimple is St. Peter's dome.

A good deal of time was spent going over the ground of the Exhibition. Technical difficulties had arisen over adopting the St. Paul's design and Lutyens was asked to do a sketch. 'I am going to do it honorarily, for Vic (Lytton)—because if I take a fee and do not get the Pavilion, it will look bad.' He was then taken by Lord Lytton and Sir Rennell Rodd, the Ambassador, to a Turin Exhibition conference. The British authorities were uneasy about the precautions being taken against fire—with all too good reason as it turned out, for in the following year the building containing the British and Belgian exhibits at Brussels was burnt. An important retrospective collection of English furniture was destroyed, the most serious loss being a set of the uncommon Soho tapestries. At Turin the Italian authorities appear to have been difficult, and ultimately Lutyens reported to the Royal Commission that the buildings were not only unfit for the proper housing of exhibits but actually unsafe. It emerged that the Italian building contractors had received no drawings and been allowed full liberty in the selection of materials and methods of construction.[1]

At this meeting (October, 1909) matters were at an earlier stage but Lutyens's comments, rarely favourable on committees, are pungent on the state of affairs:

> Appalling to think of people being fed on this kind of muck. Directly one suggests any kind of improvement one is told that the tastes of the people—the lowest ebb of peopledom—must and can only be considered—no endeavour to elevate, educate, simply a franc-holding net one has to drag about the unwashed feet of a degraded nation. During the long stupid arguments in a language I don't understand I sustained the courage of my friends by portraits of the Italians with and without their clothes etc. If there had not been some mild form of relaxation the while, I am sure there would have been high words and irremediable disasters in tempers.
>
> Old Villa (chairman of the conference) sat like some impassive elephant saying '*impossibile*'. He produced letters from Wintour to say that we only wanted a building which could stand up for the time of the Exhibition, and now we demanded as a matter of course the L.C.C. fire prevention regulations. A promise to pay the difference (by Rodd) opened all doors.

Shortly after his return to London the Rome Pavilion was put in Lutyens's charge. Writing to Baker subsequently he described how subtly the elevation in fact differed from the model he was set to copy.

> The condition to copy, i.e. adapt, the upper order of the west front of St.

[1] Report of the *Royal Commission*, p. 79.

Paul's was given me by the Board of Trade. They all thought it very like, but it wasn't a bit, which is where the fun came in for me. The whole order had to be altered, and I think it takes more architectural technique to do this, and make every other part fit in, with the design of an undoubted master like Wren. The cornice, columns, etc. were altered, the portico and pediment etc; a great labour it was but very interesting. To the lay mind a copy is good enough, but to an architect, except some tradesman, it means a very great deal of thought, insight, knowledge.

The Pavilion was of course built of temporary materials and at the opening on March 27, 1911, favourably impressed both British and Italians—which had notable results. Lutyens had made another brief visit in January 1911, on his return from South Africa, and at the later date was present both as architect and representing the R.I.B.A. 'Shall have to go in broad daylight in evening dress and an opera hat!! Too awful and ass-making,' he reported. The Dowager Countess of Lytton was in Rome for the occasion and her son-in-law visited the Sistine Chapel with her. Dr. Ashby took him to see the German archaeological establishment in Rome, when evidently the desirability of a similar British institution was discussed—which Lutyens was instrumental in forwarding. He might also have gone to Viterbo with Derwent Wood and P. G. Konody of the *Daily Mail* to see the great Camorra trial then in its earlier stages, but 'grudged the time'. On his way home he looked in on his old friends the Mallets at Grasse where Sir Hugh Lane was staying; 'a funny mixture with the Mallets.'

The last time Lutyens and Lane had been fellow guests had been at Johannesburg, staying with Sir Lionel and Lady Phillips.

§3. SOUTH AFRICA

It had originated with a telegram from Lady, then Mrs. Lionel, Phillips that he had got in Rome in 1910, inviting him to design the Johannesburg Art Gallery.

This remarkable lady, South African by birth and wife of one of the pioneers of the Rand Goldfields, was, in General Smuts's words, 'inspired by the ideals of Rhodes and Milner for the political and cultural advancement of South Africa.' She also had an innate passion for beauty and sure natural taste. At Johannesburg she was active in its development as a fine modern city; Herbert Baker had built an impressive house there for the Phillipses; and she had often discussed with him her dream of founding an art gallery, to be filled with loans from English museums and collections. She had obtained a promise of £10,000 towards this from Sir Otto Beit, and about 1908 came to England, where Sir Lionel Phillips had a house in Grosvenor Square and Tilney Hall in Hampshire, to begin collecting pictures. She may have

57. Hampstead Garden Suburb (1910). Erskine Hill and the Free Church

58. St Jude's Church, Hampstead Garden Suburb (1910) with west end as completed in 1933. The Free Church on the left, The Rectory on the right

59. RENISHAW HALL, DERBYSHIRE. Ante-room to ballroom (1908)

60 and 61. HOWTH CASTLE, DUBLIN. An added tower and the Chapel (1910)

met Lutyens in London, where Mrs. Norman Grosvenor introduced her to Sir Hugh Lane, that brilliant connoisseur, dealer, and collector, already engaged on his project of establishing a gallery of modern art in his native Dublin. Lane persuaded her to concentrate, at least initially, on buying contemporary art, and she caused something of a sensation at Wilson Steer's Goupil Gallery exhibition of 1909 by buying his *Corfe Castle*, *Limekilns*, and *A Chelsea Window*, among other works. A site was obtained for the Gallery in Joubert Park—the twenty acre central open space of the city—and a competition was held for its design among local architects. By the autumn of 1910 matters had progressed so far that Lane went out to help judge the competition. When none of the designs proved satisfactory, it seems that Lane, with Baker's agreement, suggested calling in Lutyens, in view of his work with the Royal Commission on International Exhibitions and as the coming man in the eyes of many *cognoscenti*.

Lutyens hesitated. South Africa was Herbert Baker's province, and, in addition to all the building going on at Hampstead, during the summer the extraordinary commission had come in for the £50,000 Castle Drogo on Dartmoor. Then there was the King Edward VII Memorial in the offing, Mr. Reginald McKenna wanted plans for altering Mells Park which he had acquired from Sir John Horner; the restoration and enlargement of Great Dixter and of Lowesby Hall, Leicestershire, were in progress. On the other hand the Union of South Africa as a Dominion in May 1910, had coincided with spectacular economic and industrial recovery, and seemed to open a new world of great expectations, to which his informal arrangement with Baker gave him an *entrée*. Before accepting, he therefore got in touch with him for his views, then replied that he would come, adding, 'What fun it will be!'

Baker, too fully occupied with his Union Buildings to take an active part in the Gallery scheme, had personally welcomed his coming but, it appears from subsequent correspondence, cautiously stressed the local difficulties that might be aroused by so notable an interloper from England. On this aspect Lutyens subsequently wrote to him:

> If the South African architects are on their hind legs about my going out, we can't help it—they must stay there—rampant... You did all you reasonably could (for my sake I own) to stop my coming. I have only to publish your letter to me to show that your intentions were anything but selfish.

He had been encouraged to accept the invitation by Sir Otto Beit, a supporter of the Gallery scheme; Sir Julius Wernher had further suggested to General Smuts that Lutyens should be consulted on the proposals then in a state of acute flux for Cape Town University to which Beit and Wernher were contributing half a million pounds. 'It might mean a lead to a B(aker) L(utyens) job; would you mind?' he asked

Baker (November 10, 1910). 'The thing is to block a competition for the buildings, which Beit suggested as possible. He and Wernher seemed pleased that I should have a chance of being in it.' There was also the still unsettled design for the war memorial to the Rand Regiments, the foundation stone of which had recently been laid by the Duke of Connaught, in Eckstein Park, Johannesburg.

His departure on November 19, for six weeks' absence, was made almost into an official occasion by the President of the Royal Institute of British Architects, Leonard Stokes, unexpectedly coming to see him off—with a parting gift of sea-sickness pills. His manager, A. J. Thomas, travelled down with a bundle of sixty topics requiring signature or decision. His assistant, Hall, was accompanying him with full drawing office equipment and a mass of work to be done on the voyage, including designs for Castle Drogo. A deck cabin was fitted up as an office. As the R.M.S. *Saxon* left Southampton on the somewhat speculative adventure—and his first long separation from his wife and children—he wrote to her in 'great gratefulness to the God that gave me so sweet, so dear, a helpmate, with a wit so loveable and to me a wife perfect'. Throughout his absence he kept his watch to Greenwich time 'to know what you are all doing when', and he continued the letter from day to day (until the date when the mail would coincide with his return). There is therefore a complete journal from November 19–December 17.

The voyage was uneventful except for the usual incidents and fleeting acquaintanceships of shipboard. He and Hall played a game of pretending to be in the Queen Anne's Gate office. 'I ask him for a list of the day's appointments and generally wind up by asking him to call me a taxi. It delights him.' The routine was to rise at 7, walk till breakfast at 8.30, at 10 o'clock write the home letter, then work till lunch, work again from 2 to 3.30, and after tea and another walk, till 7.30. By the fourth day out he was getting into his stride with Castle Drogo, but found working difficult: 'the swash and roar of the water and the persistent creaking distract.' He got some amusement from somewhat uninspiring and elderly table-companions but more from a school of porpoises; was put protesting on the sports committee; and applied his mathematical mind to two incidental problems. After Boat Drill:

> I wanted the Captain to measure the lengths of the sailors' arms and the waists of the old ladies on board, so to be sure they would all be saved. If a short sailor tried to save Mrs. T—, she would be lost.

The other problem was to work out the pitch of the vessel,

> from the water levels in my bath. I make out the bow and stern are moving some 32 ft in a vertical direction. The angle of the roll is more difficult to measure as the bathroom is not amidships.

On arrival at Capetown, December 7, Herbert Baker who had come especially from Johannesburg welcomed him with great warmth on board. As they breakfasted, he sketched the complicated University situation, before hurrying him off on a tour of sites and sights. In view of Lutyens having been concerned twice in its history, now with the question of its site and in 1918 as approving the design of the buildings, a short note on the University of Cape Town is required in order to appreciate the position. The South African College was founded in 1829. After the South African War it expanded rapidly, absorbing a number of other educational institutions, though the essentially Africander Stellenbosch College (renamed Victoria in 1897) continued to be its chief rival. Development of the South African College into a resident and teaching university was supported by the new Union Government under Botha and Smuts, established earlier in the year of Lutyens's visit. Just before his arrival the Government had announced the setting aside of half a million pounds for this purpose and the reservation for it of a site on the Groote Schuur estate that Rhodes had left at the Government's disposal. Simultaneously Smuts reached agreement with Otto Beit and Wernher, trustees of the will of the late Alfred Beit who had left £200,000 and a site for the founding of a new university in the Transvaal. The result was that both Sir Otto and Sir Julius promised the princely donation of a further £500,000 for the Cape University at Groote Schuur. Dr. Malan,[1] Minister of Education, had announced these financial and topographical decisions in November. Hence Lutyens's conferences with Beit and Wernher on the subject just before leaving England, and the official interest in the matter which he discovered on landing at Cape Town.

Brer Ned and Brer Bear (as they came to address one another during the course of these ten hectic days) spent the first morning seeing Rudyard Kipling's house, Woolsack, the Rhodes Memorial, and the beginnings of Cape Town Cathedral—all of which were Baker's children; lunched with General Smuts, Sir Lionel Phillips, and Dr. Malan at Parliament House; then called on the Prime Minister and Mrs. Botha at his official residence Groote Schuur. Lutyens noted 'Botha has one of the saddest faces I have ever seen', and was greatly moved by his respect for the man among whose personal possessions he thus lived, even sitting in Rhodes's chair. 'I asked him if ever in the history of the world so great a victory had been won in which there was no defeated enemy. I put it better than that; and if I could have said it in Dutch I believe he would have cried!' he afterwards told Smuts.

We may, perhaps, at this point detect the first signs of an emotional excitement —whether owing to the climate, memories of the war, the impact of new and spectacular surroundings, the discussion of great projects with eminent personages, or the combination of these factors—which is the keynote of Lutyens's record of his tour. It may have gone slightly to his head.

General Smuts asked him for his views on the University site at Groote Schuur.

[1] Father of the present (1950) Prime Minister.

The possibility was also discussed of his designing the large church projected at Johannesburg and advising on the layout of the new Federal Capital at Pretoria. Accordingly this first afternoon was spent on the slopes of Table Mountain behind Groote Schuur looking at University sites until it was time to dine with Dr., newly created Sir Starr, Jameson, leader of the Unionist Party and, as executor of Rhodes's will, one of the foremost supporters of the University scheme.

The accessibility and geniality of Union statesmen, so recently antagonists, captivated Lutyens. After breakfasting with the Prime Minister of Australia he half jokingly wrote to Lady Emily 'We must get A. J. B. to meet Asquith, to inform them of these ideas—for of such is the world here! You will find me a great Imperialist when I come home!' At Government House Lord Gladstone was not encouraging about the University project; he 'can only think in "buts"'. These were clarified soon in a guarded letter from the Minister of Education, from which Lutyens discovered how real the obstacles were, not least the Nationalist opposition. It was not till 1923, after the financial set backs of the 1914-18 war and the suicide of the architect J. M. Solomon, that building was actually begun to a much simplified design by Messrs. Hawke and Mackinlay.

After a night at Baker's holiday home on the coast at Muizenburg, which Lutyens told Lady Emily was 'a delightful little house, exactly what you would like', the two architects set out for Johannesburg. As the train carried them through the recent war zone, Lutyens found himself wishing 'it was not all so emotional, the sorrow of it creeps round me', and was enthralled by the quality of the landscape:

> O the clear bright sky, the exquisite clear softness of the light over field and sky to the east. The sunset is too colourful to be really beautiful, but the silver grays and bright blues all as clear as crystal and the purples are wonderful. Italy cannot touch it with all her mystery of the ages.

Throughout his visit the scenery, especially the quality of the light and the strange birds and beasts, enchanted him.

At Villa Arcadia, the palatial house designed by Baker for Sir Lionel Phillips on the fringe of Johannesburg, they were welcomed by Lady Phillips, Mrs. Baker, Hugh Lane, and Baker's young assistant, Solomon. Next morning Brer Ned was awakened by a voice calling through the open window and there was Brer Bear, out on his morning ride, and the vast view, over rolling veldt to distant mountains blue in the early light. In the garden he found that 'they effect the Miss Jekyll type. It is odd to see great ugly cactus growing up in a Munstead border'; he told his hostess that he found 'written on the garden wall *Mene Mene Jekyll Upharsin*'. Visitors were supposed to take things easy for the first day or two in Johannesburg owing to the 6000 feet altitude—'but I never know those sort of things; I suppose it is my enormous lungs which are big enough for two bodies.' A curious biological footnote; an inheritance, if so, from athletic Lutyens forbears which he may have shared with his brother the sprinter.

He had come to Johannesburg to design the Art Gallery, with the prospect of the Rand Regiments' War Memorial. He soon discovered the strong antipathies that flourished in the young, small, mixed, community under the forcing sun and keen air. The Municipal Council was jealous of employing any but a local architect, but appeared to be equally set against consulting Herbert Baker either. Now, forty years on, South Africans freely admit the country's debt to Sir Herbert's far-seeing and often unselfish work for architecture in the Dominion, and are proud of the buildings designed by Sir Edwin Lutyens. But at the time these undercurrents of feeling, as Lutyens noted, made his own position difficult. 'Baker is good and generous as gold and I must be careful not to hurt him however advantageous to myself. There is a meeting of the town council with Mrs. Phillips and Lane (about the Gallery). I have refused to go. I can't argue my own case.' Instead, he sat on the stoep of Arcadia and wrote of Johannesburg:

> There is this villa-decked land standing above a squalid town with here and there big buildings, a sort of Birmingham without the smoke, and every other block of buildings rased to the ground to appease some appalling angel. Then beyond, miles and miles of chimneys belching black smoke and weird cats-cradle erections—the mines. Mines of gold, the very heart of a modern world—and beyond, the veldt wasting hundreds of miles. They want me to go down a gold mine but I don't want to go down these man-made holes and see the miners and the pthysis the dust gives 'em, though water jets and every modern contrivance possible to immunise the evil is adopted. Yet it is there, and I dont like men digging for potatoes they may not eat and gold they may not spend. Yet all this! rather than not be let build marble cathedrals, and great towns to the glory of the Sun!

The site for the Art Gallery was at one side of Joubert Park, the city's central open space, gay now with flowers and lawns and shaded by a rich variety of well-grown trees, backing on the railway. Baker had envisaged to Mrs. Phillips a modest, Dutch style, building. After inspection of the site and discussion with her and Lane, Lutyens sketched a much more ambitious design. The front of the gallery proper, a low pantiled range with a portico, looked towards the park between projecting pavilions with hipped roofs each rising to a tall rectangular chimney. The walls throughout were proposed to be fine ashlar masonry, with recesses for sculpture. The principal front was shown reflected in a sunk rectangular pool. This was all more costly than the original intention, with the result that the Gallery took thirty years to complete. The last section was finished only in 1944, and the projected pool was never begun—in that dry land.

The Duke of Connaught had laid the foundation stone of the Rand Regiments' Memorial on his visit to open the Union Parliament earlier in the year. The site was on the edge of a steep declivity in Eckstein Park, a larger open space of varied contour now containing the City's Zoological Gardens. Lutyens's design (p. 211) is interesting as the forerunner of some of his 1914–18 war memorials and the earliest demonstration of his pure classicism: a triumphal archway, square in plan, with a lower arch in each flank, the whole surmounted by a flattened dome supporting a bronze figure of Victory. The barrel-vaulted central space is further lit by a square opening in the soffit on either side concealed from front and back by rectangular podiums behind the pediments over the main arches. These openings admit a beam of sunlight into the vaulted interior producing a dramatic chiaroscuro. The names of the fallen are inscribed on the sides of the arches. Lutyens wanted the site to be changed in favour of a flat one at the intersection of four avenues, and designed a setting for the monument of balustraded terraces, square pools, and flights of steps between groups of sculpture on pedestals. None of these adjuncts was carried out; but, as built, the Memorial is approached by an impressive ascent from the lower ground.

Sketch designs for both buildings had to be prepared for the respective committees; a room at Arcadia was put at his disposal as a drawing office, and on some nights he worked late on the University scheme with Baker at his office. The Gallery Committee of the Municipality came to dine at Arcadia, when Lutyens took the opportunity of giving them his 'real views' on town planning, and on the great opportunities presented by the twenty-year-old city—opportunities which, he maintained, they were frittering away. Hugh Lane was on tenterhooks lest Lutyens should be too jocular. Perhaps he admonished him to that effect. In the event he was 'very serious and earnest and they were', Lutyens considered, 'relieved to be made to dance afterwards.' He offered to go over the whole town plan with the municipal engineers and to suggest revision of the by-laws. Almost certainly he would have criticised the system by which blocks were let out for development by co-partnership companies and the planting of the avenues, which have become such a feature of Johannesburg, was let out to contractors—with the result that trees which should have been set sixty feet apart were sometimes planted at only six feet. Another theme in his lecture may be conjectured from the letter to Baker of January 20, 1911, much of which has already been quoted in Chapter VI. Its main point was his conviction that in new countries, where classical architecture was undertaken, the rules, proportions, and sections must be all the more implicitly prescribed and followed, contrary to the current belief that a colonial architecture gains character from using the classical motifs loosely and picturesquely.

This conviction of the necessity of 'super thought' in the architect building out of Europe was, of course, to be the driving power behind the designs for Delhi. But it accounts no less for the finished artistry of the Johannesburg Gallery and Memorial designs, and for the approval he was later to give to Solomon's Cape Town University designs although the latter were suspected at the time, and proved subsequently, to be too finely elaborated to be economically practicable—with the result that Solomon shot himself. Lutyens's refusal to compromise with local conditions or committees' preconceptions, if he believed them ill-founded and aesthetically immoral, lost him many commissions and earned him a reputation for extravagance. But when, despite the human or geographical factors, he won, the resulting buildings attained the standard of architectural perfection which he set himself and stand now as lonely vindications, in a chaotic world, of civilised values.

The converse of this attitude is surprising, and no less instructive. As he explained to Baker,

> in *old* countries you can use *rough materials*, where you find old men instinctively handling it from boyhood and unconsciously weaving lovely texture into it. In a new country it is impossible to expect any help of that sort in the fabric of a building. This is a point where, seeing together, we see the other's white as black!
> You say New Country, therefore Rough
> I say   ,,   ,,   ,,   Slick.
> There is in Africa no tradition on which accidents can rely, and reliance can only remain with the best *thought*—the harder and purer the better—as concerns her architecture... You get no great poetry in a pidgeon language, though you may get poetic sentiment. You cannot play originality with the Orders... Colossus Rhodes! had he realised all the labour of myriads of great men who helped to produce those Orders—he would have treated them with deep reverence.

The last sentence alludes, I take it, to a theory of Rhodes's—who had sent Baker to Rome to study classical buildings, and which Baker had presumably communicated to Lutyens—that classical architecture should be *adapted* for colonial use. In another passage in the same letter, which also discusses the perils of originality, this time in relation to gothic precedent, he criticised Baker's design for a church:

> Why spoil the swings (parabolas) of your shadows and reflected lights by pointing the arch? Why perforate your apse with lights and disturb the majesty of atmosphere on a perfect geometrical shape? There is no need for it. Westminster, Chartres, are perfect buildings built by intellectual giants, and, there, perfect poetry remains. Alter their proportions, alter their geometric (bad word for it) progression—all their poetry vanishes. Great *wall* surfaces of transparency. Now in Johannesburg you must have great surfaces of opacity, and you dont

want the wash of your reflected lights broken, [original text defective] ... a pointed arch like the jaws of a whale over a sea captain's garden gate.

As he addressed the burghers of Johannesburg and Hugh Lane over the dinner table, and the sun sank behind the blueing and empurpled veldt beyond the stoep, his discourse may have touched on these points. Its quality, if not its content, will have been similarly elliptical, elusive, beyond and above the comprehension of most of those present, but shot like the obscurity of a cloud with darting flashes of illumination; truths of his art vividly and memorably if oddly expressed. As he talked the sky itself darkened under a sudden storm and in a gorgeous phrase he recorded that there were 'great flashes that stood on end and staggered like Gods in fear'.

Both the Gallery and Memorial Committees adopted his proposals. Another day was spent at Pretoria, in pursuance of General Smuts's request for suggestions on the town layout in relation to Baker's Union Building. And there were conferences with clergy on the proposed building of a great church for Johannesburg.

A letter written after he had returned to London[1] and had discussed the design with the Bishop of Pretoria reveals his project for the church in Johannesburg to have been a remarkable one, incorporating germs of ideas which he developed thirty years later in his great designs for the Roman Catholic Cathedral at Liverpool. The Bishop's requirements were ambitious, although the site available was restricted by the street-plan, and Lutyens 'told him Wren's finding, that the voice of a preacher will not carry more than 90 ft.'. However, to meet the demand for floor-space, he proposed raising the church on an undercroft, with aisles or galleries carried over the foot-walks on arcades round three sides—a method which had been provisionally agreed to by the authorities on the spot.

> Find out, do, if this is still possible and get a resolution (poor Brer Baker) passed!! He agreed to a domed church (I suggested it with all due deference to your opinion. You can build the crypt and then if necessary cut off the dome and flat roof·it).[2]

Lutyens added that he had in mind the 'lovely plan' of S. Paolo fuori le Mure at Rome and proposed a basilican plan with five rows of columns forming eighteen-feet bays, besides the galleries over the footwalks on west and south. Then he sketched in the letter—'all too hurrid to explain what I mean'—the device used at Liverpool for lighting the aisles by clerestory windows in vaults alternately high and low: 'One into area and t' other into church. Wonderful lighting effect. With big screen wall outside to take the thrusts.' (It is significant to find him originating this system in relation to the strong light of South Africa, and that this development of vaulting was simultaneous with his uses of vaults at Castle Drogo.) The Church would have a great campanile with the *Benedicite* sculptured on its sides,

[1] To Herbert Baker, Aug. 3, 1911. [2] *Ibid.*

62. JOHANNESBURG. THE RAND REGIMENTS' MEMORIAL 1911. Original full scheme. From the drawing by William Walcot

63. CASTLE DROGO, DREWSTEIGNTON, DEVON (1910–30)

64. CASTLE DROGO, FROM THE AIR. In the original design this range of buildings was confronted by a similar one connected by a central block on the right, to form a court and extensive forecourt

65 to 67. Castle Drogo,
(65 *below*) Lower flight of great staircase.
(66 *right*) The Scullery

(67 *right*) Looking down the upper flight of the great staircase

69. CASTLE DROGO. The private staircase

68. CASTLE DROGO. Granite steps in the garden

Alternate bays, 'one into area, t'other into church'.

SKETCHES IN CHURCH AT JOHANNESBURG (1911)

beginning at the base with 'Ananias, Azarias, and Misael' and culminating at the top in a great 'O, Praise ye the Lord, Magnify Him for ever'. But he confessed to being a little perturbed lest he should get 'for ever, for ever, for ever' all down one corner for hundreds of feet. It would need working out with Baker, with whom he hoped to collaborate on it, though to his own design. At Johannesburg he found the clergy co-operative, though doubtful about funds. His jocular methods were not always appreciated. There was, for example, the Bishop of Cape Town who came to tea and wore 'an amethyst ring on his finger as big as the tea cup he offered me. Of course I tried to take the ring and he nearly spilt the tea'. Possibly, too, a Mr. and Mrs. Pim whom he met at dinner one night did not wholly relish being asked 'if there were any pimples'.

On the day after Christmas he left for Cape Town and home. It must be confessed that he had not been an unmitigated success in South Africa. Inspiring and salutary as his ideas often were, most of them were too idealistic and imaginative for men who, flattering as was their respectful attitude, were shrewdly practical, and did not always see the point of his jokes. There is some reason to suppose that he left a trail of frayed edges behind him to be smoothed over by Herbert Baker—Brer Bear, who with his accommodating architectural conscience and keen sense of practical politics was, as Brer Ned admitted, devastatingly, an excellent man on committees. But the two old friends parted affectionately, looking forward keenly, at least Lutyens did, to collaborating on the great *Benedicite* church. In the train he began a letter headed with the stars of the Great Bear, for Mr. and Mrs. Baker and their family:

> My dear Bear,
>   I loved and do love the direct simplicity of your unwavering hospitality. Not a carping or ungenerous word, to me, who must by my very nature have tried you sorely... Difficult to write to you—your kindness and good-will make words impotent things. I loved seeing you at home with your right-souled wife and your bairns. It has all made a very loveable picture in my mind.
>   The great practice you have made is remarkable.
>   It will be fun doing the church together and we are sure to have many hills and valleys to go through together over it—but it will be fun to rise through the pendentives hand in hand to the great dome that carries the vasty vault...
>   Baker, sir, I thank you.

—Then follows that grand description of Perigord beginning 'Let our church be a gathering up of all that men can do', which I have given on page 190 in connection with the Hampstead churches.

§4. GRAND MANNER

There may come times in an architect's life when the existence of several big buildings, each of which will probably stand for centuries, is decided within a few hours of one another. An extraordinary contrast then arises in the dimension of time: between the moments of executive decision and the aggregate duration of their results. This reflection is prompted by a particular twenty-four hours, April 14–15, 1911, the year which should perhaps be regarded as the peak of Lutyens's activities. Under the former date he noted, *en route* for Great Maytham, then almost finished:

> Yesterday a rush designing the Great Cross, altar, reredos and pulpit for St. Judes. Riddell and Hudson want me to prepare a King Edward Memorial

Scheme for Trafalgar Square. I sent off yesterday my Rand Regiment Memorial drawings to South Africa. I sent off plans for Drewe's revised Castle.

Then, on the 15th, he received a letter from Sir Rennel Rodd proposing the reconstruction of the Rome Exhibition Pavilion as the British School at Rome.

We have seen how the Rand Memorial and the Hampstead centre quickly compensated for the rejection of his magnificent scheme for County Hall. The three other simultaneous projects, although so different in character and outcome, are similarly linked by the bigness of their conception. Even in its reduced form, Castle Drogo represents the climax of his romantic architecture on an heroic scale; his constructive part in the creation of the British School at Rome aimed at strengthening the foundations of humanist civilisation in Britain; and the various designs for the Edward VII Memorial were essays in the grand manner itself.

The eventual reduction of the latter to a modest equestrian statue is symbolic of the insecure basis afforded by the year of George V's Coronation, despite its apparent glamour, for re-establishing the ideals of the high renaissance. The era of humanist culture initiated by the Renaissance was itself nearly spent. Yet within a few months from this April day, Lutyens was to be charged with planning the erection of Britain's greatest material affirmation of that ideal, the new capital of India. Through mounting political and financial obstacles he succeeded in fulfilling the commission and his own destiny. The building of New Delhi is to be conceived as a great pyrrhic victory for the rearguard of humanism, with Lutyens at their head, fought out before the titanic background of warring power politics. But for the present the heavens are relatively serene despite distant rumblings of war and political dissensions at home. He might well feel himself to be at the zenith of his powers, with a fair prospect of expanding opportunities stretching ahead.

The first of the three great undertakings of 1911, in point of time, was Castle Drogo, the conception period of which spreads over and links his South African visit and the works that occupied him immediately after his return. The late J. C. Drewe had first consulted Lutyens in the winter of 1909–10 on his intention to build a modern castle at Drewsteignton, Devonshire, where he had some years previously acquired an impressive outlying spur of Dartmoor. The Drewes are an ancient Devonshire family, indeed Drewsteignton means Dru-his-town-on-the-Teign, and from the sixteenth to the twentieth century had lived at the Grange, Broadhembury. The earliest recorded member is referred to in Latin documents of the twelfth century as Drogo de Teynton. Mr. Drewe, then residing in Sussex, conceived the notion of re-establishing the branch of the family on ancestral Drogo acres, and, being himself an enthusiastic amateur of castle architecture, to build, in the local granite, such a home as Drogo de Teynton might have had. One reason for Mr. Drewe's choice of this particular site, nearly 900 feet above sea level and 200 feet above the river below—a most magnificent but hitherto inaccessible situation—was that it had constituted an authentic part of Drogo de Teynton's domain.

By August 1910 Lutyens had apparently worked out a rough sketch design, for on the 3rd he wrote to Lady Emily:

> Mr. Drewe writes a nice and exciting letter. I go on with drawings. Not more than £50,000 though, and £10,000 for the garden. I suppose £60,000 sounds a lot to you! But I don't know what it means. If I look at Westminster Abbey it is an absurd, a trivial, amount, and if I look at a dear little old world two-roomed cottage it merely looks a vast and unmanageable amount. Only I do wish he didn't want a Castle, but just a delicious loveable house with plenty of good large rooms in it.

Next to a cathedral or a palace—both of which he was to be called to design—a castle used to be the peak of young architects' ambitions. Lutyens would, perhaps, have gone to its imagining without that sigh had the opportunity come ten years earlier, when he had all the Elizabethan zest that went into Marsh Court and Little Thakeham, whereas now he best enjoyed designing a Great Maytham or The Salutation at Sandwich. Yet here was one of the opportunities of an architect's life-time, and it must be seized. In the preceding weeks he had been thinking, working up a head of passion, about buildings of the tremendous kind. And earlier in the letter just quoted he had tried to resolve his mixed feelings on the matter. The following passage reveals, I think, the depth in his stomach from which Lutyens needed to conceive so organic a drama as Drogo, in distinction to the primarily intellectual source of his more humane, classical, designs. And it suggests the self-projection, or love, as he simply called it, that went into his process of conception.

> I feel so for Mrs. B.,[1] through you, for her antipathy to the big house and all it means from one point of view. I look at the big house from the other, and best, point of view:—a centre for all the charity that should begin at home and cover henwise with wings of love all those near about her that are dependant and weaker and smaller. A house with the soul of a Wilton gives me a choke of veneration, at its unending possibilities of giving and receiving love. Neither the loveliness nor the love of such can be bought, not by all the millions in the world. There! God keep the Feudal and preserve all that is best in it. Should you make all arable grass—because some by neglect grow thistles?

In the late summer of 1910, just before he started for the Cape, the site for the castle was pegged out and the line of the approach road settled, work on which was begun immediately. During the sea voyage he began working up the first rough sketches.

[1] Mrs. Cecil Baring, of Lambay.

Immensely impressive as the Castle is, it represents about a third of the vast design elaborated in the deck-cabin-drawing-office and finalised in the following April. As first conceived, Drogo would have occupied the whole summit of its heather-clad promontory, approximating in extent and effect to a feudal castle such as Richmond, built of the glittering granite as massively as Durham, and growing out of its summit like a geological outcrop. The main buildings were to lie round three sides of a courtyard open to the north, with lower wings splayed outwards towards a huge circular forecourt entered on the central axis by a massive gatehouse. The existing building, on the eastern edge of the plateau, is the east side of the court with its splayed wing extending north (p. 212). The western was to be a counterpart, while the south side of the courtyard was to be formed by an immense open-roofed hall. Since the ground slopes steeply down from the area of the intended courtyard, all these buildings were to have massive crypts, below the court level but above that of the slopes on the outward sides. The general character of the whole would have been the same as the portion built, predominantly horizontal and compact, with huge plastic surfaces of granite alternating with transomed windows, such towers as there are making relatively slight indentations of the skyline but forming masses of light and shade and so deepening the elevations. In the distant views, which are chiefly from the east and west, the appearance would have been not very unlike what it is; from the east it would have been unchanged (except in one important particular); from the west we should have seen the back of the west side instead of the front of the east side of equal length. From the south, however, instead of the end looming narrowly, there would have been the whole length of the hall, of the same height connecting with the west side. In appreciating the design of the part built, it is necessary to bear in mind that the effect of the intended whole would have been one of symmetrical balance. What appears in the fragment to be picturesque, indeed arbitrary, irregularity, however logically accounted for by the internal planning, would have acquired the extraneous justification of being part of a balanced unity. As it is, Drogo is even more of a castle, even more dramatic, for being thus an unresolved fragment. The seeming obscurity and wilfulness of its groupings and plan thus have much the same cause as the sublime irrationality produced in medieval castles by forgotten military needs, catastrophic truncations, and the domestic accretions of centuries. The sheer size of the original scheme relates Drogo to Lutyens's frame of mind at the time: to that preoccupation with big ideas stimulated by his journey to Rome just before and which was so marked during his sojourn in South Africa. One cause of the 1911 design being drastically reduced was that, at the time of the laying of the foundation stone, the owner decided that the thickness of the walls should be doubled in order to produce more completely the character aimed at. This desire, of course, doubled the cost, and it was therefore decided to postpone indefinitely the building of the west side of the court. The plan then became

L-shaped with the hall still at right angles to the east range. After the war the hall, too, was abandoned when no more than its crypt had been built which it was decided to utilise as a chapel. Then the east wing, from the present entrance tower southwards, was redesigned internally, with a revised south elevation, to be complete in itself—work on which was not finished till 1930. In early days, a large garden in front of the east side, massively terraced and bastioned above the ravine that bounds the site in this direction, was eliminated, in favour of a position on the hillside north of the Castle where nevertheless considerable earthwork was involved and has yielded admirable results. This change preserved the heather and pines as the immediate setting of the Castle, from which the walls now rise sheer. Lutyens fully approved the change and agreed that the contrast of the dark firs with the metallic granite walls and the whispering of the wind in their branches contributed to the whole effect (p. 223).

Forgetting, now, all that might have been, we must quickly look at that which is and gains in significance by our knowledge of how it evolved. The first impression, on the spot, is that Castle Drogo looks bigger than in fact it is. Therein lies part of its artistry, and the effect is traceable to the extremely subtle use of batter in the walling —not throughout but so as to produce precisely this enhancement. The same enhanced effect is produced by the slight curvature in the Parthenon and in the Cenotaph and can be noted in Lutyens's thoughts as early as his paper on garden design in 1908 (Chapter VII). For example, in the entrance tower (p. 212), the wall surface is vertical up to the string course about nine feet from the ground, then to the top of the battlements the uninterrupted surfaces of the turrets are steeply battered, exaggerating the height. The long east side, rising from the moor and bending as it goes, makes its effect by the great number of surfaces at different angles to each other, in full light, half light, and shadow, and by the main wall surfaces being battered whilst the many-windowed bay of the staircase (in the foreground of Pl. 71) is vertical. Again, at the south end (p. 223), where the sharply accentuated angles contrasting with the bay produce an extraordinary sense of almost savage strength, the height is enhanced by the batter of the east and west wall surfaces and the setting progressively back of the south end's surface, whilst the bay soars vertically.

Another source of enhancement is the degree of 'intricacy' (as picturesque critics termed the quality) that he contrived to combine with apparent massive simplicity. This proceeds chiefly from his handling of the levels, of which more when the plan is described. But it is noticeable in the sizes and heights of the windows, and in the seemingly cavernous recesses in the sides of the entrance tower, for instance; recesses each serving essential purposes in plan. The fact that the entrance court and entrance are at first floor level, too, results in unexpected courts being discovered at the lower level, as in a secret garden south of and below the tower; courts that serve to light the crypt rooms, but thus contribute to the intricacy and enhancement of the masses.

GROUND FLOOR

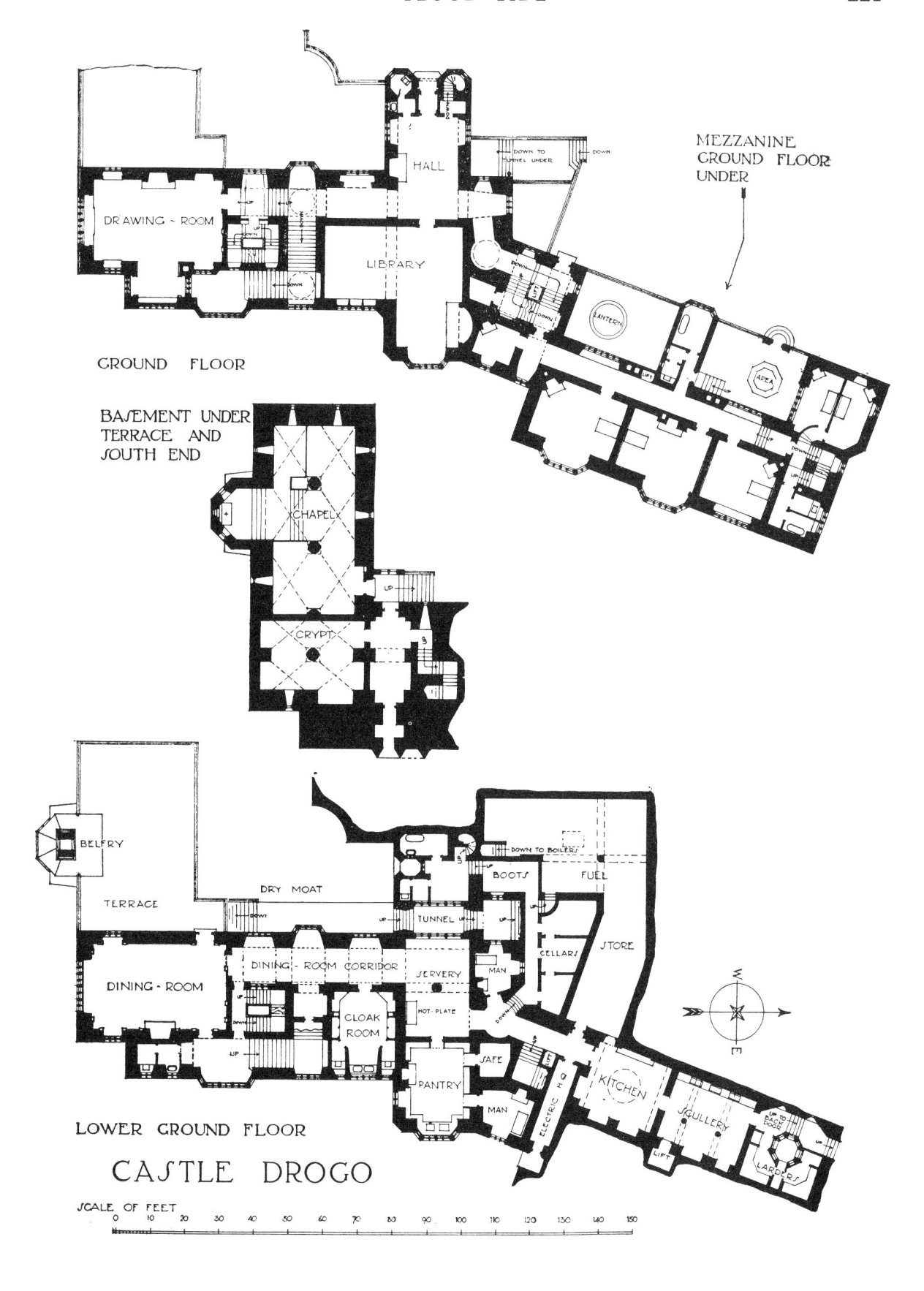

MEZZANINE GROUND FLOOR UNDER

BASEMENT UNDER TERRACE AND SOUTH END

LOWER GROUND FLOOR

CASTLE DROGO

SCALE OF FEET
0 10 20 30 40 50 60 70 80 90 100 110 120 130 140 150

The welding together of contrasting elements, which gives the design such vitality, was necessitated to some extent by the several changes in intention which, instead of their producing disorder, Lutyens turned to advantage. The contrasts were part of the original design and inherent in the nature of the site. The integrating process can be illustrated by looking at the section to the left of the entrance tower in Pl. 63. This was built 1911–14 to the first approved design and contains in its crypt several rooms, including the scullery (p. 213), executed on the 1911 scale of massiveness. This section, intended originally as exclusively for servants, became the self-contained family dwelling till the southern range was finished. It contains three floors, whereas the south half has two, and, where the ranges join, the axis changes direction.

At the point of junction is set the private staircase, and much of the fascination of the design is the way in which the problems raised by the two sets of levels and by the change of direction are here solved with apparent ease. From the plans (p. 221) it will be seen that the actual internal hinge is the circular lobby, left of the staircase, through which the corridor is turned to join the main corridor across the hall to the drawing-room and principal staircase southwards. This corridor, ten feet wide and about fourteen high, is arched, vaulted, and recessed in a series of perfect cubic spaces. At the point where it begins to ascend to the drawing-room, the staircase to the dining-room descends to the left, the vaulting of which, however, is level and joins that of the corridor in a saucer dome (p. 213). As this staircase plunges down, by shallow granite steps, the height to the vault becomes immense, so high, indeed, that two of the drawing-room windows actually look into the space at its foot, where they borrow light from a great external bow window (p. 213).

The scale of both these stairs is that of the great baroque palaces, with almost the grimness of Piranesi's imagination. The analogy is most apt to the head of the private stairs (p. 214) where the intersecting curves and receding vista of domes is directly reminiscent of the *Carceri*. A peculiarity of both staircases is that they both have apparently solid cores, containing, in the case of the private stairs, a lift, and in that of the main stairs a complete secondary flight lit by windows through the core walls. Some of the effects in these corridors and stairs are adaptations of those foreshadowed in the County Hall designs, whilst they link forward with others in the Viceroy's House at Delhi, with which in some cases they are contemporary owing to the time-lag in the building of Drogo. They are the most striking internal feature of the Castle, since living-rooms cannot be handled with such Romanesque grandeur and severity. Nevertheless the reception-rooms, with granite walls now hung with tapestries, heavily beamed ceilings, and great mullioned windows, are consistent with the *Enrico Quatro* character desired and very impressive. There are charming touches to be found in the craftsmanly handling of oak in upper corridors, bedrooms, nursery, and relatively unimportant rooms. A working portcullis to the front door,

70. CASTLE DROGO. The South end

71. CASTLE DROGO. The East side. Granite walls rising from the moor

72. KING EDWARD VII MEMORIAL. Proposed design for Piccadilly site, 1911. (Drawing by William Walcot)

73. DUBLIN MUNICIPAL ART GALLERY. Design (1913) for twin galleries connected by a bridge and colonnade across the River Liffey. (Drawing by William Walcot)

ingenious and entertaining, yet comes near to being an affectation where, emotional as the whole prodigious building is, everything else about it is logical. The ultimate justification of Drogo is that it does not pretend to be a castle. It *is* a castle, as a castle is built, of granite, on a mountain, in the twentieth century.

Not the least astonishing thing about it is that, after the first year, every stone was laid by two men alone. These two Devon masons, Cleeve and Dewdney, of course had behind them a large team of labourers, who hewed and dressed the stone from the site and, for the better stone, from Dartmoor quarries. The building was begun on contract, with a clerk of the works from London, but at an early stage his place was taken by J. C. Walker, a Yorkshireman who combined the offices of clerk of the works and master mason, making the full-size drawings etc. from Lutyens's instructions. Thus the building, which from first to last took twenty years, is not only genuine in character but in consistency, built as castles were.

§5. THE BRITISH SCHOOL AT ROME

On that eventful day, April 15, 1911, Lutyens received a letter from Sir Rennel Rodd saying that the Syndic and municipal authorities of Rome were so appreciative of the British Pavilion that they had offered to give the valuable site in order that the building should be perpetuated. The Ambassador proposed that Lutyens should 'get the Royal Institute of British Architects to buy the building and to fit it up as the British School at Rome. I must', Lutyens added, 'write to Stokes [President R.I.B.A.] and Simpson [John W.] and get it done somehow. The R.I.B.A. is hard up at present. There will be a good deal of criticism about my building and its adaptability....'

On the way to Drewsteignton, on April 20, he continued:

> Aston Webb enthusiastic about R. Rodd's proposal. He also talked about the R.A. in a nice friendly way. He will see Blomfield and others at Varnishing Day and then telegraph Rodd in my name.

This appears to have been the first step in the movement, emanating from the Syndic of Rome, which led to the reconstitution of the British School in its present form and premises. It had been founded in 1901 by a body of scholars as a School of Archaeology and had hitherto been housed in the Odescalchi Palace. During the International Exhibition there had been discussions, initiated by Lord Esher and the Commissioners for the Exhibition of 1851 (which survives as an organisation to promote Prince Albert's objects), on extending the School's scope to include students of architecture, sculpture, and painting, similar to the facilities offered by the French, American, and other foreign academies. By April, the Commissioners had got as far as putting a scheme of Travelling Scholarships before the School of

Archaeology. Lutyens had evidently taken some part in these exploratory talks since, in January, he had gone with Dr. Ashby of the British School to see the German archaeological establishment, and the fact that Sir Rennell Rodd should communicate this new development to him in the first instance implies that Lutyens had discussed the School's future with the Ambassador, who apparently did not know to whom else this important communication should be made. Actually Sir Aston Webb's contact with Reginald Blomfield directed the inquiry into the correct channel since the latter was in close touch with the 1851 Commissioners over the travelling scholarships' scheme and became one of the first members of the Council of the British School when this was set up under the new Charter granted in June 1912.

Though Lutyens was never on the Council, he was thus instrumental, if fortuitously, in establishing the School in the Valle Giulia and proceeded forthwith to devote much time and energy to its service gratuitously, at a time when he had many other important preoccupations. Not only did he make a gift of his plans and elevations for the rebuilding, and supervise its execution, involving several journeys to Rome, free of charge. He made the cultural purpose of the School his own, as amusingly described in this letter of June 8 to Herbert Baker from Bloomsbury Square:

> The FABS [an informal club within the Royal Institute of British Architects, meeting periodically to dine or visit old buildings] dined here last night—Newton, George, A. Webb, Blomfield, Carr, Watson, Gotch, Macartney, Horsley, Warren, Lutyens,—absent Stokes, Colcutt, Emerson. It was all Institute talk. We seem to have got into a muddle at the R.I.B.A., having amalgamated the Society of Architects (for Registration) without power to do so. So it may mean a new Charter. They all attacked me for not knowing more about the Institute, but I cant take interest in trade union affairs of men and build at the same time. I am afraid it is rather like my politics here. I seem to have no time to think things out—and then to utter my thoughts. You must be patient with me and instruct me. You would have been amused to have heard me yesterday cracking up the British Ideal against cosmopolitanism. That Englishmen would never become tied like the Beaux Arts men are.

The proposal involved the rebuilding in permanent form of the temporary Pavilion, and of course its replanning, in connection with which Lutyens made another short trip to Rome, May 27. He was out there again at the beginning of January 1912,[1] with draft plans for the conversion and went over the Pavilion with Mr. Freeman of Humphrey's, the contractors for the work. Writing from the British Embassy, he noted:

[1] When he met a young man, later Sir Hubert Worthington, who asked to join his office. He was an assistant 1912–13.

Ashby lunched, then palace-hunting with Evelyn Shaw [subsequently Honorary General Secretary], and a tea party at the British School. Mrs. Strong, who was once so keen, is now depressed and thinks the new building will be too far out from Rome—and is making things difficult. Ashby is keen. I have likened Mrs. Strong to a great big retriever and Ashby to a small wire-haired terrier that trots round after her.

Much of the time was spent inspecting comparable institutions. The *Académie de France* at the Villa Medici thrilled him: 'a wonderful life and tradition which I hope we may build up here.' News that other nations were to establish similar schools in the vicinity revived his vision of art as the universal bond and healer: 'I am sorry we cannot start a wide world school, with one common library.'

The building was required to provide living and working quarters for the staff and twenty-four students, the latter including holders of competitive scholarships attached to the School, and other post-graduate students admitted from the universities and art schools of the Empire. One of these was founded by Herbert Baker for a South African student and Lutyens was able to be of some assistance in expediting this public-spirited foundation. The line of the outer walls of the Pavilion was followed, the façade and portico being reconstructed in Roman cement. But the large top-lit exhibition galleries which occupied the internal space were replaced by an open garden *cortile* with cypress trees, entered from the portico across a transverse vaulted entrance hall. The space to the left of the portico became the library, that to the right the dining-hall; the west (left) side of the cortile accommodates the librarian's and director's quarters, the east side the common rooms: and seven studios are ranged along the north side. The east and west wings have two upper storeys, and the north a single upper storey, for bedrooms. Externally the building, and most of the interior, is of the simplest, with plaster-faced walls and pantiled roof.

Lutyens would probably have preferred to use stone but was reconciled by the reflection that Roman and renaissance architects had apparently not objected to plaster, 'especially if as true as Hadrian's stuff—lovely silky fibre, true to line as steel, no thumb work, keen intellect and knowledge of what to do and how to do it.' He was writing to Baker (March 3, 1911) on the subject because of the delays being experienced in starting the Johannesburg Gallery owing to the cost factor, and the question arising whether a stone-substitute would be permissible. He had always feared, he said, that the Art Gallery would have to be plaster (actually a brown sandstone was used), but protested that 'the public in their public buildings must realise their responsibilities to future generations'.

That, however, under popular government, they cannot be relied upon to do. It was the fundamental flaw in Lutyens's hope of re-creating the grand manner in the world of to-day—or even of yesterday—to design as though twentieth century democracy were animated with the fastidious forethought, or, to put it at its lowest level, the vanity of renaissance autocrats—even of the eighteenth century English aristocracy. Liberal sentiments, thrift, modesty, practical mindedness are virtues, and may be reflected in architecture of austerely functional kind, but they will not beget architecture in the grand manner; more likely demand fictitious value for little money and get the vulgar or commonplace. The greatness of Lutyens owed something precisely to his refusal—or inability—either to admit that the foundations of modern classicism rest on quicksands or to allow that to depress his creative idealism, his standards as an artist. Hence the complaints of some practical men and administrators that he was 'irresponsible', 'extravagant', 'out of touch with realities.' Had he not been, he would never have had the audacity and conviction with which to conceive and execute the last great classical buildings that, in all probability, will ever be undertaken—at least with any semblance of traditional continuity of understanding. For the next decade he was to be engaged in a continuous battle to vindicate his ideal of civilised art with perhaps the only Government still at that date endowed with the autocracy and wealth and exhibitionism required 'to realise their responsibilities to future generations' in the grand manner—namely the Government of India. In the last ten years of his life another government, similarly endowed theoretically—the Roman Catholic Church in England—was to give him another opportunity to build for future generations in the manner of the idealists of the old world. Whether the Cathedral of Christ the King at Liverpool will ever be completed to his design lies in the realm of faith. But knowledge that the opportunity for that great conception came to Lutyens serves, at this point, to give a unity to this chapter, that began with his dreams of building a great church and has traced the development of his capacity to do so.

It must end with two typical failures of popular support for conceptions in the grand manner. The building of the British School at Rome, regarded as an academy of classical design, represented a solid achievement both for Lutyens and the establishment of his ideals. Owing to the outbreak of war in 1914, the portion of the building undertaken in 1912, and planned for minimum requirements, was not ready for occupation till 1916. Subsequent additions were made in 1923 and 1938, when the original scheme was completed by the erection of the east side of the cortile.

§6. THE EDWARD VII MEMORIAL

How little foundation the Grand Manner had in popular sentiment at the end of the Edwardian epoch is shown by the sad story of the King Edward VII Memorial scheme. Soon after the death of the King in May, 1910, a fund was opened for a memorial. The large sum of money rapidly subscribed, and the spate of suggestions for its utilisation proved the remarkable extent to which the sentiments attending his accession had changed. In August the Government decided that the late King would best be commemorated by a number of local rather than by a single National Memorial, but that a proportion of the fund should be applied to a metropolitan monument. In October a committee was appointed to review suggestions for the latter, consisting of Sir Lewis Harcourt (First Commissioner of Works), Sir Edward Poynter, P.R.A., Sir Schomberg Macdonell, Lords Redesdale, Avebury, and Esher, the Lord Mayor of London, Leonard Stokes, P.R.I.B.A. and others. Over a hundred suggestions were put forward, a number of them involving a replanning of Hyde Park Corner or Marble Arch, and including such ambitious projects as an Opera House in Trafalgar Square, a central building for London University, a King Edward VII Square in place of Piccadilly Circus, a Kingsway extending Cromwell Road to the west, a new Hungerford-Charing Cross bridge scheme—indeed nearly all the perennial projects for improving London which cropped up again in the Royal Academy and County of London Plans of 1940–5. By January, 1911, these had been narrowed down to a statue with an architectural setting on the south side of the Mall or, as a possible alternative, on the Broad Walk across Green Park from the Victoria Memorial to Piccadilly. In March 1911, King George and Queen Alexandra approved a site opposite Marlborough House, the memorial to include a new bridge over St. James's Park Lake, and Mr. (later Sir) Bertram McKennal was appointed as sculptor. The latter agreed to collaborate with Lutyens but on the extraordinary terms that the architect should have no voice in the general design of the memorial itself, which McKennal proposed should take the form of a detached monument fifty-eight feet high. Lutyens's contribution was a design for a stone bridge to replace the suspension bridge and the redesigning of the intervening space on the axis of the memorial. 'Everyone says the King's Memorial will be all right,' he wrote at the time of the Coronation, 'but there is a lot of opposition; a pity it got out so soon. It is such a wonderful chance!' Actually the proposal to 'mutilate' Londoners' cherished place of communion with the ducks and flowers, and their romantic prospect of the Horse Guards', aroused unexpectedly fierce opposition and was mainly responsible for the Mall site being abandoned. Lutyens undoubtedly felt hurt by what he described as the flare up. He wrote on April 11—during those eventful days when the Drogo, Johannesburg and Rome School projects culminated and his friends were praising Great Maytham and Hampstead:

> The Tennants and Jack Pease thought the St. James's Park cry too silly and undigested and that the newspapers were mad. Jack Tennant didn't think it possible for the Committee to chuck me. But I know Committees and their methods... Riddell and Hudson want me to prepare anonymously a King Edward Memorial scheme for Trafalgar Square, at once, and they are going to boom it like anything—a sort of *cri*, a demand from the public for it.

His Trafalgar Square scheme substituted for the retaining wall on the north side of the *place* broad flights of steps separated by a balustrade in the centre of which rose the pedestal of the King's statue supported by symbolic groups. In front of the balustraded centre extended a single fountain basin. The balustrade was to be contained by pedestals surmounted by sculpture. On the east and west sides of the Square two terraces were to be formed ending in further pedestals for commemorative statues flanking flights of steps to the level of the Square. It was claimed for the design that it increased the area available for public meetings and, although it would have been costly, would certainly have transformed Trafalgar Square in the grand manner. In 1938 Lutyens's ideas for remodelling Trafalgar Square were at length given a very limited scope in the new fountains to commemorate Jellicoe and Beatty.

The Trafalgar Square scheme and another put forward by S. D. Adshead for a site in Hyde Park, were rejected by the Committee who, in July, invited McKennal and Lutyens to submit a fresh design for the Piccadilly site at the head of the Broad Walk where the Inigo Jones gate-piers from Chiswick have been placed. The artists had a meeting on the site with the Earl of Plymouth, who had succeeded Harcourt as First Commissioner of Works. Lutyens proposed a design consisting of a raised screen of columns flanked by podiums supporting bronze groups, and with a solid centre against which the King's statue would look down the Walk to the Queen Victoria Memorial (p. 224).

As an architectural memorial, the design had grandeur and distinction, but, whether on the Committee's or the sculptor's initiative, a third design was required on more economical and conventional lines—'a central object only' which Lutyens, though he had himself designed it, described to Baker as 'an ink-bottle or a clock, a cruet thing!', adding 'IDIOTS'. The stone work consisted only in a podium mounted on a high base; the King's statue, backed by the podium, looked towards Buckingham Palace; a group aptly representing 'Arbitration Quelling Strife' occupied the same position on the Piccadilly side; figures symbolising Peace and Hospitals sat on either side; and St. George coped with his dragon on top of all.

The habitués of Piccadilly, represented by their doyen Sir Squire Bancroft, complained of the way that the Memorial turned its back on that thoroughfare, as was inevitable on this site unless King Edward were to turn his back on his mother. The possibility of an equestrian statue at right angles, seen in profile within an arch in the middle of the screen, appears not to have been considered. General uneasiness at the course being taken was expressed by questions in the House. Mr. Asquith assured Earl Winterton that the land had not yet been given for the Memorial and that there would be opportunity for public discussion of the design before it was settled.

Meanwhile it is interesting to find Lutyens impressed by the rising genius of a sculptor of a very different order to his colleague. He described to Baker (February 29, 1912) going with the young South African architect Solomon (no doubt in connection with choosing a sculptor for the figure to surmount the Rand Regiments' Memorial, eventually given to Aronson) to see Epstein:

> He is enamoured of the great Egyptian and Assyrian models, but of course cannot touch their marvellous atmospheric play of surface. He has had a burst out with the ugly sides of 'manity... He himself is a nice clean earnest little man—his very purity makes his late (obscenities!) possible.[1] His ideals are sun worship and phallic worship as the primary force in man's nature. He has courage, and when he fully awakes to the loveliness of line and form he ought to do really well. Epstein might do work in the garden. [of the Johannesburg Art Gallery?]

Lutyens added that he 'nearly got the Australian building in the Strand, but am glad now as I believe I am nearly fixed up for Delhi'.

Discussion and criticism of the Green Park site for King Edward persisted desultorily throughout 1912, the view gaining ground that the 'central object' design decided by the Committee was the least satisfactory alternative. In both Lutyens's rejected designs London would have gained at least a memorial in the grand manner, which his genius would have endowed with qualities not necessarily visible to the popular critics of the sketch designs. It ended in sudden bathos when, in December 1912, the King wrote to the Committee through Lord Stamfordham, with the result that the Green Park site was abandoned and, on His Majesty's suggestion, 'the Committee will proceed to negotiate for an Equestrian Statue in Waterloo Place,'[2] for which Lutyens duly designed the pedestal.

§7. THE DUBLIN ART GALLERY

The schemes undertaken at Sir Hugh Lane's instance for the Dublin Municipal Art Gallery originated in the same spirit of civilised idealism as had the British School, the Johannesburg Gallery, and the Edward VII Memorial. This is not the time to probe too deeply into the still-unhealed wound in Irish hearts caused by the controversy over the disposal of the famous Lane collection of pictures. But the facts must be shortly told in order to give an idea of the relations between Lutyens and Lane during the years covered by this chapter, in which the temperamental connoisseur has already played some part.

Lane, son of a Protestant clergyman in County Cork, and a nephew of Lady Gregory, was born in 1875. He had an extraordinary *flaire* for expertise, which he

---
[1] Referring to Epstein's furiously criticised figures on the British Medical Association building in the Strand by Adams, Holden, and Pearson, then recently completed and now mutilated.

[2] *The Builder*, December 27, 1912.

cultivated by working as assistant and eventually adviser to Colnaghi in London and New York. Through brilliant dealing and genuine love of pictures he had soon made £10,000 with which he set up as a 'gentleman dealer' in private chambers in Jermyn Street and began forming his own collection of outstanding works of the English School and of the French Impressionists. Orpen's well-known *Homage à Manet* commemorates some of the group of artists and connoisseurs—George Moore, D. S. McColl, Tonks, and Steer—who frequented Lane's house in Chelsea. After their work together at Johannesburg, Lutyens and he 'became great sparring partners', according to Lady Gregory, who tells a story of Lane saying that he must get Lutyens to design him a room with twelve panels to contain twelve portraits of the ideal wife for him as visualised by twelve different artists—Sargent, Orpen, Steer, Kelly, Charles Shannon, Augustus John, and so on. In 1910, Lutyens laid out the garden of his house, 100 Cheyne Walk, in a pattern of two paved walks and a round pool aligned on a pair of baroque statues in niches. Lutyens agreed to accept pictures in lieu of fee—both for this and his Dublin designs. In this way he acquired various decorative and curious works, mostly of an architectural character, which gave him a lot of pleasure though they had probably cost the other little. Lane lived simply, in order to devote all his means to his collection. Lutyens, who was amused and sometimes annoyed by what he called 'his funny little Lane-headed pins which he sticks into everyone', used to say that if he sent Lane a prepaid telegram, he would bring the answer himself on foot to save the sixpence for another time. When he gave Lutyens dinner at his favourite Chelsea restaurant and extolled the excellence of the three course meal, 'wonderful for eighteen pence,' 'Wonderful,' Lutyens agreed, 'let's have it over again.' They toyed with the idea of building or restoring a great English house, as Lord Curzon, Claude Lowther, and Martin Conway were doing at Tattershall, Hurstmonceux and Allington; Lane's choice was Kirby Hall, which Lutyens said would cost him £200,000.

But the main topic at their meetings was the Dublin Gallery. In 1907 Lane had founded a municipal art gallery in Dublin to which he lent the main part of his collection of pictures, together with Rodin's *L'Age d'Arain*, the collection being temporarily housed in Harcourt House until a suitable permanent gallery should be built. In the preface to the Catalogue, Lane stated: 'I intend to present the most of them, provided that the promised permanent building is erected on a suitable site within the next few years.' By 1911 not only had no steps been taken by the authorities to implement their part of this project, but difficulty was found in keeping open Harcourt House. Lane became more and more restive at the continued delay in building the stipulated gallery, then took the initiative, in August 1912, by proposing a gallery, to be designed by Lutyens, to stand in St. Stephen's Green. The design shows an oblong building of brick and stone, with a columned portico recessed in the front towards the gardens, approached by wide steps. The flat roof is stepped up in stone on the transverse axis to the higher level of the main gallery's sky-lit roof. The brick walls are blank, with architectural niches and, in the centre of either end, a projecting pedimented feature to receive sculpture. This proposal, however, was blocked by opposition on the grounds that the building would destroy the amenities of the open space. Another site, in Merrion Square, was then considered; Lutyens giving it as his opinion that a central site in gardens was desirable on architectural grounds though Lane was in favour of a building giving direct on a thoroughfare or, alternatively, as an addition to the Mansion House. He himself admitted, however, that the latter did not give scope for a fine building which, in his enthusiasm for Lutyens's designs, he now proclaimed 'is even more necessary to Dublin than pictures. It is more than a hundred years since a good piece of architecture has been raised in Dublin'.

Feeling was now running high between supporters and antagonists of a great gallery building. Opponents, and those chiefly among the largest potential contributors to the cost, alleged that the people of Dublin did not want another picture gallery, which drew a satirical poem from Yeats 'To a wealthy man' comparing the munificence of renaissance Florence with 'the blind and ignorant town'. What cared Duke Ercole for what the onion sellers thought,

> *Or Guidobaldo when he made*
> *That Grammar School of courtesies?*
> *And when they drove out Cosimo*
> *Indifferent how the rancour ran*
> *He gave the homes they had set free*
> *To Michelozzo's latest plan*
> *For the San Marco Library...*

At a big public meeting at the Mansion House in 1913 a committee undertook to raise £23,000 by public subscription, to which the Corporation promised the balance to make up £45,000, the estimated cost of a gallery, Lane promising to find any amount required in addition. But still no site appeared to be available.

It was then that Lane and Lutyens conceived the idea that, as no land was obtainable, the gallery should be on the water—a Palladian bridge spanning the Liffey with a colonnade connecting galleries placed either end of it (p. 224). Lady Gregory thought that so daring a notion could only have been Lane's. But after the whole unhappy project had finally collapsed, he used to lay the blame on Lutyens for killing it with the bridge design. However, in February 1913 Lane was enthusiastic for it. He wrote to Lady Gregory:

> The Committee and the Press, and the principle Corporation officials have agreed to pulling down the hideous metal bridge covered with advertisements

and to build a Gallery on a stone-faced bridge. It will be the most beautiful and sensational ornament in Dublin, will in no way spoil the existing view, and bring more life to the centre of the old city.

The City Architect agreed that it would be a great ornament to Dublin, and Yeats wrote: 'I have just seen Lutyens's design—beautiful. Two buildings joined by a row of columns, it is meant to show the sunset through the columns, and there are to be statues on top.' The site was obtainable with a grant from the Corporation, without the need for an Act of Parliament as in the case of the Squares' sites. Lutyens estimated the cost at £45,000 of which the Corporation would have to find £22,000, a figure to which they agreed in accepting the design. Lane, in an advanced stage of neurasthenia, insisted that the design should be adopted and its cost made up by August; or 'no bridge, no pictures'.

The conception certainly was of fantastic beauty, and had it been executed would have made of Dublin's Georgian quays, with the Customs House at one end and the Four Courts at the other, one of the architectural wonders of Europe. But nowhere, except possibly in the St. Petersburg of the madder Romanoffs, would the expense of £45,000 for the housing of only thirty-nine paintings have been acceptable. In the explosive atmosphere of Dublin in 1913, political and religious partisanship complicated the technical, financial and aesthetic imbroglio. At its height, in August, Lane removed his pictures and sent them on loan to the London National Gallery, to which he bequeathed them in that October, though he afterwards executed an unwitnessed codicil leaving them to Dublin. Subsequently Charlemont House was acquired for the Municipal Gallery and there, Dubliners point out, the permanent building on a suitable site now awaits the fulfilment of Lane's wish. But that impetuous, testy dealer in dreams has lain in the waters of the Atlantic since the *Lusitania* was torpedoed in 1915.

The more valid objections to the bridge gallery were these: the position might be needed for a road bridge (it has not been as yet); the separation of the two galleries duplicated the staff required (two instead of one man); it would have been impossible to extend them; and the danger of humidity affecting the canvasses. In his report on the bridge scheme, Lutyens expressed his conviction that the humidity did not necessarily present an insurmountable obstacle. It was a question of fact, he stated, that could easily be tested, and asked to have the matter submitted to scientific investigation.

But it was too late, and the vision of Manet and Gainsborough joining hands against a Dublin sunset beneath a Palladian colonnade, enchanting as it would have been, was submerged almost immediately in troubles that would certainly have indefinitely postponed its completion, if they had not blown up or otherwise misused its substructure.

And Lutyens was immersed in the realisation of an infinitely grander dream.

PART II
IMPERIAL ARCHITECT

The truly classical is not foreign to anybody. It is precisely that part of tradition which does not alienate us from our own life or from nature, but reveals them in all their depth and nakedness, freed from the fashions and hypocrisies of time and place.

    G. SANTAYANA: Egotism in German Philosophy, p. 35.

Endow your Thought with Faith
Your Deed with Courage
Your Life with Sacrifice
So all men may know
The Greatness of India

(Lines proposed by Sir Edwin Lutyens for inscription on the Jaipur Column, New Delhi)

OVERTURE

AT the Coronation Durbar in December 1911, the King Emperor George V proclaimed the transfer of the capital of India from Calcutta to Delhi. The decision to build the new city can be regarded as marking the summit of the Edwardian Age's might, the peak of its progress towards the British Commonwealth ideal. The Union Building of the Dominion of South Africa, designed by Herbert Baker, was already established at Pretoria; a competition (won by an American) for the design of that of Australia at Canberra had been launched in the previous April. It was therefore felt, and justifiably, that the new capital of the British Empire in India and eventually of the Dominion of India should be made the occasion for planned architecture of commensurate majesty; an Anglo-Indian Rome. In retrospect, the splendour and political significance of that memorable Durbar, and the impressive suddenness with which so great a project as the building of a new metropolis for a sub-continent was announced, can be seen to have dramatised the undertaking from its inception, lifting it to an emotional plane; heroic indeed but one size larger than life.

The choice of Delhi was recommended by its central situation, ease of access, independence of any preponderant local community, historic prestige, and a healthy though extreme climate. The decision, however, was not based wholly, still less chiefly, on suitability, nor was it preceded—owing to the need for secrecy and quick finality—by such objective investigations as would now be demanded before so irrevocable a step was taken. It was made primarily on grounds of political expediency, into which it is not necessary here to go further than to recall its connection with the simultaneous reunion of Bengal, the partition of which under Lord Curzon had generated cumulative unrest. The gesture to sentiment, both Hindu and Moslem, represented by the return of Government to the historic capital, was strongly pressed by the new Viceroy, Lord Hardinge of Penshurst, who was determined to direct his considerable statesmanship towards restoring by every means the patriotic cohesion of all classes and races in the subcontinent. The founding of New Delhi was, in short, a measure of Imperial policy, with much reason, though possibly less wisdom, to recommend it.

If, in the narrative of Lutyens's participation in the most ambitious architectural labour undertaken by the British Empire, it is the conflict of these elements that appears to be emphasised, rather than their harmony, that is due to no intention of belittling the grand design or the immense co-operative performance that its completion represented. On the contrary, now that the immediate purpose for which New Delhi was built, and the politic needs there may once have been for circumlocution no longer exist, recognition of the stresses, internal and external, to which the undertaking was subject from the beginning enables the scope of the achievement to be appreciated in its full magnitude, and irony. It must, indeed, remain one of the greater ironies of history that the only city in which the British, never distinguished for monumental conceptions, resolved to challenge comparison with the builders of antiquity should have served its intended purpose for little more than a decade.

From the moment of its foundation the city evoked sectional antagonism, both English and Indian. The English community in Calcutta, seeing their city reduced from a capital to provincial status, did not scruple to recall the superstition that Delhi is the graveyard of dynasties. Pointing to the six previous capitals whose ruins litter the plain around that of Shah Jahan, some foretold that the building of an eighth presaged likewise the end of British rule. In England Lord Curzon led a vigorous opposition to the plan, which he estimated would cost India £12,000,000 (he was not far wrong). Among Indians themselves seditious particles and religious or patriotic bodies worked in a slow ferment towards ideals that, various as they were, had in common a profound antipathy to the system of civilisation that the new capital was designed to represent.

In the great architectural drama on which the curtain is about to rise, these, then, were the factors, physical or imponderable, which set the keynote. They are the *leitmotifs* that fate was to weave into mounting patterns of harmony or discord with the central theme of our story. Now, forty years on, it can be seen to have all the attributes of tragedy. For the spectator, whatever his political allegiance, there cannot but be pathos in the record of high ideals and disinterested endeavours that, nobly performed, have yet miscarried. From the opening of the overture with a chorus of imperial trumpets, the dissonant elements begin to make themselves heard, growing in volume and insistency as the drama unfolds. Amid these vibrations the culmination of Lutyens's life work took place, the raising in the Eighth Delhi of the most serene and one of the most extensive palaces of the world, the last splendid assertion of European humanism before the engulfing of its ideals in racial and ideological confusion. His grand conception, in the realisation of which he strained every fibre of his being, should be visualised as taking shape against a steadily deteriorating political and ethical background: such a landscape of apocalyptic scenery as the romantic John Martin had depicted a century earlier, in which doomed courts and fate-swept fanes are illumined by the glare of terrestrial and heavenly upheavals against the storms of impending catastrophe.

In mid-century, New Delhi and Viceroy's House have passed into history as scenes of epoch-ending and, it is hoped devoutly, epoch-making events. The critic of architecture can state its origins in a single sentence and pass on immediately to consider the completed work of art. But in Lutyens's life there was no such foreshortening. For its teller the shining achievement of Viceroy's House lies at the convergence of dark perspectives of obstacles and discouragements through which his progress by the light of his faith is seen to constitute a claim to greatness perhaps equalling that of the realised ideal.

The building of New Delhi is a chapter, as yet unwritten, in the chronicles of the British Empire, but equally it is the substance of the years of Lutyens's maturity. To distil its elements too drastically would be to reduce to a colourless essence material soaked in his personality. The stage is wide; the characters with speaking parts considerable and numerous; the action protracted over eighteen years in scenes far removed from the familiar. The narrative must therefore move into a distinct section in which a more circumstantial method is adopted than in the preceding. If I have attempted to set out some of its complexities and undercurrents rather more fully than a biography demanded, it is partly because Lutyens himself was at one time invited to write New Delhi's history. He never did so, but he preserved a quantity of relevant documentary material. In view of the conditions which have since arisen, that history may never be written. It therefore has seemed advisable to take this opportunity to record as much of it as could reasonably be regarded as connected with Lutyens. Nevertheless, the same method is employed as hitherto, namely to portray the architect, so far as possible in his own words, whilst engaged in the conception and realisation of one of the great buildings of our age, in relation to the other personalities concerned. For the full description of the building itself the reader must consult Mr. Butler's second volume of *The Architecture of Sir Edwin Lutyens*.

Henceforth the *dramatis personæ*, headed by the warm-hearted, choleric Sailor King, is mainly composed of high State officials. A succession of Viceroys and their wives and staffs, Secretaries of State, and the hierarchy of the Indian Civil Service take the place of the heterogeneous cast of clients and friends who have been visualised passing in and out of 29 Bloomsbury Square or consulting Lutyens in the garden of Edwardian England.

He himself, though retaining at forty-two the zest and charm of his youth, impressed contemporaries with his conviction that he had a mission to perform. He had signally succeeded in meeting the current need for a brilliant exponent of architecture who could also be trusted to attune himself to the time-spirit. In his creative work he had resisted both opportunism and imprudence. Though always impressively original, it was never so individual as to be out of harmony with current sentiment. His work at Hampstead Garden Suburb had exactly expressed the change in taste at the time in favour of romantic formalism, of which note was quickly taken by the London County Council and the Architectural Department of the Office of Works. At home he was now famous as a domestic architect of supreme skill.

During the ensuing decade his influence, in no small measure diffused by Lawrence Weaver's *Houses and Gardens of E. L. Lutyens*, became widespread, quickening American architects, and, during the war years, inspiring disciples at Hilversum and Stockholm. The English conception of a good-looking house set in a gracious garden among fine trees, which he had so variously realised with the help of Miss Jekyll, raised the standard of domestic design throughout the world. He had thus become the embodiment of the domestic outlook of the time, in no small measure because of his determined resistance to extraneous influences.[1] But still, too, he was conscious of having yet to fulfil the promise of his thirties with that great building which he believed, almost against reason, would some day evoke and crystallise his full powers—of sympathy and of integral design.

Those two potentially contradictory sides of his genius were emphasised in the *Introduction*. Hitherto his practice as a domestic architect had involved no serious conflict between them, though his relative failure in South Africa may be partly attributed to imperfect understanding of local feeling and too impetuous insistence on finite conceptions. In India we shall witness both processes stretched and severely strained. We shall be able to watch him projecting his imagination first into the Anglo-Indian atmosphere, and then increasingly into his conception of the works of art that he devised to represent the fusion. While working on New Delhi, he who had been the embodiment of English country life became an embodiment of the British imperial ideal, in order to experience in himself and so represent in architecture the rhythm of its life. But in his imagination, the elastic English conception of imperial government became fused with less elastic principles of aesthetics and design, so that a conflict developed. Not within himself, for he had completely resolved the problem in his designs; but between his finite conception and the fluid human purposes of living and administration which his work of art was required to serve.

The protagonist destined to share with him the centre of the stage requires a brief introduction at this point. For Lord Hardinge of Penshurst his Viceroyalty, assumed in 1910 and interrupting a distinguished Foreign Office career, fulfilled a lifelong ambition, namely to tread in the footsteps of his grandfather, the first Viscount Hardinge, as Governor-General of India. In addition to personal dignity and genuine executive ability he thus brought hereditary qualities to his determinationto make a resounding success of his mission. His main objective was to restore unity to a land that he found seething with sedition and Hindu-Moslem antagonism. In this over-riding purpose, in which he was signally successful, the decision to move the capital was a necessary but not more than a contributary part, calculated to provide a physical symbol of Indian nationalism achieved through and inspired by Western ideals. It is essential, in reading the ensuing chapters, to recognise that

[1] For this appreciation I am indebted to passages in an article in *The Builder*, January 7, 1944, by Prof. A. E. Richardson, A.R.A.

74. The New Delhi Planning Comission. February–March 1913. Top Row (*l. to r.*): Lt.-Col. Ogilvie, I.M.S.; T. Ward; T. Salkield, City Engineer, Delhi; Capt. Sopwith, R. E.; G. F. de Montmorency. Middle Row: Herbert Baker; J. Brodie; Capt. George Swinton; E. L. Lutyens. Front Row: S. H. Evans, assistant to E. L. L.; Capt. Roberts, R.E., Amman, assistant to Brodie

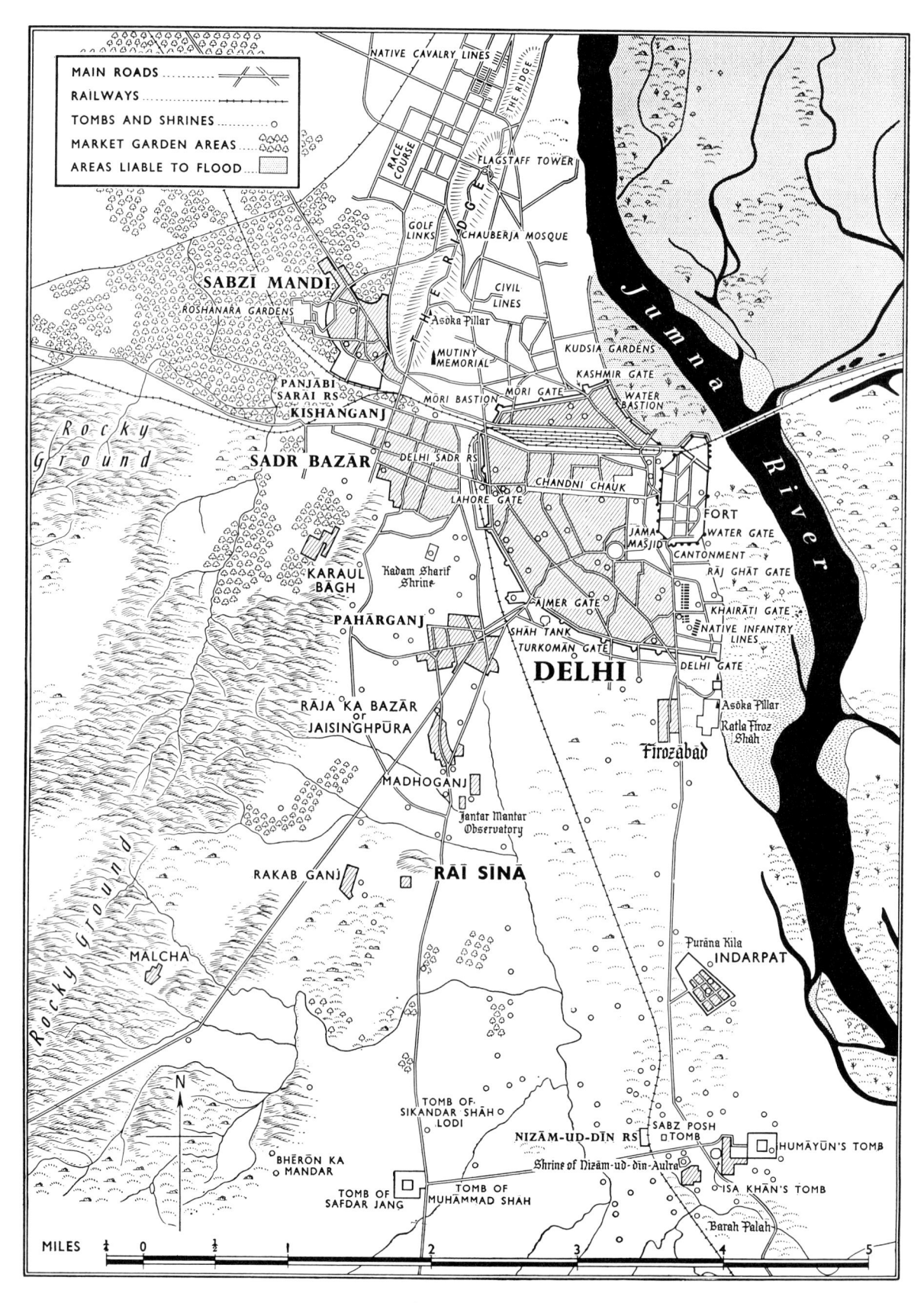

75. Delhi and its Environs. Map based on Survey of India map, specially drawn to illustrate the discussion on the site for New Delhi

shifts which appeared to his leading architect to be exasperating vacillations, frequently conflicting with the dictates of aesthetics and logic, reflected movements of the Indian political barometer as read by an astute and determined administrator. It has been said: 'If greatness lies in influencing events, then Hardinge is entitled to rank with Dalhousie and Curzon as the biggest men who filled this high office. An austere man, he won the passionate affection of the Indian princes and the confidence of the Indian people. Truly, he made the Government of India the Indian Government.'[1]

Lord Hardinge's recently published memoirs[2] present a curiously misleading self-portrait, at variance in some respects with the experience of men who served with him. He portrays himself as an autocrat individually responsible for most of the successful undertakings that he records. In the view of colleagues, however, he was, whilst strong-willed and capable of ruthlessness, by no means an originator nor a hard or proud man—the impression conveyed by his book. He possessed some aesthetic sensibilities, and at first applied them with enthusiasm to the shaping of the new city, of which he felt himself to be the father. Unfortunately they by no means always accorded with the infinitely finer sensibilities, and equally strong will, of Lutyens. The resulting clash of personalities and ideals is narrated in some fullness as constituting one of the classic conflicts in architectural history, comparable with that of Michael Angelo and Pope Julius II, or of Sir John Vanbrugh with the Duchess of Marlborough over the building of Blenheim.

There can be little doubt that the deterioration in relations between Architect and Viceroy in the latter years of his reign was partly due to the shock Lord Hardinge sustained in the attempt on his life and to the loss, a year later, of his wife. A daughter of Lord Alington and brought up in the lovely Georgian house of Crichel in Dorsetshire, Lady Hardinge appears to us through the medium of Lutyens's letters as a woman of charm, courage, and perception. In his memoirs Lord Hardinge's references to Lutyens are curt and impercipient. Yet his letters to him written during Lady Hardinge's lifetime show keen and intelligent interest in the Delhi project. Taken with the friendly relations of Lady Hardinge and Lutyens, they suggest that she often acted as the Viceroy's conscience in matters of architecture as she certainly softened some of the asperities of his character. Her death removed an influence that might have overcome the deadlock which developed in 1916 and embittered Lutyens's association with Delhi for a decade.

The third leading figure, Herbert Baker, is already well known to the reader but now comes from the wings to the centre of the stage. In the conflict of allegiances in which he became the third protagonist it was significant that Lutyens considered that it was himself who was responsible for Baker's appointment; whereas

[1] Sir Stanley Reed, *The Spectator*, May 28, 1948.
[2] Lord Hardinge of Penshurst, *My Indian Years*, 1948.

Sir Herbert maintained in his memoirs that it was due to the recommendation of his friend Sir William (later Lord) Meston and was made specifically in order to enable the Government to keep Lutyens's aesthetic idealism in check. To attempt to gloss over the animosity that developed between the two old friends would not only be to shirk familiar facts but to blur the values which Lutyens devoted his life to substantiate. Sir Herbert Baker was a conscientious, if somewhat obstinate, man of lofty ideals and little sense of humour, for whom, however, it was difficult not to have affectionate regard; he knew himself Lutyens's inferior as an architect and, as an architect, greatly admired him though regretting that he had never been to a public school. But for Lutyens, as has already been indicated, ethical virtues were of value only so far as they corresponded with aesthetic virtues; when they diverged, ethics ceased to count; the purpose of life was the embodiment of divine order in finite form, and when a man fell short in this endeavour he fell from grace, became a bad man. As time passed we witness Baker's somewhat loose idealism, summary methods, and respect for political realities assuming the colour of sins in Lutyens's eyes, till the crucial moment when the whole range of ethical values—moral, political, and personal,—are brought into conflict with the spirit of aesthetic integrity on the *glacis* of Raisina Hill. In this celebrated battle, which went on intermittently for years, Lutyens was defeated. By the canons of his art and creed, he was wholly in the right; by the rules of practical men, administrators, accountants and lawyers, Baker's position was unassailable, and Lutyens had, in a moment of aberration, put himself technically in the wrong.

In Lutyens's tremendous achievement at Delhi that controversial slope in the approach to Viceroy's House is a detail of secondary importance, and I have tried to keep it in its proper perspective. But it loomed large in Lutyens's estimation, and the gradient controversy can be regarded as one of the decisive battles in the history of planning. The classical champion's defeat by the allied forces of expediency, sentiment, function, and democracy denoted the failure of the lay mind, at the most favourable juncture in the twentieth century, to acknowledge the supremacy of the rule of order. Other scales of value were adjudged of greater importance than the aesthetic. It portended the decline of that 'humanist reaction' the ascendance of which helped to bear Lutyens to his eminence and is represented at its magnificent crest by Viceroy's House.

CHAPTER IX

THE DELHI PLANNING COMMISSION

§1. SURVEY

IN January 1912, soon after Lutyens got back from Rome, Sir Richmond Ritchie, Permanent Secretary for India, asked to see him at the India Office. The Secretary of State, the Marquess of Crewe, wished to know whether he would serve on a committee of three experts to advise the Government of India on the siting and layout of the new capital. At the interview Lutyens countered by proposing, as a condition, an assurance that he would be allowed to design 'the central buildings'. Sir Richmond Ritchie pointed out that he could not commit the Government of India, with whom the decision rested, but with that proviso appears to have been encouraging, since he forthwith took Lutyens to lunch at the Garrick Club[1] and entered his address in the Visitors' Book as 'Delhi'.

Many months were to elapse before he was confirmed in the appointment. But it is characteristic of Lutyens that, so far from hesitating, he had answered the invitation by requiring the definite appointment as architect. For this was the long-awaited moment, the crisis in the High Game envisaged a decade before, the 'Big Work that may or may not come'. Then he had decided that 'the only thing to do is to go on and be ready for it'—at a moment's notice. From the outset he evidently regarded the planning commission as primarily a means to realising his dream of some day creating the great building, to serve a high purpose, to which his whole life had been dedicated.

He supposed at first that he had been approached at the instance of Lord Hardinge, whom he had met staying at Buckhurst. Actually, it appears, Lord Crewe, immediately after the Durbar, had consulted the Royal Institute of British Architects on the appropriate appointment of an architect to the proposed planning committee. The President, Reginald Blomfield, had recommended the choice of an architect practising in India. Lord Crewe had replied there was none to whom the Government of India cared to entrust so important a work, whereon Lutyens's name was submitted. Blomfield must have been conscious of the irony of a situation in which he was constrained to recommend for such an opportunity his principal rival. Later, there is some reason to believe, he considered he therefore had a claim for consideration when a second architect was appointed to Delhi. Also he cannot

---

[1] With which Sir Richmond had a family connection, Lady Ritchie being the daughter of W. M. Thackeray, one of its original members.

but have been aware, as Lutyens was no less, that another distinguished architect, H. V. Lanchester, was at that moment in India, in connection with the large Eastern practice of his firm, Lanchester and Rickards. Indeed Mr. Lanchester seems to have lost no time in himself approaching the Viceroy upon the matter. Knowledge of this enterprising rival's presence on the spot was no doubt a factor influencing Lutyens's anxiety to stake his own claim for the Central Buildings at the earliest opportunity.

That was in the February. Until his call to Charles Street he had been occupied with the School at Rome; the protracted Edward VII Memorial schemes; large additions to Roehampton House to equip that red brick baroque mansion, designed by Thomas Archer, for a country club (destined never to occupy the building); the 'Shakespeare's England' Exhibition at Earls Court due to open in May; and his two South African commissions. Herbert Baker, busy with his Union Building, was handling the slow negotiations for these with interminable committees. In one of the series of letters involved by this collaboration, Lutyens first told Baker (February 29) 'I believe I am fixed up for Delhi... As regards the building, who does it, they wont commit themselves. There will be more than one man can do'. Then, as the idea struck him or as he decided to broach it at once, he added: 'Oh what fun if we could come together on it.'

The 'Commission of Experts, constituted by the Secretary of State at the request of the Government of India, to advise the Government of India as to the site of the new capital and the laying out of the same' was first convened at the India Office to meet the Commissioner for Delhi, Mr. (later Sir Malcolm and now Lord) Hailey. Their Chairman was Captain G. S. C. Swinton, Chairman-elect of the London County Council, a bearded, eloquent, advocate of city improvements, whom Lutyens suspected would be a charming companion but might prove something of a dilettante. The other member was Mr. John A. Brodie, C.B., City Engineer of Liverpool, who had recently won fame with his scheme for a parkway round that city. Lutyens described him as 'a great apple-shaped man full of drains', and came to have a high regard for his silence and ability. The three men were formally appointed early in March and were instructed to sail on April 1.

There followed for Lutyens a fortnight of hectic preparations and clearing up of works. 'I can scarce think of what I am doing, yet I have to and must,' is the burden of a few hurried letters. 'Sending perspectives of Johannesburg. Hope we shall meet in Delhi some day,' to Baker. 'Was at Roehampton last night. Luggage has to go to-morrow and have not got half what I want and no one to help pack,' to Lady Emily who was out of London; 'tomorrow Rome Committee, lunch at McKenna's to meet Crewe. Thursday the King at twelve. There is also a Mansion House committee on the King Edward Memorial. I do wish you were not away.'

The King received them at Buckingham Palace on March 21, when his first words to Lutyens—with reference, presumably, to one of his Edward VII Memorial designs—were, 'I want no (qualified) Angel of Victory'. His Majesty went on to speak forcibly for three-quarters of an hour on his views and wishes for the new capital. He said, Lutyens reported, that 'the Moghul was the style for India, if it was not dreadfully expensive'. The Ridge, north of the old city and hallowed by its memories of the Mutiny, was not to be built on and the planners need not feel themselves bound to the site on which the King and Queen had laid the symbolic foundation stones at the time of the Durbar. The King said 'You are going to design the buildings', to Lutyens, who answered 'Yes, sir'.

Baker also took that for granted on getting his news. He sped letters east and west to catch 'My dear Conqueror of $\frac{3}{4}$ of the Universe, ... full of the hugeness of my congratulations'. He was jubilant at the honour done to his friend but equally at the official recognition thus accorded to their common ideal—as he envisioned it—of establishing a monumental architecture expressive of Britain's imperial mission. Most people to whom architecture meant anything were impressed by Lutyens's association with the project that had caught the public's imagination. Herbert Baker expressed a widely shared conviction when he wrote to him:

> It is really a great event in the history of the world and of architecture,— that rulers should have the strength and sense to do the right thing. It would only be possible now under a despotism—some day perhaps democracies will follow... I wonder what you will do—whether you will drop the language and classical tradition and just go for surfaces—sun and shadow. It must not be Indian, nor English, nor Roman, but it must be Imperial. In 2000 years there must be an Imperial Lutyens tradition in Indian architecture, as there now clings a memory of Alexander... Hurrah for despotism! On the day you sail you should feel like Alexander when he crossed the Hellespont to conquer Asia.

Ned was duly touched by this letter when it eventually reached him. But his characteristic reaction to its heroics was to growl 'the public dont know and dont really care a dog's leg about Architecture; some like to talk about it but few can, or care to, pay'. And on March 28 when the train pulled out of Victoria Station, he, for one, did not feel much like Alexander. He had with him E. E. Hall as assistant; Brodie was accompanied by his wife, a lady of as generous build as himself. All the family had come to see them off, and old Mr. Webb from Godalming had turned up, besides A. J. Thomas, in whose hands Lutyens left his practice and power of attorney, and Sir Thomas Holderness, Under Secretary of State. In the train Ned wrote to Lady Emily:

> The train went off before I realised it was time to go and I was pushed from

the window by a lady drinking brandy. I never properly said goodbye to dear Nannie, but she will understand. I couldn't find any words.

This is just to put my arm about you and God Bless you for your wonderful and patient love.

It is all very wonderful and exciting. I cannot yet realise that I am going off to India, and shall be there in 14 days. If we do a fine thing and get our chance it will be the most wonderful thing that ever happened.

First impressions of a new land can be prophetic. At Bombay, where they stayed a night with the Governor, Sir George Clarke (Lord Sydenham), Lutyens's chief impression was of 'past mistakes, false economies, want of imagination'. He was attracted only by the Indians and the little eighteenth-century English buildings.

The old club at Bombay, with fine simple upstanding rooms, is full of the ghosts of choleric old Indian Bob Webbs who lived and died and growled with their hearts in England. The building, with all its faults, held the soul of a gentleman—a great quality and one that syndicalism don't help. India, like Africa, makes one very Tory—pre-Tory, feudal. The rot of party and votes seems like some slow sweet poison to spoilt children.

At Bombay, three native bearers were presented to them. Swinton chose the best-looking; Brodie chose the next; and Lutyens was left with 'an old scallywag dressed in an uncouth dhoti'. Swinton's smart bearer subsequently went off with all his belongings; Brodie's was arrested for murder; but Purshotum Dayal Parmar was to remain Lutyens's devoted factotum for eighteen years, and till the old man's death they continued to correspond on family and personal matters.

The Commission reached Delhi on April 15, when they were joined by their staff headed by Mr. (later Sir) G. F. de Montmorency as secretary and technical adviser, and including a Sapper officer and two clerks attached to each expert.[1] Lieutenant Chase, in charge of maps, particularly won Lutyens's affection and admiration for the miraculous speed with which he produced the necessary maps of areas insufficiently surveyed. Chase was killed early in the 1914 war before he received any acknowledgment of the debt that, in Lutyens's words, 'we and Delhi owed him.'

The party had a large bungalow as an office but on this occasion lodged at Maiden's Hotel. The heat was oppressive and the visibility clouded with the dust of ages. Mrs. Brodie collapsed with heat stroke, and Hall, with a poisoned eye, was removed to Simla where he remained for treatment and liaison with Government headquarters. An intensive survey of the whole vicinity of Delhi was undertaken at

[1] The staff, which had already made preliminary investigations, consisted of Mr. (later Sir Thomas) Ward, C.I.E., assisted by Messrs. Sale, Parker, Chance and Captains Roberts and Sopwith.

once. The daily time-table began at 5 or 6 a.m. (cup of tea and cold bath) and surveying till 9.30 a.m. in motor cars or on foot or, where that was impracticable, from elephants; 11.0 till 2.0 p.m. office; from lunch till 3.0 or 4.0 conferences or a nap if possible; then further surveying till 8.15 dinner, followed by discussions of the day's work, a visit to the club or a dinner party, and writing letters. Lutyens's to Lady Emily were in the form of a continuous journal mailed in weekly instalments.

The area to be covered ranged from suburbs clustered round the city to complete jungle across the river and arid hills interspersed with ruins on the south. The city of the Moghuls lies on the right bank of the Jumna which flows from north to south. From a point on the river three miles north of it the narrow Ridge runs in a south-westerly direction, its slopes occupied by the Civil Lines and private properties. The Durbar camps had lain in this quarter. The Ridge rises to its greatest height at its southern extremity, where it is crowned by the Mutiny Memorial overlooking the City from the north-west, after which it dies away due west of the City in a broad shallow valley thickly occupied by suburbs. South-west of these the Ridge rises again, continuing almost level in that course for eight miles where, in the neighbourhood of the vast ruins of the Kutb Mosque, it divides into two portions, one sweeping in a broad curve south-east towards the Jumna nine miles away, the other broadening towards the west into a plateau. The general character here was the same throughout—a rugged flattish surface presenting somewhat uniform sky-lines, with scanty vegetation in occasional pockets of soil. To the south of Delhi the riverain plain is serrated with outcrops flanking and rejoining the Ridge and leaving triangular valleys in between. A sketch map of the area is given on p. 242.

The Jumna has a wide sandy bed averaging half a mile broad, with a narrow stream and dry tributary creeks in the hot season, but at the monsoons floods the low lying land on either bank up to the containing bluffs which, on the west side below Delhi, have the ancient cities surmounting them. The triangle north of Delhi between the Ridge and the river, known as the Barari Plain and used for the Durbar reviews, was liable to flooding under five feet of water. All these latter areas, the flat jungle country east of the Jumna and the low-lying swampy land flanking the northern Ridge, were malarial.

The tract between the Jumna and the southern Ridge was a wilderness, used for centuries as brick-fields of which the huge refuse heaps, many forty feet high, dotted its surface and blew in fogs of dust whenever there was a wind. It is also that vast graveyard of fallen dynasties the ruins of whose cities are ranged for the most part along its eastern fringe above the river. A graphic description of this historic triangle, to which Britain was to add her contribution, is given by Sir Valentine Chirol.[1]

[1] *India Old and New*, 1921.

A couple of miles south of the city the walls of the Purana Kilat, the fortress built by Humayun, cover the site, but have not obliterated the ancient name, of Indraprastha, or Indrapat, the city founded by the Pandavas, one of those ancient Aryan races around whose conflicts in prehistoric times the poetic genius of India has woven the wonderful epos of the Mahabharata. There too, on a mound beyond Indrapat, stands the granite shaft of one of Asoka's pillars, on which, with a fine faith that the world has never yet justified, the great Buddhist Apostle-Emperor of India inscribed over 2000 years ago his edicts prohibiting the taking of life. At the foot of the Kutub Minar (eleven miles south of Delhi) the famous Iron Pillar commemorates the victories of the Hindu Emperor of the Gupta dynasty with whose name, under the more popular form of Raja Bikram, Indian legend associates the vague memories of a golden age of Hindu civilisation in the fifth and sixth centuries. The Pillar was brought there by one of the Rajput princes who founded the first city really known to history as Delhi. There Prithri Raja reigned, who lives in Indian minstrelsy as the embodiment of Hindu chivalry—the last to make a stand in Northern India against the successive waves of Mahomedan conquest which Central Asia had begun to pour upon India in A.D. 1001. In the next century an Afghan wave swept down on top of the original Turki wave, and Kutb-ed-Din, having proclaimed himself Emperor of Delhi in 1206, built the great mosque of *Kuwwet el Islam* and the lofty minaret, still known by his name, that is a landmark for many miles around.

With the monumental wreckage of these early Mahomedan dynasties, steeped in treachery and bloodshed, the plain of Delhi is still strewn . . .

—the huge fort of Tughlakubad, five miles east of the Kutb; the remnants of Firozabad built by 'the bloody King's' successor between Purana Kila and the site of Shah Jahan's Delhi; the walls and gates of Purana Kila itself and the mausoleum of Humayun; finally the city of Akbar's and Jahangir's successor Shah Jahan founded in 1638 with the building of the great Fort, to the north of these deserted capitals, and the construction of the Jami Masjid a few years later within the walled and gated city. Here the Moghul Emperors, successors of Baber and Akbar, ruled for a time over almost the whole of India. Their marble halls in the Fort reflect the magnificence of their Empire, which attracted craftsmen from Italy, but no less its slow decay until, sacked in 1730 by the Persian Nadir Shah, who carried away the Peacock Throne and countless millions of treasure, including the Koh-i-noor diamond, the enfeebled Moghul became a suitor for the protection of the British East India Company. Opposite Indrapat, on the east bank of the Jumna, Lord Lake in 1803 defeated the army of the Mahratta gaolers of the last Moghul Emperor. Then Moghul kings reigned without power in Delhi till the Mutiny in 1857.

The recapture of Delhi by the relatively small British force, in the face of four times the number of well-equipped and trained Sepoys and a vast fanatical population, turned upon the seizure and holding of the North Ridge. Every action in the weeks of confused and desperate fighting about the Ridge, which culminated in the storming of the Kashmir and Kabul gates on the north and west of the city, was burnt into the memories of nineteenth-century Britons in India, a concentrated chronicle of blood and fire eclipsing for them the blurred annals of as many centuries of lurid Pathan pomp and the majesty of Moghuls long disintegrated into dusty ruin.

In the blinding April haze of 1912, however, the three Commissioners worked for a wholly factual view of the physical features over which the centuries had battled and built and bled. Somewhere in their knee-deep dust was to be found an area of at least ten square miles for the new city and fifteen square miles for the Military Cantonment, potentially healthy and irrigable, to be acquired without disproportionate cost, and in close physical and traditional contact with the existing city, yet without disturbance to the historical and religious sites that crowded the ground. A further complicating factor was that a temporary administrative town was already in course of erection on the western slopes of the North Ridge.

During the endless arguments and discussions de Montmorency proved a walking encyclopædia, the patient methodical Brodie a tower of strength, and the mercurial Swinton something of a trial to his colleagues. Lutyens recalled one particular disputation, conducted between Brodie and Swinton whilst the three were on elephant-back, about the cost of a possible tunnel under the Ridge. 'Swinton maintained that it was cheaper to tunnel where the Ridge was low, the other that, once you tunnelled, it did not matter whether there were 20 or 200 feet above the tunnel. So acute grew the argument that Brodie said he would not be taught elementary engineering by Swinton and slid off the elephant—walking the five miles home with the temperature nearing 117 in the shade.'

Nevertheless they were unanimous in narrowing down the possible sites to four and eventually to one. At first they felt the obvious attraction to the site northwards of the city, which similarly drew every superficial student of the problem. It possessed distinct advantages. But the cost that would be involved in acquiring much fully occupied land, the interruption of the area, already cramped, by physical obstacles and the sacrosanct Ridge, and the impossibility of future expansion owing to the unhealthy condition of much of the adjoining land, amounted to an overwhelming indictment against the North Ridge. Moreover, 'the Imperial Capital should, to present an effective appearance, be approached along a line of rising ground; but here the opposite is the case and the approach from Delhi would be along a falling line towards low-lying land flanked by flooded areas;'[1] a sentence

---

[1] Report of Delhi Town Planning Committee on the Choice of Site, 1912.

probably due to Lutyens whose embryonic conception of the layout can thus be traced to these earliest days. The Commission therefore turned 'reluctantly', as they admitted, to the alternatives—but that was by no means the end of the Ridge site. The eastern side of the Jumna, and the western slope of the hills south of Delhi were both examined as possible sites but proved unsuitable.

That left the eastern slopes of the hills which overlook the river plain occupied by the ancient cities. These, with the exception of the Kutb in the extreme south, had been sited for water supply within reach of the river, but the land lying between the Delhi-Kutb road and the Ridge was virgin country unencumbered by archaeological monuments, though dotted with the inevitable shrines. The soil was good agricultural land, the villages had the healthiest history of any in the region and could not be flooded. Here a site was found that offered virtually unlimited space for expansion, yet was near Delhi itself, whence impressive approaches could be contrived. Moreover, the military authorities were satisfied with the plateau on the other side of the Ridge as suitable for the Cantonments. The land, being occupied by no business or manufacturing interests, could be acquired at relatively favourable rates. The supply of water for irrigation would be more costly than a gravitation supply but would be counterbalanced by the savings in the costs of drainage, flood-protection, and sanitary works involved on every other site considered.

The first general survey had been completed at the end of April when the Commission had their first interview with the Viceroy on his way to Simla. Discussion dealt chiefly with the Government's plans for putting in hand the building of the temporary administrative town on the North Ridge and its possible bearing on the Commission's choice of the permanent site. They were probably able to reassure Lord Hardinge that, in any event, the permanent site would not clash with the temporary site, though it was not till a week later, May 5— three weeks after their arrival at Delhi—that Lutyens wrote home 'I have made up my mind as regards site, but not how to treat it yet'.

Lord Hardinge showed himself strongly in favour of an Eastern style of architecture for the new capital. Indeed, on his instructions, the party had already spent a week-end visiting Jaipur and Agra, and been given facilities for visiting a number of private houses in Delhi.

In these dwellings Lutyens was fascinated but shocked and nonplussed by their utter inversion of every standard to which he was accustomed. Of one, belonging to an old Theosophist gentleman, he wrote:

> It was a tiny house, approached by a crooked lane 6 ft. wide, with a tinier guest-house facing it across a little court and an old house alongside for servants (4) and the cow and her calf—a nice white Brahmin beast. He had sent away his women but I gathered he only had three wives. It was all spotlessly clean

and full of ingenious and amusing devices and a very good ventilation arrangement of his own invention. There was a great deal of charm, but our host's taste was appalling and of a mad child order... But, looking on him as a child, I found him good, clean, and wise. If Ursula had arranged the doll's house with the same method, preciseness, and cleanliness, she would have had top marks.

But a rich Hindu's large new house horrified him with its squalor and filth. 'Here a naughty child played a game of stupid chaos, ugly without charm. It is not worth describing. A glad-to-be-away-from place.' At a third Hindu house, old and with incoherent additions, a wedding was being celebrated with 500 guests.

> The house was approached by a long narrow street that smelt all the smells that dirt can evoke. The entrance was covered by an awning of evergreens where a band played—pipes and tom-toms. Feasting was going on inside, in the court-yard, covered by an awning, and there was a large wood fire in one corner where everything was cooked. We went to the top of the house to look down into the court and on to the many people; and food—weird pickles, salt cakes, sweets, curries, etc. were brought to us, and lemonade in earthen pots.
>
> The complication of entertaining different castes and religions seems appalling.

He confessed that he was a long way from grasping the systems underlying these ways of life. Moslems had a central authority but Hindus seemed to have none. The problem arose acutely in connection with the shrines with which the country was larded: 'Wherever you take a line across it, several tombs and shrines are in the way.' It was difficult to trace their ownership since they were often registered in the name of the goddess or personage commemorated. For example, the second, repulsive, house that they had visited was registered in the name of 'a hideous idol with four arms and as many legs', which occupied a shrine on its ground floor.

It made improvement difficult 'without being ruthless or appearing unsympathetic; Mrs. Besant might know some good and simple way, without hurt. The great thing is to win the people's confidence and having won it never let them down'. It was not only the contrast between their ways of life and building and planning with all that Lutyens envisaged for the new city, that was weighing on his mind. He was 'harrassed by the squalid suburbs that have been allowed to grow up about old Delhi', which were valued in the Survey at absurdly high figures. The Deputy Commissioner began to frighten the planners by his estimates of compensation and rehousing costs, although Lutyens considered that £100,000, expended over a period of ten years, would suffice to clean up the neighbourhood of the new city and the purchase of the land required would pay for itself.

> Building is cheap and the native wants so little. A cow-shaped plot with a yard and a covered room, surrounded by a wall. They don't want window frames or anything of that sort, just a hole, and they live practically out of doors in their yards, and a nice mess they make of them.

A cow-shaped house, he ascertained, is one that is narrower in the front than at the back, which is propitious, whereas lion-shaped houses, wider in front than behind, are very bad and had in several cases been known to prove fatal to those who had built them.

Before leaving Delhi, Lutyens went early one morning to the Fort and requisitioned the turning on of the fountains to obtain the sight and sound effects of water falling down the sculptured cascades. The decorative handling of water was the aspect that most genuinely attracted him to Moghul architecture.

§2. THE DIVERSIONS OF SIMLA

The month at Delhi had been exploratory field work, prospecting in jungle country in the hot weather, with scarcely any society, or interruption, from outside the circle of the Commission itself. When on May 21, the party moved up to Simla Lutyens got his first, and as it proved only prolonged, taste of the heady atmosphere of the Hills. After the sweating climate of the Plains, cold nights with rain or hail when a hot bath and a fire were welcome, where you rode in a rickshaw instead of on an elephant, and you were liable to find a monkey in your bedroom, were nevertheless the least of the differences. As Lutyens put it:

> It is inconceivable, and consequently very English!—to have a capital as Simla is entirely of tin roofs, and then the tin roofs monkeying better materials and reducing the whole thing to absurdity. The hills and depths below are heroic, the building and conception of the place by the Public Works Department mind is beyond the beyond, and if one was told the monkeys had built it all one could only say 'What wonderful monkeys—they must be shot in case they do it again . . .'

The *Plain Tales from the Hills* regime was exactly sustained by the first morning, spent paying calls in rickshaws, accidentally meeting the Viceroy and Vicereine riding in the park, and accumulating social and semi-official engagements which portended an endless round of dinner and garden parties. The weeks that followed fulfilled the promise. Among his hosts were Sir Henry MacMahon (Foreign Secretary), Sir Harcourt Butler (then Education Member) Sir J. du Boulay (Secretary to the Viceroy) and their respective wives, some of whom became his warm friends. Lady du Boulay was surprised and pleased to discover that Lutyens was the husband of Lady Emily, exclaiming, 'She is the one woman I admire, for she always writes and speaks the truth, writes beautifully and speaks beautifully!' Theosophy also provided a topic of common interest with the Butlers. When it came to discussing the arrangements and accommodation of Government House, Lutyens dined with du Boulay and with Captain Maxwell, V.C., the Military Secretary. Later on he notes for instance, 'Captain Maxwell was pleased with my plans for the levée entrances etc.' His letters to his wife and to Herbert Baker from Simla constantly revert to the paradoxes of the village capital and the young lighthearted masters of the Indian Empire—*his* masters, whom somehow he has got to cajole, convince, educate, inspire, into commissioning him to give the subcontinent adult architecture, a real Imperial capital. Would any of them, charming, able athletic, and incredibly young, understand what he was driving at?

> The scenery is huge, some 8000 ft up, and looks away north to the great snow-covered peaks of the Himalayas and then down to the dusty bowels of the world, sheer giddy-making drops down to the plains, a God-made country never intended for man, too big and remote to be really pleasant to live in.
>
> India—well, man's work is so vile it depresses me, but I am pleased when I can recognize a likeness to a Hampshire down, Scotland, Italy, or some homey place! God's work, country, is always beautiful and marvellous no matter whether it is a Himalaya or a Lincolnshire Fen; and there is always that magic of it to inspire and wonder at, except the farness of it.
>
> I have no terror of the country and feel at home and like the heat and enjoy the cold. They are both amusing. But [in reply, no doubt, to a hopeful theosophical question from his wife as to whether he was not becoming conscious of a previous Indian incarnation] no, I don't feel I have ever been here before or know it a whit more than Africa. The 'horror of India' has not gripped me at all. The difficulty is to grip India.
>
> But I am awfully impressed by the Civil Service and the unselfishness of our government. The whole country is run by pleasant-blooded Englishmen, all young in the modern sense, all with responsibilities beyond their years, but all waiting for the clock to strike and tell them to go home and enjoy their pensions. Nice men, of nice feeling, but absolutely art-unconscious. It does not come within their ken at all.
>
> They will admire snow mountains with a rhodedendron in flower in the foreground, and they will go home and tie up a terracotta flower pot with a pink drapery, so I guess their admiration is not for the beauty of the mountain but for its distance and size. Its imperturbability moves some animal chord in their being. Then it is always safe to admire nature!
>
> I don't think I am 'glamoured' of India as an alltogether—it is not so good looking a country as Africa, but then I have only seen it in the dry heat, all dust

and dearth and the middens of ages blowing about. But I am happy and amused and find an enormous amount to admire and love. The natives do not improve on acquaintance. Their very low intellects spoil much and I do not think it is possible for the Indians and whites to mix freely and naturally. They are very different, and even my ultra-wide sympathy with them cannot admit them on the same plane as myself. They may be on a higher plane or a lower one than a white, but the ethics of their planes are different to ours, and for one or the other to leave his plane is unclean and unforgiveable.[1]

This characteristic analysis of the ethical and human factors of Anglo-India, as they appeared to him, summarises broadly the aesthetic problem that Lutyens felt confronting him on arrival at Simla. Its generalisations reflect his uncertainty of how the Viceroy and Delhi Committee would receive the Commission's proposals, and, indeed, of the nature of his own reception by His Excellency. He had had no personal contact with Lord Hardinge since coming to India, beyond the Commission's brief official interview with him at Delhi; and Lord Hardinge's frequently expressed view that the buildings should be of oriental character filled him with forebodings. These were intensified by de Montmorency reporting that the Viceroy was insistent on keeping considerations of site and plan separate from all architectural considerations at this stage. Lutyens was no less determined that the two aspects must be treated as inseparable and that an oriental style was out of the question, so far as he was concerned. At the same time he intended to ensure his being given the designing of Government House with, if possible, general architectural control of the city plan; to elucidate the mystery of the Government's relations with Lanchester who he discovered had been instructed to inspect the Delhi area and submit a separate report; and, if a collaborator was required, to procure the appointment of Herbert Baker. On none of these issues, fundamental to his own position, had he as yet received any guidance, nor of course, could he tell how the authorities would view the recommendation of the Southern Site in the face of the prevalent assumption that the new capital would occupy the North Ridge.

In the midst of these uncertainties came tidings of the opening of the 'Shakespeare's England' Exhibition at Earls Court, the rumour that he was being proposed for Associateship of the Royal Academy, and news that his sister-in-law, Lady Constance Lytton, had, in the cause of Women's Suffrage and under a false name gone on hunger strike in Liverpool prison in order to call attention to the conditions of working-class women in gaol. So no wonder he wrote to his wife gloomily (May 26):

> Was Earls Court in any way convincing? Exciting, the R.A.; but there is

[1] In this passage I have interpolated passages from several letters to Sir Herbert Baker into one to Lady Emily dated May 22, in cases where the same trains of thought happen to be more fully expressed or developed.

THE DELHI PLANNING COMMISSION

so much jealousy, and Poynter is so much against me that I have little hope. However, hope I will to the end, if only to keep up face.

By the same mail came a long letter from Baker, in reply to Lutyens's suggestions that they might collaborate, typical of his nature in its meticulous pondering of pros and cons. He found it very difficult, he said, to make up his mind, but as Ned might be discussing the matter with the authorities, he had talked it over with friends and sent his thoughts. Some felt that the colour problem in South Africa (where a certain Mr. Gandhi was already leading Indian opposition to the 'discriminatory' restrictions on immigration) should weigh against his connecting himself with India. On the other hand England's work in India was the greatest triumph of unselfish government in the history of the world, so that nobody should refuse the honour of having a hand in building its monument. Personally he was very unwilling to leave South Africa and his home, and could not bear heat; yet he would be free from urgent work at Pretoria in a few months' time and was chilled by the indifference to architecture in the Dominion. If asked, he would say he would only work with Lutyens; he had strong reasons for declining to consider collaboration with Lanchester, whose 'Ricardo-Frencho-Cardiff stuff' he disliked: on the other hand he felt Ned might do better with a staff of younger men—he felt he was getting an old bear and rather a blind bear. Nevertheless, 'I don't ask whether I am good enough to do the work. I realise it is easy to be a tall tree in the South African bush. But it is not one's business to reason why if one is ordered.'

Lutyens's uncertainties were soon to be resolved. At their meeting with Lord Hardinge, the Commission would have to 'sell' him their idea for the Southern Site, and, at Lutyens's insistence, agreed to obtain if possible his consent to the general question of architecture being linked with it. They therefore applied for further instructions in view of 'certain questions that had arisen', and submitted a list of points that, they understood, should be taken into consideration. These were (1) Health; (2) Military requirements; (3) Space for expansion; (4) Cost—all of which bore directly on their proposal. And (5) 'Sites for principal buildings, which necessarily involves considerations of the height and dimensions of these buildings, their architectural relation to each other, and their general relation to approaches, avenues, vistas, and open spaces'. Further points covered Brodie's field.

On the evening preceding the fateful interview Swinton and Lutyens dined at Viceregal Lodge. It was a large party including the Maharaja of Patiala, and Lutyens had little chance of speaking to the Viceroy, but Lady Hardinge invited him to 'talk architecture' with her at an early date.

In the event, the meeting lasted two hours and proved highly satisfactory. Narrating its gist, Lutyens told Lady Emily:

My special point was No. 5. When my turn came and I had to speak up, I spoke—and Hardinge agreed! to everyone's surprise. Said he quite saw my point and thought it reasonable.

So his first objective, the joint consideration of the broad architectural factors together with site and plan, was gained. More: 'he liked my first rough plan and was wise about it, looking at the general lines and not picking out details and making them difficult.'

The talk with Lady Hardinge was equally successful, and in the middle of it Lord Hardinge came in. Lutyens felt that at last he had emerged from the labyrinth of official channels on to the familiar open ground of architect-client relationship.

> I had a good talk (with H. E.) about Delhi and architecture. I am to make sketches of Government House. Lord Hardinge was quite keen and agreed with my view as to the architecture and country. He said he wanted the two cities to be one, and not two. So I scored all round, and feel very happy. I asked Lady H. about Lanchester. She said he was only coming out for a month and they had to be tactful. I asked her if there was any chance of my doing the building. She said, 'Yes of course, who else?' This don't commit the Viceroy but does, I hope, point to the mind wind.
>
> I am beginning to work hard. The amount of buildings required for Delhi is colossal! Great Fun.

In the course of frequent discussions with Lord and Lady Hardinge, Captain Maxwell the Military Secretary, and the Comptroller, Lutyens obtained in the next few days a grasp of the elaborate ceremonial and practical requirements of Government House. He was able to talk to Lord Hardinge 'as himself and not as Viceroy', and by June 3 had worked out rough plans and elevations. A quick sketch included in a letter to Baker (June 14) illustrates (p. 223) this earliest scheme for the Viceroy's House with a Great Court immediately in front of it. In the elevation it will be seen that a central dome and a portico were already integral features, with State Rooms grouped round the circular Hall forming the square body of the building. At the back the Viceroy's Wing and the King's Wing are separated by a Privy Garden deeper and narrower than as executed. The entrance front is extended laterally by lower flanking ranges from which project wings containing quarters for A.D.C.'s and the Viceroy's Secretaries.

In front of the forecourt, the Great Court extended laterally three quarters of a mile, with a Cathedral at one end and a Viceroy's Secretariat at the other; houses for the Private Secretary and Military Secretary flanked the Viceroy's House; and two colossal 'Trajan's Columns' were set in the segments of the Great Court. The approach to the Court was indicated as 180 yards wide between Secretariat Buildings attached to the Court by semi-circular ranges facing outwards, one of which was

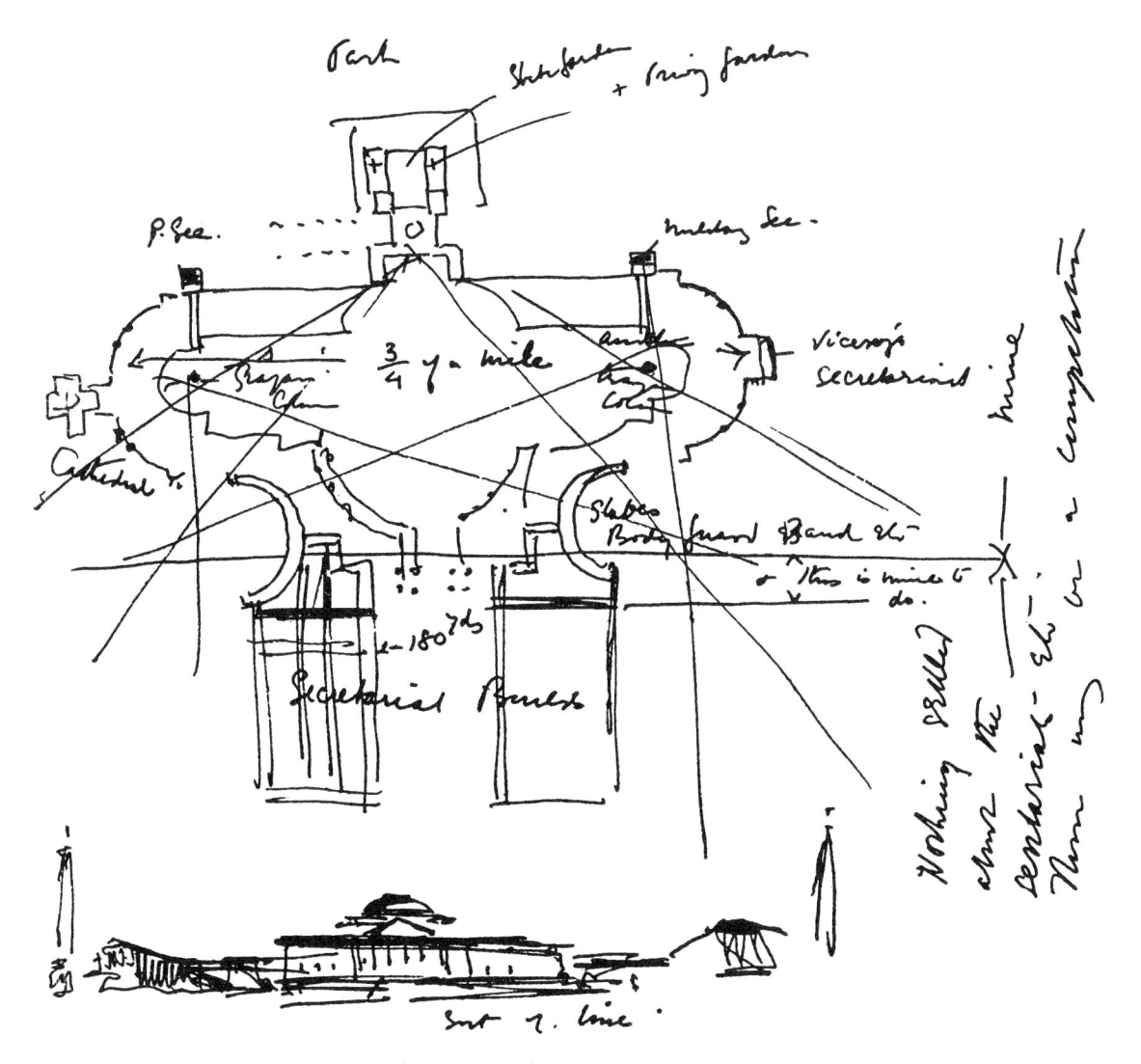

SKETCH OF ORIGINAL SCHEME (JUNE, 1912) FOR GOVERNMENT HOUSE AND SECRETARIATS ON A LEVEL SITE

described as 'Stables, Body-guard, Band etc.'. Everything above a line excluding the Secretariats was marked 'mine'.

Lord Hardinge was also able to talk freely at these interviews on the complexity of the situation, the necessity for satisfying Indian opinion, and of the varied political conditions, which in Lutyens's view, 'militate against the best—at least the best to look at.' The latter learnt of the soreness felt by officials of the Public Works Department at the new capital not being entrusted to their hands entirely; and realised that 'a fearful battle is brewing on the architectural style of the new city'.

There was indeed. Lutyens's views on the unsuitability of Indian traditional styles were fully formed, but at this stage Lord Hardinge was careful to avoid the issue which became the crucial topic of discussion during Lutyens's visit of the following winter (1912–13) when his marshalling of his case will be reviewed in its chronological place. Already, however, Lord Hardinge was so far persuaded as to admit that 'there is no absolute necessity for Government House to be of any particular style, though it is essential that the Secretariats and other Government buildings should be of a broad and simple architecture with an Oriental "motif" which should blend itself with a Government House that should be a dignified and noble monument'. (Letter to the Secretary of State, July 16, 1912). He added that he maintained that pure Eastern or pure Western architecture would be equally out of place and that 'we have to find a blend. Lutyens showed me rough drawings that he had made of what Government House might be, and I must say that as a whole they impressed me favourably'. He emphasised that he was in no way committed to Lutyens as regards Government House. But on June 6 he had written to Lord Crewe expressing the wish that he should do the work, dependent on the Secretary of State's approval.

Lutyens, whilst content at the course that events were taking, sensed that 'there is a lot of wire-pulling going on somewhere about architects'. This impression was not only due to Lanchester's being in the offing. The facts, he learnt now, were that during the previous winter, Lanchester had approached the Viceroy in Calcutta, when Lord Hardinge had asked him whether he would serve on a Planning Committee with S. D. Adshead and Brodie. To the Viceroy's surprise and without his knowledge Lanchester reported to Lord Crewe that Lord Hardinge had asked him to serve on the Committee. In order to avoid unpleasantness, he had therefore been invited to spend a month on the site and make a proposal. It appeared that he had already suggested that the design of the buildings should be open to competition, and the Viceroy mentioned this possibility to Lutyens.

But the impression of wheels within wheels was no doubt also due to the Viceroy's responsibility not only to the Secretary of State but to his Council. This supreme authority comprised such personages as the Commander-in-Chief (Gen. Sir Moore O'Creagh, V.C., G.C.B.), the Finance Member (Sir Guy Fleetwood Wilson, K.C.B., K.C.M.G.), and the Foreign Secretary (Lt.-Col. Sir Henry McMahon, K.C.I.E.). McMahon already knew Lutyens personally, and had some experience of how his enthusiasm was apt to prove expensive, having recommended him to the owner of Heywood for the designing of a garden terrace at that Irish country house. The scheme as executed, though architecturally superb, had proved very much more costly than the client had contemplated. Another Hon. Member recalled the exploits of John Lutyens, one of Ned's elder brothers, who during Army manoeuvres thirty years before, had misled Sir Frederick Roberts and 20,000 men as to the unfordable nature of the Delhi Canal through omitting to discover on a reconnaissance that it was, in fact, no more than a shallow drain at that season. The incident, with one or two others in which this earlier Lutyens had been concerned, had made a lasting impression in Indian Army circles and seems to have implanted a suspicion that there might be a family streak of that unreliability so repugnant to Government officials. These were trivial, perhaps distorted, memories; but unfortunately they cropped up at the highest level to cast uneasy shadows upon the Viceroy's mind.

Thus it came as a shock to Lord Hardinge, who had imagined that Government House would at the most cost £200,000 to build, exclusive of furnishing, gardens, stables and office quarters, when Lutyens told him (June 13) that it would probably cost £1,000,000. It says much for the confidence already established between the two men that this estimate in no way weakened Lord Hardinge's desire for Lutyens to proceed with the design.

By now the Planning Commission's Report on the choice of site was completed. It had been written by Swinton and Brodie, with de Montmorency's assistance; 'I went on with my work and looked in now and then', Lutyens said, 'when I heard words flowing at too high a cadence.' The signatories had 'no hesitation' in recommending the area south of old Delhi lying between Indrapat (Purana Kila) and the eastern slope of the Ridge. The new city itself would occupy an area of approximately 13,138 acres (20 square miles), or 13,428 acres if, as recommended, the suburb of Paharganj immediately south-west of old Delhi, was included. But in addition, for the military cantonments, water-supply, and future expansion, the acquisition was recommended of a further 29,634 acres, with 9371 acres to the west, north, and east of the old city for control of its future expansion.

The Report contained no proposals for the layout or setting of the new city, but the Commission submitted confidential suggestions to the Viceroy. I have not succeeded in tracing a definite record of this preliminary layout, but from subsequent documents its general lines and positions are left in no doubt. They come as a considerable surprise, and must be indicated, in view of subsequent developments.

Unlike the site finally chosen, which adjoins it slightly to the north-east, the proposal was for an almost level area on the Delhi side of the village of Malcha and due east of Indrapat. A main east-west avenue, some two miles long, was provided from Indrapat to Government House, whence a second vista ran north-east aligned on the Jama Masjid, and passing north of Raisina Hill—the eventual site of the Viceroy's House. This east-west axis was intersected near its middle point by a north-south avenue terminated by the site of a proposed Metropolitan Cathedral.

From what followed it is clear that this flat site, on the river plain, was chosen in order to secure relatively fertile soil for Government House and the large garden and park proposed to adjoin it to the westward, stretching to and up the eastern slope of the Ridge, which, the Committee had formed the opinion, was too barren itself for afforestation or gardening.

Although it was soon abandoned, this preliminary site had a far-reaching effect on the final relationship of the principal buildings—of Government House to the

Secretariats. It was at this stage, and with this almost level site in view, that the conception was evolved of the Viceroy's House preceded by a Great Court flanked by the Secretariat Buildings. Although the actual design, proportions, and dimensions of these three components remained fluid for some time to come, Lutyens was elaborating them in his mind all the time and never entirely departed from the original conception, made for the level site. By the time the Viceroy's House had been shifted to Raisina Hill, to be followed to that eminence by the Secretariats a few weeks later, the final design had so far crystallised that the difficulty inevitably arising from the application to a sloping site of a plan originally conceived for a level site did not immediately become apparent.

For the present, however, all was well.

§3. APPROACH TO RAISINA

During the late summer and autumn of 1912 the three members of the Delhi Planning Committee worked in London whilst their preliminary proposals were being examined on the spot by Indian government officials. Lengthy communications passed by every mail, dealing particularly with irrigation, railway communications, and acquisition of land. Brodie was primarily concerned with the first two topics, with which we are therefore not concerned; but the third, with its concomitant question of cost and consequently of sites, came to have an acute bearing on Lutyens. Meanwhile the Viceroy was urging on the Secretary of State 'the immense advantage' of Lutyens's appointment as architect for Government House being confirmed immediately, in view of the intimate grasp he had been able to obtain through his discussions at Simla, with himself and his staff, on the building's complex requirements. Lord Crewe, however, persisted in deferring the appointment pending the approval of the Commission's final report. This would not in any case be ready till the following Spring, and in the meantime was destined to undergo drastic modifications. Since no record has hitherto been made of this fluid phase in the evolution of New Delhi, this Section must include a brief sketch of it in order to indicate the atmosphere of uncertainty and anxiety, culminating in the attempted assassination of the Viceroy, in which Lutyens prepared his scheme for his greatest building.

Not only was his appointment—the condition on which he had consented to go to India in the first place—still unratified; the site of the new city, and with it that of Government House, was continually being shifted; whilst Lord Hardinge's unofficial arrangement with H. V. Lanchester now resulted in a completely different alternative layout being considered and a very real likelihood arising of the official buildings being opened to competition. Nevertheless Lutyens pressed on with the designs of Government House, setting the Queen Anne's Gate staff to scale up and draw out his sketches, 'so as in any event not to disappoint you when I come out in December,' he wrote to Lord Hardinge, 'and to prove my gratitude for all your kindness and this great compliment.' He sent, as he had promised, photographs for Lord Hardinge to see of a selection of his buildings, of which, it is interesting to note, the latter picked out the British School at Rome and the classical court of Papillon Hall, built nine years before, as likely to have most bearing on the conception of Viceroy's House.

In an interview at the end of July with Lord Crewe, when the rough sketches were exhibited but which was indecisive, Lutyens suggested the setting up of a permanent body, on the lines of the Commission of the 1851 Exhibition, to overcome the difficulties that he foresaw would be involved by changes of Ministers, Viceroys, and officials and to ensure continuity in the execution of the Delhi scheme. He proposed that the members should include Lord Crewe and Lord Hardinge, in order, as he told the latter, 'that you for your whole life would be in direction of the scheme you are responsible for initiating. The danger, I fear, is that change in the entire personel of the Government in the course of a few years will create confusion as great as was caused in St. Peters by a succession of Popes.' A committee on these lines was appointed in 1917 to supervise the furnishing and internal decoration.

In India, the Viceroy's Council had meanwhile approved the Southern Site in principle but decided to postpone the acquisition of the land pending the completion of a preliminary estimate of the cost of the new city that was being drawn up by Montmorency and W. H. Ward as regards irrigation, drainage, roads, parks, and buildings; and by Major H. C. Beadon as regards the actual cost of the land designated in the preliminary report and its tentative, unpublished, plan. This scheme had ambitiously included the environs west, north and south of Delhi in order to control the old city's expansion, besides the area to the south for the new city itself. The latter region was divided into five tracts or blocks, the position, area, and cost of which can be summarised as follows:

	Purpose	Position	Area (acres)	Cost (lakhs of Rs)
Block A	Cantonments	Extreme SW.	9,280	10·3
B	New City	S. of old city	13,428	42·2
C	Native Residential	S.W. of old city	2,542	1·3
D	Future reserve	S. of Block B	13,184	11·9
E	Preservation and Antiquities	Indrapat and riverside	4,628	7·6
	Environs of old city		9,371	24·1
		Total	52,433	Rs 9,787,482
				(£724,998)

These figures could be only approximate since, Major Beadon pointed out,[1] although the cost of ordinary unirrigated land could be taken as Rs ·80 per acre, charitably disposed Hindus and also purchasers of land for industrial development often paid very much higher prices, so that it was impossible to foresee the awards that would be allowed by the Divisional and Chief Courts, to which appeal was in all cases allowed against the Government's valuation under the Land Requisition Act. But the figures should serve at any rate in guiding the Government as to the areas which should *not* be acquired. Major Beadon particularly directed attention to the extremely high cost of the suburb of Paharganj, immediately south of old Delhi and in the northern sector of Block B. In the total cost of Block B, the 290 acres of Paharganj represented no less than 27·6 lakhs of rupees, against 14·6 for the remaining 13,138 acres. He also recommended that the remote Block D would probably not be required for at least a generation.

The significance of Paharganj lay in the preliminary layout having sited the vista from Government House to the Jama Masjid clean through the heart of Paharganj. Lord Hardinge was much perturbed by the size of these estimates. On August 1 he informed the Commission that the tentative layout was on far too spacious a scale, that the cost of expropriating the householders of Paharganj was prohibitive, and that he had therefore instructed H. V. Lanchester to make an alternative plan avoiding the suburb.

The Lanchester plan appears to have been no less extensive. It sited Government House on the level ground between Malcha and Tal Katora at the west extremity of the area, with avenues radiating thence in the direction of the Jama Masjid and Indrapat; and provided another centre at the extreme south, near Safdar Jang's Tomb, where the railway station was proposed, with another series of avenues radiating northwards. Both sets of radial avenues were intersected by streets describing arcs of varying radius centred on one or other of these two main points, with subsidiary circular features at the main intersections. By the middle of August this plan had been submitted to Mr. M. Nethersole,[2] Officiating Secretary to the Public Works Department, and Mr. C. E. V. Goument, Chief Engineer, Buildings and Roads Branch, United Provinces, who in their report suggested scrapping both sets of plans and removing Government House to the Ridge:

> Having inspected the lay-out suggested by Mr. Lanchester, we are of opinion that the site for Viceregal Lodge urgently requires further consideration. Our objection is that it lies too low to give it sufficient command of the sur-

[1] Report on the Acquisition of Land for the Imperial Capital at Delhi, August 5, 1912.

[2] Sir Michael Nethersole, subsequently Consulting Engineer to the Government of India for irrigation, humorously summed up the advantages of a southern as against the northern site for the new capital, in the riddle: 'Why cannot you have the northern site? Because dam(n) it you cant. Why must you have the southern site? Because blast it you must.'

rounding country or the dominating position it should have in relation to the new city. It is shut in on the N.W. and S.W. by the Main Ridge and bordered on the E. by Raisina Hill.

The reason for its selection appears to have been chiefly its position at the S.W. extremity of the central avenue to the Jama Masjid, which dominated the first lay-out; and secondly the soil.

The first of these reasons had disappeared, they pointed out, with the decision to exclude Paharganj; and they were convinced that it was practically and financially feasible to afforest the Ridge, covering the area of the Viceroy's gardens with three feet of soil at the rate of Rs 500 per acre per foot of depth.

Fortified by this belief, they submitted a rough plan for setting Government House on the slope of the Ridge above the village of Tal Katora, a mile and a half to the north-west of the Commission's site, with the main vista south-east to Humayun's Tomb and passing over Raisina Hill.

This recommendation was supported by Mr. P. H. Clutterbuck, Conservator of Forests, with a list of seventy-two types of trees suitable for afforesting the pockets of soil already present on the Ridge. In transmitting these notes to Swinton, Lord Hardinge requested that the whole matter of siting Government House be reconsidered. He wrote:

> To me personally the site on top of the Ridge with a magnificent view over Delhi and over the whole plain both east and west presents very great attractions. Further, I can picture to myself the approach to Government House from the plain below with terraces and gardens and fountains along the hillside that should be a reproduction in miniature of Versailles and its gardens. Such a position would appeal greatly to the Indians who would be able to point to it from miles away as the residence of the Lord Saheb.

The Committee would not, he supposed, be able to come to any decision before December; consequently he would be unable to do anything meanwhile towards pushing on the realisation of the new city. To Lutyens he wrote, August 19:

> I hope I have not shocked you and your colleagues... Can you not imagine how splendid a white Government House with red tiles and a gilt dome would look in such a commanding situation? I am still in hopes of getting Lord Crewe's assent to your doing Government House, but I have no hesitation in declaring my absolute opinion that the Secretariat and public offices must have an Indian motif. It would be a very grave political blunder and in my opinion an absurdity to place a purely western town amidst eastern surroundings. Opinion in this country is very strong on the subject. It is all very well to say that the bulk of opinion in England is in favour of the great classic tradition,

but it is not public opinion in England that is concerned, but public opinion in India. I should personally like to see buildings of a bold and plain character with an oriental adaptation. You may call it bastard or what you like, but the only alternatives are pure Indian or pure Western, and both of these I would deprecate.

He went on to enlarge on the desirability for a competition for the Secretariats. He had asked Lanchester to draw up the necessary regulations. There was little chance, he thought, of Indians producing suitable designs for the Secretariats, yet the popularity that the idea of the new capital was at present enjoying would soon evaporate if it were discovered that India was to be offered no hand in its construction beyond paying for it. Circulars announcing a competition for bungalows had already been issued. In conclusion he hoped Brodie was progressing with his plans for irrigation and water-supply, since, although the layout of the new city was thus held up, he was anxious to push ahead with the cantonments.

Lutyens had not received these despatches, only the broad decision, when he went to Balmoral to show his sketches for Viceroy's House to the King and Queen on September 8. The pleasure that this honour should have brought was therefore clouded by a state of complete uncertainty. To his wife he could merely report 'Hardinge has volte-faced altogether, nothing can be settled till after Christmas at Delhi. We are all rather concerned and fussed'. Besides not knowing whether he had in fact any official status as architect, there was the Viceroy's partiality for an Indian style to be weighed as well as the King's expressed taste for Moghul, whilst the designs intended for the lower site might have to be translated to the arid needs of the Ridge.

It was Sunday morning at Ballater. Travelling all night he had written to Lady Emily in the train and his old inarticulacy worried him:

> No news. I have only that beloved story, now old, of how much I love and want you to be home. I dont think you know when I *say* things I think; and when I write them they get fixed somewhat and a word may mean more or less of what I mean and the emphasis gets wrong.

He was to stay with Lord Stamfordham at Abergeldie Mains. Having no top hat he excused himself from attending church, the only man in a soft one, so went instead to look at the river, an occupation that always fascinated him. He noticed that suffragettes were hanging slogans on the green-flags of the golf course. Whilst waiting to go to tea at Balmoral, the Indian mail came in and he had just time to read Lord Hardinge's letter and glance at Lanchester's plan (which he criticised disapprovingly as 'pattern-making'), when it was time to go.

The party at the Castle, including Sir Walter Lawrence (who had been secretary to Lord Curzon as Viceroy), Sir James Reid, Sir Charles Frederick and Sir Herbert Samuel, were looking at the plans on the billiard table and had begun to bombard Lutyens with questions when the King sent for him. He reported to Lord Hardinge:

> Lord Crewe had been at Balmoral the week before and asked Lord Stamfordham not to allow the King to commit himself, so I felt bound not to ask any direct questions or make any statement which might have led him to make even a verbal commital.
>
> Both the King and Queen were kind about the drawings and the Queen used the word 'beautiful'.

(Queen Mary remembered their meeting at Holy Island three years before, and he reminded her of the discomfort she had experienced from Edward Hudson's cobble stones.)

> H.M. was anxious about the flag pole, which I had not shown, as to whether it could be seen from everywhere. He suggested the top of the dome, but when I explained the method of lighting the Durbar Hall [at this stage apparently by a cupola, so that a flag pole could not be attached to it] he seemed satisfied with one over the portico... H.M. said it must be the Royal Arms over the Entrance Door.
>
> H.M. had heard of the proposal to put Government House on the Ridge, which he did not like, nor could he believe it was feasible to plant the Ridge with any degree of permanent success.
>
> He said the main avenue should go to King Edward's Statue in old Delhi [in front of the S. gate of the Fort]. To give us some latitude as regards angle axis I asked him if we might move the statue using the stone he had laid as a pivot. To this he said Yes.
>
> H.M. went into the sizes of the rooms in Government House and the arrangement of his own suites and that of the Council Chamber, and seemed satisfied, saying it must not be spoiled for ha'porth of tar. He said the trees must be free and the avenues really wide.

Indeed it would appear from Lutyens's report that His Majesty approved of his views on several points then at issue between him and the Viceroy. Lutyens also reported some of the remarks he heard round the billiard table—such as that Government House looked as though it was built for hot weather (when it would not generally be occupied) and not for cold; that the building was not high enough; and the necessity of really wide avenues admitting full grown trees—and commented:

> As regards the house they evidently could form no idea of its scale in the 5 minutes they saw the drawings. Even on the old site the base of the dome came above the Ridge, and the building has been designed to meet both hot and cold weather conditions, as your Excellency knows... I answered these criticisms afterwards to Lord Stamfordham and gave him a diagram showing the relative heights of the buildings as proposed, those existing, i.e. the Jama Masjid, the Janta Mantar (observatory), a poor black, a poor white, a rich white, and also the Secretariats and Government House, in relation to the Ridge.

He then mentioned the desirability of a building Loan, which he was to advocate to successive Viceroys:

> There was a general opinion expressed that the cost of the new city should be met by a loan, and not from a surplus that might be affected by war, famine or other disaster. This of course is a matter outside any question affecting me, but I trust I am not wrong in reporting to Your Excellency all that my ears heard.

This account was preceded, in the letter despatched to Lord Hardinge by Lutyens on September 13, by acknowledgment of the Viceroy's of August 19 which, he said, had 'certainly made us sit up'. Significantly his first comment on the proposed move to the Ridge was:

> The practical difficulty of the Ridge site may be the method of an easy and 'sweet' approach to it.

As regards the covering of the Ridge with soil, he questioned whether it would not be washed away by the rains—though this could be prevented by terracing, at a cost,—'and how big and worth-while trees would be in 3 ft. of soil and how long they would live.'

The sketch designs, which he had taken to Balmoral and would send to the Viceroy shortly,

> will, I hope, show how natural and Indian a western motif can look, treated for the Indian sun *with* Indian methods applied *without* throwing away the English tradition and clinging too much to the curiosities of a less intellectual style. Except for the column I do not believe that public opinion in India would know that it was not Indian. You could employ every Indian artist, wood and stone carver in the country, to decorate and of course the fabric itself would be built

by Indians, so it would only be Indian, and India must be as open to new methods as other countries.

In another letter Lutyens disagreed with the separation of Government House (on the Ridge) from the Secretariats as increasing the distance between the latter and the Legislative Council Chamber, which was designed to be attached to Government House, thereby 'rendering us liable to the demand for a Council Chamber outside Government House'. Events were to effect both the reunion and the separation at a later date. In event of the Ridge site being adopted, he suggested the possibility of re-orienting Government House to face north-east in accordance with the King's desire that the main avenue should be aligned on the Edward VII statue and the Jama Masjid-Fort group. Lord Hardinge, however, was insistent on an east-west axis centred on Indrapat. The Viceroy had set off on October 8 on his autumn tour, to Kashmir, Rajputana, and the Central Provinces before Lutyens's sketch designs reached him.

The visit to Balmoral, approval of the sketch designs by the King and also by Lord Crewe and their dispatch to India, and now the Viceroy's tour, at length allowed Lutyens respite for his other commitments. When staying at Abergeldie he had motored over to lunch one day at Invercauld, leased for the autumn by Rear-Admiral and Mrs. David Beatty for whom he had virtually rebuilt Hanover Lodge, Regents Park, in 1910 and altered Brooksby Hall, Leicestershire, in 1911. Lord and Lady Lytton and the Winston Churchills were among the guests. Beatty invited him to fish the Invercauld waters, but he had to hurry back to London. There he had an appointment with Mr. and Mrs. Harry Maclaren (now Lord and Lady Aberconway) and Sir Henry and Lady Norman (Mr. Maclaren's sister) out of which arose his building the Corner House, Cowley Street for the Normans. Lunching the same day with Mr. Asquith an incident occurred, trifling in itself, that suddenly seemed to crystallise the paralysing atmosphere of expediency, Imperial policy, Royal reserve, and compromise which, for all the distinguished contacts that accompanied it, he felt to be stifling him. To Lady Emily he wrote:

> I was so shocked lunching at Downing Street when I commiserated with Montagu at his having to defend an action in the House which he did not like or approve of; Asquith laughed and said he had to do it every day of his life. Bah! Politics!—the greatest evidence there is of degeneracy. What can a majority have to do with right or wrong? Tossing would be a more moral and fairer method. Politics ought to be included within the Corrupt Practices Act! Whitaker Wright was a soul of honour compared to the blarney of ministers out on the cadge for votes.
>
> Oh dear, what shall I do?—they are all, every one, quite too awful for words.

The Viceroy's growing desire for a competition for the Secretariats filled Lutyens with foreboding, but also seems to have renewed in him his anxiety to bring in Baker as colleague. It becomes clear, indeed, that his pressing for Baker's collaboration varied in intensity in proportion to the imminence or recession of a competition for the official buildings.

Soon after the visit to Balmoral Lutyens gave him an account of the Delhi situation, of how 'the Government in India want a competition for the Secretariats; here they are against it', and how 'I told the King I wanted you!' Then he broke off into a discussion on the lighting of picture galleries, in connection with his design for that at Johannesburg, strongly criticising the Tate Gallery system in contrast to his own at Rome, and to the effective system at Christie's old rooms in King Street—with an opaque ceiling over glazed side-lights. The digression is worth recording (although it interrupts the flow of events which, unbeknownst to him at the time, was moving rapidly) because it produced a dictum on this subject of picture lighting.

> Those idiotic diagrams which architects and others make dont work. Light is a flood, and you might as well try to show the banks of a river, its flow and varying depths, swirls, eddies, and currents with one arrow.

In South Africa his two buildings were beginning at last to move. At Johannesburg work on the Memorial had begun and quantity estimates for the Art Gallery were coming in. But Baker wrote that the University scheme had gone into cold storage and Government House to the Public Works Department. Since his Rhodes Memorial had been successfully opened and the Union Building was nearing completion, Baker had written that:

> All seems dead here now. If I could help you by occasional visits, it would be just the great culmination for me. I have lived through three great periods here—the Rhodes, the War, and Milner. Botha has no courage left.

It was soon after receiving this communication, and when Lutyens was preparing to leave for Rome to set out the foundations of the British School early in October, that the *Times*, on October 3, published an article over Baker's signature discussing the style of architecture to be employed at Delhi. It was an eloquent article, emphasising Britain's gifts of peace and government to India and comparing the architectural opportunity afforded by the founding of the new capital to that of Byzantium. Baker advocated that it was a case neither for imitating Indian styles nor for following classical orthodoxy. The aim rather should be to build according to 'the great elemental qualities and traditions of the Mediterranean lands, which grew out of the needs of a southern climate, grafting thereon structural features of the architecture of India as well as decoration expressing the myths, symbols, and history of its people'. There were, it concluded, 'all the necessary elements, ready to the hand, of the architectural alchemist. But to the artist's creative power must be added sanity of judgment. He must avoid a Whitehall on the one hand and a Palace of Delight which might come perilously near a "White City" on the other.'[1]

The article, which buttressed, as it was intended to do, Lutyens's contention regarding the style to be adopted, yet took him by surprise. He was himself assiduously avoiding any public expression of opinion and did not entirely welcome this sudden antiphon from South Africa. It was one thing to further Baker's claims as an accompanist; another when the accompanist treated himself to a prolonged prelude on the soloist's instrument. He was nervous of what repercussions it would have on sensitive ears in India; and on his own relations with Whitehall and Simla. He had always favoured Baker as likely to be a sympathetic and tractable collaborator, but there is reason to believe that he was also in touch with Reginald Blomfield, of whose part in recommending his appointment to the Commission he was now aware. Many years later Blomfield admitted to Baker that he felt that Lutyens had 'thrown him over' in connection with Delhi. There is no further evidence on this point, but if Lutyens did ever give Blomfield any reason to expect a share of Delhi, it must have been at this period.

He seems to have convinced Ritchie and Holderness that a competition would be a mistake: yet, simultaneously with the publication of Baker's article, he ascertained that Lord Hardinge was proceeding with Lanchester's plans for a competition. The conjunction, it appears, made him decide to get the India Office's agreement at once to Baker being invited to accompany the Commission on their return to Delhi, whilst he kept Blomfield in reserve as a possible alternative. Whatever the precise circumstances, he cabled to Baker at the end of October, and Baker, on the 29th, wired back 'willingly co-operate subject difficulties explained my previous letter'.

The summons, whatever its terms (the text of it is missing) found Baker 'communing with the sad sea waves for inspiration' at Muizenburg. His reply caught Lutyens setting out for Paris to ginger up Aronson, the sculptor of the Johannesburg figures. But he had had time to inform Sir Thomas Holderness of the nature of the reply and wrote to Baker, from the *paquebot*:

> I hope we shall be created partners by force majeur. I looked up your qualifying letter (of April 26). It contained doubts and a scold for me, but nothing that need block our partnership. Lanchester is pushing his competition but his appointment has ended; Hardinge still wants a competition. I seem to have many powerful enemies, but to stand at all I must have more powerful friends.

Baker's confirmatory letter, received in mid-November, reiterated the difficulties that he foresaw to collaboration (he had meant to say 'collaborate' in the

[1] The article is reprinted as an appendix to Sir Herbert Baker's *Architecture and Personalities*, 1944.

cable; had he written 'co-operate'?): he still did not want to be parted from his family nor would he consent 'to be a sort of junior partner to do the *hot* work': he had heard that the Government were nervous of Ned on account of the tenders for the British School having come out at twice the amount of his estimate. Remember, he scolded, you cannot carry off that kind of thing with a Government, as you do with private clients, with a joke! Then, in a sentence revealing his view of the fundamental difference between them, the difference that was to lead to much misunderstanding:

> I shall find it difficult to collaborate with you. You the quicker and I the older. You rather heartless in ignoring the human side of clients, I too tender-hearted perhaps.
>
> But we agree so in principle, and if our spheres could be separate, with general co-operation, I think our work together would be for the good of the job.

He adumbrated, in a diagram, their possible spheres of influence: Lutyens's the Great Place and Government House, his the flanks of the Avenue, both architects meeting at Delhi in winter but carrying on their English and African practices in summer, with 'a supremely good practical general assistant to both of us resident in Delhi permanently'. The audacity of the scheme appealed to him, 'it accords with what I have thought idle dreams and of having some influence, through one's art, over the Empire.' So come he would. He suggested meeting in India, agreeing on their spheres of influences, then, 'You go North, I South, to work out the building of our spheres.'

Meanwhile, in Kashmir, Lord and Lady Hardinge had fallen in love with the gardens of Srinagar, of which Lady Hardinge sent Lutyens a glowing account. Assuring him Lord Crewe's delay in confirming his appointment for Government House was 'not caused by anything said from this part of the world', she added:

> I should love a Moghul garden with terraces to start from the very top of the Ridge and come to the house. We have had *such* a wonderful day and *longed* for you to be with us. Our garden here is quite perfect. I have seen less good but the same style in Persia—water running down the centre with small falls from terrace to terrace, lovely stone work and steps, lots of fountains and of course flowers. I have asked for them all to be carefully photographed for your edification. I can only tell you it was a *dream* of loveliness.

Lady Hardinge went on dutifully to back up His Excellency's decision on the virtues of the Ridge site, and when the sketch designs for Viceroy's House reached them, both wrote to Lutyens warmly approving the internal arrangements, but the Viceroy was guarded about the elevations; some he would like to see modified but postponed comment till they met in December. As late as October 29, he was declaring to Lutyens 'I do not share your doubts about planting the Ridge, as I have absolute confidence in Clutterbuck's opinion'. Within a week, however, His Excellency had entirely revised his opinion again. Swinton received a telegram 'Please ask Lutyens to prepare layout for Raisina'.

Lutyens must have been on the point of sailing for India at the end of November when he received the letter in which Lord Hardinge accounted for this change of site. He had, he wrote on November 6, been for the last two days in Delhi, and, accompanied by Hailey with Messrs. Goument, T. H. Ward, and Gordon of the technical services, had ridden over all the possible sites of Government House. The result was, he now declared, that:

> We were all of us unanimous in considering that Raisina Hill is by far the best site and that it would not be difficult to make a layout with which we should be able to cope satisfactorily. Taking off the top of Raisina Hill, we arrive at the same level as that of the tentative site. There will be a level space of at least five acres, the gardens will be terraced, while the park below will have the advantage of having some of the best soil near Delhi. The house will occupy a commanding position on all sides, while the views from the house will be by far the best that can be found. The cost of preparing the site would, according to the engineer, be practically the same as that of the tentative site. A Sikh tomb, which it is impossible to remove, will be about four or five hundred yards away... Several brick-kiln mounds in the distance could, I am told, be very satisfactorily treated by a landscape gardener. We were all unanimous.

Recalling how he himself had selected the site for Government House, Lord Hardinge afterwards (1916) reminded Hailey how,

> I went with you to examine the site and layout which had been selected. They were unanimously condemned; and on the same day you and I rode to the top of Raisina Hill and decided then that was the site for Government House.[1]

From this it would appear that the choice of the final site was made by laymen—Lord Hardinge and (as he was to become) Lord Hailey—after a somewhat cursory inspection and, although Government engineers present concurred in it, without full consideration of the architectural problems that it might involve. The references in Lord Hardinge's earlier letter to the 'tentative site' are to that at Tal Katora; those to the park and garden, to the area west of Raisina Hill, on which Viceroy's House was actually built.

> As regards the Ridge site [Lord Hardinge continued]... I think it would be a mistake to enter upon a struggle with Nature in which it is quite

[1] H.E. the Viceroy to the President, Imperial Delhi Committee, March 13, 1916.

possible that Nature might triumph in the end if our efforts flagged. Goument, who is an advocate of the Ridge site, is now I think resigned to giving it up.

Malcha, for which Swinton has a predilection, has some of the same difficulties . . . as the Ridge. It is also too far away.

I am off to Rajputana to-day and . . . shall not be back at Delhi until the State Entry on the 23rd of December.

Where do you propose to put your chimneys in your picture of new Government House?

When Lutyens and Brodie, with Evans as assistant to the former, reached Bombay on December 13 (Swinton had preceded them to Delhi by an earlier boat), they found instructions from the Viceroy to set off on a sight-seeing tour of ancient Moslem cities before reporting at the new capital. So it seemed that Lord Hardinge was not only departing from the Planning Commission's recommendation as to site but also preparing to reverse his tentative approval of a basic Western style for the buildings. An excited letter from Swinton ascribed the Viceroy's having 'gone mad on Indo-Saracenic' owing to the Ruling Princes pronouncing strongly for a vernacular style. So the Planners were back, in both senses, almost exactly where they had been in April, and only the Viceroy could make the vital decisions that they urgently needed. Lutyens, in addition, was naturally impatient for his own position to be ratified: he had devoted six months to making elaborate designs on Ritchie's and Hardinge's verbal assurances only, that he would be appointed to carry them on. He was further anxious for the Viceroy to confirm the tentative arrangements made through the India Office, at his own initiative, with Herbert Baker, whose arrival in India he supposed to be imminent. On reaching Delhi on December 20, he was therefore impatient to confer with His Excellency as soon as possible after the Viceregal State Entry to the new capital.

It was devised to be a solemn occasion, to take place on the 23rd, the anniversary of the Durbar. A distinguished company, among them Lutyens, had assembled to receive the King Emperor's representative in the Hall of Audience at the Fort, when there was the sound of a distant explosion. A bomb had been thrown from close range at the Viceroy and Vicereine's State elephant as the procession was passing along the Chandi Chauk. It had exploded in the howdah, the mahout was killed, Lord Hardinge seriously wounded. Lady Hardinge was unhurt.

A few days after the outrage Lady Hardinge asked Lutyens to breakfast at the new temporary Viceregal Lodge, in company with Sir Valentine Chirol, the personal secretary. 'Lady H. is wonderful,' he told his wife in a letter dashed off to catch the mail:

> Left alone on the elephant with one dead and one for all she knew dying man, she never lost her head. I do think she is a wonder. I showed her some

THE DELHI PLANNING COMMISSION

plans and the things I had brought out. She was so natural and simple, and then told me her story of the 'squalid incident'.

Half way down the old main street of Delhi—the people cheering wildly—an unusual thing for Delhi folk—she heard a report, not realising it was a bomb, but felt as though the elephant was wrong or there was an earthquake.

She looked at the Viceroy and saw his coat was torn, and put her hand up to close the tear—to tidy him,—when she realised that a large bit of meat (this is not her language) was sticking out of the Viceroy's uniform. The Viceroy said 'someone has thrown a bomb—go on'. She did not know how to stop the procession, and thought Lord H was probably mortally injured and another shock might hurt him again. She looked round for help and then saw only one man behind them and he was dead; so she said 'we cannot go on with a dead man in the howdah—the procession must stop'. He said 'I suppose it must', stopped it, and fainted. She beckoned Maxwell, the Military Secretary, on the elephant ahead, and does not know how he got down his and up their elephant.

The elephant behaved splendidly though slightly wounded—never ran or showed fear. Jolly beasts elephants, I love 'em. Motor cars were brought and there was much difficulty getting Hardinge off the elephant into a car. They built a scaffolding of packing cases in the crowd and lifted him down. In the car he recovered consciousness sufficient to say 'The procession is to go on and the ceremonies to take place as though nothing had happened'.

Lady H. never lost presence of mind nor did she squeal. She told me she had always been accustomed to assassinations and bombs—in Bucharest, Constantinople and St. Petersburg. When they got home, no one was there, the house empty and indeed scarce finished. Diamond, their little daughter, got beds ready, hot-water bottles etc.

They have not found the man that did it but I gather they know the organisation, and the man. My old Hindu friend, the Theosophist, said he would like to burn the man that did it. I asked if that was good Hindu tradition. The C. in C. was blaspheming helplessly on the top of his elephant, and lor! what a helpless position on top of an elephant is! The people most infuriated were the natives—Pertab Singh and the Indian troops. If they had been lining the route at that point there would have been a massacre in the house from which the bomb came. The howdah which I have seen—in Hailey's tent—is an extraordinary sight, battered to pieces and soaked in blood. And Lady H. was not touched.

I gave my presents, and the jokes had an enormous success with Diamond who immediately gave her Mother the serpent-jump-out-of-cinema-box etc.

I saw Chirol and had a long talk with him. I think things will be all right, but the bomb will delay us. The Viceroy's fixed on an adaptation of the Indian style—but I cant fight him, yet, and it just depends on what he means and what latitude he would allow. Talking to Lady H. it seemed that the suggestion is that I, Baker, and Sir Swinton Jacob—the last a walking dictionary on Indo-Saracenic art—should do the whole caboodle.

§4. THE TORCH OF SANITY

For political reasons the gravity of Lord Hardinge's injuries was minimised, but the attempt on his life was nearly successful. Though his courage and vigorous constitution enabled him to make a rapid recovery, his convalescence held up for two months the decisions regarding New Delhi which he alone could make. In his weakened condition he became a prey of irresolution as to the bearing of the new city on his great objective of engineering the unity of India. The immediate outcome was the renewed importance that he attached to a larger measure of Indian tradition in the public buildings; hence the proposal that Sir Swinton Jacob, as an authority on Indian architecture, should be associated as architect. Almost simultaneously he nearly succumbed to a public agitation in favour of the northern, Ridge, site. The final report of the Planning Commission was not due till March. In the interval, therefore, the whole character of the capital hung in the balance: between a compact 'seat of Government' consisting architecturally in a patchwork of oriental stylistic quotations, and a spacious Western garden-city plan in which the Imperial idea would be embodied by translating classic logic into the Indian medium. In both struggles the influence exerted by Lutyens proved decisive. It was, indeed, the predominance that he acquired during the early months of 1913 which stamped his personality on Delhi.

At one time and another during 1912–14 he was sent to most of the historic cities of North-Western India. To say that the time so employed was wholly wasted would be untrue. After his first and characteristically quick examination of the most notable buildings, he had concluded that Indian architecture was at too elementary a stage of evolution, spiritually and structurally, to be malleable into a work of art such as, virtually alone in his generation, he was equipped to conceive. But even while he was criticising and rejecting forms that he saw to be inapplicable to civilised architecture, he would, as was his habit, be storing in his mind notes of materials, feeling, and relevant features, or blending into his synthesis another Eastern gloss of Western truth.

For his convinced faith in Order as the visual expression of God, and in Structure, Function, and Beauty as the triune attributes of divinity, compelled him to regard the achievements of ancient Indian dynasts as the antics of adolescents: hideous barbarities, yet 'with occasional flukes into great charm such as the Taj'; but, 'as architecture, nil'. Oblique allusions in his letters show, when read consecutively, that he was forced to this sweeping denial by finding Indian building wholly deficient in that intellectual integrity fundamental to his conception of civilised architecture.

He was not concerned with archaeology, ethnology, or other 'literary' aspects of Indian architecture: 'things themselves and their own merits interest me more than how they came about. You will not get a fine art without a great artistic discipline,' and of that he could find no sign. That was the intellectual basis of his classicism. Checking it against Indian history and the evidence of his eyes, he added:

> There are no doubt great thinkers and good men; but what proof can I find that their thoughts are not as unfinished and as slovenly as the work of that other half of India that offends and distresses the eye at every turn, everywhere, wherever I have been in Native States or British territory? There is no trace of any Wren. Is there an Isaac Newton? I doubt it. Without the one you cannot have the other.

A great aesthetic can only be the expression of disciplined moral and intellectual philosophy. That conviction was now fundamental with him, the touchstone whereby to assess not only ancient but contemporary architecture. 'I feel sure,' he continued, 'it is no use blunting one's own sense of righteousness by stooping to the inefficiencies of an atrophied architecture, a long-dead impetus... Why should we throw away the lovely subtlety of a Greek column for uncouth carelessness, unknowing and unseeing?'

It was the incompetence and insensitiveness that repelled him, defects clearly revealed in the abounding ruins:

> There is plenty of veneered joinery, in stone, concrete, and marble on a gigantic scale, but no real architecture and nothing built to last. When in ruins the buildings, especially the Moghul, have none of the dignity a ruin can have that has been the work of any great period... Personally I do not believe there is *any* real Indian architecture or any great tradition. There are just spurts by various mushroom dynasties with as much intellect as there is in any other *art nouveau*. When Italians came out they brought with them their loveliness, but never anything more than two-dimension work, and they imported no architects; only craftsmen, who knew and used the Italian mouldings [here he sketched the *caveto, ovolo, ogee,* and *torus*]. The splendour of size and cost can well become vulgarity as the incentive to any art. Colour they have, as God gave them when earthquakes and convulsions made the stones,—marbles of a most lovely texture brought about by bare hands and feet (a quality our butlers once had in the balls of their thumbs and expended on our spoons). The Moghuls produced this architecture 300 years ago for a period of 150 years; but such a period, 150–200 years, can only produce an *art nouveau*: it affords no space of time for any tradition.

In an earlier letter to Herbert Baker he had explained by *reductio ad absurdum* his structural criticisms of the two chief styles, in the form of recipes:

> *Hindu:* Set square stones and build childwise, but, before you erect, carve every stone differently and independently, with lace patterns and terrifying shapes. On top, over trabeated pendentives, set—an onion.
>
> *Moghul:* Build a vasty mass of rough concrete, elephant-wise, on a very simple rectangular-cum-octagon plan, dome in anyhow, cutting off square. Overlay with a veneer of stone patterns, like laying a vertical tile floor, and get Italians to help you. Inlay jewels and cornelians if you can afford it and rob someone if you can't. Then on the top of the mass put three turnips in concrete and overlay with stone or marble as before. Be very careful not to bond anything in, and don't care a damn if it does all come to pieces.

The Taj Mahal, Fatepur Sikri, and a few of the outstanding Moghul monuments did genuinely move him, but as scenery not as architecture. He described an occasion to Lady Hardinge when he had been at Agra and seen the Taj four times within twenty-four hours under four different conditions, 'by rain, by sun, by moon, and after a hail and thunder storm.'

> Snow, at least hail, lay about and all the ponds and pools and grass spaces were deep in water. The golden leaves blown about, and all clean and sweet made a wonderful picture; the great white clouds reflected in the water made them appear as deep as the sky was high.

But by moonlight—the moment when romantic tourists are most agreeably affected—he noticed that it all became blurred and indefinite, the patterns disappeared and the arch forms merged into a fog of white reflections. To his wife, not to the Vicereine so dutifully loyal to the Moghul tradition, he added, 'it is wonderful, but not architecture, and its beauty begins where architecture ceases to be.'

It was the same with such world-renowned scenes as it had been that day when he withstood the romance of Chipping Campden, writing it off as mad and bad but for the integrity of one small window in a barn. Udaipur left him disappointed; the medieval rock-fortress of Chitorgarh near Ajmere, towering 500 feet above the plain, was to him 'barbaric ruins, a muddle of gods and chivalry. I don't think it is a good thing to see—for an architect: the romance and legends, the ugliness of it, and the courage of its people, the plethora of bestial gods and indiscriminate carving, cannot help to produce any real beauty'. The citadel of Jodhpore, approached by a many-gated and winding road, was exciting and 'some of the old houses in the town were good, the building competent; and there were some good gardens with a great lake in an older city beyond'. But the Hindu temples carved all over with gods attended by dancing ladies offended him by the apparent absence of any sense of proportion or fitness; 'there is never a sense of beauty in a consecutive line, being, or thought.' The heaped riches of treasuries and armouries left him surprised at the large proportion of rubbish, whilst the fantastic montrosity of the decoration and furnishing of the inhabited palaces gave him a perverted delight.

Lord Hardinge had been greatly impressed, on his tour in the autumn of 1912, by the great ruined city of Mandu, remote among the jungles of Holkar but in the sixteenth century the capital of a short-lived Mahommedan dynasty; particularly by the massive simplicity of some of its buildings in the so-called Pathan style. On Sir Valentine Chirol's suggestion, Lutyens visited Mandu on his way up to Delhi in December 1912, and described the place, which he reached after a long motor-drive through wild country, in more detail than usual:

> The ruins of this once great city, set in wonderful scenery and on a wonderful site, has walls four miles long enclosing jungle with a palace or a mosque here and there, with remnants of great tanks. But behind it all the building is childish, and of that quality of art so dear to the literary mind—work done in a hurry by old war-worn conquerors, ruthless and squalid, with no real nicety as the great Westerners felt it. The Durbar Hall, which seems to have particularly impressed the Viceroy, is a great stone building with sloping buttresses and a series of huge stone pointed arches which once carried a flat stone roof now fallen in. When you consider that the roof 25 ft. wide required 36 to 40 ft. of wall-thickness to support it, it becomes ridiculous, and an impossible type to adopt; and when the roof was on it would be quite dark. The other buildings are Moghul—stone treated as timber. A wonderful made picturesqueness but with no intellect. The plans are fine—but quite impractical, except as entertainment rooms for those who wear no clothes, want no furniture, and have no real reason for building except pomp and ceremony, as in, for instance, giant stairways leading to balconies where one man can squat and another precariously stand to wave a flag-fan of peacock plumes.

'To the unseeing and uncritical eye', as Lutyens generalised, these massive ruins might represent a starting point for a new Anglo-Indian architecture, in the same way that it was charmed by the Maharajah of Bikanir's new palace which, from an architectural point of view, 'would disgrace Putney Hill'. To give in to this picturesque, literary, association of ideas and attempt to graft Western requirements on to a rotten stock was unthinkable, if only because—and this was the fundamental difference between the layman's and the architect's view:

> Over all this architecture pervades a childish ignorance which, if it is corrected, so alters the style as to become unrecognizable.

On the other hand, he reassured Lady Emily:

> If they let me have a free hand I can please both myself *and* them and get at something that may prove logical enough to stand for centuries to come. But India has never had any real architecture, and if you may not graft the West out here, she never will have any.

That was his case, which he had to get the Viceroy to endorse—giving him a free hand to infuse something of the mystic and sensuous sap of the East into the virile stock of Western logic—when the assassin's missile forestalled the argument. Surprisingly soon—on January 2, only a week after the attempt on his life—Lord Hardinge interviewed Lutyens, who summed up the whole situation in a remarkable letter to Chirol. The Viceroy, he reported, seemed to be in considerable pain, but they had a long talk on the planning of the new city generally, and then, for a few minutes, touched on the question of the architecture.

> It was difficult to reach a common basis for discussion. I do not think Lord Hardinge yet realises what great architecture might be and should express.
>
> It must be constructive. Architecture will always find her noblest expression in stone. Every different material will influence that expression.
>
> Though Lord Hardinge has great taste and is certainly what one would call artistic, I do not think he realises the use of ornament in relation to construction, where it should begin and end, and what is integral and what applied. He begins with ornament instead of construction—and it waylays me.
>
> In all great styles you will find the constructional purpose is clearly defined. The system adopted is carried throughout the whole fabric, according to the logical demands of the material used. Architecture, more than any other art, represents the intellectual progress of those that are in authority.
>
> You can decorate, and the tendency has ever been, as a style developes, to increase the decoration until it encroaches on and mutilates the initial lines of construction, whereupon the style becomes debased. It has occurred over and over again. You see it here in India,—travesties of wood construction in stone, —and here they have never had the initial advantage of those intellectual giants the Greeks, who handed the torch to the Romans, they to the great Italians and on to the Frenchmen and to Wren, who made it sane for England. A ray too reached India.
>
> I should have liked to have handed on that torch and made it sane for India, and Indian in its character.
>
> To express modern India in stone, to represent her amazing sense of the supernatural, with its complement of profound fatalism and enduring patience, is no easy task.

This cannot be done by the almost sterile stability of the English classical style; nor can it be done by capturing Indian details and inserting their features, like hanging pictures on a wall!

In giving India some new sense of architectural construction, adapted to her crafts, lies the great chance of creating what may become a new and inspiring period in the history of her art.

Lord Hardinge takes my sketch and inserts windows of some particular type. This cannot be done—it is not the window I object to but an insertion which disturbs the adjacent spaces and their proportions and their relation to the whole. The whole must needs be reconsidered and designed anew. It means beginning again, which of course I do not mind, but if Baker is to work with me I should rather wait for his arrival, so as to work together.

By this you will see where I am fearful of a Viceroy's arbitrary insistence on features and insertions. He, as I can well understand, is fearful of my obstinacy. I have no wish to be obstinate, but only to serve the Viceroy, and so India, to the best of my ability.

Intolerance and impatience on Lutyens's part was precisely what the Viceroy and his counsellors had feared, some of them frankly admitted to him. But his patience with 'our lack of elementary knowledge' began to reassure them. His reasoned criticism, in this letter, of the Hindola Mahal at Mandu, probably repeats his bedside discussion with Lord Hardinge, who seems to have thought that its relative simplicity and forcefulness might make of it a pattern for Delhi. Then Lutyens came and pointed out the intrinsic lack of structural fitness—and the absurd disproportion between the gigantic buttresses and the actual purpose they were intended to serve. To the artistic layman the very massiveness of Mandu had appealed for its picturesque strength, till Lutyens pointed out its lack of commonsense.

But his definition of his own aim is as illuminating to us as it must have been reassuring, if obscurely so, to Lord Hardinge: his rejection of the 'sterile stability' of English classicism whilst preserving the sanity of its principles and adapting them to Indian sun and sentiment. In his conception of Viceroy's House, Lutyens did in fact repeat on an immensely bigger and more complex scale the process that we have witnessed at Heathcote: he reduced the classic ordinance to its elements, to reassemble them with complete integrity but with no less originality so as, in this case, to incorporate Indian (in place of Greek, or Roman, or English) sentiment. Or, as he says here, with a 'new sense of architectural construction, adapted to Indian crafts, creating a new and inspiring period in Indian art'.

The Viceroy was for a time reassured that the political synthesis at which British policy aimed in the creation of Delhi would be reflected by Lutyens with an aesthetic synthesis in the architecture. On January 7, 1913, he therefore telegraphed to Lord

Crewe for confirmation of his appointment of Lutyens, in co-operation with Baker and Sir Swinton Jacob,[1] for

> evolving and carrying out a design for Government House and other buildings of importance, while assisting Government in selection of designs for other buildings and acting generally as principal architectural adviser to Government.
>
> I have pointed out to Lutyens the necessity of adapting the designs to meet official requirements, climate, conditions, and Indian sentiment, and Lutyens realises the situation and recognizes that an adaptation of a Western style in above sense is feasible. He is ready to accept the task as defined above with the co-operation of Baker and of Sir Swinton Jacob as adviser on Indian architecture, materials etc.
>
> The combination should, I think, meet all requirements, and if you approve will you kindly approach Baker and Jacob making terms with them and inform me whether you approve.

'Satisfactory,' was Lutyens's comment to his wife, 'and admits the influence of a Western style—i.e. logic, and not the mad riot of the tom-tom.' But he was disquieted by the short-term view taken of the whole Delhi project by many officials, including Lord Hardinge. In the same letter he commented:

> The Viceroy thinks only of what the place will look like in 3 years' time. *300 is what I think of.* I mentioned 10 years in regard to something, and he said it was so far ahead that it was not worth considering! This in building an Imperial City!!

He was constantly shocked, as time went on, by the contrast between his own aim of building for eternity and the tendency of officials to be concerned no longer than with their term of service. It became particularly marked when the war protracted building interminably, and Viceroys came and went handing on questions for their successor to decide. And of course at this stage, early in 1913, Lutyens no more than anybody else could foresee that the project being initiated, great as it was, would drag on till 1930. In moments of depression, as now, amidst the excitement of Nationalist aspirations aroused by the presence of the Islington Commission,[2] Lutyens envisaged the time 'when we shall give up India and leave our people in the lurch, as they have done in South Africa. Government will get into the hands of

---

[1] This distinguished authority on Indian styles, presumably finding no scope for his wide knowledge, and desiring in any case to retire from Indian service, resigned the appointment a few months later.

[2] The Royal Commission on Public Services, under Lord Islington as Chairman, comprised E. S. Montagu, H. A. L. Fisher, and Ramsay Macdonald. The Secretary was Sir Valentine Chirol, whose consequent absences from Delhi seem to have deprived Lutyens of a personality that he had found sympathetic and helpful in making his views known to Lord Hardinge.

THE DELHI PLANNING COMMISSION

talkers, and they will be governed by phrases—as we are in England. No one will be a whit the better, and many worse'.

But with Lord Crewe's reply agreeing with the Viceroy's telegram and thereby at length confirming Lutyens as architect of Government House and principal architectural adviser, the distant clouds dissolved. For the moment the only inconvenience was that Baker had betaken himself to Rome; to investigate the housing of old paintings, he said at the time; to seek inspiration for Imperial architecture, he mentions in his Memoirs. But another sudden storm was to darken the lucid sky.

The New Delhi Commission had been busily engaged since its reassembly with bringing its final report into line with the change of site, setting Government House on Raisina Hill. Suddenly Lord Hardinge sent for Swinton—on January 17—to instruct the Committee to re-consider the Ridge north of the old city. Lutyens was naturally amazed, and Edwin Montagu, to whom he indicated the two sites in detail, took a serious view of Lord Hardinge's repeated *volte faces*.

The cause was a motion in the House of Commons initiated on December 20 by Sir J. D. Rees, Bt., and seconded by Mr. King, drawing the attention of the Secretary of State to a paper read a week previously to the Royal Society of Arts by Sir Bradford Leslie, K.C.I.E., a distinguished engineer. The picture he had drawn of the prevalence of fever in the swampy bed of the Jumna was calculated to alarm official circles. He admitted that the selected site avoided these insanitary areas but criticised it as doing nothing to remove them. From an engineering point of view, the swamps should be converted into a lake by constructing a dam a little south of the Delhi Gate and a site for the new seat of Government be found on the existing Civil Station. This circumscribed area between the Ridge and the river could then be enlarged by reclamation, giving a total area of two square miles and be capable of extension westward beyond the Ridge, if required, in the direction of the foundation stone laid by the King. This area, he maintained should be ample for all present needs. The existing buildings of the temporary capital at Delhi were good and commodious, capable of lasting as long as necessary; therefore the new city need not be built in a hurry and their replacement by permanent buildings could be gradual. On the new site this would be impossible; the new capital must be completed in entirety before occupation.

Leslie went on to suggest that the application of traditional building methods was an anachronism. The Renaissance style, as exemplified in recent Government buildings in Whitehall, no longer represented the structural methods of the present day; instead, he drew attention to the imaginative possibilities of steel structure. To insist on a Renaissance tradition would, in fact, be to cut architecture finally adrift from its real traditional foundation in the builder's—that was to say, the engineer's—art, and in the case of Delhi would be putting new wine into old bottles.

This startling premonition of modern methods of construction had no effect on the designs of Delhi. 'Chirol and Lady Hardinge both speak of a *new style*,' Lutyens had noted before Sir Bradford Leslie had published his views, 'but how?—It will want new blood to make one.' But he had already considered the possibilities of using steel, only to discover that none of suitable quality was available in India, and that its differential expansion under Indian temperatures rendered its use in conjunction with stone impracticable; and in any case, at that date, steel frame architecture had produced in England nothing more revolutionary than the Ritz Hotel.

But questions in the House on the sanitary aspects of the planning problem were calculated to throw Lord Hardinge, with his Civil Service training and in his weakened physical condition, into a fever of uncertainty. These criticisms from London were balm to Calcutta, where the newspapers paused in their attack on New Delhi to feature a campaign in support of the Ridge site, lead apparently by a Mrs. Cotes, a novelist and correspondent of London and Indian newspapers. Lutyens was deputed to beard this formidable lady, who frankly announced her intention of using all her influence with the Calcutta papers to oppose any but the Ridge site. Writing to his wife, Ned sketched the scene:

> I went at 5 o'clock by appointment and found her alone in a clean little bungalow with a post-impressionist picture over the mantlepiece to give that *dernier cri* touch. Tea things spread around and a large brass kettle cyphering—and sufficiently out of reach to give a sense of womanly bustle so flattering to a man in another's house.
>
> Her contention is that a small city to the North—a small ceremonial city with no chance of expansion—could be built, whereas a city to the South would, at the first war, famine, or other national disaster, be dropped. She says that 25 years ahead is all the Government need contemplate; anything further is on the lap of the gods.

1913 plus 25 years = 1938. Mrs. Cotes 'had no arguments or facts to substantiate her surmise'; but her intuition was not far out!

In a letter to Lady Hardinge, written in the train to Bombay on his way to meet Baker, he confessed that he was worried, if only because of 'our original bias and love for the Ridge site'.

> Only the forces of fact—cost and conditions—drove us reluctantly to the South. Architecture has nothing to do with the question; if anything the North site is the more attractive—assuring a compact city wherein every stone would tell, and, being near the river, reflections would make every penny spent look like tuppence.

Nevertheless neither Lutyens nor his colleagues doubted the unsuitability of the Ridge. The extent of ground to be occupied, and to be found only on the chosen site, was given by the size of compounds, and areas of occupation generally, which had been specified by Government and already circulated and approved by every department. He summed up the controversy—to his wife—by remarking:

> If they want a town, rather than a Garden City, I agree to the Ridge, and would be glad. But the conditions governing choice of site remain the same, namely Health. Montagu told me he has impressed on the Viceroy the necessity of providing sufficient space for the moving of all Government departments to Delhi, instead of keeping some at Calcutta, some in Simla. I am glad of this—it is a point I have been trying to push for a long time. I am glad he was here when all this took place; he regards the Viceroy's weakness and vacilation very seriously. However, Hardinge being ill and having us here, it is right to get us to show him what sort of city could be built on the North Ridge. I have been working very hard with Brodie at new lay-outs for a possible town on the northern site.
>
> But if I am in the saddle, and the Viceroy wobbles, changes, and interferes in details—it is hardly worth while giving up the best of one's life to this work. I do wish you were here to help me.

For the moment, however, leaving Swinton and Brodie struggling with the Planning Commission's final report ('Swinton loses sense in his descriptive flow of language, Brodie grammar in his struggle for expression') he felt he was about to gain an ally. He met Herbert Baker at Bombay in Lord Sydenham's launch on February 7, as Baker had met him at Capetown two years before.

The two men had not seen each other since they had separated at Johannesburg, though their correspondence had been continual, at times affectionate, and they had been working in virtual partnership. Was their meeting cordial? Lutyens's only reference to the launch gesture, in a long letter to Lady Emily, was terse: 'so that debt is over. We seem in agreement on all big points, but we shall have to consult the Viceroy about terms. One difficulty I foresee is not money terms but any form of finality in decision as to plans. The Viceroy can't decide, he don't know, and there is no one else in authority.' The implication is that there was an immediate divergence of view on some important matter and that within a few hours the danger became apparent of 'an unresolved duality' arising between two architects of equal authority.

An immediate clue to the subject of this divergence of view is given by Lutyens in a letter home a week later. At first, 'it is great fun and comfort having him,' 'he is so gentle and wise and a good fellow.' But by February 18, doubts were beginning to intrude: 'I don't think he treats architecture as seriously as I do, he makes her the handmaid of sentiment. Of one thing I am certain, a great imperial city must be laid out on lines absolutely sanitary. If for the sake of a picturesque skyline or some scenic advantage the city is misplaced, it will become yet another dead city.'

The fact, which transpired years later but so much perturbed Lutyens at this first meeting, was that Baker arrived with the preconception that the Secretariats must share the elevated site of Government House. From his historic studies of the great cities of antiquity, Baker had convinced himself that the whole official centre of Delhi should be in the nature of an acropolis. He quoted 'a city set on a hill cannot be hid.' Finding that the official site, with Government House on Raisina Hill, precluded this conception, he at first challenged the second Swinton report, just completed, on the unsuitability of the Northern Ridge. During a tour of historic cities on which the architects were despatched early in March after the Viceroy's return from convalescence, his conception of 'the picture on the kopje', as he designated it, was evidently strengthened by the ancient Indian citadels that they visited.

Sir Herbert's vision of an imperial acropolis was impressive. It was historically convincing, and its raising of the buildings destined to contain the actual machinery of government to the same level as that symbolising the Crown was in harmony with the trend of Anglo-Indian politics, with their increasing emphasis on democracy. But, since the Northern Ridge on which he had based it had been finally proved to be impractical, its adoption would involve fundamental alteration of the Commission's plan and a perilous compromise with its cardinal conception—hitherto accepted by the King-Emperor, Viceroy and planning authorities—that the domed elevation of the Viceroy's palace should symbolically dominate the layout of the city and be continually visible throughout the length of its central processional avenue. This conception had been strengthened by the shifting of the site, from that tentatively proposed, to Raisina Hill.

It is clear from long subsequent correspondence between the architects that Lutyens immediately had very serious misgivings of the compromise's implications upon the visibility of Government House from points on the processional avenue; also of the great additional expense that would be involved by the extended area of blasting and making up that would be required for preparing the enlarged level areas of the Viceroy's and Government Courts, and by the difficulty of planning buildings to fit the site and conditions. He pointed out to Baker at the time that these factors would have far-reaching consequences and mean the recasting and recosting of much of the work already done. But he agreed to the proposal. Indeed having laboured and intrigued for his friend's collaboration, he could obviously not reveal himself openly as differing fundamentally from him within a week of his arrival. Possibly at this juncture and certainly later, Brodie, who left soon after Baker's arrival, raised the question of the slope of the processional way blocking the view of Government House at some point, but it appears that both architects assured him that they would not fall into such an error.

The architects therefore addressed a letter to the Viceroy, dated March 8, 1913, in which, though it was signed by both, the proposals and phrasing are most characteristic of Baker. Before the plan of the South site was settled, and even though the Planning Report was already in the press, the signatories hoped that the relationship of the Secretariats to Government House might be reconsidered in connection with the following points:

> We are of opinion that both buildings should be raised upon a common platform, so that the approach to the space between the Secretariats and that in front of Government House should be by a dignified flight of steps, with a sloping road for processions and special occasions. Our reasons are:
>
> 1. The panorama of old cities and buildings, which is a convincing argument in favour of the South site, should be accessible to all.
> 2. The old buildings that have most impressed the imagination of mankind are those raised upon an eminence, such as those of ancient Greek cities and the Capitol at Rome.
> 3. The raised Place, denied to the ordinary traffic of the streets, would have an air of quiet and privilege.
> 4. The lifting up of the buildings on a platform seems to us an important characteristic of those we have seen in India. If we may find it difficult to copy the letter, we can at least follow the spirit of the old buildings of the country.
> 5. The four separate blocks of Secretariats shown in the first plan may not be conducive to efficiency. In the alternative now suggested these are reduced to two, which again could be connected if necessary.
>
> If the raised plan be adopted, it is necessary to move back the Secretariats to Raisina Hill, and Government House about 400 yards behind. Otherwise it would cut the traffic of the city in two.
>
> We consider that the view both from and up to Government House will be better on the raised site. If the two bottom storeys of the Secretariats are partly designed for Records and Archives and so can be placed against the raised Place, and if two storeys suffice for the superstructure, then the portico of Government House will have an advantage, as compared with the original site, of 30 ft. in relation to the road and 20 ft. in relation to the cornice of the Secretariats. The Spectator's view of the Viceroy's House must be made more impressive by the approach to it up the steps and through the piazza with its buildings and monuments, leading to the second flight of steps to the portico.
>
> The making up of the platform to whatever height might be determined (above 15 feet, at which it would closely correspond to the contours) could be done

with rubble, from the numerous old brick fields that would have to be levelled, and from a Durbar Amphitheatre which Baker suggested should be quarried from the Ridge beyond Viceroy's House. The letter concluded with a strong recommendation of this rock-cut amphitheatre which 'would appeal to the imagination, and leave a record of British rule even more permanent than the buildings of the New City'. (The amphitheatre, clearly reminiscent of that at Pretoria below the Union Buildings, was never executed.)

The sketches accompanying the letter have unfortunately disappeared. A letter of Lutyens's of the following day to the Viceroy, accompanying rough sketch elevations of Government House, refers to the dimensions of the building having been reduced after discussion with Mr. Keeling (later Sir Hugh Keeling, Chief Engineer, New Delhi, 1912–25). He pointed out that Lord Hardinge's wish at the same time for a higher dome and a heightened substructure to counteract the raised forum, made this reduction difficult. However, by reducing the relative sizes of the rooms, the cubic contents of Viceroy's House was reduced from 13 to $8\frac{1}{2}$ million cubic feet, including the larger dome. He added:

> I think the dome will look better without a cupola on the top; it will look less ecclesiastical and more in sympathy with the domes of India, and give a paramount position to the flag staff.

—on which the King had been so insistent. As regards the nature of the sculpture, he believed that if the skilled men could be found, 'the carving at the Qtub could form the basis for the capitals, bases, and other enriched work'.

Thus, simultaneously with the setting back of Viceroy's House, its original size had to undergo the first reduction to which it was subjected. By a strange, but fateful, coincidence the design had to be again reduced, at a far more complex stage, a year later at the very time when the actual angle of the gradient to the raised Place was being determined. Certainly at the later, and probably at the earlier, date Lutyens was so deeply engrossed in the process of reduction that the full implications of the contours—coming as they did within his colleague's sphere—were not immediately apparent to him.

Simultaneous with the despatch of these eventful letters, the Viceroy's Council finally decided on the Southern site. 'Any other decision would have been fatal,' Lutyens commented to Lady Emily, adding: 'Extraordinary how one distrusts any opinion but one's own in moments of crisis.' Then they were *en route* for Lucknow, where Lutyens discussed Suffragettes with the Begum of Bhopal.

> She was thickly veiled and I felt that I might have been talking, for all I knew, to Bumps, God bless her! Education is her great idea. But she said that if women in India did what the women of England do, she would stop education.

She wants to build a purdah college at Delhi, near the river so the ladies can learn to swim. I wondered whether crocodiles would interfere with purdah. I also asked her about aeroplanes; we settled that a big hat or umbrella might meet the difficulty.

Sir Louis Dane, Governor of the Punjab, put his camel carriage at their disposal —'a huge sort of charabanc drawn by six huge camels, each mounted by a man in scarlet uniform. It was built for "the Lyttons".' Lady Emily's father, first of the Viceroys, had proclaimed Queen Victoria, Empress of India at Delhi, yet found little but disappointment in Hindustan. His son-in-law, riding in his 'egregious equipage', which he found highly uncomfortable, was now duly commissioned to build his successors' palace, having performed the architect's part in determining the aspect of the city. Lytton and Lutyens, thus linked across the years no less than by marriage, alike found grief as well as establishing glory at Delhi.

In a few days the final Report of the Planning Commission was published, and Baker and Lutyens sailed for home. From Aden Lutyens told Lord Hardinge that he was working on the problem of incorporating the Indian pointed arch—the Viceroy's latest idea for adding oriental flavour—into the architectural synthesis, the successful outcome of which becomes the more astonishing the more the cross-currents at its begetting are considered.

CHAPTER X

THE EVOLUTION OF VICEROY'S HOUSE

§1. AT APPLE TREE YARD

IT WAS the middle of April, 1913, when Lutyens got back to England, after four months' absence. The developments at Delhi during the past weeks would necessitate virtually new plans for Government House being worked out during the next six months. But for the present he was completely held up for lack of definite decisions and, theoretically, by the architects' agreements with the Government being still under consideration between London and Delhi. The enforced delay, which was to last for two months, had the advantage, however, of giving him time to catch up with his work at home.

He was now an Associate of the Royal Academy. He had been elected at the end of February after a close tussle for the honour with the sculptor Havard Thomas, so Aston Webb, now President, mentioned in his letter of congratulation. In the bundle of these notes from old friends and rivals, many of which were addressed to his wife since he was still in India at the time, is one from his Father written on an odd scrap of paper, the only extant communication from the old gentleman to or concerning his son. It made no allusion to his own ancient feud with Burlington House over the Venetian Secret but simply said:

Thursley Feb. 27th

My very dear Emily,

Our fullest congratulations about Ned being A.R.A. We are all so glad of this. It is a wonderful story. Aileen wont write as I am writing
Yours truly
C. L.

Reginald Blomfield expected that he would be 'a valuable accession to our venerable body', whilst other fellow architects considered rather that it was an honour to the Academy to have his association and one that ought to have been conferred years ago; both Guy Dawber, an admirer since their time under Ernest George, and W. A. Forsyth thought so. Evelyn Shaw, his ally in the School at Rome, wondered whether Lutyens would altogether appreciate the honour, which he supposed was well meant, and suspected that the Royal Academy Council 'realise your power and influence, and whatever their feelings about your merits as an artist, would rather have you within the fold than outside'. The older generation un-

76. Perspective Drawing by William Walcot, November 1913, of the Approach to Viceroy's House between the Secretariats, with the Jaipur Column in Government Court

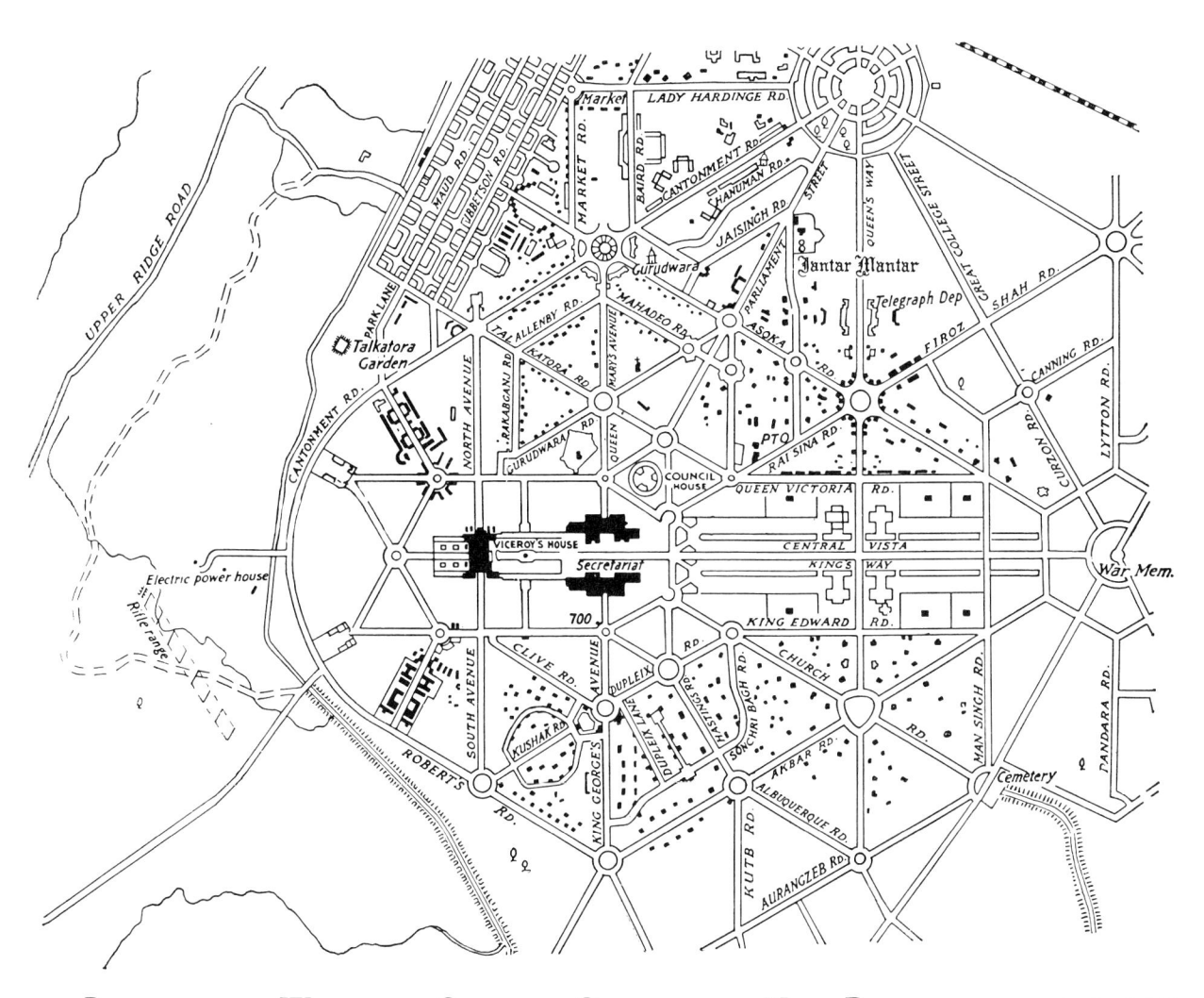

77. Plan of the Western, Official Quarter of New Delhi, as carried out
(North point at the top)

78. EDNASTON MANOR, DERBYSHIRE. (1913). (*a*) The South, (*b*) The East, and (*c*) The Entrance (West) fronts

doubtedly always had been jealous of his phenomenal rise from self-taught obscurity, securing, by means that they did not scruple to question, that spectacular succession of country house commissions, Hampstead, Johannesburg, and now Delhi. Undoubtedly he would have received academic recognition years before, but for professional jealousy. However, in view of his gratuitous work for academic art in the British School at Rome, and his appointment to design what would be the greatest classical building in British architectural history, the Royal Academy could no longer afford to withhold it. And he was pleased.

A lady for whom he was building a London house, and who had better be nameless because she pleased him less, was one of the first to tackle him professionally after his return. Ned groaned:

> She is so difficult, wants impossibilities, and never does a thing I say. She buys rubbish from Italy and wants it fitted in, then expects me to design the noses of putty cherubs in places where cherubs should never go. Makes rooms larger than the site will hold and then wants to pack in essentials anyhow. An awful client, typical of all over-reaching and vulgar minds. So I started in a cross patch mood.

He was on his way to Ireland—Dublin, Howth, and Lambay—by way of Barrow-in-Furness to choose the site of a 'distinguished guests' house' for the Vickers Armstrong Company. The ruins of Furness Abbey lay just below it and, with the great armaments works, which he was shown, raised in him a sudden sickening dread for the future of Delhi, so that he asked himself 'what avail permanent methods of construction against destruction and neglect'? Abbey House, to be a select private hotel with quarters for the Managing Director, Sir James McKechnie, took shape in the red Cumbrian sandstone as a personal rendering of Tudor tradition. To that extent it is related to Castle Drogo, but without romance. Rather grim and impersonal, as efficient as a battleship, the work caught something of the mood in which it was conceived. Yet it is animated by Lutyens's technical subtlety; and a device in its siting—the way he set the house on a slight ridge of contour so that a terrace lies before its front while the ground falls to the sides, enabling the basements to be full lighted—has an affinity to his handling of the same needs on a vastly larger scale in Viceroy's House.

The reconstruction of offices in Nottingham for the Imperial Tobacco Company led at this time to his designing Ednaston Manor, Derbyshire. But here Mr. William G. Player, the Chairman, sought escape from business into peace, and Lutyens gave him, among the level green fields, that 'dear little Queen Anne house' which he had rather have designed than Castle Drogo. Intensely personal—of Lutyens, the simplicity of its plan and of its few lines' arrangement do create the very atmosphere of repose. The three fronts to forecourt, terrace, and walled garden, are closely related yet individual, each varying the simple elements of warm brick, stone pilaster-strips, and strong cornice, bound together by one of his loveliest roofs. Ednaston fully earns Butler's tribute, in *The Architecture*, Vol. I, 'perhaps the most perfect country house that Lutyens designed. An all-round work of art, like a piece of sculpture', with that quality of total harmony found at Heathcote, Middlefield and The Salutation (p. 150).

His designs for the Theosophical Society's Headquarters in Gordon Square date from 1911 but they had been exercising him intermittently ever since. 'A nice letter from Mrs. Besant,' which he had received in February, on the heels of which a congratulatory cable had followed, had approved them finally. Lady Emily's close participation in the movement was chiefly responsible for his being engaged, and now he was occupied with the final preliminaries to building.

Then there was the gradual progress of Castle Drogo's granite walls to be inspected, the big additions to Roehampton, and Great Dixter, where the marriage of a Kentish yeoman's hall with the medieval de Echinghams' manorial hall was now consummated in one of his happiest tile-and-timber operations. The Farrer brothers' The Salutation at Sandwich was nearly finished, but their house in St. James's Square still needed attention. These wealthy bachelors took a lively interest in that part of the Edward VII Memorial—before it shrunk to the King on a horse—which had involved a stone bridge in St. James's Park. Out of their conversations now emerged the arrangement by which Lutyens was to have the upper part of the new mews of 7 St. James's Square for his Delhi Office. He had designed it as the usual quarters for coachman or chauffeur, connected to the back of the big house. But Gaspard and Henry Farrer did not require accomodation for a chauffeur (till 1924), and the accumulating mass of Delhi material was beginning to congest the Queen Anne's Gate office. The two places were within five minutes walk across St. James's Park and there was a delightful incongruity in designing a palace in a coachman's bedroom, the address of which was 7 Apple Tree Yard.

Its rustic name strikes the note of these spring weeks of 1913 which were being devoted to conceptions in refreshing contrast to the monumental embryo in India. It was, too, on a quiet Sunday in June, 'a lovely day, with a big lime tree ranging out overhead,' that Lutyens, staying with the Bensons at Buckhurst, had time to write his first long letter to Baker since they had separated at Port Said. By then they had concerted the main lines and general relationships of their buildings. But the promotion of the Secretariats to Raisina Hill, on the same level as Government House, now necessitated much closer coördination both in plan and elevation than had been contemplated hitherto. Whilst the requirements and general disposition of the Secretariats had reached an advanced stage of agreement, Lutyens's designs of the previous year were in the melting pot again. Not only was the Viceroy still pressing for the general use throughout the official buildings of the segmental arch associated with

THE EVOLUTION OF VICEROY'S HOUSE

Moslem and, he pointed out encouragingly, with Venetian architecture. But he had publicly stated in reply to Lord Curzon's allegations that Delhi would cost £10,000,000 that the expenditure would be limited to £4,000,000, of which the allocation to Government House would come only to £500,000. Lutyens had left rough sketches, reduced from his original larger conception before he left Delhi, for bulk estimates by the Engineers' Department to be made, and obviously, until their figure was known, exact dimensions and proportions, indeed the architectural form, of Government House could not be taken as determined. Further, the setting back of its site from the brow to a point well in rear of Raisina Hill must inevitably involve wholesale adjustments of plan and consequently of elevations. And it was still not impossible that Sir Swinton Jacob might be commissioned to apply Indo-Saracenic façades to Lutyens's plans.

Thus whilst Baker could forge ahead with the Secretariats on the basis of the provisional dimensions and datum lines agreed by the two architects as they crossed the Indian Ocean, Lutyens was left in a state of complete uncertainty. Their correspondence during the summer, apart from the forwarding of duplicates of all advices received from Delhi, consisted largely in allusions to the possibility or impossibility of coördinating the levels and parts of their buildings. Whenever Lutyens adjusted the north-south extent of his front in an endeavour to fit in with the limit of cost, Baker was apt to find that his east-west axes were thereby thrown out of alignment on their corresponding features in Lutyens's façade; or that some important part of the Secretariats was telescoped or had to be eliminated, involving the redrawing of the whole. He began to complain, not unnaturally.

Lutyens was growing no less weary of the continued vacillations of the Viceroy. As a result of conversations with Edwin Montagu, Birrell, A. J. Balfour, McKenna, and other political friends, his attitude was beginning to harden. He felt tempted to stage a show-down between the India Office, which favoured the monumental treatment of Delhi, and the Viceroy on this issue of the pointed versus the semi-circular arch as the basis of the Delhi designs. To his alarm, Baker appeared to be prepared to compromise (as he in fact did) on this, to Lutyens, fundamental matter. A few passages from their correspondence illustrate the situation reached in the late summer and the different attitudes of the two architects.

June 15

My dear Brer Baker,

I dont think you realise what our position is and may be in time to come, when we have to defend work ordered by Hardinge, before the new Viceroy and the India Office. I *must* write you all I know and feel or you could turn on me later and say why did you not tell me! Our difference is a small point *you* say. I think it is one of huge organic value. So do Brer Baker concede your small point and help me to my greater ideal (in my opinion).

Petitioning (August 22) to be godfather to Baker's youngest son, newly born, Lutyens continued:

> I see you still cling to series of steps with a blob on each step. You must not do this. It is banal. On no account have parabolic vaults and domes! It would take us 2000 years to get the drift of it. The Greeks might have done it—but we all [in Western tradition] got switched off to other lines.
>
> Aug. 29th
>
> The letter received from his Excellency is very disappointing. I should like to ask him to what country the Rainbow belongs! One cannot tinker with the round arch. God did not make the Eastern rainbow pointed to show His wide sympathies. Point your round arch ever so little, it ceases to be round and its quality goes. If you once let an error of that sort creep in with folk like Indians you will keep no definite control—and why start errorising?

In South Africa Lutyens had insisted that designs must be meticulous and foolproof because in a new country no tradition of craftsmanship existed to compensate for accuracy. So Western architecture in India, intended to be the pattern for centuries to come, must use only forms of uncompromisable definition. He went on:

> You say that the point is so slight that it does not matter. I maintain that an error of that sort magnifies as the years pass. It is not sane. It is mock artistry. I am glad you have carried on only an innocent flirtation with it, but feel very strongly about it and should like to fight it out with H.E. and with *you*!
>
> I wont let the 733·5 level go down, but if you put in pointed arches, the whole thing had better be put down to 690!!
>
> Talking of sentiment and politics frightens me.

Baker replied on September 26, to some of these points.

> My dear colleague who *can* write so nicely.
>
> I like your being outspoken—when it helps the cause. But don't when fighting an enemy, and when annoyed, turn and rend your friend. I by taking a rather less obdurate attitude, and recognizing the standpoint of sentiment and politics, can help to fight the arch—the devilish ones—best. You must recognize the political standpoint in a political capital, or, if you dont, the reasonableness of politicians, our masters, in doing so. And you get your way best by doing so, and showing that there are more vital things than the mere accidental shape of an arch. Ungeometrical arches and vaults in conjunction do not express a scientific logical government which the Government of India is or should be. That is the line of attack I think. Give them Indian sentiment where it does not conflict with grand principles, as the Government should do.

§2. THE GRAND MERGER

Lutyens's own synthesis of East and West, which had been forming in his mind during the previous twelve months, was now crystallising, in the course of these summer months, notwithstanding the Viceroy's hesitations, the fluidity of the plan, and the delays with the agreement contract. As Robert Byron expressed it[1]: 'whilst official opinion in England and India was demanding a fusion of national *motifs*, Lutyens sought solution on a less superficial basis. Whilst holding fast to the first principles of humanist architecture—line, proportion, mass—he discovered from the Mogul builders how these principles might be adapted to a land whose material conditions necessitate their modification. Colour and form in the Indian landscape are destroyed by the sunlight.' To provide colour, Persian tradition developed tile mosaic and marble facings, to which the Moguls added the use of the rosy, blood-red, and cream sandstones of Dholpur. 'To counteract the loss of solid form was a greater difficulty, which the Hindu architects originally solved by means of intensive ornament arranged so as to form patterns of structural illusion. [We have seen what were Lutyens's reactions to these resorts.] The Mogul builders, on the other hand, chose a more impressionist method, evolving the sweeping, blade-like cornice known as the *chujja* and the miniature roof-pavilion known as the *chattri*, whose statement of shadow, respectively mobile and static, were sufficiently pronounced to resist the refraction of light from the ground. Sir Edwin chose the Mogul method, as the more consonant with the broad lines of humanist architecture and with the genius for balance and proportion that was peculiarly his own.'

The clue to Lutyens's process of synthesis lies perhaps in two sentences, written to his colleague at this time. 'My everlasting prayer is for the greatness and help of a Wren or Newton;' but, he added, he was certain that 'if Wren had built in India, it would have been something so different to anything we know of his that we cannot name it'. Lutyens, knowing by heart Wren's English notation and the Italian prototypes of Sanmichele and Palladio, sought to think intuitively as Wren would have thought under the same fierce sun yet in the light of Newtonian principles of reason and mathematics. He must, during this summer at Apple Tree Yard, have been continually transposing into Wren-Lutyens idiom the practical, climatic, and racial factors involved. How he coördinated the immense and complex plan with the continual demands for economy that alternated with no less insistent demands for majesty will be seen in the last Section of this chapter. But here we may look over his shoulder, as would an assistant at the drawing board, and get a glimpse of the synthesis gradually evolving, through endless variants to finite form, in the elevations.

On paper, Viceroy's House is an immense square, its dimension not yet settled

[1] *Country Life*, June 8, 1931.

but some 200 yards wide and 180 yards deep, covering an area of over 200,000 square feet (Versailles covers 198,300 square feet, the Palace of Westminster 247,200). But much of that area is made up of internal courts, and almost as much again by open galleries or loggias beneath colonnades. These are his restatement in classical language of the familiar Indian compounds and verandahs; spatially, indeed, the conception may be said to be a palatial development of the bungalow, penetrated in every direction by spaces for ventilation and shade. The great lengths of frontage reinforce this analogy for, in spite of their actual height—73 feet on the north and south fronts, 57 on the east and west—they look surprisingly low, an effect increased by the emphasis of their horizontal lines. This is most marked on the east front, which looks towards the long low mass of Indrapat in the distance; for here the reiteration of colonnades, and great expanse of the forecourt, stress the dimension of length (p. 301).

It is least marked on the north (p. 331), partly because the north and south fronts are in fact loftier, since here the walls rise from a lower level, supported on cavernous basements; but chiefly because the north is the only front designed on a nearly continuous plane. The other three consist, in effect, of vast recesses between immensely wide-spaced wings the projection of which (and consequently apparent greater height) helps the illusion of low length in the range between them.

This dominant horizontality was the first characteristic of India that Lutyens determined to incorporate in his synthesis. It was far more pronounced in his Simla conception (of 1912), where Government House lay entirely on the lower level, facing a forum three-quarters of a mile wide with the Private and Military Secretaries' residences set at the ends of immensely long screens connected with the forecourt wings (p. 223). The value he attached to it is suggested in a remarkable way by his having, at a moment of crisis in the process of reducing the costs, envisaged the omission of the chief height-giving feature, the Durbar Hall dome. He wrote to Lady Hardinge 'to tell her the engineers thought the plans could be done if the dome was omitted and the upper part built plastered'. Admittedly he was then quoting a hypothetical idea of the engineers; but on subsequent occasions he confirmed that, if one or other had had to go—the embracing plan with its emphasis on succession and length, or the gleaming, copper-encrusted, dome with what Robert Byron called its 'shout of imperial suggestion'—he envisaged sacrificing the dome.

This becomes more understandable when we watch the synthesis evolving in his treatment of the elevations. Their actual length is not the only Indian element in them; their apparent length is emphasised by his inspired use of the Moslem elements of colour and cast shadow. The two-colour scheme is employed in horizontal bands only. In no case is there a vertical differentiation in colour. The rhubarb pink is used for the basements up to 13 feet on the east and west fronts, 30 feet on the north and south, thereafter in bandings on the cornices and dome. And it is the deep bands of horizontal shadow cast by the *chujjas* that are the most powerful cause of the emphasis of the fronts' length. On the 'low', east and west, fronts it is the main cornice that is developed into the *chujja*. On the 'high' fronts, however, there is an additional *chujja* at main floor level counteracting the greater element of height there.

But this feature, integral as it was to the synthesis, was not, of course, introduced arbitrarily: its functional purpose was to reduce the walls' absorption of heat by shading them from the mid-day sun. This factor of heat-absorption is a crucial one. Among the subsequent criticisms made of Viceroy's House and the Secretariats, one is that, notwithstanding the *chujjas,* their walls store and reflect heat to a disagreeable degree because Dohlpur stone has proved to be particularly absorbent of heat. If this is in truth the case, it was certainly not suspected by the Government geologists who recommended its use. But it gives, in retrospect, enormously added significance to the hitherto unrecognised fact that Lutyens originally conceived Viceroy's House as faced with marble which, of all stones, is the least absorbent of heat. He does not appear to have used that fact as an argument in favour of marble. But there is no doubt that, from his observation of Indian monuments (and for that matter of those of Rome), he instinctively and aesthetically wanted marble and abandoned it only with reluctance,[1] though at an early stage. Had marble facing been used the polychrome effect obtained by the two varieties of Dohlpur stone would presumably have been similar but of how much greater richness—and coolness!

If the horizontal elements in the elevations are predominantly of Eastern origin, the vertical are Western, except in the Ajanta Caves-like arcading of the basements (p.303). Above that level a classical ordonnance of colonnades and round arches, simple yet of utmost sophistication in their relationships, sets up a vertical rhythm beautifully adjusted to the dominant horizontal theme, and introduces a secondary balance between solids and voids. Compared to the late Georgian ratio in England, the proportion of window to wall is small; but not to the Italian. It was in Genoa that Lutyens had first realised 'the small amount of window area required to light a room brilliantly' in Mediterranean latitudes. In India it is yet less, so that the outstanding impression of these elevations is of a superbly disciplined cliff-structure. Butler (*Architecture*, Vol. II) sums up this aspect as 'perhaps the greatest *tour de force* in the whole design', pointing out how, instead of the multitude of confusedly related or reiterated rows of windows such as we might expect in a building containing about 285 rooms of every size and use ... one gets, in fact, an impression of an immense—but not cumbersome—solidity, rich with the light and shadow of colonnades and with a fenestration which breaks the solid masses exactly to the extent, and in the form, that the eye most appreciates'.

[1] 'Montagu deplores the changes of plan, reduction in sizes of the Secretariats, and the abandonment of marble.' (August 14, 1913. To H. Baker.)

But if horizontal Eastern forms and vertical Western forms may, in this much simplified analysis, be indicated as the two main elements of the synthesis, Lutyens welded them together into a new architectural substance 'so different to anything we know of Wren that we cannot name it'. Their complete fusion can perhaps best be described, in terms of modern chemistry, by saying that Lutyens reduced the two styles to terms of their atomic energy to recombine them in a new system of architectural dynamics. Robert Adam sought an analogous dynamic system in architecture and defined it as 'movement, ... that rise and fall, advance and recess of the great parts'. In Viceroy's House there are two balancing and interpenetrating movements. The one is pyramidal: every profile is markedly tapered by means of a rhythmical setting-back and battering of vertical surfaces so that every mass inclines to a pyramidal form.[1] The other is the circular movement set up by the superb uncompromisingly imperial dome. Internally this revolving movement reverberates down every corridor in vaults and domelets. Externally it is echoed in the round arches and in the lesser circular motions transmitted to the apex of each pyramid by the fountain bowls, like shallow inverted domes, which surmount them between little domed *chattris*. The conception of these extraordinary fountains on the roof of Viceroy's House, continually overflowing with water, the wealth of the East, involved an elaborate pumping system and is characteristic of Lutyens in its seeming fantasy. Yet, regarded thus as extensions of the circular rhythm of his dome—their glittering overflow sparkling in the sun like satellites of the shining copper hemisphere—and crowning each tapered vertical mass, they are seen to be as wholly essential to the architectural poetry of his synthesis as the sanity of its classic proportions and the massiveness of its undercrofts.

With this complex and unexplainable vision in his mind, Lutyens must humour the Viceroy's nagging for pointed arches, his colleague's appeals for definition of alignments and levels, and adjust his own intricate calculations to the Delhi engineers' estimates of cost in relation to cubic bulk.

In the last letter that would catch Baker before he sailed from Cape Town, written September 5, 'in the dead of night at Bloomsbury Square', he ranged over all these uncertain factors but showed, in a succession of pen sketches coloured in pink chalk, that by then he had almost finalised his synthesis in the elevations. Baker was upset by some passage in an earlier letter (which has not been preserved) in the triangular arguments over the Viceroy's arches. Ned begged his pardon:

MY DEAR BRER BEAR,
  very
I am *very* sorry, and you should not take my emphasised phraseology
  VERY
literally—so over emphasised I should have thought as to have rendered it

[1] This is emphasised in the sketch, p. 302 (*top right*).

79. VICEROY'S HOUSE, NEW DELHI: THE APPROACH THROUGH VICEROY'S COURT.
From the base of the Jaipur Column

80. THE EAST FRONT FROM OPPOSITE THE SOUTH-EAST WING

81. TWO DETAIL SKETCHES OF VICEROY'S HOUSE. A corner showing the upper and lower chujjas; and the apex of one of the wings with surmounting fountain-bowl. From a letter of Lutyens to Baker, September 5, 1913

82. THE ASCENT TO THE PORTICO, THE KING EMPEROR'S STATUE, AND THE BRONZE HORSES INTENDED TO OCCUPY THE FLANKING PEDESTALS. Drawing by William Walcot

83. VICEROY'S HOUSE. The South Court and the Colonnade of the Lower Basement

84. THE SOUTH COURT AT UPPER BASEMENT LEVEL. Looking east from the entrance of the Viceroy's wing

85. The Secretariats, Inclined Way to Government Court, and Viceroy's House, with the Great Place in the Foreground. Aerial view from the east

harmless. I would be, and am, perfectly loyal to you and fully appreciate you, and your [loyalty] to any sort of third party. I hate to distress you and you should not be. You must not let misunderstandings of this or that sort [distress you]. It is exciting, amusing, to think of your advent home again, and there will be lots of room for you in Apple Tree Yard, my Delhi office address. . .

I have tried to recast my plan, reducing it, and wired you the new measurements to-day. Order of wings is 25 ft. now; I gave you 28. You are 26·6, but I think yours should be a bit higher to counterbalance the fall in ground, so long as the portico tops anything you have in that way [i.e. so long as the portico of Viceroy's House is higher than any corresponding feature of the Secretariats]. My big order is now 32. You remember Hardinge wanted them all levelled up; there will be no great difficulty in getting our bases, as the distance is sufficient —we shall have to work them together here, and that is why an extra week will be good. . .

I got your telegram 122. I have worked at the plans since and can make 115.10½. I can't do more. We shall have to fit in other ways, but how I cannot say without your plans [here he gave a diagram with figures of the bearing of the wings of the east front of Viceroy's House on the porticos of the Secretariats, the dimension 115.10½ being the distance of the axis of the wing from the central of the three arches to the South Court]. Could you widen your buildings apart so that our porch axes come so?

Then follow the diagrams reproduced on p. 302: silhouettes of the north side of Viceroy's House showing the two *chujjas*; and of the apex treatment of a wing, showing a fountain bowl but not its attendant *chattris*, on which Lutyens wrote:

> I am leaving my top knots till I see yours—the *chattris*. I want ½ domes overflowing with water.

To which Baker replied:

> I like your continuous chujja. The line will take mine over my ground floor windows. Yes, top knots—I thought it might be *nots* with you till we meet.
>
> There is a good deal in your suggestion to widen my buildings so that my pavilions (is there a better word?) axis your wings. It would widen the view from your Portico which has been narrowing to my regret. I will work it and see. Extra cost of Plateau will be objected to? but there will be less rock to blast; 200 yards for the plateau? We could get bigger, but not very big, trees then, and a shady walk across from block to block, instead of about 120 yds, which is better?
>
> I am working on the great steps—I like the line we settled on but regret no

wider bigger massed steps. They would come very well in themselves, axial with either block; but would this not lead away from the centre—the sun of the

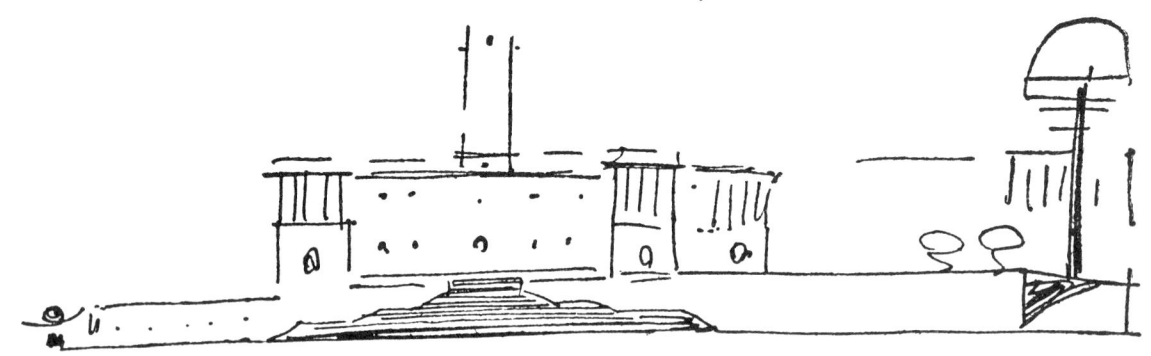

lord sahib's dome? It looks well centrifugally but I want something more centripetal, and the wider plateau may help this. But we dont want 'mosque steps' here like the Jami Masjid for the swarming millions to sit on—do we?

But if we do, they should be where they could see the procession up the sloping '*via sacra*'. Think this over will you and I will work out plans on board. Keep Walcot free for me—I should have a few perspectives and have no time here.

§3. AGREEMENT AND PERSPECTIVES

An attack of eczema and sudden access of business in South Africa delayed Baker's sailing so that he did not get to London till November 4, and they were to leave for India on the 13th. During that week the terms of their joint Agreement with the Government of India, which had been under discussion and amendment since March, had to be finally approved and signed; and the relationship of their designs to be completed sufficiently for William Walcot to make three perspective drawings which they could take out with them to show the Viceroy and Council. Much subsequently hinged on these drawings, which were exhibited at the Royal Academy in 1914; and one of the clauses in the Agreement produced the first open spark of friction between the colleagues.

The two letters just quoted show them co-operating happily on the problem to which no satisfactory solution was found: how to carry the '*via sacra*' to the higher level of the forum consistently with preserving the view of 'the lord sahib's dome' and portico and at the same time affording level and shaded communication between the two blocks of Secretariats. But it is important to note that at this stage there was no difference between them as to how it should be effected in principle.

On this basis, Baker roughed out perspective sketches during his voyage, which Walcot drew out and coloured at Apple Tree Yard. The one on which later discussions turned was a panorama of Government House appearing between the Secretariats, taken from a point in the centre of the Great Court at the foot of Raisina Hill. In this the approach ascends by a gradient at the top of which, known as Point *A*, is shown a column. It was later criticised that the picture showed much more of the frontage of Government House than appeared in the drawing made during the summer by the resident architect in Delhi from the sketches left by the architects on their departure in the spring of 1913; and, of course, very much more than can in fact be seen from that particular stance, where the gradient of the approach cuts off all but the dome of Viceroy's House. But the importance which the drawing with its artistic licence afterwards came to have, lay in the fact that Walcot had prepared it from Baker's sketches, so that Lutyens naturally assumed that it represented picturesquely the view of Viceroy's House which Baker, no less than he, intended should be seen.

It is, however, a question whether a solution of the problem of ascending an acropolis by a practicable gradient without losing sight at some point of its crowning monument, and without bisecting the area through which the gradient rises, is practically or aesthetically feasible within the framework imposed by classical planning with its emphasis on axis and symmetry. It is a question whether the full implications of lifting the Secretariats to Raisina Hill and the setting back of Government House some 400 yards in their rear were sufficiently explored before the decision was taken—somewhat hastily on the eve of publication of the Planning Commission's final report and the architects' departure.

It is curious that the same difficulty, that of fitting a symmetrical pattern to an irregular geographical conformation, introduced discord into the final discussions on the architects' Agreement. The Agreement with the Government of India provided for their joint responsibility for the work entrusted to them and for payments to be made to them jointly. The division of work between them would be a matter for their private arrangement—as was also to be the division of these payments. Before we note the method of division arrived at, the main points of their official contract, dated November 11, 1910, must be stated.

It provided that the Architects shall, (1) in consultation with Sir Swinton Jacob (as adviser on Indian architecture and materials) act as advisers to the Government of

India in all architectural matters connected with the New City, and as assessors in any competition therefor; (2) be responsible to, and receive their instructions from, the Special Committee appointed to deal with the New City; (3) prepare all necessary drawings, but (4) the Chief Engineer to be responsible for all engineering drawings. (5) The architects shall design the internal decoration and furnishings of the public rooms. (6) The Government shall establish on the work a studio of Indian arts and crafts for which the architects and Sir Swinton Jacob shall be advisers. (7) Any assistants employed by the architects shall be paid by them. (8) The architects shall visit Delhi once a year for as many years as the Committee shall require. (9) Remuneration: five per cent on the actual cost of the completed work; $1\frac{1}{4}\%$ of that amount on receipt of sketch designs, calculated on the Engineer's estimated cost, and $1\frac{3}{4}\%$ on the receipt of 'general drawings, plans, and elevations', similarly calculated in relation to the progress of ascertained expenditure. In addition, £1000 per annum honorarium for acting as general advisers as under para. 1. (10) Fee as assessors: 30 guineas, plus $\frac{1}{5}\%$ of estimated cost of the design. (11) Travelling expenses: first class steamship fares, double first class railway fares in India, a daily subsistence allowance of 30s. and a daily fee of 5 guineas while absent from home. It should be noted that Baker's early suggestion for a joint chief assistant to both architects, who would have coördinated their work and represented both in their absence, was, perhaps unfortunately, not adopted.

The Architects' mutual agreement rehearsed these heads, specifying Baker's primary responsibility for the Secretariats, Lutyens's for Government House, its gardens, and staff quarters. Any other buildings should be allotted by mutual agreement. Either party was entitled to offer advice or suggestions to the other on drawings prior to their submission to the Delhi Committee, and none should be so submitted without the other party having had reasonable time in which to communicate his views, or without, in that event, saying so. In event of disagreement the decision of the Delhi Committee should be final.

All receipts were to be paid into a joint account, to be known as 'the Pool Account', for which duplicate books should be kept in London and South Africa. From it should be debited all office expenses and 5 guineas a day when either party was absent from his headquarters 'with the consent of the other'; this to allow of a fortnight's annual visit to England on Baker's part. In view of higher overhead costs in South Africa, however, it became clear that Baker would need to draw on the Pool for expenses more heavily than Lutyens, and it was in arriving at an equitable proportion that relations became strained. Baker, in a memorandum on his relations with Lutyens (dated March, 1921) claimed that 'most difficulties in our Agreement were overcome by our agreeing, mainly on my insistence, to the principles of equal pooling of all expenses and profits—in spite of the fact that a larger share of the work thus fell on me—and of mutual trust. Lutyens, however, wishing for protection against my heavier expenses in South Africa, and my admitted policy of generosity, suggested a clause which would have tied me hand and foot to him financially. I held out that equality and trust all round was the only policy'. Lutyens agreed to this principle verbally but, according to Baker, who had gone to his home at Cobham for two days before sailing, sent a telegram 'going back on his promise' when it was too late to settle the clause before they set out for India.

The clause referred to is not available, and in any case there would be no good purpose served by disinterring this unhappy dispute were it not for the part it played in the gradual deterioration of the colleagues' relations, the light, admittedly uncertain, that it sheds on Lutyens's somewhat exacting requirements when dealing with financial matters affecting the interests of his family, and a characteristically 'naughty' letter, written from the boat *en route* for Port Said, in which he succeeded in settling the question.

The atmosphere as their two parties saw the architects off at Victoria was strained. Lutyens perceived that 'Baker is better but awfully hurt and bruised. We have not mentioned the subject, but he said something about happy days being over —which is absurd since it is only a money question and a lawyer's safeguard in the interests of my family. He is very rude and uncouth when cross—a pity, and we have so much to do together'. Writing next day to his wife, Lutyens explained his attitude. 'Baker's sulkiness has stiffened me and I feel I cannot sign for life and death any kind of clause without limit. I vowed I would endow you with all my worldly goods. The man what makes and earns must trusteewise control and cannot surrender discretion.' The fact seems to have been that Lutyens, whilst agreeing in conversation with Baker's principles of 'mutual trust', had it born in upon him by his advisers that some limit must be set to the other's indefinite claim for a higher ratio of expenses, if only in fairness to Lutyens's estate. Hence the telegram which so much upset Brer Baker. Three days later tempers had so far cooled that they could discuss the difficulty rationally. Brer Ned could report that Brer Bear 'is now digesting my proposal which I have written out in beautiful "whereas-to-before-why-not" language'. This document is forthcoming, together with a series of less legal but more wholly intelligible sets of specimen figures embodying his proposal. In the former, the fountain of Lutyens's humour plays merrily in a situation as unexpected as those other fountains that he had devised for the roof of Viceroy's House. Irrelevant as both might be thought, we see how courageously in each case he employed the unexpected to crystallise his design, suddenly turning on his power of outrageous wit to relieve a tension. The communication to his solicitor, which he gave the aggrieved Baker to approve, runs:

Whereas-tobefore-as-hereafter-why-not, I take up my pen and write. This is the agreement Baker and I are now in agreement upon as hereinafter stated—why not. Baker would not speak for days and then yesterday, the hereto-before 17th inst, the subject was opened and having exhausted it I asked if there was no alternative. He said No—so it was up to me to make a proposal —beginning the other way round i.e. I Ned or I E.L.L.

This plan was to assure either party a definite proportion of his due fees earned (oh these dreary fees!) and put a bar on possible encroachments heretobefore or behind, for of His own share a man can spend as he likes.

And that whereas and before or behind why not, it is difficult to assess fairly a limit or ratio of expenses on either or both parties hereto as before as above; and as it is no business justice to either party that by mistakes or error under or on either party those best years of his life be lost, and no increment accrue to one or other by those unforeseen circumcisions for ever greater in number and in ever increasing ratio to those foreseen—and in case of death or other like calamity to both or either one of two—of the heretobefores—why not:

So
(that we may reap)

he appended hypothetical examples. In these he proposed their pooling the two commissions. He would be allowed to spend 40% and Baker 60% of half this pool by way of expenses, dividing equally whatever balance there was. In other words, taking their total joint commission on Government House and the Secretariat buildings at £50,000, one half of it, i.e. £25,000 would be reserved for expenses, 60% of which or £15,000 Baker could spend for expenses, and 40% or £10,000 Lutyens could so spend. The other half, i.e. £25,000 plus any saving on expenses by either below the agreed ratios, would be equally divisable. In any event, half the total fees were reserved as profit. But any extra expense above 60% or 40% of half of the pool would have to be paid by whoever incurred it. Thus the portion of the pool put aside for expenses was limited, and it was in the interests of both to keep working-costs down. In its revised form the Agreement was signed by both parties on December 23, in Delhi. Baker 'agreed under protest in principle, thinking that in practice this was an extravagant estimate of any possible expenses'—and that therefore he would receive only half instead of the whole of the surplus. He did not foresee, as Lutyens had, that conditions in India were so different from those at Pretoria and that the expenses would be much in excess. Nor could he foresee that the delay due to war would inevitably throw the ratio of expenses into the 'proscribed area'. 'Nor, in addition,' Baker continued, was it foreseen 'that I would be given the Legislative Chamber—a circular building on which the expenses were altogether out of proportion to the counterbalancing work given to Lutyens in the War Memorial Arch and other Government houses—square buildings entailing repeating façades and little more'.[1]

[1] Memorandum of March 1921.

So on November 29, they arrived at Bombay friendly again. But it was not only tempers that had been frayed and battered. At Government House Lady Willingdon told Ned he must buy a new hat, 'She abused my old topee, also my dress clothes, because they are gone in the lapels'. It was his first encounter with that determined lady.

§4. ESTIMATES

December to March, 1913–14 were the decisive months in the shaping of New Delhi. Lutyens brought out with him complete small-scale plans for Viceroy's House and the designs evolved during the summer embodying his notable synthesis of Eastern and Western architecture. Baker brought similar plans for the Secretariats; and Walcot's perspectives gave an impression of how the great sweep of buildings would be related in appearance. The Government of India was anxious to begin preparations of the site, but the recent pronouncement of the Viceroy that the total cost should not exceed £4,000,000 made it certain that there would have to be further modifications of all the plans, both of the general layout and of individual buildings, before any works could be put in hand. For the greater part of the time, therefore, Lutyens was plunged in the agonising occupation of recasting Viceroy's House to accord with Lord Hardinge's demands on the one hand for a slashing of costs but for retaining ceremonial grandeur on the other, whilst he strained to maintain the proportions imposed on the building by its relation to the Secretariats no less than by its site and importance in connection with the city as a whole, and by his own monumental conception. The decisions to resite the building and at the same time reduce its cost were in fact mutually contradictory; indeed it had made the whole Government centre more costly by the immense retaining walls necessitated for the forecourts as well as for the basements at the sides of Government House. But having made his political and financial decisions, Lord Hardinge was inflexible. Since Lutyens lacked Baker's elasticity of architectural conscience and was committed to a design embodying such grand yet intricate relationships, an atmosphere of tension, with a certain guardedness in the mutual relations of architect and Viceroy, is therefore perceptible from the outset of this third visit. Lutyens complained that the Viceroy dragged political red herrings across the plans, Lord Hardinge that Lutyens's intransigence robbed him of any pleasure in his cherished project.

Among the Commission's proposals abandoned at this time was the diversion of the railway to form a new Central Station between the Old and New Cities, which was integral to the first layout scheme of the city, and with which Lutyens was concerned; and of Baker's proposal for a Durbar Amphitheatre on the Ridge westwards of the Viceregal domain. A weighty argument in favour of the latter was that its excavation would have produced the great quantities of quartzite stone required for road metal; after its abandonment the 500-year-old quarries lying between the two cities had to be enormously enlarged, thereby destroying land which has been sorely needed for extensions of Delhi. Equally the Amphitheatre would have supplied the want which was later met by the construction of the Willingdon Stadium on the avenue towards Purana Kila behind the Memorial Arch, blocking the vista from Government House—a view that was one of the chief reasons for the selection of its site.

Greatly to Lutyens's relief, however, the Viceroy expressed general approval of the architectural scheme for the acropolis group as a whole. No more is heard of Moslem-Venetian arches. Baker relates[1] that, 'We went out to the Kutab with Lord Hardinge and explained the structural origin of the early examples of these four-centred arches: and compared them with the two-centred voussoir arches of Pathan tombs. He understood, and very generously waived his opinion. Sir Lionel Earle in his Reminiscences records a legend that the Viceroy was converted by Lutyens's quip "Who designed the rainbow?"'—which, as we have seen, was an argument for the Roman arch which Lutyens had had up his sleeve since the summer. But Sir Herbert believed that he was moved by his own 'more relevant argument' on the origin of the horse-shoe arch—given in his Memoirs.

So Lutyens's synthesis of East and West was acceptable, though he did not report specific enthusiasm for it, whereas Lord Hardinge apparently praised 'the elephants on Baker's domes (I think them awful!)'. The plans of Government House, with their extraordinarily ingenious provision for the simultaneous reception of numerous guests, satisfied their Excellencies and the Military Secretary, but Lutyens realised, before submitting them to the Engineers' Department for estimating, that, under the Viceroy's new regime, 'he will not be able to do them for the money'. It is evident from Sir Herbert Baker's account of this phase,[2] that the Viceroy's apparent vacillations on the question of the relative size of Government House were in part due to his estimates of the political expediency of giving dominance to the Viceroy's residence or to the administrative buildings. There is no inkling in Lutyens's letters that he was conscious specifically of this or similar considerations. The artist's problem was sufficiently engrossing, and he merely noted that:

> When the Viceroy comes in, all kinds of difficulties crop up. It is so difficult to design even a coal scuttle well; but if they brought in politics and diplomacy, then it is impossible.

Thus, although in the previous March, Lord Hardinge had thought the dome on Viceroy's House should be taller and Lutyens had accordingly raised the height, now he 'wants to cut down my dome'. On this he remarked, unexpectedly (though it confirms the view expressed in § 2):

[1] *Architecture and Personalities*, p. 72.   [2] *Ibid.*, p. 66, *et seq.*

86. VICEROY'S HOUSE. The North Court, looking east

87. VICEROY'S HOUSE. The Open Staircase Court, looking north-west

88. THE INCLINED WAY TO GOVERNMENT COURT BETWEEN THE SECRETARIATS. Showing its effect upon the visibility of Viceroy's House from the Great Court

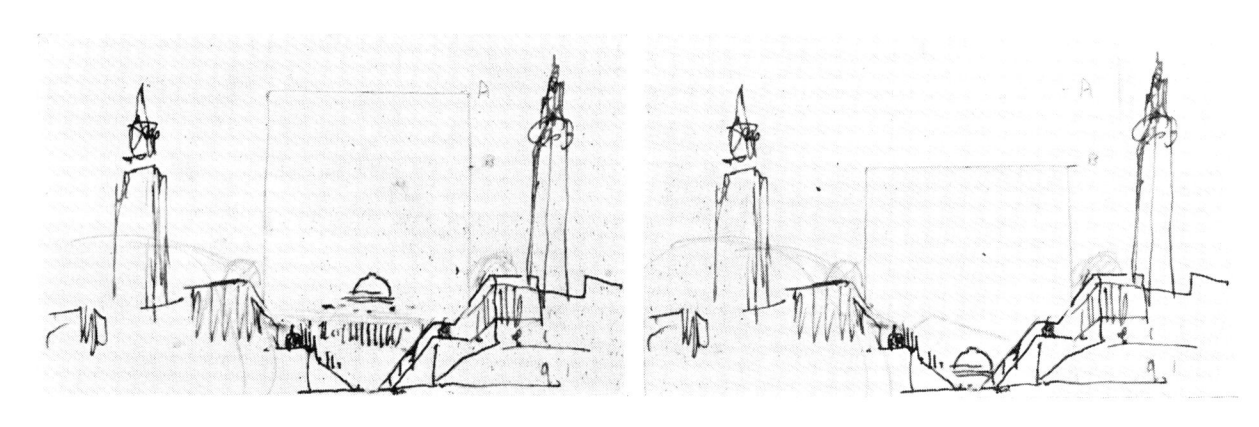

89. MOVABLE SKETCH DIAGRAM DEMONSTRATING THE ABOVE ASPECT. Prepared by Lutyens for Lord Hardinge, March 10, 1916. Shown in two positions

90. THE SCREEN TO VICEROY'S COURT. Showing relationship of the design of its wrought ironwork to the dome of Viceroy's House and the Jaipur Column. (Photo A. T. Scott)

as it is. H.E. flew a small balloon 300 ft. up in the air to see how high it would look. My dome is only 180 or so. So he said it was too high. It is all very mad.
>
> I do not mind that, but he does not realise mine is 10 ft. lower than Baker's

We will now suppose that we are suspended from that small balloon above the site of Viceroy's House, armed with Lutyens's plans of the building as eventually completed. Those that Lord Hardinge and the Engineers are examining differ from them in some important respects but are not available for comparison. We cannot therefore follow the amazing process of reduction in detail—in any case too intricate and technical an operation to be traced in this book. But the nature of the plans' alterations will emerge in the course of the narrative if we first grasp the main facts of the tremendous and complex yet superbly lucid conception. The plan is analysed in detail in Volume II of *The Architecture*, and this simplified outline should be read in connection with the impression of the elevations already given in § 2 of this chapter.

On that December day of 1913, we can see Indrapat beside the Jumna to the East, the Jama Masjid and Fort of Shah Jahan's Delhi three miles away to the northeast. To the west rises the plateau of the Ridge. Immediately below us is Raisina Hill, a rocky elongated knoll rising to some 40 feet above the plain, joined by a neck to the slope of the Ridge westwards. The summit of this hill is to be blasted off to form the level area of Government and Viceroy's Courts, the former of which will be flanked by the Secretariats along its north and south sides. Below the east end of the hill is to be the Great Place, the centre axis of which will be the principal avenue of the city, the King's Way 800 feet wide, stretching eastwards for two miles in the direction of Indrapat (pp. 304 and 502).

The site of Viceroy's House straddles the neck at the west end of the hill from north to south, so that, whilst its central mass will rest on the saddle, its sides will stand on the lower level of the plain. From the outset, therefore, Lutyens could conceive the building as having two ground levels: the lowest, the Lower Basement, being directly accessible from north and south on the general level of the city, would readily contain the multifarious service departments; the Upper Basement, continuous with Viceroy's Court and Garden, be available for the official and ceremonial access channels to the upper part of the building (p. 303). On the Upper Basement level, therefore, two large courts occupy much of the plan, connected by archways with Viceroy's Court in the front and with each other by twin carriageways tunnelling under the central mass of the main building between them. The South Court is in the nature of a deep, open, terrace over the Basement entries; the North Court is entirely enclosed (pp. 303 and 313).

This substructure supports the main floor on which the State Apartments are grouped round the circular Durbar Hall under the dome. Important persons approach it by the portico above the steps sweeping up from Viceroy's Court (p. 301).

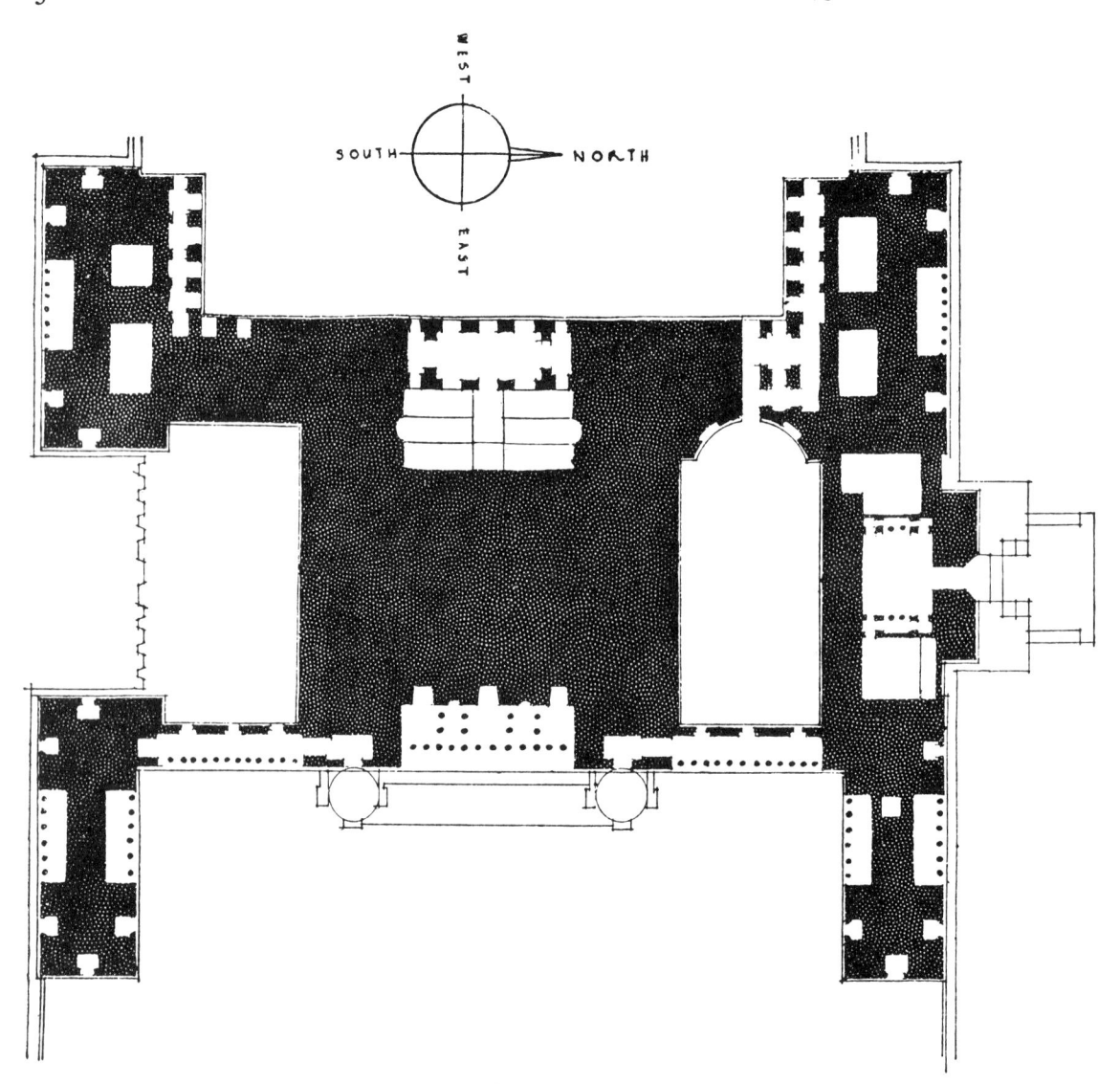

BLOCK PLAN OF VICEROY'S HOUSE AT UPPER BASEMENT LEVEL

But on its other three sides the Durbar Hall is also flanked by staircases from Upper Basement level, whilst a fourth, the Viceroy's Staircase, adjoins it on the south-west. Those on the south and north are respectively for the reception and departure on ceremonial occasions of guests not entitled to use the portico. The Western Staircase, a double flight, is contained in a court open to the sky; it is separated from the Durbar Hall by the State Drawing-room and from the West front by the loggia which occupies the centre of that front overlooking the garden (p. 313). The length of the West front itself between its wings contains the State Drawing-room and State Ballroom at either end of this loggia.

Of the wings, the south-western is the Viceroy's Residence, linked with the viceregal staircase already mentioned; the south-eastern contains suites for guests; and each is planned round two small internal courts. The early suggestion that one of these wings should contain a suite permanently reserved for the King and Queen has been abandoned. Thus the whole west front on the garden is devoted to the Viceroy's private and semi-State use. The south-east wing houses the Military Secretary and Comptroller, the north-east the Secretarial Offices, these wings being linked with the central block by corridors at Upper Basement level and on the Main Floor by the colonnades that overlook Viceroy's Court.

But whereas the two southward wings are separated by the extent of the South Court, those to the north are joined into a continuous façade (p. 331), the centre of which projects somewhat and is approached by a broad flight of steps. The entry at their head, at Upper Basement level might be regarded as the Business Entrance since it is the approach for those having business with H.E. or his staff, and adjoining it are the offices of the Viceroy's Press; over them, and filling the middle of the projecting centre, are three private courts into which look the Viceroy's Office—a kind of Cabinet Room—and that of the Viceroy's Secretary, linked with the Secretarial Offices in the north-east wing. But all this northern section of the house, devoted thus to administration, was entirely replanned in its present form in 1920–21, when it was decided that the Legislative Chamber should not be included in Viceroy's House.

In the earlier designs, including those that Lutyens made in London during the summer of 1913, the Legislative Chamber was an integral part of Viceroy's House. It took the form of a semi-circular hall the bow of which projected from the middle of the north front, its chord forming one side of the North Court. The existing Council House containing the Legislative Chambers was erected from Baker's plans to the north of the acropolis where the vista from the Jama Masjid subtends on the North Secretariat building.

In broad outline that is the disposition eventually adopted for Viceroy's House. The rectangle contained by its extreme points covers four and a half acres. But the gigantic bays formed, in effect, on three of the fronts result in the Lower Basement actually covering less than two-thirds of that area. At Upper Basement level the North and South Courts and other internal courts reduce the proportion to less than half; whilst the numerous loggias further diminish the cubic contents.

Its intricately knit character, its integrity of elevations and plan, its fusion of dramatic and utilitarian, which are brought out clearly by the analysis in *The Architecture*, set Viceroy's House among the classics of classical architecture. When we consider, too, how the elaborate functions of the plan at the various levels had to interlock with the complex aesthetic factors of the external and internal elevations, in which ratios of proportion and form no less subtle were involved, our balloon's eye view will have afforded some idea of how these virtues rendered modification or material reduction of the conception a work of extreme complexity.

This was made clear by Lutyens in a communication to the Secretary of the Delhi Committee, dated December 13, 1913, which also illustrates the kind of difficulties which he was up against. He pointed out that the arrangement of the Main Floor requested by the Viceroy for ceremonial, legislative, and private uses, alone expended more than the 8,000,000 cubic feet which had been suggested by the Committee during the summer as the total cube of the building, and at the same time necessitated a formidable excess of cubic content in the supporting basements. Contraction to any great extent, moreover, would throw the building out of scale with the approaches and with the city as a whole. The following figures, he reported, had been worked out in London:

General Cube, comprising H.E.'s Residence, Durbar Hall and surrounding rooms, Legislative Block, State Rooms, Guests Rooms and A.D.C.'s wing	8,838,503 cubic ft.
Verandahs to H.E.'s Residence, rooms and corridors over	244,751 ,,
Towers and turrets	173,519 ,,
Dome	383,046 ,,
Secretariat Offices and Flats	1,391,565 ,,
Basement, including Kitchens etc.	1,517,935 ,,
Basement under Central Block	588,220 ,,
Basement under remainder of building	2,412,590 ,,

Excluding the General Cube, the total excess amounted to 6,711,686 cubic feet; and the estimated cost for the structure alone to £536,038. The Chief Engineer had pointed out to him, he said, that the Committee had expected much more of the accommodation to be included in the 8,000,000 cubic feet than he had found feasible; and he explained the somewhat elementary fact, which the Government appeared to ignore, that:

> It is the general disposition and arrangement of the Main Floor as desired by the Viceroy that determines the size of the basements under it. Since the

original sketches were made at the beginning of this year, and which were cubed at 8,488,832 c.f., various alterations have been commanded: the dome was lowered; some 13 bedrooms and bathrooms, a billiard room, 4 great loggias, the Viceroy's Secretariat and printing press were added, and the whole of the building raised 8·5 feet.

He had therefore brought into Government House a large amount of accommodation from the indefinite category of 'staff quarters', provisionally termed Schedule B, 'so as to make full use of the great basements and to keep the plan symmetrical without sacrifice. These insertions comprised the offices of the Military Secretary and the Superintendent of the Viceregal Estates, flats for the Military Secretary, Chef, Comptroller's Assistant, Viceroy's shorthand-writer, and others; the stores for furniture and camp equipment. (The positions of some of these have been indicated; the remainder are referred to in *The Architecture*, Vol. II.) He had, on instructions, excluded the making up of the levels of Viceroy's Court and the Garden, and the filling up beneath the S.W. and N.W. wings, which would make a yet larger increase if added to the cube of the building. Moreover, to make the basement practical, four ventilation and light wells had had to be inserted which increased the superficial area of the basement, 'though to minimise it I reduced the Durbar Hall by 4 ft. in diameter and omitted four octagon halls flanking the Main Entrance'. He had also assumed that water supply, sanitary fittings, heating, refrigeration, and lighting etc. could be provided at a rate which would be covered by £77,592; and that the foundations and buildings up to the level of Viceroy's Court would not be included in the £500,000. This assumption, though bold, was reasonable since the work involved resulted from the Government's resiting of the house, so, he maintained, should not be included in the cost of Government House. But he warned the Committee, even so, that:

> The Chief Engineer's estimate prepared from my drawings shows that the accommodation asked for, and the limit of cost, are incompatible with reference to the general layout of the New City—

i.e. the extent and size required for Viceroy's House in relation to the layout of the city centre, and the accommodation specified by the Viceroy, could not be obtained for £500,000.

To meet this excess he suggested that either the greater cost must be faced; or the rate reduced 'so as to leave the inside of Government House as a carcase, which, if well built, might be mighty fine in effect'; or the size of the building be reduced. 'It would be possible to reduce the scale by a ratio, without altering the arrangement of the plan, which would bring it nearer to or within the prescribed cost;' but 'a reduction of the scale would affect the planning of the Forum and also the scale of the

Secretariat buildings which are at present designed in due relation to Government House'.

Between mid-December and mid-January Lutyens succeeded in virtually recasting Viceroy's House. On the 21st he wrote home that he had been too busy to keep up a daily record, being at work 'on what are practically new plans'. In his view, Lord Hardinge would 'make any sacrifice to keep the cost down so that he can stick to his guess estimate'. He almost despaired of reintegrating the vast and complex conception so as not only to accord with departmental and ceremonial requirements, and with the financial limitation, but also to preserve the coherence of the architectural symphony which, as yet, he alone was in the position to visualise. Yet, incredibly, he succeeded. It is, however, worth recording his resentment of one detail of the reduced plan thus forced upon him, because it was often adduced subsequently as a criticism of his planning in general: namely the distance at which he had now to set the Vicereine's sitting-room from her bedroom. In 1916, long before the walls had risen but when controversy upon the approach gradient to Government Court had already begun, he referred to this unfortunate necessity in almost the very words employed twenty years later by self-styled critics:

> My argument, when Government House had to be reduced, that the Vicereine had to mount 45 steps and traverse an additional 300 feet to go to Her Excellency's Sitting Room and her Bedroom was waved aside with the same insistence as is now adopted to save an official a small percentage of additional exercise.[1]

He was so dejected by what seemed to him short-sighted folly that he wrote letters reporting the situation to Edwin Montagu, Lionel Earle, and others, which, however, he tore up. Then he wrote to Lady Hardinge reporting that the engineers considered that the plans approved by the Viceroy might be carried out if the dome was omitted altogether and the upper part of the walls faced with *chunnam*—the Indian plaster that, as a material, Lutyens by no means objected to. Rome, as he had seen, was largely of stucco, and he had been prepared for the Johannesburg Gallery to be stucco-faced. The Vicereine immediately visited him at his office in apparent distress at his 'black letter', and begged him 'not to make criticisms and difficulties'. He replied that Lord Hardinge must understand that there was a point beyond which he could reduce no further. To his wife he wrote that the place should be called Bedlampore:

> It is like composing an opera when they leave out the fiddles and all but one wind instrument, and leave you a banjo with one string, the Viceroy's drum, a triangle, and a cornet perhaps—but they save one skin of the drum.

[1] Note on Lord Hardinge's letter to W. M. Hailey dated March 13, 1916.

He maintained that the economies bore particularly hard on him, since 'they cut essentials in Government House but dont grudge monies to the Secretariats'. A constant nightmare was that the reduced designs would be thrown irretrievably out of alignment with the Secretariats, which for the same reason were coming disproportionately large, whilst Baker, in his view, was being less helpful than he might have been. He felt that his collaborator, instead of facing difficulties, was prone 'to slur them over, which I cannot bear doing without a fight. I think it only honest... He is so used to cheap work and getting over difficulties in a slovenly way. He wants to get on and build; I say, work on until it all fits and makes a competent scheme—a few months wont matter in fifty years time'.

The Secretariats, nevertheless, were being reduced, though proportionately less than Government House. Baker had been joined by his South African partner, F. L. H. Fleming, and together they brought his plans within the sanctioned figure early in the new year. They received official approval, after which Baker declined to endorse proposals to the Committee for adjustments. For his part, he has recorded:

> I watched silently and with admiration Lutyens's tenacity in his fight with the Viceroy and the Government; a difficult position of conflicting loyalties, as I probably alone knew how the immense mass of building in relation to floor area contributed to the expense of his plan. Finally, working with amazing skill and energy, he reduced his plan, and it was accepted.[1]

The revised Government House design was sent in on February 23. The Delhi Committee were extremely sceptical of the costs being reducible within the official limit and, it would seem, were sympathetic to Lutyens personally and to his contention of the unwisdom of cutting unduly costs which must be faced eventually. Lutyens maintained, of Lord Hardinge's policy, that it was unwise politically 'and his methods liable to lead to great complaints hereafter of the estimates having been exceeded'. Keeling, the Chief Engineer, in the end agreed to exclude all the cost of heating installations from the estimate at this stage, in order to bring it within the limit. Preliminary figures suggested that if the upper floors (above the red sandstone) were faced with *chunnam* the cost would come within the limit by £16,000; and if with stone would exceed it by £25,000.

There was an important conference of the Committee on the site one Sunday morning at the beginning of March, with the Viceroy, Hailey, Montmorency, Keeling, Nicholls the Government Architect, Maxwell the Military Secretary, and

---

[1] MS. Memorandum, dated March 1931. This memorandum, and that dated March 1921 from which quotations have already been made, were among the papers put at the author's disposal by Sir Herbert Baker. The earlier one was no doubt prepared at the time of the final discussions of the Gradient question (see Chapter XIV, § 1); the later in connection with a strongly critical article by Robert Byron in *Country Life*. In both Sir Herbert gives his account of his relations with Sir Edwin since their collaboration in S. Africa, with special reference to the Processional Way at New Delhi.

the two architects. 'The Viceroy sat for two hours on Raisina Hill, talking to Hailey,' Lutyens averred. 'We might all not have been there, and the others were very cross at having their Sunday spoilt. Then they looked at the plans. The Viceroy now wants to enlarge the plans again—but there is no money. More quality to go somewhere. However, a new Viceroy may be worse.

'Monday. I started new plans for the West wing. They seem to come along but will cost more...'

Baker's remark, in the passage quoted above, of conflicting loyalties, expresses the dilemma in which Sir Herbert undoubtedly found himself at this stage. To what he termed the 'imperial conception' he devoted as much toil as Lutyens and a firmer grasp of practical and administrative problems. Schooled under Rhodes and Milner rather than under Wren and Newton, his ultimate allegiance was to statesmanship and he recognised all too clearly its paramountcy over art. Delhi, to him, as to the great majority of Englishmen, was a great British political conception. To Lutyens Delhi was all that but more: the opportunity for the expression in harmonious and logical form of the Divine Spirit, wherein the compromises and adjustments of policy were subordinate. With him there was no conflict of loyalties though there might be, and was, agonising effort in reconciling their demands.

Is it invariably possible for the genius of man to reconcile humanist aesthetics with practical mechanics, in this instance of government and geology? That question was inherent in the decision to set Government House at the back of Raisina Hill, approached up the escarpment and across a level 'forum' between the Secretariats. The laws of optics were likely to be brought into conflict with the laws of aesthetics, and the conflict was imminent.

The decisive meeting of the Delhi Committee on the layout and reduced Government House plans was held on March 16, 'so you won't know the result till I get home,' Lutyens had told Lady Emily. Neither have we, therefore, his personal record of the result. Notwithstanding that the outcome is clear from other sources, the lack of his own version is unfortunate since it is no less clear that subjective influences were weighing unusually heavily on him at this time when decisions were made and plans signed which were to affect his work at Delhi permanently.

His health, hitherto so good, was causing him anxiety. He had had a haemorrhage that made him realise that he must get home without further delay. The weeks of frustration and intense application in reducing and redesigning had thrown him into a mood of unusual dejection with India in general and the Government in particular. He was wearied, he owned, by the underlying carelessness, fatalism, cruelty and filth of the East, and convinced that 'my lack of school training puts me out of real sympathy with Bureaucracy—the spirit of compromise. Barrie was quite right when he said I should find Governments always aiming at second best'. Now he felt himself almost beaten, and, in the concentrated effort to preserve his conception

THE EVOLUTION OF VICEROY'S HOUSE

of Viceroy's House essentially intact although dismembered, he seems momentarily to have lost interest in the routine of official procedure.

This assumption, I am convinced, accounts for his failure, at this point, to appreciate the full significance of a certain minute which he undoubtedly did sign between March 16 and 21, when he and Baker left Delhi. The Committee duly approved his revised plans and the Engineers contrived to adjust the costs to the Viceroy's satisfaction. At the same time the architects were required to sign a declaration that there would be no further alterations to either plan such as would prevent building operations beginning on the foundations of the Secretariats. Blasting on Raisina Hill, to level its crest, had in fact already begun early in February.

Together with the plans thus finalised was, it appears, a document determining the gradients of the lateral approaches to Viceroy's Court, and of the King's Way from the Great Place to Government Court between the Secretariats. After discussion and experiment a gradient of $22\frac{1}{2}$ was selected, but since the exact levels of the Great Place were left to be determined finally in the following year, the question of the final gradient of the King's Way did not, in Lutyens's view 'become practical'. He therefore regarded the angle selected as in the nature of 'useful *data*, giving us limits as to maximum gradient'.[1]

Since the inception of the existing scheme in 1913 when, with Baker, he had prepared a sketch of the three buildings on Raisina Hill as they would be seen from the Great Place, he had visualised the portico of Government House, i.e. the façade above the red sandstone foundations, being continually visible from the avenue over the crest of the slope between the Secretariats. There was no doubt in his mind that Baker, in whose area the actual slope occurred, was equally clear on this crucial point, since the façade was so shown in the perspectives by Walcot the preparation of which they had supervised together at Apple Tree Yard. Though he might privately criticise some of Baker's designs and his general attitude to architecture, he did not for a moment doubt his loyalty as collaborator, least of all to the preservation of the principal view of Government House—the *clou* of the entire conception of New Delhi.

Therefore, ill, tired, dispirited and preoccupied, and confident that his colleague would in any case notify him if any development in the Secretariat area threatened to injure his central conception, he put his signature with, we must suppose, perfunctory attention to the minute referring to a gradient of $22\frac{1}{2}$. Baker, for his part, assumed that Lutyens had accepted this angle of ascent, and the consequent masking of Government House over some length of the approach, as an inevitable consequence of the site. It is curious, however, and was to prove highly unfortunate to their future relations, that Sir Herbert did not apparently happen, even in casual conversation, to refer to the change thereby brought about in their original joint

[1] Letter to H. Baker, January 27, 1916.

conception. Lutyens naturally did not do so, since, so far as he knew, no change was involved. It is the more curious since Baker himself recorded an occasion—and there must surely have been many others—when the subject could scarcely have been left unbroached were there not some tacit reason for avoiding it. In the memorandum on their collaboration (written in March, 1931) Sir Herbert recalled:

> On our voyage homeward we worked upon our designs and it was then, I think, that Lutyens asked me if I would agree to the column which the Maharajah of Jaipur had given, shown at Point A, i.e. in the centre of the Secretariat Court, being moved to the centre of the Viceroy's Court. I agreed, thinking with him that it would be more valuable there as it would be seen on its side axes, north and south [as well as from east and west]. He said nothing of the effect of moving an object from the top of the gradient—which was also approximately Point A.

It is a reasonable interpretation that Lutyens 'said nothing' because, in moving back the Jaipur Column, he was implying to Baker that he intended it to remain near the top of the gradient, that is of a gradient at a much gentler slope bisecting the Secretariat Court with the Jaipur Column visible at its termination. This is confirmed by his having mounted the column on a pedestal high enough to counteract its distance from the top of his gradient. In that case, Baker's agreement will have appeared to him as assent to the gentler, longer, slope. Lutyens, who repeatedly denied that the finality of the $22\frac{1}{2}$ gradient was made clear at the time of his signature, would not necessarily have mentioned the angle of slope in connection with the position of the column; for him, the slope followed the column, and he used words sparingly and obliquely in connection with his designs. But had the two architects been in full sympathy, it is almost inconceivable that Baker should not at this point have said, either 'Will not the top of the column look funny peeping over the crest of the slope?' or 'I am sorry that our perspectives have not worked out quite as we intended', or words to that effect. Either of such remarks would have awakened Lutyens to the real situation in time to retract his agreement to the gradient. But, for reasons which have had somewhat painfully to be indicated, they were not apparently on chatting terms at the time as regards their work. Nor can it be denied that Baker had a vested, if sound architectural, interest in a short, steep, gradient, since it would enable him to devote a large extent of Government Court to a level space uninterrupted by the ascending cutting—greatly to the convenience of the Secretariats' officials and to the functioning of official ceremonies. So he also said nothing. There was no reason why he should—Lutyens had signed the minute and Baker had no reason to suppose that its significance had escaped him.

It has been necessary to examine thus carefully the circumstances in which the architects' misunderstanding over the gradient arose, since the result, besides constituting a blemish in the realisation of the Delhi conception, became a recurrent and embittering theme in Lutyens's relations with future Viceroys and, above all, with his colleague. It is possible that neither architect ever entirely understood how it had arisen. It is only by the collation of numerous documents, and their study in the light of events and of the architects' mutual relations at the time, that this conclusion has been reached.

Another no less sad conclusion was at hand. With them on the boat was Lady Hardinge. Lutyens's admiration of her gallantry throughout the crisis of the Viceroy's attempted assassination, when, as he put it, 'the Viceregal crown rested on her shoulders,' had been unbounded. It was to her that, on some occasion of penitence, he had made the often quoted apology 'I will wash your feet with my tears and dry them with my hair. It is true that I have very little hair, but you have very little feet'.

Even during these fevered weeks when his professional relations with Lord Hardinge were tense, he had dined and had 'happy pleasant talk with H.E. and HER'. Lutyens had noticed lately how ill she was looking. Worn out by her indomitable spirit, Lady Hardinge died in the following July, a few months before her eldest son succumbed to his wounds in Flanders.

CHAPTER XI

VISHVAKARMAN

THE atmosphere of the summer of 1914 in England, beautifully caught in the pages of Sir Osbert Sitwell's *Great Morning*, still pervades a few of Lutyens's later country houses as palpably as it does Maurice Baring's '*C*', Stephen McKenna's *Sonia*, and Saki's satires. Its essence, distilled but pungent like old *pot pourri*, is perhaps most distinctly sensed in Lutyens's miniature, Queen Mary's Doll's House, made for that purpose afterwards. To appreciate the unfolding of his life, it is helpful to be able to imagine if not to remember the feeling, however faintly, of that summer in London, since it was the culmination of the age that produced his most characteristic architecture; the age of which, indeed, his architecture is among the most evocative and complete expressions. For him, immersed in the designs of Delhi which at that time it was intended should be largely completed by 1918, there can have been little leisure. Baker also had his office in London that summer, and they worked together industriously. His most interesting new commission was that for the building of St. Martin's Church, Knebworth. This brick building, though never completed, is of considerable interest for its duplicated arched aisles.

But apart from works in hand at Ednaston, Abbey House at Barrow, and Castle Drogo, the most numerous demands on his invention were for alterations and additions, most of which must have induced melancholy since they were to his own earliest works. Lawrence Weaver's imposing folio *Houses and Gardens by E. L. Lutyens* had been published by Hudson at the beginning of the year, 'and it does make me hot,' he wrote, looking at his copy in India. 'I do wish he had not mentioned Delhi so often and—oh dear—it is just a catalogue of mistakes and failures: clients who when I first started—I don't mean Chippy of course—did not know enough to direct, and afterwards not enough to be led.' His early Surrey mannerisms made him self-conscious. New bathrooms for Hudson at Lindisfarne and Herbert Johnston at Marsh Court were another thing. But changes at Orchards, even though it was the building that had enabled him to marry, now embarrassed him. And Chippy (Arthur Chapman) had actually sold Crooksbury—with all its ghosts of Bumps and Barbara Webb; and the new owner insisted on transforming that garden front of 1898, his first adventure into Wrennaissance, to the now fashionable olde-worlde-oaky. If he would not do it, somebody else would, so rather than let alien hands dismember his first-born, he hardened his heart and plunged in the adze himself.

This last summer of the old world was also to be the last at 29 Bloomsbury Square, the lease of which expired in September. The scenes for sixteen years of that strange but on the whole so happy and so fruitful partnership were being finally dismantled. Seven days after war was declared he wrote in lurid jest:

> the drawingroom and schoolroom at Bloomsbury Square have been bombarded, and the diningroom will have been by the time you see it, so, darling own Emmy, don't look at any room but our sitting room.

The 'mens', as the children had called the office downstairs, had of course already moved to Queen Anne's Gate or Apple Tree Yard, their place being taken by the children's school-room. Barbara and Robert by now went to a school at Hampstead; but Ursula, Betty, and Mary, with a number of friends, were being educated under the auspices of the Parents National Educational Union, forming in effect a small private school at Bloomsbury Square, later in the new house. This was to be nearby, the second from the north end of the west side of Bedford Square. It has since been re-numbered but it was then No. 31. When it had been settled upon, Lutyens had remarked, 'do you realise the luck of numbers? 7 Apple Tree Yard, 17 Queen Anne's Gate, 29 Bloomsbury Square, and now 31 Bedford Square: all log numbers, i.e. not divisible'. He devised interesting and expensive effects for the new house, such as the front hall papered in tin-foil. But nobody really liked it, and the family verdict was that it was soulless.

So, perhaps, was that most brilliant Season of an age in which, as Osbert Sitwell felt, 'happier, wealthier, wiser every day, we were being conducted by the benevolent popes of science into a Paradise, but of a most comfortably material kind; a Paradise where each man and woman . . . even if not destined for angelic honours, could at least aspire to the monetary honours of a Rockefeller or Rothschild.' Though so preoccupied, Lutyens must have partaken of its intellectual and physical refreshments. Since the family were at home till July, we have no letter-diary of his doings. But 'redecorations at the Berkeley Hotel' in the catalogue of his works at least shows that he was contributing to the comfort; and the vermilion skirting boards in some of its bedroom passages is a still visible relic of his touch. A kitchen wing to the most haunted house in Sussex, Brede Place, for Mr. Moreton Frewen, Winston Churchill's brother-in-law, perhaps came to him through Lady Randolph and her connection with the Shakespeare's England Exhibition. Granville Barker, whose season of Shakespeare at the Court, with Norman Wilkinson's and Albert Rutherston's *décors,* was making theatrical history, came to Lutyens for redecoration of the auditorium. Barrie, E. V. Lucas, Knoblock, Lane, and Nicholson at Rottingdean, were among his cronies. His aversion to opera was not so great that he was not sometimes to be seen in Lady Cunard's box or in her gatherings of the witty at 20 Cavendish Square, and in Mrs. Charles Hunter's *singerie* drawing-room in Old

Burlington Street or at Hill Hall, with George Moore, Sargent, and Tonks. He liked Tonks, because, once motoring home together from Mrs. Hunter's, the painter had told him he had 'met Father and been rather thrilled by him'. Then he was always made much of by Lady Horner, whether at Mells or her house in Buckingham Gate, where besides all her (and almost his) Jekyll relations, he would meet Grey, Haldane, the Asquiths, and most of the members of the Liberal Cabinet, whilst Edward Horner brought the flower of his doomed generation.

But for Lutyens the bitter out-scented the sweet in the savour of these months, partly because they cover the period of his closest association, through his wife, with the Theosophical Society and Mrs. Besant. The connection between him, with his strong sense of intellectual tradition and discipline, and the dynamic mysticism of this extraordinary woman, a stormy petrel to most of the institutions which he supported, was one of the oddest interweavings in his life's tapestry. Indeed it assumes the aspect of predestined pattern when we realise that in 1879, when he was ten, Annie Besant had publicly disapproved of the establishment by Disraeli and Lytton of the Empire of India as forcibly as she was to denounce, as inadequate, the reforms proposed by Lord Hardinge and embodied in the Montagu-Chelmsford declaration of 1918. When we narrated how Ned Lutyens fell in love with Emily Lytton in that Victorian drawing-room nearly twenty years ago, it was remarked that Fate seemed to be taking a hand in his destiny by thus linking the unknown young architect with the daughter of Disraeli's first Viceroy. 'As Faith wills, so Fate fulfills' he had inscribed upon the Casket representing his self-dedication. We have seen his faith being fulfilled in full measure. But in these summer months Fate too, in the person of Mrs. Besant, came stalking out of the past to be present as the curtain fell upon the age's climax.

The origin of this link, or rather cleavage as it proved, between husband and wife has been noticed in connection with the house at Varengeville which he had designed for M. and Mme. Guillaume Mallet. It was there and inspired by Mme. Guillaume, that on a visit Lady Emily had decided to join the Theosophical Society. Soon afterwards she made the acquaintance, which ripened into devoted friendship, of Mrs. Annie Besant, the Society's President, and began to throw increasing energy into the preaching and teaching of Theosophy. Lutyens was attracted to it also, owing to its broad attitude to religion and proclamation of the fundamental unity of all faiths, a view which expressed his own convictions. Though he was frankly sceptical of Theosophy's occult elements, its pantheism strongly appealed to him, and Mrs. Besant's work for regenerating the Indian peoples coincided closely with his own desire formed by his search for Indian artists and craftsmen for the building of Delhi. Mrs. Besant, for her part, recognised his genius, calling him playfully *Vishvakarman*, the divine builder, and making him an honorary member of the Society.

When therefore she decided to meet the Society's expanding needs by building a headquarters in London—with the help of some wealthy members among whom incidentally was Lutyens's hostess on his yachting trip to the Baltic, Miss Dodge—it seemed natural that he should be appointed as architect. It was decided in 1911 to erect large quadrangular premises surmounted by a cupola and with fronts to Gordon Square and Tavistock Place from Lutyens's designs (p. 331)—but against his counsel. As the capital available was not large, he had advised beginning on more concise lines, designed for gradual expansion. But the Committee, possibly relying on higher sources of advice, did not accept their architect's. Unfortunately, too, the Society's affiliation with Fabianism led to their embarking on the experiment of building with direct labour, without a contractor, and employing only members of trade unions recruited into a specific Guild. Lutyens vigorously disapproved to his wife. 'I do not think it right to ask a man his political tenet before you give him work. All Churches are apt to be bullies, and I think this is a case of Inquisition.' There were objections to the authority to be exercised by his Clerk of Works, and he foresaw this idealistic experiment leading to waste of the limited funds when, instead of the simple task of dealing with bricklayers and masons, it came to enrolling the technical specialists required for the building's later stage. Yet his fertile mind, even whilst he was at loggerheads with the committee and its representative on the job, was ready to devise to his wife a workable guild system for modern building:

> The only practical system is to form a guild of foremen (say) representing the various trades, bound by guild rules affecting wages and quality of work, and then extend the principle with sub-foremen down to the men, keeping them together and in touch with a central body or committee. It would be essential to lasting success that each member of this body should have been through at least one building trade himself. The present (Theosophical) Committee knows nothing about building... But it has nothing to do with me—except your interest and concern; though it is doing my reputation no good amongst the Art Workers Guild people, not that I mind that—much. The thing is to get on, insult no man so that you lose his good will and his interest in his work, and dont have a man as boss who exposes his building ignorance with practical workmen.

He pursued the train of thought generated by the relation of religions, socialism, and his aspirations for the arts, a few days later, when war had been declared and, sanguine as men were in 1914, every road led to a question mark.

> I cannot believe that any good can come of war. The only chance for [humanity's?] real confident advance is through intellectual strivings of efficiency in the arts. Of course being in an arena, I think architecturally... The great Greeks should be our example. I believe they *were*: but they were really a

minority only, the upper classes. We want that spirit throughout democracy, plus that which Christ taught and which, except by a few cranky saints, was never assimilated by states and their churches. I dont mean cranky in any abusive sense—but cranks never help things forward, rather 'tother way.

I do not believe, for instance, that it is any use my going out, even if I had the gift, to preach, but by the excellence of one's work and ambition one can lead men to higher and better things on parallel lines to one's own.

This private belief of his, for which he found expression only at rare moments of stress, but which inspired his whole life, was, as we have noticed elsewhere, the conviction of true artists that the faithful exercise of their art is itself religion and must, for the artist, precede religion. On another occasion the sight of 'Baker immersed in a large tome on Religion and Art translated from Italian with a preface by Mrs. Strong', moved him to reflect:

Judging from the illustrations, the connection cannot be proven. I wonder if they have not put the cart before the horse; that a body with the power of penmanship would not far better prove that *art comes first*. It is the failure of godship that turns men to words and rituals to give expression to the middens of their failures. They will not face the discipline that any real art entails.

Similarly with liberal democracy, and yet more with the socialist's ideal of equal mediocrity:

Governments have no real courage. They forego the best as Utopian, try diplomatically for the second best and fail, covering it with a third rate result.

The welfare of the greatest number means no man is really happy. And there will be no happiness until every man can do his best in the work he best likes doing. The happy man is he whose interests are in games and sports, with a regular salary and a pension assured. And he growls! A happy man is the agriculturist on good land favoured by God's weather and climate and who cannot read or write:—I believe the Turkish villages in East Europe reach the greatest sum total of human happiness!

Perhaps this moody nihilism represented Lutyens's innermost political conviction, but it is difficult to visualise him finding much happiness himself in a society of subsistence farmers. But already the age of Edwardian aristocracy that, with all its shortcomings, had shaped him and best fitted his genius, was in its death throes, and the century of the happy pensioned sportsman was dawning, through the darkness of war.

91. VICEROY'S HOUSE, NORTH SIDE. As redesigned in 1920 after omission of Council Chamber

92 (*left*). THE JAIPUR COLUMN. Diploma drawing. (By courtesy of President and Council of the Royal Academy)

93 (*right*). DESIGN FOR THE THEOSOPHICAL SOCIETY HEADQUARTERS, GORDON SQUARE (1911)

94. SKETCH BY LUTYENS OF A BRAHMIN BULL

95. ELEPHANTS AT THE CORNERS OF THE NORTH ASCENT TO VICEROY'S COURT. Carved from designs by C. S. Jagger

CHAPTER XII

FIRST WAR YEARS

§1. THE END OF THE SUMMER

'SO war was declared last night. I heard it at the Athenæum, too late to telegraph you. Crowds singing outside—an offshoot from the Buckingham Palace crowd. Walked home.' He frequented the club often in those early August days 'to get the news'. He had been elected to the Athenæum in 1907 when he had been tickled to notice a particularly elderly member, ninety years old, whose name was Young. 'I have seen to speak to to-day and yesterday,' he wrote on the 6th, 'Lady Randolph Churchill, Harold Baker, Benn, McKenna, Lady Horner, Runciman, Samuel, Custance, Saxton Noble, Lord Roberts, Prothero, Lionel Earle and Aunt T (Mrs. C. W. Earle). Lord Sydenham says the war will last 9 months, Chirol profesies a year, Kitchener says 3 years. The only thing I can do is to carry on, and induce all others to, but we must be careful, and we must all learn to do something of real use. No room for cranks! Nearly the whole of my office has volunteered. I think Robert might join the Boy Scouts.' He spent the week-end with the Jekylls at Munstead House, where the McKennas were staying. 'I saw Bumps, she is in the Hut;' a week later she was busy 'making wonderful shirts and kitbags'. At the 'Other', a dining club, he met both Kitchener and Churchill and sat up talking war with Riddell, Col. Jack Seely, and Waldorf Astor. These contacts gave him a clear and by no means optimistic insight into the strategical situation.

'Delhi will go on all right, I think,' he had ascertained by the 24th. 'Player has dropped his tobacco factory, but goes on with his house (Ednaston); Sitwell has stopped his golf club-house (at Renishaw).' But Herbert Johnston had decided to complete what he was doing at Marsh Court. Another day 'Granville Barker lunched with me, to look at my sketches for his theatre, seemed heartened, and liked my original ideas. Dined with Marie Tempest and Graham Browne in a luxurious house, which Nicholson a great friend of theirs painted and wanted me to see. Amusing but useless talk. Have been at Mells, Lady Horner had seen Lord Haldane, who had no bad news. So many people are waiting with awful anxiety on the casualty lists—the 12th Lancers have suffered badly... After dinner went down to say good-bye to Mrs. Congreve [wife of General, later Sir Walter, Congreve, V.C.] off tomorrow as Red Cross nurse to Ostende'. Then one night in early September, while the heirs of the Edwardian Age were meeting their destinies at Mons and the great Russian Rumour had all London by the ears, he met one of the men of the future.

>After dinner I walked all down the Mall with Col. Branker of the Air Force, with a view to disguising London by falsifying the directions of streets etc., by rearranging the lamps and putting lamps in odd places. Several policemen took a good deal of passive interest in us.

The Air Age had begun, and this must have been one of the earliest discussions of its peculiar art form of camouflage.

Building ceased gradually, but, though the quantity of work was less, he had to do more and more of it himself now the young men had joined up, and a complete standstill with all private work was only a matter of time. The Theosophical Headquarters was eventually abandoned half-finished, to be completed to a different design after 1918 by another architect for the British Medical Association, to whom the Society had sold the site. For its income was much reduced by the war's unifying effect on divided minds. On this topic Ned wrote, a little sharply, to his beloved theosophist: 'Yes, the Germans undoubtedly have belief and faith in their righteousness. Our only chance is belief and faith in ours. Now the die is cast, it is no use having open minds.'

Had it not been for Delhi, the financial outlook for a now middle-aged architect with a large family, though he consorted with the leaders of his time, was not pleasant. On Raisina Hill, too, construction of the vast foundations was to go on with ever diminishing resources till the nations closed in their grapple for life and work was closed down in 1918. In the familiar, dreary, half light with which war suffuses the arts of peace, our vision would presently be almost restricted to the two architects doomed to share the same quarters year after year among the paralysed foundations of their joint labours, were it not for the occasional flashes generated by the overcharged atmosphere in the tent, and for an altogether unexpected and more genial burst of sunlight from outside the warring world.

§2. DELHI 1914–15

The rigours of a voyage under war conditions—beginning from Tilbury on December 4, instead of via Brindisi—were lightened by William Nicholson being of the party. Lutyens, finding him with no prospects of earning a living in war-time England—even the King's shilling—undertook to arrange for him to paint the Viceroy's portrait. Besides a cargo of shells there were on board Aubrey Herbert, George Lloyd, and Leonard Woolley, also, though he did not join the group, a young man named T. E. Lawrence, all bound for Egypt. 'We play chess fast and furious, with the chivalry of Balaclava; very bad chess but great fun.' Lutyens was to see a good deal of the future Lord Lloyd, but not of Aubrey Herbert (brother of Lord Carnarvon of Tutankhamen fame) nor Woolley, destined also to fame. He sketched verbally 'that most curious unsoldierlike trio that ever bore arms':

Herbert—mad, blind in a qualified sense, a Maurice-Baring-wit of courage and unexpectedness.

Woolley, born of a parson, Oxford manner, archaeologist and humanist. He was tried in a Turkish court and found their game was a remand to keep his credentials. So he whipped out a revolver and, pointing it at the judge, demanded his papers. The Court cleared except for the pistol-pinned judge who quakingly released his papers and let him go. He has had wonderful experiences in Syria etc [before the war] and been surveying Sinai. Hence he is on the staff of this Turkish expedition.

Lloyd, cursed by the prefix George. A Tory demagogue. His mannishness tempered by streaks of niceness and gentleness and by a life-long friendship with Herbert. Knows Baghdad and them parts.

After the warriors had been dropped at Port Said, Ned and Nicholson got up a Christmas pantomime, introducing Father Christmas, a Pudding, Columbine, Clown and so forth. 'Nicholson is very good at making the rhymes. I want to get an Indian (old Mr. Gupta, Prime Minister of Baroda, is on board) to play the part of the Pudding. It would save grease paint—but we are too conscious yet of our respective colours. Baker is absorbed in ethical subjects.' The chess tournament went on all the way to Delhi, where they arrived on Christmas Eve, Ned and Nicholson passing a pocket board up and down between their sleeper berths. The portrait of Lord Hardinge, full length in his robes, was duly begun. The Viceroy, driving his own car, called on the architects when Nicholson was lunching at their camp. Whilst Lord Hardinge was talking, Lutyens looked round wondering if Nicholson was still there. 'On the sofa I saw a rug and from under the rug protruded a pair of boots. He was asleep! The Viceroy was much amused. But he is a pathetic creature and has felt his boy's death'—within a few weeks of his wife's.

Over the Christmas holiday the architects were the guests of Sir Harcourt Butler, one of Lutyens's most frequent hosts at Simla and Vice-President of the Viceroy's Council, for a tour of Lucknow, Benares, and the Buddha country round Gaya. Lutyens most appreciated the last, 'charming, green, pleasant hills which, if at all like what Buddha saw, proves him to have been a man of taste and discretion.' There was, too, 'grotesque, but refreshing and refined,' one of Asoka's columns, 'the emperor who apologised to the conquered for the waste of war'; and at Buddha Gaya 'one of those wonderful Asoka rails which I admire most of all India's work—a great stone fence which Asoka built round Buddha's shrine to protect it. The Shrine itself, a restoration built by the British.' Similarly at Lucknow it was not the awful Moghul buildings of the King of Oudh nor the modern institutions, little better, but 'some beautiful trees and the old Residency built in fine English manner, that were most refreshing to see, dignified without ostentation'. At Benares they were up early and went down river in the Maharajah's paddle boat worked by 8 men. The most wonderful prospect in all India—the hosts of multicoloured people bathing, the great steps, temples, many of them sinking in the mud, their foundations being washed away by the river. Bulls, cows, donkeys, dogs—mangy ones—goats, people washing, praying, bobbing, exercising, meditating, fakirs, priests, every sort of black body doing every sort of thing—a kaleidoscope of gesture and colour, the lovely morning light over it all.

After breakfast I went down to the Theological College and talked Theosophical Building with Mrs. Besant. I introduced Baker who seemed much impressed but sceptical of the theories of Karmah and the whole Hindoo philosophy—but he is curiously matter of fact and unimaginative on these lines. His world is bounded by the range of a pom-pom gun.

Then we went to view the Temples. Oh my! The dirt, filth, and the impossibility of bull, cow and monkey worship and oh the stench and hideousness of everything. Barbarism in terms of evil smelling slime. A Juggernaut car to squash the whole thing seemed logical and desirable. It will be a relief to be able to contemplate Buddha after the Hindoo terrors.

The main temple of Gaya town he admired, a really pleasant building in a kind of black quartzite carried on many columns surmounted by a dome. The party was entertained by the monks till, garlanded with chains of jasmine and marigolds, they entrained again in Sir Harcourt's saloon coach. On the return journey to Delhi, Lutyens

had good talks with Butler. He says the Government have got cold feet over costs and there will be no chance of more money now. They will spend later on. This is bad policy. Meantime I have to cut down grievously to make a start at all.

But at least 'Hailey, Montmorency, and all from H.E. downwards' were unimpressed, indeed wildly angry,

with a certain Professor Geddes who has come out here to lecture on town planning—his exhibits were sunk by the *Emden*. He seems to have talked rot in an insulting way and I hear he is going to tackle me! A crank who don't know his subject. He talks a lot, gives himself away and then loses his temper.

With this advanced patrol the New Architecture was making its circuitous, but evidently well advertised, reconnaissance of Raisina Hill, using contours and existing buildings for cover instead of marching majestically up the processional way in the logical and honest British tradition. Professor Patrick Geddes,[1] like his disciple Lewis

---

[1] See *Patrick Geddes in India*. Edited by Jaqueline Tyrwhitt, with an Introduction by Lewis Mumford, and a Preface by H. V. Lanchester. Lund Humphries, 1947.

Mumford, came to preach the ideological basis of a new, biotechnic order, using a strange vocabulary for strange conceptions. 'The central and significant fact about the City is that it functions as the specialised organ of social transmission. It accumulates and embodies the heritage of a region and combines in some measure and kind with the cultural heritage of the larger units, national, racial, religious, human'— a conception now lucidly self-evident to the citizens of London and Berlin but one which the imperialists of Delhi may perhaps be pardoned for having misunderstood. Lutyens gathered that

> One of his ideas is that all the roads of a city should be in old nullahs. He says people don't walk out when it rains!! Well, if they went by nullahs they couldn't. He also lays down the law about *Serais*; says that the coolie lines here are incestuous and wants to separate the men and women. I must say no money is wasted, but they are given water-tight sheds which they divide off as they require. They come, some for a few days only, with wives, sisters, cousins, aunts, grandmothers, and children, and maintain their family lives and traditions. He wants to break up families and prevent women taking their babies out to work etc. He is also voluminous over the Secretariats, says that the Records should be kept in the buildings since to divorce the Law Maker from the Historian is immoral: all this from seeing a small scale plan showing the 'Record Office' in one place and 'Secretariats' in another. He never asked about the accomodation for Records provided in the Secretariats.

However, the Voice crying in the foundations of Megolopolis soon moved on, his place taken by the Delhi Committee. 'Satisfactory preliminary talk' Lutyens noted; 'they take a more practical interest in things now, which is good and gives us a lot to do. I feel we shall earn our 10 guineas a day this year. They are very nice and understanding but cannot afford to see the essential difference between an arch carried on posts of sufficient calibre and those that have a bilious (thin) feeling: and in elevation on paper they do look alike. Nor do they think it matters what the sweeper sees at the back door. Personally I hate to expose omissions and defaults even to a feather-numbered sparrow!'

Baker recorded[1] that it was during this visit 'that Lutyens first raised the question of the Processional Way, but then suggested only the widening of the view (by substituting steps for the great platform of my design) forming, as I argued, a great sloping stadium in the place of Government Court. The question was not strongly urged then—in fact he helped me with the design of the levels at the bottom of the Processional Way [presumably those of the Great Court at the foot of the slope, which were settled at this time] as it is now designed and built; and he acquiesced in the approval of the Committee of the slope of the Way through the medium of the

---

[1] Memorandum, March 1921.

full-sized models which were built and which he, I, and the Committee inspected together'.

§3. CASTLES IN SPAIN

The Duke of Peñaranda, younger brother of the Duke of Alba, had asked Lutyens, whom he used to meet with Lord Wimborne at Ashby St. Ledgers, to design a palace on a remote manor of his estate near Toledo. On a morning towards the end of June, 1915, Lutyens therefore found himself in the Palacio de Liria at Madrid. 'Travelling by night I have seen very little of Spain, and very little of the Palace except my own rooms,' he wrote on the 23rd. One hall, he had noticed, was hung with memorials to the great Viceroy of the Netherlands, his armour, banners, and the superb tapestries which he took campaigning; another with portraits of the Empress Eugenie, a member of the family. There were some good portraits of the Stuart Kings of England and Scotland, who were also ancestors, so that 'when Alba was at school in England he was called Stuart; he is also Duke of Berwick'. The Duke of Peñaranda motored Ned into the town 'to buy guide books and to buy a motor himself for the rough roads, to save his Rolls. He did not get one, so is hiring one that looks as large and comfortable. Multitudes of servants, first class French cooking, but the only really Spanish thing was a most excellent ham, the best I ever tasted'.

It was all rather like a dream, and seems the more so to us since this letter, which explains neither how or why he had been transported out of the war world, is the only record of this visit. The roads to the site seem to have proved too bad even for the hired car's inferior though massive constitution and a regular expedition had to be organised to take place in October. But no doubt requirements and accommodation were discussed and rough sketches made.

A week later Lutyens was in a train going from Turin to Genoa, to make arrangements for closing down work on the British School at Rome. Again we do not know how he got there, whether direct from Madrid; but in Turin he had some time to wait, which he spent in the picture gallery. There are not many records of his thoughts on pictures—though his visits to Spain will yield some—so his impressions *en courrant* may be quoted:

> Two delightful pictures by Giovanni Griffier,[1] a name unknown to me; one of an English house by Wren, garden by Le Nôtre; and Lambeth. Van Eyck of the Passion, a panorama of many scenes, each a Station of the Cross. St. Peter's cock shown as a peacock, a new idea to me but probably a just view, with the harsh cry of the bird. Wonderful names and frames but nothing held me. The picture I liked most was an unfinished Italian Adoration. Its charm to me was

[1] Jan Griffier 1645–1718; in England 1668 and 1687–1718.

that it was out of its frame, leaning against the wall of an empty gallery. It had human interest at once, and the spirit of reverence became accessible,—the feeling that the painter might have walked in at any moment and been cross at one's looking at it.

In London that September he saw his first Zeppelin raid, on his way home to Bedford Square from the Athenæum. The family were still in the country but he found the panic-stricken servants in the wine cellar. He told them that the safest place was to 'stand under the door lintel of a main wall, and if a bomb falls near you fall flat on your face at once'. The family should practise doing so as a game. But he could not imagine how the staff had got hold of the wine cellar key.

The second journey to Spain, on which he would actually get to El Guadelperal where the palace was to be built, had been elaborately planned with the help of Sir Thomas Holderness of the India Office to enable him to catch the P. & O. at Gibraltar. There would then be a week in Egypt as the guest of Sir Henry Macmahon. So this year he would be away for five months. On the way he stayed with the Mallets in Paris—now a queer family, M. Guillaume gone royalist and perpetually acting royalty, Mme. Guillaume expecting instantly to hear that her son was killed, Mme. Grunelius, her mother, lodging them in a house given over to war works, and old Monsieur henpecked and without a room to sit in. However, they all went to see the captured German guns at the *Invalides* and had tea among lovely *revue* ladies at Rumpelmeyers. The Alba chauffeur was to have met Ned in Paris but failed to turn up. However, after two nights and a day in the train—which made him feel he really ought to have a valet, 'travelling so much for other people on business leaves me no energy for my own affairs'—he found himself deposited outside the big iron gates of the Liria Palace in the grey dawn.

They swung open, and the dream began again, a kaleidoscope of tapestries and armours, the pink uniforms of the King's Councillors, Goyas, Tintorettos and Velasquez ('I do wish Robert could see the Velasquez and realise what attainment can mean'), five Dukes and the Prime Minister to luncheon. The Prado and Aranjuez, The Escorial, 'a wapping great palace, all very simple and no fraudulent construction as our Government to-day insists on. Motley's *Dutch Republic* helped me to realise the power of which it was the centre; the gardens very pleasant, thick cut box hedges in knots, stone niched walls, and gravel.' After individual buildings, people begin to materialise:

> Peñaranda is a charming person, 33, young, simple in a nice way, full of fun and life. Alba (his brother) is a grandee of Spain thirteen times over, so he could sit in 13 seats in the Senate if he had as many situpons. He has only one, and as it happens he prefers his seat in the Deputies. He has given me a ham, which I shall give to the Viceroy.

In the intervals of seeing Madrid, Lutyens worked in his room on the designs of the palace and at transforming his sketches to a metre scale. The Duke did not expect to begin building till after the war, but there was much preliminary work to be done; besides the preparation of the plans, a water-supply had to be constructed and accommodation for the building staff to be put up. Under the most favourable circumstances the palace could not be begun for two years.

The plan was to motor to Toledo, then on to stay the night with the Duke and Duchess of Santonio (the 'Duchess Sol', Peñaranda's sister); next morning to get as far as possible in the car then ride to the farm, which was called Elgordo, where they would spend two nights.

Of Toledo ('terrible lunch, waiters all venerable Don Quixotes') Lutyens gave a rapid *apperçu* of the setting in a loop of the Tagus crossed by the fortified bridges, and the most notable buildings, crowned by the great palace.

> The Cathedral, where the dead hand that lays its weight on Spain is seen in flesh of very flesh, the fat priests, cannot be compared with northern cathedrals, but the wealth and elaboration is certainly impressive: great coloured windows and most marvellous profusion of heraldry, partly hidden by great gilt reredos and in front of them great iron grilles and grilles again in front of the choir. Precious stones, marbles, inlaid woods, carving. The large illuminated books must take two men to lift. Each generation piling on the last some elaboration making a temple so sombre, so mysterious, that you can only think of the poverty stricken country outside with sadness.
>
> They seem to have had good architects, and Philip II was a purist. Grand conceptions but weak in architectural technique, and when they leave the Doric order, which by the way they run to death, they come awful croppers. They seem to have had no men of the calibre of Mansard the elder, certainly no San Michele, nor a Wren.
>
> The two bridges across the Tagus belong to Alba. He used to get the tolls but they have been given up yet he has to keep them in repair. His only recompense is the protection of the bridges themselves, which are remarkably lovely—towers at each end, great buttresses and four small arches, one of great span, all in granite.

Then away along a frightful road that stretched across the plain till it stood up to the horizon like a chimney. The condition of the roads made him realise what the British had done for India. But he could not make out why they did not halve the width and so save enough money to keep up a narrower road well—as Napoleon had in France. And so to Ventosilla:

> An old house added to by their own labour, direct and shamelessly shoddy —rambling, comfortable and as English as they can make it. A sumptuous tea,

with a delightful Irish nannie presiding. Santonio and his Duchess are keen only on country life. Independant of everything and everybody they breed mules and pigs, preserve their game, make their own electric light and power for their own machinery—A Lambay in a sea of Spain.

There is a delightful priest, father confessor and estate agent, loving the hunt and the shoot and spends the day in breeches and gaiters. For dinners he appears in his cassock. An adernoidal tutor. Motors in plenty. A delightful battery of servants, all friends of the family, each one a host in himself. Furious wood fires.

Each little boy has a recess by his bed as an altar, a chapel where saints, martyrs and Mother Mary stand in full panoply of Rome.

Dinner. Uncomfortable dining room—huge table with many faces round it, scratch lot of servants, food very different from Liria. Sideboard covered with pots and pans and silver, so untidy as to give me the feeling they were moving house.

Duke gouty, sport and farming. She very small always in breeches, more like a boy, though in the evening appeared gowned like a Byzantine queen in baroque jewels—some very good pearls and a net of gems for head gear. Dogs everywhere.

Transparencies and pictures a great success with the children, especially with the priest.

A gaunt bedroom and yet more gaunt bathroom.

Next morning they set out in a huge Mercedes for Elgordo, crossed the Tagus by a frightening private ferry, and bump-bumped along the roads, 'goats, sheep, black and white, galore, and the arid country made an Old Testament picture, very like India. And here we killed a dog, such a dear fuzzy shepherd dog.' About 20 kilos from Elgordo they were met by a guide, a heroic creature with sheepskin cloak mounted on a regular Rosinante and carrying a loaded rifle. There they left the main road.

I was quite calm thinking nothing could be worse, but the road now proved to be just a track made in sandy wastes by mule carts. Up, down, precipice to right of us, precipice to left. Other guards joined us and galloped on regardless of our difficulties, attempting to show us the way.

Elgordo village, of 1200 inhabitants, is perched on a gentle mound, approached by knee-deep ruts not cobbled but bouldered. A barren, gaunt church, and Peñaranda's granaries (the rents are paid in grain). The property apparently belonged to the Empress Eugenie.

The whole population had gathered in a small piazza, the crowd's picturesque squalor emphasised by three gigantic ducal footmen in livery who had been sent on in advance to prepare quarters, which proved to be extremely primitive. After lunch the party set out on horse-back—though Lutyens who had had visions of an agonised ride with his trousers rucked up to his knees, had the doubtful luxury of a seat in the bailiff's cart. The sky was overcast, the country got even worse, and they looked at possible and impossible sites till dark when it came on to rain. The evening was spent by the Duke in receiving his tenants and their wives, none of the latter of whom appeared to be on speaking terms with one another. Then to a night of extreme discomfort and squalor.

But next morning was brilliant with the whole panorama laid bare—forests of old ilex, the Tagus at their feet, a range of mountains beyond a plain to the south, snow capped giants to the north.

> The Priest—a kind of Bumps in orders—rode about searching for brick earth, lime, and sand and returned gloriously happy having found all. There are Roman ruins near by. On the site I want are great heaps of stones evidently collected by some ancient for a building never started—perhaps a Moorish fort before the reconquest or a Roman one before that. No tool marks were in evidence on the granite. A surveyor from Madrid came out and I showed him where and what I wanted as to levels etc. There are two possible sites: one on a cliff over the river with a curtailed view of snow mountains; the other high up with great views all round but no shelter whatever and no view of the Tagus. I want the lower, where the trees grow big and the river runs and you get views beneath the spreading branches. The local people and the priest say Hill-top—it will look so fine and be so well seen!! The forest abounds with pigs—nice clean God-made pigs that live on the sweet acorns of the ilex.

Next morning they returned by the same route, visiting a tile factory in a church and a mill with jolly great terra-cotta jars ten feet high full of fermenting wine, and reached Madrid the day following. The Duke of Alba showed Lutyens his archives, including Christopher Columbus's Atlas, letters from Henry VIII and Queen Elizabeth, and countless treasures. Then he left for Algeciras to catch the P. & O. and finished his letter after a very bad night in the train whilst waiting for four hours in a downpour at Bobadilla Junction.

The designs of El Guadelperal were completed in 1917, and preliminary works, including the construction of 14 miles of road and the building of a small temporary house for the Duke, were begun in 1918. The tradition of the site's Roman occupation was confirmed to the extent of a prehistoric dolmen coming to light on it which involved finding another position for the building. The work, almost as great an undertaking as Viceroy's House, was still in its early stages when the Spanish Civil War brought it to a halt and the Liria Palace was burnt, together with much of Toledo.

§4. EGYPT

'O$\overset{M}{\underset{Y}{}}$—my cartouche! Here I am at Cairo after a night journey from Thebes.' Lutyens was writing on November 16, a fortnight after leaving Gibraltar. He and Baker, whom he joined on the boat there, had stayed at Malta on their way, but the letter about it is missing, probably sunk. Five submarines were reported at large after they left Malta and Ned 'comforted many people by telling them we had already sighted and passed four'.

A few extracts from his impressions of Egypt are given, consecutively, since, even to such hackneyed although sublime monuments his penetrating eyes and idioms bring fresh significance reflecting unselfconscious light on himself. His host from early Delhi days, Sir Henry MacMahon, now High Commissioner for Egypt, was absent with Lord Kitchener (on preparations for the Gallipoli landing). The architects were looked after by Lady MacMahon and his Secretary, Mr. (later Sir Ronald) Storrs.

'The Cairo mosques are much better built than anything I have seen in India. They are remarkable, with qualities of real building, and not that love of Dicky (shirt) front order so loved by the Moghuls. Fine conceptions finely wrought. The Bazaars good too, the closed streets with serrated gleams of brilliant blue sky. In the Museums, with the Director, saw much that was beautiful, much that was odd, and those pathetic and horrible mummies that I hope some day will be reinstated in their tombs amongst the writings on the walls intended only for the eyes of the Gods, to their own great comfort.

'To the Pyramids, till a good sunset. I never realised they stood on a plateau. The Sphinx . . . that speaks what all true men feel. With these colossal monuments the weariness of it, the ruin and destruction, the eternal strife is very saddening. And it goes on perpetual, in both worlds.

'Luxor: One of the obelisks before the Pylons was given by Menelek to the French and is the one now in the Place de la Concorde. How any moral man could give or take such a gift is beyond the dreams of reason.

'A huge mud-conceived temple in stone and granite, ruined and despoiled. A dreadnought beached.

'Karnak: A good deal of the work is without imagination, like noughts added to a cheque; but much that was lovely, much that was impressive; and the vast labours spent marvellous.

'The Valley of the Kings: We crossed the river before the sun rose behind the Luxor temple. To the west all was pink above the gray waters. Met on the other side by donkeys, mine large, white, and called *Train de luxe*. Only like a train when it trotted and then like a train off the rails. Every now and then it brayed and I felt I was riding a lion in asses' clothing.

'It grew hotter and hotter. Saw several tombs of the Kings, and though it was thrilling I felt ashamed in the presence of the old long-dead bodies. It can't be right to fill museums [with them] to amuse the curious. The wonderful colours as fresh to-day as when painted 4000 years ago.

'Queen Hatsupa was evidently an economist—and a suffragette ... delicious drawings, extraordinarily true and observant, especially of the things that had not been conventionalised by the priest-craft. I liked best the funeral temple of Rameses III, a fine big place, most impressive. The cartouches and hieroglyphics extraordinarily deep cut and a good sense of colour left. There seemed to be Assyrian influence in the profiles of the building. Then to the two great Colossi that overlook the Nile. They have corkscrew channels inside so that in some winds they make noises and the priests used them as oracles.

'The Ancient Egyptians were great god-fearing children playing with huge toy bricks, and then telling their stories in picture words with no adjectives. So occasionally they rose to a very high level of accomplishment. They had little thought of this world but to meet the terrors of the next and assure a perpetual happiness.

'The Pyramids by moonlight looked monstrous large and made me wonder if the very hills were built by men of a race of giants to the Egyptians as they are giants to our times. Yet with their material magnitude there seems to be some spiritual motive as great and as impressive and marvellously mysterious.'

When he resumed this most diversified of his passages to India, something happened that struck him as curious. It was not that, among the passengers, there was a party of bookies from England in search of unrestricted racing in India. There was thick fog in the Suez Canal, during which the liner ran aground, being eventually towed off by a French cruiser. Lutyens made a few sympathetic remarks to the Captain:

> but was rather astonished when an officer came up to me later and said the Captain would like to speak to me in his cabin, so I went up to the bridge. He showed me his chart and his report, and how it all happened.
>
> He was quite calm and took it as a matter of fact that his career was ruined.
>
> I wonder why it is I get the confidence of working men, who cannot write, or write well ... seldom of the men who write and base their lives on other people's words. ...

§5. DELHI 1915–16. THE GRADIENT CRISIS

Lord Hardinge's Viceroyalty having been extended, he was still at the helm when the architects reassembled at Delhi in December, 1915 and remained till after

FIRST WAR YEARS

their departure in March, 1916. The war was at a crisis. Their arrival coincided with the Viceroy's order, under strong pressure from London, for the unfortunate advance on Baghdad which resulted in the disastrous seige of Kut and the 'mismanaged' withdrawal down the Tigris; there was bitter fighting on the Frontier, and conspiracies were discovered in Delhi and elsewhere. Lord Hardinge says[1] that his own health was beginning to deteriorate seriously, and Herbert Baker was ill, at times seriously, during most of this visit. Though immune from the stresses of war, the camp on Raisina Hill had its own inherent tensions which shortly became acute.

All over India construction work was being closed down for the furtherance of the war effort. At New Delhi the axe fell less heavily as yet. Lutyens described the position as 'estimating goes on; schemes gradually get sanction, and then go on as money provides'. Work already undertaken continued but no new operations were sanctioned unless in some way contributing to war potential. One result was that Lutyens could apply himself immediately to some of the important matters of detail and organisation for which there had hitherto been little time. The eventual need of architectural sculpture raised questions of the forms and symbols to be employed, which required to be determined or designed; and of finding or training sculptors, out of which issued the much larger question of forming the centre for the training of craftsmen which was laid down in the architects' agreement with the Government.

They all bore on the great column, donated by the Maharajah of Jaipur to commemorate the Coronation Durbar (p. 331). Robert Byron has described the exquisite ornament:

> The slender pillar, assisted by a pedestal set on a double base of red, rises to a height of 100 ft. Upon it rests a white egg from which, secured by a brass hoop, burgeons a bronze lotus. Finally the calyx of this flower balances on its very tip a six-pointed star of glass, diurnal reminder of the Indian orders of chivalry. The star is 15 ft. in diameter and 148 ft. above the ground.[2]

It was to have been erected in Government Court, at 'Point A', but as has been narrated Lutyens had moved its destined place back to Viceroy's Court. Point A will crop up again in this Section. In the winter of 1915–16, however, the importance of the column lay in the money for it, 2 lakhs of rupees, being available. This would enable work on it to be begun, if the craftsmen could be found. Unfortunately it transpired that this sum, worth some £14,000, would not suffice for a column of the proportions and character designed by Lutyens; and the generous donor had his own views on the decoration of its red sandstone pedestal. Instead of the symbolic reliefs of the King in State and the Royal Arms with Indian suggestions as proposed, H.H. preferred a bas relief of the King as he appeared at the Durbar, which Lutyens opposed. This kind of question recalls the large part played—as testified by Lord

[1] *My Indian Years.*   [2] *Country Life*, June 27, 1931.

Hardinge's memoires[1]—by ceremonies and decorations in the Viceregal routine; and necessarily therefore in the decoration of the Government buildings. The Viceroy took a close interest in the Royal Insignia to be incorporated in sculptured decoration, and discussed with Lutyens models that the latter had had prepared. Armitage, the sculptor, had taken pains to ascertain from the India Office and Heralds' College the Orders worn by Their Majesties at the Durbar, but the Viceroy insisted that only Indian Orders should be represented.

Baker, who ever since their week in Egypt, had been laid up with 'gippy tummy', during convalescence had been working on heraldry for the Secretariats. Lutyens whose ensuing comments suggest a principle of permanent relevance to the architectural rendering of symbols, mentioned that his colleague had been

> very busy making out emblems for India, Provinces, and indeed all the Dependancies of the British Empire—the Rose, Leek, Five Rivers of Punjab, etc. I maintain that an architect should always design in three dimensions. It is his job. That is why I want to give the Star of India [on the Jaipur Column] six points, since five wont be seen from all views as an entity; and yet it can be applied to a coat or shield. Any animal (except a flea or a sole) is all right. In Europe you can always use a figure and emblazon your bearings on a shield, but an allegorical figure is not possible in India.
>
> Architecture should begin where literature (words) leaves off, each depending on the other. It always has in *great* periods.
>
> Baker says it [designing the symbols] is very difficult. I fear it is, and all the more worth the doing. It wants a Shakespearean wit to ordain symbols which will hold the people to them and hold water too.
>
> It is certainly the duty of the architect to go the one better and stick to his three dimensions, and let the painters and writers do the others. I would rather see an orb, which means power, surmounted by a star of six points (which can be drawn flat or round).

Sir Herbert Baker, in *Architecture and Personalities*, has also recounted the value which he came to attach to well conceived symbols. Lutyens respected his enthusiasm, and frequent success in using them, but criticised his tendency to make them two-dimensional or simply inscriptions. Indeed, in an unkind mood, he remarked that Baker was most successful as an architect 'when he has plenty of texts he can put up'

Symbols naturally raised the question of sculptors to execute them. This year a beginning was made with assembling and training the Indian craftsmen who would be needed as the buildings advanced. Lutyens refers to trying a man on a *galli* (pierced stone screen) and another, a Brahmin, on modelling an elephant—probably

[1] *Op. cit.*

in connection with the high reliefs (p. 332), eventually carved by C. S. Jagger, at the corners of the retaining walls of Viceroy's Court formed by the north and south ascents.[1] He had always been enthusiastic for making the building of Delhi the opportunity for establishing a training centre of craftsmanship, a kind of technical university, not only for carvers and painters but engineers and plumbers; and not merely for immediate needs but as the missing counterpart to the immense material and intellectual benefits brought to India by the English. For he felt strongly that whilst the raj had suppressed abominable practices, given India the finest engineering in the world, medicine, sanitation, and virtually abolished famine, it had destroyed the Indians' arts—'though not more than we have done in England', he added characteristically. Lutyens, to whom Mrs. Besant's work for developing India's conscience appealed precisely for its bearing on the re-establishment of conscientious workmanship, kept the ideal of the Delhi Centre very near his heart throughout his Indian years. As it was, however, especially in war-time, 'they are training clerks, and nothing else; and they learn all our evil bureaucratic tricks and little else.' A prime instance of babuism occurred at this very juncture, when he found that a specification being circulated for the staff houses contained the injunction, due evidently to an Indian clerk, that 'no drawing-rooms in any new house shall be rectangular'.

So when the Education Member of the Viceroy's Council, Sir C. Sankaran Nair, going over the site with Lutyens, asked him if he thought the establishment of such a school, if only for three months in each year, would be practicable, he adumbrated a complete scheme. The proposal had recently been put up to the Viceroy who first approved and later rejected it, so that the following outline, contained in a letter to Lady Emily, is probably a version of his official memorandum on the subject:

> A school to promote the fine arts in connection with the building of the new Imperial city of Delhi would be devised to raise the level of endeavour and make the principles taught in the lecture-room visible and practical. It should comprise:
> Masons: work on vault and dome building, walling, carving, sculpture, fine brickwork, and tile mason's work.
> Carpenters and Joiners, including woodcarving, cabinet work and furniture.
> Smiths: metalwork in brass, iron, copper, bronze, gold and silver; from gate grilles and chandeliers to girders.
> Marbleworkers; inlay and intarsia.
> Clock work; orreries, astronomical instruments.

[1] Lutyens often mentioned his fondness for elephants and made many comic sketches of them. That he made drawings for these sculptures is suggested by the beautiful one of a Brahmin bull reproduced for comparison, on p. 332.

Gardening: horticulture and botany.
Painting and decoration.
Sanitation, drainage, plumbing.
Fine writing, inscriptions.
Carpets, weaving, tapestries, curtains, embroidery.

To train hundreds of men to be so employed, happy and contented in their work, accorded with his conviction that 'there will be no happiness in the world again until every man can do his best in the work he best likes doing'. He recognised that at first the provision of good teachers of so many subjects would be difficult. It would be essential to exclude politics. The object should be:

> to form a permanent tradition in the creation of beauty, as applied to everything and to every use, which, when achieved, can but promote the glory of God and follow the great example given by that love and perfection with which all created matter is endowed.
>
> Boys would learn to rely on themselves and on their work, and become citizens in the good sense of the old Guildsmen—so different from the modern trades unions where quality of work is sacrificed to protect the man.
>
> The Guild and patrons would automatically protect and encourage the good craftsman; as of old, the bad craftsman, men not qualified to enter the Guilds, would have to be protected [maintained?] by the public, but not by the Guilds; and there should be places to fit all grades of ability—down to lunatic asylums.
>
> The *Prix de Delhi* men should receive Government commissions; prize students could be employed in helping their seniors; and in time a benevolent circle might be formed, with this Indian School at Delhi spreading its influence and labours over the whole Peninsular.
>
> You will say that it is all material. But it is a far surer foundation, to build spiritual sympathy and understanding on, than politics,—though it may cover a small field of the world's labours.

The miner and the machinist, he admitted, presented difficult problems: 'the man who works in the dark, and the machinist except when engaged in the creation of machines, seem to be occupied with ungodlike operations.' Government, he concluded, should take over from trade unions the onus of determining a living wage. It could not be settled by voting; and so long as members of Governments continued to be educated only in dead languages, little would be achieved. Rather they should be taught their duty to their fellow men as their first objective; and equally political interferences with professional men, debasing their work, should not be tolerated.

96. Viceroy's House. Lower Basement Colonnade (1921)

97. Junction of retaining wall of Viceroy's Court and South Secretariat (1917)

98. Lower Basement of Viceroy's House (1917). Looking west over foundation of the Staircase Court and centre of West Front

99 (*above*). Miss Gertrude Jekyll. By William Nicholson (1920). (National Portrait Gallery)

100 (*right*). Ursula Lutyens. By William Nicholson (1916). (Viscount Ridley)

Even in its most limited form, of a training school connected with the building, this vision never materialised. But it illustrates the idealism of Lutyens's mind, the idealism that he set himself, and realised, in architecture; an ideal demanding an almost superhuman and disciplined loyalty to aesthetic excellence; but at once indefinite and somewhat inelastic in application to practical problems. Within a few days the application of the ideal vision to practical realities was to arise in the issue that dominated the remainder of the 1915–16 session at Delhi.

During January the angle of the gradient of the King's Way as it ascended Raisina Hill became visible. Work on its construction was now being begun and Lutyens realised for the first time, with a shock of dismay and incomprehension, that it was being constructed at the angle of maximum steepness discussed two years ago, and without reference either to him or to its effect upon the visibility of Viceroy's House. He immediately prepared a careful section, not having been furnished with one by his colleague in the interval, and verified that:

> In the view from the Great Place [at its foot] Government House would be obliterated and both the Jaipur Column and the large dome, if built, would be awkwardly truncated.

In a private letter he hinted at the arising dispute by remarking 'Baker curiously tiresome and numb as to what lines and levels are right in landscape work', and complained that he could not get him to discuss the effect, revealed by the section, of the gradient upon the visibility of Viceroy's House. In order to bring the matter to an issue before the Delhi Committee, he wrote a formal letter to Baker roundly asserting:

> This is not satisfactory collaboration.
> There is yet time to avoid these grave defects, so that the original idea we agreed and expressed in your own perspectives is maintained.

At the same time he set out the circumstances leading up to this situation, which have been given in Chapter 10, §4. His fundamental complaint was that he had been largely if not entirely instrumental in procuring Baker's invitation to collaborate at Delhi; that, on Baker's pressure, he had agreed to the setting back of Government House from Raisina Hill in order to share the eminence with the Secretariats; and that Baker had assured him that the visibility of Government House would not thereby be affected as from the processional approach: on the contrary, Baker's perspectives, exhibited at the Royal Academy, had shown its front unobscured. He himself had been careful not to interfere in Baker's sphere of responsibility, confident that the latter would observe the spirit of this assurance; and in view of this confidence, and of the adjacent levels being still undetermined, had incautiously signed a minute affecting the maximum gradients to be employed.

Now Baker informed him that he had signed his agreement to the actual angle of gradient and that he had nothing to do with the surroundings of the Secretariat. Sir Herbert in a letter to Hailey (March 18, 1916) enables us to see how, meanwhile and perhaps throughout, he had come to the conclusion that the practical and social value of a level expanse of Government Court outweighed with him the scenic value of a continuous sight of Government House:

> Whether the Acropolis idea of our original conception was right or wrong, now it is there it appears to me inconceivably unwise to cut the raised court in two by a continuous deep cutting or to cut it away in endless and useless steps. To do so would have 'mistake of conception' and 'change of plan' writ large over it for all time.

Quite apart from the merits of the contention here urged, which is generally agreed by impartial opinion to be sound, the use by Sir Herbert of these expressions is, indeed, astounding! Who had changed whose plan? On what is the mistake of conception writ large but on the macadam of the steep gradient?

Baker maintained[1] that he had frequently explained to Lutyens his need for a level expanse in Government Court: Lutyens that he had only agreed to the gradient on the condition of a model of the whole emplacement and its approaches being made. It is impossible to elucidate how the misconception arose other than by the regrettable supposition that, their relations being what they were, Lutyens had made no great effort to understand Baker's point of view, and Baker, the more he became convinced of the benefits of a level Government Court, refrained from stating his case fully and frankly to Lutyens lest the latter should revoke his inadvertent agreement to the gradient. Sir Herbert's position was technically unassailable. But Lutyens came to feel, with increasing bitterness, that he had been double-crossed, scored off. Unfortunately it would not be surprising if a hundred little barbed sallies on his part, and indeed larger differences such as their quarrel over terms and his outrageously comic letter to the lawyer settling it, now that they came home to roost, found the once green and flourishing tree of Baker's friendship leafless and brittle. The last paragraph of this section seems to confirm that the latter was not insensible, now, that the laugh was with him.

Before the matter came up before the Committee Lutyens took into his confidence Lady du Boulay who was wife of the Viceroy's Private Secretary and, since Lady Hardinge's death, H.E.'s close friend. She 'was very sympathetic and duly shocked'. Sir James du Boulay visited the site next day to verify it for himself and expressed himself as 'horrified', but pointed out that a decision must rest with the Viceroy who, Lutyens considered, was 'unknowing and all but unapproachable on matters of physical effect'.

[1] Memoranda 1921 and 1931.

FIRST WAR YEARS

Yet he was not without confidence that the Committee would revoke the gradient decision. It had recently been reconstituted, with Sir Claud Hill representing the Public Works Department, and worked more efficiently instead of 'everything having been done, till now, in watertight compartments'. It had recently accepted his design for the layout of the Great Place. At a meeting in mid-February he therefore recapitulated the substance of his letter to Baker, the latter substantiating his rebuttals point by point. But his general case was that the work under construction did not fulfil 'the advertised, exhibited, and agreed intentions'.

The Committee took the view that Lutyens's proposal involved a departure from accepted plans, 'carrying the termination of the slope back to a little east of the railings dividing Government Court from Viceroys Court'; whereas Baker was claiming that 'the pitch of the road is inherent in the nature of the raised platform which was agreed to as a basis of the Plan for the central buildings in 1913'; and that 'in a two mile vista a prospect which for part of the distance hides and then reveals itself again is rather an attraction than otherwise'. Baker added, in his evidence, which Lutyens regarded as mean of him, that any change would involve very considerable expense in blasting and building walls and pulling down portions of the front east walls already built. This, the Committee ascertained, would cost between 20,000 and 30,000 rupees (some £2000), and concluded that there had been no departure from the original proposal. Were the gradient altered, Government Court would 'practically disappear', the privacy of Viceroy's Court be intruded upon by being made visible from the Great Court, and the proposed prolongation of the gradient and its retaining walls constitute a serious inconvenience.

> In short, without discussing the artistic merits of the alternative picture, the Committee feel that the extra expenditure would produce a result involving serious material and administrative disadvantages and cannot be justified.

Thus the Delhi Committee rejected any alteration, primarily in order to save £2000, and, specifically, without considering the aesthetic implication. Lutyens learnt through du Boulay, to his chagrin, that Lord Hardinge was equally opposed to any alteration. 'It is a cruel shame,' he commented to his wife; 'I shall have to insist on its going to the Government of India to get my objection put on record, and then I shall have the odium of explaining to everyone that Baker's perspective is all wrong. Hardinge doesn't really care a bit, so long as something is done for his estimate.'

The Viceroy, occupied by the manifold engagements of his last weeks of office, did not receive Lutyens for a month. Meanwhile the latter saw him, in public, not as the arbiter of Delhi's and India's destinies, but as a pathetic, bereaved, rather little man. He was engaged in opening the Lady Hardinge Medical College and Hospital for Women at Delhi—initiated by his wife and erected since her death at the cost of £100,000. Lutyens described the ceremony, adding:

> But O, the ugliness of the building. Everyone realised it but no one cared. H.E.'s position having to talk about Lady Hardinge was pathetic. And the big state chair was so high that his legs swung—like a child's.

Each architect, with the other's cognizance, submitted their views in writing. Lutyens, apologising for troubling His Excellency at such a time, yet insisted that the matter was of such importance that he would be failing in his duty if he did not draw attention to it. He continued:

> I have, by the Committee's showing, made a great mistake in signing a plan which committed them to a gradient such as can only, in my opinion, produce an ugly and clumsy effect. I made this error in good faith.

Having designed the Courts at either end of the area in question, he had assumed that the intervening portion would be designed in sympathy and so as not to obstruct the view of Government House which was the 'original, logical, and right intention'. The Committee had not officially shown him the Government Architect's perspective drawing, so that he could have protested three years ago. In any case, such a question should not be decided, as by the Committee, entirely on grounds of cost. He insisted that 'in an architectural composition of three great buildings, with two Towers and three Domes', the decision should be made upon their relationship, not upon factors connected with a particular point of detail.

He asked the Viceroy to postpone decision, unless he should be convinced now, till a model could be made and submitted. If the gradient were reduced, it would be possible to eliminate steps from Government Court altogether, and the Secretariats could be connected by covered ways entered from the cuttings, so that people passing from one building to the other would only have the width of the roadway itself to cross in the open. 'This would not materially interfere with the lines of Mr. Baker's Secretariat gardens, a detail which he considers essential.' He admitted that these passages may further increase the extra cost of the altered gradient, but 'in a matter of this importance I do not think an extra cost, small in its relative percentage to the total cost of the buildings, should prohibit the rectification of the present line'. He was convinced that much greater outlay would be involved later, when rectification of the line would be demanded.

Baker limited himself to objecting that the proposed 'covered ways' did not remove the inconvenience of stairways giving access to them from the Secretariats; and that, if the roadway was carried up in a cutting, processions using it would see little, when between the walls of the sunken road, of the Secretariat buildings. 'After much thought,' he concluded, 'I still feel, as I have felt from the beginning, that the present plan is an inherently good one both from an aesthetic as well as from a practical consideration.'

Lord Hardinge interviewed Lutyens on March 10—the day after, he tells us in his memoirs, that he had received a telegram conferring on him the Order of the Garter. Lutyens made notes of their conversation, from which the interesting point emerged that the setting back of Viceroy's House from the crest of Raisina Hill had been against Hardinge's own wish. Once that was done 'it did not matter whether it was seen from anywhere as is could not be seen from everywhere'. He denied that cost was the prime consideration, complained that Lutyens had brought no alternative plan, and, when he produced one, said it was to a different scale and that anyhow he only looked at plans which had been agreed by both architects. Nor would he consider a model, which would be too costly. Lutyens offered to defray the cost; but that it could not be ready before he left India. Lutyens 'submitted to him a moveable diagram showing the effects produced as planned and in relation to Baker's official perspective' (p. 314): a deadly serious application of his playful transparencies. But 'H.E. would not consider my contentions and suggestions on their merits. I do not consider that my plan has been heard'.

The Viceroy proceeded to expand these views in a full communication to Hailey, as President of the Delhi Committee, dated March 13. He again emphasised how the difficulty was inherent in the setting back of the House from the point that he had himself selected. He recalled to Hailey how

> You and I rode to the top of Raisina Hill and decided that that was the site for Government House. My idea had always been that it alone should be on Raisina Hill, the Secretariats on the lower ground. The architects however conceived a scheme which they thought better ... and that Government House should be thrown further back and thus share with the Secretariats the dominant position in the new city. I remember pointing out that this would be the result; but as the architects pressed their scheme, and as I considered it to be a fine one from an architectural point of view, I accepted their views. From that moment, the idea that Government House should be seen from every part of the city vanished. ... The idea that it should be seen without interruption along any particular road was never raised, and I remember that it was perfectly obvious to me, as to everyone else, that the crest of the hill would naturally obscure the view of Government House on the processional road for a space of rather less than half a mile from the foot of the hill. This to me was of trivial importance, once the idea of the visibility of Government House from every side had been surrendered.

This remarkable assertion can be qualified by recalling that one person at least, who might be expected to have shared Lord Hardinge's knowledge, namely Sir James du

Boulay, his Private Secretary, was, as has been noted, 'horrified' when Lutyens pointed out to him, a few weeks previous to this date, the fact so long obvious to Lord Hardinge.

Regarding Lutyens's specific proposal, the Viceroy adopted Baker's argument:

> From an aesthetic point of view such a cutting, which will have the appearance of a glorified railway cutting, presents to my mind very serious objections, since the architectural value of the Secretariat buildings will be entirely lost from the moment one enters until one leaves the cutting, while the fine courtyard which, according to the present plan, will exist in front of them, will practically disappear. It will only be possible for a visitor to obtain a good view of the Secretariats when he arrives at the end of the cutting adjoining the gates of the Viceroy's Court, by turning and looking back. This means the complete disruption of Government House and the Secretariat buildings as a harmonious whole which, I submit, is a most important object of attainment.

He shared also Baker's view of the inconvenience and costliness of connecting passages, even if served by lifts. 'It should most certainly be rejected,' he added. In conclusion:

> My own feeling would be, in approaching Raisina Hill from the direction of Indrapat, that it would be pleasant to have a fine vista in the distance of the Secretariats with Government House in the background, but that, on approaching Raisina Hill, the attention of the mind should be diverted in pleasant anticipation of the fountains and other works of architectural art that one expects to find in the forecourt [? those designed for the Great Place], and while mounting the incline the attention should be diverted to the Secretariats and the treatment of the plinths until one arrives expectant on the summit of the crest and finds almost the whole of the Secretariats and Government House laid out before one. This I regard as the true and natural frame of mind and one that I have always anticipated. Unless my memory deceives me, my impression is that the piazza of St. Peters at Rome, which is comparable to the platform comprising Government and Viceroy's Courts, has no vista on any road by which it can be approached, while the dome of St. Peters may be said to dominate Rome. I see no reason why the dome of Government House should not do the same in Delhi without a continuous vista on the processional road.
>
> These are my views, and having carefully supervised the new Delhi project from its very inception, I have considered it necessary to place them on record, and to state my opinion that the decision of the Delhi Committee appears to me amply justified.

There was no immediate reply possible, but in a letter to Sir Valentine Chirol, a

Member of the Viceroy's Council, Lutyens replied to Lord Hardinge's fallacious argument from St. Peter's, and the analogy of a railway cutting.

> A railway is such an odd idea to occur to anyone! I have done *so* many gardens. It is a cruel invention. There are famous Italian gardens where slopes have been used with good effect; and the Forecourt at Versailles, which has a bigger rise, does not give a railway effect though it has carriage ways up to projecting wings.
>
> I agree with Lord Hardinge that in approaching Raisina Hill it would be pleasant to have a fine vista of the Secretariats and Government House. But from the avenue the Secretariats *cannot be seen*—at point B they are hidden by the trees of the avenue and the towers will only be seen from the Great Place; whilst for more than half its length Government House and the Jaipur Column are spoilt by truncation, finally to disappear.
>
> It is not right or fine that the central object of a vista should disappear and reappear. An avenue stops at its first break and the stop should have a designed termination, not an ever varying one.
>
> The dome of St. Peters dominates the city only when seen from the famous seven hills. Bernini designed a road direct from his great Piazza to the Tiber. The line of this road exists. It is a misfortune it has not been cleared. The last Syndic told me he hoped to do it.[1] The great criticism of St. Peters is that the dome disappears behind the huge narthex. It would be seen from Bernini's Road. The obelisk would never (!) disappear; nor does the dome after obliviation reappear like a Jack in the box.... I cannot draw the same conclusions from it as Lord Hardinge. As an example, it condemns the very thing he and Baker contend for.

In a postscript he scribbled the first form of a bitter joke which he subsequently circulated with considerable effect: a drawing of the Star of India surmounting the Jaipur Column as seen from the Great Place, with the caption 'No dogs must be allowed on the ramp' (p. 358).

Both architects left Delhi shortly after this. Lutyens intimated that he would be willing for the question to be submitted to arbitration, but Baker refused. At one moment Lutyens had thought of resigning but, apart from every other consideration, he was too inveterate a fighter to contemplate retirement, and his armoury was far from being exhausted. On the boat, during 'a very jumpy journey owing to the number of submarines in the Mediterranean', the architects argued ineffectually. 'Baker says I will not stick to Point A [the original site of the Jaipur Column near the top of the gradient]; I say he will not face the fact of Government House not being seen as shown with deliberation in his drawings.' When Lutyens told him that

[1] This has of course now been effected.

he proposed to bring the whole matter before the King, Baker 'laughed heartily, and said I could not see a joke against myself. I own I do not see where the joke comes in'.[1]

NO DOGS MUST BE ALLOWED ON THE RAMP

[1] Letter to W. M. Hailey, April 2, 1916.

CHAPTER XIII

CENOTAPH

§1. HALF-WAY HOUSE

THE summer of 1916 was remembered by the children for its happiness. In retrospect, it was an island of serenity in the grey war years, on which the family were all gathered together as they used to be at Bloomsbury Square and in a way, as it turned out, that they would never be together again. The children were all too young for the carnage of the Somme to have reality for them; but Barbara, Robert, and Ursula were old enough to be conscious of atmosphere and surroundings and personalities, and these all seemed what they should be when one is young, but so rarely are. One reason was that they were living in one of Father's favourite houses.

The Lutyenses had been lent Folly Farm, near Theale in the Kennet valley, by Mrs. Merton its new owner. The weeks spent there represented the nearest approach they ever attained to the ideal of domestic happiness that, long ago, Ned had envisaged for his bride: the little country house with a trim garden for her and some fishing for him. The building was of sufficient distinction for them to have their friends to stay, and the place afforded all the resources to occupy the children as they should be at their age in the country. He himself was inwardly gnawed by anxiety and frustration—by the inevitable paralysis of architecture at the peak of the war, by the drain on his savings when the children needed more spent on them than ever, and by the sickening sense of having been double-crossed during the past weeks at Delhi. Somehow that defeat must be avenged, the wrong course on to which Hardinge's bureaucracy and Baker's obstinacy were forcing his design must be righted. Yet for the nonce and by luck the semblance, if not substance, of his dream had come true, and he was happy there. These summer evenings at Folly Farm fulfilled the picture that was always in his mind, wherever he might be, in train, or ship, or tent, when he ended his home letter to Emmy with some such form of the familiar sequence as 'my great love to Barbararie, Roberti boy, her Ursulaship, Betty my own, Mary Mine, dear Nanny. Bless them all and most darling yourself. Your very own loving Nedi'.

Two years later another of those half-dreams, half-vows, of his courting days was signally fulfilled: the winning of worldly honour for Emmy and Ned, which he had used to picture with a knight in armour riding forth to prove his lady's faith in him. Yet within a few weeks of his receiving the accolade of knighthood he must write to her, remembering these summer weeks perhaps (though the name Folly Farm may have acquired an ironic bitterness): 'the only chance for cohesion is a garden, a farm, ponies, etc. But it is a chance I have lost.' By then, the war had nearly disintegrated their family life, even when apparently crowning his worldly ambition, and as nearly as it had shattered the civilisation that he represented. In another twenty-five years his world would lie in ruins indeed, though by then, all passion spent, husband and wife were reunited as closely as though their cohesion had never been strained.

This chapter, which covers the closing years of the war, will end with Lutyens at the summit of his powers, acknowledged the first architect of his age, and with the genius displayed in his most brilliant single feat universally acclaimed. But it will also have to note the beginning of that process of recession: in his personal life from the ideals that he had set himself in youth; in his world from the humanist ideal. There will, however, be no kind of recession in his powers as an artist. On the contrary, the twenty-five years of his greatest successes will yet lie before him. What we shall miss is the unity of artist, man, and age, which has, perhaps, been the most notable aspect of this story hitherto. Henceforth the artist will hold consistently on his quest for the geometrical quintessence of perfection, the man cloak disillusion with his kind by increasing recourse to levity, and the world be forced to set out on untried paths in search of life. Not inaptly, therefore, may this chapter in Lutyens's life which tells of ideals realised but illusions lost, be named from his memorial to the spirits of those whose earthly part is buried elsewhere; and this section of it, which begins with the end of his youth, be entitled Half-way House.

Folly Farm itself, like Crooksbury, was one of his most intimate buildings, in which he had been able to portray his developing sensibility. The miniature Wren-naissance house of 1905, the colour of ripe strawberries and bloomy plums, had been expanded in 1912 with that barn-like wing and cloister of brick arches rising from a pool (p. 130); a combination that still pleased him by its wit. Most of his early buildings made him sad now, but this one bore not only being revisited but lived in with old friends. Even Bumps was coaxed away from Munstead Wood and, after doing a little gardening by force of habit, would take off her hob-nailed boots to play the pianola. William Nicholson, back from India, stayed for weeks beginning paintings. He had been commissioned to decorate the dining-room at Folly Farm and began the now legendary *trompe l'œil* in bistre and greys of bird-cages and bell-pulls among red lacquer windows and a shadowy frieze of china plates, of which, owing to the indifference of a subsequent owner, the *Country Life* photographs alone survive. He also began seven portraits of Ursula. Six came to premature ends, but the seventh (p. 350) is the portrait of her wearing a bearskin that belonged to a fancy dress got for some party in Apple Tree Yard. He eventually finished it, dashing in the inquiring, round-eyed, face in little more than half an hour. Next year Nicholson became Lutyens's neighbour in what had been Lord Strafford's stable at 11 Apple Tree Yard.

Other personal happenings marked this year as the half-way post for Lutyens. His father, the old Captain, passed away and with him the Venetian secret; and Lutyens was elected to the Garrick Club, that genial *rendezvous* of men who enjoy talking to each other, in which, when he got used to it, he spent so many of the happiest hours of his later life. He was proposed by George Frampton, the sculptor, seconded by Alfred Sutro, the playwright, and supported by Orpen, Col. Newnham Davis, W. J. Locke, Norman Forbes-Robertson, George Alexander, and G. R. Halkett. And in Lady Cunard's box at the Opera, he was introduced to Lady Sackville, who afterwards dropped him at Bedford Square and noted in her diary how delightful she had found him.

The later war years, by slowing down and finally stopping work at Delhi, constitute a half-way mark in that respect also, though not chronologically. But as yet Lutyens, so far from foreseeing the static years, threw most of his energy into a 'plot' to expedite and gain a greater measure of control over operations by taking advantage of the change of Viceroys.

During the course of the summer of '16, the King and Queen began to take increasing interest in Delhi. It is impossible to say to what extent Lutyens was directly responsible for Their Majesties' concern, though it will be remembered that on the boat returning from India he had recently told Baker that he would have to bring the matter of the gradient to the King's notice. A contributory factor was no doubt Lord Curzon's renewed opposition to the cost of Delhi and the pressure brought by him on Austen Chamberlain, the new Secretary of State, to abandon the undertaking. However it came about, that summer Queen Mary paid a visit to the Delhi Office at 7 Apple Tree Yard in order to inspect the plans. The Queen noticed that the designs had been greatly altered from those submitted and approved at Balmoral three years previously, expressed a fear that, as a result of the economies effected, the State suite originally intended for their Majesties' use would now be inadequate; and, with her personal interest in furniture, inquired how the arrangements for furnishing Government House were progressing.

§2. INTERIM REPORT

Queen Mary's visit to the Delhi Office was the prelude to Lutyens having interviews with the King and the Secretary of State at which he was able to express his opinion on the unsatisfactory state of affairs and make his own proposals for their future conduct. They can be grouped under the heads of Furnishing and the Control of Architectural Design.

From the first he had pressed for the establishment of a school for Indian craftsmen in conjunction with the building of the capital, and the institution of an annual *'prix de Delhi'* on the lines of that of the British School at Rome. The outlines of his proposal to Lord Hardinge were summarised in Chapter XII, §5. The selection of appropriate models of furniture and decorations was to be entrusted to committees of experts in India and London, and he was urging their appointment on Lord Crewe as early as August 31, 1914. The former, he had suggested, might consist of the Viceroy, Hailey, de Montmorency, and Lord Carmichael—the last then Governor of Bengal and a man of exceptionally well-informed taste; the latter, of Lord Crewe, Lionel Earle, Hugh Lane, Sargent, and Lady Horner 'who knows the rules of comfort and the needs of a great house'. Among the first duties of the London committee should be to select models of old and modern furniture for reproduction by Indian craftsmen. If the garden of Government House came under its scope he recommended the addition to its membership of Sir Herbert Jekyll and Miss Ellen Wilmot. Nothing had come of it at the time but the scheme of committees was now resuscitated by the India Office which agreed to the formation of a Delhi Advisory Committee.

On the larger issue of architecture, Lutyens's correspondence with Hailey, as Chief Commissioner for Delhi, throws some light. The latter welcomed the King's interest in the new capital as a trump card to forestall proposals to close down building operations any further, but as regards the Queen's criticisms that the State suite was now too small, he pointed out that, with the foundations now finished and the basements well advanced, Lutyens might find it difficult to effect any radical change. With this Lutyens agreed (October 17) but made a suggestion that should be recorded as a matter of historical interest, illustrating it with a thumb-nail sketch-plan.

This proposes a range of Royal Apartments set in front of the west, garden, front of Government House, to which it would be connected by corridors or colonnades enclosing a garden court. 'It is', he remarked, 'the only way I see to provide for a King Emperor's wing, on a level with the main floor, and providing a garden up to that level, to satisfy their Majesties. Their Excellencies' present rooms would become guest rooms.'

At the same time (October 18) Lutyens sent a communication to Lord Stamfordham, for the King's consideration, strongly criticising the Government of India's handling of New Delhi and putting forward a proposal for the control by the Crown of further developments. He sent Hailey a copy of the document.

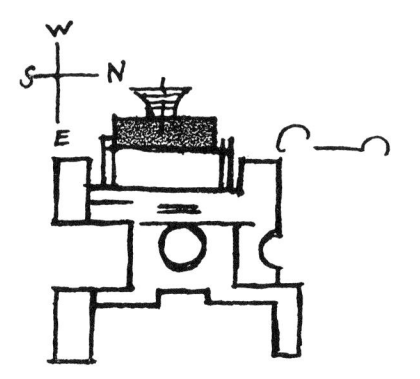

SUGGESTED ADDITION OF A STATE SUITE TO WEST FRONT OF VICEROY'S HOUSE

His complaint was that estimates had been framed according to political exigencies, ignoring architectural requirements, and in water-tight compartments so that money saved in one could not be expended in another without the Secretary of State's sanction for which there was reluctance to apply. The allocation for Government House, he stated, had from the outset been incompatible with the requirements demanded by the Government of India, and, rather than make application for sanctioning larger expenditure, the plans had been reduced despite their having been approved by the King. Every category—Secretariats, Drainage, Irrigation, Railways, Staff accommodation—had suffered alike, whilst the £1,000,000 allotted to unforeseen contingencies had remained an accountants' dream. It was by such methods, Lutyens alleged, that final decisions had been reached in every case, and not, therefore, in the best interests of the work. The initiative, he bluntly pointed out, really lay with the Chief Commissioner for Delhi, 'a most excellent man but, as a Treasury man, his first and final idea is to sacrifice size and quality so as loyally to adhere to the original (lay) Estimates and to avoid appeal to the Secretary of State.'

He then proposed to Stamfordham: 'What I should like to see is the King taking over the initiative for Government House, its furnishing, gardens, and staff quarters,' and for Government House specifically a Committee presided over by the Queen in person. In any event he wished to be given the right to appeal to the King directly against decisions which, as architect, he considered detrimental to the permanent dignity of the conception. He then suggested the building of the additional western range of State Apartments. It will be noticed, however, that he had not yet referred to the alteration of the gradient, which we may regard as Lutyens's implicit objective in this remarkable proposition. That was to come.

A fortnight later, November 4, he was received at Buckingham Palace. He spread out in the dining-room the drawings and perspectives of Government House, plans of the layout, photographs of the Secretariat designs and others. Writing to Lord Chelmsford, he described the King and Queen as having gone carefully through all the drawings; and remarked:

> The King realised that the plans of Government House were not the same as Their Majesties had already seen and approved, and said that they should not have been altered and reduced without his being consulted and his consent obtained. His Majesty commanded me in future to write to Lord Stamfordham on matters concerning Government House etc.
>
> The accommodation, thickness of walls, and number of bathrooms were criticised; that there was no Sitting Room for the wife of the Viceroy attached to their Bedroom Suite; and that this Suite was too far removed from the Private Sitting Room. Their Majesties remembered the original plans which had the Viceroy's Bedroom, Sitting Room, Office etc *en suite*. I pointed out how some of their criticisms might be met.

His Majesty regretted that Marble was not used for the façades of the Palace, that the Marble Statues of the King and Queen given by the Maharajas Bikanir and Gwalior would not look right against a stone building and will have to be reproduced in stone or bronze; His Majesty preferred bronze.

The King approved the water basins on the Palace roofs and the Horses as emblems flanking the Statues. His Majesty was very emphatic on the importance of using monoliths for the Columns throughout the Palace.

As to the cost, it did not matter how long the Palace took to build, so long as it was, when built, worthy of India and its purpose, and if money was not forthcoming now, parts might for the time being be omitted and façades left unfinished as is usual in Italy, until such time as money was available to complete them.

I pointed out it would be feasible to omit the façades if they were faced with marble on completion, but not if faced with stone.

His Majesty objected to the rise in level from the Great Place masking and impairing the dignity and approach to the Palace, which should be the one predominating building of first importance in the new Capital.

That the Staff Houses & Quarters, Stables and Gardens with their Terraces, Walls, running Waterways etc., as being part of the Palace, should be built of stone, or material to match, with all due dignity to the Viceroy's Establishment as a whole.

The Bungalows and official residences in the New City should be built well and made to conform to the dignity due to an Imperial City.

That the design and erection of Government House was a question of first importance and personal to their Majesties.

One does not know which aspect of this document is the most surprising: George V's remarkable memory, according to Lutyens, for quite minute details in plans that he can scarcely have had time to memorise three years previously; or Lutyens's delightful ignorance of the constitutional position of the British King Emperor. He had gone to a great deal of trouble to secure this trump card. Alas, it turned out to be the Joker, and the laugh would still be with the more sagacious and therefore all the more provocative Brer Baker.

However, with this memorandum of his interview in his pocket, Lutyens set out for Delhi with high hopes of being able to assert his authority as principal architect with the new Viceroy. The journey, at the end of 1916, was again *via* Spain and seems to have been the most adventurous of his war-time passages to India, as it was also destined to be his last. But Lutyens's account of it is missing. From oblique references it appears that, in getting to El Guadelperal, he 'was upset in a Rolls Royce and the ferry across the Tagus sank', then in the Mediterranean his ship was shelled by a submarine for an hour and forty minutes. He got to Delhi at the beginning of January, 1917.

§3. DELHI 1917-19

Encouraging changes had taken place. On Raisina Hill there was at last something to see. The great retaining walls of Viceroy's Court were approaching completion—the south side considerably more advanced than the north. The east end of the south wall was up to the coping at the point, known locally as 'the Bakerlootyens junction', where it joined the basement of the Secretariat (p. 349). The lower basement of the S.E. wing of Government House was half-built, and the vast piers of the Kitchen Loggia, to support the South Court, were rising; by the end of 1917 their corbelled capitals, carved with Lutyens's mute bells, were in position (p. 349). The greater part of Government House was reaching Upper Basement level. Its catacombs, partly blasted out of the rock, partly brick-built, looked like a gigantic maze from the vantage point of the staging at Durbar Hall level (p. 349). In this photograph we are looking west and excavation in the foreground is for the foundations of the West Staircase; the sheds beyond occupy the position of the Garden. The garden front was not yet above ground; the north side was reaching Lower-Basement level. In every direction trolley-lines criss-crossed, penetrating into the basements, and there was a regular railway siding for the unloading of materials near the foundations of the north-west wing. It had taken five years to get thus far, but now people who came out to inspect the works began to be impressed.

The new Viceroy, though reticent and reserved, contrasted agreeably with his formidable predecessor. Lord Chelmsford had, indeed, been serving as a Captain in a Territorial battalion in India prior to his sudden translation to the position to which, in view of the critical situation, some had expected that Lord Kitchener would be appointed. Before leaving India the previous year Lutyens had, with Lord Hardinge's permission, drafted a letter to Lord Chelmsford on the gradient question, in which he offered to have models made at his own expense to illustrate the points at issue. In it he had frankly stated:

> I regret that absorption in my profession has prevented me realising the rules that control bureaucratic methods; but I fail to see why posterity should suffer from an error made in good faith through ignorance of methods outside the philosophy of my profession as an architect. In any event, may I ask that my Protest is officially recorded.

If this letter, which exists only in a MS. draft, was sent, no action appears to have been taken upon it.

His first encounter with the Viceroy also began rather unfortunately. The elderly office car carrying him to dine at Viceregal Lodge broke down in a low suburb of the old city:

> I was stranded. I phoned Government House and they promised to send a car to my relief. So off I went walking to meet it. I walked at least 2 miles, when I was lucky enough to pick up a 2nd class Tonga. I never met the car. I got to the house about five to nine (dinner at 8.15), found no one in the portico, so I walked in; no one in the Hall, and I walked on; no one in the inner room, so I walked . . . but the band was playing, so I entered the dining room. They had reached the pudding stage. Chelmsford was very friendly and my place was kept by Lady C's side. . . I told her I heard she did not like puns. She said she loved them, but I was good and did not make any.

Lutyens had already sent copies of his memorandum of the interview with the King to the Viceroy and leading members of the Delhi Committee. Lord Chelmsford now assured him that money was the only difficulty and that it had been largely due not to the Government of India, but to Lord Hardinge. He had to point out, however, that neither he as Viceroy, nor the Government, nor the Delhi Committee could take any action upon the substance of Lutyens's memorandum, since his conversations with the King had been in the nature of a private interview. If he wished to pursue it, Lutyens must raise the matter with the Secretary of State. This he now proceeded to do, having hoped it would not be necessary in view of Austen Chamberlain's indifference, as he regarded it, to the architectural aspect of Delhi. We hear nothing further of direct intervention by the Crown in the raising of Delhi. Lutyens's *démarche* had failed.

But he acted on the King's command to be kept in touch with proceedings, reporting to Lord Stamfordham on the situation as he found it at the beginning of 1917. He mentioned that the estimates for the superstructure of Government House, which had just been completed, came to £80,000 in excess of the sum allotted. Part of the excess, he expected, was in respect of decorations which it would prove possible, and legitimate, to omit.

Five principal houses for the Viceroy's Staff had to be cut down in size and quality.

The Stables were to go on, but in brick or mud, plastered and whitewashed, unless Chamberlain approved more worthy methods of construction. He said, 'I told Lord Chelmsford and Sir Claude Hill that Imperial Delhi should be built in Levée dress rather than in overalls.' Bungalows in course of erection for gazetted officers were of inferior quality and some would have to be pulled down.

Lord Chelmsford had approved the principle of an advisory committee for the furnishing of Government House.

He went on to outline the possibility of the omission of the Viceroy's Council

Chamber from Government House, as in fact followed from the constitutional changes proposed a year later in the Montagu-Chelmsford Report. At this stage the suggestion was put forward by Claude Hill, without divulging the real reason, on grounds of economy, meeting the Royal criticisms, and the possible future needs of the Council. It is interesting to find both Lutyens and Keeling, the Chief Engineer, at once agreeing to the change, and Lutyens accurately foreseeing the architectural outcome:

> This would eventually entail an important building, costing more money. But it would add to the dignity of the scheme as a whole, since economy in the Secretariat Buildings has resulted in their terminating one of the main avenues of the new city in a very ugly and awkward fashion.
>
> These new Council or Parliament Buildings would be so placed that they would mask the Secretariats and might in themselves make a worthy termination of the important road that leads direct from the railway station.

A rough sketch plan in the letter shows a circular building, as erected, on approximately the site occupied by Sir Herbert Baker's Legislative Chamber. That its designing fell within Baker's and not his province resulted from an arrangement come to at this time.

The two colleagues were not getting on together any better. But Lutyens was, he wrote, working hard, from 9 a.m. till 11 or 12 at night, going out little. He had only two assistants left in the office, Wands and Barrett, and gave a good deal of time to helping Nichols, the Government Architect and his native assistants. He himself was occupied with details and estimates for Government House and 'my piéce de resistance, the gardens of Government House' the earthworks of which the Committee would be able to put in hand in event of masonry building having to be closed down. Both architects were also working on designs for the houses for the Viceroy's Staff.

Welcome reliefs were visits from Baker's friend of Pretoria and Round Table days, Lionel Curtis, then working independently on the constitutional problems which the Viceroy and Edwin Montagu were to review with such thoroughness later in the year. Lutyens found Curtis 'charming and amusing, and easily amused; very unlike old Baker who lives in the furrowed clay of his own despondency. Curtis makes me walk, and every day now I take long walks and—don't rub it in!— I feel much better spirited and hearted for it. Standing all day at my work takes it out of me'.

When the alternative schemes for the staff bungalows came up before the Committee, Lutyens's, as he expected and intended, came too expensive, and Baker's 'bungle ohs!' as he contemptuously termed them, also too high but possible. After some animated discussion, Lutyens suggested his being relieved from 'the anguish of designing jerry-villas' in return for responsibility for all buildings along the State Approach, including 'Point B'—the intersection of the north-south Queen's Way with the King's Way, and the newly proposed site of the All India War Memorial at the next intersection eastwards. He was much elated at this exchange and mentioned that he had already made sketch designs for one of the four big buildings to flank Point B—intended to comprise the Ethnological Museum and the Record Office.

This re-alignment of their spheres of influence brought Lutyens the great Memorial Arch (the buildings at Point B never materialised except parts of the Record Office), but equally set the Legislative Chamber in Baker's area.

Another cheering development was that the Government decided to allocate an additional £130,000 to Government House and to release the reserve fund for essential purposes. But none of the funds so obtained were to be applied to altering the levels of the Approach 'during the present time of war'.

Designs for the garden of Government House were completed and submitted in February. When Government House was intended to stand on the lower level, Lady Hardinge had visualised a Persian type of garden with water-courses and cascades descending the slope to the west front. On the actual site the terrain available consisted of the rocky neck connecting Raisina Hill to the Viceroy's Domain—the latter an area of 330 acres on the lower slopes of the Ridge. It was in the Domain that the Bodyguard and Stable lines were to be situated, terminating diagonal vistas, with the Private and Military Secretaries' houses, and the bungalows for the Viceroy's Staff, somewhat further off. Hence the concern that Lutyens felt for their worthiness to form part of the intensely humanised landscape that he envisaged.

In the space intervening between the Domain and the west front of Government House he was instructed to design a Moghul Garden. This, by its nature, involved terraces, waterways, sunk courts, and extensions of the great retaining walls at the sides to create the level area required. For the present he was allocated 'sufficient money to plant some shrubs and no more; it is too Alice-in-Wonderlandish for words. But it will come in time'.

This is the origin of surely one of the most highly wrought pleasaunces ever laid out; a wonderful affirmation of the power of intellect over nature, in this case an arid, treeless, rocky, and inhospitable nature. The miracle that in time he worked, creating ten acres of brilliant mosaic compacted of intersecting canals, fountains splashing on tiers of red sandstone water-lily leaves, paved alleys, squares of lawn, plats of flowers, and geometrical groves of trees, was as yet a mirage of the future. But during the three lean years before he returned to Delhi, during which Government House scarcely progressed at all, it proved possible for the immense amount of spadework and making up of ground to be carried on, so that, when Viceroy's House was at length occupied, its garden was established.

As time went on it became clear that no fresh building work would be undertaken before the end of the war. The demand for detailed drawings for Government House therefore ceased, and Lutyens was required only to wait, before returning home, for the revised estimates to be worked out and a decision to be reached on the extent of the stoppage. But he wasted no time. He described to his wife how,

> As I am paid 5 guineas a day for advice alone, I fill every spare moment designing something that may or may not be. It helps the Government to formulate instructions, focuses their needs, and I am able to lay down principles affecting the scale and treatment of various sites and positions.

Among buildings for which he made sketch designs now were the Cathedral, the Ethnological Museum and Record Office, a proposal for the War Memorial, diagrams for the location of Rajahs' palaces, and the treatment of the setting of the ruins of Indrapat. 'Unless these are foreseen and formulated,' he wrote to Stamfordham 'the result will become a tangle of undigested ideas, and the fiasco, as I consider it, of the approach to Government House will be repeated.

> As regards the proposed War Memorial, I hear it is suggested that it should take some utilitarian form. This, I think, will be a great opportunity missed. Utilitarian objects should be provided in any case in due time as a duty. But to commemorate this great war a structure should be erected where, independant of creed and caste, all India may commemorate her great men, who have served their King Emperor and Country, now and for all time.
>
> It would surely do more to give pride of country, unity of service, than the erection or endowment of a scheme that can only appeal to a limited class—as against all India.
>
> This is a question if I may venture to say so, that His Majesty should decide and in his name call for subscriptions which, judging from the success of the Queen Victoria Memorial at Calcutta, should be very large.

In the coming months he was to be engrossed, to the exclusion of almost all else, on work for the Imperial War Graves Commission, culminating in the Cenotaph. It is interesting to note that this forcible expression of opinion, which was no doubt not lost upon the home authorities, was first made by Lutyens in connection with the germ of his great War Arch at Delhi.

In the same letter he put in a plea for the retention as Chief Engineer at Delhi of Hugh Keeling who was due to retire in December. He wrote:

> Mr. Keeling has had the work here in hand since its beginning, and is a first class man whom, from the sum and nature of his experience, it would be difficult to replace. I hope some way may be found to retain his services, since New Delhi may suffer greatly.

From the beginning of their association in 1912, Lutyens had got on well with the big, imperturbable, engineer. During the first Estimate crisis of 1914 Keeling, whom the successive recastings of Government House involved in labours no less gruelling than they did Lutyens, maintained unruffled calm and rendered immense service to the architect, not least in soothing and reassuring him. Lutyens had learnt his complete integrity and that his loyalty to the great conception could always be trusted. Sir Hugh Keeling, as he became, was fortunately retained in his vital post till 1925.

Lutyens left Delhi on April 8. During the summer the planting of the trees of the King's Way was begun, making the potential avenue, 800 feet wide, look startlingly immense; the garden estimates went forward; but winter work was restricted to drainage installations and the building of clerks' quarters. In August Lutyens sent out revised designs for the upper floors of Government House with the Council Chamber omitted from the north side. But in November he was much exercised by a rumour, which proved baseless, that the Government envisaged the north side repeating the south. He asked Montagu, who by then had succeeded Chamberlain as Secretary of State, to use his influence against the proposal.

Montagu was then at Delhi. In the previous August, shortly after Chamberlain's resignation on the publication of the Mesopotamia Report, he had taken over the India Office and, having made the historic definition of British policy as the granting of self-government to India, proceeded in person at the head of a Commission to draw up, with the Viceroy, a report on the most practical way of carrying that policy into effect. In his diary,[1] kept for the information of the Prime Minister, Mr. Lloyd George, he recorded a visit to the new capital in company with Hailey (November 14, 1917), noting with remarkable perception:

> I am impressed by the superiority of Lutyens over Baker. Lutyens shows distinction of architecture and novelty of idea which is very refreshing, and is obvious although the basement storey and the lay-out is practically all that has been done. I am glad to think there is a prospect, by increasing his pay, to keep Keeling, the engineer-in-charge—a wise thing. I sympathise with Lutyens in that for some distance the view of Government House along the main avenue will be obscured, but it is too late to alter this... I am again impressed by Hailey's competence, but his optimism and the way he smoothes over all difficulties is rather specious.

It had been already decided that the architects should not come to Delhi for the cold weather 1917–18. At the beginning of January Hailey wrote to Lutyens:

> We have got as far as we can with Government House. It is very melancholy to see New Delhi hanging fire in this way; we can't, as a matter of fact,

[1] *An Indian Diary*, by Edwin S. Montagu, 1930.

even spend our full annual allotment, as we cannot get materials. The railways are so congested with war stuff that they can't send up stone and lime, and every day one sees fresh restrictions on traffic. The Moghul Garden seems to me the kind of thing the Committee might like to deal with. The whole scheme costs a lot; but we shall have to get on with the terrace near the house whatever happens.

Hailey, 'the most immaculate of official minds' as Lutyens termed him, was himself due for promotion after more than six years as High Commissioner (though in the event his term was extended for a year); de Montmorency, the Assistant Commissioner, went to an appointment in the Punjab; and other members of the team were being transferred.

In February, 1918, Hailey reported that 'the Viceroy's Court is getting on well and begins to look like a reality; you can at all events see the shape of things now. But the delay is depressing'. One problem was the shortage of cranes; the few there were in the stone yards were commandeered by the Munitions Board. Baker's bungalows were going up, as an experiment, but Keeling complained bitterly that one of them contained a passage only 3 feet wide, an unseemly width for a man of his bulk and, as he said, 'frankly impossible for a really big man.' A start was also made with Lutyens's house for the Viceroy's Private Secretary, for which the cost had worked out favourably.

The new Indian Constitution, providing for a Chamber of Ruling Princes, was expected to lead many of them to erect residences at Delhi. Lutyens and Baker had, during their last visit, made recommendations on the extent to which the Government should regulate the style and type of these buildings. It was now approved that the architects employed by Chiefs should be required to place the focal points of their designs, and also servants' quarters and stables, in assigned positions, and that gateways and external walls of compounds should be so located and designed as to agree with the general layout.

In July, 1918, as a result of the War Conference held in Delhi, restrictions were intensified. Work on the central buildings was to be closed down altogether at the top level of the basements, which would ensure against damage to work already completed and enable building to be resumed expeditiously. The only constructions permitted were buildings that could be used for the accommodation of extra Army Headquarters, military establishments and additional troops. Consequently it would be unnecessary for the architects to come out for the 1918–19 season.

Temporary lines to be erected for four additional battalions would not affect the New City, but bungalows for their officers would be needed and it was proposed to press on for this purpose with the houses for the Viceroy's Private and Military Secretaries (by Lutyens) and the Bodyguard lines, together with a number of other bungalows. Hailey wrote to Lutyens that this would keep the much reduced establishment busy for eight months, and that, besides getting the work done at the Army's expense, 'it will enable us to push on with tree planting and some of the garden.' The restriction did not apply to private owners, so that it was hoped that a certain amount of private and commercial building might get done, though none of the Ruling Chiefs were expected to build as yet. In 1919 construction of the Ethnological Museum was deferred. The standstill continued in force till 1921–22. By then the Montagu-Chelmsford reforms had so far transformed the Constitution that expenditure on the new city was thenceforth controlled not by the Viceroy's Council but by the Legislative Assembly; and by that date the Chief Commissioner, to whose untiring work New Delhi and Lutyens owed so much, had also been transformed from head-poacher into head-keeper: Sir Malcolm Hailey, Financial Member of the Council.

§4. WAR GRAVES

In June, 1917, almost as soon as Lutyens returned from India, the Director of War Graves, General Fabian Ware, invited him, together with Herbert Baker and Charles Aitken the Director of the Tate Gallery, to visit France in order to give their opinion on the arrangement of military cemeteries and the nature of the monuments to be placed in them. The Imperial War Graves Commission had been instituted in May, and was considering the policy to be adopted. It was not till the following February that the broad lines of this were settled, largely on these three advisers' recommendations. And of the three it will be found that Lutyens, with his characteristic percipience, was chiefly responsible for the principles followed. It was, for instance, still undecided whether individual graves should be marked, if so by what means; whether private memorials would be allowed; and the nature of any standard official monuments.

Early in July, therefore, he found himself billetted in a chateau close to British Headquarters at Montreuil. Fellow passengers on the boat had been J. M. Barrie, visiting the grave of George Llewellyn Davies, and Owen Seaman, editor of *Punch*, on his way to 3rd Army H.Q. Each day the party motored great distances inspecting field burials and temporary cemeteries, so that it was not till the 12th that Lutyens had time to write his impressions to Lady Emily. The letter intimately reveals the compassion of his nature, in a way that his long struggles at Delhi and activities elsewhere have tended to obscure. It is important, too, as recording the train of emotion and thought for which he was to strive to find expression, with growing intensity, during the two ensuing years, and which culminated in the monument by which his name is most widely remembered. It may therefore be given almost in its entirety:

The 'cemeteries'—the dotted graves—are pathetic, especially when one thinks of how things are run and problems treated at home. What humanity can endure, suffer, is beyond belief. The battlefields—the obliteration of all human endeavour, achievement, and the human achievement of destruction, is bettered by the poppies and wild flowers—that are as friendly to an unexploded shell as they are to the leg of a garden seat in Surrey.

It is all a sense of wonderment how can such things be.

Men and Lorries—motors without thought of petrol. Fat horses and thin men, all in the pink of condition. Great in size beyond imagination, and all so inexplicable that it makes writing difficult—and one dares not mention names of places etc.

One is seeing very little of all there is to be seen—we are not allowed very near the front,—but that little is ominous of what lies beyond. A battlefield with the blurred trenches, the position of a machine gun marked by its litter of spent cartridges, the ruined tanks, the rough broken shell-hole pitted ground you assume was once a village, where a small bit of wall of what once was a church may stand but nothing else.

The half-ruined places are more impressive, for then you can picture what a place might have been.

The grave-yards, haphazard from the needs of much to do and little time for thought—and then a ribbon of isolated graves like a milky way across miles of country, where men were tucked in where they fell—Ribbons of little crosses each touching each across a cemetery—set in a wilderness of annuals,—and where one sort of flower has grown the effect is charming, easy, and oh so pathetic, that one thinks no other monument is needed. Evanescent, but for the moment almost perfect,—and how misleading, I surmise, is this emotion, and how some love to sermonize.

But the only monument can be one in which the endeavour is sincere to make such monument permanent—a solid ball of bronze!

For miles these graves occur, from single graves to close-packed areas of thousands, on every sort of site and in every sort of position—the bodies laid to face the enemy—in some places so close one wonders how to arrange their names in decent order.

The question is so big, so wide, that the most we can do is to generalise.

General Ware, the Director, is a most excellent fellow and very keen to do the right thing without fear or favour of the present sentiment. with a preference for the most permanent and perfect.

The Mess here is delightful; a terrible chateau does not spoil it. A good view and fine trees. France—as France—is altered, becoming gentler and more sympathetic simply because they have not the labor to cut the trees so hard.

> I am now starting for [Abbeville, name deleted], tomorrow we go again to battlefields, to a scene of obliterated villages, scarred soil, destroyed tanks etc.

Within a month his emotions had crystallised. The idea of permanence and sincerity expressed in this letter by 'a solid ball of bronze' had taken finite architectural shape. He advocated to the Commission that in every British cemetery should be:

> one great fair stone of fine proportions, 12 ft in length, lying raised upon three steps, of which the first and third shall be twice the width of the second; and that each shall bear, in indelible lettering, some fine thought or words of sacred dedication. This stone should be, wherever circumstances permit, on the east side of each cemetery and the graves lie before it, facing east, as the Army faces now.[1]

He also strongly advocated equality and uniformity of treatment of every grave, with headstones of uniform pattern. By mid-August Miss Jekyll had written to him at length, endorsing his Great Stone conception, and Lady Emily, writing from her mother's house, Homewood, threw herself into the discussion in its support with unaccustomed warmth, explaining:

> it appeals to my side of life, as houses don't. I see so much true symbolism in it. I do hope you get it through. I am also entirely at one with you about equality of sacrifice, and all who die, no matter from what cause, should be honoured. I think it is awful that the wife of a man shot for cowardice gets no pension: after all, he is equally lost to her, and by Government orders. I think it barbarous.
> P.S. Too funny, Bumps and Lady Sackville together!

It is not clear how and where these two ladies came together, the 'fairy god-mother' of his youth, and the other who was to give him as much, though very differently, in his middle age; or whether they were only together in supporting his monumental idea. In any case that question belongs to a later section of this narrative, but the jangling chord is struck in that postscript by his wife.

At first there was a possibility that Lutyens might be appointed architect-in-chief for all War Graves, and he was asked whether he could afford it, since it would involve his giving up much private work. By the end of 1917 he had intimated that he would not be able to accept the appointment, no doubt on the grounds of time and finance. He also ridiculed the notion of being given the rank of temporary Captain, and having to wear a belt for a sword, a tool that he did not know how to use.

There ensued strenuous canvassing of support for the Great Stone as against the specifically Christian symbol of the Cross; and for the plain standard headstone rather

---

[1] Quoted in *War Graves*, Report to the Imperial War Graves Commission by Lt.-Col. Sir Frederick Kenyon, November 1918, in which it is stated that this suggestion was made by Lutyens 'at an early stage'.

than differentiated designs. Lutyens rallied William Nicholson, Auckland Geddes, General Macready, and Reginald Blomfield to the Stone, which Fabian Ware also supported strongly. The latter also favoured Lutyens's design of the headstone rather than that of Herbert Baker, who appears to have been the chief advocate, with the Earl of Selborne, of the Church of England's desire for the Cross.

Thus the familiar differences of the two architects of Delhi were transferred to the War Graves Commission by the irony of their eminence. The basis of their opposition was the same. Lutyens, thinking in terms of architectural form, conceived an abstract shape of intrinsic beauty and therefore, he maintained, essentially spiritual, 'irrespective of creed or caste,' as he had said of the proposed All India Memorial. Baker relied more on associated ideas to inspire memorials that should reflect specifically religious sentiment. The underlying antipathy of the two men no doubt contributed to the intensity with which Lutyens began to oppose the Cross, so that a moment came when he exclaimed, 'I am beginning to believe the Cross is the great anti-Christ of prophecy!' But his own pantheism, coloured as it was by Theosophy with its comprehension of all spiritual beliefs, added moral fervour to his aesthetic conviction. The controversy continued to be fought up to Cabinet level, when the form of a National War Memorial was discussed and Alfred Mond told Lutyens that it was most painful to hear the bereaved Lord Selborne pleading for the Cross. Lutyens replied 'I wish a few had pleaded against it to make folk realise the inherent cruelty of the *forced* Cross'. In the early stages he was fearful of the effect which political considerations might have upon the War Graves Commission's decision. Characteristically, having come to his own, he was uncompromising on its absolute rightness. In the event, the Commission did compromise, no doubt wisely. Whilst accepting 'the idea and symbolism of this great memorial stone', they resolved that it lacked definitely Christian character and also the idea of self-sacrifice, demanded in the cemeteries of a Christian Empire; whilst the Jewish, Mahommedan, and Hindu faiths also desired the inclusion of their religious symbols. They therefore recommended that, whilst all cemeteries should include Lutyens's Stone of Remembrance, there should be associated with it the Great Cross of Sacrifice in Christian cemeteries and such symbolic structures as were required elsewhere. Among adjuncts that had been suggested were lych gates and rose gardens. Lutyens was opposed to rose gardens as essentially impermanent, and the Commission considered lych gates meaningless in cemeteries in which, by their nature, no further burials would take place. But some forms of shelter were naturally needed, and Sir Frederick Kenyon advocated small cloisters or colonnades. In all cases, however, he concurred that 'permanence should be the note of our cemeteries'. The Report also envisaged the need for collective battle memorials, at Ypres, the Somme, Arras, Messines, etc. It recommended the division of the cemeteries into groups assigned to a principal architect who would design certain cemeteries himself, with a corps of younger architects working under him; and proposed, as principal architects, Lutyens, Baker, Blomfield, and Lorimer, with Macdonald Gill to advise on lettering, and D. S. MacColl and Charles Holmes on general aesthetic questions.[1]

A carven Stone
And a stark Sword brooding on the bosom of the Cross,

as described by Kipling in his poem on the King's pilgrimage in May, 1922, are associated in the majority of the cemeteries. The Stone of Remembrance, a monolith weighing 10 tons, with the inscription 'Their name liveth for evermore', was set in all the larger cemeteries.[2] In the Stone he worked out a much more subtle form than that briefly described above. The system of optical corrections, or entasis, which he applied to the planes of the monolith was, if not the first, the most notable instance of his applying this exquisite principle to an apparently simple form. He said of the Stone:

> all its horizontal surfaces and planes are spherical, parts of parallel spheres 1801 ft. 8 in. in diameter; and all its vertical lines converge upwards to a point some 1801 ft. 8 in. above the centre of these spheres.[3]

It is largely this complex geometry, which he derived from Professor Hamblin's study of the Parthenon, that gives to Lutyens's Stone a mysteriously vital force. Its most sensational application was to the Cenotaph, but having once mastered the method, he applied variants of it to many of his later buildings and to all his memorials, which thereby acquire their unique and moving quality. He was alone among modern architects in combining the faculties required to manipulate this infinitely subtle system of visual overtones. We have noted his emotional impulse, which he summarised as 'a solid ball of bronze'; but he alone united the cast of mind and sensitiveness of eye with the endless patience necessary to conceive, rationalise, and obtain the accurate execution of, such exquisite refinements.

§5. 'BEKNIGHTED'

The analogy of Lutyens's mind to a crystal sphere cut in facets, each reflecting a complete image as its surface caught successive sources of light, has been used before in this book. It expresses the essential unity of his many sides, but also a seeming lack of connection between them which puzzled some people. And it suggests, not inaptly, the extent that it depended for its surface glitter on external illumination.

---

[1] *War Graves, op. cit.*, January 24, 1918.

[2] Both Lutyens and Blomfield designed Memorial Crosses, but in order to implement the principle of joint responsibility, the Commission usually placed Blomfield's Cross in cemeteries containing Lutyens's War Stone, and Lutyens's Cross in cemeteries designed by other architects.

[3] Quoted in *Imperial War Graves Commission*, 6th Report, 1926.

Without the stimulus of fresh contacts and fresh problems to tackle, he was prone to depression and boredom. Who is not? But boredom was so strange to him that at times he seemed to lack the resources to withstand it which less lucid minds perforce cultivate. At every other period of his life he had had more to do than seemed humanly possible. Now he had too little, apart from Delhi which though infinite was at present inhibited. A crystal, however prismatic, throws no light of itself in darkness, but the gleam of a star, the flicker of a will-o'-the-wisp, may be magnified through it to a rainbow.

The winter of 1917–18 was the darkest of the war. We now know that when the sun rose upon the world of architecture it was to usher in a new era of changed values, revised ideals, among which humanism would count for progressively less. Certain individualists would be highly civilised, some capitalists exceedingly cultured, but architecture generally would be increasingly tinged with the proletarian ideal of efficiency. A new generation of architects would arise who knew not Wren though respecting his Olympian shade. For Lutyens the new day was to bring honours and reputation beyond his dreams, but as the greatest architect of the immediate past rather than the leader to the future. In these dark months of inactivity he might, conceivably, have foreseen the revolution that was to take place, and, with his extraordinary assimilative powers, have transferred his allegiance from the ancients to the 'cranks'—as he had regarded the prophets of the modern world. But those who have followed the narrative of his development can perceive that such a readjustment, involving betrayal of his faith, was outside his nature. And during that winter, when his own lights were low, he was visited by a particularly effulgent will-o'-the-wisp.

He was conscious, in the gloom, that since those serene summer days at Folly Farm, with which this chapter opened, the framework of his personal life had been wrenched askew. His wife had evacuated the children from the danger of air-raids to the hills of Church Stretton in Shropshire, where they remained till the end of the war and Lady Emily paid many visits. The Bedford Square house was shut up but for a couple of rooms. So he had no settled home, a fraction of a wife, scarcely any family, no new work, Delhi almost dead, a rapidly falling bank balance, and the old nightmare of debt confronting him. Over all hung the interminable waste and agony of war.

Lady Emily was preoccupied, too, with the situation created in the Theosophical Society by Mrs. Besant's launching of the Home Rule for India League. At the beginning of 1917 Mrs. Besant had been elected Chairman of the Indian Congress and initiated a vehement campaign for Dominion status within the Empire. A passionate royalist and imperialist, she believed that a self-governing India, in co-operation with Britain, would set an example capable of transforming the East if not the world. In the light of after events it may be justifiably contended that, had

Dominion status been granted to India immediately after the War, the bitterness of the ensuing twenty years would have been avoided and India have remained united. Both the Indian and Home governments, however, took the view that India was not yet ready for self-government and answered the agitation by the repressive Rowlatt Acts. At this point Mrs Besant and the rising influence of Gandhi parted company. She and her liberal Indian friends agreed to apply Gandhi's weapon of passive resistance, but to the Rowlatt code alone. Gandhi, on the other hand, preached resistance to all British legislation.

The crisis came in the summer. Mrs. Besant was 'interned', confined to her residence at Ootacamund near Madras, whereupon Congress agitation in India was redoubled. 'It makes ordinary work difficult,' Hailey confided to Lutyens; 'everyone is on a soap-box, gesticulating.' The War Council met at Delhi, confirming the cessation of building and cancelling the architects' 1918–19 visit. Montagu announced the impending reforms and his forthcoming visit to India. In England the Home Rule for India League was formed with Lady Emily as one of its leading figures, and its inaugural meeting was held at the Lutyenses' house in Bedford Square. *The Times* of the following day published a leading article entitled 'A Mischievous Movement'. Lady Emily, not unjustifiably, was gratified at having provoked attention in such eminent quarters.

At this juncture, Edward Hudson, with his forthright adoration of Lutyens, wrote to his wife pointing out bluntly how wrong she was, having an architect of genius as her husband of whom she should be taking great care, to involve herself in political movements which might well do him the greatest harm. Mrs. Besant, equally sensing the possible repercussions of the meeting in Bedford Square on Lutyens, also wrote from Ootacamund that if he objected to his wife's connection with the Home Rule League she must resign from it. Under the double pressure she did so.

Marital relations, though mutual loyalty was fundamentally as strong as ever, were undeniably becoming frayed. The Home Rule League, the children's absence, the lack of a home and the frustrations of Delhi combined to cool the domestic atmosphere to a temperature lower than it had ever been before. All the more at this time Lutyens must have needed warming and cheering, the interest of new work and that stimulating consolation which in his youth Barbara Webb, Gertrude Jekyll, even Princess Louise, had given him.

Since the previous summer he had been finding this, and more, through quickly ripening friendship with Lady Sackville. Their first encounter at the Opera had been followed by frequent meetings, to which each brought equal enthusiasm, to discuss a house she proposed to build at Hove and plans for another in London. Lady Sackville was convinced of his genius, adored his quick sketches of ideas, which miraculously agreed with hers, and, an important point with her, thought he would prove amenable to her often capricious requirements. For his part he not only found in her company the stimulus and warmth that his life was lacking, but was undoubtedly attracted by her.

He was now nearing fifty. A younger man[1] has described Lady Sackville as she was at this time:

> Though now middle-aged and fat, the lines of her face were pretty with an almost classical prettiness, and her expression could be extremely seductive. The long, hollow, hooded upper lids ... displayed eyes, rather prominent, of living, changing but rather shallow fire, for to all her gifts she had given a material direction.

Half-peasant, half-aristocrat, with the sparkle of her Spanish mother, a famous dancer, she could radiate fun or create a scene in her bilingual Anglo-French, and equally command with the instinctive charm of a long line of Sackville forbears (since her father was Lord Sackville's uncle). She was, in 1917, still mistress of Knole though her relations with her husband were becoming strained. She was also mistress of an excellent cook and of remnants of the fortune left to her in 1913 by Sir John Murray Scott, estimated at nearly half a million and comprising the residue of Sir Richard Wallace's superb collections of works of art, though by now she had succeeded in dissipating the greater part of it. Miss Sackville-West's portrait of her mother[2] describes affectionately, though not uncritically, the make-belief world to which her immense faculty for delusion gave temporary reality; her voracity for fun; her combination of reckless extravagance and incredible economies; her ingenuity for turning everything to a purpose wholly different to that for which it had been intended; and her delight in the improbable and unexpected; her acquisitiveness, too, of anything that glittered and glowed, from lumps of amber or lapis-lazuli to—crystals. One might say that all Lutyens's more engaging, if more superficial, facets scintillated in such a radiance as she emitted, and the brighter he sparkled the more she desired his companionship. Among her methods of getting rid of her fortune was a passion for acquiring, decorating, enlarging, and then changing houses. For this she found in him an enthusiastic and tireless collaborator, whose labours 'for love' she rewarded with lavish gifts as between friends.

In the autumn of 1916 and again in the following summer after his return from Delhi, they met constantly, conferring on plans, in her London house, at Knole and Hove. Occasionally Lady Emily and one or other of the children, or her daughter and son-in-law, the Nicolsons, were of the party. But usually she had him to herself, when they made sight-seeing trips visiting Hever or Bodiam or Lullingstone, the Colefaxes at Old Buckhurst, and Miss Jekyll (who was immediately charmed by Lady Sackville) at Munstead. At Hampton Court one day they ran into Roger Fry.

---

[1] Sir Osbert Sitwell, in *Great Morning*, p. 223.   [2] *Pepita*, by V. Sackville-West, 1937.

'Searching for inspiration?' Lutyens asked him: 'Good heavens, no!' answered the prophet of Post-Impressionism.

Though plans and places continued ostensibly to be the topics they discussed, an enchanting friendship had been established that warmed quickly to an affection and was to obsess both for a decade. The relationship cannot be traced with any fulness since little material data for it exists. But the part it played in Lutyens's development must be suggested at this point. B.M. (*bonne mamman*), as she was known to her friends, undoubtedly brought him great personal happiness (and endless worry) besides aesthetic stimulus, at a time when his earlier sources of happiness and stimulus were obscured. But B.M. was a queen among escapists, and it was his more superficial talents that she directly evoked. Had he been subject, during these years, to a less frivolous and more responsible influence, his whole attitude to the actualities of post-war conditions might well have been different. That he was fully conscious of them, but revolted from the prospect, is evident from a letter to his wife that he wrote sitting alone in the Athenæum one August night of 1917, in a mood of profound dejection. He was then intensely aware of darkness, malaise, emptiness and of the cleavage that was deepening in his allegiances.

He had, he said, found a large parcel at his office containing pipes, a pouch and tobacco, from Lady Sackville, who had written that she wanted to enlarge her new house still more in spite of the advice he had given her that twenty-five years of heavy taxation lay ahead. He tried to tell his wife something of topics common to them both: Mark Fenwick was thinking of building cottages at Abbotswood; Miss Jekyll approved the Great Stone. But tonight they did not mean much. He could think only in the empty club, of his empty home, of 'the beastly waste of war, the loss of life and happiness, the church faces that mask animal instincts, the moral fences in which one can have no real faith knowing as one grows older how they are created'. He was talking round the point, but in a moment he blurted it out: 'we do, especially I, manage my life badly somehow.' Then he sheered off again to contemplate the black void where architecture should have shone, seeing instead bureaucracy in India, divided counsel and compromise at home:

> an awful quagmire of hideousness and discomfort ahead: a million cottages to be built by a Government that can only work through compromise, leaving its conscience in the hands of accountants... A cottage cannot be 'good' if the man building it is not happy and content in his work. [Could a Viceroy's Palace be?] Beside that fact, pay (so long as he can live) matters little.
>
> The Government's building rules, which they are to make, will be based on obsolete Acts. To save themselves trouble and get a 'procedure' they will determine costs before they ascertain essentials. They will treat their professional advisers as being dishonest and in the process make them so. Those in final

power will be appointed for their very want of special knowledge, and be more influenced as to whether there is a d in knowledge than in the subject matter in which they have to deal, design, decide...

It would be the sordid wrangles of Delhi interminably over again. All the argument over the War Graves question made him feel sick and 'perturbed' his work. He must give his time free, of course, so that, besides creating worry, it was no financial compensation for not going to India. That knocked out £1000, and he could not see how he would make it up, since no work was being done in England and everything in India was going so slow (consequently the small percentage of fees due to him on the little that was being put in hand was being diminished and postponed). Yet he had to work just as hard, indeed harder, since there was little office help to be had. However, the War Office had released his Delhi assistant, Barrett, to return and help on Indian work.

But, O, Emmie, money is difficult. I don't know what I shall do. Only I can make it, and war stops everything. I don't think I *could* last two more years; it would take *all* my savings. I don't see how closing down Bedford Square would help; I still owe money for getting into the place. I do wish it had been a better house...

That autumn, however, 31 Bedford Square was sold, and no substitute being found to suit all requirements, the Lutyenses moved into a succession of furnished houses. The gloom was little lightened by the setting up and occasional meetings of the Delhi Advisory Committee on the decoration and furnishing of Government House. It was constituted in May, 1917, with Lord Crewe in the chair, Lady Minto, Lord Hardinge, Lord Carmichael and Sir Cecil Harcourt Smith, as a Standing Committee to advise the Secretary of State, and to consider schemes for internal decoration submitted by the architects; but was not empowered to give them instructions nor to communicate with the authorities in India. Yet it was to receive a grant of £2000 a year for five years with which 'to purchase articles of historical interest or artistic merit'. Models of some of the State rooms were made to aid its deliberations.

In connection with the Committee's work, it was also proposed that an exhibition of Indian Arts and Crafts should be organised, to be held either in Delhi or in London. A complicating factor was that a large proportion of the furniture and decoration must necessarily be of Western character. The Committee disapproved of Lutyens's aim of encouraging native labour to execute such work, since Indians would thereby be led away yet further from their own traditions. They therefore proposed limiting the exhibition to such Indian contributions as carpets, textiles, pottery and tiles, carved and inlaid stone work. The project, though it involved Lutyens in considerable correspondence, received little encouragement either in Delhi or London, and came to nothing, its place at South Kensington being eventually taken by an exhibition of War Memorial designs old and new. Yet it is suggestive, in connection with Lutyens's ambitions for the furnishing of Government House, to catch flickers from this facet of his activity reflected in another, as when we find him using the great increase in the value of Sir Richard Wallace's furniture collection at Bagatelle as an argument, in a letter to Hailey, for the Government of India investing in valuable pieces at war-time prices; and Sir Thomas Holderness, the Permanent Secretary for India, being invited with Lutyens to a week-end at Knole. For Lady Sackville was generous in furthering the designs of her friends, and also regarded herself as having a flair for dealing in objects of *vertu*.

Probably the letters exchanged almost daily, when they were apart, by these strange allies had already begun; between the celebrated architect and the famous hostess, McNed and McSack as they now called one another. His new nickname had originated by his writing to Miss Barbara Jekyll (now Lady Freyberg), the daughter of Sir Herbert and Lady Jekyll, on her engagement to Francis McLaren, that, since her sister was married to Reginald McKenna, one must obviously be Mac something to be loved by a Jekyll and signing the letter McNed. B.M. took up the joke and insisted on joining the clan as McSack, calling the Nicolsons McHarold and McVita and so on. None of the McNed and McSack correspondence has survived. But possibly a specimen of its more jocular contents is afforded by the unexpected confusion of two facets in a letter to Lady Emily—who had long since ceased to be much amused by his puns—written in the train between Bordeaux and Hendaye on January 1, 1918. It was, one imagines, such characteristic Neddity that was among the qualities that attracted, because they amused, McSack. The date is significant, since he knew that, in the morning papers, his name had appeared among the Knights in the New Year Honours. The occasion of the honour, which, among architects, was shared at that time only by Sir Aston Webb and Sir Thomas Graham Jackson, recognised the quality of his work at Delhi (on which Edwin Montagu had testified to Lloyd George), and his gratuitous services to the War Graves Commission.

Thus the new knight, suffering from a heavy cold and a temperature, spent his vigil and greeted his Lady. It was, he told her, snowing heavily as the train neared the Pyrenees and he was alone, having lost the travelling companions with whom he had beguiled the night journey from Paris—a French airman with a 'nice star-dusted face' and an American copper magnate who had thought his curious idioms typically English. Another American fellow-passenger had earlier asked him if he were not Lloyd George. 'I said, Yes, I am. *American*: Well I guess you have put me in a difficulty now. *Me*: Not of my seeking, I assure you.'

> The little lady on my right enjoyed it enormously and I found she was a traveller in veilings. I am sure she sold lots of veilings by the unveiling of her

101. THE STONE OF REMEMBRANCE ('WAR STONE'). Erected in Imperial War Graves Cemeteries; designed 1917

102. DESIGN FOR PROPOSED TEMPORARY WAR SHRINE IN HYDE PARK, AUGUST 1918

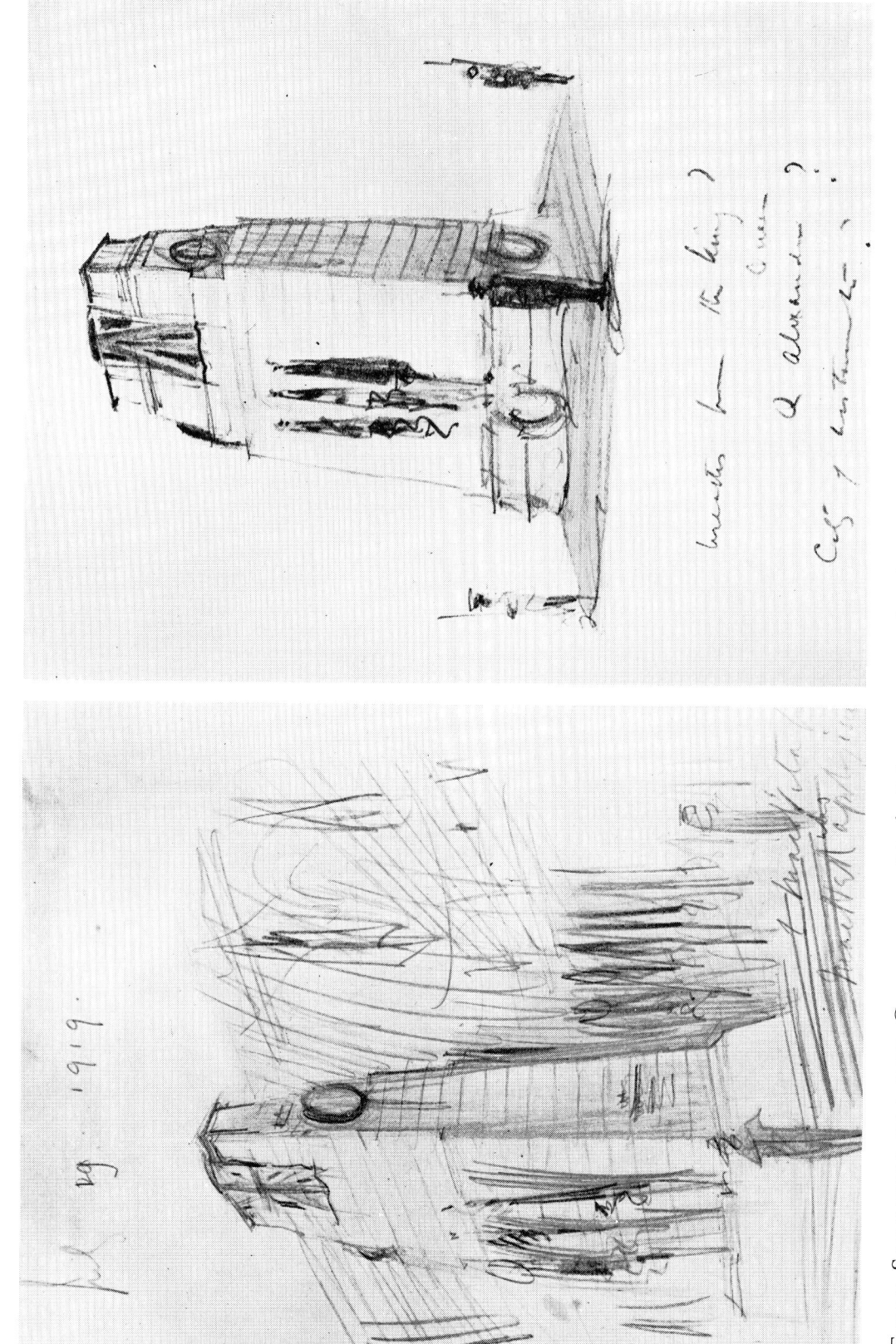

103. First Sketches for the Cenotaph. Made July 19, 1919, the day on which Mr. Lloyd George invited Lutyens to design 'a catafalque'. (*Left*) For the Hon. V. Sackville-West (*reproduced by her permission*); (*right*) For Sir Frank Baines (*reproduced by permission of Mr. A. J. Pitcher*)

sleek little eyes. A little lady what travelled and was merry at it might prove a solution of many difficulties. I wonder what you would say?

My cold is immense and I use up handkerchiefs per kilometre. At the Bristol (Hotel, Paris), nature having forsaken me for 2 whole days, I asked the waiter for a '*verre de selles Epsom*'. He brought me an *œuf à la coque*! I humbly ate it, and, wonderful to relate, nature suddenly returned to me, immediately—such is the action of God, who cares for people who are children. My request for Epsom salts was taken as a prayer. Now if I was properly grown up I should, on the next occasion, ask for an egg, but then it would be with dire or contrary results without doubt.

I hope you admire my philosophy. However, I got rid of pains and creeps and surges of giddiness which constitute the 'flu, and the fever too—flew.

I wish I was at home to see the papers.

On eventually reaching the Liria Palace, he continued:

When God says s'no'w he seldom means yes, but yes it is—now. 32 hours late and oh what a journey. We were snowed up at Avila, 3 hrs from Madrid, snow banks in front, a derailed train behind, our fuel for warming the carriage failed, the lights went out, and there for hours on a mountain top I waited, getting hungrier and colder hour by hour. Finally we got back into Avila station but the *Fonda* (restaurant) was so extraordinarily unappetising that one did not get fonder of ones food—you see I can still joke.

I felt thoroughly be-knighted!!

It snows and snows and snows, I with a fearful cold in my snose—it was all s'nose, as my *mouchoir* s'knows too well!!

When, on reaching Madrid, he was met by an emissary from the Duke of Peñaranda, he feared the poor man must have been waiting a very long time; and when, after a cab-drive through the petrol-less capital to 'this Opulent house', he was immediately served with an excellent omelette, opined that 'they must have been turning out omelettes in preparation for my advent every $\frac{3}{4}$ of an hour for a day and a half!'

This visit to El Guadelperal—they all seem to have been made in mid-winter—had to be effected by train and mule team owing to the petrol shortage. It was necessitated by Peñaranda's decision to proceed at once with the adaptation, heating and drainage, of a small house in the village for his immediate use. It was therefore the most prolonged of Lutyens's visits—nearly a fortnight—and was repeated two months later when a clerk of the works—Hinton—was sent out from England. Peñaranda had been absent on his arrival at Madrid, but the ducal family were assembled in full force, with guest grandees, when he left on the journey home, still in jocular vein:

> The first Duke I call Duke, the second Duque, the others Duquoques (a joke). At the station was old Osma—going to Paris to see his to-be-dead-in-a-week wife. He is a pompous little ex-Minister who has a brilliant collection of *objets d'art*—or 'Dart nots'. His wife is notorious as he is for infidelities.

The journey was rendered particularly excruciating by Sir Edwin Lutyens having been entrusted by a bemused Embassy with the Foreign Office Bag. He consequently detected a Spy in a sinister looking Belgian who seemed suspiciously anxious to share his sleeper. Eluding him, the temporary King's Messenger decided to share berths with a man who looked like a Spanish groom but admitted, after the train had started, that he was in fact a German. Ned was horrified:

> All I could say was *Vraiment. Comme il est curieux.* He had the lower berth, but I made him take the top, and I put my Bag beyond and below in that crevice that the *lits* of these *waggons* make.

The German was frighteningly obsequious, but Ned, in the lower bunk, listened to every squeak of the springs above, until he fell into a deep sleep. He awoke ultimately to find the Bag, his money and passport—where he had put them. The Spy turned out to be in the fruit-preserving business and to be expecting to make a fortune by an invention 'to bake and powder cabbages, potatoes, apples etc; which powder, with water added, reconstitutes itself as cabbages, potatoes, apples etc. He intended to go to America, and told me how I could make £5,000,000'.

Lutyens always had the knack of picking up the most extraordinary travelling companions, and perhaps this little man (his suspicions of whom, very real at the time, seemed ridiculous afterwards) is now the Dehydrated Vegetable King of U.S.A., and has been feeding Europe with the dessicated fruits of the invention thus imparted on that nightmare journey through Spain.

§6. NATIONAL MONUMENT

The holding, though at desperate cost, of the Germans' Spring offensive, and awareness of the imminence of the Allies' 'Big Push', destined to surge across and beyond the battlefields of '15, '16, and '17, quickened hope. But the sense of coming deliverance had the effect, rather, of unnumbing the ache in the world's heart. The cumulative emotion of thankfulness shot with grief seemed choked by lack of means for its expression. As the fourth anniversary of the war's beginning came, a temporary War Shrine erected in Hyde Park brought a measure of relief, most moving in its evident efficacy, to this pent-up flood of feeling. People of every sort and condition lined from dawn till dark to lay their pathetic tributes before it. No great thing in itself, its meeting of millions' need was deeply impressive. Sir Alfred Mond, First Commissioner of Works, was prompted, in the words of a contemporary,[1] 'to call in Lutyens as admittedly in the highest rank of living designers,' to produce a more fitting monument. A generous citizen, Mr. S. J. Waring, offered to defray the cost. The erection was required to be temporary and removable, to meet the current need without forestalling a possible future national war memorial, yet to be in itself of good proportions, lucid in purpose, in symbolic accord with the nation's solemn mood.

Though now forgotten, Lutyens's design for the Hyde Park Shrine is important as bringing to an issue the trends and events traced earlier in this chapter. It represented the first public trial of the extent to which the undenominational type of memorial, which he advocated, accorded with national feeling. The proposal for the Shrine produced many letters to the Press in favour of religious symbolism. Would the War Graves Commission, to which the handling of the monument was committed, be able to sustain the official view that it should consist in the Altar, symbol of remembrance, and not the Christian Cross? Besides, it would be Lutyens's first public work since his knighthood brought him to general notice, the first to be exhibited of all the war memorials that followed, and the experimental step in the evolution of the Cenotaph (which made its erection unnecessary). The strength of feeling which the appropriate form for official memorials had evoked in him during the preceding twelve months has already been noted. Though it is characteristic of his approach to all his works, it was the more marked in these early memorial designs because they gave him outlet for the emotion that he shared deeply with everybody else at the time, and, moreover, gave him something to design of immediate need. The free functioning of his creative faculty was essential to his well being. Its inhibition, with consequent sense of frustration and boredom, was unsettling his private life, resist it as he might. But the spiritual quality of his memorial conceptions was also the side of his work into which his wife could enter equally. Thus they reinforced the bond uniting them by all the elements of greatest value in his personal life. In this sense they were in a way a substitute for a home, and so possess a double symbolism, as free expressions of the strongly mystical side of his nature, and as representing the positive pole in the conflicting attractions to which he was subject at the time.

The design for the Shrine (p. 383) consisted in an altar raised on a platform with steps in front and flanked by two pylons formed of four square piers and surmounted by a large fir-cone. Before the altar was a ledge for offerings. Altar and pylons were to bear inscriptions. In describing the design to Lady Emily (August 30, 1918), it was the nature of the inscriptions which most exercised him. His characteristic observations have a perennial bearing on this always thorny problem:

[1] Sir Martin Conway, in *Country Life*, September 21, 1918.

The two pylons represent God and Man. The War Stone is flanked by these monolithic watching-pavilions, glorified sentry boxes, carrying fir-cones —emblem of eternity. On these buildings will be carved your text:

IMMORTAL	ETERNITY
God created man in	And made man
His own likeness	in the image of
to be immortal.	His own eternity.

Below the platform on which these structures and the great stone rest is a bench approached by six steps, and a landing where wreaths may be laid.

There is [the question of] the inscription for the stone.

Kipling: 'Their bodies lie buried in peace but their name liveth for evermore.'

Kenyon suggested the latter half would do. But what are names? Even that is too long to bear repetition thousands of times round the world's circumference.

You want a word—like Go losh.

Though it suggests gums and slippers now, it will mean the thing in the years to come.

Your other text, 'You live and die, and die and live,' does not appeal to me —sounds helpless and hopeless and has the rhythmical action of a barrel organ.

'(To those) (These are they) that came out of great tribulation.'

'(For these) The Trumpet shall sound on the other side'

Barrie's 'All's Well'

Nicholson, 'To the brave.'

'Peace be with you'—too churchy and Christian. There might be fine things in Bunyan.

I was glad when I found both Waring, the donor, and Mond anti-cross... The question is coming to a head, and if Kipling says the ukase the Royal Commission will say yes.

I want one phrase, one word, and the same to ring the world. OPQRST is what I have put on the model—six consecutive letters from the alphabet. A long inscription would not have the same effect. Or use initials (like the splendid SPQR) of a phrase set out at length at the back of the shrine.

The Altar was to be exactly the same as those designed by him for the Cemeteries. Hence the importance that he attached to the inscription and his reference to its 'ringing the world'. In the published sketch of the Shrine Lutyens set the word AMEN on the Altar. Six years later he had a long talk with Rudyard Kipling on the subject:

He said my Great War Stone (hating the word) was an inspiration and looked well no matter where it was placed. The only mistake I had made was to have an inscription on it. Even my proposed Amen. It was Kipling who made them put on 'Their name endureth for ever'.[1] Even that was cut down from a longer proposition he had made. It was nice of him.

That summer a few unimportant private commissions came in to enliven the office. He had already fitted up the 'pent-house' flat on a top floor of the Adelphi, the eyrie overlooking the river to which J. M. Barrie had retreated after the break-up of his marriage. The 1918 jobs included alterations and garden work at Breccles Hall, Norfolk for Edwin Montagu, whose Report now appeared, confirming the changes at Delhi foreshadowed during Lutyens's 1916–17 visit. A whole set of Delhi designs were now lost in transit by the ship being torpedoed. Private memorials, among them those for Billy Congreve at Chartley, Sir Bryan Leighton at Loton, and at Muncaster, involved a good deal of travelling. More friends, or their sons, were killed. Barbara, now a debutante, was some company for her father in London, but seemed, he thought, tired and depressed. Robert enlisted in the Royal Flying Corps, thus further, if inevitably, emphasising the breaking up of the family circle. Looking ahead, it seemed to the father that the only chance for cohesion would be a garden, farm, and ponies, the chance that he had lost. He wished he had bought Hundridge—a beautiful little Queen Anne house in the Chilterns. A little bitterly he wondered whether the Theosophical Society ever thought of the home and the happiness of home. Having none, he enjoyed Royal Academy Varnishing Day business ('the architects have decided to elect Scott') and such week-end parties as one at Hever where, besides the Astors, there were Lady Cunard, Lady Diana Manners, with Duff Cooper, Lord Ribblesdale, Vansittart, Edward Knoblock and Sir Sefton Branker.

Soon the Armistice threw London into November carnival, conjuring up visions of a return to pre-war conditions—the only peace that most people could imagine. McSack suddenly abandoned her other schemes and bought a house in Sussex Square, Brighton, to which shortly and inexplicably she added the two adjacent. These she required McNed to join into one palatial abode. Her daughter has described how she set about trying to convert these great echoing mausolea into a habitable dwelling, at a cost, by her own admission, of over £50,000. A windowless cavern of a basement was transformed to a playroom for her grandchildren on wet days; a passenger lift and central heating (which could never be used because it consumed a ton of coal a day) were installed; a dining hall formed by demolishing walls, capable of seating a hundred guests, though she never had more than two and in any case took all her meals in a loggia.

[1] Actually *Their name liveth for evermore*; Lutyens's forgetfulness on this 'literary' point is typical.

In all these activities she had the co-operation of an architect who seemed to have been specially created to suit her. She and Sir Edwin Lutyens together were the richest comedy. That most delightful, good-natured, irresponsible, imaginative jester of genius could keep her amused by the hour, as, with his pencil flickering over the paper, and the jokes pouring endlessly from his lips, he flung domes and towers into the air, decorated them with her monogram, raised fountains and pavilions, paved garden walks with quartz and marble, and exercised all the ingenuity which she so well understood. Of course they squabbled. There were times when he tried loyally to restrain her extravagance. There were times when she worried him almost into his grave. There were times when he irritated her, for underneath all his flippancy he held certain standards from which, as an artist, he would never depart.

'You understand nothing of the *grammar* of building,' he would say in despair; 'now look, I'll show you . . .' but she would never look and would never even attempt to understand.[1]

Early in the New Year, en route for El Guadelperal, he had a sight of the longer carnival of the Paris Peace Conference. His new friends looked after him—Harold Nicolson got him a room in one hotel, Princess Bibesco one at another, and somebody gave him the new experience of being asked if he were any relation of Barbara Lutyens. Nicolson took him to lunch at the Majestic, the British Delegation's headquarters where he saw 'everyone one knows: to speak to, Lord Reading, Smuts, Montagu, Alan Parsons (Curzon's secretary), Lionel Curtis, Sir Henry Wilson, Birrel, Arthur Balfour, and the man I met in Jermyn Street who wants to build 5000 cottages (I still don't know his name)'. He was admitted to the Conference itself where he noted with a shade of satisfaction that Lord Hardinge, as Under Secretary for Foreign Affairs, seemed to play a very small part; then dined in company with Nicolson and Augustus John, after which both, with the hotel concierge, accompanied him to the station to get a seat in the Madrid express. (They found him one in a non-corridor coach full of Americans smoking cigars. 'Too cold to open the window, but I had my sleeping bag and slipped off my boots, so everyone who avoided my boots trod on my feet. However, it was fun in some ways.')

He had scarcely got back from Spain when he was due to sail for South Africa to report on the designs for the new University of Cape Town. In 1910 he had helped to choose the site on the Groote Schuur estate and had hoped then that Herbert Baker and himself would be commissioned to build the University. Delhi and the war had ended that prospect. J. M. Solomon, a disciple of Baker and an architectural idealist was given the commission. After a tour of European and American universities he had returned in 1917 full of enthusiasm for the unparalleled site

---

[1] V. Sackville West. *Pepita*, p. 260.

and the great building that he was to design, though there were some who questioned whether he would be able to confine his undoubted artistry within the limits of the funds available. Baker, for whom the post of consultant had been reserved, declined it on grounds of preoccupation with Delhi and War Graves, so Lutyens was invited in his stead.

Solomon had intermittently worked in Lutyens's office when in London and now received him as his guest at the Woolsack, the house built by Baker for Kipling, in which he now lived ('A nice little house, but full of schoolboy errors, a sort of early me,' Lutyens commented). After intensive examinations of site and plans, Lutyens reported 'most excellent, and I can suggest no better way for economy or effect'. Solomon's achievement must have been of a high order to earn such praise from Lutyens. Unfortunately it proved to be a case of Viceroy's House over again. The initial cost involved would be a million and a quarter, of which only half was available. Although at the time, on the crest of the Peace boom, the prospect of finding the balance appeared good, rumours of economies in prospect were rife. Eventually the Government agreed to advance the £750,000 needed. But either the suspense, or the strain of effecting reductions, or the dread that he was unequal to the technical responsibilities, unhinged the architect's mind. Solomon shot himself at his home, eighteen months after Lutyens's visit.[1]

The circumstances of the tragedy were so nearly analogous to those recurrent on Raisina Hill that we are not unjustified in reflecting upon the moral toughness required in an architect who aspires to build greatly.

It was on July 19, not long after his return to England, that Lloyd George sent for Lutyens and told him that the Government required a 'catafalque' erected in Whitehall, to be ready for the Peace Celebrations to be held at the end of the month. The great procession, including the Allied leaders and contingents of every unit and nation, would at this point do honour to the Fallen. Consequently, Lloyd George explained, the design must be of the undenominational type already approved by the Government in connection with Lutyens's Great Stone for the war cemeteries and Hyde Park Shrine. In view of the short time, a fortnight, available for its construction, it must be a temporary structure, and the design be produced immediately. Its temporary nature may have suggested the word catafalque to Lloyd George, as connoting 'a temporary stage or platform erected by way of honour in a church to receive a coffin or effigy'. Lutyens, with one of his flashes of simultaneous intuition, memory, and visual perception, perhaps saw, in the split second before he answered, 'the poppies and wild flowers that are as friendly to an unexploded shell as they are to the leg of a garden seat in Surrey.' It is certain that he saw the seat, a massive rustic podium made for Miss Jekyll at Munstead twenty-five years ago, with Charles

---

[1] Work to a simplified design was not resumed till 1925, with Messrs. W. Hawke and J. McKinley as architects in association with C. P. Walgate.

Liddell remarking that it looked like the Cenotaph of Sigismunda, then explaining that a cenotaph is 'a monument erected to a deceased person whose body is buried elsewhere'. So he replied to Lloyd George: 'not a catafalque but a Cenotaph.'

The design was completed that day, and examination of a sketch which he made in the evening shows that it corresponds almost exactly to the Cenotaph as originally erected. In the sketch the wreath is one stage higher than in fact, and the infinitely subtle entasis of every surface, which gives the monument its magic quality, is exaggerated.[1] The plotting of these lines of course took considerably longer, involving frightful calculations based on Hamblin's measurements; and filled a manuscript book of thirty-three pages.[2] Templates had to be cut for every surface, in itself a work of utmost delicacy. But it can be said that the commissioning, conception, and rough though finite design of the Cenotaph took place within six hours; probably less.[3]

In narrating this quick sequence, several statements have been made which should be substantiated. Lutyens told me, and later repeated at my request, the train of thought that led him to propose the name Cenotaph to Lloyd George instead of catafalque. Lady Railing (then Miss Clair Nauheim and working in the office) was a witness of the time Lutyens took with the drawing. And Mrs. Harold Nicolson (Miss V. Sackville West) says that he came to dinner that evening still in a state of great excitement and drew for her in pencil and coloured chalks, on the back of an advertisement, the sketch reproduced (by her permission) on p. 384.

On the great day itself vast crowds beheld the legendary figures who, still mounted high on fame, had led the nations to this victory, riding at the head of contingents from every unit and country of their commands. As the procession moved down Whitehall the paeons hushed, and in the silence, punctuated only by the tramp of marching legions, marshals and men saluted the Dead as they passed by the Cenotaph. Unveiled that morning, the unfamiliar pylon, with its strange name and mound of wreaths heaped at its base, was all that remained substantial when dusk fell upon the pageant.

[1] The Cenotaph contains no vertical or horizontal lines. The four corners if produced upwards, would meet at a point about 1000 ft. above; all the horizontal lines are radials of circles, from a common centre at 900 ft. below ground. The joints of the masonry are the thinnest possible, no more than $\frac{1}{16}$ in.; a great feat of masoncraft.

[2] So Lutyens informed the Hon. Mrs. Harold Nicolson to whom I am indebted for the information.

[3] As this page goes to press, I have received a parallel but amplifying account of these events from Mr. A. J. Pitcher, then Office of Works Architect in charge of Peace Procession decorations. He writes: 'One of the provisions was to be a "saluting point" in Whitehall. At the last moment it was decided to appoint an architect in private practice to design this feature and my chief, Sir Frank Baines, was asked to get in touch with Lutyens. Sir Frank called on Lutyens late the same afternoon and when the matter had been briefly explained, Lutyens took a sheet of notepaper and produced a sketch in less than a couple of minutes. At 10 o'clock the following morning the half-inch and full size working drawings were in our hands and were handed over to the contractor the same morning.' Mr. Pitcher preserved the sketch (p. 384) and a half-inch drawing. Sir Frank Baines's interview was evidently in the afternoon of July 19, after Lutyens's with Lloyd George.

CENOTAPH

The tumult and the shouting dies,
  The Captains and the Kings depart,
    Still stands Thine ancient sacrifice . . .

The long lines of people stretched to add their homage for many days. Though few, it may be, were in the mood or were qualified to analyse the intrinsic qualities of the memorial, it was instantly acknowledged to give form, in some mysterious way, to the emotion of which it became the central symbol. Its acclamation as a masterpiece by the more percipient was instantaneous. The evening found it recognised as constituting already an historical monument that must impress even those with no knowledge of how it came to be or what great occurrence it portended. Dispassionate inspection confirmed not only its astonishing rightness for its purpose, but to its particular site, and the extreme distinction underlying its apparent reticence and simplicity. We, who have followed its creator's life no less than its gestation, can recognise in the Cenotaph the simulacrum of Lutyens's unique combination of attributes; a consummate work of art embodying not only the poet's intuition, the mystic's creed, the great architect's mastery of the subtleties of his craft, but the man himself with his sweetness, directness, and inarticulacy. In the Cenotaph we see indeed, more clearly than in any other of his works because it is so concentrated, what Lutyens was. Its inception, equally with the finished result, is the perfect instance of the working of his genius, and could have been achieved by no other process. A greater problem cannot be imagined as set to any man: to design, at a moment's notice, such a simple thing yet one of such immense significance, both in intention and, as has proved to be the case, in effect.

Among the innumerable messages of congratulation that came to him, Lutyens valued a characteristic note from Barrie:

2. Robert Street, Adelphi
6. August 1919.

My Dear Lutyens,

　　The cenotaph grows in beauty as one strolls down alone o' nights to look at it, which becomes my habit. I stand cogitating why and how it is so noble a thing. It is how the war has moved you and lifted you above yourself. I think it was Milton who described poetry as 'thoughts that voluntarily move harmonious numbers'. This is a harmonious number and I feel proud of it and you.

Yours sincerely,
J. M. Barrie.

The cascade of press cuttings continued for days, the great majority expressing the public desire for the Cenotaph's permanence, exactly as it stood, even to reproducing in bronze the four guards who had been mounted with reversed arms at its quarters. The official view, whilst agreeing to its reconstruction, at first stipulated that it must stand on another site, owing to interference with traffic, regardless of the fact that the design was so evidently, though subtly, related to its site. On the morrow of the ceremony, acknowledging Mond's congratulations, Lutyens emphasised some aspects of the case for permanence, which need to be recorded lest any future proposals should be made for its alteration:

> Personally I should like the monument to be where it now stands; if in Portland stone, with all the refinement digestion can invent to perfect it.
>
> The site has been qualified by the salutes of folk and allied armies. No other site would give this pertinence. Whitehall is a processional road although already barred by the Duke of Cambridge's statue. By altering the refuges, a wider pavement round the Cenotaph would be good, and to avoid people falling over the lowest step, the first step [should be raised] to the level of a seat or bench.
>
> Many have suggested to me to place bronze figures, representing sentries, round it. This I would greatly regret: it would prevent living sentries being posted on days of ceremony. The position where the sentries stood might be marked with incisions on the pavement.

Lutyens intended the banners at the sides, and the Union Jack which, surmounted by a laurel wreath, was draped over the symbolic sarcophagus at the top of the Cenotaph, to be reproduced in carved and painted stone. It is to be noted that the draped flag is shown as integral to the design in his first sketch. Only unwillingly did he consent to actual banners in the one case, and the elimination of the draping flag above. The authorities did, however, resist the appeals of the symbolists that the emblems of the Empire's various religions should be carved upon the Cenotaph.

Work on the permanent monument was put in hand in October, as Lutyens was setting out for Delhi, and was completed in time for the second anniversary of Armistice on November 11, 1920. Mr. Lloyd George wrote from 10 Downing Street on November 17,

> to thank you on behalf of the Cabinet for your fine and generous service in designing and building the memorial which has become a national shrine, not only for the British Isles but also for the whole Empire.
>
> The Cenotaph by its very simplicity fittingly expresses the memory in which the people hold all those who so bravely fought and died for the country. How well it represents the feeling of the nation has been amply manifested by the stream of pilgrims who have passed the Cenotaph during the past week.
>
> The Cabinet is anxious that you should know how much they appreciate the fine work you have done, and how grateful they are to you for it.
>
> Yours sincerely,
> D. Lloyd George.

For the next eighteen years (when the date was transferred to the Sunday next following the anniversary) the usage of the Two Minutes Silence, perpetuating the hushed salute of the victors, was observed throughout the British Empire at the eleventh hour of the eleventh day of the eleventh month. Focussed upon the Cenotaph at its core, that global envelope of silent ether extended the monument's form to infinity. Those moments of simulated eternity seemed to intensify, as year followed year, the spiritual vitality of the Cenotaph's almost imperceptible curves; a vitality, however, that, when the sea of sound came roaring round it again, was discovered afresh to reside in the design. The seeming miracle that he had achieved was reaffirmed in 1946 when the impossibility of repeating it was acknowledged by inscribing the dates of the Second World War with those of the First.

Yet he had envisaged the feat a dozen years before, when he had written to his wife:[1]

> There is that in art which transcends all rules—it is the divine (I use poor words)... To short sight it is a miracle. To those of a little longer sight it is Godhead. If we could see yet better ... there is no ploy which cannot be lifted to the divine level by its elevation as an art.

In the Cenotaph he might have been setting himself to demonstrate, in clearly apprehended form, that obscurely phrased truth that, indeed, underlies all his works though less patently in some than others: that the highest spiritual conception can be equated by consummate art.

His performance translated him almost overnight to Olympian status in the eyes of fellow architects. The seemingly effortless perfection of the Cenotaph set a standard of excellence to which thereafter (for a time) they recognised that they could aspire. Gone for good—in all save his most inveterate or intimate antagonists—were the doubts and jealousies of his genius. He stood as the supreme living architect of British Empire, reincarnating, if not surpassing, 'that incomparable young man' Sir Christopher Wren.

Elated and humbled by his triumph, he wrote as the day closed to his absent wife and children, sending to each his special love 'on this of all days':

> To all the blessing of God. And prayers for a complete home, with all it means.

---

[1] See Chapter VI, § 4.

PART III

'SO FAITH FULFILS'

... a mind sustained
By recognitions of transcendent power,
In sense conducting to ideal form.

WORDSWORTH, The Prelude, XIV

INTERIM PORTRAIT

THE subtle perfection of the Cenotaph had opened people's eyes to qualities in the Architect, indefinable but as genius, for which Wren alone seemed to afford a comparison. As the decade advanced he was raised in the estimation of many to a yet higher and more solitary pedestal when it became apparent that at New Delhi he had achieved a feat unattempted on such a scale since the completion of Versailles, which as architecture his palace surpassed.

'One had never seen before, and will never see again, anyone who resembled this singular and delightful man,' Sir Osbert Sitwell[1] records of him at this time. 'An expression of mischievous benevolence was his distinguishing mark, as it was of his work. He would sit, with his bald dome-like head lowered at a particular angle of reflection, as his very large, blue, reflective eyes contemplated a view, a work of art, or something particularly outrageous that he intended shortly to say.'

'The years pass,' wrote E. V. Lucas in 1924,[2] 'his eyes grow merrier, his spectacles ever rounder, his head loses a hair here and there; but he is still undefeated, still an eternal child, an apostle of beauty and thoroughness, a minister of elvish nonsense. He builds a New Delhi, eighty square miles of palace and avenue; he builds a Queen's Dolls' House, an affair of inches but such that Japanese cherry stone carvers could not excel. His friends were legion; his mind was electrically instant to respond to any sympathetic suggestion; he never broke his word; he never let you know if he was tired; and with it all he was out for fun.'

William Rothenstein's drawing, done in 1922 and reproduced in the Frontispiece, is the best factual likeness of him in the early 'twenties. The artist has penetrated behind the 'elvish' façade to bring one the fine, classical, bone-structure and wide eyes, here unsmiling. His contours are becoming more rounded and smooth. A spherical motif begins to be his own caricature of himself and is emphasised by the horn-rimmed spectacles that exaggerate the round-open eyes beneath the dome of his brow that is heightened by the receding but still curly hair, turning from dark to grey. It is the eyes that one remembers, and the finely chiselled pointed nose. John's portrait (p. 401) seizes on both features, but one did not notice so beak-like a nose as in this portrait. It also gives him a yellow colour, whereas his complexion was a clear and healthy pink. His neck, too, was shorter, seeming the more so because of the deep upright white collar that he invariably wore. Yet, if glimpsed suddenly, the portrait gives an uncanny likeness for an instant.

[1] *Great Morning*, p. 19.
[2] *Everybody's Book of the Queen's Dolls' House,* ed. A. C. Benson and Lawrence Weaver.

His expression reflected very little variation of mood. He can best be described as looking happy, with those exceedingly sharp, open, quizzical eyes that twinkled when joking but missed nothing, so that, although he seemed not to have looked about him, he was apt to surprise one by remarking on aspects of people and things not readily apparent. Even when searching for a word or concentrating, he never frowned. Instead, his eyebrows might lift and the half-smile become abstracted. What one most clearly remembers of an encounter was his hands—perfectly observed in the John portrait—exceedingly fine, firm, and almost never still. As expressive as the faces of others, his fingers would grope for and then grip an idea, rapidly feeling or outlining its shape before he seized the virgin pad with which to illustrate it. The Dulac drawing (opposite) most exactly represents his expression as one remembers him henceforward, but omits the significant hands. Whatever they are doing is coming out right; were there any difficulty there would be a slight tension about the nose, as is suggested by comparison of the two snapshots taken a good many years later (p. 402). All four of these well illustrate the hands.

These observations preface the narrative of Lutyens's Olympian years. He was now a legend. His authority and genius were unquestioned. He seemed above the turmoils and trends of the day. Personally, he was wholly unaffected by his immense success and reputation, apparently remaining, as these descriptions by friends stress, ever young and unpredictable.

But it was not only outwardly and in intellectual capacity that he was expanding. The third element in him, the spirit that nobody knew, the existence of which is scarcely implied in the impressions quoted, had waxed in power and scope during the years of conflict. His power of sympathy enlarged his spirit in proportion to the scope and nature of the works into which he projected his faith, and which it was given him to endow with the unalterable proportions and lineaments of fate. This aspect of his personality will henceforward assume ever increasing significance, as he projected his spirit into the conception of the amazing Cathedral designed for the Roman Catholic See of Liverpool, of a new City of London, and of the union of science and art in a new theory of architecture.

At the end of Part II we left him setting out for India after completing the Cenotaph. There his most sustained endeavour was still not yet half-way to realisation. We take up the story on his return to New Delhi.

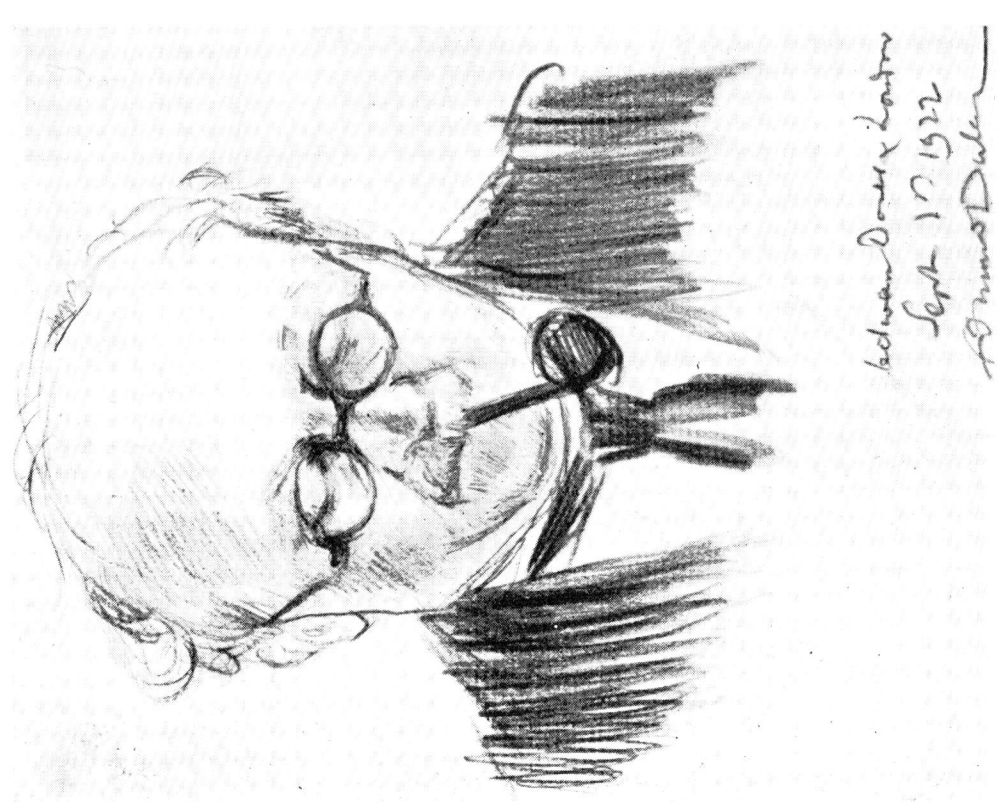

104 (*above*). Portrait Sketch by Edmund Dulac. 'Sept., 1st 1922, between Dover and London'
105 (*right*). Portrait by Augustus John, about 1920. (In the possession of Viscount Ridley)

106. LUTYENS IN HIS SIXTIES. Four snapshots illustrating characteristic attitudes and expressions

107. NEW DELHI: THE MILITARY SECRETARY'S HOUSE. Designed by Lutyens and occupied by him during his later visits

108. LUTYENS AND HIS BEARER, PERSOTUM

109. WITH E. V. LUCAS, 1920

110. AIR VIEW OF NEW DELHI LOOKING WEST. In the foreground the War Memorial Arch and the King's Way; the Record Office is visible at the intersection of Queen's Way—the only one built of the four buildings projected at this intersection

111. THE ALL INDIA WAR MEMORIAL ARCH. Foundation stone laid 1921; dedicated 1931

CHAPTER XIV

DELHI RISING

§1. 'IF YOU CAN BEAR...'

BEFORE New Delhi was begun, Lutyens had forecast to Lord Hardinge that Government House, which the latter had guessed should cost £200,000, would cost a million pounds. He was to prove almost exactly right. Hopefully, Lord Hardinge had adopted the Public Works Department's figure of a total cost for the whole city of four million, another guess, based on optimism and non-existent plans. Ever since, operations had been embarrassed by the grossness of the understatement. Keeling's first detailed estimate amounted to six million, with a reservation pointing out that no authority had been able to lay down precisely what the estimate ought to cover. In 1921–22 the large additions necessitated by the Constitutional changes, the growth of Government personnel, and the rise in building rates increased the estimate to eight million, which in the end rose to ten million. No less illusory was the period of four or five years originally reckoned for the construction.

From the end of the war till the beginning of 1923 the whole undertaking hung in the balance. Junior staff and the army of operatives, dispersed during the war, had to be reassembled; the basis of costs had to be entirely revised; public opinion became alarmed, so that the project was subject to continuous hostile criticism; and the change-over from Viceregal to elected Indian control following the Montagu-Chelmsford reforms produced an atmosphere of uncertainty. Moreover the unrest generated by the continual agitation of Congress for Swaraj, and Gandhi's non-cooperation campaigns, slowly worsened the political atmosphere. A sense of crisis became endemic.

Between December, 1919 and January, 1923, Lutyens spent in the aggregate nearly a year in India. There was little concrete to show for it, but they were months of intense office activity, revising, recasting, and, in the event, preparing for the relatively rapid progress eventually achieved. Government House hung fire until early in 1923 the report was issued of the Committee of Inquiry appointed by Lord Reading in 1922, to examine progress in construction and to report on any necessary changes in the general plan of the capital, under the chairmanship of Lord Inchcape, and consisting of British and Indians of independent views. Lord Reading subsequently told Lutyens that the inquiry had been undertaken largely to counter the political and financial criticism, through ascertaining and publishing the facts, in order to provide an independent basis on which the increased estimates could be sanctioned by the Indian Legislature. But meanwhile, and until the latter found its political feet, supplies and outlay for Government House, the spectacular heart of the capital, had to be restrained, and, in the event, integral features of the original plan of the city were abandoned.

But others were added. The new Constitution itself involved transforming the architectural landscape. The Legislative Assembly having replaced the Viceroy as the arbiter of India's destiny, the building of its Chambers, on a site not provided for in the layout, and completion of the Secretariats for the Civil Service, must take precedence over the Viceroy's residence.

Lutyens's chief architectural preoccupation was therefore the reshaping of the north side of Government House, previously to have contained the Viceroy's Council Chamber, into extended Viceregal offices; and the All India War Memorial Arch at the eastern end of the processional King's Way. In the earlier months he was also completing designs for the group of large buildings at the junction of Kings Way and Queens Way intended to contain the Record Office, Medical Research Building, Ethnological and War Museums: and his scheme for a terminal Central Railway Station with adjacent shopping centre to form the connecting hinge between the old and new cities at the point later known as Connaught Place. The Record Office was estimated to cost £42,500, the Medical Research Building £150,000, and the War Museum £20,000. After the first had been begun, the erection of all three was postponed indefinitely for reasons of economy.[1]

The design of the All India Memorial Arch was approved in March, 1920. Its purpose was twofold: to commemorate the 70,000 Indian soldiers who had fallen in the war; and specifically the British and Indian soldiers killed on or beyond the North-West Frontier, whose graves are unmarked. Their names, 13,516 in number, are inscribed on the faces of the main piers of the Arch and on the walls of two small courts formed under the lateral arches.

The possibility of a great Indian war memorial in this situation had been accepted as early as January, 1917. Its designing, however, followed the War Stones and Cenotaph. Thus stylistically and chronologically this huge monument (p. 404) is a significant link between Lutyens's pre-war and post-war modes. We can detect in it the first large-scale development of his monumental geometry, to be carried to such refinements in the 'twenties and 'thirties. Now, as then, he began with a simple dimension, 30 feet for the width of the main east and west arch, two and a half times which gave him its height. Multiples or fractions of this unit of 30 feet prevail

[1] These four buildings were to have been externally similar but in some cases to have contained more than one unit or function (thus explaining the apparent differences in cost). The Record Office, visible in Pl. 110, has a stone façade facing east. The Ethnological Museum was intended to incorporate an existing small building containing wall paintings etc., brought from the Gobi Desert by Sir Aurel Stein. No progress was made with it.

throughout. The height to the spring of the side arches in 45 feet (span 17 feet); the east and west fronts are just 90 feet wide, as is the height to the cornice. The fronts therefore form almost exactly a square, with a superstructure proportioned by the other fractions, giving a total height of 139 feet. The plan, on the other hand, is the 'ideal rectangle'—approximately 92 feet × 56 feet; and the faces are insensibly diminished by a succession of seven set-backs between the base and the main frieze. It is the combination of these mathematical proportions and visual corrections that give the monument, as to all his later works, a recondite but palpable vitality. In the attic, means were provided for maintaining a perpetual column of thin smoke, to glow by night.

The site and design of the new Council House to contain the three Chambers of the Legislative Assembly formed the main subject of discussion at the beginning of 1920. Baker proposed a three-winged plan with a central dome over a great hall in the centre. Lutyens succeeded in obtaining the Delhi Committee's agreement to his original suggestion for a circular building as more satisfactory to the angles of the street plan and as the termination of the main avenue of approach from the north-east. The case for enclosing the three Chambers in a circular perimeter formed of columns and a screen wall was strengthened, as Sir Herbert Baker has admitted,[1] by the need for more accommodation than his original design provided. The foundation stones, both of the Chambers and the Arch, were laid in February, 1921, by the Duke of Connaught, deputising for the Prince of Wales, when he inaugurated the All India Legislature following the first elections. The building was opened in 1926. The auspices of the former occasion were darkened by the bitterness engendered by General Dyer's volleys at Amritsar, the Duke's serious illness *en route*, and by the rival demonstration staged by Gandhi in the old city. Nevertheless, Lutyens pointed out to the Duke, in the basements of Government House, his device by which the capitals of the columns comprised little bells at their angles, the bells that, according to legend, are heard to ring when a dynasty passes but in this case, being of stone, he remarked, could never ring.

In the new Assembly little time was lost before attacks began to be levelled at most aspects of the new city. Mr. Sarma, the newly appointed Indian Minister of Public Works, however, won Lutyens's admiration by his defence of his Department and the conduct of building operations, although both Indian and British critics clamoured in the newspapers. These attacks reached their climax at the beginning of 1922. Besides the cost, they assailed the climate and geographical location of Delhi. Privately, Lutyens admitted that the location of the capital had been hasty, too much influenced by sentiment, and should have been determined by scientific planning. But he regarded such an objective method of approach as 'impossible to achieve under any democracy', requiring 'an autocrat with a wisdom and fearlessness

[1] *Architecture and Personalities*, p. 75.

of judgment too rare to be within the range of practical politics'. Thus he foresaw that the scientific planning of new towns, to be effective, must necessitate wide compulsory powers. When in 1911 he and Baker had been corresponding on the Delhi project, they had supposed that the Government of India exercised such autocratic powers. A generation was to elapse before a government dared apply in England the directive compulsions which lay beyond the scope of capitalist Edwardian democracy even in most autocratic form.

The financial situation was complicated by the awkward fact that the Government had to confront the Legislative Assembly at its first session with a Budget deficit involving unprecedented calls on the Indian taxpayer. In order to encourage the Assembly with the possibility of completing the central buildings rapidly and cheaply, and so to voting the necessary funds, Hailey, now Finance Member, revived Hardinge's and Chelmsford's idea of finishing the upper storeys of Government House in plaster, and pressed Lutyens to agree. He refused, pointing out that the time saved in erection would be offset by the time spent in making new drawings and estimates; and the reduced initial cost by the continuous expenditure on maintenance. In any case, stone was essential for the structural portions, including the staircases which were designed as part of the walls, and equally for all mouldings, linings, cornices and architraves (or, to look well with plaster, preferably marble). Meanwhile, quarrying, plant and establishment charges would run on. Instead of making false economies of cost and time by using inferior material, Lutyens urged the floating of a loan to be taken up by banking houses. £5,000,000 at 6% free of Income Tax would be repayable in 40 years by an annual disbursement of £323,000 principal and interest, and so remove New Delhi 'from the yearly political arena of the Budget', whilst giving a new confidence to contractors and craftsmen. 'Give your new parliament the chance of proving its wisdom,' he retorted.[1] Lutyens had always pressed for a building loan. His proposal had met with approval at Balmoral in 1911, and informally been endorsed by Montagu subsequently. A recent visit to Bombay had impressed him with the success of the £10,000,000 loan raised there by the Governor, Sir George Lloyd, to finance his great scheme of foreshore reclamation and city extension. He urged the Viceroy designate, Lord Reading, to discuss a loan with the Secretary of State. However, nothing came of it and the new capital continued to be financed by instalments, henceforth of £500,000 annually.

Attention was drawn to the *impasse* at Delhi by the publicity attending the Prince of Wales's visit to India in January, 1922, itself far from a success. *The Times, Morning Post,* and *Observer* published antagonistic articles under such titles as 'Historic Monument or Folly?', 'Delhi's Costly Glories', 'Marble Halls and Bad Government'. In an interview given to *The Statesman* of Calcutta, Lutyens strongly deprecated newspaper criticism as merely making matters more difficult for all concerned, and

---

[1] To Sir Malcolm Hailey, January 17, 1921.

replied personally in the *Morning Post*. He emphasised that the only economical policy would be to carry through the scheme with confidence and practical foresight. The climate of Delhi was unjustly maligned. He was entirely satisfied with the site, though he considered it 'a pity' that Government House would not be seen from positions on the main avenue. He replied to the *Morning Post's* wild allegations that the cost to date was £20,000,000 by accurately stating it to be £5,600,000. 'If only the people took less interest in politics,' he concluded, 'and more in creative art, India would be in a happier state.'

But the whole financial position needed adjustment, owing to depreciation of the rupee as compared with sterling from 2s. to 1s. 4d., and the all-round rise in costs due to increasing bureaucracy. Taken with the long delays in building, it was involving the architects themselves in actual loss under the terms of their 1913 Agreement. In November, 1921, a supplementary agreement was therefore signed, providing, in lieu of the remuneration then assigned on a percentage basis, the payment to the joint architects of a lump sum of £195,000. The date of completion of the works and of the payment was fixed at December 31, 1929. Up to date, it appears, they had received £60,000, of which, by their mutual Agreement, their share of personal income between 1913 and 1921 had been £15,000 each. Henceforth, the gross remuneration would be £18,000 a year till 1924, £19,000 in 1925, £16,000 in 1926, decreasing by £1000 annually to £8000 in 1929. Provision was made for the scheduled works taking a less or a longer period to complete. Till 1925, therefore, each would receive £4500 per annum net personal fee, dropping to £2000 in 1929.

Throughout the years now under review Lutyens was preparing to obtain redress of Lord Hardinge's refusal, and Lord Chelmsford's war-time evasion, of reconsideration of the Gradient question. This was still regarded as a matter for the Viceroy's decision alone and therefore was due to be brought up when Lord Reading succeeded Lord Chelmsford in the season 1921-22. In 1920 it had been arranged that Lord Carmichael should state the case for revision to the Home Advisory Committee. For this purpose Lutyens prepared a series of drawings, explaining them with comparisons of the scale, as that the distance from the Memorial Arch to Government House, about 1¾ miles, corresponded roughly to that from Notting Hill Gate to Marble Arch; and from Government House to the Great Place below the Secretariats (half a mile) to that from Buckingham Palace to Admiralty Arch. From the Memorial Arch to the Great Place (just short of 1¼ miles, compare Marble Arch to Oxford Circus) the ground was level and Government House remained in full view. The gradient then rose abruptly to 1 in 20 (St. James Street is 1 in 30) for a distance roughly equal to that of Pall Mall from the Mall at St. James's Palace. From the Great Place only the upper half of the dome would be seen; during the ascent it would disappear almost entirely and, moreover, the Secretariats on either side be hidden by the flanking walls of the ramp. He therefore proposed the extension of the slope to the centre of Government Court, and its widening by lateral flights of steps 'to give more dignity to the view of Government House and to show the Secretariats to greater advantage'. He admitted that the alteration would be costly, much more so than when he had pressed for it previously, but much less than at some future date when, he felt convinced, public opinion would demand it.

Baker, whom the Committee interrogated, explained his opposition on grounds of the cost and delay, the danger of blasting operations to adjacent masonry, the heat of sunk flights of steps such as Lutyens proposed, and the practical inconvenience to the staffs of thus separating the Secretariats. But, he said, he based his objection on higher architectural reasons. The existing disposition expressed a definite idea, namely the giving of dignity and importance to the actual mechanism of Indian democratic government, as represented by the Secretariats, raising their personnel above the proletariat in the Great Place below, and to a level with, though divided from, the privileged *enclave* of Viceroy's Court beyond. He conceived that it would be rather an insult to the new Government of India if the amenities of its servants were subordinated to the occasional requirements of Viceregal processions—occurring perhaps once in a decade. In discussion, he said that he had no objection to the alteration on abstract architectural grounds, but to do so would be to change fundamentally the notion that he conceived to be embodied in the central buildings. Expense was also a vital factor, since Government was cutting down his Legislative Chambers and the money could be much better spent on them. The Advisory Committee's record of the discussion was transmitted to Delhi.

Before going out to India at the end of 1921, Lutyens stayed at Balmoral where the King appears to have confirmed his preference for Lutyens's proposal. In the following February Lord and Lady Reading, attended by Lord Willingdon and Sir George Lloyd, met Lutyens (who also had a party of friends with him) on the site. Lutyens took the occasion, though an informal one, to raise the issue with the Viceroy. He recounted the episode to Lady Emily, then staying at Adyar with Mrs. Besant:

> I spoke very calmly. George Lloyd was emphatic about it; Willingdon charmingly neutral with a bias for doing the right thing. I lunched with H.E. on Monday and spoke again, giving him the King's message.
>
> The Committee meeting is on Friday. Pray for me. I do hope I win my level way, for our and India's sake, but they are terrified of money.

The meeting appears to have been indecisive, for Lutyens continued to press Reading for a decision whilst the Inchcape Committee was in Delhi—in view of the financial cost of the operation; and emphasised that, if his appeal was refused, Government House would need to be redesigned, to overcome the slope's insult, at a far greater cost than that of the changing of the gradient. It is not clear whether he informed the Viceroy of his intention to resign if the decision was given against him, but he certainly discussed the step with Keeling and with his wife, and had already threatened to do so to Baker when the subject was before the London Committee.

Baker had appealed to him as one good sportsman to another:

> Is it not rather a childish attitude to say that just because you can't always get your own way, you wont 'play' any more? I have given way to you in nine cases out of ten when we have differed, and raised no criticism in many more. When the Viceroy asked me last March if I wanted to reopen the question of the Legislative Buildings, which had been decided against me and in favour of your ideas, my answer to him was that he, as umpire, had given me 'out', and it was not for me to reverse his decision. Cannot you play 'cricket' too?[1]

But Lutyens was not a cricketer, nor could he regard architecture as 'giving expression, in its highest aspirations, to human and national ideas'—as Baker had explained his own creed to Lord Reading on the same issue—in other words, as a department of administration. He did distinguish, with the absolute clarity of a child, between values that, as an artist, he held to be true and those that were compromised by expediency and were therefore, he held, false, dishonest. He stated his fundamental divergence in the criticism that his colleague 'spoils everything by some mental reservation which, in practice, produces bad, undigested, design'. To compromise in this way was, for Lutyens, equivalent to sinning against the Holy Ghost. He felt the need of resigning on practical and moral grounds no less. Owing to the impossibility, under the circumstances, of collaborating, it would not be fair on India for the architects of Delhi to be mutually antagonistic. 'I can work if there is a fair prospect of conversion to my view, my original plan and essential lines,' he confided to his wife. But, on top of the rising costs of Government House, the implied snub, if his appeal was rejected a third time, left him no alternative, he felt. If so, he would publish a statement in *The Times* to clear himself of responsibility 'for Baker's mess'. Resignation would affect him seriously financially but 'you have always been brave about money', he told his wife. 'I have a few years left and must cut myself off from such a fiasco as this. I am up early, and sleep little, but feel happier and relieved at my decision. But I won't act over quickly.'

His wife, fortunately no further away than Madras, received the letter in time to convince him that his duty to India and architecture lay in fighting on, seeing Government House to the finish, however grievous the wound in this minor, if vital, joint in the grand conception. He eventually took heart from her and his friends' persuasion, provided that it would be made clear that responsibility for the gradient was not his but was due to the Government's parsimony. It is evident, however, that

[1] June 30, 1920.

the deciding factors with the Government were the practical and political considerations.[1]

The decision was, in the event, referred to the Secretary of State, who informed Lutyens in June, 1922, that the Government of India declined to reopen the question. Acquainting his ally Lord Carmichael with the verdict, Lutyens added: 'Hailey said that the rejection was on the score of money. I wish the G.O.I. would state that, for, until they do, it looks like an ugly thing agreed on as being beautiful.' By then, his natural resilience had so far reasserted itself as to enable him to avert his eyes from the scene of his 'Bakerloo', as he termed his humiliation and to concentrate on the immense task of completing Government House. But he never forgave his colleague, whose Secretariats, as they rose, intensified his architectural disappointment. For the remainder of their collaboration the atmosphere in the architects' mess at Raisina was strained, and apt to be highly embarrassing to visitors and even to assistants.

At the beginning of 1923 the report of the Inchcape Committee confirmed Hailey's remark. Describing the Viceroy's Court and Central Vista as 'in the main ornamental in purpose', it maintained that 'expenditure on them should be kept rigidly within the provision sanctioned'. In other respects, however, Lutyens could rejoice that the 'Axe Committee' had left him alone; indeed fortified him. The Report stated that up to March, 1923, the total gross outlay on the city would aggregate 841 lakhs (£$5\frac{1}{2}$ million), leaving 531 lakhs (£$3\frac{1}{2}$ million) to be expended on works already in progress, 'the lines of which cannot, with any regard to economy, be altered at this stage.' Government House was spared altogether, with the hope expressed that the full 10 lakhs (£66,600) allowed for structural and marble work would not be fully expended. The War Memorial Arch was to be treated as distinct from the building of the city and therefore excluded from the gross estimates.

By the time the Inchcape Committee's Report gave the all-clear, the reorganisation of the supply problems which are noted in §3 of this chapter were being overcome and the walls of the central buildings could at last begin to rise above their Upper Basement level.

§2. PLACES AND PEOPLE IN INDIA

Among Lutyens's papers is a folder containing miscellaneous skits and lampoons by various hands groping for the comic side of these embittering and inhibited years. In his own hand is this extract from Gibbon (Vol. iii, p. 247, ed. J. B. Bury) whom he had taken to reading on his sea voyages:

> Perhaps the pride of the ministers whose business was seldom interrupted by reflections might reject as wild and visionary every proposal which exceeded the measure of their capacity and deviated from the forms and precedents of office.

[1] See Lord Hailey's letter to Sir Herbert Baker quoted in *Architecture and Personalities*, p. 66.

To his friend Sir Walter Raleigh, better known for his works on English literature than for the satirical humour that drew him and Lutyens together, may be due a ballad introducing sundry notabilities at Delhi that begins:

> *I sing of a city uprising*
> *Like the newest of Aphrodites*
> *From a jungle of tombs and temples—*
>   *A City of Dreadful Knights,*

There are allusions, among others, to the then Finance Member, Sir William Meyer, and to Lutyens in these typical verses:

> *There's a loan-ly descendant of Midas*
> *Who gilds where his hand alights*
> *And compels the admeyeration*
>   *Of the City of Dreadful Knights . . .*

> *But the last and the choicest spirit*
> *To scale the Olympian heights*
> *Is that migratory Puck who designed*
>   *The City of Dreadful Knights.*

Raleigh's initials are attached to an amusing and not wholly obscure *Ballad of William Pottinger*, describing an architect whose 'lowly modest ways' and readiness to agree with members of committees earned him golden opinions and the commission to design a university:

> *And now the five committee-men*
>   *All round the board were ranged*
> *To give advice upon the plans*
>   *And how they should be changed.*
> *O, in stepped Willing Pottinger*
>   *The blandest of them all;*
> *A fairer spoken gentleman*
>   *Ne'er stepped into a hall!*

> *Then out spoke one committee-man*
>   *And he spoke bold and free;*
> *'This porch' says he 'is twelve foot high;*
>   *I'd have it twenty three'.*
> *And out then spoke another one,*
>   *Says he 'I think it best*
> *To take these gables facing south*
>   *And turn them to the west'.*

And last of all the wise Chairman
　　Whom nothing did escape,
'The building seems all right,' says he,
　　'But I do not like its shape.'

Then gentle William Pottinger
　　With modest mien began
To applaud the ingenuity
　　Of each Committee man.
'And I, if I may be allowed
　　To speak my mind,' says he,
'With all the changes you suggest
　　Most fully do agree.'

There were, no doubt, festive gatherings at which such sallies would be appreciated, though many more where they would not be and the brightening must be extempore. The period is not recorded when, at a Viceregal dinner party, a nervous curate named Western was among the guests. Noting that he was being neglected by his neighbours, Lutyens lent forward during a pause in the conversation and, addressing him in a loud voice, remarked 'Excuse me sir, but may I ask if you are related to the Great Western?' Sir Osbert Sitwell, in telling this anecdote,[1] imagines 'for an instant the young man's eye pondering whether Aunt Isabel or little Wilfred could justly be claimed as the Great Western, and then the outraged buzz of conversation rescuing him and carrying him off to pastures of convivial delight', and justly accounts for the sally's apparent cruelty by Lutyens's perception that only by means of a profound shock would the curate's neighbours be made to take pity on him.

This method of approach was called by Lutyens 'jaw-dropping', and was used frequently with startling effect but only with those whom he wished definitely to befriend, or never to see again. A more harmless device for thawing atmosphere is illustrated by an occasion when, dining with the Military Secretary to Lord Chelmsford (Col., now Sir Ralph, Verney) some guests arrived who did not know their host and hostess (who happened to be in another room). Lutyens instantly stepped forward and played host, introducing another guest as Mrs. Verney. The comedy worked well until people got the giggles and the Verneys came in, when it became very complicated. 'But we all sat down to dinner with no stiffness left at all,' he added (unnecessarily) in describing the evening. He depicted his own embarrassment when a large party of guests arrived, whom he had forgotten that he had invited, with 'I was in my boots quite chin high with shock'.

---

[1] *Great Morning*, p. 21, where the curate's name is spelt Weston, which slightly obscures the pun in print.

At Delhi his quarters were now in one of the big staff bungalows (p. 403) not yet required for their destined occupants. There he had the unaccustomed luxury, after the makeshifts of earlier years, of three big sitting rooms, with seven bedrooms and bathrooms, which thenceforward enabled him to bring his wife to India on several occasions, and to entertain many friends. Indeed, he found the big barely furnished rooms were grim without people; and domestic pets, though numerous, were not always satisfactory. There were a succession of cats, but a porcupine was voted more of a pest than a pet; he lived in a hole all day, demolished a whole garden if he could, and only appeared in the dark, when he was not necessarily welcome. Then Lutyens had the idea that some green and blue parrots would furnish the house cheaply and of course decorate it, 'for,' as he wrote to Ursula, 'you could not take your eyes off a loose parrot, so you always had a perfect picture in view, all coloured. I told Persotum to get me six. He bought me one, which I paid for with a nip and scarlet skull! Then he brought me a cat. That's how one's bearer keeps one in order.' On an earlier occasion he had told Ursula: 'An elephant is coming to stay with us—he will bring his own trunk. The Union Jack is to show his war sympathy'. 'Jolly beasts, elephants,' he always told the children, his letters to whom portray many. 'I saw one having a drink the other day; the water was poured down his nose, like this'. But another time he told them a story of how:

> I went for a ride on an Indian dancing horse and was getting along quite nicely until we met a huge elephant and the horse shied and I so nearly came off. Then it swung round, galloped away, and—horror—I found the elephant after me and felt its hot breath between me and the saddle!! Just as I was getting home the elephant caught my horse's tail. But luckily for me the tail came off just as I got home.

The faithful Persotum had correspondingly prospered and promoted himself. Soon after taking up his new quarters (before the parrot arrived) Lutyens described himself seated sahib-like at ease one evening, with:

> Insects, flies, bugs, beetles and whatnots tap-tapping against the walls and ceiling and tink-tinking against the lampshade. The ching of a beetle in the fan —a silence—then the wob on floor or wall. Ching, wob, and an insect soul has crossed the bar. Bar! happy thought. '*Koi hai*—soda please.'
>
> Persotum met me with his grandson, and has provided himself not only with new tidy clothes but a complete fitment of Odol smile—a revolution in his appearance.

When he was given the Military Secretary's house, he entertained a great deal. One unusual feature of its furnishing was a dinner table of which the middle consisted in a blackboard. A piece of chalk was laid beside each guest so that everybody could draw on the board at any moment of the meal.

One of his first guests was E. V. Lucas, on a busman's holiday in India, whom Lutyens tried to persuade to use his witty pen in a description of New Delhi. Lucas blenched at the mass of complicated material (as well he might!) but applied his humour to a more congenial topic—a tiger shoot in which the two artists took a passive but enthralled part. Sir Harcourt Butler, now Governor of the United Provinces, invited them to join an outing on which the other guest was Lord Goschen, Governor elect of Madras. The party left Lucknow one Saturday evening, travelling in the Governor's train to a point near the Nepal border where elephants and beaters met them under the Chief of Police, Kumar Bum Bahadur Sha,[1] who was in charge of operations. Lutyens was detailed to Bum Bahadur's elephant as a non-combatant. The intended quarry was *gond* (swamp deer), and the ground a jungle of lagoons and swamps adjoining a river among areas of tall yellow grass. Lutyens delighted in the great herds of deer encountered (only a stag with an exceptional head would be shot at), and was beginning to count up the species he saw— black buck, peacocks, bitterns, florikens (a rare form of bustard), various hawks, eagles—when his elephant 'tapped the ground with her trunk and gave a ventriloquial whinney, indicating the presence ahead of some carnivore'. The excitement was great when a tigress was presently sighted, and Lord Goschen got in a shot. Bum Bahadur commanded *cello, cello*, hurry, hurry; the elephants were marshalled into the deep grass till only the turbans of their crews were visible, 'and we up in the howdahs stood out like boats tossing on this yellow sea.' Fires were lighted to supplement the insufficient complement of elephants, and, as the unbeaten area grew smaller and smaller:

---

[1] The spelling, as throughout the following anecdote, follows the text quoted.

the elephants got more excited, tore up the grass in front of them, mahouts objecting and seconding their elephants' remonstrances, yet my Bum was obdurate and drove them on and in. A wounded tigress is no joke: at every push the elephants squealed, the trapped beast—as yet invisible—growled and snarled, and everyone shouted, hollared, and facing us were the flames roaring sky high.

I was sorry for the beast—she was dying, but no one dared go near her. She growled, snarled, tried to move and now and then swallowed with a cat-like gesture—humanising her at the last.

On the return journey, E. V. Lucas wrote what purported to be a 'minute account' of the day. Lutyens sent home a copy of the narrative with a note that Lord Goschen and he were going into partnership with a libel action against E.V. as a result. An extract still reads as comically as that delightful humorist's *Wisdom While you Wait*:

10.	a.m.	Departure for the chase. Lutyens makes his will.
10.15.		Lutyens sees hog-deer
10.16.		Hog-deer sees Lutyens and swoons. Goschen shoots hog-deer.
10.45.		Lutyens's latest pun overheard by Gond, who sinks into a coma. Goschen shoots Gond.
11.0.		Bum Bahadur calls for his cello
11.1.		Lutyens says he doesn't like playing second fiddle (faint laughter).
1.10 p.m.		Sensational entrance of tigress and Gond. Goschen fires at Gond and hits tigress, who takes cover. Lutyens and Bum Bahadur begin drive.
2.40.		Hearing that there is danger, Lutyens hides behind Bum Bahadur.
2.50.		H.E. shoots tigress in shoulder and head.
2.51.		Lutyens says 'Shoulder heads!' Death of tigress.
2.53.		Goschen takes careful aim and shoots tigress.
2.54.		Renewed death of tigress.
2.55.		Tigress shot again by Goschen.
3.0.		Bum Bahadur having had enough of the howdah acts as mahout.
3.1.		Lutyens says 'Here's a howdah do!' Goschen mistakenly refrains from shooting Lutyens.

Though so little progress was perceptible at Delhi, 'there is an enormous amount of building going to be done all through India' Lutyens reported in 1920, 'especially under the Reforms. Is it going to be our swan song? I only hope it may be a good song, well sung, to our and India's dignity.' He was in much request for services or advice from Ruling Princes, Provincial Governors, and in connection with War

Memorials. Consequently, with his annual passages to and fro, his existence resembled the migratory Puck of the poem rather than the static capital. In March of 1920, after a night journey involving two changes, he was at Lallgarh, as guest of the Maharajah of Bikaner, probably to discuss H.H.'s proposed palace at Delhi. He described Bikaner as 'an oasis, a great fort with a town packed round it, in a desert,' but found difficulty in giving a coherent description because a carnival was taking place below his bedroom window, which was situated below that of the Maharajah's ladies. Dancers and singers in red and gold robes were performing to an unholy din of tom-toms. His room, he discovered, had a mysterious gallery high up in it from which 'the ladies can watch how an architect gets into bed. What can I do to impress them as a strong silent man? Slow deliberate actions and beautiful gestures would, I think, impress them most—but my rounded face and form are not conducive to that'. Before leaving Delhi, he added, he had attended a fancy-dress garden party at the Claud Hills: 'everybody had to go as a bird or insect—I went as myself, a rare bird. I met three Brahmins and said to one old gentleman "I suppose if you touch me you will have to wash yourself all over". He grinned, then broke into a laugh, said No, and shook both my hands warmly.'

He returned home from Delhi this year by way of Jamnagar (in the Kathiawar peninsula), Bombay, Madras, and Colombo. The journey to Jamnagar began on such a glorious evening, 'a ball of gold and a ball of silver balanced on either side of the train,' that he opened all the sixteen windows of the Jam Sahib's luxurious railway carriage and fell asleep watching the star and moonlit plain. In the night he was awakened by a strange noise and found that thieves had climbed in and thrown all his luggage out on to the line. Persotum got the train stopped and the luggage collected, or 'I should have arrived at Jamnagar—where the red carpet was apparently spread out for me—with nothing but my pyjamas'. The red carpet turned out to have been laid for the British Resident; nevertheless the Jam Sahib—none other than Ranjitsinghji—proved to be an ideal client, with whom Lutyens was to have cordial professional relations for a decade. The occasion of this visit was discussion of his plans for the Jam Sahib's house in New Delhi, a new palace in course of erection at Jamnagar, and replanning of the prosperous city itself. His Highness wanted to pull down part of the town wall, indeed had already begun to do so, but offered to rebuild it if Lutyens thought fit. As to the new palace, 'I could only advise him to pull it down, cut his loss, and begin again.' But he was unusually impressed by the old palace:

> There were some wonderful paintings, and one room had been left untouched for two or three hundred years. No one would enter or clean it because of a murder committed there long ago. I went in. The old Jam's bed was just as it was, all falling to pieces, the quilted stuff on the ceilings and a great red painted

blotch on the wall, stuck all over with stamps of gold to appease the goddess for the crime. I offered to clean it up. The Jam Sahib wants this all modernised but I persuaded him to leave it, protect the old paintings, and use it as a State Museum.

Lutyens became very fond of this State, Nawanagar, with its invigorating climate and scenery, and lively people 'looking as though they lived to live instead of living to die—an Indian habit'. As he got to know it better he judged it the best run State he knew, owing to the enlightened policy of its ruler in forcing down rents, thereby attracting or retaining subjects, and developing the facilities of its seaport. Lutyens's town planning improvements were well advanced in 1928, when he last visited Jamnagar, and the Prince continued to consult him respecting the antiquities. Among his specific designs for H.H. is the pedestal and setting for Heseltine's statue of the first Jam Sahib, mounted on a specimen of the famous Kathiawar breed of horse.

At Bombay, where he conferred with the State architect of Baroda on a library that he had designed for H.H. the Gaekwar, he said that he had given Sir George Lloyd:

> a lot of advice on his land reclamation scheme for Back Bay. I think I shall be roped in to do the extensions of the city. I have pleaded for a Venice, with sea ways and lagoons, instead of the bay being filled in completely and no fun. It would be a glorious scheme.
>
> Mrs. Besant was at Bombay, and came up to Government House, but I was keeping an appointment in the town and missed seeing her.

The Bombay extension did not come under his hand and was less imaginatively handled. Two days later he was in Madras, whither Lord Willingdon had invited him to advise on replanning.

The oldest British settlement in India, scene of Clive's first steps towards the Empire for which Lutyens shaped the short-lived final capital, surprised and attracted him. The old East India Company houses appealed to him by their sincerity:

> with the souls of gentlemen and none of that horrible eurasian architecture that our modern sentimentalists promote. But O the people!—scallywags, awful faces, to me degenerate. I have seen Adyar in the distance. Willingdon adores 'naughty Annie', and it is amusing to have her hobnobbing with Governors.

But again he missed meeting her to renew their old friendship.

Architecturally, the problem at Madras was the haphazard siting of the old buildings, set in compounds of unmanageable size. Lutyens observed with regret that, in the past, no advantage was taken of the waterways and rivers intersecting the low sandy ridges in which the city had grown up. The proposed replanning involved a new Government House facing Adyar across the river, the one in the city becoming the Secretariat, conversion of the Georgian Assembly Hall for public functions, and the building of a new Council Chamber to match it, besides a War Memorial Hall. The existing plans disclosed 'a passion for domes and towers':

> Three huge buildings are in prospect, all in a row, each surmounted by five domes, but each building distinguished by originality as though that were a virtue. Then there are the existing buildings, all with towers and domes eurasian in style and of that particular vulgarity which the English occupation of India has for its monument!

Lord Willingdon having been called away, and his deputy refusing to commit himself to definite instructions, Lutyens felt it unnecessary to make more than broad suggestions. He was, however, given permission to spend £50 on architectural books for the Public Works Department architects, who, he found, had none. Wherever he went, Lutyens made this request. It is significant that those he selected were limited 'to those that Wren could have had access to—for what use is it to buy any books he did not know, until we are able to do better than he? The tons of art publications might just as well go into the sea—save for record'.

When he was at Madras, he received a telegram from Sir Harcourt Butler inviting him to submit designs for Lucknow University and state his terms. The prospect excited him: there was 'a river to deal with there, and a very understanding Chief, full of human wisdom and of Solomon wit'. The Lucknow scheme was to get as far as the drawings stage, involving visits in 1921 and 1922. But in the end both the University and the Madras Plan petered out, so far as Lutyens was concerned.

In a temperature of 110° in the train, and stripped to the buff, he was playing patience on the night journey southwards from Madras, when the onrush of a great thunder storm swept the cards—a cherished pack lent to him by E. V. Lucas—down the track; his second mishap by open windows. The two days he was in Ceylon ended in magnificent stormy sunsets, the great cumuli gold, the grass and trees blue, with the tree tops sunlit gold, the sky a deep indigo of a colour he had not seen before. His business at Colombo was the War Memorial. On the Column voted by the committee he persuaded them to replace the usual angel with 'a brazier to burn petrol and make a column of smoke by day and of fire by night'. The old Dutch architecture struck him as finer in feeling and design than any the British had achieved, free from the faults of vulgarity and mental unction to one of which if not both the English seemed always prone. Big brass shields in the Dutch Church, intended to be filled by generations to come that never came testified to the unfulfilled faith of those earlier empire builders. He reflected again on faith when, in the native quarter, an ornamented juggernaut was dragged among the dark-skinned, naked crowd to a tornado of tom-toms and he saw with horror:

112. VICEROY'S HOUSE FROM THE NORTH-EAST, DECEMBER 1921

113. SECRETARIATS AND COUNCIL CHAMBERS, c. 1926

114 and 115 (*opposite page*). A Picture Letter for the Children. Undated but, from its theme, perhaps connected with the office in Apple Tree Yard, i.e. the early 'twenties. It is typical of many such letters and represents comically the quality of Lutyens's spontaneous drawings.

and

This is what they looked like

& they died & looked like this.

Dead

and in heaven they looked like

just two little cherapples

116 and 117. TWO TYPICAL COMIC DRAWINGS FOR CHILDREN. 116 (*above*) 'Lays Majesty'. 117 (*below*) 'Commanding the Northumberland Light (very) Infantry'

a really beautiful—he was ascetic to look at—young man covered with dust, garlanded with flowers and naked but for a loin cloth, writhing on the ground where he had prostrated himself under the gaudy temple and its wheels had gone over him... He was charming to look at, and I cursed the priestcraft—and wondered why it is the Archbishop of Canterbury did not induce his flock to throw themselves under brewers' vans.

After just over two weeks journeying since leaving Delhi he picked up a boat for Port Said, and spent his last remaining rupee answering a telegram just received from his eldest daughter announcing her engagement to Captain Euan Wallace.

Two years later a professional visit to Jammu, with plans for General Raja Sir Hari Singh, yields us a somewhat indiscreet picture of the dynastic situation in Kashmir at that time. Amid breath-taking scenery and architectural squalor, Lutyens found the young, progressive, and unorthodox Heir Apparent at loggerheads with the aged, opium-eating, orthodox Hindu and misanthropic Maharaja, among whose testy habits was the firing of guns at intervals through the night when His Highness prayed. 'It is a mercy they have not this habit at Buck House,' he wrote:

> I see him at 4.o'clock this afternoon—his best time. His worst is 5.o'clock when he gets wild and cat-like furies. He joys in other peoples sorrows and quarrels, loves funerals and hates marriages. He gave a mint of money to the war but his pleasure was really when our, and his, men got a knock. That he enjoyed hugely as a good joke. The old man won't have a bath or w.c. in the house, but washes seven times a day; is building two terrible houses but does nothing to ameliorate the condition of the people.
>
> Yet I think Hari Singh is probably rather hard on the old man. Though he has declared him his successor, he has also appointed a spiritual heir, who will inherit his private property. As Hari Singh has over a million of his own, he don't care, and says it will save him the nausea of having to drive a nail into the old gentleman's head when the gods call him to their own.

Unfortunately Lutyens's account of his interview with this eccentric Prince is missing.

When Delhi was nearly finished the Maharanee of Cooch Behar accepted Lutyens's invitation to stay at his bungalow:

> She was very considerate, left her sepoys and other servants at the station so as not to embarrass us, and her two boys with their tutor at Agra. So she arrived with 2 bearers, an ayah, and a charming eunuch...
>
> I did not get to bed till nearly 2.o'cl. At about 5 o'c I was awakened by a

great noise and the Nawab Sahib shouting 'Thieves'. I rang up the Police. 'No policemen can be sent unless you send a chit,' says a baboo voice. After nearly an hour they arrived.

The Maharanee had been asleep, when she became conscious of a man in her room feeling her all over and one hand on her throat. She awoke and said 'Who are you? Go away!' whereupon the man decamped. Her watch was gone, her room in disarray, everything unpacked and lying about, and they had gone off with £60,000 of jewels, and all her clothes and saris. Her pearls she had been wearing and put in a drawer, casual like. It was to find them that they had been groping over her.

The Maharanee was most extraordinarily self possessed, really brave and helpful, a regular Roman matron. I felt wretched; could do little but calm Persotum. The abject terror of the chowkidars and their cringing attitude shocked me.

But this alarming incident was as exceptional as its social occasion in the routine of life in the bungalow as ordered by the excellent Persotum. Ladies of quite another kind came to the bungalow once a week when Lutyens was at Delhi, for he gave a standing invitation to spinster residents at the Hardinge Hospital to spend the evening there. It was a kind thought on his part, much appreciated, even though he was never there to act as host. But the normal visitors, apart from travelling friends, were officials and colleagues. On one occasion, Pandit Motilal Nehru, father of the first Prime Minister of India, came to lunch. Lutyens liked the friendly old Nationalist, enjoyed his wit, and took him over the buildings.

He said that if Gandhi had been here, he would certainly have brought him too, though Gandhi deplored the waste of money on architectural piles. I said it was all Indian work, and much better worth doing than spinning; that India, where she once led in the fine arts, is now deplorably behind the times, with half baked statesmanship and agitation the only live thing. I told him of our search for Indian materials that would wear, and the hopelessness of it. He said he had not thought of building as an education to the Indian mason craftsman.

So I hope to get him interested.

He wears a black coat and white jodhpurs, on which I drew buttons, so that he looked exactly like an English bishop—and told him that was all he was fit for if he did not help India in her material needs.

Did Nationalist leaders, inspired by the sage simplicities of the Mahatma, perceive the wisdom also of the eccentric composer of Britain's 'swan song' and their future capital?

§3. FACTORS AND FIGURES

Most encouraging of the 1922 Committee's conclusions was that additional machinery should be acquired to make better use of the stoneyards and materials in hand. Building throughout was largely controlled by the rate at which the stone for the central buildings could be produced and dressed. Though the nature of the materials used has been alluded to briefly, and although their supply came under the Public Works Department, Lutyens's problems were so closely involved with this aspect of operations, particularly at the stage now being considered, that a short review of this basic factor is required. In the period of paralysis a great deal of energy was applied to preparing the way for the smooth delivery of materials when operations should again be stepped up and when, with the closing stages, their range and variety greatly extended. If this aspect of his architecture is not dealt with in relation to Lutyens's work in England, conditions in India were so unique (the organisation evolved having disintegrated subsequently), that for the sake of historical record a summary of the facts is desirable.[1]

The whole constructional responsibility for the new city remained with Sir Hugh Keeling, whose knighthood in 1923 acknowledged the outstanding technical services, established by the Committee's investigations, which he had rendered to New Delhi since its inception, and continued till his retirement in 1925. He was then succeeded as Chief Engineer by Sir Alexander Rouse, previously Superintending Engineer in which capacity he was followed by Mr. J. L. Sale, with Mr. T. S. Malik as Executive Engineer for Government House. The latter, a stalwart Sikh who never flinched from assuming responsibilities, eventually became Sardar Bahadur Sir Teja Singh Malik and Chief Engineer of the Central Public Works Department.

The architects' office till 1925, known as 'Raisina Mill', was a long single-storey building adjacent to a set of similar buildings occupied by the Public Works Department. In the middle was a large room used as a joint mess, flanked by two wings in one of which each architect had his office. They had also slept in these, till in 1920–21 Lutyens was allotted the Military Secretary's bungalow which he used till 1929. Meanwhile, in 1925, the office was shifted into the North Secretariat, by then partly completed and occupied, and from 1926–29 to the South Secretariat. Lutyens's staff normally consisted of a resident representative and resident assistant, with his own travelling personal assistant who since 1916 had been invariably E. E. Hall. In addition there were from four to six Indian draftsmen, who were nothing more than tracers, squatting on their stools, often on the table. His first resident representative (1915–20) John Greaves, remained there single-handed during the later war years,

[1] In this section I am indebted to the assistance of Mr. J. L. Sale, C.I.E.; to his unpublished paper on 'Contingency in the Construction of New Delhi'; to an article by Sir Alexander Rouse published in the *Indian State Railway Magazine*, February, 1931; and to information supplied by Mr. A. G. Shoosmith, O.B.E.

when A. G. Shoosmith succeeded him and remained till 1931. Till 1920, Lutyens brought with him an assistant from Apple Tree Yard each year, S. H. Evans in 1912, J. M. Wilson 1913–16.[1] In 1920 E. C. Gentry became resident assistant till 1928. Thenceforward Hubert Wright came from Apple Tree Yard, where he had been in charge of the inscriptions on the Memorial Arch, to help Lutyens with the finishing stages. He became Lutyens's most trusted assistant, having his details at his finger tips. In addition there were a native *chaprassi* or messenger whose chief duty, when not praying, was to lift the curtain for people entering the office; and a *chowkidar* or night watchman who dusted the drawing boards and slept outside the office door, trusting to his prestige as a blood-thirsty Pathan to keep away any who might deem an architect's office worth robbing.

When at Delhi, E. E. Hall was the main connecting link with the Engineers' Department, especially as regards service-installations and throughout at Apple Tree Yard, handling the routine business of ways and means, accounts, and materials, in which he was indispensable.

The stone employed at Delhi is the Vindhyan, belonging to the upper Bandar strata, used by Akbar and Shah Jehan at Fatehpur Sikri and elsewhere. Besides its virtues of workability and endurance, this stone has been put to most astonishing uses, including beams up to 30 feet span; and lintels and slabs of 16 feet span are common. The quarries originally selected were to the south of Delhi, in Dholpur State for the white and buff varieties, in Bharatpur for the red. Private enterprise was so ill developed at Bharatpur and disputes so numerous that before long operations were concentrated at Dholpur, where both colours were available. But it was the more remote from rail communications, so that 15 miles of light railway and 5 miles of sidings were laid down by Government engineers and quarters built for the staff and workmen. The scene of operations was a rocky desert, miles from civilisation, infested with outlaws, and a veritable inferno in hot weather. The difficulties of labour supply were enormous. No less than eleven quarries had to be abandoned after heavy development expenses, owing to the quality of the stone not coming up to expectations. Progress was also hampered by the fact that the original piece-work contracts proved unduly restrictive by specifying all dimensions on quarry orders with only 10% margin on the cube. This involved rough dressing at the quarry and, as prices rose during the war, the small contractors began to give up. The cost of transport for 150 miles rose proportionately. After the war, therefore, detailed quarry orders gave place to general orders specifying so many lineal feet of a given depth. Akbar's methods of quarrying still prevailed. In 1917 the question of improving on

[1] In 1920–21 he brought out a versatile old Etonian and ex-airman, Herbert Ward, one of the first prisoners of war to have escaped from Germany and a trainer of fighter-pilots. Supposed to work on the Record Office drawings, he acted rather as social A.D.C., staying in Lutyens's bungalow. Abandoning architecture for sculpture, he subsequently disappeared from the world of art; a regrettable loss of a notable personality.

these methods had been taken up with a view to opening a deep-faced quarry. But tests revealed no continuity of colour and quality and, until a great deal of expensive machinery and more methodical working were introduced, the traditional method had to be followed.

By 1922 a third of the stone had been delivered, approximately a million cubic feet. The Committee's recommendation for expediting work therefore meant that plant could be purchased and the number of railway wagons increased. By these means the output gradually rose to 40,000 cubic feet of dressed stone per month, reaching the peak of nearly 60,000 in 1926 when 3500 stone masons were being employed. The total quantity of 3 million cubic feet of dressed stone used in the Central Buildings involved the actual transport of nearer 6 million cubic feet weighing 400,000 tons for some 200 miles in all. The stoneyard at New Delhi was the largest in the world. From one end where the rough stone was delivered, to the other where it passed, still by rail, to the site, measured some 2000 feet, its buildings covered 22 acres and at the period of maximum activity it was turning out 2500 cubic feet of dressed stone a day.

Stone masons were assembled from all over India. But, much as was the case in medieval England, many were small agriculturists by caste and left the works in spring and autumn to attend their fields, with the result that at these seasons half this army vanished. It had the further result that the cessation of operations extinguished the short revival of a great and ancient tradition in stone craftsmanship. However, these men, trained locally to the European system of proper working drawings and templates under British foremen, and given good models, succeeded in turning out for five shillings a day carved and moulded stonework that invited comparison with that of European professionals. The credit for the training and the very high class of work produced was due to W. B. Cairns, M.B.E., who was in charge of the yard from 1915.

The local quartzite of the site, which it had been hoped to use largely in the buildings, was found at an early stage to be not easily workable, and suitable only for large blocks or for rubble. The projected amphitheatre in the Ridge at the west end of New Delhi, in the excavation of which the quantity required for building would have represented a very small proportion, was abandoned for that reason. But large quantities were used for road-metal and concrete. During the war the prohibitive cost of cement in India curtailed the use of reinforced concrete, and 're-inforced brick' came to be used as a substitute. The need for obtaining a satisfactory type of flat roof and ceiling at a cost approximating to jack-arch roofing was important owing to some 40 acres of flat roof being involved in the New City, and 18 acres in the Central Buildings alone. Roofing represented about one-sixth of the cost of the average residence, which was (as Lutyens frequently complained) very restricted. It was believed that reinforced brickwork provided the solution, but a few years' experience revealed the inherent deficiencies of the method and a good many bungalows justified Lutyens's gibes by having to be replaced. After the war, however, the Indian cement industry made rapid progress, so that by 1921 the use of reinforced concrete and the ordinary hollow-tile T-beam became standard for roofs and floors. The position of reinforced concrete was assured by the introduction in 1928 of Indian rapid-hardening cement, which played a valuable part in the last stages of completing Government House.

The carcase material throughout was, of course, brick. An astronomical quantity was used—some 700 million, nearly all produced at twenty-two Government kilns. It was generally supposed that the clay in the neighbourhood of Delhi was too sandy to make good bricks, but suitable earth was found to the south of the site, connected by railway. The soil of Delhi, however, is highly saline and consequently salts in the brickwork backing of the Central Buildings began gradually to produce discolouration in the stone facing; black on the white stone, white on the red. This chemical problem had not arisen in the historic cases of the use of Dholpur stone which, at Delhi, had been backed with quartzite.

The only stone imported, with the exception of the Royal Foundation Stones, was that for the floor of the Durbar Hall, in particular the Rosso-Porforico marble procured from Italy, since it was found impossible to obtain stone from India of the size and colour specified. The marbles of India are of an infinite and beautiful variety, and were used extensively in Government House. But most of the quarries were undeveloped or inaccessible, and of many samples submitted it was found that pieces no larger than the samples were obtainable. The white marble most used was that from Makrana in Jodhpur State, also from Alwar. The green was procured from Baroda and Ajmere, the grey from Marwar, and the yellow for the columns of Durbar Hall from Jaisalmere. The latter had to be carried slung on camels for forty miles over sandy desert, which limited the size of blocks. When the camels struck work, lorries were employed, but their carrying capacity was small over the trackless desert and their life short. Pink marble was obtained from Alwar, Makrana, and Haripur. In all about 100,000 cubic feet of Indian marbles were used.

Given the scale and magnificence demanded by the Government of India for New Delhi, the total cost of £10 million ultimately expended, so far from being excessive, appears astonishingly moderate, including as it did all the services of a large modern town. Of this, Government House itself accounted for £877,136 (128 Lakhs), or £1,253,000 including the garden and Staff Quarters. With regard to the frequently pressed claims in favour of the maintenance of Calcutta as the capital, the cost would probably have amounted to more in the end, when the vastly expanded needs of Government had been met. Building rates at Delhi were infinitely cheaper and the cost of the land negligible compared with what would have been demanded at Calcutta. Figures of comparative costs as between individual buildings, given by Sir Alexander Rouse, set

    Government House at Rs 1. 4. 6 per cubic foot.
    Secretariats   0. 11. 7
    Legislative Buildings 0. 12. 3
    Bungalows   0. 4. 3

At the rates prevailing at the time, a good stone-faced office building in London would have equalled about Rs. 4 per cubic foot. The cost of stone as between Delhi and London was in the ratio of 6 to 14 Rupees, and of brickwork 32 to 100. Whereas the whole of New Delhi cost £10 million, the two-thirds of County Hall, Westminster, erected cost nearly £5 million.

CHAPTER XV

THE TWENTIES

§1. 13 MANSFIELD STREET

SOON after the Peace Celebrations and before sailing for India in October, 1919, Lutyens was dining with Mr. Willie Bridgeman, later Lord Bridgeman, in his Adam house in Mansfield Street, near Portland Place. By the end of the evening the homeless months were virtually ended, for it turned out that Mr. Bridgeman wanted to sell the house which Lutyens, after a quick taking stock of its graces and spaces, was equally anxious to buy. It was another 'log number', like those of all the other houses he had possessed. Its gentlemanly front, with contemporary fan-lit doorway, enclosed a plan resembling that of 29 Bloomsbury Square, though the scale was larger, and there was a mews attached at the back. This was to be his home till his death, the background for his most kaleidoscopic years, the 'twenties.

The decade between the Versailles Treaty and the economic collapse of 1929–30, which saw the spectacular but as it proved unstable recovery of liberal capitalism, was a no less well-defined period in Lutyens's life. Delhi was officially completed at the end of 1929, the year in which his achievements culminated in the commission for the Roman Catholic Cathedral of Christ the King at Liverpool. In 1931 his lease of the office at 17 Queen Anne's Gate ended and, the Delhi office having been transferred in 1924 from Apple Tree Yard to 17 Bolton Street, both departments then moved to 5 Eaton Gate. Till then Mansfield Street also periodically served as a third workshop—for Queen Mary's Dolls' House and, in the early stages, for the Cathedral. Thus its white classical staircase, with dark scagliola pillars and black wall-panels, is the appropriate setting against which to visualise the comings and goings of these years expended by Lutyens at a white heat of creative vitality. In this chapter it is attempted to catch some reflection from the facets of his personality lingering upon Mansfield Street's white walls. In the next chapter we will undertake the no less elusive task of co-ordinating the high-pressure output and routine of the Queen Anne's Gate office.

His prayer 'for a complete home, with all it means', uttered on the evening of Cenotaph Day, seemed answered. It meant much to him to know his children were happy around the house although he might not see much of them individually. He wrote each in turn the affectionate, enchantingly illustrated letters from which some of his drawings have already been reproduced, or told ridiculous stories which they loved (pp. 422–3). As they grew older these stories became more sophisticated

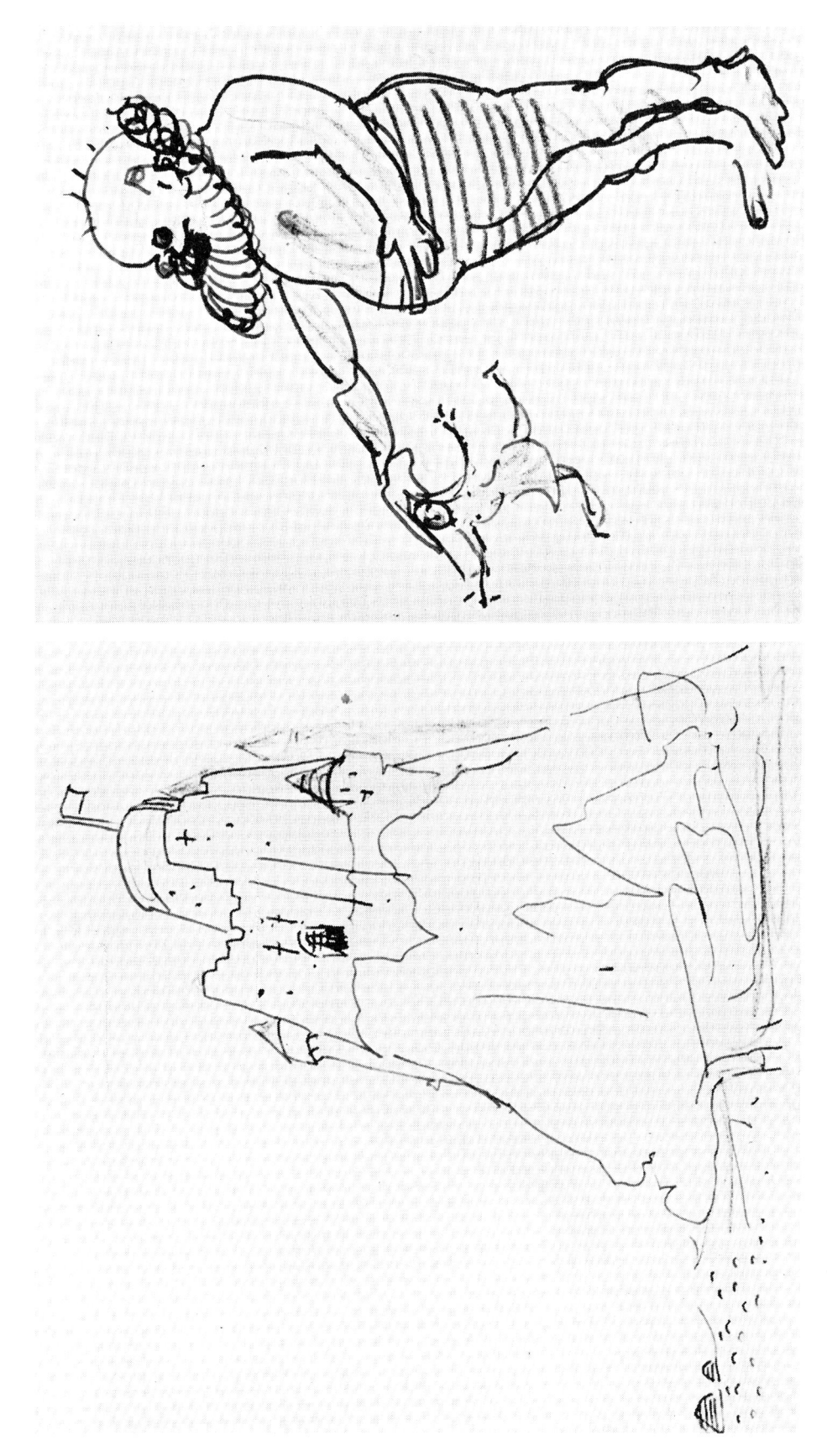

118 and 119. Ghastly Castle, and the Giant Who Ate Up Little Girls. See The Story of the Ghastly Greedy Giant, p. 437

120. How to Draw Horses. 'What could I do? with two more legs.'

121. Equine Hexagon,
formed of six horses

434

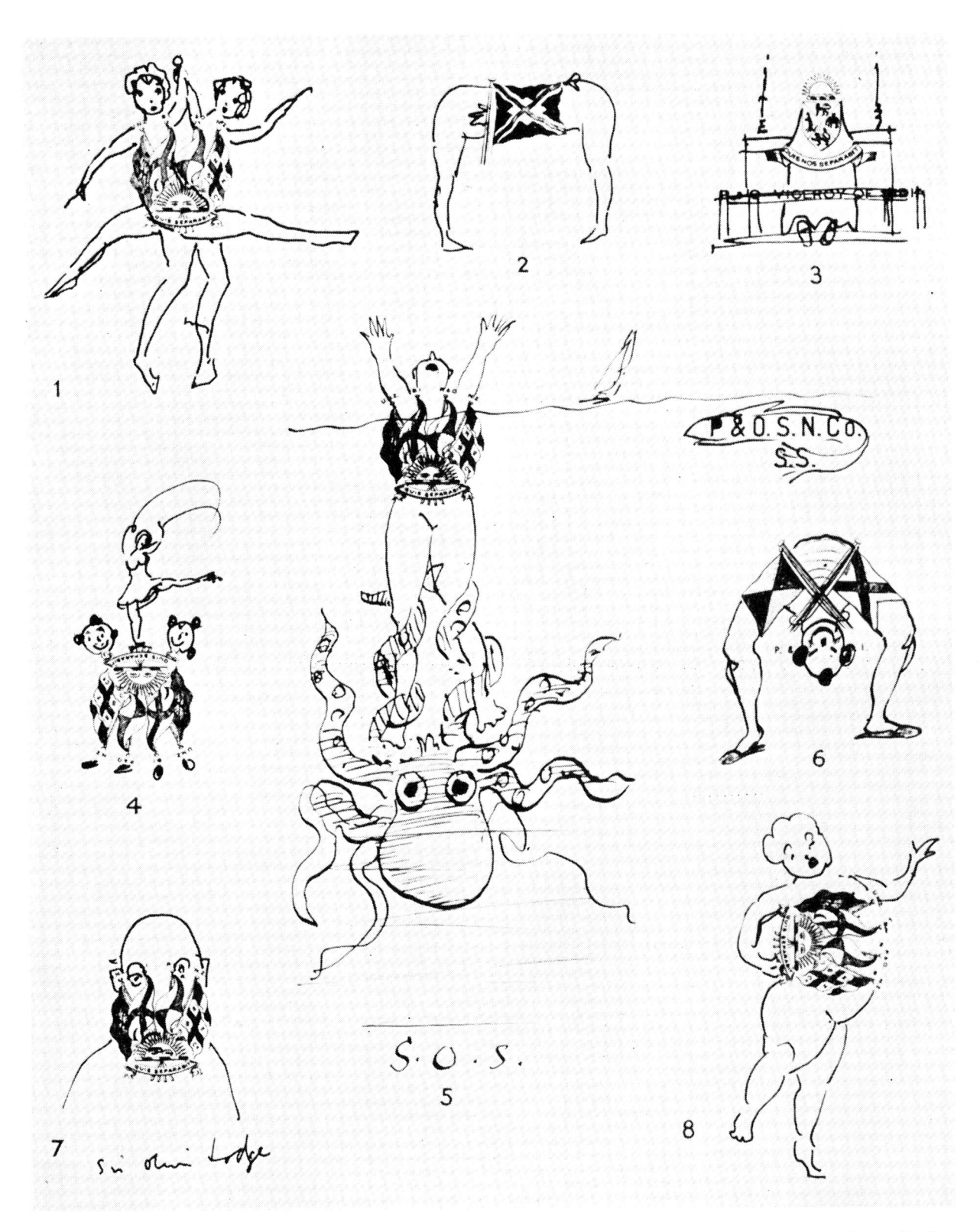

122. DOODLES. Devised on journeys from the letter headings of P & O, Union Castle, and other shipping lines. The captions given are Lutyens's, but in many cases none exist or are needed: 1. The Jolly Sisters. 2. Two People in one cabin trying to put on the same shirt. 3. Cantuar prays for them at sea. 4. and 6. Here we are again. 5. S.O.S. 7. Sir Oliver Lodge. 8. The mosquito caught

123. DOODLES. 1. Breakfast in bed. 2. ——. 3. ——. 4. The tiger is an awful beast. 5. A Bombay duck left on the beach to rot. From a letter of advice to A. G. Shoosmith: 6. 'Be as Solomon'. 7. 'Avoid *Shikar*'. 8. 'Avoid the social'. 9. 'Be a strong man'

THE TWENTIES

too, such as the one about the Ghastly Greedy Giant which he sent to Ursula from Delhi in 1917. It begins with a description of a Christmas Party given by Lady Hardinge. Then:

> Once upon a time there was a great ugly hungry giant that lived in a great granite castle shouldering high on a great granite mountain, around whose feet water lashed and boiled, and the rocks arose so steep that it was difficult to get up and too dangerously easy to get down.
>
> That which was considered the most forbidding habit in which this great giant indulged was the eating up of little girls; and the other that he only wore bathing drawers [p. 433].
>
> Mondays, Wednesdays, and Fridays he had a little girl for supper. Tuesdays, Thursdays, and Saturdays a little boy. On Sundays a curate because of the day. You see he was a Christian, whereby, unfortunately for him, he came within the laws and moral obligations of the civilised state wherein lay his castley seat.
>
> Now, the Lord Mayor and his council of Ghastleyton near to Ghastly Castle passed a resolution and made a good-by law to say that wherein and out certain persons devour little boys, girls, and curates, it was not to be—why not. So the poor old ogre began to starve, and he got so thin that he could whistle in and out through his own key-hole, without opening the door.
>
> So there was a mass meeting to promote a society, and one was formed with many and most influential people: a Giant's Protection Society, with the liberty of feeding the object. For he was an awful object, and through starving became quite abject. And the upshot of it all was, the Mayor and his council rescinded their resolution and allowed him to eat the ugly little girls and boys and silly curates. There were very few ugly children and he soon ate them—but oh how tired the poor giant got of eating curates.
>
> Curates curried, curates boiled, curates fricasseed, roast, fried, and dried, till he could eat no more.
>
> Now, he had to use a church spire for a tooth pick and this is how the end came. By pure misadventure he swallowed a weather-cock which changed with the wind inside him and made such a tangle up of his personal machinery that he died.
>
> And everyone was very very sorry. And they buried him amongst the bones—those that were not turned into stock—of all the little children and curates he had ever eaten.
>
> His wife, whom it has not been necessary to mention (she was not a suffragette) until now, died of grief.
>
> This is the scene of Ghastly Castle and the graves. [p. 433 *left*]

He was always encouraging and teaching them to draw. He believed in their education through the exercise of eye and hand and ear; that is as potential artists rather than as readers or mechanics. That accounts perhaps for his refusing to let them learn so automatic a habit as typewriting. On the other hand he also refused to let Ursula, who showed some promise as an artist, go to an art school, maintaining that a woman's place was in the home. This was the source of his often-quoted opinion on the Future of Women in Architecture: 'it depends on what architect she marries.'

These anecdotes are typical of his relations with his children. He adored playing with them, and, when they showed interest in some aspect of his own world, he would let his imagination and knowledge play around it with delight, and often with no little profit, for them. When he had one to himself, as when Barbara was old enough to come to stay with him and Hudson at Lindisfarne, or Robert went with him to stay at Knole, or Ursula and he went off on some expedition, he fondly accepted them as adult artists. When, a little later than the time we have reached, his youngest daughter Elizabeth kept house for him at Mansfield Street in her mother's absence, he sometimes entered keenly into problems of musical composition with her. Elisabeth, the musical genius of the family, was working on the technique of the twelve-tone scale, and he was sufficiently interested in the mathematical problem involved to say: "Why not a twenty-four semitone scale"? It was a grownup stage of the games and stories through which he had sought to lead them when they were little into his own world of the imagination.

He was supposed not to have time or inclination to be bothered with their personal problems, so there was almost a conspiracy of silence to keep from him knowledge of what was going on. Yet he possessed a wisdom about affairs that, had he been consulted more, and his advice when given more frequently taken, would probably have benefited them all. And he had a strange intuitive understanding of what was happening. One of his daughters has said that, although she never did confide her problems to him, she always became aware that he knew them, and by some uncanny perspicacity would say, sometimes allegorically, the one thing that helped. He would not face being the cause of unhappiness in others, particularly his family. And as he shrank from 'scenes', setting great store by courtesy, he was never prepared to assert his will over his wife's.

No sooner had the family moved into Mansfield Street than it began to disperse. In 1920 Barbara married Captain Euan Wallace whose election next year as Member for Rugby initiated a brilliant political career. Then in 1921, Robert, who after demobilisation had gone up to Cambridge, threw up his university career to enter journalism on becoming engaged. It is not necessary to digress into the romance beyond saying that it involved all the psychological relations alluded to above. The situation created a breach between father and son which took long to heal, much to their mutual loss, for the son's help in interpreting the outlook of his generation to the father might well have been valuable, as eventually proved to be the case.

This gentleness, or weakness, or fundamental detachment from everybody, in his nature resulted in his giving no less affection to his wife, although he found he had enough of it to spare for others. He brought her the same degree of love as in the Blumenthals' drawing-room when he first saw her, hated to see her brow creased with care or concentration, and wanted to make her laugh happily. For twenty years she had been rather the children's mother than his wife, then the suffragette, then the theosophist and journalist. Apparently ignoring his own almost complete absorption in his profession and her almost complete inability to share in it, he still irrationally craved her undivided attention. He always had, he told her, the hope of winning her back from 'the cranks', to his own eccentricities (as she might regard them), or somehow to adjust himself to hers. His picture of the young architect and his bride in the Little White House, the design for which was rolled up in the Casket on the mantelpiece, was open in the cabinet of his heart, with her spinning (if, inspired by Gandhi, spin she must) 'wonderful fine linen for my marvellously designed tables!— and we purr, not spar, when together'—he wrote to her. Now Mansfield Street offered a fresh chance of realising that elusive, and actually impossible, ideal. From Delhi, when the family had moved in, he wrote to her 'yes, we will have little dinner parties. Of course I am shy, too, and shyness reacts on me worse than you, because I give offence by being loquacious. Your silence is better. We might have rehearsals, because that side of life has a good deal of play-acting in it'. But somehow there was never time for those rehearsals, and meals, if they were alone, passed in silence for the most part, each absorbed in a book or the newspaper. And when there were guests, these were apt to find the performance very under-rehearsed and to experience a sense of strain in adjusting themselves to two such manifestly different minds at either end of the table. Yet he, at least, was content that she should just be there, endured agony when he must leave her, and was always pressing her to accompany him to Delhi, as she did on eight occasions. In the bungalow there, though he was as pre-occupied as ever and she was often away at Adyar or staying with Lord Lytton during her brother's period as Governor of Bengal, relations were subtly easier. He told Ursula how happy her mother was in India, to the degree even of laughing at his jokes. He had her to himself, free from household cares, cranks, and children.

Yet, for all his thirst for her presence and love, it is doubtful if he ever declined an invitation to lunch or dine out in order to spend the time at home. The habit of regarding parties as professional engagements, leading to new contacts and possible work, was too deeply engrained. Besides, it economised, in theory, rested the servants, and Lady Emily had always encouraged him to go out on his own, claiming that her absence made her the most popular wife in London. So, Mansfield Street and his fundamental shyness notwithstanding, Lutyens became one of the most sought-after diners-out in the London of the 'twenties. His wit and unconventionality were already proverbial. A lunch or dinner at which he was present was assured of being memorable for something. And in the very wide circle of his acquaintances, he did no doubt establish a good many useful contacts besides making new acquaintances. The conception of Queen Mary's Dolls' House grew out of a dinner party, as will be narrated in the next section. Incidentally, it was at about this time that, as an obscure young man, I first began to meet him at Edward Hudson's house where Suggia would sometimes enchant us (and more particularly our host) with her magic 'cello and saturnine, but laughing, majesty. On one occasion Sir Martin Conway, tousled and beetle-browed, came in late and, as he stood looking for a seat, Lutyens drew him down to sit on his knee, embraced him cello-wise with one arm and sawed an imaginary bow across his body with the other to a rhythm different to Madame Suggia's the while. Lunching one day with Sir Arthur and Lady Colefax at Argyll House he met Mme. Melba. The circumstances of their encounter are typical both of his social technique and peculiar susceptibility to women of spirit and physique. They had been briefly introduced and he found himself sitting opposite to her. For some reason he decided that it was a case for the conversational opening that he termed jaw-dropping. So in a pause he looked blandly across to her, as to some shy nonentity, and asked 'And what do *you* do?' The pause became a silence, while Melba finished her fish and sipped her glass. Then suddenly she burst out superbly into the first bars of Mimi's song, snapping, as she ended abruptly, '*That's* what I do!' Which might be thought to have been her last word to him; but it was observed that they left the house together. The friendship thus formed became a devoted one and lasted till the end of the great diva's life.

In the same key is the anecdote of a client, Lady Cooper, for whom, at this time, he was altering 96 Cheyne Walk. Expressing regret at the mess the builders were making of her house, Lutyens politely asked what *would* she do. 'I suppose', she replied with the air of one enduring much bravely, 'I must be an ostrich and bury my head in the sand.' He looked at her quizzically through his round spectacles, then said, 'And have you very beautiful tail feathers?' Cardinal Gasquet, no more than Melba, was one to be jaw-dropped, and in the following passage can be judged to have won the point. Lunching with Mrs. Patrick Campbell at Sir George Lewis's, at Rottingdean, Lutyens turned to the genial Cardinal with a serious expression and said, 'Tell me, Your Eminence, when you are Pope will you be Boniface or Innocent?' With equal gravity the Cardinal replied 'Pius'.

From Rottingdean, too, he wrote (August 14, 1921), that he had been 'drawing a lot of pics for Winston Churchill to show him how to sketch and get shapes'. Mr. Churchill was evidently commencing his art studies, and Lutyens showed him how, from two elongated loops, he could produce either a boat or the brim of a hat; or from three eggs the body of a horse and, by multiplying globular forms, a classical female figure. Some of his drawings connected with horses will be found on p. 434.

Most of his own entertaining was done at his clubs, the Garrick now for preference. There had for some time been yearly Delhi dinners for which he took some trouble collecting his allies home on leave and from the India Office. Latterly a group of his friends used to entertain him on the eve of sailing. E. V. Lucas wrote amusing verses for that of December 5, 1920, beginning:

> *We're here to be jolly, we're here to be fed,*
> *But most for the honour and glory of Ned,*
> *Who's sailing this week to the land of the ele-*
> *phant, tiger, monsoon, Ranji, curry, and Delhi...*
>
> *There are workers who have to be ready to start,*
> *Who must be 'in the mood' for their science or art,*
> *With every appliance at hand and utensil:*
> *But all Neddy needs is six pipes and a pencil.*
>
> *With these he is happy, provided for all,*
> *With these inspiration is ever at call:*
> *In the street, in the train, during soup, he'll begin it—*
> *Your home or your tomb—and its done in a minute.*
>
> *He's always the same, as he draws or he chaffs,*
> *And everyone likes him and everyone laughs,*
> *From his fellow R.A.s and his ministrant Hindoos,*
> *To the tortoise who died that his eyes might have windows.*

On other occasions E.V. got George Morrow to make a drawing à propos this yearly event. The collection of these entertaining pictures became one of Lutyens's cherished possessions.

In 1921 he received the highest honour that his architectural colleagues could confer: the Royal Gold Medal of the R.I.B.A. But the only architectural gathering that he attended regularly was that of the F.A.B.s—a club of the Royal Institute that dines and makes an architectural outing every summer. His fellow members were apt to find him an uncomfortable companion, because the last thing he ever wanted was to talk professional shop. They admired and respected him, and he would have liked to have their friendship, (at least of those whose work he approved), but he would generally talk above—or below—their heads. 'Why don't you like me?' he suddenly asked one of them on such an occasion; a man who had been his pupil and who venerated him intensely. One reason was that few felt they could meet him on equal ground, and all that they might be suddenly struck by a barb of unintentionally yet none the less stinging humour. And, respectable men, some of them did not relish his play. On a visit, for instance, to Castle Acre in Norfolk, where there is an almshouse of which the inmates wear red cloaks and sugar-loaf hats, he upset the decorum of these grave signors being entertained at tea, by capering round the table draped in an old red curtain with a tea-cosy on his head and waving a warming pan.

None of his friends had been more delighted than Lady Sackville when he got the Mansfield Street house. Knowing the state to which the war had reduced his finances, she lent him £5000 towards the premium required, and added, in lieu of fees for recent plans, a set of Soho tapestries. Various pieces of furniture followed, and then the first and only motor car that he ever possessed, a Rolls Royce that arrived complete with a chauffeur of her own choice. Lutyens christened him James, so as to be able to say 'Home, James'; but made it quite clear to the family that it was *his* car, for his professional use. In her generous, if possessive, way Lady McSac took up his children and often had one or more of them to stay or for a meal, sending them home with a present. One day she took Elisabeth in the car with her on a round of all McNed's London buildings. Pulling up in front of his little Midland Bank in Piccadilly, then just finished, she asked a constable if he knew who was its architect. On the officer saying that he regretted he could not tell her, 'Then I'll tell you,' she rejoined, 'it is by the great Sir Edwin Lutyens, remember that,' and drove on. Their visits generally ended in some kind of scene, embarrassing to the young, and the children, though fascinated, were in considerable awe of her. Or she would arrive at his house draped in magnificent furs and resplendent in jewelry, beautiful and imperious. On these occasions she always brought Lady Emily some small gift, too, such as a couple of carrots in a tin, for her vegetarian larder.

At the end of the war she had suddenly left Knole and her husband, impelled by what revulsions in her unpredictable Spanish blood, to take up permanent residence in her Brighton houses and Hill Street. As permanent, that is, as anything could be with her. Early in the 'twenties she sold, at tremendous loss, the Sussex Square houses and bought a small one on the cliffs at Roedean, overlooking the sea and exposed to the full ventilation of the gales. She also got rid of Hill Street and acquired 182 Ebury Street, the genial old brick house in which Mozart had lived when in London. MacNed was regularly bidden to little luncheon and dinner parties, and she was upset if he did not make time to see her for a few minutes most days when they were both in London. The move to Roedean opened fresh vistas for exercising his ingenuity. Till well on in the 'twenties, they continued to enjoy each other's company. Each fulfilled a vital need in the other, though, towards the end of the decade, McNed began to find her *exigence* increasingly tiresome.

For rows, always inseparable from her friendship, multiplied and lengthened. She was becoming more exasperating. It may be untrue to say that she suffered from delusions, but as she got older and poorer the streak of parsimony in her developed into mendicancy, and vagueness into preposterous suspicions. Unable any longer to give, she exercised incredible ingenuities to get. With MacNed it had often not been clear which of her presents to him she regarded as tributes of affection and esteem, and which represented professional fees. The loan to buy Mansfield Street had long since been repaid. But various bits of furniture were gradually reclaimed, then the tapestries, though he pointed out they had definitely been given in lieu of fees. (After her death her daughter duly returned them to Lutyens.) To the last, however, he succeeded in maintaining that the car was a payment in kind for several thousand pounds worth of fees due. Their meetings, which had grown fewer, had by now ceased altogether. As the 'twenties passed into the 'thirties, husband and wife could discuss together the curious case of Lady McSac and how best to treat those sad, importunate, but still magnificently inaccurate, letters which continued to arrive from time to time.

He found before then, or rather renewed, an exquisite source of happiness through beauty in the motherhood of his elder daughters. The state and process of motherhood was holy to him, exciting in him, a middle-aged man, an almost feminine emotion of wonder, delight, and love. He had always admired those *enceinte* figures, whether in reality or the medieval pictures of mothers-to-be, equally with the Madonna-and-Child type of composition. The lines moved him aesthetically as the maternal functions stirred him emotionally. Any curtailment of the physical and spiritual beauty of the mother and child relationship was abhorrent to him. As he grew older he was moved the more by the beauty of children—though ogres might eat ugly ones. The birth of Barbara's sons had begun to reawaken these feelings in him, largely dormant since his own last fatherhood. After his beloved Ursula's marriage to Viscount Ridley, the news of her confinement pierced him with an emotion more maternal than fatherly. He recalled her own birth when, hurrying home from Ashby, he had found:

> a long thin wife with her past swelling alongside of her in bed, and such a funny little thing was that once big belly-swell—and that sore, pointed, bald, littlest bit of humanity was you, and I was so apologetic for being somewhat perhaps a party to our new raw babe... I often wonder why your arrow-shot clove my heart. Perhaps in a previous incarnation I was your wife, and the 'mother' in me begot the memory of a husband (you), in those days when Mrs. Besant was prancing in the battle front and everything was possible. Instead of the flying dream, when with slight effort I rose beyond the reach of all, and none could catch me, the flying dream comes again but it is I who cannot—but only just fail to—reach the grail I want, and that is you my darling.

This testimony, expressed so curiously, of an almost mystical emotion, yet throws a little beam of light into the recesses of a mind where, as in some unexplored cavern, a genius dwelt. Though from it issued the crystalline stream of his art, sparkling with invention and joy, there would come, too, dreams and gusts of emotion that frightened him, when he was alone, unoccupied.

So to the utmost he must live at the front of the cave, designing, jesting, scintillating, and, even when sitting at home with the wife who understood or at least accepted his peculiarities, doing puzzles or playing patience, till sleepiness slowed his thoughts.

§2. QUEEN MARY'S DOLLS' HOUSE

The impression of Lutyens's personal life during the 'twenties, attempted in the last section, would be misleading if regarded otherwise than as a composite picture put together from grains and fragments rescued from the torrent of his creative output during those years. Yet as though his practice in England and India were not sufficient drain upon his imaginative vitality, he must needs also make himself responsible, at the beginning of the decade, for designing and assembling the most elaborate model ever made of a completely equipped palace. The colossal toy, with the production of which nearly 1500 people were involved one way and another, belongs to the personal aspects of Lutyens assembled in this chapter rather than to the narrative of his achievements as architect contained in the last and to be resumed in the next.

The Dolls' House is, indeed, the historical microcosm of the early 'twenties, the immediate post-war years of economic and mental readjustment. Their paralysing effect on Delhi has been observed. At home the paramount needs of housing and the redeployment of industry—the building of a land 'fit for heroes to live in' as the contemporary slogan expressed it—were hammered into the nation's conscience, though with less deadening insistence than on the shattered Britain of 1945. So, also, the period required for recovery from the war was proportionately less. The Government announced that at the end of five years, in 1924, there would be held a great British Empire Exhibition, to celebrate, and 'sell', the nation's industrial convalescence. Meanwhile, however, and oppressively so in the first years, taxation rendered virtually impossible resumption of the kind of building to which Lutyens had been accustomed, and very doubtful the survival of the social class and aesthetic standards on which his practice had been built. Hence arose the notion of recording a rich house of 1920, in miniature complete to the smallest detail, such as exists of no other epoch, to be set against the gargantuan reinforced concrete vulgarity of the Wembley Exhibition.

The idea occurred at a dinner party given in that year by Sir Herbert Morgan, at which Princess Marie Louise, Lutyens, and, it seems, E. V. Lucas were present. Somebody remarked that we do not really know how they furnished and lived in a house of Queen Anne's, still less of Queen Elizabeth's time. Now, with a host of

125. QUEEN MARY'S DOLLS' HOUSE. The Centre of the front raised to show the hall and staircase

124. QUEEN MARY'S DOLLS' HOUSE. The drawer at the side of the base contains the garden (see pl. 130)

445

126. THE QUEEN'S DOLLS' HOUSE. The Queen's bedroom

127. The Dining Room in the Queen's Dolls' House

128. THE QUEEN'S DOLLS' HOUSE. The Grand Staircase

129. THE LIBRARY, stocked with miniature books

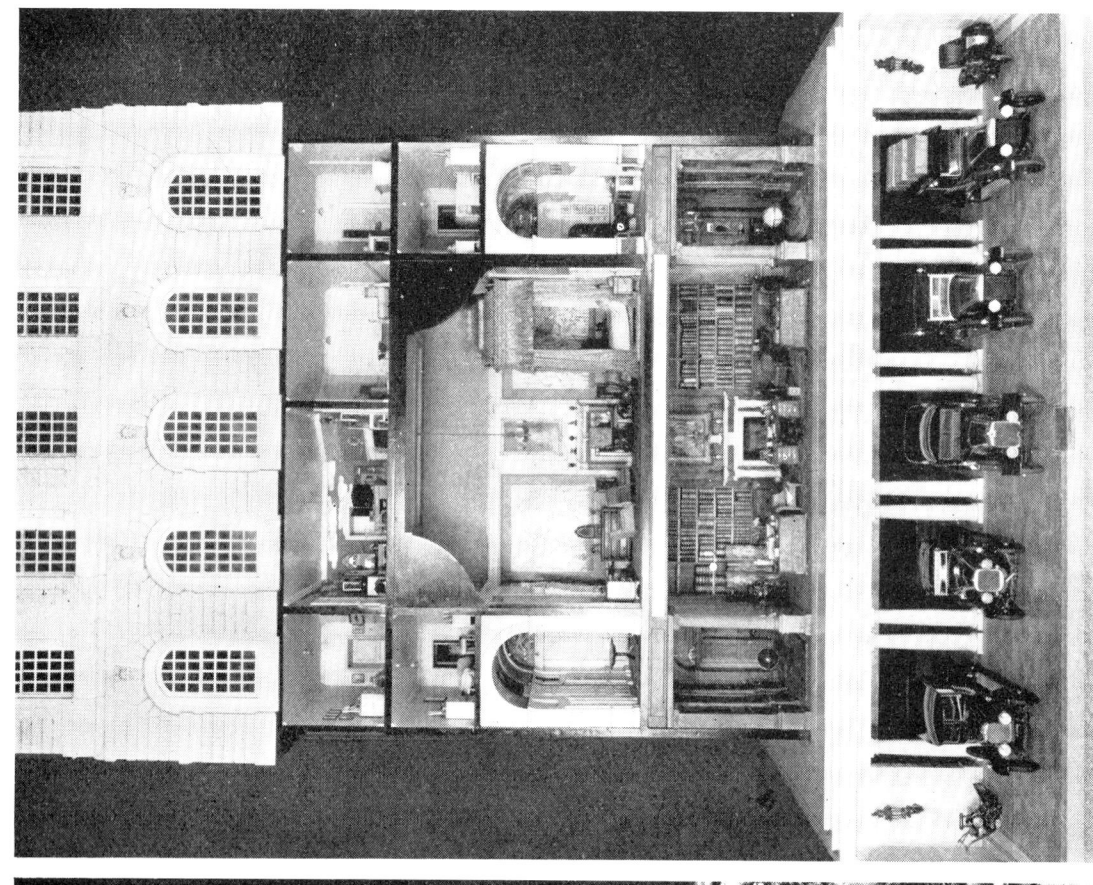

130 and 131. SIDES OF THE QUEEN'S DOLLS' HOUSE. Showing (*left*) the garden, and (*right*) the garage, library, King's bedroom, and, on the top floor, the Princess Royal's room, Queen's sitting room, night nursery and nursery bathroom. The upper mezzanine contains two servants' bedrooms

skilled artists and craftsmen inactive, the way of life of another great age was passing away. Let it be portrayed exactly, at a scale of one inch to one foot, for the delight of children and historians for ever. Whose was the original idea is forgotten, but before the end of the evening Lutyens had roughed out a design and method of procedure, and the Princess had undertaken to ask the Queen to accept the model as a tribute by many hands to the affection felt for Her Majesty by the British people. For amidst the ruin and disruption and vast imponderables of 1920, the domestic virtues of George V and his consort shone as a steady light in a dark world. Their home-loving simplicity had added a new and delightful attribute to the conception of monarchy which they had signally upheld through five frightful years. A desire was widespread, if undefined, to give some permanent shape to the emotion that on Armistice Day, and subsequently, drew tens of thousands to the forecourt of Buckingham Palace. The idea of giving Queen Mary the best dolls' house in the world had just the element of monumental unexpectedness which catches the imagination of the English, yet the aptness, it was realised, that would delight her, whilst enabling a great many people to contribute. No one would be called on to spend much money, but hundreds their joy of work, and that which was a labour of love would carry real pleasure to its recipient. 'One of the pleasantest things about the Queen's Dolls' House', A. C. Benson afterwards wrote of it, 'is that it has not been got together by the overwork and anxiety of a few, but by the enjoyable and willing cooperation of many delighted designers, craftsmen, and donors.'

That was true, up to a point—the point where the innumerable lines of organisation, design, selection, and fitting together converged in Apple Tree Yard and later in the dining-room at Mansfield Street where the 'building' was finished. 'The project could never have been carried out', Benson observed, 'without a presiding genius who had within his powers both efficiency and a keen sense of fun. Such a combination could be found nowhere better than in the person of the architect, Sir Edwin Lutyens.' E. V. Lucas was more emphatic. Without his creative mind, he affirmed, 'the House would most probably never have been built at all and certainly would not be the miracle of fine workmanship that it is.' No attempt at a detailed description of the Dolls' House is contemplated. A large octavo volume of 250 pages is devoted to the subject,[1] besides the catalogue of the library which fills another.[2] The list of donors, of monetary or material contributions, numbers about 500; that of artists who decorated it, 60; and who contributed miniature works for the library, 600; whilst some 250 makers and craftsmen are listed. But an indication of its nature is necessary for those who have not seen it (pp. 445–8).

The house is 102 inches long on its main (north and south) fronts, $58\frac{1}{2}$ in. on

---

[1] *The Book of the Queen's Dolls' House*. Edited by A. C. Benson, C.V.O. and Sir Lawrence Weaver, K.B.E., with 92 plates of which 24 are in colour. 1500 numbered copies. Methuen 1924.

[2] Edited by E. V. Lucas.

east to west. The façades—the main one recalling the centre of Hampton Court's —were described by Lawrence Weaver as 'a delighted deference to the greatness of our greatest, Sir Christopher Wren', which, in the interior, is 'joined with a sharp perception of the convenience that to-day's science has showered upon life'. The façades and roof are, in fact, a wooden case which is raised by electrical mechanism to reveal the rooms within. The house proper stands on a base 116 in. by 72 in., which is 39 in. high. This is divided into a lower portion containing 208 drawers made to contain the dolls. The upper portion of this base serves various purposes: it contains the electrical transformer breaking down normal current to the 4-volt system of the house's lighting circuit; and a tank to receive the waste of the water system. On the west front a drawer with falling flap contains the garage, complete with six cars the antiquated appearance of which—the latest thing in their time—impresses one most of anything, perhaps, with the time that has elapsed since those days. The eastern end extends similarly to reveal a garden terrace.

In the internal arrangement Lutyens, with complete seriousness, played the difficult game of planning a symmetrical house of four elevations. The only liberty taken with the rules was the assumption that the Royal Doll Family had no visitors to stay and few servants living in. The main internal feature is the Grand Staircase Hall filling the centre of the north front, with floors of white marble and lapis lazuli and walls painted by William Nicholson with a really magnificent design of the expulsion of Adam and Eve from Eden watched, as he put it, 'by their pets'—the entire animal kingdom. Beyond the hall is the kitchen, to the west the library, and to the east the dining-room with adjoining pantry, separated from the hall by a scullery and service corridor respectively. Above the scullery the strong room, at the southeast corner, contains behind steel grilles the Dolls' Crown Jewels. On the main upper floor, level with the head of the grand staircase, the Saloon fills the east side, its ceiling painted by Charles Sims with youths in a bold lattice pattern, its walls hung with rose-pink silk. Opening off it the Queen's Wardrobe, divided into domed compartments, gives into the Queen's Bedroom in the centre of the south front: a lovely apartment in blue silk damask with a ceiling by Glyn Philpot of sombre golds and black. The Queen's Bathroom, vaulted and decorated not unlike her Wardrobe. communicates with the King's Bedroom, decorated in crimson and gold.

The second floor is devoted to the Nurseries, the Queen's Sitting-Room, Linen-Room, and household adjuncts which fascinate with their perfection of equipment no less than the miniature elaboration of the State apartments with their tiny thrones and portraits and sumptuous furnishings. The most astonishing of them all is the Library, 45 in. long, 21 in. broad, and $15\frac{1}{4}$ in. high, panelled in Italian walnut, and containing 350 leather-bound volumes specially written by the most eminent hands, a number of ancient printed books of the same scale, and microphotographed editions of the leading newspapers and periodicals.

The labour of specifying, organising, and collecting the components was to some extent distributed over a committee under Sir Herbert Morgan. Lady Jekyll managed the kitchen stores, Gertrude Jekyll the garden, Francis Berry of the St. James's Street firm the cellar, George Muntzer—Lutyens's principal upholsterer—held the office of honorary decorator, A. J. Thomas superintended the engineering. The draughtsman was F. B. Nightingale, and Miss Clare Nauheim with Miss Beatrice Webb shared the secretarial work in Lutyens's office. Parnell and Son of Rugby made the structure, for which Robert Hudson of that firm was primarily responsible.

But it involved Lutyens himself in a great deal of detail, apart from the designing. He insisted, and took endless trouble to secure, that everything should, in fact, work. The only exceptions are the motor cars and the smaller toilet fittings—the latter owing to the physical property of viscosity in fluids. But the lifts work; and so does the major plumbing, as he delightedly demonstrated to Queen Mary on one of her frequent visits to inspect progress.

From the first Her Majesty took a keen interest in the project. The Queen, he wrote in the summer of 1921,

> ... writes that she is nervous as to how the Dolls' House opens.
> She wants to be able to open it herself, so that she can play with it without calling servants. Can you see the Queen going hush hush to play with the dolls!

In the same letter he said he had received the first estimates for any of the furniture: 13 State portrait frames, £50, which he had sent to Mrs. Marshall Field: and £30 for the ivory cradle for the infant prince, sent to Mr. H. Konig (for whom he was designing the garden temples at Tyringham). 'These are the first attempts to land a fish,' he added,—to apply the method he had envisaged of obtaining contributions to the costs of components. One file of his Dolls' House correspondence has survived. In it there is a characteristically painstaking letter from Miss Jekyll (March 17, 1923) asking about the colouring, and exact proportion of the upper moulding, of garden pots—one inch high!—with the pottery's attempts at which she was not satisfied. No doubt he dealt with it succinctly. And there is a series to Nicholson urging him on with the staircase murals. The dates of Nicholson's replies are uncertain since he had a way of heading his letters 'Here. Now,' continuing 'I say Ned, I am sorry to seem such a sluggard but its not for want of working. Can you give me all August? ... I shall be in our Tree next Monday' (i.e. at Apple Tree Yard); and compensating for a certain uncertainty with such a pictorial signature as that on p. 452. It was all part of the fun—and the efficiency—of the colossal trifle. And when at last, after three years' toil the fairy palace was assembled complete in the dining-room at Mansfield Street, there was the fun of gently shocking Queen Mary by demonstrating its sanitary workings, or replying to her inquiry why the pillowslips in the Doll Queen's bed were embroidered infinitesimally M.G. on one case, and G.M. on the other: 'For "May George?" ma'am, and "George May!"'

Whether or no that anecdote is apocryphal, Her Majesty graciously wrote in her own hand to Lutyens on June 24, 1924, asking him to accept a photograph of herself 'in remembrance of the trouble you have taken concerning my beautiful Dolls' House', and continuing:

> I know how much thought and care you have expended upon this wonderful work of art which is such a joy to look at, and I, as the proud possessor of this house, can never be sufficiently grateful to you for having given so much of your time in order to give me pleasure. The crowds of visitors to the Dolls' House at Wembley are a proof that the public do appreciate your work.
>
> With many many thanks
> Believe me
> Yours very sincerely
> Mary R.

PICTORIAL SIGNATURE OF WILLIAM NICHOLSON TO A LETTER TO LUTYENS

§3. ON PASSAGE: INDIA, PARIS, NEW YORK

The passages to India were mostly occupied with drawing and other work. Hall no longer accompanied him, as in the early years, but was sent ahead to make his path straight. Generally he contrived to get a deck cabin or similar commodious apartment for his floating office. On the outward voyage in December, 1920, however, he had to use the chart room. He wrote from Port Said:

> The difficulties of work have raised my dandy, and I have worked hard. But lord! how I sweated in that little red hot room at the top of the ship, up and down and the slip-slap on the windows and the big steering wheel moving mysteriously and the engine bells ringing amidst all the hub and dub of a chart room. Then my table was glass, to protect charts under it—not conducive to draftsmanship.

It was an exciting voyage. Not only had he with him two new assistants, A. G. Shoosmith and Herbert Ward, the former destined to be his representative and companion at Delhi till Government House was completed; but also an important client, who had already approached him about reconstructing a big country house in Yorkshire. Mr. (subsequently Sir Amos) Nelson was eastward bound on business connected with his cotton mills at Skipton, near which he had purchased the imposing but undistinguished Georgian mansion of Gledstone Hall. A local Lancashire architect, Mr. Richard Jaques, had been instructed to make plans for its reconstruction. Later, Nelson proposed to his architect that he might care to be associated with one of wider reputation, and Mr. Jaques suggested Lutyens, whose work at Heathcote was well-known to both. Thus had begun a very successful collaboration. Both architects had already worked on the plans, but it was arranged that Lutyens should complete his share with the client on the ship. 'So I have to keep his interest to a pitch higher than the toss of the waves!' he remarked of their conferences in the chart room. Both seem to have been so much elated by the process that the subsequent estimates for the reconstruction showed that its cost would be pitched up too. It was therefore decided to build a new and smaller house on a new site, the agreed plans for which were not completed by the two architects till 1923. Sir Amos got the kind of house he wanted, which Mr. Jaques assures us is a Lutyens house, whilst Lutyens acknowledged that he adopted many of his collaborator's proposals yet was freed to devote himself to the succession of other works which each year brought—perhaps contrary to his expectation when he had committed himself to the Dolls' House. Among these were the headquarters office of the Anglo-Persian Oil Company—Britannic House; the Midland Bank branch office in Piccadilly (also in collaboration), continuation and extension of the Theosophical Society's building for its new owners the British Medical Association; half a dozen country-house additions or reconstructions, a sequence of war memorials and cemeteries, and such trifles as London alterations and stands for Wembley Exhibition. So there was material for thought and work, on top of Delhi, to occupy every sea voyage. Too much, indeed. Though he would say that it was a wonderful rest to get away, in the next line he would write that he was reading Gibbon from 12 to 1 at nights and often from 4 till 5 a.m. 'which brings sleep'. And when he could not read, he had taken to playing interminable patience as a sedative.

He also invented about now, and henceforth practised assiduously, a remarkable kind of doodle (pp. 435-6). Taking the embossed heading of the ship's notepaper, he used the Line's crest or burgee or whatnot as the starting point for a 'pic'—the abbreviation he generally used for his illustrations to letters. They were invariably of a farcical, surrealist, character and executed with assured speed. The number is only less astonishing than the variety of these fantasies, in which the P. & O.'s rising sun badge was worked into tigers and elephants and Indians and ladies or whatever oddity the pattern suggested to him at the moment, with scarcely a repetition of the same theme. Sometimes the doodle had some bearing upon a passage in the accompanying letter. But quantities were drawn on otherwise blank sheets for sheer love of nonsense. Whilst the P. & O. series preponderates, and therefore gives most opportunity for appreciating his fertility for variation on a theme, the devices of other Lines were evidently welcomed as fresh starting points.

On one of his last passages to India (1928-29) he wrote that he had 'done a house in a large double cabin' given him for his work, but had also been co-opted by Sir Atul Chatterjee and a group of distinguished Indians to a committee for the restoration of Benares. But to him, as with all committees, 'they talk and talk their culture but are blind, blind. You can talk to English engineers without bringing in the ancient philosophies of King Arthur and the Knights at Table.' As a solace he turned to the Maharanee of Cooch Behar, for whom Robert, by then established as an independent architect, was undertaking some work, and invited her to stay with him in Delhi ('though she seems only really interested,' he thought, 'in Bridge at 2s. a point.') The somewhat embarrassing outcome of Her Highness's visit was narrated in the last chapter.

But on a trip to Paris, in the summer of 1922, his habitual, if occasionally disconcerting, affability to ladies had a characteristically charming ending. He was on War Graves business, and having picked up at St. Omer Major Goldsmith, his assistant for the French cemeteries, had gone to Brussels for a conference at his stoneyard with M. Swarle, the contractor for Etaples. Then he caught an afternoon train for Paris where he was to stay with Miss Elsie de Woolfe (later Lady Mendl) at her Versailles villa. He found there a house-party including Mrs. Vanderbilt, and M. and Mme. Balzan (the latter the former Consuelo, Duchess of Marlborough), gathered to witness a great fête in the Palace that night. Miss de Woolfe had got him a ticket by representing him to the authorities as Architect to the King of England, she said.

> It was rather thrilling, certainly moving, passing through the crowds of French people into the great forecourt, the palace blazing with light, figures looking absurdly small crowded in the windows overlooking the approach. The Russian Ballet was being given in the *Gallerie des Glaces*, extraordinarily well done, a continuous performance without break or curtain, and the old

ceilings and decorations were once again alive with light. How Louis XIV would have loathed the modern crowd. His State bedroom was 'lived in'—as green room and piled high with wigs, ballet-skirts and all the properties of the Ballet. Afterwards there was a great supper and fireworks, the gardens too wonderful in the moonlight, full of people yet not too busy.

I led a revolt against the supper, so we all went home and had a little impromptu supper at the Villa to ourselves. I got off with Anne—Mrs. Vanderbilt. How could I know this dear old lady, exquisitely dressed, was held in awe and reverence and treated as a Queen in New York? She had a necklace of black pearls and diamonds which, for want of conversation, I admired. They were really a bit too much for me. But she asked me, would I like one—a black pearl!! I answered that I would rather have her face! She gave a great squeal of delight—and we got off. Everyone much amused by my taming of Anne, though I still wonder if she really meant to give me a pearl!

After breakfast next morning on my verandah, several of us walked to the Little and Great Trianon with private keys. I enjoyed that but was saddened by the neglect and ruin into which the place is falling; and the place was full of ghosts. Mme. Balzan was walking through a week or two back when she tumbled on Marie Antoinette and her ladies, all in crinolines and hair on top. It gave her a fearful turn, till she discovered it was a cinema in course of being taken.

'Anne' would not believe that ivy hurt trees, so to prove how, I put my arms round her elegant form and gave her a death squeeze to show how it was done. It made a great impression on the onlookers besides on Anne herself. It was then I learnt of her standing and reputation, from the general impression of amazement and amusement. I believe she is approaching 70, and she has a Theosophic mind which you would appreciate.

For dinner arrived Miss Elsa Maxwell! and Hugo Rumbold who brought his Versailles film of Marie Antoinette, which the Armenian chauffeur ran in the ball room—mostly used by Miss de Woolfe (aged 60) for her health drills. She gave me an exhibition of them to a gramophone—on a mattress, in tights, with an india-rubber corset and a jumper extraordinaire—next morning before I left. More of an acrobat than a woman!

In Paris he discussed preliminary questions of layout for the Memorial to the Missing of the Somme, at Thiepval (the undated rough sketch for which, p. 479, may be of this time), with M. Bigot the French Government architect. 'He could talk no English and you know my French! but we managed a very satisfactory conversation with rather doubtful conclusions.' Then he went to Molyneux to see his 'very good, wonderful' doll, for the Dolls' House, 'but it must be seen in the house before I give my verdict,' before leaving to meet Goldsmith at St. Quentin.

All the time El Guadelperal was not exactly progressing but proceeding. After the discovery that the site originally chosen for the Duke of Peñaranda's inaccessible palace occupied that of a prehistoric arsenal stuffed with flint knives and arrow-heads, another had been selected two miles away. A well was dug, a water-tower and filtration plant built, miles of pipe-line laid, a good many miles of road constructed, and a brick-yard established. The Duke's intention was to get all the outside work begun or completed before beginning on the house itself. Accordingly stables, dairy, workshops, and an electrical generating plant were next built, the last to supply the whole estate with light and power. A sunk garden was put in hand, with arrangements for irrigation. Then, a sensational event at the time, the Duke married, and it became an urgent matter to erect a nursery wing for the infant duke—'for Penny's Halfpenny' as Lutyens expressed it. He visited La Caceres, as it was called, on the way out to India in 1924 and 1926, if not in other years as well, but no adventures are recorded.

He was to meet Mrs. Vanderbilt, the distinguished object of his affable temerity, next at her New York house. In 1924 the Institute of American Architects honoured him by conferring its Gold Medal upon him. At the time there appeared a possibility of his having to go to Australia in connection with the Australian National War Memorial at Villers-Bretonneux which he was required to carry to completion. But it was found possible to transfer to him the drawings and materials of the work already done without the necessity for his going to Melbourne, so he was able to cross to New York to receive the Medal at the Annual Convention in April, 1925, and to combine it with preliminary discussions with Sir Esmé Howard, the British Ambassador, of the scheme under consideration by the Foreign Office and Office of Works for building a new Embassy in Washington.

To say that the visit, of less than a week, to the United States was a nightmare of mounting horror for him is not to impugn the kindness and hospitality of his hosts or the very real admiration that he evinced for much of what he saw in New York and Washington. But he was haunted by the expectation from him of a public speech before a very large and entirely unknown audience, amid circumstances of much pomp, as well as by the virtual certainty of being required to deliver sundry speeches to lesser, preparatory, gatherings, and of facing the ordeal by journalists administered to eminent entrants to the United States. To one of Lutyens's constitutional shyness and complete inability to speak extempore—to whom any public utterance was terrifying and only to be made after hours of careful preparation—the frightful prospect was scarcely redeemed by the novelty, honour, and practical promise of the journey. It began inauspiciously with Dr. Inge—'the gloomy Dean' —three priests and two corpses aboard S.S. *Homeric*—which the P. & O. crews, he recalled, termed 'God-botherers'. Sure enough dense fog hung over the Hudson, blocking out the celebrated view and delaying them thirty hours. However, he was grateful to Dr. Inge for drawing all the reporters on arrival so that he landed in peace and, having an I. A. (immediate attention) certificate from the Embassy, dispatch.

A deputation of architects received him, led by Mr. Harvey Corbett, who in the ensuing days earned his undying esteem and gratitude, as will appear. The atmosphere was formal until Lutyens broke the ice by remarking to a very serious architect as they walked through the dock buildings 'Ah! So this is McKim's great railway station!' His companion gravely corrected the misapprehension and promised he should see the Pennsylvania Station later. To which Ned retorted 'I think I have your goat, sir'.

> Roars of laughter and then it all went famous and chitter-chat, quips, jibes, and arm-in-arms.

Somebody motored him round New York, where he was impressed by the traffic-management, but regarded the method as applicable only to a grid plan. Then he was received warmly by 'Anne' Vanderbilt 'in a very small and very charming house: she has shut up her big Fifth Avenue house owing to troublesome daughters who marry indiscriminately and get twins immediately'. And in the evening had his first fright at a large dinner of architects where Dana Gibson and Cass Gilbert made witty speeches, and 'I got out of it, or rather into it, very lamely—but lor' how I hate it'.

Next morning to Washington, and, with his habitual train-fever, a long time in which to admire McKim's great railway station: 'a colossal hall modelled on the baths of Caracalla, 150 feet high, of no use, great waiting rooms right and left which lead to another great iron-roofed hall from which stairways descend to the trains.' Confinement in the waiting-room, listening to the echoing announcements of other trains, pending that of his own, kept him on tenterhooks, and he got hopelessly entangled in a ninety page Sunday newspaper. His bewilderment, on at length taking his seat in the right train, was turned nearly to nausea by the super-heated perfume of super-scented women in the hot car where he could not smoke. He betook himself to the ante-room of a third-class lavatory where he could open the window and light his pipe. At 12.45 he queued up for lunch, reaching the restaurant at 1.30 when he selected from a huge menu an omelette, a steak, and coffee. After a very long time a huge omelette, a colossal steak, and a great pot of coffee arrived all at once. He couldn't look at the omelette, ate half the steak, and got back to his humble seat at 3 o'clock to look out of the window:

> The countryside is dreadfully untidy. Little white houses of wood stuck down anywhere, no gardens, are squalid and distressingly unhandsome. The dog-wood was in flower, and cherry blossom. But for a flowering tree here and there, the country seemed a waste of tears.

Washington station proved to be 'another great pompous building, built in the spirit of advertisement'. But the plan of the city was fine—though not so fine as Delhi—and the buildings far better: 'public patronage is alive where at Delhi it is nil.'

> The Lincoln Memorial is a great thing, but placed too close to the Washington Obelisk, which again blocks everything, so big is it. They should have put it across the river, but there it would have been in Virginia which sentiment forbade. A glorious thunderstorm came on and the marble colonnade of huge dimensions, the ink black sky, and vivid coloring of trees and red roofed buildings made an impressive spectacle.

He stayed at the Embassy in kindly and relative peace, examined the proposed site, and had long discussions with Sir Esmé and Mr. Brooke, his collaborator to be, spending an afternoon at Mount Vernon—'so charming, so pathetic, and all so small'. The Chairman of the American Fine Arts Commission came to dinner. That body, it seemed to him, was 'much more authoratative and less sentimental than the Commission recently established in London' (of which Lutyens was a foundation member). 'Mr. Moore answered all my criticisms of Washington by saying "yes, we are going to do it". They are spending £10,000,000 (not dollars) to put the plan right!'

It was Tuesday mid-day when he got back to New York, where Alfred Bossom (whom he called 'Abraham') lunched him in an atmosphere of gothic tapestries and wax candles high up in a sky-scraper, and he found himself sitting next to 'a charming curious lady' who turned out to be Miss Elsie Janis, the actress. He dined with her and her mother, an old lady who talked endlessly, feverishly, and spent the rest of the evening between Miss Janis's dressing-room and the front of her theatre.

Next day he got back to the architectural world, sight-seeing and inspecting offices in charge of Corbett, with a Convention entertainment in the evening. The opulence of American architects overwhelmed him. Then his troubles began. He was presented to the Architectural Convention, but got out of replying to the address of welcome by saying that, having been only a few days in America, he could not speak American so that Corbett would reply for him, which he did with acclamations. The same dodge worked with equal success at the Town Planning Convention next day, and Corbett rescued him a third time after the Institute's (dry) dinner on the Friday. As he listened to his spokesman he commented to himself:

> *Maître Corbett, sur une arbre perché,*
> *Tenait dans son bec—Lutyens.*

But he could not so escape the final ceremony. He had drafted a speech, with the help of Beresford Pite (who was attending the Convention), which Lady Betty Fielding, aged nineteen, had typed for him at the Embassy.

The whole lot of us went to the Metropolitan Museum where we mustered, on the top floor. They all put on robes, there was a standard-bearer. We were marshalled at the top of a great staircase going down straight into the Great Hall, packed with folk. The band burst out in a blaring march and the standard-bearer goose-stepped down the staircase lined with folk. Then the President in robes, and then me in dinner shift, with Davis who was once Ambassador to us, followed by about 40 robed gentlemen, marched down and round the hall where we stood with the dais and the braying band behind us amid clapping people. Then folk passed and for an hour I shook hands with strangers, 'glad to see you.' All sorts of people I had heard of, but they weren't half gone by when a halt was called and we went up on the dais.

Everybody standing, and I, poor me, before a huge Union Jack. The President spoke a Eulogy and gosh!! called to me and put the medal round my neck—a great and very beautiful golden disc. Then up gets Mr. Davis and he spoke a *most* moving eulogy on what I had done—in the Cenotaph, all very upsetting, and then I was all of a quake and more miserably moved than can be described. I asked the President if I could read my speech, to which he assented. Then I was committed!

It took ten minutes. I had much better not have read it, but just said thank you as best I could. But off I went, and it got worse. I found myself trembling, but could steady myself by pulling the paper I was reading from hard. Then I was frightened that if I pulled as hard as I was pulling, the paper would burst. And I was thinking of every sort of terror as I read.

At last it was over. No one could hear me, which was something. The band played God Save the King and the Star Spangled Banner, the procession reformed, went up the grand staircase again, and in the muster room I reached peace.

Then Corbett motored me down to the docks where I got on the steamer about 11.30... My cabin is surrounded with the bottles of whiskey they were always giving me and which I shall bring home as a trophy, of rum-running and my abstinence.

It was an ordeal.

Corbett had said that though I had never told him my impressions, he knew what they were; that I thought America the most wonderful country I had ever seen (though I had not been out of New York) and that New York was the most wonderful city (though I had only seen Fifth Avenue) etc.

But it is a wonderful place.

Alive, keen, friendly.

Great achievement and alive only to make achievement.

The scale they can adopt is splendid.

> The sky-scrapers are growing from monstrosities to emotions of real beauty, and the general character of the work is of a very high standard indeed, far higher than anything on the Continent or England.
>
> They are all children with gigantic toys, growing, I believe, to equally gigantic manhood.
>
> But the place does want tidying up and pulling together.

He was back in Washington in October, 1928, seeing something of J. B. Fagan, Miss Fay Compton, and Somerset Maugham at Gilbert Miller's country place, before becoming immersed in the Embassy building's early stages (he seems to have moved much in theatrical circles when in the States). And again in May, 1930, for the moving-in, 'pushing around soporific folk' whom 'Office of Works stringency, lack of funds, correspondence, estimating and re-estimating, have thrown into a kind of mental paralysis, making them dog-tired of the job. It is a pity, so to have spoilt a good job'. Then he was too wearied and disappointed himself with Whitehall's cheese-paring, to have so much zest for the lighter side of travel. Besides, he was turned sixty himself, the 'economic blizzard' had hit the States, and was freezing credit at home. The 'twenties were over.

CHAPTER XVI

QUEEN ANNE'S GATE

§1. THE LUTYENSIAN MODES

BETWEEN 1919 and 1930 inclusive, some ninety works emanated from the head office, at it was called, at 17 Queen Anne's Gate. They ranged from quite minor alterations of town houses to great city buildings, from country house gardens to the new bridge over the Thames at Hampton Court and the British Embassy at Washington. Besides, he designed about ninety Memorials, from inscribed tablets to the Memorial to the Missing at Thiepval. That amounts to 180 works, comparing with some 165 (excluding the few Memorials) designed in the twelve years 1903–14. The output of the Delhi Office cannot be numerically computed but should be added to the 180 if we would compare the quantitative output of his practice in the two periods. Some of the memorials required only a single drawing, and some works were in collaboration or were projects never executed. But others were of much greater bulk and complexity than any of the earlier period (except of course the early schemes for Delhi). Though results obtained by this kind of arithmetic are of doubtful value, it is suggestive to suppose that, if he had expanded his London office instead of being absent from it for some three months in the year, he might theoretically have produced a further forty-five works in the 'twenties (i.e. one quarter of 180) making 225. Having regard to the fact that Lutyens was designing *continually*, it is probably not misleading to compute the Delhi Office's output as almost equivalent to that missing complement of forty-five works.

The quantity, however, though exceeding that of any other noted English architect, including Wren, is less significant than the quality and variety of his work. No detail of this was ever delegated to an assistant. Every adjunct, however small, in each undertaking, was personally designed or specified by him; and no drawing left the office without his personal approval of it, or before (in most cases) it had been repeatedly revised. Regarded chronologically, this creative flood is perplexing in its abundance. It can of course be considered by categories: country houses, additions and alterations, garden work, public memorials, personal memorials, city buildings, ecclesiastical works. These, however, are little more suggestive of his evolution as artist during these years of intense application than the chronological list. What we need is a means of notation representing not the kinds of buildings so much as the architectural keys in which he was composing. In Part I we roughly distinguished between his romantic and classic veins. Since then, two phases of profound experience have greatly enriched his range and technique of expression. The years of sustained application at Delhi have exercised his classical muscles so that they possess a power and suppleness given to no contemporaries and few predecessors; a quality that might be described in Bergson's phrase as *élan vital*, restoring youth to the classical forms. But the buildings in this category are still denoted visibly by Orders, so it must be called a kind of classicism, for which is suggested the term Lutyensian, on the analogy of Palladian. Lutyensian Classic is characterised by an original yet intensely coherent use of the classical canon, taking many apparent liberties with its traditional forms and ratios, but producing results unmistakably related to Humanist prototypes. His first important essay in this mode was Heathcote; his masterpieces in it are Delhi, of course, though there modified by the necessity of Indian qualification, and the Midland Bank, Poultry, in London.

But parallel to the evolution of Lutyensian Classic, his monumental work with the War Graves Commission produced a type of design in which classical notation was gradually reduced or eliminated, retaining the elements and proportions, to which he added subtleties of entasis, visual compensation, and curvature by means of a basically simple but complex geometry, that was likewise often implicit, not expressed. In these late works, of which the prototype was the War Stones and the first great manifestation the Cenotaph, he carried the art of architecture into a realm unvisited by any save its supreme exponents. His most complete extant monument in this key is the Thiepval Arch; but it is most fully developed in the still unexecuted designs for the Cathedral of Christ the King at Liverpool, which occupied him during the years beyond the period covered in this chapter. This category may be named the Elemental.

We thus obtain four categories applicable to Lutyens's matured modes: that vernacular, poetic, early vein, which we have termed generally Romantic; the typical 'Wrennaissance' of his middle period, which at this stage we may describe as Lutyens Traditional; Lutyensian Classic; and Elemental. Yet, since he never repeated himself and, even when designing in an early vein, was expressing his mature conviction and experience, these categories can at best be indicative only. The spirit underlying the Lutyensian and the Elemental permeates the Romantic and Traditional works of the 'twenties and 'thirties, endowing them with its *élan vital*. But provided with this framework we can at least sort out in brief compass the most notable of the 180 works of the 'twenties.

§2. WORKS OF THE TWENTIES

In the Romantic key, Castle Drogo, resuming its baronial advance after the war, affords the *basso continuo* throughout the 'twenties. One only of the three originally intended sides of its court had been partly built and was now to be slowly completed, the proposed great hall adjoining at right angles being now omitted and its undercroft formed into a chapel. Of this time therefore is the dramatic design for finishing the narrow south end of the building and the layout finally adopted for garden terraces constructed among granite outcrops of the hill-top (pp. 223, 214). Begun a year before Delhi, the construction of this most romantic of Lutyens's original conceptions covers the same period, being completed simultaneously after exactly twenty years.

Similarly at Ashby St. Ledgers, in August, 1921, Lord Wimborne was roused to renewed activity by a recent party for the Prince of Wales when, according to Lutyens, there was such 'a terrible squash that he is going to add lavishly in spite of the hard times'. The work consisted in a new wing more individual than his earlier additions and in that simplified but subtle version of Tudor tradition exemplified at Castle Drogo. Thence, he wrote, he was posting to Devon, where a wing was being added to Mothecombe, a traditional house in an idyllic combe on the coast near Ivybridge, belonging to Mr. Alfred Mildmay; and Captain N. L. Colville was enlarging and modernising the Tudor manor house of Penheale, across the Cornish border, to contain his ever growing collection of beautiful possessions. As at Ashby, the problem was to provide a considerable number of additional bedrooms and office quarters without challenging comparison with the seventeenth-century granite manor house. He contrived it with his invariable originality and sureness, evolving a group dominated by a four-storey tower and lying about a court, which, with something of Drogo's character, is invisible from the front of the old house yet combines with it in feeling and mass in more distant views. At Clifford Manor, near Stratford on Avon, a Wren house had been added to a medieval timbered grange, but in 1918 had been burnt (p. 465). The brick walls of the Wren portion were standing and, save for a slight raising of the stone-slated roof, Lutyens re-created it exactly, though replanning the interior and recasting some of the rooms. The timber wing had to be entirely rebuilt and he handled the traditional materials so that, whilst the stranger may suspect nothing, the informed eye perceives at once the hand, that could be so self-effacing, which reshaped Great Dixter and had first demonstrated its technique at Munstead.

In 1920, the adding of a chapel, St. John's, to his Church of St. Jude at Hampstead imposed on him his own tradition of Edwardian days, as did also, a little later, continuation of the Theosophical Society's building, by then sold to the British Medical Association. Then, in 1921–22, he was invoked by Reginald McKenna to match his skill with that of Wren himself—in the little building which the directors of the Midland Bank proposed to erect adjoining St. James's Churchyard in Piccadilly. Though in collaboration with the corporation's architects (Messrs. Whinney, Son, & Austen Hall), the gem that resulted is wholly due to Lutyens. Using Wren's materials and technique, and keeping the three-storeyed, slate-roofed cube in sensitive abeyance to the church, he infused the design with that freshness, subtlety, and aptness of which he alone held the clue. A characteristic refinement not generally noticed is the concealed gutter just *above* the eaves—providing for the disposal of rain-water without interfering with the delicate profile of the cornice; a method that he had confided to Baker in a letter twenty years before.[1] (See opposite page).

McKenna now requested his friend to build up Mells Park, Somerset, another victim of defective electric or heating installations which led to the burning of so many old houses in these years. Lutyens was not given a free hand and the result is not especially notable. Mells Park must not be confused with the manor house in the same village, in which (the remains of the original Jack Horner's house) Lutyens had unobtrusively helped his beloved Sir John and Lady Horner to establish themselves. There, now, in the splendid church adjoining, he designed for them one of the most moving of his memorials: that to their son Edward, killed in the war. It stands in a small side chapel, a pedestal surmounted by A. J. Munnings's bronze statuette of a mounted cavalry officer, the modern cavalier.

But at Ashwell Bury, on the chalk edge of Hertfordshire, in a commission having much in common with that of Mells Park, Lutyens worked a minor miracle. A dull white brick exterior of vicarage type was transformed by him with limewash, an overhanging cornice, and proportioned windows into a distinguished yet still simple design, and a staircase and drawing-room formed of a Lutyensian spaciousness *in parvo*, as though a fragment of the Viceroy's Wing at Delhi.

Each of this selection from Lutyensian tradition and romanticism of the early 'twenties is to a greater or lesser degree a notable work of art in itself, though two only were free-standing new conceptions; and each is to some extent infused with the new Lutyensian and Elemental qualities. These appear as a distinct if not immediately definable air of intensity and completeness. More obviously, we notice the absence of water-pipes and gutters (they are concealed), a pyramidal movement produced by diminution, stepping back, and the batter of wall planes giving *élan* to apparently traditional shapes, the vitality of mouldings, and the inter-coherence of every motif. There were no loose ends, nothing left to chance.

Now we come to the four outstanding expositions of Lutyensian classicism, in which this supple strength and intense completeness of design were fully developed. In almost every respect these creations are unacceptable by modern standards of architectural puritanism. They were extravagant of cost, space, and materials, they were designed for the pleasure or enhancement of individuals or individual interests, they display no new methods of construction or concealed them by classical veneer. But though they no more 'express the present', as the present conceives itself to be, or even as the 'twenties hoped themselves to be, than does a full rigged ship, they are as challengingly lovely as those proud vessels will ever be. For in those transitional

---

[1] At the time of writing the opportunity exists of completing this Wren-Lutyens composition by rebuilding the bombed vicarage to balance, and echo, the Bank at the opposite side of the churchyard.

132. CLIFFORD MANOR, STRATFORD-ON-AVON. Reconstructed 1919 after fire

133. THE MIDLAND BANK. PICCADILLY BRANCH (1922)

134. BRITANNIC HOUSE, FINSBURY CIRCUS. Initiated 1920

135. THE MIDLAND BANK, POULTRY. Initiated 1924

136. GLEDSTONE HALL, YORKSHIRE (1923). The approach and entrance front

137. GLEDSTONE HALL. The Staircase

138. The South Front and Sunk Garden

years nobody, as Mr. Butler puts it, quite knew what expressing the present meant. To many of middle age the 'twenties seemed that they might fulfil Edwardian promise of restored humanism. The end was no doubt coming, but till it came let us live, they said, as fully, as well, as handsomely as we can, and build so that we leave at least a memorial of the civilisation we inherited and perfected. In the Dolls' House Lutyens epitomised that view, even while embodying it to full scale in Britannic House; the Midland Bank, Poultry; Gledstone Hall; and the Tyringham temples. The first two may be taken together, since they followed chronologically (1920 and 1923) and, though the results differ greatly, were successive developments from the same premise, namely a palace of modern commerce. In both, the pyramidal movement sets the basic rhythm of the elevations; but it is the contrast in the means employed to produce it that is most significant.

Brittanic House, headquarters of the Anglo-Iranian Oil Company, fronts west on Moorgate Street and south-east on Finsbury Circus. The façades are similar (p. 134) but it is the elliptical one to the Circus that controlled the planning and dominates the imagination. It is endowed with tremendous *élan* by the progressive settings back and inwards of the wall surfaces, and by the upward diminution of the voids and main masses, towards a steep unbroken sweep of grey roof. Between the arched and rusticated ground storey and the seventh, the setting back amounts to six feet. The upper half, where the Directors' rooms are disposed, breaks into a Corinthian Order between immense arched windows, the sumptuousness of which extends downwards in rich interlacings of sculpture. The building is of course steel-framed, but gives the effects of powerful solidity and movement. This baroque excitement echoes up the remarkable staircases—a memory perhaps from those at Genoa that filled Lutyens with envy for their spaciousness. This series of ascents from ground to fifth floor leaps, from side to side of the Circus front's axis, through inclined 'tunnels' that link high barrel-vaulted halls spanning its lower and uppermost flights. It is as if three of the great staircases of Viceroy's House (to be described in the next chapter) were superimposed, and reminds us of those earlier, romantic, ascents at Lindisfarne and Castle Drogo with their hanging galleries, but with marbles replacing granite, and utmost suavities their bulk. Over all, there are staff dining-rooms and kitchens contained in the roofs, fully lit by clerestories at the back. Of the offices (the building also contains Moorgate tube station) it can be said that they are as practical as in most other palaces of commerce. But those others are not in 'one of the City of London's finest monuments, a cousin of St. Paul's Cathedral',[1] at which one can look for half an hour, watching the splendid life in that sunlit arc and seeming to experience music.

Britannic House is that Edwardian cynosure 'a raging beauty', decked, though with a new look, in all the armoury of classical opera. The Midland Bank has the un-

[1] A. S. G. Butler, *The Architecture,* Vol. III.

voluptuous, intellectual, allure of her sisters in the 'twenties. Around the Mansion House several young ladies of Threadneedle Street were already making their *débuts* in expensive gowns not always concealing their mercantile ancestry, when, a few yards along Poultry, Mr. McKenna introduced his, that at first sight might seem but an addition to their company. But far more has been expended on this débutante in refinement than in splendour. The Midland is radiant in what Lutyens called (Chapter 19, §2) architectural colour, and Mr. Butler terms most learned line, with a little exquisite sculpture (p. 467).

For the firmness and commodity he had associated with him Mr. Laurence Gotch, F.R.I.B.A., and was thereby freed to devote himself to the delights of architecture. Externally this building is, with little doubt, his most *learned* work. It is no exaggeration to say that it develops and refines the principles of classical design to a point seldom if ever reached before. Although the building is steel-framed, the whole is designed to stand as if of masonry unsupported.

The general character gives the same impression of strength and richness as Britannic House, and there is the same appearance of the upper works receding. Yet there is here little applied ornament, and the fronts are actually set back only as many inches as, in the other, feet were sacrificed. Above the rusticated Doric base rises a front essentially modern but treated in a human way sympathetic to the stone of which it appears to be built. But the originality and subtlety of both these elements takes Mr. Butler[1] several pages and numerous detailed drawings to analyse. In that base, Lutyens demonstrates his extreme development in the refining of his favourite Order, and went a great deal farther in that respect than Palladio. It involved recasting the whole Order to a stouter proportion—thereby running counter to his own earlier precept, à propos Heathcote, 'You cannot play originality with the Orders'—unless you have attained that plane of mastery on which the elements of architecture can be transmuted.

The buttresses of the upper part are married to the horizontal lines below by an exquisite device introducing a scallop shell. Then his magic—that effect of recession—begins to work. The buttresses have horizontal rustication—one would say all the way up. But, looking more carefully, one notices that from time to time it leaves off, and that the vertical plane recedes ever so little—actually one inch. In fact each course is also an eighth of an inch less in height than the one below it and the channels are reduced correspondingly. The wall space between the buttresses, too, if followed up, is seen to recede on its own, though the surrounds of the windows maintain the vertical plane. The windows themselves tend to diminish in width and increase in height as they ascend. Simultaneously the front contracts as it rises, leaving those cut-off corners in which Reid Dick's boys grasping geese symbolise Poultry—or the geese that lay golden eggs, it has been suggested.

[1] *ibid.*

The effect of this virtuosity is that the whole elevation is vibrant with life. It seems to shape itself upwards and backwards like a living thing, with a rhythm of moving beauty. It also makes every other rusticated façade in the world, including Brunelleschi's Pitti Palace, over which Ruskin raved, look heavily unimaginative. We can see in it, besides, Lutyens's transition from Classical to Elemental architecture taking place: the most ancient Order, the very conception of Wall, dissolving and being reconstituted before our eyes.

To descend to matters of planning and communications now would be an anti-climax. Suffice it to say that the ground plan joins with complete lucidity two irregularly alligned fronts (the other is in Princes Street). But a few words must be given to the Banking Halls, with their gorgeous green Verdite columns (quarried somewhere in Africa), and to another great staircase, in both of which the effect is of princely richness without there being a suggestion of vulgarity: a feat of most sensitive skill. Indeed, as Mr. Butler observes, the building should be treasured as a national monument.[1]

The circumstances in which he made the designs for Gledstone, for Sir Amos Nelson in collaboration with Mr. Richard Jaques, have already been mentioned (Chapter 15, §3); and for its analysis the reader must consult Mr. Butler. Yet here no less we must form a quick impression of this Lutyensian peak, which is as worth preserving as the Bank just described. Set in a dip of a spur of the Yorkshire Moors, this little palace contains but seven bedrooms (with six more for servants in a wing), and is approached in simple state through a lace-like grille into the oblong forecourt framed by square lodges. All the diagonals seem to converge on the portico straight ahead, yet the eye is most conscious of the high steep stretch of roof, hipped at the ends and without bellcast, its diminishing slates brought all the way from Gloucestershire. Its steep angle of 54·45° is emphasised by the gentler pitch of the lodges' and wings' roofs, and, as we look, we become conscious that the walls are inclined slightly inwards and the depth of each course of the creamy stone diminished too. And we begin to feel the effect of the strangely tall narrow windows, in relation to the high portico and horizontality, which brings something of the France of Louis XVI into Yorkshire (p. 468).

In the second movement, the garden front, the tempo is changed from quadrille to pavane, one might say. The house becomes more intimate, with casement windows and loggias, and the stately measure that hitherto it has sustained is transferred to far-projecting terrace bastions, flanking pools on the centre axis, of which the furthest is a round mirror in a masonry frame half surrounded by curving steps, built up from the slope at the head of which stretches the house. This garden structure, supporting a distant prospect (and in plan carrying on the lines of the forecourt),

---

[1] Lutyens also designed for the Midland Bank, the Leadenhall Street branch (1928) and the remarkable King Street building in Manchester (1929), both in association with Whinney, Son & Austen Hall.

is softened by a Jekyll planting scheme and is actually the Lutyensian rendering of the site-contours which others might have smudged with little retaining walls and crazy steps, but which he made the occasion for monumental garden landscape.

The Gledstone sonata's third movement takes us indoors. The rooms are almost austere in their simple rendering of the stately theme, though in fact light and liveable. The austerity is largely due to Lutyens having, in the communications of the ground floor, worked out fully here his favourite conception of a classical interior rendered in black and white. The hall, the arched corridors, and the final *cadenza* of the marble staircase (with black coved ceiling), are lined, skirted, and paved in black and white. The staircase is made particularly grand by the alternate black and white marble steps being carried, in the lowest flight, across two, instead of one, third of the total width and the whole width of the archway opening to it: the device which, carried out in oak on a modest scale, has such impressive effect at Ashwell Bury and re-appears in the Dolls' House (p. 468).

For all its lavishness of design and thought, there is nothing luxurious about Gledstone. It is the conception of the English country house, as an art form, raised to its highest pitch, and thus ministering to the spirit rather than to the body. So, too, at Tyringham an architectural landscape and two temples of exquisite form were conceived not as ends in themselves but as an ideal setting for civilised life, means to the apprehension of truth. Soane designed the house, subsequently much altered, to which the owner, Mr. F. A. Konig, desired to append a garden for the recreation of the spirit and the body through the exercise of both. This may sound sentencious, but how else can one describe a garden of formalised landscape embodying long waters flanked by a bathing house of temple form balancing a shrine dedicated to parental memory and music? Comparable motives underlay the heroic landscapes of Stowe, near Tyringham, and here, in another age, another if lesser Stowe might have taken shape. Equally, in other hands, a glorified swimming bath, bathing cabin, and cocktail bar might have eventualised. But it was neither pictorial poetry nor self-indulgence, but the humanist ideal of equal provision for physical and spiritual health, which set the theme; an ideal which the architect held with as much conviction as the client, and expressed not in terms of the picturesque or the trite but of fitting classic design.

Two long pools twenty yards broad stretch successively a distance of 150 yards from the house alligned on the dome surmounting it. Between the pools is a causeway containing a round basin between a pair of pillars surmounted by creatures spouting water. Lawns, contained by clipped yew hedges backed by tall elms, flank the water, and at either end of the causeway stand the temples (p. 477).

They are similar, square in form, with an arch beneath an engaged pediment on each face, of the local stone and a facing of a white crushed-stone compound; their slightly cruciform plan is stepped back above to carry a white concrete dome which echoes that of the house but repeats in miniature that destined for Viceroy's House. The bathing pavilion, corresponding closely within to its elevations, affords eight cubicles in its corners. The other, we now observe, at first sight identical, is prolonged behind by two diminishing squares like the choir and sanctuary of a tiny church. This it is, a place consecrated to the apprehension of Divine Truth not through religion but through music and architecture. A Latin inscription dedicates the building 'in memory of our fathers and to the Supreme Spirit author of the universe all parts of which are led upwards to Him in perpetual progress to ever higher spheres'. That faith is qualified elsewhere, however, by another legend. 'Seek truth,' it runs, 'but remember that behind the new knowledge the fundamental issues of life are veiled.'

The west door opens into the square nave, to which eight columns, carrying the dome, give a cruciform plan, and whence two barrel-vaulted compartments extend eastwards. The columns are of green scagliola, the square pillars behind them of black, the floor of grey, white, and black marbles, the altar, beyond the next compartment, of malachite scagliola and white marble. The place glows with structural colour. But where is the music? Its source is concealed where we might least expect it: beneath a wrought brass grille that serves as floor to the second compartment, where walnut stalls give the semblance of a choir. Down there are ranged the pipes of an organ of which the keyboard is at the lower level beyond the altar. One uncovers automatically on entering this temple, not only because an altar is associated with consecration but because the act of reverence is instinctive when confronted by the design, so sincere, so noble, so spacious, so instinct itself with reverence yet withal so genial.

The monumental idea of this garden might have been devised for Lutyens's mood at this time, for only he was capable of creating the work of art that it became. In the Music Temple, a shrine of the humanist faith, the last master of humanist architecture matched the uniqueness of the opportunity with its unique beauty. The Tyringham undertaking translates into terms of the landscape garden, with its humanist traditions, the aesthetic conception that Lutyens had been developing from the inception of Delhi and, for a decade, in his work for the War Graves Commission. The scale and classic technique are those of Delhi in miniature, the idealism that of the commemorative monuments, of which the most notable introduced landscape considerations.

The great base hospital cemetery at Etaples, of which travellers from Calais have a view, is the most impressive, with its banner-flanked pylons surmounting arches reared up white from the long terrace against a screen of dark firs. Even more so is the approach to it from the road above, where a gap in the firs frames the sharp outline of the Cross and, passing it, flights of steps descend to the terrace, suddenly unfolding the whole cemetery and, beyond, the wide estuary and the Channel. The long line of the terrace, approached from below by converging flights of steps, could not be parallel to the lines of graves owing to the lie of the land, which also presented difficulties at the ends of it. Lutyens brilliantly related these symmetrical and asymmetrical elements. At first, the stone banners of the pylons (such as he had envisaged on the Cenotaph) were criticised for their unfamiliarity. But the profound sense of stillness which their motionless folds gradually produce on the mind, makes itself felt on observers and critics (p. 478).

There are characteristic gate-houses at Warlincourt and Grevilliers, the pair of brick loggias at Daours, the Australian National War Memorial at Villers-Bretonneux for the whole of which he became responsible, the Memorial to the Missing in the great R.A.F. cemetery at Arras. Besides the Faubourg d'Amiens Cemetery, Arras, and Bard Cottage, Boesinghe (Belgium), for which he was also responsible, he supervised many others designed by junior architects on the staff of the Commission for which he continued to act as one of the three Principal Architects. Cenotaphs were designed for Bermuda and Hong Kong, monuments of other form for Colombo, Southampton, Leeds, Leicester, Manchester, Northampton, Norwich, York, and the classical shrine to the Mercantile Marine on Tower Hill, London; besides numerous smaller places. The Arch and its approaches at Leicester is one of the more spectacular in appearance and setting. In his varied designs the hall-mark of Lutyens is unmistakable though difficult to define succinctly. In each case apparently simple forms, founded on the classical ratios, build up a mass that moves the observer by its implicit qualities of proportion and profile. He rarely introduced sculpture; in his War Graves monuments there is no symbolism apart from that of the forms themselves which became progressively more abstract. This monumentality of pure architecture culminated in the Memorial to the 73,357 Missing of the Somme at Thiepval.

The form of the Memorial can be said to have developed from its purpose of recording this terrible list of names. This might have been done by inscribing them on the walls of the cemetery. But the site (a position that had been held with great obstinacy by the Germans) on a crest in the bare rolling downland, seemed to demand a monument sheer on the skyline without enclosures. In the Delhi War Memorial Arch Lutyens had provided for the commemoration of 13,516 names on the flanks of the main arch and in the two courts formed by the intersecting subsidiary arch. At Thiepval more than three times as many names were to be inscribed. He may therefore have been led to the basic conception of the Memorial to the Missing by the idea of multiplying the surfaces available for inscription by multiplying the number of arches. That is to say, by subdividing the four blocks, formed in plan by a greater and a lesser intersecting arch, by two smaller arched tunnels parallel to the greater, and two arched passages parallel to the lesser, forming sixteen squares in plan. Whatever its origin, that is the practical basis of the design which he evolved by his characteristic method of clinching his first empirical conception by analysing and rationalising it. The result is a solid geometrical composition of four sets of arches of progressive dimensions, each set contained by its rectangular structure. In addition to the stepped, pyramidal form automatically produced, and the batter of the superstructure, two other typical features are noticeable near the summit (145 feet high): the alternate set-backs on the fronts and sides; and the recessed centre to the highest attic, here flat and angular in harmony with the rest of the structure (p. 479).

This, built of small reddish French bricks and stone, chiefly Portland, is impossible to describe, however shortly, without enumerating some rather complicated proportions that underlie this unique monument's character of enduring significance. But since, as Mr. Butler emphasises, 'this work is on the highest level of Sir Edwin's invention', some of the dimensions that he cites must be quoted. The two basic progressions followed throughout are that the arches are all of his favourite ratio of height to width ($2\frac{1}{2}$ times); and that the block containing each set of arches rises to the height of the springing of the arch in the preceding block.

The width of the main arch that runs from east to west is 35 ft., giving the height to its spring as 70 ft. To the block containing it he added supporting blocks on north and south to the height of the spring of arch No. 1. In the two sides thus formed there is a north to south arch 20 ft. 3 in. wide. Thirdly, the east and west supports of No. 2 arch are extended in these directions to form four blocks which are pierced from east to west by tunnels 13 ft. 6 in. wide. Finally these blocks are extended north and south for a distance of 7 ft. by blocks (27 ft. high) from which passages 9 ft. wide burrow right through the building and through the supports of No. 1 arch. The faces of these intersecting archways, tunnels, and passages are all lined with stone slabs inscribed with the names. A matter notable to students is that, in these progressive arches, Lutyens did not simply enlarge the architraves proportionately; they were deepened by a corresponding multiplication of their members.

There is sublimity in this great abstraction of pure architecture. To the emotional mind, its multitude of arches may represent portals to the four quarters of the wide horizon, ever open for the spirits of the lost. That imaginative aspect is of the kind that may well have been in the Architect's mind, as certainly were its visual qualities of mystery, of texture, and of deep sharp shadows. But it was axiomatic of his Elemental mode of design that the motivations of heart and eye must be subordinated to and disciplined by the mind; their promptings be the effects of certain forms combined in some ratio or science that it is for the architect to ascertain, leaving nothing to chance. Thenceforward, especially when he began to develop the principle of progression, first applied here, to the designs of his Cathedral, Lutyens was often engrossed by the possibilities thus opened up for an aesthetic systematised by the scientist's practical accuracy.

At Thiepval the landscape setting was so naturally elemental that no problem of its handling arose. The conception of monumental landscape design envisaged at Leicester, and worked out in garden context at Tyringham, received fullest expression in his designs for the Dublin War Memorial, initiated 1930 (p. 478). This is in the nature of a garden in which the levels, steps, and beds of flowers, accented with obelisks and pergolas and fountain basins, create a scene in itself monumental if it could be approached as intended. It lies above the Liffey opposite Phoenix Park and the integral feature was to have been a new bridge on the axis of the Memorial. This, like his Lane Gallery bridge, has not been built, so that the garden is somewhat inaccessible and has to be approached from the back. Nor has the design, made in 1926 at the instance of Gaspard Farrer, for a bridge in St. James's Park to replace the suspension bridge that, though graceful, was recognised to have a limited life (it now has to be propped up). In this connection we may cite the highly Lutyensian memorial lodges and gate-piers at the entrances to Runnymede, presented to the nation by Lord Fairhaven. These charming pavilions, erected in 1930, are related to those that he designed, but which also were not built, on the abutments of his new bridge over the Thames at Hampton Court.

The adjacent Palace here introduced monumental and landscape relationships of the delicate nature which Lutyens was best qualified to handle. The lodges, integral to his design, were his scenic acknowledgment to his master, of whose spiritual presence Lutyens of all men, at this spot, could not but be intensely conscious. Their absence is regrettable, but does not affect the beauty of the subtle curves of the three arches.

This summary of his more notable work during the 'twenties is grouped roughly according to the postulated categories, akin to keys in music, in which Lutyens can be regarded as having been simultaneously composing during these years of almost incredible creativeness. Their number, variety and intensity imply the white heat at which he worked, but only a prolonged account of each undertaking could convey their most extraordinary characteristic, namely the personal quality of the design of every part, achieved in almost all cases by continual revision. In attempting to trace, moreover, the development from his own 'tradition' to his individual classical, and thence to his Elemental mode, very numerous lesser works have been omitted. These tended to sustain his traditional manner, and can be divided between small country houses and adaptations, and those London buildings in which he applied the principles of his tradition to the problem of modern urban architecture.

The former generally give the impression, by their homely atmosphere and the attention evidently paid to niceties of finish, of having been due to a leisurely specialist in this class of work. The old Grange at Rottingdean, where William Nicholson had lived and which Lutyens did up in 1919 for Sir George Lewis, typifies his peculiar blend of sympathy for good existing work with zest for his own. The brick and flint and weatherboard additions at the back of a stucco-faced Georgian

139. TYRINGHAM PARK, BUCKINGHAMSHIRE (1924). The park layout and temples

140. TYRINGHAM. The Bathing Pavilion

141. Interior of the Temple of Music

142. ETAPLES: IMPERIAL WAR GRAVES CEMETERY

143. DUBLIN WAR MEMORIAL (1930)

144. THIEPVAL: THE MEMORIAL TO THE MISSING (1925)

145. An early, possibly the first, conception for the design before its rationalisation

147. Staircase, 42 Cheyne Walk, Chelsea (1930)

146. Westminster Housing Scheme, 1928.
North elevations to Page Street

parsonage were small in extent—the adding of a service wing, the remodelling of hall and dining-room, the paving of a court and garden walk—but of the kind which demand great care to do well. His treatment of the big hall formed by Nicholson in the body of the house is no less characteristic: the boarded floor painted in black and white chequer-pattern, walls and ceiling glossy apricot, as a background to old furniture and rugs (p. 490).

In 1927 Edward Hudson bought another country retreat—a derelict moated manor house under the Downs at Plumpton in Sussex—and claimed Lutyens's services to make it habitable. A pair of lovely weather-boarded cottages with tall brick chimneys was built, screening the site from the approach and containing an arched entrance in the middle, which led to an oaken footbridge carried on slender arches (p. 490). Hudson never occupied the moated house, preferring the oak and whitewash of the mill cottage and to enjoy its view up the chain of lakes linked by ingeniously contrived cascades. He now recommended Lutyens to Magdalene College, Cambridge, for building the projected Benson Court on a site across Bridge Street and contained by the river. The westernmost of the three ranges intended has alone been built. This impresses by its unassuming firmness of brick and modest stonework. A footnote to its ancestry, which stems from Munstead, is that the Bursar, Mr. Peel, then lived at Middlefield, and converted his colleagues to their choice by placing a copy of Weaver's book in Combination Room.

Lord Revelstoke (his old friend Cecil Baring of Lambay) got Lutyens in 1930 to design what might be called a small country house—for it stood in its own grounds—24 Cheyne Walk, Chelsea. A few years later it was pulled down and the site engulfed by flats. Like a miniature Middlefield externally, inside it was a Gledstonian gem enlivened with architectural wit of late Delhi vintage. There were walls papered with posters, sheets of *The Times*, and bookbinders' marble-paper, varnished, against which stood out the exquisite silhouette of a white Lutyens chimneypiece. There was a piece of wall furniture made to contain a Chinese landscape roll which was slowly moved through its frame by the mechanism of two clocks, themselves of enchanting design, perched above its ends. But the *tour de force* was the staircase. A spiral, the underside of one of its treads coincided with the entablature of a doorway beneath it—itself identical with the other ground-floor doorways. The apparently fortuitous effect was a perfect instance of Lutyens's lightly worn skill, for the achievement of the 'coincidence' dictated the staircase's width, angle of ascent, and the number of treads, and in its turn was controlled by the height of the lower storey. Yet the three-dimensional design was made to look so easy and inevitable that its complexity appeared only when one paused to think about it (p. 480).

The Benson Wing (his only sample in Cambridge), the Y.W.C.A. Central Club, Great Russell Street, and the British Pavilion at the Antwerp Exhibition were all designed in 1928 and represent aspects of Lutyens tradition. At the same time his collaboration was invoked by the Westminster Estate to apply the influence of that tradition, as distilled by him from the broad tradition of English architecture, to the blocks of flats and offices that then were beginning to change the character of the West End. Other architects were generally responsible for the plans and structures, Lutyens for the elevational character. Grosvenor House, Park Lane (1926) was followed by Terminal House, Grosvenor Gardens (1927), Hereford House flats, Marble Arch (1928), Aldford House, Park Lane (1930), Brook House (1932). They all display some aspect of the principles embodied in his great city buildings: for example, though few are aware of it, the windows of Grosvenor House are progressively diminished. By such means he sought, with no little success, to retain the scale and language of Georgian town architecture for mass housing.

But the most notable application of Lutyensism to this twentieth-century need is the Westminster Housing Scheme. The City Council commissioned him to undertake this slum-clearance and rehousing operation for the very poor in 1928, when he was at the height of his aristocratic career; the first block was opened in 1930; and a few years later Page Street, which runs through the area from east to west, was lined with the standard units for some 300 yards on both sides (p. 480). Each U-shaped block, of six storeys, contains thirty-five flats ranging from one to four rooms, all of which have at least one window facing south and a kitchen facing north or sufficiently shaded by the concrete access galleries. The plans, reproduced in Volume III of *The Architecture*, show how efficiently he systematised the essentials of minimum housing. The *emotional* stimulus, corresponding to conditions of site in a landscape setting, was evidently the need for pervasive light in this depressing locality. To obtain brightness of appearance under all weather conditions and despite extreme austerity of form, he resorted to contrast of colour by using light grey bricks, Portland stone, and a high grade Portland cement retaining its whiteness, in conjunction with the fenestration. Subjecting these elements to the same geometrising process as that applied to the elements of, say, the Thiepval Memorial, he arrived at the chequer-board pattern which makes this regiment of cubes unique in housing. The austerity is softened by a batter in the walls of six inches from base to parapet, a diminishing progression of the windows, concealing of pipes behind the galleries, and beautifully designed little shop-pavilions and gatepiers between the blocks on the street frontages.

'Nobody else', observes Mr. Butler, 'would have had the imagination or courage to do anything so odd yet so successful.' Twenty years after their erection they illumine their neighbourhood, and the most valid criticism is that some of the rooms are over-windowed. Housing sentimentalists, however, have tended to regard this apparent subjection of human needs to a geometrical ratio as implying in Lutyens a lack of 'social conscience'. How that virtue of the heart is to be combined with the intellectual one of tidiness that Lutyens set himself (and here achieved so signally) was a problem which assailed him some years later when he surveyed the untidiness of socially conscious suburban layout from the air.

All the trends that we have denoted and followed in this chapter are combined in his handling of the Washington Embassy, for which F. H. Brooks of Washington was the architect on the spot, and the late Harry Wardman, of the Wardman Corporation, the builder from his specifications. The site's slope gave opportunity for dramatic use of the levels, whilst its 'P' shape—narrow at the approach end, widening beyond—presented just the kind of difficulty that stimulated him. The representative nature of an embassy suggested, particularly in the garden city of Washington, a traditional English character—country house Wrennaissance. But its official status, no less than American Colonial memories, justified a strong classical element. Finally the significance of the building rendered a certain monumentality essential. The functional problem was to serve the Embassy's two distinct purposes on this restricted site and within this aesthetic combination; those of the Chancery, and of the Embassy proper, the latter uniting the social and private requirements of an ambassador. Prominent among the social requirements was that a large proportion of the site available should be reserved as a garden for receptions, and a ballroom with the requisite circulation be provided in the Embassy.

From the outset he found that the 4-acre site, with its restricted approaches, and the funds available to meet the high cost of building in America, barely sufficed for covering these needs with the appropriate amplitude and dignity. The land was obtained by exchange of the old Embassy site on Connecticut Avenue and was therefore dependent on the value obtained for the latter. Not till the building was finished was the frontage on Massachusetts Avenue extended by further purchase of land. These original limitations must be remembered in view of the criticisms subsequently made that the accommodation is cramped. It could scarcely have been foreseen in the 'twenties, certainly not by the Treasury mind, that the business of the Washington Embassy, or more exactly the Chancery, would increase in extent and complexity to the degree witnessed in the 'forties. At the time, the primary need was a dignified residence for the Ambassador, capable of providing hospitality on the scale of an English country house, attached to a Chancery of which the Foreign Office specified the accommodation required and likely to be required. The relative importance of the two parts of the building at the date it was designed are accurately reflected in the view of them from Massachusetts Avenue: a forecourt enclosed on three sides by the Chancery, above the flat roofs of which the end of the Embassy is seen rising beyond (p. 489). Had the wider frontage been available at the time, and the extension of business been foreseeable—assuming also a more liberal financial outlook—the whole setting out would have been different, but could scarcely have been more effective.

Given the conditions in force, Lutyens's handling of them was one of his cleverest feats. He planted the Embassy proper on the high ground at the further end of the site, where space was available for its garden and service quarters. Its front looks south-east, commanding a view over the city from its portico. This use of the slope secured the dominance of the Ambassador's residence over the Chancery, and brought its ground floor on a level with the upper, main floor of the Chancery set on the lower end of the site. It also provided the solution of the problem of access.

Approach to both buildings had to be from the same direction, the north-east, from Massachusetts Avenue, where the Chancery must also be accorded the maximum frontage. The raising of the Embassy enabled Lutyens to bring the approaches to it round the back of the Chancery to an entrance in the basement of the Embassy at the point where the two buildings are linked at the higher level (ground floor of Embassy, first floor of Chancery). The link is, appropriately, the Ambassador's study, accessible from both residence and office, which is in the nature of a bridge, forming a *porte cochère*. Beneath this is the principal entry to the Embassy, with a broad double staircase ascending to its ground floor. At their head these staircases give into a corridor running the full length of the building, with drawing-room and dining-room at the further end, the Ambassador's room on the bridge at the nearer. In mid-course this corridor passes between the ballroom, occupying the middle of the building, and the garden portico, which together form the centre axis of the Embassy proper.

The elevations of the latter are reminiscent, in their reliance on the structural elements—wall, roof, chimney, window—of Chelsea Hospital. But they are given the Lutyensian quality of intensity by the steeper angle of the roof (p. 489) rising from the deep stone frieze without cornice projection. The effect, characteristic of all his later work, is to add an expression of alertness, keenness, tautness—as of a face with wide open eyes and brows raised—to the firm, sane, balance of the mass as a whole. In this sense, the Washington Embassy expresses the nature, almost one might say the appearance, of its designer with extraordinary faithfulness.

It also expresses, no less truthfully, the plan already outlined. The most ingenious feature of this was the handling of the entrance, which is expressed by the dominance, on the Chancery axis, of the Embassy's side-elevation, where it is seen above the raised pediment over the Chancery entrance in the centre. Here the ground slopes gently to the Avenue, and in this, the public, view the composition is balanced between the tall terminal pavilions which soar over the Chancery's flat roofs. These pavilions have not only a basement but an attic storey and steep-pitched roof, further stressed by a single culminating chimney stack. These twin exclamations contain, in their upper storeys, the caretaker's flat and record storage respectively. Aesthetically they illustrate Lutyens's axiom that, in a design on a sloping site, dominating mass is required at the lower end. He never expressed the axiom, which is fundamentally scenic and picturesque, with such forcible result, except at Castle Drogo. So these emphatic terminals, culminating the last big work of his most productive period,[1] are rooted in the Surrey countryside of the 'eighties, with the shade of Randolph Caldecott

far, far away
With his horse and his hounds in the morning.

§3. THE HEAD OFFICE

Such is a selection from the most prolific years of the man who produced more work than any English architect since Wren; work that is signed in almost every line and moulding, and which no other contemporary could quite match, though many tried. How did he do it, employing only, with two or three notable exceptions, a quite ordinary, young, semi-trained, and frequently changed staff? In New York he was astonished by the affluence of architects, and, whilst he genuinely admired the scale of their work and the quality of some of it, used to sum up his general impression as 'thousands of everything and nothing in particular'. The contrast between it and his work was as great as between the spacious, efficient, admirably equipped offices of American architects and the austere makeshift of 17 Queen Anne's Gate.

The office had moved in 1911 to this outwardly fine Queen Anne House which, however, preserved none of its original detail within; was, indeed, almost bare. For most of the war the place had been sublet, work being doubled up with that of the Delhi Office in Apple Tree Yard, until 1919 when it reopened. Of the attractive team whom we met in Bloomsbury Square, none had remained continuously with Lut, as they called him, except A. J. Thomas and E. E. Hall, the latter now manager at Apple Tree Yard. The rest were established in practices of their own, had disap-

---

[1] The criticisms levelled at the Washington Embassy from both practical and visual aspects have been amusingly expressed by Harold Nicolson (*Spectator*, May 28, 1948):

> There are few architects for whose work I have greater esteem.... He did, it is true connect the Chancery building with the Ambassador's study by a bridge which casts a gloom over the main entrance. [But] he failed to provide the Ambassador with any private sitting-rooms, with the result that two of the bedrooms have had to be diverted for this purpose. He failed to provide '*dégagement*', with the result that at an official reception the guests cannot leave the building without having to push through the later guests as they arrive. And he constructed an enormous central corridor which, although a magnificent architectural achievement, diminished the space essential to the state dining-room and drawing-room.... The garden front is of impressive design; but the Chancery block is internally inconvenient and externally a cramped and pitiable affair, and, since it faces the street, the whole building presents an ungainly appearance to the outside world.... Sir Edwin was apt to introduce into his architecture those private jokes which rendered him so adorable as a companion. He thus inserted into the main staircase a small window through which the Ambassador's children might peep at the guests; that was an amiable device. Yet when Sir Ronald Lindsay first took up residence he found that every cupboard in the house (and there were hundreds of them) possessed a different Chubb lock and that the keys which fitted these locks bore no indication of the cupboard to which they belonged. It took several days of hard work before a single cupboard could be opened. And my word how Lutyens laughed!
>
> [The confusion of the keys can scarcely be laid at the Architect's door.]

peared, died, or been killed. Among assistants, the oldest inhabitant in 1919 was George Stewart, who had come in 1911 and was to remain on the establishment to contribute his unique experience to the authors of these records. But S. H. Evans had returned, with a wounded arm, to the war-time office, which had mainly consisted of J. P. Nightingale, H. A. N. Medd, C. H. James, Garrett, Wands and Miss Nauheim. The post of secretary to Lut continued, as in the past, to be filled on short tenure till the coming in 1922 of Miss Beatrice Webb, stalwart, cheerful, single-minded, and tirelessly efficient, who remained till there were none but she and Stewart. Last, but first to be encountered at Queen Anne's Gate, there was Mr. Tribe, a former bus-driver with that calling's robust humour, who lived with Mrs. Tribe in the basement and performed the functions best perhaps described as groom-porter.

There were two rooms on each floor. The ground floor front was Thomas's, Miss Webb ruled in the back. In the first-floor front the hard core of the office worked, with Lut's office adjoining at the back. Two or three smaller rooms on the floor above were occupied by the floating population of young draughtsmen, never more than five or six at a time.

In the first-floor front room the same spirit prevailed in the 'twenties as at Bloomsbury Square, if never so rampageous. The industrious Stewart worked away at country houses, always helpful to newcomers but not responsible for them. Garrett was engaged entirely on memorials. Absorbed and mysterious, revelling in subtleties, his work was particularly apt to arouse the ire of the 'old man', from whose room he would emerge injured and indignant, to receive little sympathy from his colleagues. Evans, working on gardens, but soon to set up on his own again, perhaps remembered the early days too well to associate himself wholly with the new team. Yet they had their glee club, and, round the immense table that occupied the middle of the room, all assembled for the tea-break, when cakes would be provided on birthdays or by the odd sweepstake winner. The day officially started at 9.30 and ended at six, but few of the men were clock-watchers. Leading assistants commonly and ungrudgingly left only in time to catch the last train home, and when there was a 'panic' might spend all night in the office. A 'panic' was an intensification of the high pressure at which, for all its superficial air of genial camaraderie, the office was expected, and unquestioningly impelled, to function by Lutyens's unsparing, dynamic, almost hypnotic, force.

Outside the office he might appear as jester, dreamer, schoolboy, or in the light of any of the facets whose colours diversify this narrative. But in the office he was at once all of them and none. He was wholly himself, incandescently serious though emitting sparks of feeling, irritation and humour. He worked, which with him meant drew, or rather scribbled—inventing, experimenting, correcting, revising, or scrapping—at a white heat.

Punctually at 10 o'clock he would arrive, call for Tribe to pay the taxi—until

James and the Rolls came into existence—then, advancing with his very short, quick, almost dancing steps, preoccupied and benign-looking, be heard calling impatiently in his muffled, nasal, tones for Thomas and the day's appointments. He might be detained for quarter of an hour by technical discussions with Thomas, but rarely allowed him more before trying to slip up to his room to get on with whatever he had in mind, if possible unobserved by the queue of assistants waiting to catch him. It was a repellantly barren place, his room. He had torn out its chimney piece and was content with the large open wound and generous fire which was left. He worked with his back to this at an antiquarian board, to the right of which Tribe had arranged six pipes, already filled, and a new box of matches against his coming. These he smoked, or rather lit, or affected to light, almost continuously, the consumption of matches rising with the pitch of his concentration, so that at the end of the morning Tribe, judging from the mess, could report, or not, 'the old man didn't arf panic this morning'. In his room there was another board in the window at which an assistant was sometimes privileged to work. But the rest of it was a sea of drawings among which the devil, he would complain, was always hiding the rubber and compasses. There were no drawings or pictures hung on the bare white, rather grubby, walls. The occasional client penetrated to this room, with considerable astonishment, but tradesmen, builders, or craftsmen seldom.

But there was a steady stream of assistants bringing the results of the previous day's, or it might be night's, work for his approval, or rather emendation, since he rarely passed any drawing in every detail. He always saw the author of the drawing himself, however junior. Each man was directly responsible to him and so, each knew, for some part if not the whole of every Lutyens conception. He never went round their boards or inquired how jobs were going, but it was the routine that at every stage they should be brought to him for revision or questions. He would explode loudly and frequently. He was never completely satisfied with everything and was always liable to have had second thoughts himself involving entire recasting of a drawing or many drawings. For some assistants it was a daily ordeal to face what must often have seemed to them his abuse of an honest effort. At least one nervous youth so much dreaded the interview that he had always to wash his clammy hands before entering. Garrett, perhaps because his memorial work involved Lut's most complex and subtle conceptions, was liable to the most severe criticism. No doubt Lutyens was often sorely tried by his devoted, but human, slaves. His letters from Delhi alone exist to record his aspect of the process, which functioned similarly there, and occasionally betray impatience at what seemed to him his staff's reprehensible requests for leave. But always after a particularly stinging assault he would relent and say, 'That's all right me boy. I'm not angry with you. It's the job.'

It was also the method. By making these ordinary men the instruments of his extraordinary faculties, thus bringing each into the closest possible communion with his creative emotion on some part of a conception, this method made them subject to his own impatience with himself. He never himself made a finished drawing now, and nobody now saw him use ink. Though such a masterly draughtsman, and his little explanatory sketches a delight, he worked, occasionally, on a rough full-size, but generally on squared paper plentifully figured or, once a drawing existed, on a 9-inch strip of rolled tracing paper. The preparation of these rolls, which had a homely name, was another of Tribe's chores. In addition, there were his pocket pads, the 'virgins', which he used for recording impromptu notes and ideas. Equipped with these, then, and working in a slough of loose tobacco, spent matches, bits of india-rubber, and unwanted instruments, he sat or stood to deal with the succession of drawings laid before him by assistants, one of whom, W. A. S. Lloyd (who for some months worked at the board in the window) we may now accompany.

> To start you off, [says Lloyd] he would give you a squared paper draught or one or two scribbles on virgins, always basically dimensioned. You would then go away and thrash it out, with the aid of Batty Langley ('The Bible'),[1] or, if you were very raw, of the hints of someone a little older in the office, and the precedent of an earlier job. Back you would go for more instructions, sometimes merely to be told to 'go and do it again', but generally to have the rough places made a little smooth, a little not always explained, by pushing, pulling, and adjusting of balances.

These emendations, however, would be made not on the drawing but on the tracing rolls, usually a succession of alternatives, the strip getting longer and longer until the final variant was approved and ringed round. Off the draughtsman went again to incorporate the amendment.

> You were generally fairly clear from your original instructions of the elements of the composition, of the essential rhythm of the pattern, and, even if this sometimes led to fantastic fractions, the basic reason was always simple. There were certain elementary rules which, once seized, had to be applied throughout the whole building or composition. For instance, all window-panes had to be identical in proportion, generally in that of a square to its diagonal in height. If the key arch of a design was, say, $1\frac{1}{2}$ squares to the spring, all others would echo or fundamentally change that ratio. The nearly similar was not accepted. All mouldings, with the exception of an occasional cyma, were set at an angle of $54 \cdot 45°$ to the horizontal, thereby attaining a true $45°$ on the mitre. Roofs followed suit, being only as it were major mouldings.
> In earlier days the angle of his roofs was $51 \cdot 5°$, that of the pyramid. But the angle of $54 \cdot 45°$, being that formed by the relation of a square to its diagonal,

---

[1] *The City and Country Builder's and Workman's Treasury of Designs*, or *The Art of Drawing and Working the Ornamental Parts of Architecture*. Edition of 1750.

148. WASHINGTON: THE BRITISH EMBASSY 1926. Entrance front

149. GARDEN FRONT OF THE BRITISH EMBASSY, WASHINGTON

150. PLUMPTON PLACE, SUSSEX (1927). The 'Gatehouse' containing cottages and the bridge over the moat

151. THE GRANGE, ROTTINGDEAN. The main sitting room as redecorated 1919

and ruling as it also did in rectangles, was adopted and rarely departed from in the last 30 years. 'Never' is a word Lut would not accept. He made his rules but was not a slave to them and would shake the purist by occasional arbitrary and unexplained departure from them.

The 'spent curve', as he called it, was anathema. All mouldings were built up of arcs of various simple constructions. This also applied to domes, niches, etc., the semicircle never being allowed, except in the arch, to complete itself. He thought continually in three dimensions, if not four, and set no store by a drawing other than as a statement of intention. 'Don't portmanteau it' was standard criticism of an over-crowded elaborate drawing. The facts must be set out without confusion for the simple.

He worked entirely by relation of parts, thereby involving all in extraordinary fractions. An instance notorious in the office at the time was the diminishing height of the rustication blocks on the Midland Bank, each of which was to be a mathematical fraction less than the one below it and involved a diminution by the amount of ·273 recurring of an inch. He would admit of no approximation in the drawings, on the plea that plenty of inaccuracies would creep in without beginning in the office. 'About! I dont know what you mean by "about",' he would say. At any time he was prepared to alter his fundamental unit if he saw a better, thereby jettisoning all drawings to date and thereby causing all-night last-minute 'panics' in the office. Three times in my three years did I spend all night in the office, and we frequently left only to catch the last train home.

The most complete set of drawings prepared in and sent out from the office at one time was the remarkable set of sixty-eight sheets prepared before 1927 for the Washington Embassy. English architects are apt to have their American colleagues held up to them as examples in this respect. But this masterly product of Queen Anne's Gate created something of a sensation even in the land of streamlined offices and meticulous detail.

He himself never worked late now, or missed lunch at the Garrick, the Athenæum ('I like to wash my hands between two bishops' he would say of the latter), or with friends. In the afternoon he went to the Delhi Office and much the same procedure would be repeated, though there the staff was apt to be larger and, the overall pace being more measured, there was less liability to panics. Or he had to go out to a job or a conference. He always grudged time spent away from his drawing-board and never believed that his assistants were really working unless they were at their boards. But he was exceedingly punctual at all appointments, and expected clients and others to be equally so, having probably created a minor panic in the office in order to gain the time to absent himself. When Hore Belisha, then Minister of Transport, arrived at a conference for which Lutyens, the contractor and several others had been kept waiting, and observed cheerfully 'Ah! Quite a Cabinet Meeting,' he rejoined coldly 'but much more intelligent'. On the other hand, if he were in the wrong, he would confess it as disarmingly as he had on that occasion to Lady Hardinge. At a meeting on the site of the Midland Bank in connection with Ancient Lights owned by adjoining properties, Sir Reginald Blomfield was among the representatives of the latter. Lutyens, finding himself in error on some complicated issue, said nothing but stepped towards Blomfield, turned his back on him, lifted the tail of his coat, and bent forward.

His departures for more extended expeditions were attended with considerable flurry. There were feverish calls to Tribe to ensure that his bag contained the requisite quantities of virgins, tracing-rolls, paper, matches, tobacco, and such plans as would be required, and, if the journey was by train, a mad rush to enable him to catch it with a very wide margin; for he was addicted to train fever. It was when he was out of the office that he did the greater part of his conceptive thinking. Many designs originated on the return journey from sites, and problems would solve themselves in the course of committees to which he was listening with only half an ear, or at home. The solution, scribbled on a virgin or the back of an envelope, would be produced next morning for some assistant to disentangle. It might be a sketch drawing, or ratio of proportions noted in figures, that had thus suddenly become finite.

His ideas were always elementally simple at bottom. It was their working out and relating with the absolute lucidity that he demanded which involved endless revision. Endless it was apt to be, especially in his later years, when the responsible assistant had to exercise his own judgment as to where to halt the process by insisting that the drawings had to be sent off tomorrow. Otherwise Lut might continue indefinitely elaborating or simplifying the pure mathematical relations in which he delighted, those proportions in circle, sphere, square, cube, square and a half, square to diagonal, double square, and no 'about' about it.

Similarly with materials, he was delighted if, at the outset, their substance or optimum dimensions would give the basic character or unit of a design, as is illustrated in this letter to A. G. Shoosmith, written on P. & O. paper (with elaborated heading[1]) and dated February 13, 1928, à propos his representative's commission to design the Cantonments Church at Delhi:[2]

My Dear Shoo,
    Bricks!
    A building of one material is for some strange reason much more noble than one of many.

[1] Namely, depicting the moral injunctions 'Be a strong man', 'Avoid Shikar,' 'Avoid the Social,' 'Be as Solomon and brick your church in terms of cubits.' (See p. 436).

[2] This elementally forceful little building is undoubtedly one of the finest modern brick churches.

It may be the accent it gives of sincerity, the persistence of texture and definite unity.

The Romans used brick most magnificently, and used bricks 3 ft. long.

I have used bricks 3 ft. long in England. They cost about £5 each, the difficulty being to dry them and lift them about prior to burning.

In India there should be no such difficulty in the hot weather and a big brick goes further than a little one. Q.E.D.

Make your bricks 12 in × 6 in × 2
18 × 6 × 2
24 × 6 × 2
30 × 6 × 2
36 × 6 × 2

If you must cope, use thinner bricks, i.e. tiles.

A cement wash will keep moisture out better than a thick cope of cement, which cracks. Then cement is so liable to fissure, and I know if cement ever gets smeared on pavement you can never get it off.

Dont use, whatever you do, bricks on edge or any fancy stuff. It only destroys scale and promotes triviality.

Try bricks of varying thickness. 3 inches at the base working up at the top of your tower to 1 in. thick. They are just as easy to make as any other shape, and £5 will cover the cost of all moulds.

The Romans did it! Why should not Britons?

You will get a fine wall, and their mass, proportion, with precious fenestration, will do the rest.

Get rid of all mimicky Mary-Ann notions of brickwork and go for the Roman wall.

I hope you get that pavement right in H. E. Council's Court.

Homage to the mem-sahib Shoo.

'God sees it,' he would exclaim when taxed with setting detail where no man could view it. But, as Lloyd justly adverts in quoting the phrase, 'he took God for a gentleman only interested, as he was, in the visual aspect of a building from all angles but not over curious of how it stood up.'

For the office dealt only in surfaces. Lut was not interested in what held the building up or composed the core, heated, or drained it. He left generous tolerances in these respects, and Thomas or collaborating architects and builders put in the stuffing and bones. All his buildings could have been built of the materials on the face [and he would have regarded them as 'noble' had they been], but he did not really mind, or recognize, the supporting steel, or concern himself greatly with the bonding of the thin bricks he liked using to the common backers.

He had the most vivid imagination of the life that was to walk his houses, but little sympathy with the confused multitudes that would occupy the pigeon holes of large city blocks, and his work showed it. He worked as a sculptor, painter, or modeller, and like them did not worry about the armature inside the cast, the weave of the canvas, or the quarrying of the stone.

'It takes a very great man to jump all these obstacles, and still run true,' concludes this former assistant, repeating in different words the identical verdict of those earlier Lutyens men given in Chapter 7. Lloyd, like Milne and Hannen twenty years before, distils Lutyens's genius finally to 'the true spirit', 'truth,' and reflects:

We in our turn, and our children after us, will tackle our chances in different ways. But we can learn from Lutyens's work to seek simplicity, never to compromise with 'good enough', never to forget the driving rhythm, to salt pomposity with humanity, and to look at work 'as God sees it', all round.

CHAPTER XVII

THE FINISHING OF VICEROY'S HOUSE

GOVERNMENT House was scheduled to be completed and occupied by the end of 1929. But at the beginning of 1928 that looked scarcely possible. By the end of 1926 the walls had reached chujja level; in 1927 the chujjas and roofs were being constructed and by the end of the year the wings were fairly complete. Indeed the south-east wing was fully finished at the end of 1927, when it began to be used for storing furniture. The main portico long lagged behind, owing to the precedence accorded to the Legislative and Secretariat Buildings for the white Dholpur stone, exceptionally large blocks of which were required for the drums of the portico columns. However, these were put in hand in 1927 and were finished by the end of that year. By 1928, therefore, the building was covered, including the inner dome of the Durbar Hall, thrown in 1927.

The outer dome was not begun till 1928. A very valuable economy in its construction, worth some £7000 which could therefore be expended elsewhere, was due to the initiative of J. L. Sale, Superintending Engineer. Lutyens had designed a brick cone, of the type used by Wren for St. Paul's, to carry the apex of the outer dome. Sale prepared a drawing demonstrating the possibility of doing without the cone. The drum of the dome consists of an inner and outer wall or skin. He proposed a reinforced concrete deck roofing the drum, tied to the inner dome, and also tying the skins of the drum together. The weight of the outer dome would rest on the inner skin of the drum (inclined slightly inwards) but also be distributed to the outer skin by means of the reinforced decking. Lutyens, after exhaustive examination, adopted the system. An advantage of the deck is that it provides a strong and level floor for the removable glass lid closing the eye of the inner dome. The strength of the construction permitted the centering for the outer dome to rest upon it and thereby enabled the Durbar Hall to be cleared so that work on the marble veneer could proceed during 1928.

Despite the delays imposed on Government House, after the completion of the Legislative Buildings and Secretariats in 1926–27 its construction went rapidly ahead, thanks to the devotion and energy of all concerned. But there was a time in 1928 when, to Lutyens's impatience, the progress, especially with the marble work in the Hall, was exasperatingly slow.

§1. QUESTIONS OF CRAFTSMANSHIP

His complaints were justified regarding the backwardness of the furniture and decorative fittings. For fifteen years he had been urging successive Viceroys and Secretaries of State to establish the Delhi School of design and craftsmanship for these purposes, had sat on innumerable Delhi Advisory Committees at home, and designed himself nearly every piece, clock, fitment, in the House. The school had never materialised, but under a cabinet-maker with the gift of leadership, Mr. F. Harding, a remarkable team of Indian cabinet-makers had been trained, who only needed materials. When the rooms were eventually being furnished, the first table made at Delhi came to light and was put in a place of honour. It was a table enamelled in blue and gold, and, seeing it again, Lutyens recalled how, when it had been proudly shown to the Vicereine of the time, she had exclaimed 'Oh, how very ugly!' Disappointed, he had told the Viceroy how it had been hoped to present the first piece made at New Delhi to Her Excellency. 'In a few minutes the Viceroy returned and told me what a beautiful table he and Her Excellency thought it. But I said I could not offer anything to her that she so greatly disliked.' The memory rankled.

The wood most extensively used was of course teak. But for the decorative furniture, padauk, shisham, ainee, blackwood, poon, koko, walnut, and ebony were also used. For making five- and seven-ply boards the assistance of the Forest Products Institute at Dehra Dun was of service. But the climate of New Delhi was particularly hard on furniture. Owing to its variation from 115°, with very low humidity, to almost complete saturation at 90° and to a dry cold at 30°, no timber, however hard and well seasoned could fail to move. The furniture most affected was the antiques imported from England.

The seasoning plant ordered at the beginning of Lord Irwin's Viceroyalty (1926) did not come into operation till 1928, so that much furniture including nearly all that for the State rooms, was not finished till after 1929. But the new Viceroy infused his keenness into all ranks so that the craftsmen performed prodigies within the limited time.

Lutyens said that he had received welcome help in this direction from the late Dr. Kennedy North, whom he had first met in connection with the Queen's Dolls' House. This versatile expert on the arts and the care of pictures was invited to Delhi by the P.W.D. to advise on technical and chemical aspects of craftsmanship, more particularly as bearing upon plasterwork in the new capital. As confident as competent, he seems to have put everybody's backs up, but got results by taking pains to show the right way of doing things, how to mix paint and put it on, how to make plaster and run fine mouldings. He was a born buffoon, but what he taught was remembered. The resident cadre managed to keep up this standard, much assisted by H. F. Wilson, the foreman carpenter and joiner, who was put in charge of all decorative finishings. During his unconventional investigations North reported discovering sundry skilled craftsmen, including a family at Lucknow possessing the wood blocks of the old India printed cottons. Lutyens was impressed by the quality of workmanship North had obtained, noting that 'he has found men who execute all the crafts I want for Government House; information I have tried to get from the Indian Civil Service for 13 years. I am very pleased and happy with what he has achieved'. As an example, however, of the kind of difficulties always arising, the printed fabrics were duly ordered from the Lucknow family, and the old blocks were used, but the colours and printing were so crude that they were useless. The craftsmanship had died for lack of discriminating patronage.

Lutyens was especially anxious that the weaving of the carpets for Government House should revive the standard of design and technique of the great Persian period. It was partly in this connection that he had gone to Kashmir, where some of the finest carpets were made.[1] For the Durbar Hall the design selected was a copy of a Persian Royal Garden carpet of the sixteenth century, fragments of the original of which were lent by Mr. H. D. MacLaren (now Lord Aberconway). Similarly for the other State Rooms, sixteenth and seventeenth century Persian originals were loaned so that not only the patterns but the dyes and materials should be reproduced and so revive standards of the age of Shah Abbas. The carpets occupied over 500 weavers two years. It was estimated that those for the Durbar Hall, dining-room and drawing-room alone contain 279,000,000 knots and that 7000 miles of wool was used. There can be no doubt that working on these carpets exercised, as Lutyens intended, an edifying influence on the designers and weavers employed and that, as works of art, they will be held by future generations of Indians in as high regard as, for instance, the precious collection of seventeenth-century Indian carpets preserved at Jaipur.

The possibility of Indian artists being employed to execute mural paintings in Government House, and to adorn the dome of Durbar Hall particularly, was considered. Lutyens frequently visited the Art Schools at Bombay, Calcutta, Lahore, and elsewhere, examined the local Schools of Architecture, and followed the progress that was being made on the paintings in the Secretariats. He was opposed to mural painting unless very carefully related to the design of his important buildings, as we have seen in connection with St. Jude's Church, Hampstead, and came to the conclusion that contemporary Indian work was fundamentally out of key with the conception of Government House. One of the Indian painters who applied for employment set forth his merits with no little confidence. Lutyens wanted to reply to his letter:

My Dear Michael
    (May I drop the Angelo?) I thank you so much for your letter. The only remark I can make is what a pity it is you cannot design, draw, or observe.

[1] The leading makers were Hadow's of Srinagar and Stavides of Lahore.

But he was advised not to. The only room painted in Government House was the Council Room where the decoration, designed by Percy Brown, Curator of the Victoria Memorial Hall, Calcutta and executed by Munshi Ghulam Husain, was restricted to pictorial maps.

In compensation for these and other worries he was sustained by the most sympathetic of the Viceroys with whom he had been engaged. He spent Christmas 1926 with Lord and Lady Irwin at Barrackpore, where the Crown Prince and Princess of Sweden were also staying, and was immediately delighted by the informal family atmosphere. He noticed, for instance, that after dinner, whereas another Viceroy, after the ladies had retired, would have sat in his chair smoking his cigarette and waiting for the men to be brought to sit at his right and left, 'Wood stands and waits, not sitting himself till his guests are seated.' He was invited to stay at Viceregal Lodge, Delhi, and it immediately became evident that there was a better spirit abroad. He found the Viceroy helpful and personally anxious to get things done, Lady Irwin businesslike and with imaginative taste, so that questions of furnishing, decoration, picture hanging, etc., could be settled amicably and immediately. As the House neared completion one or other was somewhere about the place almost every day. The furniture models chosen by the Advisory Committee and made in England were by then in production, with further pieces brought from England by Lady Irwin to be copied. Owing to the extremes of climate, some fell to bits; but it had cost little, and could be cheaply replaced. Continual difficulty was met with in the choice of fabrics for curtains and upholstery. The materials were Indian, and many of great beauty, but there again durability was not their common virtue.

There were incidents of light relief. He amused the Viceroy, who had asked the purpose of a very small room, by explaining it had been designed for Lord Hardinge's dog. He took much trouble in getting made, for use on fitting occasions, a trick bed which would tip its occupant on to the floor. He amused himself by designing a series of electroliers for the nurseries—simple but delightful painted wooden things embodying the kind of subjects he pictured in his letters to his children—four galloping ponies, four praying angels, and, the most ingenious, four hens and chicks with, hanging from each bracket, an egg which spills its yoke as the bulb of the light. Some of these are illustrated, with a sketch, on the opposite page. The nurseries, at the top of the Viceroy's wing, gave him welcome scope for play. One of them has a floor patterned in red and white for games of chess or backgammon. Being grouped round an internal court, the nursery gallery looking into it had to be fenced for safety with a screen. Into this he worked his idea for decorating his bungalow with parrots by introducing into each side of the screen an exquisite cage for a parrot.

'But this is our lightsome mood,' he confessed. 'The rest is solemn furniture; firedogs, fire-irons, fenders, clocks, lamps, stuffs, panelling, mantelpieces—no two

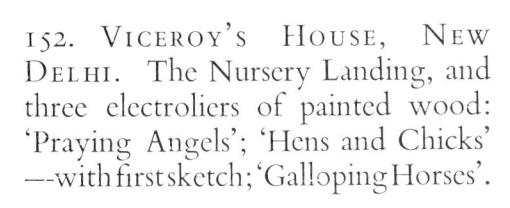

152. VICEROY'S HOUSE, NEW DELHI. The Nursery Landing, and three electroliers of painted wood: 'Praying Angels'; 'Hens and Chicks' —with first sketch; 'Galloping Horses'.

153. NEW DELHI. The Round Walled Garden at the west extremity of the Viceroy's Garden

154. ONE OF THE TWO BIG FOUNTAINS NEAR THE HOUSE AND THE SOUTHERN CANAL. The fountain, of red stone, is conceived as three tiers of water-lily leaves. On the skyline to the left is the stone framework for a bosquet

155. SOUTH RETAINING WALL OF THE VICEROY'S GARDEN, 40 feet high, and a gazebo

156. PART OF THE GARDEN FRONT OF VICEROY'S HOUSE

157. Air View of New Delhi, from the West. The analogy of the garden pattern to an intricate Persian carpet is evident. In the foreground, the Round Garden is contained by a ring of nurseries, bothies, frame-yards etc. The King's Way and War Memorial Arch in the distance

mantelpieces in the house are alike.' As these (some of which are illustrated on p. 514) and the immense quantity of marble-work gradually came into place, visitors became increasingly enthusiastic. 'You would have purred,' he wrote to his wife of what some of them had said.

He himself began to tire physically now, if as dynamic mentally as ever. He admitted that he was generally worn out at the end of each day with the continual walking involved by routine inspection. It took three to four hours to go round the House itself, not including the Viceroy's Press in the north side, the domestic quarters, kitchens, bungalows, and the garden. Often he went the round twice a day. But he had to admit that it looked well, simple and dignified, 'a gentleman's house, and, though original, it is, in that it is built in India, for India, Indian.' He was told it was twice as cool as the Secretariats.

§2. THE MOGHUL GARDEN

An unfailing coadjutor, of whom he could not speak in terms too high, was W. R. Mustoe, O.B.E., of the Horticultural Department, responsible for all planting since 1922 and now pushing forward the finishing of the garden. In the Safdar Jang nurseries every type of tree and shrub that would grow at Delhi was propagated; five hundred varieties were established in and about the city; and the enormous quantities of roses required were only matched by their beauty. Where there had been a desert in 1928, by January of 1929, were

> masses of beautiful roses, the tanks run and reflect and ripple, and my rainbow in the deep fountain has come off—a vivid rainbow. Children *can* find its end! Last night it gave a lunar rainbow. The roses are wonderful, the mignonette scents the whole place. I am making a butterfly garden—of all the plants butterflies like.

Mustoe or Sale would breakfast with him nearly every day. One morning the former was almost in tears owing to a sudden frost in the night having worked havoc with his annuals. On another morning a veterinary surgeon, 'a sort of St. Francis who lives with birds and beasts,' came to advise on the placing of nesting boxes for birds in the garden. Some of the fountains took a good deal of coaxing before they would play. One of them which refused to respond finally exploded geyserlike whilst experiment in control of the water levels in the channels was in progress, enveloping its creator in mud.

The 'Moghul garden' that with Mustoe's help had thus at length been brought to beauty is as impossible to depict in words as a great Persian carpet of which the pattern was inspired by similar compositions (pp. 500–2). It is invisible except from the west windows of the House, being raised above the adjoining plain on its retaining bastions which prolong those of Viceroy's Court. The skeleton is formed of four waterways, two north to south, two running east-west from square basins immediately below the windows of the House. In these basins and at the four intersections are most singular fountains consisting in three tiers of huge red sandstone discs inspired by the giant leaves of the Victoria Regia Lily. The foam of the central jet, which rises to twelve feet, splashes on their slightly recessed surfaces and pours through slots in their margins to the next tier and the next, the general effect being horizontal rather than vertical. From the four waterways a network of lesser channels playing about many kinds of round, square and lozenge-shaped stepping-stones, extends at what may be termed the water-level of the garden, its central area. This is patterned with red sandstone edges and plots of lawn alternating with chequered flower beds. At the upper level, five steps above the waterways, a complementary pattern of paved walks and stone-boxed beds, the walks carried over the channels by unparapetted bridges, superposes a secondary design which is carried round the whole as its frame. The two levels, emphasised by the fountains and the luxuriant colour-masses, counteract any impression of flatness. It is a vast carpet that one sees, but by this means it is given thick texture even under an almost vertical sun. In the evening, when the long level mass of the House throws its shade over the nearer lawns, the patterns in the carpet spring into relief as each runnel and bed catches its own ray and throws its own shadow. The trees, set in geometrical groves for the most part round the edges but also near the House, have now grown to emphasise the third dimension which was only implied at the time by the sense of texture. On the axis of the dome and enclosed by these jewelled parterres lies the Vice-regal lawn for the receptions which were the social *raison d'être* of the garden.

By now, too, flowering creepers have clothed what were very curious features provided for that purpose on the West boundary: a skeleton tower at each corner, and masonry hoops contained by pylons flanking the flights of steps descending to sunk tennis courts beyond. In the middle of the west end the central vista passes between walls to the circular privy garden (p. 500), surrounded by a double wall (the interspace for gardeners' purposes), and containing a round pool. Here the massed segmental flower beds offered the butterflies the refreshment to which Lutyens referred. Incidentally he had projected a butterfly garden for Lady Sackville in one of her numerous projects a decade earlier. It is the end, an ultimate secret retreat, of the colossal linear conception that begins two miles away at the Memorial Arch (p. 502).

From the north and south sides of the main garden, bastions project supporting rose gardens from which the eye can range over the domain stretching in semi-circle westward to the skyline of the Ridge, or over the city landscape north and south. Between them, at the foot of the wall, gardens of clipped box and herbs make cubic designs remembered by Lutyens from his sight of the Escorial it may be (p. 501).

§3. OPEN HOUSE

At the beginning of 1929, less than a year before the Viceroy's entry to the House, much was still unfinished. In Viceroy's Court (p. 511) the wrought iron of the screen was being erected, and was not completed till 1930. None of the white sculptured elephants and lamps surmounting the piers were erected till after the House was occupied. The long masonry tanks and fountains flanking the approach were holding water. But though the marble effigies of George V and Queen Mary took their place beside the portico, the pedestals above the steps for the bronze horses were, and are still, empty. In the centre of the Court, the Jaipur Column, commemorating the 1911 Durbar and initiation of the new city, still lacked its capital. The monument, 144 feet high (p. 331), has a white sandstone shaft of only seven feet (average) diameter, which is spined with a drawn steel tube to give additional support to the crystal star and bronze lotus surmounting it and weighing five tons. This tube is anchored to the reinforced concrete core of the base. The exquisite elasticity of the structure is indicated by the observation that the tip of the star is liable to oscillate up to six inches in a stiff breeze. In 1929 the temperamental carver Giudicci was still cutting the bas-reliefs on the base, which C. S. Jagger had modelled. The star was not put in position till 1930.

Though the projected buildings on the Kingsway were non-existent, the War Memorial Arch was rising for its dedication in 1931. In place of the Cathedral intended to fill a prominent place in the early plans, the Church of the Redeemer had been built on another site from the designs of H. A. N. Medd, formerly in Lutyens's office and now Baker's principal assistant.[1]

Nomenclatures and dedications occupied his thoughts not a little as his labours neared their end. With the exception of churches' dedications, to which he attached deep significance—perhaps desiring to visualise for Whom precisely he was designing—he set no store by names and inscriptions in the early stages. Indeed the reverse, since he once pointed out that God asked Adam to name the beasts *after* He had created them, whereas some architects seemed to him, as he put it, to name their animals before starting to create them. But the subject was raised in February, 1929, by the King's decision that Government House should be known as Viceroy's House. Lord Irwin also asked for inscriptions for the Jaipur Column and the Viceregal Thrones. Lutyens described how he and friends had 'combed the Psalms and Proverbs', without success, and he had himself written a number of such sentences for the thrones; and for the Jaipur Column the noble words that are prefixed to Part II of this book:

---

[1] The church has now been raised to a Cathedral. It was due to Lutyens that the site for it was moved from the official quarter to one more accessible. He selected Medd's design in preference to one by an assistant in his own office.

> *Endow your thought with faith*
> *Your deed with courage*
> *Your life with sacrifice*
> *So all men may know*
> *The Greatness of India.*

Lord Irwin distilled from this the conciser version used:

> *In thought faith in word wisdom*
> *In deed courage in life service*
> *So may India be great.*

For the thrones, Mrs. Shoosmith helped him with suitable inscriptions, from which Lord Irwin chose, 'Wisdom resteth in the heart of him that hath understanding,' from *Proverbs*.

In these early months of 1929 the outer dome of Viceroy's House, symbol and hub of his whole conception, sprang from its drum and was curving to its eye. Its reinforced concrete shell took shape, upon the centering supported upon the deck of the lower dome, within eleven weeks. The copper casing of the dome, however, was not laid till the following year. During the ensuing heat of 1929, the under surface of the inner dome was rendered and the final polishing given to the marbles of its walls and floor. The last stone on the eye of the outer dome was laid in April, 1929, eighteen years from its genesis and seven months before the appointed day, by Lord Irwin in the presence of a select company who had been hoisted aloft for the short but vertiginous ceremony. Lutyens was not present, having already returned to England.

But we may imagine ourselves perched on that vantage point, one morning in December, 1929. Our situation was almost identical when we supposed ourselves suspended from Lord Hardinge's balloon at this very point in 1913, surveying the arid contours of Raisina Hill. But, where then was a wilderness of rock and scrub and spoil heaps are now acres of roofs and courts and canals, eighty miles of tree-planted roads, the living carpet of a Moghul's garden, numberless offices, bungalows, and the appurtenances of the Indian capital radiating about our eminence. From Viceroy's Court below us, through Government Court and then beyond the fountains of the Great Place, the 800 feet wide perspective of Kings Way stretches eastward to the Memorial Arch beyond which the antique walls of Purana Kila, now surrounded by the beginnings of a considerable park, overlook the waters of the Jumna.

A car mounts one of the slopes guarded by the red sandstone elephants into Viceroy's Court, and, passing between the long eastward-reaching wings of the House, disappears beneath an arch in the red plinth of the façade, to emerge in the South Court. The Architect is about to make one of his three-hour tours of the palace. We will accompany him with the winged feet of imagination which speed time and space.[1]

To-day he has no business in the vast lower basement where the kitchens, ranged just beneath the court in which he stands, are reached by tradesmen through the cave-like arcades that support the court's southern parapet, and whence lengthy brick-vaulted corridors conduct to bakeries, sculleries, dairies, wine-cellars, all kinds of stores, the boiler room, workshops, and ultimately to the Viceroy's Press in the north side. Nor does he turn to his left towards the entrance to the Viceroy's residence in the south-west wing—though we shall have a sight of that self-contained house later. The car might proceed forward, into one of the two arched tunnels beneath the main block, and, depositing him like a guest to a State function at one of the entrances *en route*, come out into the North Court and so emerge through another arch into Viceroy's Court again.

Instead, he returns on foot the way he has come, to the east front, and ascends the cascade of steps to the great portico of twelve unevenly spaced white columns, three deep in the centre. They have the basic type of his Delhi capital, many variations of which can be noticed within (p. 512). The doors open, at the head of a further flight of steps, to the transverse Vestibule 40 ft. high, half as wide and nearly twice as long, lined with the marble used throughout the corridors, i.e. the white Makrana figured with grey, brown, yellow, blue and pink. From the vault hang three bronze lanterns 6 ft. high (p .512).

We are now on the Main Floor. Were our visit *en prince*—for this *entrée* was to be reserved for Highnesses—we should move forward immediately into the presence of the King Emperor's representative beneath the Durbar Dome. Instead the Architect turns to his left into one of the two arched and saucer-domed corridors, 21 ft. wide and 210 ft. long, paved with grey and white marble, that run either side of the Hall (p. 513). He glances into the State Supper Room in the south-east corner; but follows the corridor westwards to the landing of the South Main Staircase. This, balancing a counterpart north of the Hall, is of the white marble enclosed in the red sandstone structure of the lower storey, with arches supporting its vaulted ceiling. From the crown of that hang two colossal bronze lanterns, inside each of which three men actually worked on the wiring as it hung (p. 513). From the landing three arches give into the Hall.

Three State Drawing-Rooms now cut the axis of the corridor. The Architect turns into the middlemost of them, the State Drawing-Room (p. 514), which adjoins the west periphery of the Hall and is a barrel-vaulted gallery 108 feet long, with

---

[1] *The Architecture*, Vol. II contains a comprehensive analysis and description of the interior of Viceroy's House, related to its conception as a whole. For the full appreciation of Lutyens's master-work this close relationship must of course be studied in the plans, and its perfection of treatment in the detail drawings, there included. The description that follows here aims only at conveying the general character of the plan and apartments, so many allusions to the evolution of which have occurred in this volume.

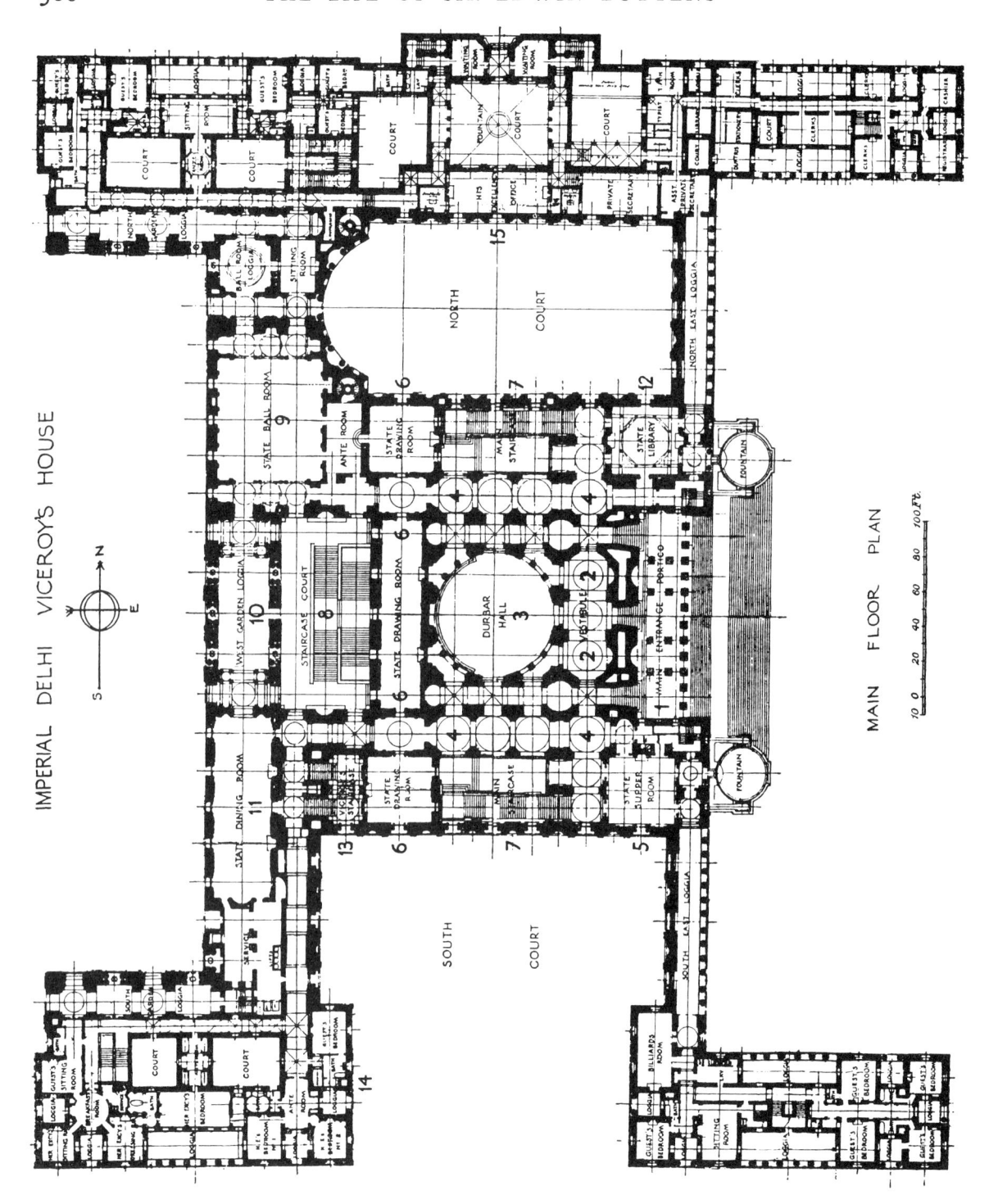

1. Portico. 2. Vestibule. 3. Durbar Hall. 4–4. North and South Corridors. 5. State Supper Room. 6–6. State Drawing-Room. 7–7. North and South Main Staircases. 8. Staircase Court. 9. State Ballroom. 10. West Garden Loggia. 11. State Dining-Room. 12. State Library. 13. The Viceroy's Staircase. 14. The Viceroy's Wing. 15. The Viceroy's Office.

two fireplaces and ranges of white marble pilasters, the intervening wall covered with cloth of gold. The room contains some of the most graceful and intricate furniture designed and made for the House. One of the most gorgeous of the Kashmir carpets runs its length, bordered by an Indian pattern of grey and white marble, and lit by four of the loveliest of the palace's crystal chandeliers. The five windows in its western wall overlook the Staircase Court, open to the dark velvet of the Indian night—a Veronesque conception (which we shall return to enjoy). With the open colonnades of the West Loggia beyond it, this internal court serves to separate the State Rooms which we are exploring from the Viceroy's State Suite that occupies the main floor of the west front. We will reach this in a moment from the further end of this exquisite gallery, by way of the North Corridor. But first we are led across the latter into the northern of these three drawing-rooms. Like its south sister, it is square, and panelled in teak which in this case rises only about two-thirds of its height, being surmounted by a high coved ceiling. Its rounded form is echoed by the room's rounded corners, silver sconces glitter against the panelling, and the sense of homeliness engendered (in contrast to the marble magnificence hitherto) is fulfilled by easy chairs and sofas.

The North Corridor is prolonged to the Garden Front as a lobby to the Ballroom from which it is separated by three arches repeated beyond the dancing floor by those of a counterpart. Here guests could meet separated from the dancers whose dresses and uniforms looked the brighter against the walls of white marble and old English mirrors beneath the glow of six crystal chandeliers. The walls above the marble, left plain to strengthen this contrast, were subsequently enlivened by misplaced painted decoration.

At either end, the Ballroom gives into loggias in the west front. That to the north is square, with an eye to the sky in its coffered roof, and affords possible access to the Guests' wing through the North-west Garden Loggia. But the sensational moment here is when, from a short corridor that we have crossed unnoticed, we suddenly catch a glimpse inwards, across the North Court, through an answering aperture in its east end, along one of the tanks of Viceroy's Court aligned transversally on the loggias of the Secretariats in the distance. That exact and tremendous perspective is one of the datum lines over which Lutyens and Baker sweated blood in the earliest months of Delhi: not merely so as to give this peep, but to ensure the perfect architectural adjustment of their spheres of which this is an almost incidental aspect.

From the south end of the Ballroom, beyond the lobby by which we entered, opens the great loggia that occupies the centre of the Garden Front. This is the most enchanted of all these architectural lungs that interpenetrate the palace and which Lutyens elaborated from the common Indian verandah (p. 515). Of cream stone, with patterned grey and white marble floor, it has a barrel vault 65 feet long and is prolonged between arcades by lower vaulted extensions. Its long sides are supported by columns coupled in depth, giving great majesty to the perspective. Between them, fountain basins set in the cills cool the air and between those on the west the Staircase Court (thronged with guests to the ball) is seen below.

Continuing southwards we reach the State Dining-Room (p. 514), formally entered from the end of the South Corridor. This hall for banquets is one of the most impressive in the palace, owing to its proportions: 104 ft. long, 34 ft. wide and 30 ft. high—almost a triple cube. The pilastered teak wainscot, hung with full-length portraits of Viceroys, is barely half its total height except at the ends. At the south end it includes a great alcove for the Viceregal plate (above which is a musicians' gallery), rising to the upper cornice that divides the unpanelled area of the wall from the ceiling cove. This unpanelled area was intended by Lutyens to be painted with formal decoration, where it is felt to be needed. Even so, the room's height is offset by a range of superb chandeliers that seem to flicker in the grey and white crystalline triangles and cubes of the marble floor.

Beside the South Corridor where it enters the State Dining-Room another leads south into the Viceroy's Wing, passing the head of the Viceroy's Private Staircase. The smallest of the four important stairways, this is yet the most bewitching, for, ascending beneath arched vaults of grey marble, the white marble steps are flanked by overhanging troughs of water, lined with black marble, which add a magical quality to the visual satisfaction produced by the architectural perfection of the ascent (p. 516). The flow from lions' mouths and the ripple of the waters is controlled by a concealed device, the adjustment of which was a delicate operation.

We can notice no more of the Viceroy's Wing than to realise that it is a complete country house in itself on four floors. It has two internal courts, into which His Excellency's summer office looked (whereas the adjoining winter office faced south). On the floor above, Her Excellency's bedroom looked both ways, on to a south loggia and into the Courts. The rooms can be described as of the satisfying quality, simple yet personal, that Lutyens gave to so many country houses, and each distinguished by an individual chimney piece. The Viceroy's Wing has its own garden loggias looking north over the two great fountains against the House.

Our way back lies through the suite of Private State Apartments—designed for the Viceroy's personal entertaining—which occupy the upper basement of the central block on the garden side facing west. Behind them, a corridor connects with the Guests' Wing; in front, their windows look directly over the main fountains. First comes the dining-room, beneath but only half the length of its State counterpart and thus easily served from the kitchens. It is a panelled room, entered from a marble lobby, cooled by large wall fountains, through two arches flanking the fire-place (a device Lutyens perhaps derived from William Kent, and used on other occasions). The Drawing-Room beyond is a long, rather lower, room, typically English, with

158. NEW DELHI: VICEROY'S HOUSE AND VICEROY'S COURT AS COMPLETED (1930). The white domes visible on the left are those of the Bodyguard lines

159 and 160. VICEROY'S HOUSE. (*Left*) Under the main portico. (*Right*) The Vestibule immediately within it

161 and 162. VICEROY'S HOUSE. (*Left*) The South Main Corridor. It runs from east to west, south of the Durbar Hall. (*Right*) The South Main Staircase

163 and 164. VICEROY'S HOUSE. (*Left*) The State Drawing Room, looking North. The windows are lit from the Staircase Court. (*Right*) The State Dining Room, which overlooks the garden

165. VICEROY'S HOUSE. The Garden Loggia. Between Ballroom and State Dining Room, overlooking the Staircase Court and the Garden

166. VICEROY'S HOUSE. The State Library

167. VICEROY'S HOUSE. The Viceroy's Staircase. Cooled by water-troughs lined with black marble

168. VICEROY'S HOUSE. The Durbar Hall

169. NEW DELHI COMPLETED. Portrait group in Moghul Miniature style by Mrs. A. G. Shoosmith

the stone external pelmets to the french windows as the only exotic note. Then, in the centre of the front, comes the lower west Garden Loggia, really the main way of egress to the garden and equally to the Staircase Court. Beyond it lay Her Excellency's Private Sitting-Room, Office, A.D.C.'s room and H.E.'s Study.

The Staircase Court (p. 313) can only be really appreciated in terms of colour. Grand in scale (111 ft. long, 53 ft. wide) and faultless in dignity, it is the red sandstone of its lower half and ascents, the cream of the arched and pillared main floor walls, then the reflected light upon the soffits of the far-overhanging cove that partly roofs it and frames the cerulean or starry sky—these, with the deep diagonal shadows and massed greenery in tubs—which make of it one of the most memorable spaces in the whole building. Leaving it by one of the arched ways at its corners we find ourselves in the Western Carriage-Way, and so emerge into the North Court. The centre of it is occupied, as is the open South Court, with fountains of almost abstract sculptured forms. The apsidal west end adjoins the Ballroom; the north side contains the Viceroy's political offices approached from the north entrance; with the Press premises below it. Adjoining, the North-east Wing is occupied by a sequence of lesser offices (p. 313).

But we must turn back to the Main Floor, mounting this time by the North Staircase (which resembles the southern), for we have missed the most beautiful of the four State Rooms set at each corner of the Durbar Hall. This is the State Library. Photographs are as inadequate to represent the form of this room as that of Wren's St. Stephen's, Walbrook, which it resembles. It is square, but given circular character by the dome carried on eight arches, four of which span rectangular recesses (to door, windows, and fireplace), and four semi-domes. Twelve columns make an inner square, four at the angles supporting the semi-domes, eight the arches of the main dome. A continuous cornice follows the cruciform figure thus produced, but the marvellous floor of grey, white, and yellow marbles is inlaid in patterns of interlacing circles. The rectangular 'aisles' provide ample space for all the books that are likely to be studied in so entrancing a room which rivals in miniature magnificent baroque libraries (p. 515).

So we return to the Vestibule from which we started. But this time, having made the round of this enormous, intricately yet so exquisitely co-ordinated, concert of palace and country house, printing works, warehouse, and Imperial headquarters office, we will no longer skirt but enter its climax (p. 517).

The impact of the Durbar Hall, however approached, is immediate, overwhelming, and utterly silencing. From the huge eye whence light streams from the dome of this white Pantheon, the human eye falls abashed to the gleaming floor, seeking where to begin appraisal. 'The pattern of the floor alone is so huge,' Robert Byron felt, 'as to leave the entrant breathless, almost frightened to make his first two or three steps. In its glacial porphyry surface the jasper reflections of the encircling columns are intersected by broad white bands and curves edged with black, two of which lead, direct as an arterial road, from the entrance to the thrones.' The walls are cased in white marble to a height of 42 ft. where the dome begins to spring, 72 ft. in diameter, 77 ft. 6 in. high. Four apses, two on the west, two on the east, have coffered vaults the archivolts of which cut into the dome. But these voids are bridged by the entablature ringing the Hall and carried across them by the shafts of yellow Jaisalmer marble with white bases and caps. In the attic storey small square windows diffuse soft light through marble *jahlis*. The dome itself, wholly white and plain, lifts to the eye that can be covered, but not closed, by a great glass lid, and at night is flooded with light from hidden sources, and by four lamps of white marble standing in each apse. Between the western pair towers the gorgeous canopy of the thrones, that are dwarfed by its cascade of crimson velvet.

'In any light,' Mr. Butler has written, 'this temple of imperial power has an elemental quality. It reproduces no other round interior but surpasses all in a faultless distillation of their handling of the dome.' As a summary, too, of the impression abiding after this fleeting tour of Viceroy's House, his verdict cannot be more justly or concisely expressed: 'Nowhere did Lutyens slip from the high standard of design . . . he set himself. It is not a matter of rich elaboration, nor is there ever a suspicion of that vulgarity into which lesser men might have been led. It was a case, rather, of doing everything as perfectly as possible yet all the time on a balance between common sense and the urge of a continuous inspiration.' Some of Lutyens's works can be criticised for their exaggeration of what Mr. Butler calls access areas at the expense of rooms. Here there are the most magnificent corridors and staircases but also equally superb rooms juxtaposed in graded splendour.

'An individual and peculiarly English splendour expressing, perhaps for the last time, the spirit of humanist aristocracy in the language of a dwelling,' was Robert Byron's epitome. Lutyens, he said truly, had placed the Viceroy 'in a setting whose qualities of exact judgment and independent invention are the qualities that have made English Viceroys of India great. It is Lutyens's confidence in the ability of his line and mass to justify his love of novelty which places him in succession to the great architects of the Italian renaissance and the English eighteenth century'. From the point of view of this narrative, with its recurrent theme of will achieving the vision conceived by emotion and intellect, the significant word in that judgment is 'confidence'. As faith had willed through seventeen years—indeed near fifty, since that day when the boy Lutyens had first mustered the confidence to assert his own rightness against overwhelming authority, and proclaimed his life's purpose to become an architect—so now, notwithstanding the outrages of fate, it was fulfilled.

The days preceding the formal opening of the House, when everybody would be in top hats to receive their Excellencies, and the Municipal Council would present an address, were chaos. Lutyens, with a heavy cold, described it as:

like an Exhibition. It is impossible to conceive they have been at it 17 years. Contretemps follow each other from hour to hour. The English foremen work day and night. If it had not been for this handful of trained craftsmen I cannot imagine what would have happened. The Indian foremen agree there is not nearly enough supervision. 3000 panes of glass have been broken and 500 keys stolen, besides doorknobs and window-fastenings. I keep on exploding and stopping to blow my nose.

Monday the 23rd was a morning of white mist, in which the booming of distant salute guns heralding the Viceroy's arrival masked another explosion. An attempt, echoing that on Lord Hardinge when enacting the transfer of the capital to Delhi, but mercifully ineffective, had been made to bomb Lord Irwin's train. The ceremony proceeded, 'then H.E. went up the stairway to the great portico, where I and others were presented to him. At a given signal the doors were opened (there was no key, as there was no lock). They went into the House, and for the first time in 17 years the House was closed on me.'

Yet there were endless little things remaining to be done which, since everybody proceeded to take ten days' holiday over Christmas to recuperate, seem to have devolved on the Architect and the Vicereine to do largely by themselves. On the last day of the year Lutyens was writing to his wife grumbling furiously at this vacation, when a note from His Excellency was delivered.

> My Dear Lutyens [it ran]
>   This is just to congratulate you warmly on the K.C.I.E. which the King has conferred on you in the New Year Honours List. Anyone who has seen the wonderful achievements of New Delhi knows how well you have deserved this honour, and it is a particular pleasure to me that it should have been just after our entry into our new house. Lady Irwin joins me in sending you our warmest congratulations.
>   Yours sincerely and gratefully,
>   Irwin.

'Now that's a surprise!' the Knight Commander exclaimed, 'coming just as I was telling you of my troubles. I suppose, but don't know, I can wear a ribbon and star' (and sketched himself, thus bedecked, in the margin). Continuing his worries he said the Government of Hyderabad had approached him with a great scheme which, he guessed, would involve his coming out to India yearly for the rest of his life, should he accept it.

That summer he was in Washington again, for the opening of the Embassy, and there learnt of the proposals, contained in the Simon Report, for Provincial Autonomy through the decentralisation of Indian Government. 'So those enormous

Secretariats will become almost empty,' he supposed, and the old wound ached for a moment. In January of 1931, he and his wife came to Delhi for the official opening of the new Capital. With them were Edward Hudson, with a *Country Life* photographer (the late Mr. E. Gill, who then took nearly all the photographs of New Delhi reproduced in these volumes). Among the Viceroy's distinguished official guests were Lord Hardinge and Captain Swinton. We have no record of the meeting, on the scene of their joint conception, between the former Viceroy and his Architect who shared so many memories, and, had they lived another fifteen years, would have shared such bitter disillusion; but Swinton paid full tribute to the completed conception at the birth of which he had presided.[1]

Nor, since the recipient of his journal was with him, have we Lutyens's account of the celebrations. But his wife wrote to the children her impressions of their coming to Viceroy's House. It is moving for its simple directness, its properly admiring pride, and its characteristic grasp of the human rather than the architectural significance of the experience. Through her inexpert eyes we may catch glimpses of the culmination of her husband's life more vivid, although partial, than a more knowledgeable report.

She described the thrill of driving up the great Kings Way and seeing the House appear. 'All is so changed on the last years that it is like a dream—the trees grown, the wonderful Arch up.' But, now that all was finished, the 'great crime'—as every Lutyens must hold the slope between the Secretariats to be—was the more glaring. Seeing it now, she more fully understood 'Father's rage at the spoiling of his life's greatest work by the silly slope'. Nevertheless, and 'despite the niggling economies' of the Government of India, 'this remains a colossal and most wonderful achievement and should make Father's name go down to history as one of the architects of all time. Hudson is so moved that he can hardly keep from tears. He said to me yesterday "Poor old Christopher Wren could never have done this!"'

The union of Eastern and Western atmosphere was most remarkable, 'yet all is original, nothing copied.' The grand simplicity seemed to her the outstanding quality of it all, though with such a wealth of beautiful detail, everything appropriate to its setting. 'And everything—furniture, fire-backs, clocks, doorhandles—designed by the single mind.' As for the garden, it was a paradise. 'Though so formal, yet everything has grown up so quickly, and flowers are set in such masses, producing a riot of colour and scents, that, with the fountains playing continually, there is not the least sense of stiffness. The round garden beyond beats everything for sheer beauty and is beyond words. No photograph can convey it, nor the effects produced on the House by the *shadows*.'

There had been a dinner of ninety guests; 'it was, of course, deadly.' But they had assembled in the Durbar Hall, dined in the State Dining-Room, and it had given

---

[1] His appreciation of Viceroy's House is quoted by Butler, *The Architecture,* Vol. II.

the opportunity of seeing the great rooms lit up. And with all the splendour of the great official building, the atmosphere was yet not formal. 'The Viceroy is such a great gentleman that all the pomp just slid off him. Even I felt happy and at my ease. Father was indeed lucky to have had such appreciative and charming people as the Viceroy and Vicereine for the inauguration of the House:' and Lady Emily's heart went out to Lord Irwin for his recent unconditional releasing of the Congress leaders. If only his policy of affording India Dominion status had been supported by the Home Government, 'all the trouble and bloodshed of the past year would have been avoided.'

And perhaps immeasurably greater bloodshed and tragedy, leading to the sundering of India and the abandonment of Viceroy's House to become, it is said, a medical school and museum. Leaving it, as he thought for good, Lutyens confessed afterwards 'I had not the nerve to say good-bye to Irwin. I just walked out, and I kissed a wall of the House'.

CHAPTER XVIII

CATHEDRAL

§1. AESTHETIC SCIENCE

IT was eighteen months before that surreptitious parting kiss for Delhi, and some time prior to his sailing to prepare the Viceroy's reception in his House, that the vision of a yet greater dome first appeared to Lutyens. Into the model and drawings for its realisation he was to put not only the technical experience of his lifetime but the materials for a science of architectural aesthetics. The crystallisation of his theory in the drawings for his Liverpool Cathedral, published and analysed in *The Architecture*, Volume III, make of them architectural documents of great intrinsic importance, embodying as they do his most important contribution to the future of architectural aesthetics. But there are constant allusions to, and fragmentary illuminations of, this developing philosophy to be found in his spoken or written expressions henceforward, from which it will be attempted in this and the following chapter to constitute an outline of his conception in relation to the narrative of his later years.

In the autumn of 1929, the Washington Embassy was building, much-discussed blocks of flats were changing familiar London skylines, and Thiepval's vaults rising to propound a new theorem of monumental mathematics. He had also accepted the Ministry of Transport's invitation to design a combined road and railway bridge at Charing Cross which would enable that station, reconstructed, to remain on the north bank. In doing so he had thrown the weight of his reputation into the scales against that of the combined architectural societies, including the R.I.B.A., confederated to preserve old Waterloo Bridge by obtaining the removal of the railway station and bridge altogether and the diversion of through traffic from 'Rennie's masterpiece' to a great new road bridge at Charing Cross.

The issues involved in the Waterloo Bridge controversy need not detain us longer than to note that Lutyens did not share this admiration of the old bridge (he regarded it as 'jerrybuilt' and inadequate). But the unexpected alignment of the first architect of the age in opposition to the official policy of his profession, coming on top of his known dislike of the Institute's measures for the training and registration of architects, produced a considerable sensation. It led to the realisation that he occupied a position of splendid, if puzzling, isolation in national architecture.

His resignation from the Royal Institute, soon after reaching Delhi in December, 1929, appeared to confirm this isolation, and that at a time when both the profession and a bewildered public were becoming divided by the great 'Modern' schism. The new word Functionalism, and the equally strange name Corbusier, were on the lips of every young architect whose imagination leapt in prodigious parabolas of reinforced concrete.

The resignation from the official camp of the arch-traditionist, as the younger generation looked upon him, raised among some of them momentary hopes of being able to acclaim him the leader of their's, even while the last granite blocks were being hewn at Castle Drogo, and Delhi was in the frenzy of completion. At this juncture Lutyens surveyed the prospect in the company of some of these young men. But whilst he made clear his impatience with the limitations of professional training and practice, equally he preached a gospel of idealistic discipline, of transcendental tradition, to which few of his hearers were prepared to submit themselves.

'The calamity we both acknowledge,' he told them, 'is the separation of our great profession into Engineers and Architects. The Engineer, in the vanguard of necessity, has no responsibility to any law pertaining to ideal vision; he is free from tradition and is wagged by no tail either of poetry or sentiment. Yet the Forth Bridge has the qualities of a gentleman. Its great gesture laughs at detail. Unconscious of tradition it leaps to its objective. But the Architect is shelved like a bottle of flavouring on a kitchen dresser, to be used in small quantities as taste demands. Architecture appeals to the few, and they view it from every angle of literary and archaeological taste. None have acquired, nor are there any means of teaching them, the laws and science of ideal vision. The controlling patron is trustee for monies and values, but beauty has no legal status. The public does not care, accepting with equanimity disfiguring advertisements, petrol stations, and Peacehavens. Yet I am convinced the *country* is full of dormant genius, only needing a patron to awaken it. All great periods of architecture have one common and essential denominator: Unity in the measured tread of their rhythms; nothing left to chance. Method, Scale, Rhythm, based on realities and observed with the rigidity of Music, are necessities to all great architecture. Einstein tells us that Time is a fourth to the three spatial dimensions by which we live. A fifth must be the Grace of God, possibly within all men. Its smallest module may be—a gentleman! If Engineers studied the laws of beauty as keenly as they study those of stress and strain, and had the grace to make the essential sacrifice, they would oust the Architects from the pedestal that they seem anxious to vacate. Architecture, like music, requires an orchestra of many men and instruments. In the days now past they played to the baton of the Master Builder. Tradition was their sap, working within them as does the blind sap that within its structure creates the cypress or the beech. Shall we ever "conduct" again, without further loss of sap, the iron posts and beams, deep girders spanning great widths and carried by stanchions, to some rhythm and code of entases, and so recover beauty?'[1]

[1] From an article published in 1926 and an address to the 'Tomorrow Club', 1932.

In every address that he was called upon, with increasing frequency now, to deliver, he groped for words, to which the effort imparted at times the quality of poetry, in which to embody this conception that was taking shape in his latest, 'abstract', works such as Thiepval. Its working, its sap as he termed it, had been shaping what we have called Lutyensian Classic, then assumed Elemental form in that breath-taking Arch of the Missing. The enunciation and practice of this gospel of Aesthetic Science, as it may be termed, engrossed him till the end of his life. It was indeed the consummation, the distilled Theory, of his architectural achievements. But he lacked the didactic skill for its setting forth in words—which in any case he mistrusted—and almost despaired of being understood by those who alone had the power and means to enable its demonstration in architecture.

The essence of his theory of Aesthetic Science is that Classic architects have approached a solution of its problems but have failed to give reasons for their conclusions. Variations of solution are merely attributed to various masters, without analysis of the reasons for them. Beauty is an absolute quality, governed by the product of natural and scientific laws, governed by ascertainable facts unaffected by standards of taste or sensuous associations. 'The brain should excite the senses to appreciation rather than allow the senses and their attendant phrases to placate the mind.' The Greeks possessed knowledge beyond present apprehension. What reason determined the curvatures of the Parthenon? What is the scientific reason of Nature's unfailing but infinitely subtle grace? Even illiterate craftsmen, in his own recollection, possessed something of this natural, divine, 'sap,' enabling them to create beauty apparently independently of the classical or any other formulae, yet, if analysed, probably obeying an instinctive if obscure measure of rhythm.

But, in a distracted and vulgarised age, deprived of intelligent patronage and with a Royal Institute of British Architects that, in his opinion, was becoming a trade union rather than a learned society, how to set in motion the research by which alone these secrets (embracing perhaps but infinitely exceeding his father's Venetian Secret) could be extracted?

Humorously but with intense seriousness—and with that curious hint (in its references to dignitaries of the Roman Catholic Church) of pre-vision that sometimes chose his words for him—he imagined himself a Pope of Art:

'My Cardinals should lay down formulae of beauty as sincere as those laid down for strains and stresses by Engineers. For the only means of solution I see is that some sort of Chair should be founded to search and inquire into the laws of nature's beauty as they affect the eye. I should like to see the curves of tree-stems analysed. The geometry and impulsive forces of crystals, the genial sphere, curves simple and in three dimensions, must be explored, and the facts so obtained be related to the facts known, scientifically or empirically, to architects since Egyptian and Greek times. Codes verified and uttered with authority must influence the critical faculties of the multitudes and give them some consciousness of what they see. Surely God, in His creation, (to small human sense) is blind, as sap within the tree. Yet we, beholding Nature, see Him and adore.'

These were among his thoughts and preoccupations when, dining with Alfred Sutro (his sponsor at the Garrick Club), he met the Archbishop of Liverpool. Dr. Downey referred to his intention of building the Metropolitan Cathedral projected by his predecessor. 'What fun for you,' said Lutyens, and, recalling the conversation, added: 'We discussed Cathedrals generally; later he wrote asking me to go and see him at Liverpool with reference to his Cathedral. I was surprised and certainly as pleased, dare I say, as Punch. I think Dr. Downey had in his mind that, in so much as the Anglican Cathedral was being built by a Roman Catholic, his architect should belong to the Church of England. I thought it to be an excellent idea. "Why not?" said I. I went to Liverpool and arrived just before lunch. I was shown into a large dull-gloomed room, and waited, feeling nervous and rather shy, till in came His Grace—a red biretta on his head and a voluminous sash around his ample waist. (Later he reduced his weight by 8 stone, no mean achievement). He held out a friendly hand. His pectoral Cross swung towards me, and the first words he said were "Will you have a cocktail?"'

The late Bishop Keating of Liverpool had begun the acquisition of land in the vicinity of the existing Pro-Cathedral near the Adelphi Hotel. But at the time of Dr. Downey's succession a much larger and magnificent site was made available by the closing of the grim mass of workhouse and infirmary occupying nine acres on the summit of Brownlow Hill. This eminence is part of the semi-circle of low hills that encloses Liverpool about a mile from its river centre. At one point on it, called St. James's Mount, rises Sir Giles Scott's Anglican Cathedral. About half a mile northwards, and slightly higher, was the workhouse site, approached directly from the centre of the city where lie St. George's Hall and the Pro-Cathedral. Thus, were the site obtained, the two Cathedrals when seen from shipping in the Mersey would loom on this ridge silhouetted against the sky. Archbishop and architect inspected the site. It was evident from it that the church would need to be approached from the south, with its liturgical east to the north, whereas that of the Anglican Cathedral is to the south.

Thus Dr. Downey's vision from the outset involved departure from ecclesiastical precedent, in choice of site no less than of architect. In the latter he may well have been influenced, as Lutyens modestly averred, by his being an Anglican, in view of Liverpool's reputation, in the early years of this century, for sectarian bitterness second only in that respect to Belfast. But the Archbishop envisaged no common cathedral. His ambition was to found the greatest modern Roman Catholic Church in Christendom, second in extent and majesty only to St. Peter's. What conversation had passed between him and Lutyens at Alfred Sutro's table we cannot tell. But a perceptive mind that had been following his progress from Delhi, through some of his works of the 'twenties to his designs of Thiepval, and that had chanced to hear or read his adumbration of an aesthetic science, must have been strongly disposed to behold in Lutyens the ordained instrument of that mighty dream. They 'discussed cathedrals generally', and from that discussion must have emerged, through the joke-screen, to so keen a mind as Dr. Downey's, the essentially spiritual nature of Lutyens's emotion; his long-cherished dream of designing a great building of which the one dominant purpose was the praise of God; his comprehensive, if surprising, grasp of liturgical forms and usage; and the inexhaustible creative vitality still clamouring for expression. Twenty years ago Lutyens had confided to his friend '*au fond* I am horribly religious, but cannot speak it and this saves my work'. Two years ago, hearing the men's voices in the Garrison Church at Gibraltar joined in singing *From Greenland's Icy Mountains*

> brought all that Mother believed and felt and taught me flooding back, the mysteries of the child's conception waved again, so I am feeling very sentimental and want you here with me,

he told his wife. 'But it is all beyond my reach, whether too high or too low. I only know I shall reach its level again.'

Now what, by that last sentence, did this strange man mean? 'I shall reach that level again.' That he would reattain faith at some later period? That in death he would become as a little child again? Or, by some mystic premonition, that he would be called to praise God in conducting, as the supreme exercise of his 'ideal vision', such an architectural orchestra, such a 'Unity of method, scale, and rhythm', as in his dreams he had always believed would fall to his lot? We cannot tell, and in the next sentence the schoolboy in him added:

> Two thousand years of goody-goody and look around—there is little else but baddy baddy, and the most successful seem to crow on dunghills!

Now, standing in front of the derelict workhouse on Brownlow Hill, great rhythmical forms rose before his eyes, forms that some master of prose whose name he had forgotten had translated into unforgotten words:

> a gathering-up of all that men can do, with fifty roofs, blank walls like precipices, and round arch after round arch, architrave after architrave. It is like a good and settled epic, or better still it is like the life of a healthy and adventurous man who, having accomplished all his journeys and taken the fleece of gold, comes home to tell his stories at evening and to pass among his own people the years that are left to him of his age. It has the experience, growth, and intensity of knowledge, all caught up into one unity. It conquers the site upon which it stands.

He had written out those words in 1910. As faith wills, so fate fulfils—it seemed.

§2. THE VISION OF UNITY

When he sailed in December on his sixteenth journey to Delhi, for the exacting weeks of preparing for the Viceroy's entry to the House, his mind must have been full of this tremendous but yet secret project. Not the obliquest reference is made to it in his private letters, for the option on the hill site was not yet secured. As soon as its acquisition was announced the enthusiasm for it, of Liverpool Roman Catholics, enabled its cost, £100,000, to be quickly raised, and the work of clearance was at once put in hand. The design in its broad lines and much essential detail, involving many conferences, took him the better part of a year. Provisional plan and elevations were released to the Press in September, 1930, but although the plan has remained essentially unchanged, comparison of the sketch perspectives then published with the model exhibited at the Royal Academy in 1934 reveals that all above the main roof level in the 1930 design had been provisional—as Lutyens emphasised at the time was the case—and was fundamentally redesigned. The foundation stone was laid with much pomp before a temporary High Altar protected by a domed shelter, itself a structure of some beauty and over 80 ft. high, on June 5, 1933. By 1940, the crypt Sacristy flanked by two chapels in the north end, and the Archbishop's Chapel beneath the site of the High Altar, were completed, and other parts of the crypt and foundations were in use—as air raid shelters. The materials employed, and to be employed, are grey granite for the plinth, cornices, other dressings, and for the casing of the dome. The rest of the building will be of long thin Roman-shaped bricks $1\frac{1}{2}$ in. × 24 in., pinky brown in colour, the virtues of which he had commended to Shoosmith a year before. Already 4,000,000 bricks and 40,000 cubic feet of granite have been laid, 70,000 tons of earth been excavated including 18,000 tons of hard rock which had to be blasted out. With this massive material reassurance, though proportionately it is slight, of the vast structure's ultimate reality, we may look at the 1934 model and plan, in order to obtain some conception of the unparalleled edifice in which we may believe, as an article of faith, that Lutyens's genius will some day—he set it two centuries hence—be at last displayed at full scale.

The conception is now complete, worked out to $\frac{1}{4}$ in. scale before his death, of infinitely the largest, most original, and most perfectly integrated church ever to have been projected as a homogeneous whole by a single architect. In scale, in boldness of imagination, in awe-inspiring drama and yet intellectual consistency, the prodigious conception surpasses, in all moderation, any product that has been carried to this stage of completion by any mind applied to the aesthetic science in recorded history. The Cathedral of Christ the King at Liverpool is indeed 'a gathering up of all that men can do'. When built it will be the greatest church in Christendom.

These are indeed superlative claims, which it cannot be within the scope of this

Life to substantiate fully, even were it possible in brief compass. An adequate verbal impression can only be conveyed by constant reference to the complexly lucid plans and by describing in detail each vast component, a feat that Mr. Butler has signally performed in Volume III of *The Architecture*. But the claim must be made good in general terms, since in its superlativeness lies the nature of the claim which has been implicitly made of the reader throughout this narrative and explicitly by Mr. Butler: that Lutyens was the greatest artist in building that England has known. As concisely as may be, therefore, the theorem and rhythm, with the main features, of the design must be indicated, since they constitute the grand expression of Lutyens's theory, outlined in the previous section, which was the distillation of his life's work.

Though here we have only the model (p. 535) and a plan (p. 532) the dimensions represented give a notion of the conception's size by comparison with St. Peter's, Rome, and St. Paul's, London. But first we may imagine ourselves ascending Brownlow Hill a century, it may be, hence and the vision realised, though now the fabric of a dream. A cliff-like mass of pinkish buff brick laced with grey granite looms before us. In the centre of its south end confronting us, a portal arch 145 ft. high, and seeming more by reason of the stepping back and batter of its face and sides, soars between two lesser arches, its stepped gable surmounted by a huge effigy of Christ the King. From a distance we can see above and beyond this frontispiece, some 400 ft. above ground, stepped-back cubic masses supporting so vast a dome, encased in the silvery granite, as never swelled in Europe or Asia, though recalling that of London in sweetness of outline and exceeded in actual girth by some in India. As outliers of its buttressing cubes ascend on either side twin elongated bell-towers, slender in elevation from the south, but from either flank discovered to be near as broad as the transept portal above which each stands; for these belfries, christened by their creator Law and Order, and removed from the approach-front where they conventionally belong, crown the short but notably broad transepts that, in a distant view, widen the extent of the front. In the elevations of these transepts the southern portal is repeated. The intervening expanses of nave wall, almost windowless, batter appreciably as they rise to some 120 ft. from steeply battered granite bases ranging between 30 ft. and 60 ft. high, according to the slope of the ground level. At their summit, and again some distance below it, they are bound by deep courses of granite. Moving towards the north (the liturgical east end) there comes into our sight, above the tiered cubes of the silhouette, such a spire as Wren might have set above a city church, and, as we move further northward, a balancing fellow on the opposite side; but here dwarfed to the stature of a *flèche* by an apse separating them and by the strangely changing form of the dome-mass now darkly marshalled behind them. From the point we have now reached, the north-west (the liturgical north-east), the structural logic of this architectural mountain begins to become apparent. Each cubic mass is seen to proceed out of, or be related to, others below or adjacent. The elusive shapes of the dome's supporting masses reveal themselves as four Y-shaped buttresses projecting far from the vastly rotund and exceptionally lofty drum, and rising from a square base or terrace, the parapet of which is pricked with twelve slender columns supporting statues of Apostles. From our stance, too, we can see descending steps to the crypt, and, turning leftwards, the rectangular façade that, arched and pavilioned at its summit, forms the north end. From every point on our circuit, but from here particularly, the tapering mountainous silhouettes have seemed at first sight arbitrarily if sublimely romantic, but now reveal themselves as logical emanations from a plan of intricate and, in Blake's epithet, awe-ful symmetry.

In the dome's exquisite shell and cupola, Lutyens's veneration of Wren is evident; and we may recall his poor opinion of 'that pimple', St. Peter's. In the 1930 description, it was projected to be cased with stainless steel; a choice perhaps attributable to the ecclesiastical authorities, since, in subsequent references, Lutyens declared himself strongly opposed to the use of light-reflecting materials on general principles, and he evidently set himself with fervour to explore the possibilities of granite, carried on a brick skeleton, and hailed his solution with joy.

Now for the dimensions of the fane around which in vision we have moved. The length of its body from South Portal to that flat north end is externally 680 ft.— roughly 225 yards, comparing with St. Peter's 715 ft. and St. Paul's 510 ft.; across the transepts, from East to West Portal, 400 ft. (St. Peter's 450 ft., St. Paul's 250 ft.). Height, to the top of the Cross on the Dome is 510 ft.—St. Peter's 450 ft., St. Paul's 366 ft. The best way to appreciate the height of the body is to visualise London buildings of 80 ft. sheer frontage set beside it; they would come up to about the lower of the granite string courses (the one above the lower portal arches). Grosvenor House's roof pavilions would reach to the parapet of the main walls. The internal diameter of the dome is 168 ft., the biggest in Europe, comparing to St. Peter's 137 ft. and St. Paul's 112 ft. But these dimensions, and the mountainous symmetries that they qualify, are still in the nature of 'effects', not fully accounted for until we discover the logic of their cause. For nothing, it must be emphasised again, in the conception is arbitrary. Its romanticism, loosely akin to Gothic and Byzantine structure, is coldly, mathematically, intellectual in cause; the logical product of a scientific aesthetic applied to national, structural, and liturgical tradition. The controlling formula is concisely expressed in Lutyens's own words, which may be prefaced by pointing out that the system of progression is an application of that developed in the Thiepval Memorial but that here the arch dimensions used in the body of the church are in the very lofty proportion of 1 to 3, or three circles (elsewhere in the building it drops to $2\frac{1}{2}$ or $1\frac{1}{2}$). He said:

> The conception of the Building as a whole is one of progression. Arches running east to west are 15 ft. wide and 45 ft. high; they carry arches running

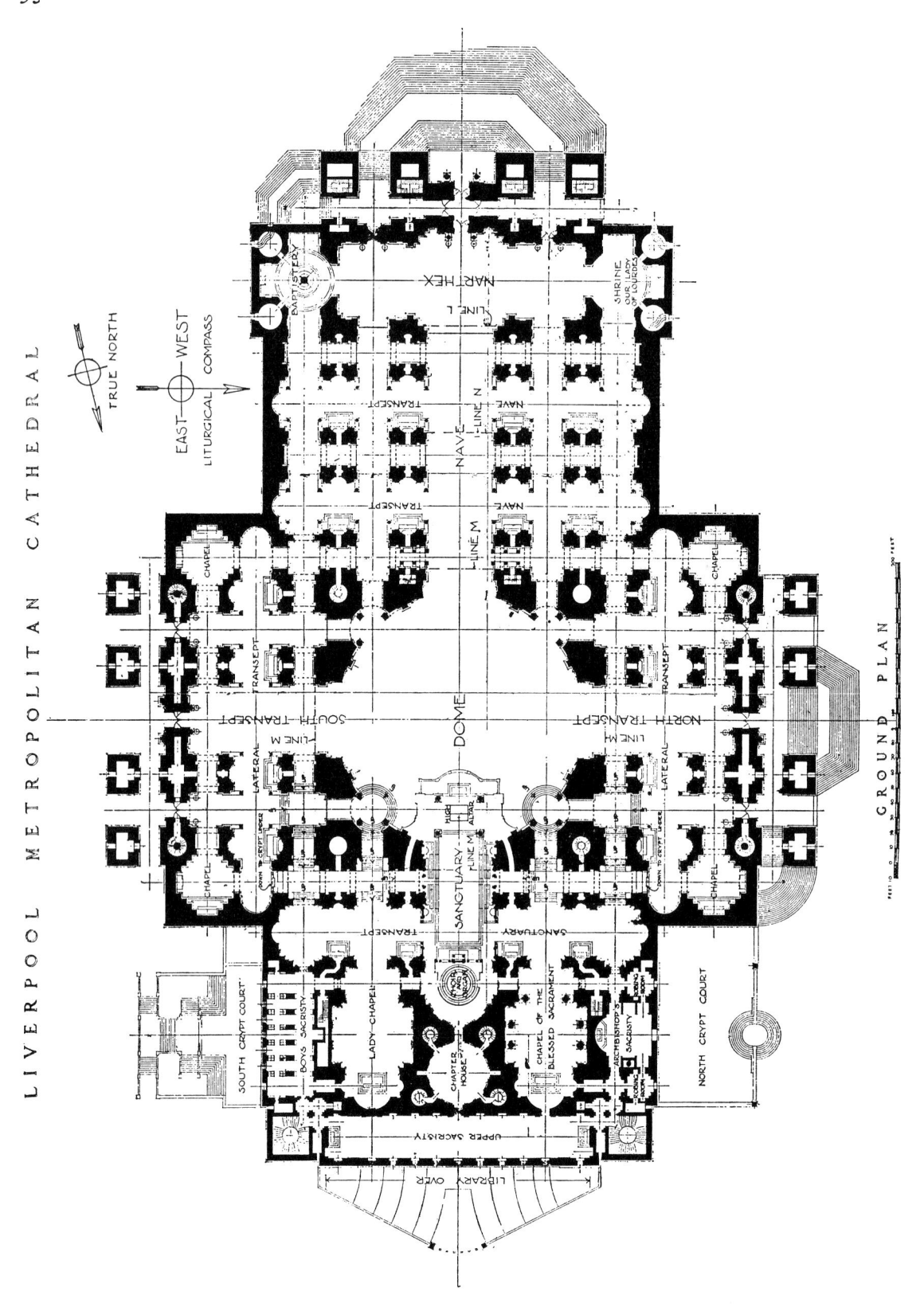

LIVERPOOL METROPOLITAN CATHEDRAL — GROUND PLAN

north to south 22 ft. wide and 66 ft. high; which in turn carry arches running east and west 32 ft. wide and 96 ft. high, carrying the main vaults 46 feet wide and 138 ft. high, and growing in crescendo to carry the great Dome 168 ft. in diameter, covering a height of some 300 ft.

The exterior is an amazingly cogent expression of the plan given by these dimensions and of the structural means of its execution as handled by Lutyens in his final, elemental phase. In the North Portico the 15 ft. spans (that run across the plan) are the arches in its returns. The 22 ft. spans are represented by the lateral arches, the vaults of which are carried northward as the inner aisles. The 32 ft. spans, forming the nave arcade, are not represented externally but their height is hinted at by that of the four bastions which form the upper part of the portico and are, in fact, the terminating buttresses of the arcade. The 46 ft. span provides the central arch, the crown of which (145 ft. high) expresses externally that of the main vault of nave and transepts. The recurrence of the external arches in the same position in the transept porticos is accounted for by the transepts repeating at right angles the progression of the liturgical east-west axis.

Similarly the Y-shaped buttresses of the dome and the square mass on which they stand, which confer so protean a silhouette on the culminating massif, are the external expression of Lutyens's greatest tour-de-force in the planning of the Cathedral. The two-fold problem confronting designers of domed churches is the aesthetic one of relating the circular form of the dome to the rectangular masses below: and the structural one of supporting the dome in such a way that the piers do not obstruct the internal axes. At St. Peter's, Michelangelo failed to solve the second part of the problem: the nave aisles are terminated by the piers. At St. Paul's Wren procured continuity for his aisles in both directions but notoriously at the cost of his dome's stability. At St. Peter's the external relationship has always been open to criticism: at St. Paul's, Wren relied upon the simple combination of circle and rectangles to provide by itself a satisfactory geometrical relationship so far as visible from ground level. Its simplicity is the virtue of its inherent structural defect.

Lutyens has planted his drum on what is, in effect, four solid triangular masses of masonry (forming the outwardly visible square mass) of such great dimensions that the inner aisles of nave and transepts can be carried through them on both axes. The weight of the dome is distributed over these triangles by four buttresses, of the same height as the drum, which are bifurcated into eight and break gradually forward to the plane of the triangles' outer sides, thus extending the stress to the arcades of the *outer* aisles of Nave, Sanctuary, and Transepts. Within, the segments or curved hypotenuses of these triangles carrying the dome are so wide between the four great arches that they can each contain a semi-dome of the 32 ft. span beneath which the 22 ft. vaults of the inner aisles converge. By this means is avoided the muddle that

Wren got into by trying to bring his eight dome-arches, of unequal widths, to equal height. Lutyens, indeed, has combined the simplicity and majesty of St. Peter's with the romance and interest of the long vistas of St. Paul's. Incidentally, too, the spandrils between the great arches and above the semi-domes will, as he said, give a great opportunity for the painters of to-morrow.

It is notable that the solution externally of this double problem—of stability and circle-square relationship—occurred to him after 1930, for in the preliminary elevation the drum was supported by eight shallow buttresses based on the arcades of the *inner* aisles, and critics at the time commented upon the unsatisfactory relationship of circular drum to rectangular base. Its solution by this means, with such visually powerful and original result upon the silhouette of the total mass, constitutes the supreme application of his last, the Elemental, mode of design and construction, originating in the War monuments, developed in the great city buildings, and exemplified at Thiepval.

We cannot linger within, save to draw attention to a very few causative forms and consequential effects. The interior combines the dark and lofty mystery of Nôtre Dame with the amplitude of Santa Sophia beneath the dome, and the classic stateliness of St. Paul's in its handling. The Nave and main Transepts, 138 ft. high and 46 ft. wide, have two sets of aisles 66 ft. high and 22 ft. wide, divided from it and from each other by arches set in pairs and alternately 96 ft. high by 32 ft. and 45 ft. by 15 ft. Thus the cross vaults run at alternate levels. This enables side chapels to be set in the thickness of the arcades formed by the double arches, and the higher vaults to be lit by windows from light-wells above the lower vaults.[1] The pilasters throughout are of the Delhi Order.

The Sanctuary projects southwards into the dome-space, and is some 12 ft. higher than the main floor level. The High Altar beneath a baldachino is perched on this platform's forward edge, so that the celebrant faces the congregation from beyond it. At the further end of the Sanctuary is set the Archbishop's Throne. Behind it, filling the remainder of the Apse, a great circular depression sunk in the floor contains both choir and choir-organ, developing the acoustic experiment made in the Temple of Music at Tyringham. Beyond the Apse is the round Chapter House, flanked by the Lady Chapel and Chapel of the Blessed Sacrament marked externally by the twin spires. Beyond and containing these on either side are ranges of sacristies, staircases and lifts to Crypt, and rooms for the many services of a Metropolitan Cathedral.

We have omitted much in this cursory view: beneath the High Altar the chapel, already in existence, where Archbishops are buried, the doorway to which from the Crypt is a 6-ton monolith wheel 8 ft. in diameter and 9 in. thick which rolls with a

---

[1] He adumbrated this kind of vaulting system as early as 1911 in connection with Johannesburg Cathedral. *See* page 210.

170. METROPOLITAN CATHEDRAL OF CHRIST THE KING, LIVERPOOL. The Model: Scale 1/48. Total height 510 ft. Materials, silver-grey granite and pink-buff brick. In this view from the liturgical north-east (actually north-west) with a transept and its surmounting belfry on the right, the sacristies backing on the sanctuary to the left, 'the elusive shapes of the dome's supporting masses reveal themselves as four Y-shaped buttresses projecting far from the vastly rotund and exceptionally lofty drum, and rising from a square base'

171. HALNAKER HOUSE, SUSSEX (1936)

172. CAMPION HALL, OXFORD (1937). The entrance

173. MIDDLETON PARK, OXFORDSHIRE (1937). Entrance front

noble rumble to close and open; the floors, warmed from beneath, of polished cast iron where not of marbles; the Confessionals built into the walls of Istrian stone; and far up round the base of the outer Dome, a cloister, where priests can read their Office, 15 ft. wide by 30 ft. high, opening to an outer terrace 170 yards in circumference overlooking city and sea and river 440 ft. below.

But taking our departure by the south doors, we must halt in the space that will be the prelude to all within: the Narthex. This space, itself bigger than some cathedrals and occupying the width of the portico, through the side arches of which it is entered, has a vault 150 ft. high intersecting the nave vault of equal height. At its east end is the Baptistry, at its west a chapel to be dedicated to Our Lady of Lourdes and at its angles spaces for four other chapels or chantries—one, Lutyens hoped, for the children of the street or the Penitent Thief. Its five inner portals, guarded by great grilles of precious workmanship, give into the vistas up Nave and aisles to High Altar, Lady Chapel and Blessed Sacrament Altars. This Narthex will never be closed but, warmed and lighted, be open as a refuge to the destitute. And in the piers of the huge arches are telephone boxes, police and first aid stations, and those easements necessary to great congregations in the flesh but so uncommonly provided by designers for the spirit.

§3. PILGRIMAGES AND ALLEGIANCES

The nature of transcendental elements in architecture more and more engrossed his thoughts; of those impulses, defiances, inspirations, through which artists unconsciously become sometimes subject to a 'great immeasurable cycle of law'. It was a mystery that had always fascinated him. As long ago as 1908[1] he had called these intimations 'a miracle to short sight; to those of a little longer sight Godhead; and if we could see yet better, facts may be revealed before which the very God as we conceive him will fade dim. It is that which should bring all arts—Architecture, Sculpture, Painting, Literature, Music, into sympathy'. In the evolving theory that we have called his gospel of Aesthetic Science, and in the vision of this unity taking shape as his Cathedral, his faith was gradually being fulfilled, though he was aware that himself would never see his partial realisation of it, still less the new Organic Architecture, the perfection of which in the distant future was now his mastering belief. He held this faith with the passion and conviction with which others embrace religion. It was his religion. The quest of its mysteries to him was the search for God. His self-projection into the spiritual life of the Cathedral assimilated him to the priests of the Church whose servant he had become. As he had grown into an enlightened imperialist whilst absorbed with New Delhi, so he was now filled with devoutness. The greatness of the vision within him gave him a spiritual stature that

[1] Chapter 7.

could somehow be sensed. Not that his friends found him more distant, or the priests any nearer their fold. The more he became the architectural mystic, the more carefree and facetious he seemed in ordinary life and the less liable to embrace the faith to which he ministered. But his spiritual and aesthetic absorption in the Future Architecture (as the religious mystic is preoccupied by the Future Life) must be remembered in order to make complete sense of his later years.

Meanwhile, he had never actually seen the Parthenon, in the riddle of whose curvatures and entases lay, for him, the clue, or one of the clues, to absolute beauty. So he and his daughter Ursula set out on an odyssey together, in August, 1932, which would take them to Pompeii, Athens, Constantinople, Cyprus, Baalbec, Damascus, Jerusalem and Cairo. He had a sheet of glass framed in the way he had devised in boyhood, through which to look at all the famous buildings they would see. Except for his cruise with Miss Dodge and the Jekylls in the Baltic, twenty-five years ago, it was his first protracted holiday since his honeymoon in Holland. Father and daughter called it their Marmalademoon and kept a joint diary.

It is an oddly desultory record. Both sought rest rather than zest on the little Messagerie (he called it Menagerie) Maritime boat that they boarded at Marseilles and were in the mood to love only the highest if and when they saw it. Ideal vision set a fastidious standard of appreciation, enabling them—as Mr. Tilney's theory of picturesque beauty had fortified Miss Morland to dismiss the whole city of Bath—to write off many famous cities as unworthy of investigation. Yet it was a pilgrimage—including sixty genuine pilgrims bound with their priests for Jerusalem, besides a couple of retired Scottish builders on holiday who were much impressed by their distinguished fellow-traveller—though disillusion proved to be its goal.

They didn't think much of Vesuvius. Pompeii had evidently been a pornographic Blackpool, depressing in its abundance of bad design. 'It was all second rate. Some of the brickwork was good and well done, but the applied decoration was just stupid and ill thought out, and they had no Masters working in the town. The town without doubt created Vesuvius and it was the town alone that blew the bloody place to bits—or God's good judgment'—Lutyens interpolated in the diary.

So to Athens, 'a despicably ugly, squalid, uninteresting jerry-built bungaloid growth.' The barren greyness of the Acropolis was the next shock, then the Parthenon's casual, undramatic, siting and pathetic ruin. Was this uninspiring, literally blasted, fragment the epitome of architecture? Ursula saw her father becoming 'desperately depressed, thinking of the futility of all endeavour while God or man destroys so ruthlessly that nothing remains but dirt and squalor'.

> The most tragic spot I ever visited, [he described it to his wife] heartbreaking to see the utter valuelessness of all human endeavour. The Parthenon was there, all I knew it to be, but oh so little of it. No one silhouette was per-

fect, the restorations being attempted are woeful. It is a glorious remnant of what has never, at its best, been a unit perfect in itself. The craftsmanship, the cutting of the marble, was superb, but the work is not so convincing when it comes to the bonding of the external angles of their cellas. The Erectheon and Temple of Wingless Victory are very disappointing; the Temple of Theseus a box and little more. The Parthenon has no relation to its site, no dramatic sense such as Romans had. The site must have been chosen by extraneous causes—the settling of an eagle, a prophet's dream.

I looked at it long, and the more I looked the more depressed I became. The design is full of cunning and requires months of patient labour with accurate instruments to determine the method prompting its design. It was destroyed for its beauty by man, as God surely destroyed Pompeii for its bestiality and common labour.

He told architectural students at home that whilst seeing the Parthenon he was conscious only of the tragic waste. Yet even so, no one could say it was dull; even the pain it produced was not dull. It was the profound labours and creative force expended on its design as an entity within itself that challenged imagination.

No more than four stones are alike, and only two of those are interchangeable. It was designed without allowance for chance. The mind creating it was, in the artistic sense, blind as is the sap within forest trees. I can imagine the scientists of old defying the creations of their artist friends and designing the Parthenon to prove that by science alone real beauty can be achieved.

But at the time, it is evident, he could not resolve the reactions to the Parthenon of his dual nature, his romantic emotionalism and his intellectual idealism, the alternating and periodic fusing together of which was a process of his genius. The former comes out in his discovery that the Greeks had no sense of dramatic siting or pictorial relationships, qualities as fundamental in his English scale of values as the design's organic unity in that of his idealism. Very little acquaintance with Hellenic scholarship, or with the motives of romanticism, would have prevented his disillusion. But he brought to the Acropolis the virgin mind of the artist. He turned with relief to two little brick Byzantine churches, and to the romantic landscape of Attica with the setting sun gilding the Parthenon as the boat carried them away.

The war memorials on the skyline of Gallipoli were only more monuments for decay, in his disillusioned eyes; and the magnificence of the approach to Constantinople did not alter his desire only to see Santa Sophia. At last they entered her, through the narthex bescaffolded by Professor Whittemore. Lutyens's description in the diary is:

Lovely detail—panelled marbles of too much variety had all been polished. Some extraordinarily childish, from a design point of view; the caps of the pilasters terminating the colonnades just eked out to fit (Wren would have had a Roman fit), and the geometry of some of the vaulting in the angles of the main octagon was curiously uninventive. They had craftsmen, a patron, a great geometric idea; but in that, as the guides reported, it was built in seven years with three architects, it looks as though, in an intellectual way, it might have been built by seven architects in three years.

> We have seen great Architecture—great ideas—but no one thing complete. Ruined, either by God (and He may be forgiven) or by Man—for the reason (God be Willingdon!) that he knew better. He only wanted difference, and that his own.

The relevance of that last bracketted quip will emerge in due course, but here it may be interjected that Lutyens's brooding on the futility of architectural idealism in the face of God's and man's destructiveness is largely accountable by the news that was beginning to reach him of alterations to Viceroy's House by Lord Irwin's successor.

So the cruise continued, in perfect weather and imperfect company. Rhodes, restored by Mussolini, a clean place at last with trees and flowers and a lot of new buildings 'not particularly good but intelligently sympathetic to the place'; Cyprus ('nothing to see here; father didn't go ashore'); a glorious drive over the Lebanon to Baalbec. Of the Temple of the Sun 'the scale was magnificent, but the Architect was a man of little skill in the craft of Architecture, loading everything with needless ill-placed ornament, a collection of features and broken cornices unhappy in their spacing and positions and ill-proportioned'. Damascus 'thrice damned—dirty, dusty, dreary'. Miles of Biblical country, Jordan, Sea of Galilee, Cana, and Nazareth at evening, quiet and clean and sweet-smelling. At the Casa Nova Hotel, run by Franciscan monks, Lutyens asked (luckily of a foreign monk) 'how many times do I ring for a virgin?' Then grief and horror for Jerusalem, where the only two good things were Sir John Burnett's British War Cemetery, a beautifully kept relief to the slop and squalor around, and the convent of the Ecce Homo, not for its architecture but for its clean sweetness and the Mother Superior's gentle holiness. Everywhere else dense filth, quarrelling sects, warring buildings each towering over its neighbour. No reference, unaccountably, to the Dome of the Rock, but this Lutyensian comment on the environs:

> The old villages with their simple horizontal lines forming terraces in themselves, intertreed, are charming, and with a new town built on the surrounding hills they would adorn and give point to the old city with its mass of features jewelled within a simple and gentle setting. Ecce Homines.

At Cairo the Pyramids had not changed since 1916, but the mystery of the Sphinx had been deflowered by the uncovering of its paws. So pleasantly and uneventfully homeward, passing at Etaples 'the British monument awaiting its destruction in the coming war'.

As a tail-piece to the record of 'our Marvellous Marmalade Moon' Lutyens set this tribute to his daughter:

> Receipt against boredom and other ills.
> Take, without dilution, large doses of Ursie, and continue the treatment. An intoxicant that has no evil effects and stimulates the heart.

Next year he went on a real pilgrimage from Liverpool to Rome, in the company of the Archbishop, Monsignor Adamson, Mr. Doyle the contractor, and a train-load of the devout. His purpose was twofold. To obtain the Pope's approval of the plans for the Cathedral; and to interview a Prix de Rome scholar who had 'gone modern'. It was a very uncomfortable journey, and after dutifully processing round St. Peter's for some time, he managed to slip away in order to roam about by himself, while 'the great church was still full of chant and song, these thousands of folk singing different hymns in different languages; and an effect not unpleasant, like a gigantic musical beehive'. Then the same process at St. Paul's Without the Walls. Next morning, in tail coat, Orders, and hard shirt, with the Archbishop and the pilgrims to see the Pope. After waiting for three hours he was received, knelt, and on instruction kissed St. Peter's Ring. His Holiness discoursed to him for some time in Italian, saying (he learnt afterwards) that he had seen and admired the plans and was glad that the Lady Chapel was to be built first, since people in England appeared to have forgotten the existence of Our Lady. Then an impressive thing happened. Among the pilgrims in the Hall of Audience was an Indian with his Eurasian wife and a baby that had fever. The Pope asked for the baby to be brought to him, saying 'Suffer little children to come unto me'.

> The mother and babe climbed the steps of the throne and the Pope laid a very large and apparently heavy hand on the baby's head and blessed it. The mother nearly fell down the steps but the Pope leant forward to help her, and gentlemen of the Court led her to safety. The pilgrims were thrilled—for the sick baby was cured, temperature normal!

Afterwards Lutyens produced his plans to be 'vetted ritualistically'. It turned out, he told Lady Emily, that:

> all I had proposed was wonderful and perfect; I seem to have known all and every particular of the adoration of Our Lady. This comes from having a wife I love! So I know instinctively how to Hail Mary.

Following this highly satisfactory interview came the more difficult one with the student. His handling of it, and advice, are typically humane and illustrate the theory of aesthetic science applied to a common problem of the 'thirties. The young man at the British School, of which Lutyens was a Commissioner,

> had gone off on the German-Corbusier tack, bored with having to go through a course of measuring ancient buildings to no useful purpose as they have all been measured a hundred times before. So he and two other students are collaborating to design a Dominican Priory in the new nude style, grammarless and cheaply adjectived. I criticised fairly freely, but was fearful of driving the boy to extreme rebellion. I shall have to report it all to the Commissioners at home. But afterwards I got him alone for two hours.
>
> He had won the Prix de Rome, accepted it and all it involved, to carry out its articles. At his age, 22, discipline was invaluable, and in after life he will get a lot of it, so it is just as well to learn patience when young. I advised him to measure up some ancient building suitable to his purpose, then, for his thesis, take the building and translate it, whilst maintaining the proportions, to a modern building.

The great architect may have given the young student the gist of a lecture that he had delivered at New College, Oxford, earlier this year (1933):

> It is not a bad scheme to memorize a design in figures and dictate it to a fellow student to draw out, who can return the compliment. It is an exercise requiring accurate thought and expression, wherein nothing can be left to chance or to a dexterous twist of the pencil. The blind sap of knowledge alone can lead beauty to a height beyond the power of the human eye to reach—the eye becoming merely the servant of the mind. Even so the architect of the Parthenon must have used his brain to create beauty.
>
> In design ratio is essential, and that ratio must be maintained throughout the trajectory of the intention; without the deviations claimed by doubting eyes and verbose taste.
>
> Do not anathemise the column. Do not despise 'the orders'. I appreciate the boredom of their registration—their true purpose is no longer acknowledged. But they are the analysis of the work of past masters, and are, at the most, but the skeletons of their traditions. They should be studied and used with understanding, imagination, and invention. For no two masters used them alike, each differing in his own interpretation.
>
> To copy any one sequence literally is liable to create a mere collection of dry bones.
>
> Nor is it, in any way, imperative to use columns or other forms, when foreign to the purpose of a building. The river front of Trinity College, Cambridge, shows how Wren evolved an astylar treatment.

There is never any forced originality in the great art of building. History shows that 'return' is of more importance than blind adventure, and it is on the lines of intelligent evolution that the best service can be rendered. It will need the collective efforts of at least three generations to regain the human quality lost by architecture in the last hundred years.

So, he repeated, have faith, measure, translate.

His own allegiances were so firm and so manifestly devout, he was so plainly an artist of giant stature, that irreverent architectural students and reverend Fathers accepted him with equal delight and respect. Possibly with the latter, however, there was something of the wisdom that Anatole France depicts in the story of *Le Jongleur de Nôtre Dame*. For his part, self-projection enabled him to out-Pope the Pope in architectural imagination and personally he obviously felt *en rapport* with the dignataries of the Roman Catholic Church as he had never felt with those of his own; a maternal, Irish Catholic, streak in him, perhaps, that had always secretly and now openly rebelled against the Protestant puritanism of his father. Archbishop Downey and his Monsignors entered happily into the spirit of the joke when, in earnest conference, he loosed a clockwork mouse over the plans of the Cathedral. In proposing a toast at the archiepiscopal table, Lutyens could raise his glass and proclaim:

> *'Here's to the happiest hours of our life*
> *Spent in the arms of another man's wife!*

Gentlemen, our Mothers.' Or, in the course of being conducted by Cardinal Bourne over Westminster Cathedral, in the early days of his Liverpool work, his guide was not scandalised when he pointed to the words *Ave, Ave, Sancte* on the walls of the Lady Chapel, asking, 'Tell me, Your Eminence, do two 'Aves make an 'Oly?' Father D'Arcy S.J. recounts a favourite conjuring trick that Brother Ned (the term is apposite again) used to demonstrate on a stranger, bidding him hold a matchbox, so, in his left hand, so; watch it carefully; now put the right hand over it; then raise the left knee, further, further; ending with 'Now, do you feel your leg being pulled?' But Father Ronald Knox, asked on first introduction to Brother Ned, 'Do you know it is a scientific fact that when you cut a carrot its temperature drops?' was quite equal to the question, replying, 'Yes, and when you cut a friend his temperature rises!'

In 1934 he received the honorary degree of Doctor of Law at Oxford. After a rehearsal of his merits by the Public Orator, a witty verse was sung to the tune of *Good King Wenceslas*:

> *This is where we raise a shout and burnish our escutcheons.*
> *The better to reflect the glory of Sir Edwin Lutyens.*
> *Mighty things he can erect from a Doll's House to a Dam, Sir.*
> *He's George's Royal Architect and Mary's little Lamb, Sir.*

*At Delhi in the mystic East Sir Edwin's star is rising,
And Jumna's plain is fair again with forms of his devising.
So don't be nervous, little Lut, and do not stand so shyly;
A gorgeous figure you will cut, when advertised by Reilly.*

Some of these pleasantries were connected with the building of Campion Hall, Oxford, for the Society of Jesus, the preliminaries to which, however, had been accompanied by a very unpleasant episode. The Society had for some time been contemplating expanded quarters, and had obtained a design from an architect for enlarging their house in St. Giles's. The plans were apparently not entirely satisfactory, and Lady Horner suggested to Father D'Arcy that he should ask Lutyens to give a confidential opinion. The opinion was unfavourable; 'Queen Anne in front, Mary Anne behind,' whereat Father D'Arcy asked whether Lutyens could recommend another young architect for the work. 'If you put it like that,' he replied, 'there is nothing I would rather do myself.' For a time the matter lapsed, till a new site was obtained, off St. Aldates, when Lutyens agreed to provide designs, undertaking to keep the cost within the original figure. There ensued a complaint from the previous architect of unprofessional conduct on the part of Lutyens. At the formal inquiry the charge was unanimously dismissed.

Campion Hall consists of two ranges at right angles enclosing the old garden of Micklem Hall, which forms the third side. Owing to the restriction of the site the building had to be high and is seen only in sharp perspective, so that, with the need to incorporate Micklem Hall, regularity of elevation was neither possible nor called for. The design, using local rubble with Clipsham stone for dressings, must therefore be of that picturesque order stemming from Munstead—indeed recall the joke about Miss Jekyll's house resembling 'a monastery of the time of the Heptarchy' (p. 536). Whenever in his later years he used his romantic mode, any sentimental looseness there had been was replaced by the ordered scale and rhythm of the 'aesthetic science'. The façade and angle to the street presented by the chapel are austerely simple, almost devoid of windows, yet, within the limitations imposed, display a sensitiveness of handling and a massive reserve which grow upon the observer. Its virtues are the negations of that striving for effect, that 'advertisement', which Lutyens so often reprehended now; and are more noticeable when this modest building is compared with other recent contributions to Oxford architecture of the same materials and intentions. There is a more exquisite simplicity about the barrel-vaulted chapel where, with roughly rendered plaster and natural oak woodwork, strong colour is concentrated in the lighting pendants and Brangwyn's panels. An obvious instance of the interbreeding of Lutyens's later with his earlier stylism is the occurrence of the Delhi Order in the columns of the baldachino filling the apse. The Spanish artist J. M. Sert offered to fresco the Chapel as a gift if he were commissioned to decorate the vaults of Liverpool Cathedral. Lutyens, however, as on other similar occasions, objected to mural decorations that he was not in a position to control.

His principles affecting colour in mural decoration and stained glass are contained in these two extracts from addresses relating to the Cathedral but no less applicable to this and others of his buildings.

> On the plaster surfaces of vaults and domes I hope to see lots of black—an important factor in all impressive decoration.
>
> In our climate the sun is not strong enough to give, by contrast, the dark glowing shade essential to the success of mosaic.[1]
>
> In the Cathedral, the greater volume of light will be through windows invisible from any normal position. The sills of the great windows in the Narthex and Transepts will be in view some 120 ft. above the floor. They may be blazoned with cypher, emblem, or heraldry, but then with great restraint.
>
> The glass generally I propose to keep clear, so that the passing clouds may be seen and give, by their movement, an impression of great stability to the vaults of the massive structure. The shrines or chapels in the thickness of the walls will cry aloud for glass whereby no outside movement may distract.
>
> In general, windows in their sequence should be the work of one mind by one community of craftsmen, endowed with one cadence of colour, and that restricted; of one intention to a common focus, by which I mean that the eye remains constant and is not consciously forced to expand and contract to meet the demands of sight.
>
> I think perspective should be avoided, and no sense be given as of space beyond the picture plane common to the glass itself.
>
> The scale of the figures should be kept small. Those large, holy, haloed Saints, bearded, and packed in grotesque stone crocketted niches, that bring outside in, should, in my opinion, be avoided. Complete separation should be maintained between man's work within and nature's work without, and the window be treated more like a page of fine script with illuminated initials, so that it promotes the same attitude of vision as pertains to a picture book; rather than that of a painted landscape.
>
> The Chinese method of isometric drawing is one by which the eye is not waylaid by misguiding perspective. The design remains constant to the surface it adorns.
>
> I often wonder why black is not more frequently used. If you want great dignity in decoration, use black. It is conducive to magnificence.
>
> I feel it in my bones that, as in jewelry, glass should never be made to look like jewels. Sir W. Richmond's Byzantine kaleidoscopic windows in St. Paul's

[1] To the Architectural Association, 1932.

Cathedral are to me somewhat distressing. Even in the churches in Greece and in the Mosques in Constantinople, that type of glass seems to burn with a deliberate intention to destroy the fabric, and to put the mosaics into the corners of correction.[1]

On quitting the Royal Institute he accepted the Presidency of a recently founded body, the Incorporated Association of Architects and Surveyors. At their annual gatherings its President delivered himself of some of his best remembered pleasantries, such as 'Doctors, unlike Architects, can bury their failures'.

Having himself entered architecture through a country builder's yard he had never been happy about the prevailing system of architectural education:

> The city student has too easy access to the solutions of problems, and learns the solutions before he can absorb the problems. He is too easily influenced by passing foreign fashions. In due course he goes gaily forth, full of knowledge but with no real sympathy with or understanding of the country, which he seems eager to destroy to prove what may be but an architectural slogan.[2]

This conviction had long coloured his relations with the Royal Institute. After the setting up of the first Architects' Registration Council following the passage of the principal Rigistration Act, he visualised the need for a new architectural society that should be open to all registered architects irrespective of sectional interests, and be primarily concerned with the day to day professional interests of its members, whilst establishing the title and qualifications of registered architects in public estimation and protecting the public against unqualified practitioners. Accordingly in 1933 the Institute of Registered Architects was formed with Lutyens as its first President. Though the 1938 Act has made registration obligatory, the I.R.A's accession of numerical strength has justified the soundness of his contentions.[3]

Other changes had taken place in the background of Lutyens's practice. Both offices were moved, in 1931, to 5 Eaton Gate, a large house taken in expectation of work on the scale of the 'twenties. There the Delhi drawing office was on the top floor, the 'Cathedral room' occupied the first floor. But the economic depression of the early 'thirties, of which one effect was that the building of the great church proceeded on a very much smaller and slower scale than had been expected, from the outset rendered Eaton Gate unnecessarily large.

In 1935, A. J. Thomas's long service of thirty-three years with Lutyens ended. For most of that time, if not from the beginning, it had been understood that Thomas was free to take work on his own account. Lately this had increased to an extent which, in Lutyens's opinion, interfered with the discharge of his duties to himself.

---

[1] To the British Society of Master Glass Painters, May 18, 1933.
[2] Presidential Address to I.A.A.S., 1931.   [3] *See* The *Daily Telegraph,* August 25, 1933.

The remarkable position that he had come to occupy in Lutyens's office was taken by no successor, had that been possible or desirable. Though a steady stream of work passed through, it never attained the proportions that rendered a successor necessary. The empty rooms, however, were put to an appropriate, and satisfactory, use when in 1936 they were leased to Robert Lutyens, now already established in independent practice. This geographical *rapprochement* of father and son, after some degree of estrangement for a dozen years, was a source of happiness and benefit to both. The position of a great architect's son who intends to follow the same career is not an easy one if he also is of independent spirit and not content to follow from the outset in an established path; the more so if the father is not accustomed to working with a partner. In the circumstances, Robert Lutyens's determination to make his own professional way unassisted was an honourable one and had met with considerable success. But both came to feel the artificiality of their separation. Their reunion followed Lord Jersey's commissioning the latter to build a new house at Middleton Park, near Bicester, and expressing the hope that the younger architect would consult his father when preparing the designs. The outcome was a collaboration on much the same lines as that at Gledstone. The son took much of the burden of discussion and all the weight of execution off the father's shoulders, but Lutyens contributed from the abundance of his invention and experience to an extent which justifies Middleton being regarded as the last of his series of great country houses. Technically it is interesting as demonstrating how the luxurious requirements of the time—a dozen bathrooms, with accommodation for numerous visiting valets and maids—could be met within the framework of the aesthetic science without a water-pipe or a window conflicting with the symmetrical unity (p. 536).

It had been intended to use the materials of the rather undistinguished Georgian predecessor of the new house, but in the event the golden Clipsham stone was used; and, as owner's requirements grew, so a modest intention developed into one of the largest private houses with which Lutyens was ever concerned. There are features in the design which link it with Gledstone and Washington, notably the use made of four little houses for staff to dramatise the approach, each a cube with pyramidal roof culminating in a central chimney stack; in the emphasis on the tall narrow first-floor windows; and in the pronounced pitch of all the roofs. And there are affinities to Campion Hall in the analogous but more elaborately subtle application of craftsmanship to the same stone. Without going into these intricacies and those surmounted in the plan, Middleton can be indicated as an impressive realisation, on the plane of domestic architecture, of Lutyens's 'ideal vision'. Here he had an appreciative patron and an ingenious partner who between them enabled him to work out that 'unity of method' which he was carrying further in the drawings and model for Liverpool Cathedral.

In the mid-thirties the full scheme for the Midland Bank, Poultry, was completed in two phases; and Sir Roderick Jones, for whom he had done up the Grange at Rottingdean, commissioned the Reuters and Press Association Headquarters in Fleet Street (1935), in association with Messrs. Smee and Houchin. It was his most 'modern' building, but in the design of the entrance front there are refinements as advanced as in the Poultry bank. Bombing of some adjacent buildings has temporarily revealed the care he took to relate the almost invisible east façade to the adjacent steeple of St. Bride's Church. It was one of those courtesies that, in those hustling days, few would observe; but which, as he used to say, 'God sees.' In adjoining Salisbury Court, 'The Cogers' shows how Lutyens built a public house.

Much of his most characteristic skill went at this time into work at the opposite extreme of his architectural range. The trustees of the picturesque Devon village of Cockington put in his hands the design for the village inn, the Drum. He was given a free hand to use simple traditional materials of good quality, and with the local stone, oak, and thatch produced that often sought but rarely found delight, the ideal country inn. In a bridge to carry a road over the Pilgrim's Way, near Guildford, he returned to the very scenes of his youth and enjoyed the opportunity to use the oak and Bargate stone of his earliest Surrey houses, handled now with no less cunning but with an assurance which he had not always shown in the 'nineties. Then in 1936 his old friend Reginald McKenna came to him again to build a new house adjoining the ancient flint ruins of Halnaker, on the Sussex Downs near Goodwood. This, again, should be described as a collaboration, since not only had McKenna already sketched the plan he wanted, and chosen its materials, whitewashed brick and Sussex tiles, but Lutyens's colleague on the Midland Bank, Mr. L. M. Gotch, was associated in the administrative part of the work. To the superficial eye, Halnaker reflects, near the end of Lutyens's astonishing trajectory, the inspiration of its beginning, in the roofy whitewashed idealisations of Randolph Caldecott. But more careful inspection, as also in the case of the standard small house designed at Chobham, Surrey, for Messrs. W. H. Colt in order to demonstrate Canadian red cedarwood, shows unmistakably the master hand that left 'nothing to chance' and gave its inimitable touch to the smallest component. At Halnaker, for instance, that most ordinary utility, a wall-ventilator, becomes a tiny work of art when fashioned from fragments of roofing tiles.

Seen out of relationship to Lutyens's main preoccupation, these reversions to his youthful manner might suggest an ageing man's reminiscences. In fact, each was the product of its site or other conditions, though no doubt they constituted pleasant diversions from more exacting and uncreative disciplines. Chief of the latter was his appointment in 1935 as Consultant to Sir Charles Bressey in the preparation of the Highway Development Survey (Greater London), of which the outcome was the 'Bressey-Lutyens Report' in 1938. The terms of reference required a plan providing for the needs of the next thirty years in the 1821 square miles of the Greater London

Area. An incident of the assignment was a flight over London—Lutyens's first and only adventure into the air.

He did not enjoy it, mistrusted committing his 14 stone of weight to the heavens. But the aerial view of architecture fascinated him.

> I could scarcely believe Hampton Court could be so small. My bridge from the air looks ever so much better than any others—why? I know, but I shan't write it. But it was odd. Hatfield, North Mymms, dwellings and developement. One knew at once whether a good architect or a bad had been at work. Very refreshing, knowing one was looking at things from what one might call God's point of view.
>
> The amount of green was striking; the amount of garden allowed to the average houses, and the countless tennis courts. All very interesting and perplexing, making the world a difficult place to keep tidy and *soignée*. The simplicity of Hampton Court, its childlike planning, surprised me. The deliberate waywardness of all else was bewildering—the incoherent mess and undirected endlessness was the last chapter of Revelations.

His part in the Survey was to advise upon the architectural aspects of the proposals made, as when recommended routes cutting through built-up areas might create unprofitable and untidy sites of irregular shape defying architectural treatment and unsuitable for modern buildings. Paragraph 54 of the Report, in which several characteristic turns of phrase suggest Lutyens's hand, besides the sentences quoted as his, outlines the town-planning policy that has since been developed from it:

> In many parts of London the area occupied collectively by streets, alleys, and courts is extravagantly large and nothing but advantage would accrue from the creation of larger building blocks served by streets spaced at wider intervals. . . . 'Special care should be taken to give proper architectural form to the roundabouts. It is all-important that the building lines adjacent to these, as well as the buildings themselves, should form parts of a well-considered architectural design. . . To achieve well-designed sky lines, careful consideration should be given to the prosceniums of the streets that converge upon them. It is desirable that the design of any one roundabout should be controlled by a single mind.'

Lutyens contributed the sketches of typical roundabouts included in the Report, and collaborated closely with Sir Charles Bressey in the lines recommended for specific new streets.

Memorials of old friends and contemporaries provided constantly recurring occupation now. There had been the Lord Cheylesmore monument in Embankment Gardens (1928), Lord Northcliffe's at St. Dunstan's-in-the-West (1930), the tomb for Edward Hudson's family at Hampstead (1931). In the autumn of 1932 Sir

Herbert Jekyll died, and that winter Gertrude Jekyll passed peacefully away with the last roses. Lutyens had helped to persuade her in 1920 to allow Nicholson to paint the portrait (p. 350), for which she would only spare her rest time after dusk. So the painter applied some of the daylight that she grudged for herself to a portrait of her boots. Both masterpieces were acquired by Lutyens who gave them to the Tate Gallery. After her death he was anxious that both should be transferred to the National Portrait Gallery, of which he was a Trustee; but a decade has to elapse after a person's death before a portrait is eligible for the national collection, and boots, even when such speaking likenesses as these, must be left outside. His memorials at Busbridge, Surrey, to the Jekylls, sponsors of his early success, were erected in 1934. It must have been about 1930 that Lord Birkenhead had teased him about reported short-comings of the Washington Embassy by saying that, but for these, he had been going to ask him to design his memorial. Lutyens was nettled, so replied that he had already an idea for it. What was it? 'A rolling stone,' he retorted. Within a year he had to devise the altar tomb for this sparring-partner in Chorlton-cum-Hardy churchyard, which suggests something of the statesman's exuberant spirit in the lively baroque forms of its sculpture. In 1933 he designed Melba's memorial for Melbourne, another singer's, Conchita Supervia, in 1937, the Aldrich Blake monument in Tavistock Square (with Lady Scott), and Lord Grey of Falloden's (with Reid Dick) at the Foreign Office (1936). J. C. Drewe's, his faithful client at Castle Drogo, had been designed in 1932, H. J. Tennant's of Great Maytham, in 1936, and Lord and Lady Revelstoke's plain altar tomb was set up under the rampart of Lambay. At Knebworth he devised the grave of Nanny Sleath, his and the family's mentor for forty years, in 1939 where already Mrs. C. W. Earle (Aunt T) and his nephew Antony, Lord Knebworth, had been commemorated by him. In 1936 he designed the George V Memorial at Windsor and, with Sir W. Reid Dick, the tomb in St. George's Chapel to the King with whom he had had such long and friendly consultations over Delhi.

He had already designed the King George V Memorial and fountains at Delhi, to the cost of which H.H. the Maharaja of Kapurthala was a generous contributor. But since 1931 his connection with the Government of India had ceased. Lady Willingdon, when her husband succeeded Lord Irwin in that year, had expressed to Lutyens warm appreciation of Viceroy's House. But before long rumours began to arrive that not only various uncompleted works, agreed to be finished, were being countermanded, but alterations being made, and integral features being moved, without reference to him. Jerry-built development on the outskirts was proceeding uncontrolled, threatening to make the approaches to New Delhi as squalid, he feared, as the Old City. A Stadium, originally mooted in commemoration of Lord Irwin's viceroyalty but eventually named after Lord Willingdon, was to be sited on the central axis between the Memorial Arch and Purana Kila. And important buildings such as the Reserve Bank, Supreme Court, and Federal Chambers, on the character of which he felt not unreasonably he should at least be consulted, were projected. Hall wrote on his behalf in 1931, to Col. Hastings Ismay (now Lord Ismay), Military Secretary to the Viceroy:

> I have been informed that the Government of India consider that the work can be safely entrusted to the Government Architect, since the number of buildings will not be great, and presumably do not see the necessity of submitting these to Sir Edwin for criticism. It is apparently not realised how important it is that the Architect responsible for the general layout, and particularly of the Kings Way, Memorial Arch, and Sunk Garden at Purana Kila, should be consulted on the type of building to be erected on such an important site. Two years ago Sir Edwin was approached, and thought that, whilst it would be quite possible to formulate a scheme for the stadium on that site, great care would have to be taken in designing the buildings in order that they should in no way spoil the effect of the Memorial Arch and the walls of Purana Kila. It is quite impossible for another architect, however good, to know what was in the mind of the original designer.

But these formal requests had no more effect than his own personal appeals, such as this to Lady Willingdon:

> Rumours grow like weeds. The latest is that Your Excellency is glazing in the loggias, which is possibly true but would lead me to pray for a just fire.

(The Viceroy's room had recently been slightly damaged by fire.) The ventilating eye of the Durbar Hall dome had been closed by a solid covering whence to hang a chandelier. The sculptured elephants were removed from the screen of Viceroy's Court to serve as ornaments of the garden, where unauthorised cypress and other trees were being planted. Decorations were introduced into the House where he had studied simplicity. The Vicereine's favourite colour scheme was preferred to the architect's, leading him to refer to her with increasing frankness as the 'mauvey *sujet*'. His facetiousness, however, concealed a bitter astonishment that the creations, great or small, representing near twenty years of an artist's lifework, could thus carelessly be contorted, mauled, ignored. But this disillusion pierced deeper than his feelings for his own work, as we have noticed in his melancholy brooding upon the Acropolis. Such an exhibition of indifference to the artist's vision, displayed by government or individual, conjured up a prospect of the denial of every tenet, the destruction of every rhythmic arch, in the cathedral of his creed, by an internal or external proletariat that deliberately repudiated the Western tradition of art.

A story that can aptly end this chapter has been told me by my colleague. Lutyens and he were returning together one night from the City and Guilds of

London Institute Art School in Kennington, at which Lutyens, as visitor in architecture, had been talking to the students. On the way back he had spoken feelingly of his anxieties for Viceroy's House. He had, he said, written to the King on the matter, who had spoken to the Queen, who had written sharply to Lady Willingdon, who had taken no action. On reaching Mansfield Street about midnight, he had invited Butler to look at the Cathedral model, which at that time filled the drawing-room. As they examined it, Butler says, Lutyens 'became as it were transformed and with a kind of anxious humility explained the design, with special reference to the section of the nave which, he pointed out, provided the unit of the design. Butler was deeply moved by this first, mid-nocturnal sight of the mighty conception, but more so, he relates, by the appearance of the man beside him, so changed from the eminent, sociable, laughing Lutyens of a few minutes earlier. He saw for those moments the creator, without his protective mask, utterly absorbed and serious, contemplating his greatest creation, humbly, because he saw that it was good.

CHAPTER XIX

AS LIGHT FELL SHORT

§1. LAST JOURNEY TO INDIA

IN October, 1938, Lutyens left on his eighteenth passage to India. The new Viceroy, the Marquess of Linlithgow, wished him to report formally on the restoration of Viceroy's House to its condition in 1931 and on any works agreed but not executed for its completion. And there was a projected processional arch and layout at Jaipur, designed in collaboration with Robert in 1937, the site of which needed to be inspected.[1]

At this time the word 'black-out' had been already introduced into the vocabulary of internal decoration. In England, all but the most optimistic were discouraged from undertaking architectural ventures above ground, though time had been bought at Munich. However, during the preceding twelve months Lutyens had been working on the designs of the National Theatre (South Kensington site) in collaboration with Mr. Cecil Masey; and, among other things, on a housing scheme on part of the country club of Ranelagh. There was a storm on the Cathedral committee at Liverpool, directed to obtaining more rapid progress with the building of the crypt walls by, if necessary, omitting the granite. Since the basement was designed to consist entirely of granite, Lutyens remarked that it was like exhorting a knitter to get on with a sock and leave out the wool. The Archbishop, he heard, had lectured the committee on the difference of the Cathedral from ordinary buildings and insisted that the architect must be supported, not hampered. The specification of granite held good. There was faith, therefore, in the Church.

During the familiar voyage he learnt further details of Lady Willingdon's alterations from Lord and Lady Linlithgow, who were fellow passengers. It was hot when he arrived at Bombay on October 24, and, no longer attended by accustomed henchmen, Hall or Persotum, he had difficulty with the Customs. An official seized a tin case, declared as containing plans, with the statement that none might be imported till fumigated. Lutyens remonstrated that he had brought or sent them into India for thirty years without this precaution being deemed necessary, and they were plans for the Viceroy and Government. 'Plans!' replied the Inspector, 'I thought you said plants!' It was all very hot-making. His train, leaving at 8.15 p.m., was due to

[1] The Maharaja had commissioned this scheme from Robert Lutyens, in connection with which he had gone to India in 1937 but proposed that his father be asked to collaborate. The designs (never executed) included fountains of which each jet sustained a ball as if by magic. The drawings are signed jointly.

reach the station for Jaipur at 2 o'clock the following afternoon, whence he would have a three-hour motor drive to his destination. He wrote a letter from a new hotel at Bombay which had 'all the terrifying paralysis of the modern touch', though it was better, he owned, than the 'Indoshamiana style'. It was nearly his last joke. Long before the letter reached his wife, his son received a cable dispatched from Jaipur, October 28:

> Regret inform you Sir Edwin is suffering from patch pneumonia. State Doctor reports he is progressing favourably as can be expected.
>
> Maharaja.

Another followed, stating progress was normal 'though naturally condition is regarded serious. Crisis expected two or three days'.

His two elder children, Barbara Wallace and Robert, made preparations to fly to his bedside should his condition—he was in his seventieth year—give cause for more serious anxiety. However, further cables, from the Viceroy's Military Secretary as well as from the State Doctor, were reassuring. On the 31st, no complications had developed; on November 1, the crisis was past and temperature normal; on the 2nd, 'condition very satisfactory, convalescence starting, no further cables necessary.' Sitting on the verandah of the State hospital on November 1, he wrote, unsteadily, of how it had happened, beginning '$\begin{smallmatrix}\text{O}\\\text{My}\end{smallmatrix}$ trapped!'

For a decade he had been increasingly prone to colds, and, veteran of innumerable train journeys, 'train fever' had nearly been the end of him. After the sticky heat of Bombay, the night was cold; in the antiquated sleeping car he could neither get the window to shut nor discover how to switch off the fans. It became very cold, then a grotesque nightmare of shivering horror. He had too few clothes on the bed, and those were continually blown off by the draught. 'Almost naked I shivered over the clothes that fled me and held them lest they escape me again. With dawn came realisation of complete exhaustion.' He managed to leave the train, but, already feverish, the long motor-drive, involving a river crossing, finished the night's work. When he reached Jaipur he was delirious, and was immediately put to bed in the hospital 'with two nurses, night and day, or wet and dry'.

He was evidently well tended, making a very rapid recovery. Before he left on the 7th, he was climbing walls and ladders with 'Jai', seeing all he needed for the work in hand. But the two nurses accompanied him to Delhi, where he was met by A.D.C.s and conducted to Viceroy's House.

That evening he went all over the garden with Lady Linlithgow by moonlight. It had grown up amazingly, though the bigger trees still had far to go. Next morning he was up at 6.30, wandering about in his 'dreggy', but kept a promise not to go up yet to the State rooms. On the ship he had owned to be rather dreading

AS LIGHT FELL SHORT

the sight of 'all the putrid mischievousness'. But, once back in the great familiar House,

> my thrill to be here gave me a choke, and, perhaps being a little on the weak side, tears are very near the surface.

A stenographer was detailed to accompany him around the premises, recording all Lady Willingdon's 'vagarious vagaries', and his own intentions, executed and unexecuted. Many of these had already been attended to. W. R. Musto, who had planted every tree and knew its name, was summoned from his present station at Jodhpur. Together the old allies spent several days on the gardens and avenues, tracing from the original plans 'the amazingly ingenious destruction of tidiness', that had taken place, and noting the trees that, barely established, had been cut down for sundry reasons. 'I have got rid of all the silly cypresses,' he wrote: 'they won't grow at Delhi; at the Villa d'Este, yes, but in India detestable'. The white elephants introduced into the garden had already gone back to their gate-piers. Day by day for a week he perambulated 'dictating facts, comments, criticisms'. On Armistice Day he attended the ceremony at the Memorial Arch, beyond which the Willingdon Stadium now blocked the view to Purana Kila. One day he devoted to driving round and round Delhi. Another to the old city, where he noted that, by continual changes of policy, the Indian administration had missed the opportunities of betterment created by the building of the new city. 'If they ever get control of New Delhi, it will be done for.' But he was delighted to see that the great avenue of Kings Way had become popular with Indians for evening walks, with the space round the Arch packed with cars 'of them that take their walks'. He completed his report, though he found it a considerable effort. 'But I think they will do everything and put the house back as I left it.' The proposals for Federation were raising the possibility of the Government needing another great building, for which he said he was going to make sketches. He was asked to write the whole history of the designing and building of Delhi from its inception.[1] During his visit he came in for two Viceregal dinner parties. Lord Linlithgow had brought a quantity of fine family plate with him, so that the long table and buffets of the State Dining-Room made a fine show. He revisited No. 1 Bungalow, where he had lived for so many seasons. He went back to the stone which, on leaving the House in 1931, he had surreptitiously kissed, 'and rubbed the place very gently with my pocket hanky.'

He looked up many old friends, English and Indian. Then in Bombay, Persotum, now a feeble old man, came to meet him. His grandson, at one time in Lutyens's office, was now well established in the Viceregal drawing office. Lutyens and his

---

[1] A page and a half of typescript describing the preliminary meetings of the Survey Commission may be the beginning of this. The history got no further and the notes are incorporated in Chapter 9.

bearer had corresponded regularly, exchanging family news, and their rencontre was an emotional one.

The journey, that at one moment had appeared likely to take him further than anybody had expected, resulted in another reunion. Before leaving Delhi for 'Homemily', he received the letter written by his wife on first hearing of his illness. During the forty years of their marriage, tides had ebbed and flowed and ebbed again, exposing rocks that neither had suspected when they had set sail with their Casket, and carrying both to unexpected places and people. It may be supposed that now the tide flooded high again for, writing to her from the boat, with 'the long journey nearly at an end', he finished a letter of deep affection with expressions of gratitude 'for all you have said—I have it in writing'.

§2. PRESIDENT, ROYAL ACADEMY

He got back at the beginning of December, to appearance none the worse, though his silvered hair was now quite white and made a venerable halo to his still rubicund and merry face; and he wearied more easily. A few days later, on Sir William Llewellyn, President of the Royal Academy, reaching the age limit of seventy-five, he was elected his successor, being then himself three months short of seventy. He had been a full Royal Academician since 1920, when he had deposited as his Diploma work the design of the Jaipur Column, and been scrupulous in his attendance of council meetings, also taking his turn, as one of the architect Academicians, as Visitor of the R.A. Architecture School.

Since this side of his work is almost unknown, it is appropriate to consider it at this point, carrying on the allusions that have already been made to his theory and practice, more particularly in Chapter 16 and Chapter 18. He recognised the shortcomings of the R.A. School as regards architecture but had taken his responsibility none the less seriously, as is shown in a letter of September, 1924: 'I teach all day, correcting drawings and explaining what is wrong and why, within my limitations.' The exacting standards that he applied to his own work and to all building did not, however, prevent him being a kind, if stern, critic of young men's work. On the contrary, his conviction of the necessity for evolving tradition made him add restraint to his natural humility in appraising their efforts. His loathing for Ruskin was largely due to the latter's confident laying down of the law: 'look how he broke up years, centuries, of effective teaching by his language and formulated ideas of how things should look. You go in for thought-forms,' he continued, in a letter to his wife:

> so do I, but I have to put my thoughts into practical form and make one breath of thought fit with another to materialise them. Even after years of practice it is

extraordinarily difficult, and entails endless endeavour and rectification, to get thought-forms, with all my training, to fit and materialise.

Directly you become a teacher you cease to teach, in that you cannot practice. Teaching can only be slow, and the modern pupil is avaricious for 'knowledge'. They can only quote and formulate—a method that leads to a collapse at the first ditch. You can teach nothing (to speak of) in a generation.

'No one is too old to be a student,' he told them at one of the annual Prize Givings (1939). 'There is no finality but in corruption,—and then who knows but that honey may ensue? As we age and climb the crags of knowledge and the rocks of experience, the wider are the prospects of discovery and the higher the peaks of possible achievement. I am not going to indulge in the pleasure an old man takes in criticising the young. Your best critic is your own growing power of observation and inner conscience.'

Nevertheless there may here be grouped together a few of Lutyens's aphorisms and observations on architecture, delivered at various times and many of which, in addition to those already quoted, he imparted whether in this form or by implication to students:

TRADITION. We cannot get rid of the body of tradition, murder it as we may.

By tradition I do not mean the hanging of Roman togas on Victorian towel-horses.

Tradition, to me, consists in our inherited sense of structural fitness, the evolution of rhythmic forms by a synthesis of needs and materials, and the avoidance of arbitrary faults by the exercise of common sense coupled with sensibility.

The best old work was composed. Few modern buildings seem to have a feeling of growth: in them the forms and details appear to meet as strangers, and their phrasing to consist in little more than an initial and a mark of new and complete interrogation.

A thing is not vulgar because it is common.

In an age of living art you are unconscious of beauty; it is an atmosphere.

The old is to the modern as is Vermeer to a poster.

RHYTHM. My generation believed that the measure of man's architecture was man, and that the rhythm of a building should correspond to the rhythms familiar in human life.

All architecture must have rhythms that affect the eye, as music does the ear, producing vibrations in the brain. (Cf. Chapter 18, §1: 'all great periods of architecture have one common and essential denominator: Unity in the measured tread of their rhythm.')

The rhythm of modern architecture is rarely genial. It is either a wearisome staccato or a confused medley like the tuning of brass bands.

Is the rhythm which modern architecture expresses that of the proletariat in the mass—crowd psychology in place of the conversation of a civilised man?

GRAMMAR. I require of a building, as of an individual, that a statement should be made gracefully, perhaps with distinction and humour. Many modern buildings, to me, are just shouting very loud and quite unintelligibly. I catch a phrase here and there, recognising a scrap of English or Italian, may be. There is vitality, heaps of it. But there seems to me no grammar and little sincere effort at style.

I feel about the new mode of building that it has been easy to design because there is, as yet, no grammar.

LIGHT. Light is the most important element that architects have to compose with. Any building material that reflects light should generally be avoided. By its reflecting surface it destroys all homogeneity between the street or landscape and the building.

Glass as an essential material has to be used, but I prefer its use in moderate sizes and faceted so no sheet of glare is produced. Areas of glass alone do not give serviceable light. Deep window-reveals which reflect, distributing a diffused light, give the most kindly illumination. Modern construction denies us this great quality.

I have an enormous admiration for the Crystal Palace. Lord Grey said to me 'We are going to buy it for a great Imperial purpose. What would you do with it?' I said 'Put it under a glass case'.

COLOUR. The colour of buildings has both a chromatic and a sculptural sense. You cannot go far wrong in building-colour if you use local materials.

The most remarkable instance I know of colour in masonry, in the sculptural sense, is the basement windows in the Banquetting House, Whitehall. Inigo Jones must have had a knowing eye for colour to have put four stones, instead of three or five, across the openings in the podium wall, thereby maintaining the sculptural colour of his masonry. I have yet to meet an architect who has noticed this invention.

Vanbrugh used his weighty materials as a pigment, and the sky his canvas, with a brush too wide to allow any niceties of detail. Surely Mammon was his Zeus.

There is wit, and may be humour, in the use of material.

London is a brick country, and the dirt of London is its glory. St. Paul's would not be half as beautiful if you whitewashed it.

Our climate is the architect's colour and he must acknowledge it, play up to it.

STEEL & CONCRETE. New materials cannot change the outlook, for the *principles of design* have been, and are for all time, unchangeable.

Shall we ever 'conduct' again the iron posts and beams, with which we build, to some rhythm and code of entases, and so bring beauty in their train?

SPACE AND FORM. The thin walls obtainable by using steel construction are worth while, if only to watch your client's face glow with joy at winning a few square feet of carpet.

But I crave for soft thick noiseless walls of hand-made brick and lime, the deep light and reflecting reveals, the double floors, easy stairways, and doorways never less than 1 ft. 6 in. from a corner.

The waste of space that, unwittingly, creates that most valuable asset, a gain of space.

To get wide rooms, do not build them so low as an American gentleman built his dining room, so low that he could only have soles for dinner.

Architecture, with its love and passion, begins where function is achieved.

The period when he set the subject for the students came to be regarded by them as the highlight of the course, and the evenings that he attended the School, it is said, were not only a great help architecturally for all concerned but, as one might expect, full of humour, amounting to hilarity. Many students still treasure the inevitable little sketches made on these occasions.

With Arthur J. Davis he was the most active Academician on the joint committee with the Royal Society of Arts for the Exhibition of British Industrial Art held at Burlington House in 1935, to the planning of which he gave much time and care. One of the exhibits was an elaborately decorated and equipped bathroom. The exhibiting firm demurred at introducing a specified object within the chaste walls of Burlington House. Oliver Hill, the designer, therefore inquired of Lutyens whether there was any objection to including the *bidet*, receiving the lightning if not perhaps illuminating, reply, 'Biddy good-bye and go!'

In the February after his election past and present members of his office staff, including some old pupils and assistants, entertained him and the family at the Café Royal. He would like, he told them, to call them his children, but that would involve too many explanations to his wife. The true word, he felt, should be mothers, for surely one and all of them had freely given their life blood to him and his interests. He recalled personalities and incidents of his early practice already recounted in this narrative, and ended by saying that were he elected Pope, he should not be more surprised than he was when elected P.R.A.

It is pleasant to be able to record that reunion was not limited to this circle. The breach with the Royal Institute of British Architects was healed and he returned formally to open the memorial exhibition of drawings by his contemporary in Ernest George's office, Sir Guy Dawber. When he was proposed as P.R.A. Sir Herbert Baker, with whom he had kept on distant terms since the final gradient crisis at Delhi, wrote from his home in Kent welcoming his candidature and offering his support. It was a typically generous gesture, since Lutyens had certainly not facilitated his former colleague's resumption of practice in England, nor become more charitable regarding his subsequent achievements. But Baker wrote:

> I should like to vote for you for the sake of our old friendship which I enjoyed so much; and forget all the soreness and the harm—as one must in the assurance and peace of old age.
>
> Such a lovely sunrise and thrush singing. Do you remember the sunsets we saw from the old Roman road in Shropshire?
>
> Yours as of old . . .

Lutyens replied appropriately, signing himself 'ever as once was, Ned Lutyens'. In the course of the ensuing correspondence Baker showed himself to be thinking along parallel lines to Lutyens on the architect's opportunity of bringing the arts closer together, and suggested poets being eligible for the Royal Academy. It was their ancient bone of contention and Lutyens replied, as he had told the other a hundred times, 'we must be our own poets,' going on to explain the plan that he already had it in mind to apply his Presidency to putting into effect.

He was the fifteenth to hold that office since Sir Joshua Reynolds, and the third architect, his predecessors having been James Wyatt and Sir Aston Webb. As President, Lutyens added to the respect which his fellows felt towards an unquestionably great creative artist, an evident keenness to discharge his responsibilities fully, under the guidance of Sir Walter Lamb, the Keeper and Secretary. 'The Lamb is my shepherd, I shall not want,' he reassured himself, and 'Am I doing all right?' he would whisper occasionally to him at Council or Assembly. In fact, he not only brought to the position the valuable virtues of industry, fair-mindedness, and the humility of the true artist; but made his short and difficult term of office the most vital, as regards architecture, since the academy's foundation.[1] Whilst he did not presume to interfere in the work of the hanging committees, it was nevertheless noticeable at once, that, as he claimed in his speech at the Academy Banquet on April 27, 1939, many works of a fresher and more enterprising character, including a larger selection by younger and less known artists of conspicuous talent, were hung. For, as he went on to emphasise:

> All great art is secret, and can only speak through its own medium. So who am I to lay down the law, beyond a prayer for sincerity? The most untutored

[1] It was in the summer preceding his election as President that Augustus John, following Sickert and Stanley Spencer, had resigned from the Royal Academy in protest at the policy of the Hanging Committee.

174. THE FLOWER HUNT. The drawings of this and three following plates, in pen and chalk, are extracted from a MS of eight pages, a complete page of which is reproduced on page 565 The story which they illustrate appears on page 576.
1. Fox-glove. 2. Dog-rose. 3. Hornbeam. 4. My Pæony and the pack. 5. Miss Tree on her chesnut, 'Conqueror'. 6. Miss Lily Waters

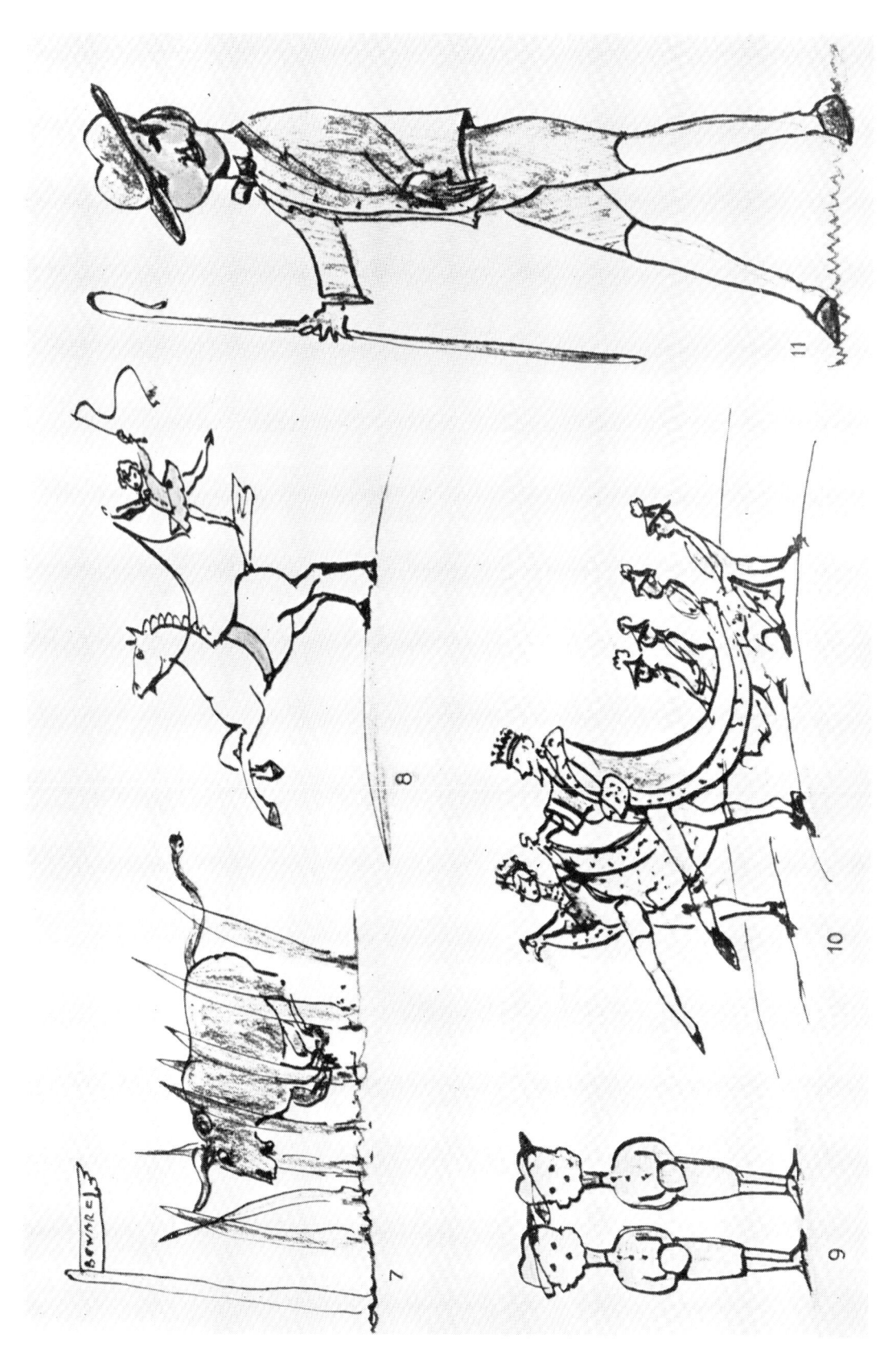

175 and 176 (*on opposite page*). 7. Bull-rush. 8. On her Mare's Tail. 9. Two Miss Whych Elms—which is which? 10. Lords and Ladies. 11. Miss Primula Primrose. 12. Mr. Lion—a dandy at hunt balls. 13. The Freezias. 14. Catkins. 15. Columbine. 16. Ragged Robin. 17. 'If the Foxglove don't play try-thomas with a red hot poker'. 18. Portrait presented to ME by the hunt

563

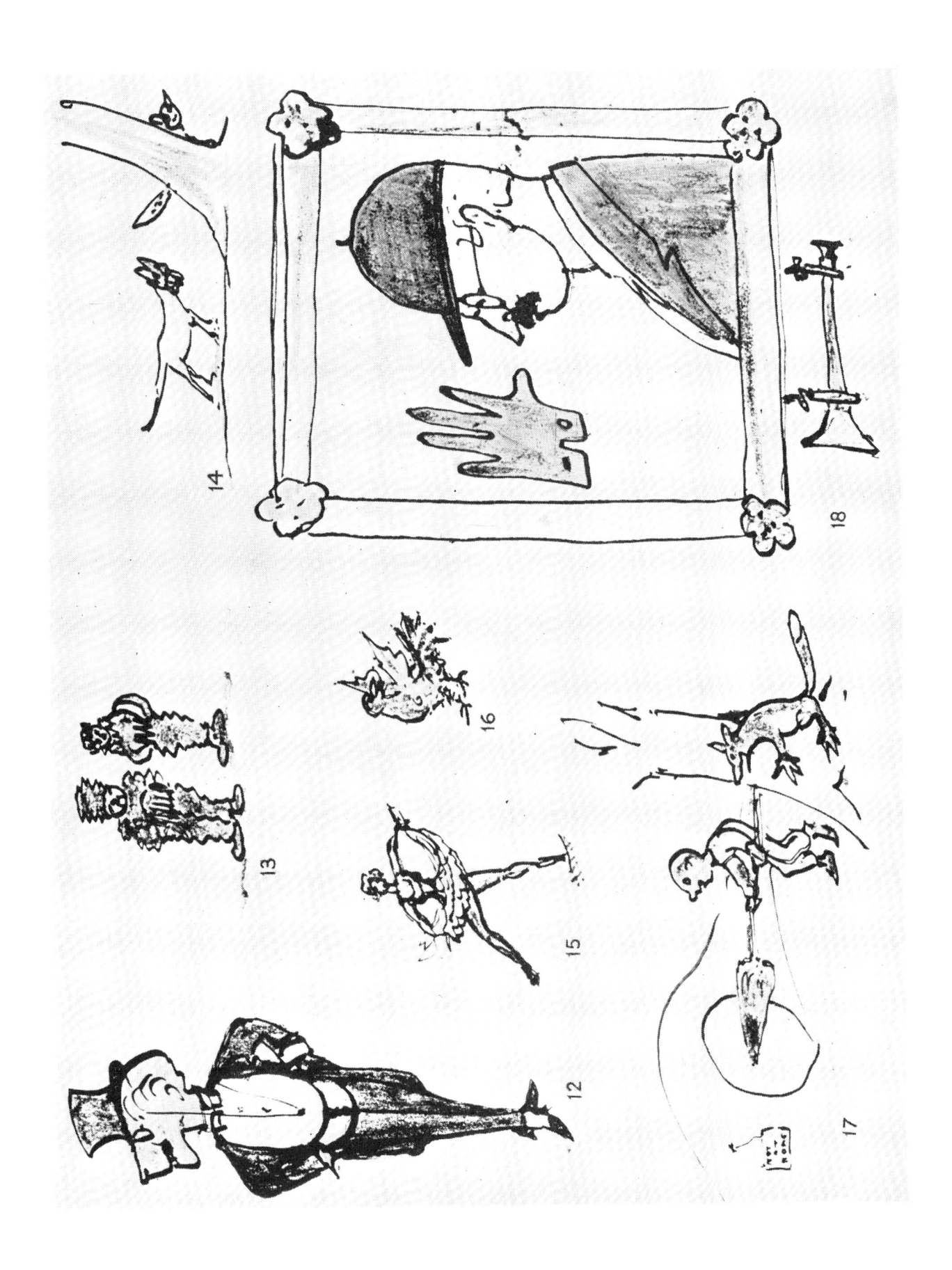

177. 'Here we all go! Tally Ho!' 'The scent is heavy—in fact its scent-per-scent—all in a garden grown. The last Rose-dog got a glove from the fox. Snowdrops, dripping, shed snow to restore the melted Freezias. Love in a mist—the end of all good stories—the Elms bewitched'

may hold honest convictions. Therein lies his strength: in the fact that he *does* not know—does *not know*.

He had never been so clever as to join in the perennial jibes at the Academy which, though it might have recognised his abilities sooner, had accepted his earliest works and rejected none. He had too sincere a respect for sound workmanship, and too strong a belief in the cumulative value of transmitted tradition, not to recognise the Academy as serving an essential social and aesthetic function. His personal fastidiousness might limit his appreciation to the very small number of living painters who combined the sensitiveness and restraint of William Nicholson, and, as he put it privately, painted like gentlemen. But he was too well aware of the value of public opinion and of the nature of official channels, not to respect the institution as the essential, if cumbersome, vehicle of the nation's aesthetic conscience. Moreover he saw in it a means, and was determined to use his Presidency as a platform, towards furthering his 'ideal vision' of establishing the aesthetic science.

He therefore devoted the greater part of his Banquet speech to an appeal in general terms to the Government and public spirited benefactors 'to finance a School to promote a philosophy of real beauty'. The Academy schools afforded the necessary premises. But the existing School was framed, he recognised, for a system of office pupilage, now extinct, and was next to useless. He estimated the capital necessary to reconstitute the School at £100,000. The fund for which he appealed was to endow, as a first stage, a Prize of London, analogous to the Prix de Rome, to enable the winners to live 'the spacious life', and to conduct researches on those absolute values in which aesthetics and science would merge. He mistrusted his ability to outline the full conception, on which, as we have seen, he felt very deeply, in an after-dinner speech, remarking that he would divulge his plan only to those that gave. But he indicated its nature clearly by pointing to the Pythagorean inspiration of the Parthenon, and Wren's debt to Newton. 'I hope,' he went on, 'a similar *entente* between the Royal Academy with the Royal Society may be devised to analyse and formulate a creed of beauty.' That was his purpose: to give practical reality, by means of research scholarships, and a reorganised Academy School, to his conviction, outlined in Chapter 18, that the future of the art of architecture must lie within a realm governed by laws scientifically formulated out of the raw material of physical, natural, and aesthetic properties.

The course of events decreed that the resources of science should be directed to holocausts of destruction, instead of to such constructive researches. Such public works as the Jellicoe and Beatty Memorial fountains for Trafalgar Square, the Staines by-pass bridges, and the Cromwell Road extension, were put into abeyance. Before the last alterations to the garden at Ashby St. Ledgers were finished for Lord Wimborne, that faithful admirer was himself laid beneath a memorial by 'that architect fellow, Lutyens', as he teasingly used to describe his ally of thirty-five years.[1] Another echo came from Spain. El Guadelperal, its Duque having been murdered in the Civil War, had been abandoned unfinished. But the Duke of Alba now applied to Lutyens to rebuild the Liria Palace, damaged in the siege of Madrid.[2] In January, 1940, we get a glimpse of him trying to arrange for the portrait of Miss Jekyll to be extracted from the Tate and transferred to the National Portrait Gallery; attending a Fine Arts Commission meeting with the awkward job devolving on him of indicating to Tait the modifications required by the Commission in the design by the latter for the building in Parliament Square on the site of the Westminster Hospital; and then talking to Sir Fabian Ware on the new War Graves:

> I said keep the same headstones, the same monuments, i.e. extend the existing cemeteries where possible, and the new ones to be on the same lines, with the same War Stone. In a hundred years time 1914 and 1939 will all be part of one war. It is certainly the same sacrifice for the same cause.

But he was under no illusions on man's vastly increased means for destruction, nor on the effects of a long war on artists and the arts. As soon as it began he set about reshaping the scheme for instituting the 'Prize of London' School. His first optimistic idea was to obtain through Parliament the payment of a percentage of all war-time expenditure on government contracts for the support and employment of artists on work of longer-term importance. 'Brave words,' he wrote to Baker, remembering the inscription on his own marriage Casket, 'enable men to ennoble fate by nobly bearing it; but they do not feed wives and children.' During the winter, as it became clear that no public funds would be available, he obtained the King's sanction for the setting up of the Royal Academy Planning Committee, 'to study the architectural problems which will arise in the development of London after the war.' Promises of help were obtained from the Minister of Transport, the London County Council, and town planning authorities. Besides architects invited to collaborate, representatives of the Metropolitan Police, and of road and rail transport were enrolled, with Sir Charles Bressey as Vice President and Lord Keynes as financial adviser. H. Austen Hall was appointed co-ordinating secretary, and throughout the Committee's existence Mrs. Martin Buckmaster discharged the laborious task of rendering and co-ordinating the detailed plans on a master plan of the whole area covered.

The conception, preceding by several years the official City, County, and Greater London Plans, of mobilising architects, engineers, and their allies to prepare a long-term scheme for the eventual replanning of London on ideal lines, had long been in his mind. In an address delivered in 1933 he had visualised the formation of a

---

[1] With regard to Lord Wimborne's memorial, 'I have written to Alice W. to say all is well and that my only sorrow now is—that the churchyard will be so beautiful that she will die to be buried there.' (Letter of December 13, 1939.)

[2] Now being built to Lutyen's design.

body for this purpose, just as, a decade before the launching of his appeal for the Prize of London, he had outlined their alliance in the 'aesthetic science'. He had proposed on that earlier occasion, a statutory termination of all London leases at agreed values in 99 years' time, enabling the appointed authority thereafter or earlier to put into effect the reconstruction schemes devised meanwhile. Unauthorised buildings erected in the interval would be subject to this limited life. He instanced the determination of the bridgeheads of Paris in the time of Louis XIV as an example of such long-term town-planning, so that when railway bridges were required in the nineteenth century they were erected without conflicting with it; and the Architects' Plan devised during the Revolution from which the Haussmann plan had developed. Under his scheme, he continued:

> With Bridgeheads determined, new and wider roads planned or laid out, buildings could be designed of height proportionate to such widths, and skylines be settled in relation to focal points.

He then—this is still in 1933—adumbrated this new city of the atomic future, in terms that give shape to the aesthetic science that he conceived would govern its architecture, and which must controvert any suspicion that Lutyens was a conservative thinker, however averse he was to undigested design. High above the houses steel or beam light-masts, tapering to 1500 feet and painted in many colours, would stand to warn aeroplanes of regulated flying-height, and rays would light the wings of those that infringed the regulations. All roofs would be flat for helicopter landing. Houses would be heated by the urban authority, and light be so cheap that it need never be turned off, only veiled when inconvenient, or possibly turned on and off automatically by the action of some ray. Every dwelling would have television and so its own theatre. The dwelling house will be noiseless and, he believed, small windowed—a refuge from the glare of day and the blaze of night, depending for all general working purposes on artificial light—as he had found was already the case in American banks where windows are ignored except for architectural effect. Rooms would be air-conditioned and so lit that the hand and pen throw no shadows.

'The split atom,' he foresaw, 'may split our present civilisation, to be joined again to serve man's need. Perhaps, too, the soul of Archimedes will return to Earth to lead men to that inexpressible beauty that lies in the atmosphere of the Gods, to be won by methods mathematically expressed.'

The Royal Academy Plan for London, the first instalment of which was published in October, 1942,[1] rather relied upon the Wren-Newton aesthetic than that visionary forecast. Taking the Bressey-Lutyens Report on Highway Development for its basis, Lutyens emphasised, in a foreword, that Report and illustrations were not a town-planning scheme in the technical sense. They were put forward as an

[1] *London Replanned*. 'Country Life', 1942.

ideal, practicable but tentative, with the object of stimulating the imagination of those who would eventually be responsible for the work of reconstruction. Its main concern was 'to present a plan for London's material, social, and aesthetic requirements as conceived by architects; to solve some of the major problems of design; and to state the case generally for an architectural approach'. Among its leading principles were that the minimum unit of design should be the block; that matters of scale, skyline, ordered siting, and balanced frontages cannot be left to individual caprice; that back and side elevations must be no less carefully considered than fronts, and the distant view no less than the close-up. With regard to height of buildings, these should be controlled not by a standard regulation but according to the angle of light measured from the opposite side of the street, and carefully avoid the visually unsatisfactory angle of one-to-two (imposed in Kingsway). A no less important factor was internal lighting, so that light-angles would, in effect, impose a zoning ratio, greater height being allowed in proportion to the width of adjoining streets or open spaces.

This vital formula, which has since been incorporated into standard planning practice, was not developed very far in the first Academy scheme, nor were designs for traffic centres and shopping centres worked out so fully as in the second Report.[1] But the challenging conception of enlarging the precincts of St. Paul's Cathedral, with a southward vista to the Thames, was first given expression in it. Equally the designs for restoring Covent Garden as an amenity centre, for the approaches to the British Museum, and for the environs of the Tower of London, conjured up the visual possibilities. This was the plan's primary purpose, and a great deal of really valuable thought was given to working out detailed proposals for the shapes of sites, road-junctions, traffic centres, etc. created by the Bressey highway network: proposals which future planners could with advantage examine. The reasons for the Royal Academy Plan's failure to exert more immediate influence than it has lie primarily in the lack of data available (in the middle of the war) to the small body of designers. Had the scientific and social data been available, or had Lutyens lived until it was available and been able to communicate to his team the principles of his theory, the opportunity was propitious for working out his conception of the aesthetic science as regards town planning. Another cause of its failure to be adopted by an impoverished post-war nation was the extravagant lengths resorted to for attaining monumental axial symmetry in a city of which the aesthetic essence is its picturesque irregularity. On this aspect, however, may be quoted the later comment of a leading authority on city planning, which is applicable not only to much subsequent English post-war town planning, but to Lutyens's principles of layout as a whole:

> As Ruskin pointed out, if we are to appreciate the picturesque, we need the

[1] *Road, Rail, and River in London.* 'Country Life', July, 1944.

contrast of regularity. The late Sir Edwin Lutyens's plan for London took this into full account. It was a plan in the grand manner, and its best features should have been incorporated in the worthy but unimaginative official plans which followed it.[1]

§3. IN A GREEN SHADE

The Planning Committee had not been working many weeks when, in April 1940, its convener succumbed to a second attack of pneumonia complicated by thrombosis. He was taken to convalesce at Beechwood, a little house at Lavington, beneath the Sussex Downs, belonging to Barbara and Euan Wallace. By the beginning of June (it was immediately after the evacuation from Dunkirk) he seemed fully recovered. The thrombosis, though insignificant in itself, had raised fears, of which he was aware, that it might prevent him working. After a few weeks, however, it was evident that there would be no disablement, though his never very distinct speech and writing were somewhat impaired. As soon as he was fit he resumed work in London, returning to Beechwood, where his wife remained, for week-ends.

That was the summer of the fall of France and the Battle of Britain. In the tense atmosphere of London during these boding months it was a tonic to meet Lutyens at the Garrick Club, serene and jocular as ever, and now full of the progress being made with the Plan. The fellowship of colleagues working beneath the baroque painted ceiling in the Palladian dining-room of Lord Burlington's house, on an apparently great constructive scheme, must have meant much to him. It was certainly a sedative to discuss façades and vistas over a glass of port with him, whilst he scribbled the skyline of his new London on a virgin, when the sky was hourly bringing forth destruction. Sometimes he would be lunching with one of his surviving friends—occasionally William Nicholson, or Sir Saxton Noble; or with Robert now returned to the R.A.F. With them there was no need for taut cheerfulness. The sharing of old ties, however tangled and frayed and relaxed by stresses of catastrophe, made for good company enough.

With Saxton Noble he had used to play an entertaining game in the 'thirties, which the architect at least had taken seriously. It was that Noble wanted a large house which he could not afford to build, so Lutyens designed him a very large one, bigger than Viceroy's House, with a great hall, vestibules, portico, a lovely chapel, a picture gallery, armoury, saloon, library—all of yew hedges and waterways. There were to be two great staircases in ruin, which would form rockeries, and a steward's court and room that would be the only part actually built, to serve as a comfortable small house 'but just a bit pomposo', as he described it. In the great forecourt there

[1] Christopher Tunnard, Associate Professor of City Planning at Yale University, in a letter to *Country Life*, September 3, 1948.

would be a monument 'to those who fell paying taxes—all rather good fun, and in its way quite lovely and, it may be, loveable'. It had all been drawn out in plan, and seeing the two old friends together in that apocalyptic summer, recalled to me summer days ten years before, when I had motored Lutyens down to Somerset for a weekend. He had brought the plans of the green mansion with him, to discuss the planting of the rooms with Mrs. Norah Lindsay, that enchanting gardener, at Sutton Courtenay where we had spent a July night. Reading his account of the outing has recalled incidents by me forgotten or never observed, and impresses again with his extraordinarily acute observation. He wrote of that romantic garden and house:

> Sutton Courtenay lies level with the Thames alongside the Asquiths' Wharf. Great trees, level waters, and a soil that grows abundantly ancient yews and wonderful flowers. The beds all wide—too wide for what is called practical purposes, unmanured, the dead and dying things mix with the living in a riot of glorious beauty.
>
> The house old, older than one would believe, and really admirable, but so littered with odds and ends—squalid, aping the luxury of the millionaire, dirty and oh so untidy.
>
> After dinner a moon and fitful walk following Mrs. L with an electric torch, trying to find out where and how to turn off the fountain, so we might have baths in the morning.

The rest of the tour had been for me sheer delight and for him seems to have been something of a *recherche du temps perdu*. We called on Lady Horner at Mells, who welcomed her beloved Ned affectionately among a mist of grandchildren, and he showed me the Munnings monument to Edward. In the medieval manor house of Cothay we stayed with the son of the lady whom he had asked about her beautiful tail feathers; then, being so near Hestercombe, he must see how the grandest of his early gardens looked. In twenty-seven years the vistas and terraces overlooking Taunton Dean and the trees around his great orangery had grown up nobly and made him feel he must be '190 years old at least to have planned so hoary and old a place'.

We had crossed Salisbury Plain, ever joyful to him, and dropped into the valley of the Test, 'one of God's kindest and most gentle of His creations,' when he resolved he could not pass so near Marsh Court without looking up Herbert Johnson. There we were pressed to stay the night, and Lutyens listened to the organ played in the ballroom that was the latest addition to his *tour de force* in chalk-building of the South African war period. He saw the mulberry tree that he had planted now reaching to high windows, the Breguet clock that he had bought cheap for the billiard room, and talked far into the night with our host, who had called on him no less unexpectedly thirty years ago the night before Edward VII's coronation, to discuss the furnishing of these very rooms.

AS LIGHT FELL SHORT

Watching Lutyens, whom one could never regard as an old man, refreshing himself beneath the Zoffanys in the club coffee room, as the sirens wailed yet another Alert, I remembered our talking as we left Marsh Court next morning, of his youth in the cottage at Thursley, of Randolph Caldecott's visits and drawings, of his excitement with the buildings of Philip Webb in those days, and of how the Cenotaph had originated in the garden at Munstead. Our journey into his past had put him into a rare mood of reminiscence, and how often in writing this book have I not regretted that, at that and other times when we were together, I could not make better use of those moments! Had I possessed a fraction of the knowledge of his eventful life which it has since been my fortune to acquire, what innumerable gaps in it might he not have filled for us! And how embarrassed we should both have been. For example, it appears that when I set him down at Eaton Gate at the end of our outing, he had found a letter from B.M. saying that if he did not pay her some extraordinary and imaginary sum of money on which she was counting, she proposed to write to this and that eminent person about it.

Sifting the layers of memory in these last days of 1948—1941, 1931, 1921, back to 1901, 1891, then the unrecorded years at Thursley and Onslow Square—gardens form the connecting background rather than buildings; the lovely sequence from Miss Jekyll's at Munstead to the enamelled carpets of Delhi; gardens of which the geometry left nothing to chance yet the forms and colours of nature were given their freedom, and the shapes of trees seen to greater advantage for their humanised surroundings. These elements, and the light suffusing them, had, one recognised now in retrospect, been his first love since his boyhood when he had begun memorising their relationships through his portable picture frame; and remained a prime inspiration of his creative invention. Delhi itself, and his vision of the new London, might be interpreted as majestic gardens.

During that summer of imminent invasion, whilst Britain's battle for survival was being fought in skies of cloudless blue, the Lutyenses' dream of the little white house had come true at last for a few months. To be together somewhere less remote from London than Lavington, they decided to hire a caravan, which was parked at Knebworth. Actually they never slept in the caravan, being hospitably received in the manor house, but it was none the less a spirited idea. Then, as autumn approached, Lady Emily arranged to lease Ockham Mill, on the Surrey Wey, from which Lutyens was able to travel up and down daily by bus or car. Ockham Mill was the first and only country home, not forgetting Folly Farm thirty years before, that he had had the leisure to enjoy with his wife. The old idyll lived again. The owner, Lady Stokes, had converted the waters and orchard of the old mill into an Eden which Miss Jekyll would not have despised. Lutyens described the quaint house as 'an architect's holiday—nothing fits, only hides itself in unexpect places. It reminds me of those old fashioned ladies who have great charm but are quite worthless'. But the sunsets through the trees and across the water, in that flat countryside, stirred him; and he pottered happily along the banks of the mill-stream watching for a fish to rise.

But, disregarding the noise and risks, he continued to spend many nights in London in spite of his family's protests. At Mansfield Street, where Mr. and Mrs. Tribe—for so long the caretakers of Queen Anne's Gate—were installed in the basement, there was a shelter of sorts for him to sleep in during raids. But Robert, working at an R.A.F. Group Headquarters in London, pointed out the insubstantial structure of the house and begged him to sleep in the Langham Hotel where he had a room. In the middle of September, when there were heavy raids nightly, he was particularly insistent, holding out as a bait an evening to be spent in Robert Byron's company. However, after a heated argument with his son, Lutyens eventually decided to stay in the house, slept in his own room till gun-fire began, then went down to the shelter as a heavy explosion shook the building. Soon after he had installed himself below there came a furious ringing of the bell, and Robert and a friend presented themselves, somewhat dishevelled. The Langham itself had been struck by a large bomb that had, fortunately, failed to explode, but which resulted in the wardens turning everybody out of the building. Recounting the experience,[1] Lutyens wrote:

> Poor dear Robert was fearfully crestfallen and apologised to me. I said it was just a bet. I had betted on Mansfield Street, he on the Langham, and this time I had won! I think we will get accustomed to it all, except to a direct hit: and then the chances are that one would be unconscious of it. You would wake up and, if in heaven, ask your neighbour which hymn it is; if in hell, which hunting or rollicking drinking song? Apart from these interruptions I slept very well and finished the night, as I began it, in my own bed.

During 1942 he stayed in London, dividing the time between the office, now installed at the back of Mansfield Street, and Burlington House. Work at Liverpool, and all building now, had been closed down, but, with the ever faithful Miss Webb and Stewart at hand, completion of the quarter inch drawings was pressed on. The family, dispersed in the country, were safe. But on his seventy-second birthday he had to apply himself to the melancholy task of designing the headstone and setting of his son-in-law, Euan Wallace's, grave in the churchyard at Lavington. In the yew-hedged enclave, before long, four of the five Wallace sons were laid beside their father. Day by day he laboured on in the little lonely office. To a friend who visited him he admitted, after showing him the great Cathedral sheets with their meticulous detailing of domes and vaults and shrines, that he never saw anybody now. The

[1] To his wife. It should be said that, although away on this occasion, Lady Emily immediately returned to London, never to leave her husband again except for a few weeks' treatment in hospital at Newcastle.

architect who for so many decades had found the days too short to speak with all the unending procession of draughtsmen, contractors, and clients, who had spent half his life hurrying from place to place, been the friend of beautiful and witty women, of governors and princes, was left to himself at last. His daughter Ursula kept up a correspondence with him over a projected garden for her Northumberland home in the problematical future, and on a scheme for building a new general hospital at Newcastle after the war.

He began conceiving, that preliminary process of projecting his imagination into the furnishing of the hospital. At the end of 1942 he wrote to Ursula:

> It is very difficult, well nigh impossible, to make a sketch for so complicated a scheme as a General Hospital... What I would like to have is not a plan but a series of diagrams to show the relativity of the various needs. The size and number of wards—by size I mean the number of beds in a ward or wards, the cubical contents necessary for a patient, men, women. Its baths, lavatories, etc, house-maids' closets, mess rooms, kitchens. The operating theatre, or theatres— ear, eye, bone, bowels, etc—should be top lit? The disposal of contagious offal. ... Terraces for sunbathing and loggias.
>
> What I need would be a series of diagrams showing the requirements and relationship of each to each. Rather similar to a family tree.

He was appointed joint-consultant with Sir Patrick Abercrombie for the re-planning and reconstruction of Hull. Sir Patrick tells me that he performed very useful service in loosening up the imaginations of the committee. At one meeting he impressed on them that the level of the whole city must be raised several feet; at another that, since the site was so flat, an artificial hill or acropolis should be formed of war-debris.

So the weeks passed. One never saw him other than alert and seemingly cheerful. One afternoon in the spring of 1942 I looked in at the room at Burlington House, where the President was bent over a sea of plans. In the courtyard, the band of an American unit, recently arrived, was playing rousing music. Lutyens, with beaming face, seized me round the waist and waltzed me half way round the room, with much the same *élan*, I suppose, that forty-five years before had astonished his future wife in Victorian drawing-rooms.

Such an instance of his persistent vitality can be compared with the general directions that he addressed to his fellow planners, by conference or correspondence. He urged on them that 'the centre of the Empire should be not only spacious but well poised, and planned majestically'. To one colleague who pleaded that the irregularity of the historic conglomeration of Westminster presented analogies to the unwritten British Constitution, he admitted the difficulty of devising a worthy plan for Parliament Square but insisted that, by courageous demolitions, it could be very much more effectively balanced. The ruthlessness of some of his proposals was partly due to the expectation of much heavier war damage than was in fact sustained, and to the Plan's looking to a relatively distant future. But it must be confessed that the impulse of imperialistic symmetry outweighed with him the factors that he had recognised as linked together in aesthetic science, which, as regards planning, seem likely to develop a wholly different conception of city landscape, democratic, irregular, picturesque. Forty years ago he had hesitated, after his additions to Crooksbury, on whether to follow the winding path leading to 'democratic' design, or the symmetrical vista that ended at Viceroy's House. In 1940, as in 1912 and 1898, he turned to the right, where the promptings of the yet unformulated aesthetic science whispered 'left'. It is perhaps significant that the colleague who had now pleaded for asymmetrical design at Westminster was his old combatant, Herbert Baker.

Nevertheless, the leadership that he was exerting in the arts, both as P.R.A. and Planner, with his vision of unity, supplemented in its restricted sphere the spiritual *élan* exerted in those dark years by the great Prime Minister—whom he had once instructed in drawing. His schemes were idealistic, his counsel that of perfection. In the squalid makeshift and pathetic materialism of war, many more were heartened by his courageous spirit than, perhaps, agreed with or saw much likelihood of realising his visions. Like the young men who had entered his office as callow youths, to leave it with an ideal of conduct and performance, they were influenced, if obscurely, by the fact that here was a man of inflexible faith in the beauty and graciousness of life; in self-respect. The acclamations were therefore widespread and sincere which greeted the conferring on him, in the New Year Honours of 1942, of the Order of Merit.

It was the first time that an architect had received this most distinguished of honours, limited to twenty-four living members and conferred 'for exceptionally meritorious services in Our Army and Navy or towards the advancement of the Arts, Literature, or Science'. Immediately preceding recipients had been Lord Baden-Powell, Sir Arthur Eddington, Lord Chatfield, and Sir James Jeans. Of the Press comments on the occasion, one of the more apt and epigrammatic was 'his work's shortcomings are on the plane of vogue and whim, its virtues are for all time'.

Soon after his investiture he wrote thanking his grandson, Nicholas Ridley, for his congratulations:

> The actual Order is a wee little locket-shaped medal worn round the neck. From behind you see nothing at all except me. You're proud of me—and I am proud of you! So? do two prides make a fall?

and signed himself 'Your Grand-O-Man, Grandfather'. He never had an opportunity of wearing the O.M. in public, but it lived in a drawer in his office, and once or twice he hung the 'little locket' round his neck for his secretary's benefit.

AS LIGHT FELL SHORT

A letter to his wife in the following February refers to the address he delivered at the funeral of Sir William Llewellyn, his predecessor as P.R.A., and pictures his routine in this last year of his active life:

> I gave my first sermon in St. Paul's Cathedral, a few short words on Llewellyn. It all went off all right. Then I went to the R.A. to see how Mrs. Buckmaster [was getting on], and answer letters with Lamb etc. That's all my news. I'm fairly free for this week.
>
> I slept last night from 10.30 till 7.30, which was good. My cough is better ... I am working on my Cathedral again. The Archbishop thought my drawings beautiful. He endorsed candles as the only lighting to God's altar. I have reminded him that St. Peter's is entirely lit by candles, and King's College Chapel.
>
> I want my Cathedral lit by candles. You need wondrous few. The big nave at St. John's College is lit by four candles and isn't it glorious and mysterious! The choir is alone well lit, in that every chorister has a candle.
>
> But they want electric light, and flood lighting at that.

The cough to which he referred, the first symptoms of his fatal illness, had begun to afflict him towards the end of 1941. He dismissed it lightly at first, to those who sympathised, by saying that, in a motor accident in which he had been involved on one of his journeys to Ockham a year previously, he had swallowed his spectacles. He tried to allay his coughing by smoking less, then began to cough blood. This distressed him, but more for its inconvenience than for its dangerous significance, and he worked on in spite of it. His medical advisers now subjected him to an X-ray examination in which he participated with a detached unconcern. This revealed a slowly growing cancer of the bronchial tube, though he was not informed of this diagnosis. But he was counselled not to tax his strength, and to rest.

During the hours of enforced inactivity he had leisure at last to elaborate the picture-stories which he had used to interpolate into letters, first to his wife, then to his children, and now to his grand-children. Their more finished drawings show how vividly he was remembering in his old age the picture books of his own childhood illustrated by Kate Greenaway and Caldecott. These stories also represent, in their astonishing puns, Lutyens's fertility in this line of humour, that fascinated his more hardened friends, but which is rarely so effective in quotation as in its context. A letter for Amanda (his daughter Mary's child) dated October 14, 1942, could only be done justice to by reproduction in colour, since it is a fantasy on flower-names, with the drawings tinted in chalk. Notwithstanding the technical problems involved in reproduction, however, he must tell the story here, since the light from this facet in the darkening, blacked-out, Mansfield Street house is so engagingly typical of the embers still glowing there. It is also adorably comical. The numerals refer to drawings reproduced on pp. 561-3.

Amanda, bless her, sent me drawings by her own hand of some Red Dog Roses. Whether it was their sweet scent which she strewed around that started me out hunting, but—

The roses became hounds—Red Dogs (2). Then by putting two and two together I soon secured a pack.

To hunt the Fox-Glove (1). As we hunted only in wet or damp weather, we provided master fox with gloves to keep his feet dry, more or less!

I called for my Paeoni, unhung my horn from its beam and my crop from under its stone—an odd place to keep it—but there it was! (3)

My Paeoni and the pack, horned and spurred complete, all out for a lark! (4)

Then we must describe some of our blooming Field. There was Miss Tree, on her Horse, chestnut in colour, called the 'Conqueror', with four white stockings which the horse kept up with Blue ribbons (5). Conqueror is saying 'how can I get on without rains my dear?'—a mystery to Miss Tree! 'Which way now?' says Conqueror.

Miss Lily Waters, an exotic sportswoman whose only fear was of getting her feet dry (6).

Miss Primula Primrose, somewhat bilious looking—she never rode a horse because it made her feel Dizzy. And unlike Miss Waters, to keep her feet dry she wore Colts Feet (11).

In course of the Hunt, beware of the Flags, for the Bull may Rush out at any minute (7).

And don't the Ragged Robins sing! (16).

Laurastinus *var* Ridleyamos came out on a Mares Tail (8) and though the tail is last, she always came in first at the kill!

Catkins (14) were uneatable to the Rose dogs—that's why Laurastinus always carries a whip, not for the mare but for the hounds.

Lords and Ladies form the glad throng (10). Then there were the Freezias, who came warmly clad, lest their hearts melt at the sight of a kill (13). They are dressed in firs.

A great difference to Columbine, who is awfully negligée (15). A careless little thing!

Then there are the two Miss Wych Elms—ever know which is which? However both are bewitching (9).

Mr. Lion, a Dandy, who only appears at the Hunt Balls (12). He's very proud because he can trace his descent from Ass-per-a-grass.

[In the next drawing the pun may be difficult to see for its point is the notice 'Not at home' hung outside the fox's earth.]

If the Fox-glove dont play, Try-thomas with a red-hot-poker (17). The little fox laughed to see such sport.

Here we all are! Tally Ho! The scent is heavy—indeed it's scent per scent —all in a garden grown.

[A whole page is devoted to the hunt in full career, (p. 564), with at the bottom, reading from left to right.]

The last Rose-dog got a glove from the fox. Snow drops, dripping, shed snow to restore the melted Freezias. Love-in-a-Mist—the end of all good stories: the elms bewitched.

[And on the last page:]

Portrait Presented to ME, by the Hunt (18).

He was working, too, at a succession of newspaper articles and addresses. His strength would fail before he reached their end, and his never very legible script would become indecipherable even to his secretary. But typed drafts of them were made, which he continued to work over. He was seeking to develop by this means the conception of the aesthetic science as applied to replanning problems and architectural education. Their insistent theme, that 'to achieve true beauty is a science', has already formed the subject of sections in this and the previous chapter, where it has been sought to explain the means by which he had been carried to this conclusion, so much at variance, to the superficial view, with the reputation based on his earlier work. But since these fragments are in effect his last words we should ponder their message again in this place.

He addressed himself to an audience of artists and scientists whom he had convened 'to break the ice that lies between us, with a cup of wine. We artists need the help of the scientist to drill us through some common language to a sense of that accuracy and truth which alone can produce beauty. Mere formulae and algebraical expressions will not help us.

'Now gentlemen, we must combine to establish a great school. I want sometime, somewhere, your help with which we may begin to analyse, to prove, and thereby to know, the forces and restraints that, to an intellectual mind, compel beauty.

'Through the study of nature, of the growth of plants and trees, is one way by which we can arrive at sources of beauty, for translation into facts and figures. Art without the sap of science is a disease.

'We architects, for our part, will have to make use of new materials in meeting modern needs. But in doing so we must not overlook our own great tradition of building, evolved to suit our culture and climatic conditions. It is an impossibility for a beautiful city to be planned by architects who are not steeped in the atmosphere, tradition, and culture of their own country. We do not want foreign cities built on English soil, like disfiguring warts on a fair face.

'The designing of a city will take as long as the city takes to build. But it is difficult, in the first instance, to imagine a perfect city without a perfect river, of fresh running water, a thoroughfare for the trade and enjoyment of the citizens. With the help of Engineers we could make our river clean again. Avenues, parks, and gardens should adorn its banks, joined by bridges that cross with grace and of which the bridgeheads are not necessarily symmetrical but assimilated.

'The steep north bank and the flat southern bank of the Thames need different treatment. The warehouses and docks must not be unmindful of their position, but have the elements of beauty, which their reflection duplicates.

'Shopping streets and shopping centres should be narrow, preferably running from north to south, and be free from fast-moving traffic; some might be enclosed as arcaded courts. The old squares, now sorely disfigured, can set the example for residential planning; they too should be free from fast-moving traffic. For this there should be raised roads, separating it from local traffic.

'In the ideal city advertisements, covering façades with personal opinions and mechanised devices, and murdering all civic propriety, deserve the death sentence. A right-minded public should be educated to boycott the wares they advertise. No trade sign should be higher than 12 ft. above pavement level.

'There must be laws to protect our cities from the speculative builder. The primary question we shall be called upon to decide is whether we shall allow vested and monied interests, architectural ignorance and utilitarian philistinism to wreck our unique opportunity for creating beauty, not only for our own sakes and of posterity, but as a compliment to the world's Author'.

Though his strength was ebbing, he presided at R.A. Councils till May, 1943, including the hanging of the Summer Exhibition in April. Through the summer he continued to get himself dressed and down to the office to work on the last Cathedral drawings and the Hull report. When he was no longer able to stand at his drawing board, a board was contrived to fit across the arms of a carrying chair procured to move him from bedroom to office, though he would not use it for that purpose. Still the strip of tracing paper travelled over the drawings, from summer into autumn and the first winter days, bearing the last trickle of that flood of figures and variant treatments that had been issuing from him for fifty years. The young men, who had transferred the vanguard of that endless procession of perfecting to the final drawings of little country houses in Surrey, were now themselves elderly gentlemen, or dead. Across a larger board had passed the teeming inventions of his middle years, the agonies and triumphs of New Delhi, the evolving geometry of the Cenotaph and its elemental offspring, and there the conception of the aesthetic science had taken shape in the mathematical progression of the Cathedral's arcades. Still the true spirit must be in all things, though only God might see the moulding, high up in clerestory or the semi-darkness of the vault, on which the failing pencil was now ensuring that nothing should be left to chance. The war would surely end this year, then building would begin again and finished drawings sufficient for ten years' work at least must be completed. As Stewart took over each finalised tracing, this necessity was impressed upon him. The drawings must go on without delay to be ready for the end.

He was determined to be present at the Royal Academy General Meeting and Assembly on December 7, 1943, since he had not been able to attend a Council since the Spring. He wrote to Ursula on December 13, how much he had enjoyed meeting his colleagues. He had forgotten, he said, that at the last Assembly of the year the President offers himself for re-election, or otherwise. However, he had been duly re-elected, though next year he would reach the age limit.

> Its an awful bore being in bed. I am missing a great deal. I long for warmer weather, to give my cough a chance. If I was raised to a peerage I should call myself Lord Cough of Cough. I am tired of bed, yet Mother won't let me get up.

At Christmas there were children and grandchildren, but though a bottle of Hock was opened to celebrate the day, there could be no party, for now his wife was in bed, too, with influenza. Yet he was able to sip a little of the wine with one of his sons-in-law. Though too weak to work, he had probably intended to, for he had had some of the Cathedral designs brought up to him. They were arranged round his bedroom so that his eyes could range over every part of the great church in which his imagination had now dwelt for nearly as long as Viceroy's House had taken to build, still, in his mind, testing, checking, verifying the truth as set forth in the vision that he must now bequeath to future generations.

So the moment, that had been in his thoughts on the night before he married the woman still beside him, came: 'the time for us to part, when silence, just silence, will be my medium of expression.' Indeed, he could not speak. But there was no need, for he lay surrounded by his true medium of expression, the designs of his greatest work where, emblematical of the Three Persons in One God whom he served, 'experience, growth, and intensity of knowledge were all caught up with one unity.'

On New Year's Eve, 1943–4, his son recorded:

> Father lies adying. Propped up in his St. Ursula bed he sleeps his life away, in a bedroom hushed and tidied up at last, the silence only broken by his troubled breathing. The massive dome of his head, sunk on his breast, surmounts a frame so wasted of strength, that even when he emerges to a partial consciousness he cannot clear the strangling fluid from the lungs. The transparent, emaciated hands close and unclose aimlessly, revealing surely a distress of mind which drugged stupor cannot banish. The spirit resists expulsion from its only tenement; the unavailing heart beats on.

It is hard to accept the merciful verdict of modern medicine. The inescapable impression remains that the unarmed soul is contesting with bitter anguish for possession of the body it is unready to resign: a sense of familiar nightmare in which the will is powerless to avert catastrophe. We awaken from evil dreams. Only death is eternal.

He died on New Year's Day, in his seventy-fifth year, without pain.

In death the true spirit, that he had sought and served and guarded in life, was imprinted upon his face. Those about him saw no longer the familiar rubicund countenance, the blue eyes twinkling through their horn-rimmed windows and defying dullness by a thousand devices. They beheld a face that they had never seen, from which the superficial contours had fallen away to expose the features of the spirit which had been within.

> His face in death, a little fierce and bitter, seemed free at last from all necessity of evasion. Later, with his lips slightly parted, he looked more himself, although reduced and strangely transfigured. It was the countenance of genius.

Though the great forehead remained unchanged, the nose, proud and sensitive, now assumed fastidious dominance. The memory of a smile still seemed to linger about the wide, tenderly chiselled lips, now clearly seen, and had left happy wrinkles at the corners of the eyes. Death's emaciation revealed the jaw of one not of great physical strength, jutted slightly forward by enthusiasm and will, to the affectionate but firm, gentle, chin.

But we have seen that beautiful and gentle spirit before, when, watching, through his parents' eyes, a little boy playing beside the River Wey, we fancied their expectation of his becoming poet, priest, or artist. It would be true to say that he had become all three, having experienced the intuition of the poet, the technical growth of the artist, and a spiritual intensity sometimes transcending the mystic experiences given to priests, all caught up with the one unity that is Architecture.

The funeral service took place in Westminster Abbey on January 6. The King was represented by Admiral Sir Basil Brook, the pall-bearers being the Earl of Lytton, Viscount Ridley, Robert Lutyens, Sir W. Goscombe John, R.A., Mr. Sidney Lee, R.A., Mr. W. Curtis Green, R.A., and Mr. W. Russell Flint, R.A. The Insignia of the President of the Royal Academy were carried by the Treasurer, Mr. Vincent Harris, R.A., and the Keeper and Secretary, Sir Walter Lamb, K.C.V.O. Close behind followed Sir Herbert Baker, K.C.I.E., R.A., now partially paralysed, walking with Lutyens for the last time.

His ashes, contained in an urn designed by his son, were placed in the crypt of St. Paul's Cathedral.

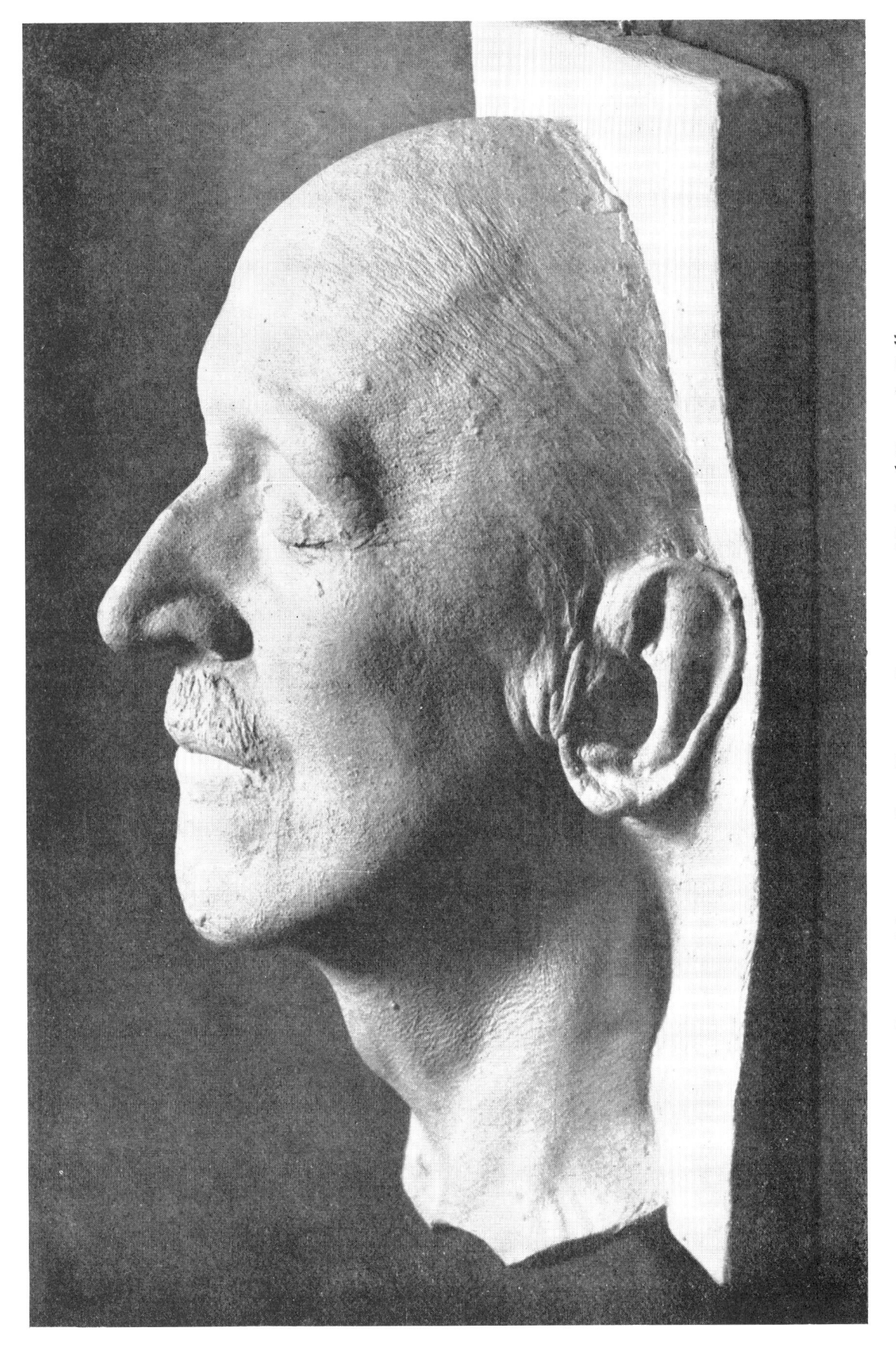

178. Death Mask of Sir Edwin Lutyens. National Portrait Gallery

CONCLUSION

LUTYENS AND THE ARCHITECTURE OF THE FUTURE

HIGH as was Lutyens's reputation, the studies of his work and life, now concluded, will have failed of their purpose if they have not shown him to have been a greater artist, a finer spirit, and a profounder thinker than was recognised during his lifetime by any but a very few. The analyses of his work in *The Architecture* have revealed in it an integrity, a range of imagination, and a combination of feeling and strength which surely substantiate Mr. Butler's claim that Lutyens was the greatest artist in building whom Britain has produced. The selection of his designs illustrated constitute the largest and most imaginative addition made by a single mind to the classics of English architecture for two centuries, and which, it is not too much to prophesy, will be studied and emulated so long as architecture is conceived as an art.

His relative stature among the memorable architects of history must be left for posterity to determine. The estimate struck by historians of the scholarship of architecture will, we do not doubt, be very high. Among practitioners it may well vary from age to age according to the direction in which architecture develops, and to whether architecture is regarded as an art or a branch of science. His contemporaries were convinced that he was the most creative architectural genius this nation has known for two hundred years, but one who was so entirely engrossed in his art that he never developed a quite adult contemporary sense of professional responsibility. The younger generation of architects go further in their criticism. While acknowledging his genius they censure him for withholding, in their view, any contribution to the development of a 'real' architecture. This point, which Mr. Butler has discussed, will be considered here.

As an Appendix to our studies, which have largely accounted for these tributes and imputations, the authors of his *Life* and *Architecture* jointly seek to clarify the nature of Lutyens's legacy to posterity. We claim that the analyses of his later designs now published, taken in conjunction with his own disconnected elucidations of his theory brought together in this volume, do constitute the materials of a legacy for the future, potentially as valuable as his contribution to the classical body of architecture.

The validity of any such conclusions must, it is owned, depend upon the course of events. We confess that the extraordinary cessation of building which has intervened since his death, indeed for a decade in Britain, has given a sense of unreality to the process of formulating even a provisional estimate of the applicability to the future of what Lutyens so signally achieved. Not only architecture but the world is in a state of flux to which, however, the paralysis of normal activities perhaps gives exaggerated significance as regards architecture. Yet when we consider that a commensurate cessation of building has occurred in English history probably only during the years of the Civil War, and previously in the decade of the Black Death, on both of which catastrophes ensued a far-reaching change in the character of national architecture, we shall not be disposed to minimise the results of the present interregnum. Already the number of architects capable of designing in his medium has diminished, and the craftsmen trained to execute such work are dying.

The gravamen of young architects' complaint is that Lutyens did not greatly concern himself with the economics, construction, and social planning with which they are largely preoccupied and which they regard as the only real bases for design. That, instead, he took those foundations for granted and elaborated upon them idealised conceptions employing a scale of values which they do not admit but which to him was absolute. Nurtured as he was in traditional English sentiment and reflecting, with singular completeness, the romantic idealism of the race, a disillusioned generation label him and those whose faith he shared—in the contemptuous way by which dry little tickets are attached to the arteries and members of the body politic— as representatives of 'the Humanist Survival'.

The first item in this complaint is little more than the petulance of students that an artist of heroic calibre has not bequeathed to them a manual of his art. The latter, on the other hand, goes to the root of the ethical foundations of contemporary thought, on which the attitude to all human activities, the arts included, must be based. The phrase 'humanist survival' not only means that the notion of humanism must fail to admit the full implications of the Scientific Revolution, but implies that that revolution, produced by the discovery of new sources of energy, is complete and thereby extinguishes the validity of humane values.

At this middle point of the twentieth century, however, the world stands aghast at the realisation of what those full implications do mean. In the light of Hiroshima we have glimpsed the truth that scientific materialism has always been, is, and will be disruptive of humane civilisation, which is the only genuine kind of civilisation the world has ever known, unless controlled and applied through the medium of humanist ideals.

This round assertion is made not forgetting the many and great conveniences which science, physical and otherwise, has contributed to civilisation, but equally remembering the inconveniences. To give a few obvious instances, science has greatly prolonged the expectation of life, whilst, however, reducing the probability of it owing to failures of the human factor. It has added enormously to life's comfort whilst diminishing its enjoyment. The scope of knowledge has been so vastly increased that no single mind is capable of bringing it into intelligible focus. Science has at last established the nature of reality by depriving it of meaning, and dissipated superstition by dissolving the concept of God into a cloud of doubt.

The mortal peril to humanity of thoughtlessly accepting these conveniences (with their inherent disadvantages) as constituting a philosophy of life is now becoming apparent. For the implications of this disruptive materialism, baldly stated, are that 'human beings are nothing but bodies, animals, mere machines; that the only really real elements of reality are matter and energy in their measurable aspects; that "values" are nothing but illusions which have somehow got themselves mixed up with our experience of the world. . . . The political consequences of this "nothing but" philosophy are clearly seen in the widespread indifference to the values of human personality and human life so characteristic of the present age'.[1]

In the realm of art and architecture its consequences are the same, indifference to the values of the human spirit and human life. The aesthetic values of the past are held to have been illusions. The power of inspiration or guidance by a spirit, however lofty, and whether divine or human, is suspect if not rejected. In the name of faithfulness to realities the delicate fabric of relationships, allusions, and overtones, which constitute civilised art, is stripped away, revealing primeval chaos.

The effect of this glance into the abyss, the opening of which threatens to be the culminating achievement of the scientific ideal, is to establish that, if civilisation is to survive, it can only be through mastery of these disintegrating forces by the human spirit, which our anthropomorphic intelligence aspires to regard as comprising elements of the supernatural, the cosmic, in a word, God. The process of reintegration must begin by accepting the assumption that the world is the product neither of determinism nor chance exclusively, but is concerned with a spiritual purpose. Without that assumption humanity has no third alternative to delivering itself either to the modern worship of the State, or to the now discredited faith that science is inevitably leading it towards a material Utopia round the next corner. Without this means of self-detachment from mass error, and of self-union with an eternal spirit to which certain immutable values belong, humanity may well possess as little wish as it at present has expectation of surviving the clash between complete materialism and entire empiricism.

Although it has been necessary to range somewhat far in taking a brief but not wholly superficial view of the background of architecture's future, we are here concerned only with the bearing of this argument upon architecture when we come to consider the means of reintegration. Architecture, having been tied to the Law of Gravity and the use of man, has been saved from the more extreme manifestations of

[1] Aldous Huxley, *Science, Liberty and Peace*, 1947.

disintegration reflected in some other arts, although the denial of humane values has proceeded to equal lengths in extravagant theories. Amid the present flux of ideas it is possible to detect two poles of architectural thought around which reintegration is being attempted. It is certainly helpful to recognise in these two poles our old friends the classic and romantic principles.

One, represented by the school of Le Corbusier, can be described as the principle of fitting human needs to a finite intellectual system, cellular in character, standardised in type, politically autocratic, aesthetically classical.

The other, less powerful, to which the names of Mumford and Frank Lloyd Wright attach, stands at the opposite extreme, and envisages a reshaping of social, aesthetic, and structural forms to fit the natural proclivities of the human organism; politically democratic, aesthetically romantic.

These rival, or complementary, conceptions of the basis of architecture have, of course, persisted from the earliest times. But till the middle of the nineteenth century architecture was nourished by their interaction or alternation. Both are capable of producing an architecture. But the plain lesson of history is that, whether in the sphere of the arts or society, no greatly enduring achievement has been attained without some degree of synthesis between the intellectual, if materialist order of the one and the imaginative empiricism of the other.

But we have stated the conviction that the essential medium of synthesis (the 'third alternative') between the extremes of dogma represented by these architectural poles is man's recognition of the spirit and the existence of certain immutable values appertaining to the spirit.

The fundamental respect in which Lutyens differed from other notable architects of this age was his conviction of the existence of these absolute values (beauty, truth, human dignity), and his identifying them, in his last phase, with a system of mathematical proportions. In the light of our elucidations of this system as exemplified in what we have termed his Elemental Mode, and of his efforts to bring about an alliance of artists and scientists 'to formulate a creed of beauty', it is seen that his theory and practice were ultimately directed precisely towards reintegrating architecture by a synthesis of intellectual and empirical concepts on the basis of accepting faith in a spiritual yet finite idealism. In other words, belief in the existence of absolute beauty and absolute truth as qualities produced by natural and no less by scientific canons, and governed by ascertainable facts, unaffected by fashion or by association of ideas.

Conventional architecture, he admitted, is too heavily encumbered by tradition, sentiment, and archaeology to advance appreciably itself towards the possible synthesis that he envisaged, though in its transmitted lore is contained data of the greatest value for the process. Engineering, on the other hand, with which he broadly equated the new emancipated architecture, although it was free from the clutter of tradition, admits 'no responsibility to any law pertaining to ideal vision'. But if, he reiterated, 'the laws of beauty were studied, in nature and art, as keenly as the laws of stress and strain,' and the constructor 'had the grace to make the essential sacrifice', i.e. of unfettered utility, to ideal vision, then a valid architectural synthesis would begin to evolve.

No student of architecture, whatever his allegiance, can deny Lutyens's axiom that 'all great periods of architecture have one common and essential denominator: Unity of Rhythm, with nothing left to chance'.

Nevertheless there is a very widespread suspicion of the principle of applying canons of proportion to functional design, as is well expressed, and countered, in the following passage:[1]

> There will always be those who believe that any attempt to rationalise in the arts will make the exercise of aesthetic abilities mechanical, and that where logic steps in inspiration flies out. These fears are almost certainly needless. Artists have in all ages shown themselves ready and able to work contentedly within systems of rules whether imposed by religion or social conditions or by academic authority, however arbitrary such rules may have been....
>
> This process, moreover, is not as illogical as it may seem, for there is no doubt that the eye can detect a great many geometrical relationships, and the spectator usually derives at least some satisfying sense of order wherever a design conforms to a law, even if that law be merely arbitrary.
>
> But in this age of rationalisation most of us will ask for something more, and there is at the moment a very pressing need for a systematic analysis of visual effects on which could be based a theory of composition something better than purely empiric.

Lutyens stated the same conclusion, with greater force and scope, as 'Method, Scale, Rhythm, based on realities and observed with the rigidity of Music, are necessities to all great architecture'. It was to ascertain the basic realities, which artists could distil and relate to their medium, that he aimed to establish his Research School of scientists and architects. The 'creed of beauty' that he believed would result, would thus be a synthesis of material and empirical science with aesthetic intuition. But whilst the scientist would assemble the basic observations and facts conditioning a form or combination of forms, it was, Lutyens insisted, for the artist, with his instinctive sympathies, to interpret the formula into visual shape.

A 'Humanist Survivor', with his countryman's upbringing and romantic tem-

---

[1] From a paper by H. Lewis Curtis, F.R.I.B.A., in the *R.I.B.A. Journal*, February, 1949, discussing the late Manning Robertson's theory of Functional Proportion as outlined by A. Leonard Roberts, F.R.I.B.A., in the January, 1949 issue.

perament, he initially suggested natural forms as most likely to provide the raw material for research. On the other hand, in his last years, he undoubtedly encountered at least the embryos of new architectural forms, the products of social and technical factors, which, as such, represented the postulates of civic science, awaiting the synthesising process of translation into aesthetic grammar.

An outstanding instance of how the application of scientific methods to problems of town planning has produced new shapes for aesthetic formulation is afforded by the types of 'zoned' city buildings evolved for the Ministry of Town and Country Planning by Professor W. G. Holford and also embodied in the Final Report on *Reconstruction in the City of London*.[1]

These diagrams, unlike the somewhat arbitrary conceptions for 'machines to live in' or the empirical romanticism of Lloyd Wright, are the results of technical studies from many angles. They are skeleton forms dictated by converging graphs representing necessities: angles of light and illumination, the dispersion of street-noises, optimum density in relation to street-capacity for transport, correlating the results so obtained with angles of sight, building height, and ancient monuments. Their relating of realities to architectural form gives to these diagrams the authentic reality of the traditional basic forms of temple and bridge, with none of the arbitrariness of 'functional' or empirical hypotheses. Part of the synthesising process, for the urban buildings of the future, has thus been effected. But as yet they are raw cubes. The third stage of the synthesising process must be to endow their component masses, their stepped silhouettes, their bold projections and re-entrants, with Method, Scale, Rhythm, equally based on realities and observed with the rigidity of Art. Thus the synthesising process envisaged by Lutyens for the formulation of a genuine modern architecture awaits the final stage of transformation into works of art.

The truly remarkable thing in the case of these new basic forms for city buildings, arrived at by primarily scientific methods, is their approximation to the architectural forms evolved by Lutyens in his Elemental Mode assisted by his geometrical system. In the Thiepval Memorial he rationalised geometrically a complete system of proportions applicable to a building of this disposition. The Thiepval ratios have, of course, nothing to do with human habitation; it would be inappropriate to apply them literally. But, once the artist has determined his unit of design, the system of progression evolved by Lutyens is ready to his hand.

To some extent, too, the systematised progression and step-backs in some of Lutyens's other city buildings, seem to have been premonitions for the future. Mr. Butler's analyses make available specimens of the formulae which architects who are prepared to design grammatically as artists, rather than crudely as exhibitionists or

---

[1] *The Redevelopment of Central Areas*, H.M. Stationery Office, 1948. *Final Report to the Improvements and Town Planning Committee . . .*, by Dr. C. H. Holden and Professor W. G. Holford, 1947.

propagandists, can now take as affording 'classic' standards of rhythmical design. The principle thus demonstrated is applicable to all architectural conceptions.

We can now, indeed, recognise that the Thiepval Memorial, the Poultry bank, and the designs for Liverpool Cathedral (which gives such tremendous aesthetic effect to closely similar structural postulates) constitute forward bases, of great cogency, established by Lutyens's genius as starting points for the advance of the Humanist tradition into the questionable future. They embody in architectural language his 'true spirit', his faith in accumulated knowledge, his insistence on unity based on reality, and his humanity. In their systems of composition founded on visual effects they supply the ideal corrective to an architecture floundering between pure empiricism and 'nothing-but' utilitarianism. They dispel pessimism by the vitality with which they illumine his text

Architecture, with its love and passion, begins where function ends,

and his personal motto 'By measure we must live':

Metiendo Vivendum.

INDEX

*Buildings designed or altered by Sir Edwin Lutyens

*Abbey House, Barrow, 107, 293, 326
Aberconway, Lord, 269, 497
Abercrombie, Sir Patrick, 573
Adamson, Mgr., 541
Adshead, S. D., 230, 260
Adyar, 410, 419, 439
Agra, 252
Aitcheson, Professor, 85
Aitken, Charles, 372
Alba, Duke of, 338, 340, 566
*Ammerdown, Somerset, 124
Anglo-Persian Oil Company, 453
*Antwerp Exhibition, British Pavilion at, 481
*Apsley End, 71, 98
Architecture and Personalities, quoted, 17, 25, 35, 271 n., 312, 407, 412 n.
Architecture, contemporary, bearing of Sir Edwin Lutyens's work on, 583 et seq.
Architecture of Sir Edwin Lutyens, The, quoted or referred to, xvii, xix, 164 n., 192, 239, 294, 299, 315, 469 n., 470, 471, 475, 482, 520, 530, 588
Architectural Association, address to, by Sir E. Lutyens, 545 n.
Argyll, H.R.H. Duchess of, 25, 36, *see also* Louise, Princess
Armitage, sculptor, 346
Aronson, sculptor, 271
Art Workers' Guild, The, 17, 329
Ashby, Dr., 169, 200, 226
*Ashby St. Ledgers, 94, 108, 194, 443, 463, 565
*Ashwell Bury, 464, 472
Asquith, Rt. Hon. H. H., 230, 269, 328
Athenaeum Club, the, 182, 333, 491
Athens, 538
Australian National War Memorial, 456

Baalbec, 540

Baker, Sir Herbert, xv, 17, 20, 25, 44, 74, 139, 140, 141, 163, 172, 179, 181, 197 n., 200, 203, 209, 210, 237, 243-4, 246, 270, 275, 276, 285, 288, 306, 310, 336, 367, 372, 390, 407, 560, 566, 574, 580; *see also Architecture and Personalities*; his appointment to New Delhi, 243, 246, 282; his conception of, 247, 286, 296; his relations with Lutyens, 180, 308, 310, 321-4, 337, 351, 364, 367, 410-11; *see also Architecture and Personalities*
Balfour, the Rt. Hon. A. J., 172, 295, 390
Balfour, Gerald (later 2nd Earl Balfour), 38, 50, 61, 73, 144, 172
Balfour, Lady Betty, 36, 49, 144
Balmoral, 266, 267, 408, 410
Baring, the Hon. Cecil (Lord Revelstoke), 114, 218, 481, 550
Barnett, Canon, and Dame Henrietta, 118, 187
Barrie, Sir J. M., 39, 114, 151, 165, 168, 322, 327, 372, 389
*Barton St. Mary, E. Grinstead, 127, 128
Battersea, Lord, 36, 68, 72, 75, 146, 155
Beadon, Major H. C., 263
Beatty, Admiral Earl, 193, 269
Bedford, the Duke of, 186
Bedford Square, No. 31, 327, 377, 378, 381
Beechwood, Sussex, 569
Beit, Sir Otto, 200, 203, 205
Belleville, Mrs., 106
Benares, 335, 454
Benson, A. C., 449
Benson, R. H., 167
Berkeley Hotel, 327
Berners, Lord, 98
Berry, Francis, 451
*Berry Down, 58, 71, 72, 146, 151
Besant, Mrs. Annie, 172, 218, 253, 294, 328, 336, 347, 377, 378, 410, 419

Bharatpur stone, 428
Bhopal, Begum of, 288
Bigge, Sir Arthur (see Stamfordham, Lord), 177 n
Bikanir, Maharajah of, 279, 364
*Binfield Lodge, 71
Bird, Sir William, 168
Birkenhead, Earl of, 550
Birrell, the Rt. Hon. Augustine, 295, 390
Blackburn, Ernest, 103, 173
Blomfield, Sir Reginald, 96, 136, 143, 175, 225, 226, 245, 271, 276 n., 375, 492
Bloomsbury Square, No. 29, 66, 143 et seq., 239, see also Lutyens, Sir Edwin, offices of
Blow, Detmar, 14, 136, 180
Blumenthal, M., and Mme Jacques, 36, 73
Bombay, 248, 408, 419
Bossom, Alfred, 458
Botha, General, 205, 270
Boulay, Sir J. and Lady Du, 254, 352
Bourchier, Rev. B. G., 192
Bourne, Cardinal, 543
Brabazon, Hercules, 36
Brangwyn, Sir F., 544
Brassey, Capt. Harold, 178, 193
*Breccles, Hall, Norfolk, 389
*Brede Place, Sussex, 327
Bressey, Sir Charles, 548, 566
Bressey-Lutyens Report, 567
Bridgeman, Lord, 432
*Britannic House, London, 453, 469
*British Medical Association, 231 n., 334, 453, 463
Broadbent, carver, 124
Broadway, Glos., 170
Brodie, J. A., 246, 247, 248, 251, 257, 260, 261, 262, 266, 274, 285
Brooks, F. H., 458, 483
*Brooksby Hall, 269
Brown, Percy, 498
*Buckhurst Park, 107, 156, 245, 294
Buckmaster, Mrs. Martin, 566, 575
Buddha Gya, 335
Builder, The, 22, 137, 240 n.
Burlington House, 569, 572, 573
*Burrows Cross, Shere, 71, 75
Busbridge, Surrey, 71, 550
Butler, A. S. G., xvi, xvii, xix, 135, 469 n., 470, 471, 475, 482, 520, 530, 552
Butler, Sir Harcourt, 254, 335, 416, 420
Byron, Robert, 321 n., 572, quoted 297, 298, 345, 519, 520

CAIRNS, W. B., 429
*Calcot Park, Berks., 97
Caldecott, Randolph, 8, 27, 39, 72, 87, 127, 189, 485, 548, 571, 575
Calcutta, 238, 284, 285, 497
*Campion Hall, Oxford, 544, 547
Canadian red cedar-wood, 548
Capetown Cathedral, 74, 205
Capetown, University of, 203, 205, 209, 270, 390
Carmichael, Lord, 362, 381, 412
Casket, the, 41 et seq., 56, 57, 60, 100, 172, 328, 439, 556
*Castle Drogo, 107, 197, 203, 204, 210, 217-25, 293-4, 326, 462, 469, 485, 525, 550
Cathedral of Christ the King, see Liverpool Cathedral
*Cenotaph, the, Whitehall, 25, 369, 376, 391-4, 459, 462
Ceylon, 420
Chamberlain, Rt. Hon. Sir Austen, 361, 366, 370
Chance, Sir William, 71, 74, 86
Chapman, Sir Arthur, 18, 86, 95, 151, 178, 326
*Charing Cross Bridge Scheme, 524
Congreve, Lady, 333
Congreve, William, 389
Connaught, H.R.H. the Duke of, 204, 208, 407
Conway, Sir Martin, 232, 387 n.
Cooch Behar, Maharanee of, 425, 454
Cook, C. A., 71
Cooper, Lady, 440
*Copse Hill, Glos., 178, 193
Corbett, Harvey, 457, 458, 459
Corbusier, Le, xvii, 525, 586
Cotes, Mrs., 284
Country Life, 25, 95, 96, 98, 100, 105 n., 108, 139, 143, 162, 522, 567 n., 568 n., 569 n.
**Country Life* Building, 124
County Hall, London, Competition, 137 et seq., 176, 179, 217, 222
Courtauld Thompson, Lord, 144 n.
Crewe, the Marquess of, 245, 246, 260, 262, 263, 267, 281, 282, 295
*Crooksbury, 18, 19, 25, 41, 61, 84, 86, 94, 100, 151, 326, 574
Cunard, Lady, 327, 361, 389
Curtis, Lionel, 367, 390
Curtis Green, W., 580
Curzon of Kedleston, the Marquess, 232, 237, 238, 243, 267, 361
Chelmsford, Viscount, Viceroy of India, 363, 365

Chesters, Northumberland, 103, 120, 151
*Cheyne Walk, Chelsea, No. 24, 481; No. 96, 440
*Chinthurst Hill, Surrey, 26, 53, 86
Chipping Camden, 169, 278
Chirol, Sir Valentine, 249, 274, 275, 279, 280, 282 n., 284, 333, 356
Chitorgarh, 278
Churchill, Lady Randolph, 193, 327, 333
Churchill, Rt. Hon. Winston, 155 n., 327, 333, 440, 574
*Chussex, Walton-on-the-Hill, 135, 136
City and Guilds of London Institute Art School, 551
Clarke, Purdon, 85
Classicism, see Lutyens, Sir Edwin, Architecture of, development towards Renaissance classical
*Clifford Chambers Manor, 94, 463
Clutterbuck, P. H., 265
Cochrane, Mr. H., 125
*Cockington Inn, Devon, 548
*Cogers, The, Fleet St., 548
Colefax, Lady, xvi, 379, 440
*Colombo War Memorial, 420
Colt, Messrs. W. H., 548
Colville, Capt. N. L., 463

DAMASCUS, 540
Danes, The, Herts., 45, 57
*Daneshill, Hants., 105, 113
D'Arcy, Rev. Father S. J., xvi, 543, 544
Davis A. J., 559
Dawber, Sir Guy, 17, 136, 290, 560
*Deanery Garden, 84, 95, 97, 100, 101, 106, 161
Dehra Dun, Forest Products Institute, 496
Delhi, 238;
    Ancient Cities and monuments of, 249, 250, 252, 254, 261, 264, 265, 268, 269, 288
    King Edward's statue, 267, 269
    Malcha, 261, 264, 274
    North Ridge, 247, 248, 249, 251, 252, 256, 265, 276, 283
    Superstitions connected with, 407
Delhi, New, 123, 217, 231, 462, 537, 550
    All India War Memorial, 368, 369, 375, 474 (see also War Memorial Arch)
    Architects' agreement for, 306, 307, 308, 409
    Architects' remuneration for, 308, 310, 409
    Architectural style of, 252, 256, 259 et seq., 265, 268, 270, 274, 276, 281, 282, 289, 295, 366;
        Indian elements incorporated in, 297–9, 312
    Assistant architects, etc., at, 308: Barrett, 367, 381; Gentry, E. C., 428; Greaves, John, 427; Hall, E. E., 427, 428; Harding, F., 496; Mustoe, W. R., 503, 555; Shoosmith, A. G., 428, 453, 492; Wands, 367; Ward, H., 428 n., 453; Wilson, F., 496; Wright, Hubert, 428
    Bodyguard lines, 368, 371
    Cantonments Church, 492
    Cathedral, 261, 369, 505
    Central Railway Station, 311, 406
    Chief Engineer at, 308, 319, 321
    Church of the Redeemer, 505
    Civil Lines, 249
    Climate, influence of, on design of, 237, 268, 297, 298, 299, 496
    Committee of Inquiry, 405, 410, 412, 427
    Competition proposed for design of, 262, 266, 271, 308
    Completion, intended date of, 326
    Coolie lines at, 337
    Cost of, 295; estimates of, 311, 312, 318, 319, 321, 336, 364, 366, 368 et seq., 405, 408, 409, 412, 431
    Council House, 407
    Criticisms of, 405, 407, 408
    Delhi Advisory Committee, 362, 366, 381, 409, 496, 498
    Delhi Committee, the, 263, 308, 318, 321, 322, 337, 353, 366
    Delhi Order, the, 507, 534, 544
    Dholpur stone, 428, 430
    Durbar Amphitheatre, 288, 311, 429
    Engineers' Department, the, 312, 428
    Ethnological Museum and Record Office, the, 368, 369, 372, 406 n.
    Foundation stone of, 247
    Government Court, 286, 288, 315, 323, 337, 351, 353
    Government (Viceroy's) House, site and design of, 258, 265, 273, 282, 286, 287, 295, 297 et seq., 311, 312 (see Viceroy's House below)
    Gradient to Viceroy's House, problems connected with, 262, 265, 268, 286, 287, 288, 306, 307, 320, 322 et seq., 337, 351, 363, 364, 365, 370, 409, 410 et seq., 418, 522, 560
    Great Court, the, 307
    Great Place, The, 315, 323, 353, 357
    Hardinge, Lord, policy on, 274, 281; see also Delhi, New, architectural style of
    Jami Masjid, 306, 315
    King's Way, the, 315, 323, 368, 370, 406, 522
    Loan for, Sir E. Lutyens's advocacy of, 268, 408

Delhi, New
  Medical Research building, at, 406
  Military Cantonment, at, 251, 252, 261, 263
  Official opening of, 522
  Plan, Lay-out, of, 252, 258, 261, 264, 286, 288, 295, 322, 357, 406
  Planning Commission, 246, *et passim*
  Public Works Department, 259, 405, 496
  Purana Kilat, 312, 506, 550
  Queen's Way, 368, 406
  Raisina Hill, 244, 261, 265, 273, 283, 286, 295, 307, 315, 322, 365, 506
  Secretariats, 258, 261, 265, 267, 268, 269, 270, 287, 294, 295, 300 *n*., 305, 311, 315, 317, 321, 337, 346, 367, 406, 410, 495, 503
  Site of, 249 *et seq.*, 252, 257, 262, 355; costs of acquisition of, 263; early alternatives for, 258, 261, 265, 267, 268, 269, 272, 284; problem of land proprietorship in, 253
  South Ridge, 252, 261, 264, 265, 274, 288, 311, 315, 504
  Stable lines, the 368
  Stone yards, 371, 429
  Tree planting and trees at, 265, 268, 273, 305, 368, 370, 372, 503, 504, 555
  *Viceroy's House, 18, 123, 222, 244, 281, 472, 540, 553, 569, 574, 579 (*see also* Government House); *Chattris*, 300, 305; *Chujjas*, 305; Cost of, 262; Council chamber, 317, 366, 370, 406; Craftsmen and craftsmanship at, 288, 308, 328, 345, 346, 347, 348, 361, 381, 429, 496, 521; Dates fixed for, stages in building, 409, 495, 503, 505, 506, 520, 521; Design of, approved, 323; Design of, evolved, 281, 288, 298, 299, 300, 305, 315, 318, 319, 320, 321 (*see also* Plan and Arrangement); Dimensions of, 288, 295, 298, 305, 317, 318; reduced, 288, 295, 298, 311, 319, 320, 321, 336; enlarged, 319, 322; Dome, 288, 298, 300, 306, 307, 312, 319, 351, 495, 506; Durbar Hall, 315, 319, 497, 519, 523; Fountains at, 364, 503; Furnishing of, Lady Irwin and, 498, materials for, 496, 497, State Suite, 361, 362, 381, 496, Textiles, 498; Gardens of, 272, 367, 368, 370, 371, 503, 524, 554; Garden loggia, 509; Interior described, 506 *et seq.*; Jaipur Column, 324, 345, 351, 357, 505, 556; Lady Willingdon, and, 550, 551, 553, 555; Marble proposed for, 229, 300 *n*., 364, 408; Materials of, 297, 298, 299, 320, 364, 408, 427, 428, 429, 430, brick, 430, stones, 297, 428, marbles, 429, 430, 530, proposed, marble, 229, 300 *n*., 304, 408, plaster, 408; Nomenclature of, 505; Nurseries, 498; Opening of, 521; Opinions and technical descriptions of, 283, 284, 299, 318, 363, 506, 520, 522; Perspective designs for, 306, 323, 324; Plan and arrangement of, described, 298, 305, 315, 317, 506 *et seq.*; Plaster finish, proposed for, 408; Portico, 305, 507; Progress of, in 1917, 365, 370, in 1918, 370, 371, stopped, 371, in 1926–28, 495, 505, delayed, 406; Royal Suite proposed, 317; Sculpture at, 345, 346, 364, 505; Staff Houses and Bungalows, 319, 364, 366, 367, 368, 371, 415, 427, 430, 555; Viceroy's Court, 315, 319, 353, 365, 410, 412, 505; Viceroy's Wing, 464, 498, 510
  War Memorial Arch, 310, 312, 368–9, 375, 406, 412, 434, 505, 550, 555
  War Museum, 406
  Willingdon Stadium, 312, 550, 555
  Work on, closed down, 1918–22, 371
Democracy and architecture, 228, 247
Dholpur quarries, 297, 428
Dickenson, Oswald, 179
Dodge, Miss Mary, 179, 329, 538
Dolgorouki, Alexis, Princess, 125, 126, 128, 167
*Dormy House, Walton Heath, the, 127, 136, 168
Downey, Dr., Archbishop of Liverpool, 527, 541, 543, 553, 575
Doyle, Richard, 9, 541
Drewe, J. C., 217, 550
Dublin, 293; Municipal Art Gallery, 186, 231 *et seq.*; Sir E. Lutyens's designs for, 232 *et seq.*; War Memorial, 476
Duckworth, Gerald, 39

EARLE, MRS. C. W., 85, 146, 172, 333, 550
Earle, Sir Lionel, 85, 312, 320, 333, 362
*Eartham, Chichester, 167, 168
*East Haddon Hall, Northants., 71
*Eaton Place, London, No. 94, 72
Eden, Mrs., 90
*Ednaston Manor, 293, 326
Edward VII, King, 105, 118; coronation of, 106, 121, 156; Memorial to, 191, 203, 216, 228, 229, 230, 231, 246, 294
Egypt, 343
El Guadelperal, Spain, 339, 340, 341, 342, 364, 385, 390, 456, 566
Elwin, the Rev. Whitwell, 38, 147
Endsleigh, Devon, 187

Epstein, Jacob, 231
Escorial, The, 339, 504
Esher, Lord, 225, 229
*Etaples, 454, 473, 541
Evans, S. H., xvi, *see also* Lutyens, Sir Edwin, Office of
Evans, the Rev. W. H., 72
Evill, N., xvi, *see also* Lutyens, Sir Edwin, Office of
Exhibition of 1851, Commissioners for, 225, 263

FAIRHAVEN, LORD, 476
Farrer, Gaspard, 137, 294
Fatehpur Sikri, 428
Fenwick, Mark, 101, 119, 169, 380
Field, Mrs. Marshall, 451
*Fisher's Hill, Woking, 98
Fleming, F. H., 180, 321
Flockhart, 88, 137
*Folly Farm, Berks., 94, 113, 125, 126, 136, 168, 359, 360, 377, 571
Franklyn, Mrs. A. S., 108, 128, 168
Freyburg, Lady, 382
Fry, Roger, 379
*Fulbrook, Farnham, Surrey, 71, 72, 146

GALLWAY, MARY, 4, *see* Lutyens, Mrs. Charles
Gandhi, Mahatma, 257, 378, 405, 407, 420, 439
Garrick Club, the, 245, 361, 441, 491, 527, 569
Gasquet, Cardinal, 440
Geddes, Patrick, 336
Geddes, Sir Auckland, 375
Genoa, 196, 299
George V, King, 176, 194, 237, 246; and Queen Mary, 191, 266, 361, 449; coronation of, 186, 217; on New Delhi, 267, 410
George VI, King, 566, 580
George, Sir Ernest, 18, 137, 157, 180, 226, 290, 560
Gertrude Jekyll. A Memoir, 24
Gide, André, *quoted*, 78
Gidea Park, 187
Gill, E., photographer, 522
Gill, Macdonald, 376
Giudicci, sculptor, 505
Gladstone, Lord, 134, 206
Glasgow Art School, 85, 127
Glass Painters, British Society of Master, addressed by Sir E. Lutyens, 546
*Gledstone Hall, Yorks., 453, 471, 472, 547
*Goddards, Abinger, 85, 87, 97, 127, 192
Goodhart-Rendel, H., *quoted*, 35 n.

Goschen, Lord, 416
Gosford, 120, 128, 151
Gotch, Lawrence, 470, 548
Goument, C. E. V., 264, 273, 274
Gravetye, Sussex, 75, 175
*Great Dixter, Sussex, 193, 203, 294, 463
*Great Maytham, Kent, 135, 136, 142, 192, 216, 550
Great Morning, 326, 379 n., 399 n., 414 n.
Gregory, Lady, 232, 233
*Grey Walls, 98, 99, 137, 189
*Grosvenor House, London, 482
Grove, Archibald, 58, 71, 151
Guthrie, Miss Aemelia, 26
Gwalior, H.H. the Maharajah of, 364

HAILEY, LORD, xvi, 246, 273, 275, 320 n., 321, 336, 362, 363, 370, 371, 372, 378, 382, 408, 412 n.
Haldane, Lord, 328, 333
Halifax, Earl of, xvi, (*see* Irwin, Lord)
Hall, H. Austen, xvi, 566
*Halnaker House, 548
*Hampstead Garden Suburb, 186 *et seq.*, 190-2, 216, 239, 463, 497
Hampton Court, 125, 379, 461, 549
Hannen, Nicholas, xvi, 165, *see also* Lutyens, Sir Edwin, Office of
*Hanover Lodge, Regent's Park, 193, 269
Harcourt, Sir Lewis, 229
Harcourt-Smith, Sir Cecil, 381
Hardinge, the Hon. Diamond, 275
Hardinge of Penshurst, Lord, Viceroy, xvi, 240, 243, 245, 252, 254, 256, 259, 262, 271, 274, 280, 284, 344, 362, 365, 381, 390, 521; Indian policy of, 237, 240, 366; on site of Government House, New Delhi, *quoted* 265, 273; determined site of, 273
Hardinge, Lady, 243, 254, 257, 272, 274, 284, 320, 325, 362, 368, 492
Hardwick Hall, Derbyshire, 176
Hare, Augustus, 137, 156
Hari Singh, Gen. Raja Sir, 425
Hawke and Mackinlay, Messrs., 206
Hawkes, Mrs. C. P., xvi, 5 n.
*Heathcote, Ilkley, Yorks, 113, 128, 139, 161, 163, 167, 168, 179, 281, 294, 453, 462, 470
Heaton, A., 67, 68, 144
Hemingway, Ernest, 128, 163, 168
Heseltine, P., 419
*Hestercombe, 113, 125, 128, 167, 570

Hever Castle, 108, 379, 389
*Heywood, Ireland, 260
Hicks, Sir Seymour, 152
Hill, Lee, 97
Hill, Oliver, 559
Hill, Sir Claude, 366, 418
Hillingdon, Lord, 85, 88, 89, 162
Hoare, Walter, 105
Hodgson Burnett, Miss, 137
*Hoe Farm, Hascombe, 26
Holderness, Sir Thomas, 247, 271, 339, 382
Holford, Professor W. G., 588
Holy Island, 167, 168, 176, 267; see also Lindisfarne
*Homewood, Knebworth, 72, 104
Horne, Edgar, 96
Horner, Edward, 328; Memorial to, 464, 570
Horner, Sir John, 192, 203, 464
Horner, Lady, 328, 333, 362, 464, 544, 570
Houses and Gardens by E. L. Lutyens, 96 n., 240, 326
*Howth Castle, 192, 293
Hudson, Edward, 25, 95, 96, 98, 105, 106, 124, 127, 137, 141, 143, 167, 176, 182, 186, 229, 326, 378, 438, 440, 481, 522
Hudson, Robert, 451
Hull, Yorks., plan for, 573
Hunter, Mrs. Charles, 327
Huxley, Aldous, 585 n.
Hyderabad, Government of, 521

IMPERIAL TOBACCO COMPANY, THE, 298
Imperial War Graves Commission, the, 369, 372, 376 n., 381, 382, 387, 388, 462, 473
Imrie, G. Blaire, 88
Incorporated Association of Architects and Surveyors, 546, 546 n.
Inge, the Very Rev. W. R., 456
Institute of American Architects, 456
Institute of Registered Architects, 546
Irving, Mrs., 72, 153
Irwin, Lord, Viceroy of India, 496, 498, 505, 506
Irwin, Lady, 498
Islington, Lord, 282 n.
Ismay, Lord, 551

JACOB, SIR SWINTON, 276, 282, 295, 307
Jackson, Sir Thomas G., 137, 382
Jagger, C. S., 347, 505
Jaipur, 252, 497, 554
Jaipur, Maharajah of, 553

James, William, Mr., 99, 104, 137, 157, 159
James, Mrs., 157, 159
Jamnagar, 418
Janis, Elsie, 458
Jaques, Richard, 453, 471
Jekyll, Gertrude, xvi, 6, 23, 39, 40, 46, 48, 72, 73, 74, 85, 95, 108, 143, 146, 174, 206, 240, 288, 326, 333, 342, 360, 374, 378, 379, 451, 472, 544, 549, 550, 566; *quoted*, 24 *et seq.*, 153; collaboration with and influence on Sir E. Lutyens, 24 *et seq.*, 71, 75, 125; her boots painted, 550; portrait of, 549, 566
Jekyll, Col. Sir Herbert, 24, 71, 84, 85, 86, 90, 125, 152, 179, 362, 549
Jekyll, Lady, 451
*Jellico and Beatty, Trafalgar Square Memorial, 230
Jersey, Earl of, 547
Jodhpur State, 430, 555
*Johannesburg Art Gallery, 186, 200, 203, 204, 207, 208, 227, 270, 320
John, Augustus, 232, 390, 399, 560 n.
Johnston, Herbert, 100, 326, 333, 570
Jones, Inigo, 104, 122, 138, 140, 196
Jones, Sir Roderick, 547

KAPURTHALA, H.H. THE MAHARAJAH OF, 550
Kashmir, 425, 497
Keeling, Sir Hugh, Chief Engineer, New Delhi, 288, 321, 367, 369, 371, 411, 427
Kelly, Sir Gerald, 232
Kenyon, Lt. Col. Sir Frederick, 374 n., 375, 388
Kilkatrine House, Inveraray, 72
*Kingsway, Offices of *The Garden* in, 179
Kipling, Rudyard, 181, 205, 376, 388, 391
Knebworth, Herts, 38, 76, 192
*Knebworth, Golf Club, 135, 136
*Knebworth, St. Martin's Church, 326
Knebworth, Anthony Lord, 550
Knoblock, Edward, 327, 389
Knole, Kent, 90, 382, 442
Knott, Ralph, 138, 141
Knox, Mgr. Ronald, 543
Konig, F. A., 451, 472

La Mascotte, 108
Lahore, 497
Lallgarh, 418
Lamb, Sir Walter, xvi, 560, 580
*Lambay, 94, 99, 101, 105, 114, 122, 127, 192, 293, 341, 550

Lanchester, H. V., 138, 246, 257, 258, 260, 262, 264, 271, 336 *n.*
Landseer, Sir Edwin, 4, 6, 19
Lane, Sir Hugh, 186, 200, 203, 206, 208, 231, 232, 234, 263, 327
Langley, Batty, 488
Langton, John, 113
Lawless, the Hon, Emily, 41, 71, 75
Lawrence, T. E., 334
*Le Bois des Moutiers, Varengeville, 147, 172
Leslie, Sir Bradford, 283
Lewis, Sir George, 440, 476
Lewis Curtis, H., 587 *n.*
*Lindisfarne, 99, 100, 106, 127, 141, 162, 166, 326, 438, 469
Lindsay, Mrs. Norah, 570
Lindsay, Sir Ronald, 485 *n.*
Linlithgow, Marquess of, Viceroy, 553
Liria Palace, Madrid, 338, 339, 342, 385, 566
Little College St., Westminster, House in, 98
*Little Court, Tavistock, 187, 193
*Little Tangley, 26
*Little Thakeham, 87, 101, 103, 122, 162, 173
*Littlecroft, Guildford, 98
Liverpool Cathedral, 190, 210, 228, 400, 432, 462, 524, 527-8, 541, 545, 546, 572, 579, 589; Building dimensions, and ratios of, 529–533; Lighting of, 575; Model and design of described, 529–37, 552
Llewellyn, Sir William, 556, 575
Lloyd, Lord, 334, 408, 410, 419
Lloyd, Nathaniel, 193
Lloyd, W. A. S., xvi, *see also* Lutyens, Sir Edwin, Office
Lloyd George, David, 185, 370, 382, 391
Lloyd Wright, Frank, 586
Loch, Lord, 53, 61, 63, 71
Loch, Lady, 38
London County Council, 119, 123, 168, 239, 246
London Replanned, 567 *n.*
Lorimer, Sir Robert, 108, 376
Louise, Princess, Duchess of Argyll, 25, 36, 45, 68, 71, 72, 73, 74, 98, 176, 378, 444
*Lowesby Hall, 178, 193, 203
Lucas, E. V., xvi, 166, 327, 399, 416, 420, 441, 444
Lucas, Seymour, 194
Lucknow, 288, 335, 416, 420, 497
Lumb, T. B., 97

Lutyens, Sir Edwin
BIOGRAPHICAL
Ancestry etc., 3; Capt. and Mrs. Charles, 4, 5, 6, 18, 19, 37, 62, 290, 327; children of, 5, 6, 14, 18, 62, 207, 260
Birth of, 6; engagement of, 44, 48 *et seq.,* 57, 71, 328; marriage, 76; children of, 147, 154, 171, 177, 359, 432, 438, *et passim*; homes (ideal), 43, 45, 63 *et seq.,* 101, 141, 172, 173, 439, 571, (*see also* Offices of); health of, 6, 322, 503, 554, 575, 578; honours, degrees, etc. of, 290, 382, 441, 456, 521, 543, 556, 574; death of, 580
Beliefs of, 140, 181 *et seq.,* 244, 276, 322, 328, 348, 375, 395, 411, 537; in Discipline, 277, 330, 525, 542; in Humanism, 277, 472, 473, 543, 557, 589; in tradition, 525, 543, 557, 577
Opinions of: bureaucracy, 347, 365, 380; colour, 147, 198, 206, 298, 471, 481, 497, 545; Guilds, Socialism, 329, 330, 348; motherhood, 443; Newton, Sir I., 174, 277, 297, 565, 567; paintings, 338, 339, 565; public speaking, 456, 459; punctuality, 491; Ruskin, 556; scenery, 198, 206, 255, 336, 373, 539, 570; sentiment, 123, 169, 171, 181, 277, 279, 285, 296, 346, 373, 411, 586; U.S.A., 459 *et seq.*; water, rivers, etc., 10, 95, 100, 173, 178, 254, 267, 272, 419, 503, 572, 578
Personal Characteristics of, 144, 145 *et seq.,* 155, 161 *et seq.,* 170 *et seq.,* 186, 432, 438, 486; reads Gibbon, 412, 453; social conscience, 482 (*et seq.*), 584; social technique of, 159, 227, 414, 439, 440, 455
Professional Relationships of, with Sir Herbert Baker, 17, 21, 95, 123, 180, 181, 203, 204, 205, 207, 210, 216, 227, 244, 246, 247, 255, 256, 257, 270, 271, 272, 285, 295, 296, 300, 309, 321, 324, 351, 367, 374, 411, 412, 560; Lord Hardinge, 243, 258, 263, 280, 285, 295, 300, 311, 320, 522; Royal Academy, 20, 26, 290, 556, 565; R.I.B.A. 226, 441, 524, 526, 559; *See also* Jekyll, Gertrude; Offices, Partnership
ARCHITECTURE OF
Abstraction, trend towards in, 114, 124, 135, 141, 174, 400, 462, 464, 471, 474–6, 526, 533, 534, 546
Classical, his development towards, 77, 83, 104, 113, 119, 121, 124, 128, 151, 462, 526;

Lutyens, Sir Edwin
ARCHITECTURE OF
'Lutyensian', 462, 464, 470, 476; methods of handling, his, 120, 133-5, 140, 200, 208-9, 318, 462
Drawing, his method and aims in, 9, 487 *et seq.*, 491, 542, 578
Geometry of, 128, 174, 296, 346, 376, 475, 481, 482
Materials, instances of his craftsmanship in, or opinions on, 98, 492; brick, 87, 105, 108, 113, 126, 136, 137, 189, 193, 475, 493, 558; chalk, 100, 101; chimneys, 87, 88, 94, 96, 99, 101, 108, 126, 128, 136; glass, 558; granite, 219, 531; plaster, 134, and cement, 227, 482, 493; steel and concrete, 493, 559; stone, 29, 86, 87, 170, 544, 547; texture, 83, 99, 115, 126, 209, 474, 475, 493; in new countries, 209, 296; tile, 86, 87, 104, 116, 127, 136, 139, 193, 548; timber, 31, 32, 86, 87, 105, 222, 463, 544, 547; modes of, 476; ratios in, 164, 177, 376, 391 *n.*, 470, 475; romanticism in, 78, 104, 114, 217, 462, 544; synthesis of Eastern and Western in, 280, 281, 297, 300
Romantic impulses in, 78, 104, 114, 217, 462, 544,
NEW DELHI
Appointment to, 245, 260, 262, 274, 282, 290
Council House, 407
Craft Centre, proposes at, 347
Criticises handling of, 362
Gradient at, admits error in, 354
Influence on character of, his, 276, 361, 369
Resignation at, considered, 411; *see also* Delhi, New
OFFICE AND ORGANISATION, 21, 163 *et seq.* 461, 487-8, 492, 559
Assistants of, 485: Alwyn, G., 162; Ayrton, Maxwell, 98, 161; Barlow, W., 21, 93, 162; Baynes Badcock, E., 93, 97, 113, 119, 154, 161; Coleridge, J. D., 98, 161; Dalton, 93, 98, 113, 119, 144, 161; Evans, S. H., 98, 162, 274, 427, 486; Evill, Norman, 98, 161; Farquharson, H., 98, 161; Garnett, 486; Goldsmith, 454; Hall, E. E., 162, 204, 247, 248, 427, 452, 485, 551, 553; Hannen, Nicholas, 98, 162, 165; Hinton, 385; Huddart, R., 161, 162; Hughes, 179; James, C. H., 486; Lee, J. S., 161; Lloyd, W. A. S., 488; Marchant, R., 161; Medd, H. A. N., 486; Milne, Oswald, 98, 103, 162, 165; Nauheim, Miss C. 451, 486; North, J. L., 161; Phipps, the Hon. Paul, 98, 161, 162, 165; Severne, N., 98, 162; Stewart, George, 572; Thomas, A. J., 98, 113, 161, 162, 204, 247, 451, 485; Tribe, 486, 572; Wallich, 162, 165; Wands, 486; Ward, W. H., 161; Watney, 179; Webb, Beatrice, 451, 486, 572; Wilson, J. M., 428; Wright, Hubert, 427; *see also* Delhi, New
Offices: 7, Apple Tree Yard, 294, 297, 305, 327, 361, 428, 432, 449, 485; 29, Bloomsbury Square, 144, 161 *et seq.*, 327, 485; 5, Eaton Gate, 432, 546; 6, Grays Inn Square, 18, 19, 36, 40, 45, 62, 93; 17, Queen Anne's Gate, 182, 204, 262, 294, 327, 333, 432, 485, 486, 572; 13, Mansfield St., 432, 449, 451, 551, 572
Office output, 461; system, 163, 164 *et seq.*, 461, 487, 488, 492
Partnership, forms of, 93, 179, 309, 310, 547, 548
Staff Dinner to, 21, 559
THEORY OF ARCHITECTURE OF
'Aesthetic Science', the, 524, 526, 529, 531, 544, 547, 565, 567, 574, 577, 586; Absolute beauty and, 526, 538, 539, 577, 586; engineering and, 525, 526, 586; 'Ideal Vision', 525, 528, 547
Architectural education, 557, 565, 577, 587; grammar, 558
Architecture, contemporary, his reference to, 525, 542, 554, 557, 558, 559, 587; his principles of xx, 22, 103, 116, 120, 133, 135, 164, 166, 174, 280, 470, 471, 475, 482, 484, 488 *et seq.*, 493, 525, 526, 531, 542, 545, 549, 557, 558, 559, 568, 573, 574, 587, 588, 589
Architecture and Poetry, 166, 209, 560; and Time, 282, 321, 525, 529
Town Planning, views on, 123, 208, 408, 419, 420, 458, 549, 567, 568, 573, 578

Angelina, his bicycle, 3, 9, 40, 43
Cenotaph, name, 391; Lloyd George and, 394
Furniture, early designs of and views on, 63 *et seq.*, 147
Gardens by, 87, 96, 101, 107, 116, 124, 125 *et seq.*, 173, 174, 232, 463, 471, 472, 571
Garrick Club and, 361, 441
Lectures, addresses by, 526, 542, 557, 560, 575
Liverpool Cathedral, and, 528

Logic of, 208, 225, 280, 282, 295, 296, 321, 322, 411, 491, 494, 529, 578
Rainbow, the, on nationality of, 226
Sackville, Lady, and, 378, 380, 442, 571
Versailles, fete at, and, 388
War Memorials, factors affecting his conception of, 369, 373, 461, 474, 476, 566
Wren, Sir Christopher, referred to by, or as an influence on, xxi, 108, 121, 123, 138, 140, 174, 189, 190, 277, 280, 297, 300, 340, 377, 420, 531, 533, 540, 542, 565, 567
Lutyens, Lady Emily, xv, 36, 38, 55, 143, 146, 151, 171–2, 246, 254, 324, 374, 378, 411, 439, 442, 522, 579; Sir Edwin's relationship with, 46, 144–6, 168, 170, 204, 247 *et seq.*, 285, 328, 360, 378, 380, 382, 387, 395, 438–9, 444, 556, 571
Lutyens, Robert, xvi, 4, 144, 154, 164, 326, 333, 359, 389, 438, 454, 547, 554, 569
Lutyens, Ursula, 171, 253, 326, 359, 360, 415, 438, 439, 443, 538, 541, 573
Lyon, Thompson, 85
Lyttleton, the Hon. Alfred, 99, 137, 188
Lytton, Bulwer, 38, 49; Countess of, 46, 47, 49, 56, 59, 170, 200, 269; Lady Constance, 38, 172, 256; Robert, 1st Earl of, 7, 37, 48, 59, 194, 196, 199, 269, 289, 328, 439; Victor, 2nd Earl of, 38, 580

MACDONALD, THE RT. HON. RAMSAY, 282 *n.*
Macdonald, Sir Schomberg, 229
Mackail, Denis, 151
Mackenna, the Rt. Hon. Reginald, 203, 246, 295, 333, 463, 464, 470, 548
Mackennal, Sir Bertram, 229
MacMahon, Sir Henry, 254, 260, 339, 343
Madras, 411, 419
*Magdalene College, Cambridge, 481
Malan, Dr., 205, 206
Malik, Sir Teja Singh, 427
Mallet, M., and Madame Guillaume, 85, 172, 200, 328, 339
Mandu, India, Ruins of, 279
Mangles, Harry, 24
Mansfield St., London, No. 13, 432, 439, *see* Lutyens, Sir E., Offices of
*Marsh Court, 87, 98, 99, 100, 101, 122, 161, 162, 326, 333, 570
Mary, Queen, xvi, 449, 451, *see also* George V, King; and Queen Mary's Dolls' House
Masey, Cecil, 553

Maxwell, Capt., 255, 258, 275, 321
McColl, D. S., 232, 376
McKecknie, Sir James, 293
Medd, H. A. N., xvi, 505 *n.*
Melba, Mme., 440, 550
*Mells Manor, 192, 328, 464, 570
*Mells Park, 203, 464
Mendl, Lady, 45
Michelangelo, 140, 174, 533
*Middlefield, Cambs., 133, 135, 136, 192, 294, 481
*Middleton Park, Oxon., 547
*Midland Banks: King St., Manchester, 471 *n.* Leadenhall St., London, 471 *n.*; Piccadilly, London, 442, 453, 463; Poultry, London, 462, 470, 491, 492, 547, 588
Mildmay, Alfred, 463
Milford House, 7, 39, 44, 67, 144, 146
*Millmead, Surrey, 108
Milne, Oswald, xvi, 163, *see also* Lutyens, Sir Edwin, Offices of
Ministry of Town and Country Planning, 588
Ministry of Transport, 524
Mond, Sir Alfred, 375, 387, 388
*Monkton, Sussex, 104, 105, 121, 128, 151, 157, 159, 162
Montagu, the Rt. Hon. E. S., 269, 282 *n.*, 283, 285, 295, 300 *n.*, 320, 367, 370, 378, 382, 390, 408
Montagu-Chelmsford declaration, 328, 367, 372, 405
Montbrison, Mme de, 108
Montgomery, Field Marshal Viscount, 105
Montmartre, 85
Montmorency, Sir G. F. de, 248, 251, 256, 261, 263, 321, 336, 362, 371
Morgan, Sir Herbert, xvi, 444, 451
Morris, William, 14, 39, 83, 187
Morrow, George, 441
*Mothecombe, Devon, 463
*Mount (now Amesbury) School, Hindhead, 105, 124
Mumford, Lewis, 335 *n.*, 336, 586
Munnings, Sir A. J., 464, 570, 580
*Munstead Corner, 26; House, 23, 71, 152; Wood, 18, 28, 72, 74, 115, 146, 148, 156, 463, 544, 571; 'The Hut', at, 25, 28, 40, 85
Muntzer, George, 168, 451

NAIR, SIR C. SANKARAN, 347
*Nashdom, 113, 125, 126, 167, 179
*National Theatre, South Kensington site, 553
Nauheim, Miss Clair, 392, *see also* Railing, Lady

Nawanagar, H.H. the Jam Sahib of, 418
Nazareth, 540
Nehru, Pandit Motilal, 426
Nelson, Sir Amos, 453, 471
Nethersole, N., 264
*New Place, Shedfield, 113, 127, 167, 179
Newcastle, General Hospital, 573
Newgate Gaol, old, 25, 120
Newton, Sir Ernest, 136, 226
Nichols, Government Architect, at Delhi, 321, 367
Nicholson, William, 23, 24, 25, 120, 127, 327, 333, 360, 375, 450, 451, 476, 549, 565, 569
Nicolson, the Hon. Harold, xvi, 379, 390, *quoted*, 485 n.
Nicolson, the Hon. Mrs Harold, xv, 379 n., 392
Noble, Sir Saxton, 333, 569
Norman, Sir Henry and Lady, 269
North, Dr. Kennedy, 496

OCKHAM MILL, SURREY, 571, 575
Olaszi, Bodrog, Hungary, 178
Old Basing, brickfields at, 105
Onslow Square, London, No. 16, 5, 18, 48, 62
Ootacamund, 378
*Orchards, Godalming, 71, 75, 85, 146, 192, 326
Orpen, Sir William, 232, 361
'Other' Club, 333
*Overstrand Hall, 85, 87, 88, 97, 98, 147

PALLADIO, ANDREA, 128, 297, 470
*Papillon Hall, 106, 121, 126, 162, 263
Paris Exhibition, the (1900), 84, 89, 98, 146, 194
*Park Hatch, Hascombe, 20, 86
*Parliament Chamber, Inner Temple Hall, 193
Parnell and Son, 451
Parthenon, the, 376, 526, 538, 565
Pasture Wood, 88
Patiala, Maharajah of, 257
Patrick Geddes in India, 336 n.
Peñaranda, Duke of, 338, 385, 456
*Penheale, Cornwall, 463
Pepita, 379 n., 390 n.
Perigord, 190
Peterborough, Bishop's Palace, 71, 73
Phillips, Sir Lionel, 80, 205, 206
Phillips, Lady, 206
Philpot, Glyn, 450
Phipps, Hon. Paul, xvi, *see also* Lutyens, Sir Edwin, Offices
'Picturesque', the 78, 121
*Pilgrim's Way, Bridge over, 105

Player, W. G., 293
*Pleasaunce, The, Cromer, 72
*Plumpton Place, 105, 481
Plymouth, Earl of, 230
Purshotum, Payal Parmar (referred to as 'Persotum'), 248, 415, 426, 553, 556

Quality Street, 151, 165
Queen Mary's Dolls' House, 326, 432, 440, 455, 469, 472, 543; described, 449 *et seq.*; origin of, 444

RAILING, LADY, xvi, *see also* Nauheim, Miss Clair, and Lutyens Sir Edwin, Offices
*Rake House, Milford, 72, 98, 153
Raleigh, Sir Walter, 413
*Rand Regiments Memorial, Johannesburg, 186, 204, 207, 208, 217, 231, 270
Ranelagh housing scheme, 553
Reading, Marquess of, Viceroy, 390, 405, 408, 409, 410
Reconstruction in the City of London, 588
Rees, Sir J. D., 283
Reid, Herbert, 17
Reid Dick, Sir William, 470, 550
Reilly, Sir Charles, 544
*Renishaw Hall, Derbyshire, 175, 192, 333
*Reuters and Press Association Headquarters, 547
Rhodes, Capt. Ernest, 71
Ricardo, Halsey, 74
Richardson, Prof. A. E., 240 n.
Riddell, Lord, 98, 229
Ridley, Viscount, 443
Ritchie, Sir Richmond, 245, 271
Roberts, A. L., 587 n.
Roberts, Capt., 248 n.
Robertson, Manning, 587 n.
Robinson, William, 23, 75, 83, 96, 153, 175, 179
Rodd, Sir Rennell, 199, 217, 225
*Roehampton House, 246, 294
Romantic tradition, the, *see* Lutyens, Sir Edwin, Architecture of Romantic impulses
Rome, 287, 299, 320:
*   British school at, 217, 225, 228, 246, 263, 270, 272, 293, 542;
*   Exhibition, British Pavilion at, 194, 199
*Roseneath, Dunbartonshire, Inn at, 56, 71, 72, 146
*Rossall Beach, 97, 98
Rottingdean, 327, 440
Rouse, Sir Alexander, 427, 431

Royal Academy, 4, 62, 63, 290
Royal Commission, International Exhibitions at Turin and Rome, for, the, 186, 194
Royal Commission on Public Services (Islington Committee), 282 n.
Royal Fine Arts Commission, 458, 566
Royal Institute of British Architects, 226, 245; Journal, of, 587 n.
Royal Society of Arts, 283, 559
*Ruckmans, Oakwood Park, 27
*Runnymede, 476
Ruskin, John, 14, 28, 78, 121, 169

SACKVILLE, LADY, 154, 361, 374, 378, 380, 382, 442, 504, 571
Sackville-West, the Hon. V., see Nicolson, the Hon. Mrs. Harold
Sale, J. L., xvi, 248 n., 427, 503
*Salutation, The, Sandwich, 135, 137, 192, 294
Samuel, Lord (Sir Herbert), 267, 333
Sanmichele, 128, 140, 297
Santa Sophia, 534
Santayana, George, quoted, 235
Santonio, Duke and Duchess of, 340, 341
Sargent, J. S., 232, 328, 362
Savoy Hotel, 97
Schultz, G. Weir, 17
Scott, Sir G. Gilbert, 389, 527
Scott, G. Murray, 85
Sert, J. M., 544
Shakespeare's England Exhibition, 193, 246, 256, 327
Shaw, Evelyn, 290
Shaw, Norman, 17, 20, 67, 119, 121, 123, 126, 137, 187
Shoosmith, A. G., xvi, see also Delhi, New, Assistant architects, etc., at
Shoosmith, Mrs. A. G., xvi, 506
Sickert, W. R., 560 n.
Simla, 248, 254, 255, 262, 285
Sir Edwin Lutyens: An Appreciation in Perspective (1943), 4, 154 n.
Sitwell, Sir George, 175, 333
Sitwell, Sir Osbert, xvi, 8, 176, 326, 379 n., quoted, 379, 399, 414
Sleath, Miss ('Nanny'), 550
Smee and Houchin, Messrs., 548
Smith, Mrs. Eustace, 135, 177
Smith, Hatchard, 103
Smith, Logan Pearsall, 23, 30
Smuts, Field Marshal, 200, 203, 205, 390

Solomon, J. M., 206, 231, 390
*Sonning bridges, the, 98, 105
Sopwith, Capt., 248 n.
Spectator, the 243 n., 485 n.
St. Bride's Church, London, 548
*St. James's Park Lake, bridge over, 229, 294
*St. James's Square, No. 7, 192, 294
*St. John's Institute, Tufton St., 125
St. Paul's Cathedral, 62, 138, 161, 530, 533, 534, 545, 568, 580; windows in, 545
*St. Peter's Home, Ipswich, 98
St. Peter's, Rome, 263, 356, 357, 530, 533, 541
Stamfordham, Lord, 177 n., 266, 362, 366
Starmer, Walter, 192
Stephen, Leslie, Vanessa, Virginia, 39
Stevens, Alfred, 121
Stewart, George, xvi, 572
*Stoke College, Suffolk, 71
Stokes, Leonard, President R.I.B.A., 225, 229
Stokes, Lady, 571
Storrs, Sir Ronald, 343
Strong, Mrs. Eugénie, 227, 330
Suffragette Movement, 288
Suggia, Mme, 440
*Sullingstead, Hascombe, 27, 36, 58, 61, 71, 124
Sutro, Alfred, 527
Sutton Courtenay, 570
Swinton, Capt. G., 246, 248, 251, 257, 261, 273, 274, 283, 532
Sydenham, Lord, 248, 285, 333

TAVISTOCK, 186
*Temple Dinsley, 135, 139, 142, 178, 193
Tennant, H. J., 108, 136, 229, 550
Theosophy, 85, 172, 252, 255
Theosophical Society, 328, 389; Headquarters, Gordon Square, 294, 329, 334, 453, 463
*Thiepval, Memorial to the Missing, 455, 462, 474, 482, 526, 528, 588
Thomas, A. J., 546, see also Lutyens, Sir Edwin, assistants of
Thursley, 4, 5, 14, 17, 18, 62, 571
*Tigbourne Court, 96, 97, 161
Toledo, 340
Tonks, Henry, 232, 328
*Tower House, Mayfield, 71
Tunnard, Christopher, 569 n.
Turin, Exhibition, 199
Tweed, John 121
Tyrwhitt, Jacqueline, 336 n.

UDAIPUR, 278
Unwin, Sir Raymond, 186, 188

VANDERBILT, MRS. 'ANNE', 454, 456, 457
Verney, Col. Sir Ralph, 414
Versailles, 125, 298, 388
Victoria, Queen, 49, 73, 89, 118
Vinci, Leonardo da, 140
Vindhyam stone, used at Delhi, 428

WALCOT, W., 306, 307, 311, 323
Wales, Prince of (later King Edward VIII), 408
Walgate, C. P., 391 n.
Wallace, Capt. Euan, 425, 438, 569, 572
*War Memorials, 420, 424
*War Shrine, proposed temporary, in Hyde Park, 386 et seq., 391
*War Stone (the Great Stone), 373, 374, 375, 376, 380, 389, 391, 462, 566
Ward, Sir Thomas, 248 n., 263, 273
Wardman, Harry, 483
Ware, Gen. Sir Fabian, 372, 373, 374, 566
Waring, S. J., 387, 388
*Warren Lodge, 39, 61, 192
Warwick Castle, 155
*Washington, British Embassy at, 456, 483, 485 n. 491, 521, 524, 547
Waterloo Bridge, 524
Weaver, Sir Lawrence, *Houses and Gardens by E. L. Lutyens*, 96 n., 240, 326, 450
Webb, Sir Aston, 119, 137, 143, 225, 226, 290, 382, 560
Webb, Barbara (Mrs. Robert), 6, 18, 23, 25, 36, 39, 46, 50, 53, 67, 76, 85, 154, 326, 378
Webb, Miss E., xvi, 572
Webb, Philip, 14, 17, 26, 83, 571
Webb, Robert, 7, 39, 61, 144, 247, 248
Wellesley, Lord Gerald, 179
Wernher, Sir Julius, 180, 203
West Dean Park, 157
Westminster, Duke of, 36, 53, 72, 74
Westminster Cathedral, 190
Westminster Housing Scheme, 482
*Whalton Manor, Northumberland, 135
Whinney, Son & Austen Hall, Messrs., 463. 471 n.
Willingdon, Lord, Viceroy of India, 410, 419, 540, 552
Willingdon, Lady, 311, 550, 551, 552, 553, 555
Wilmot, Miss Ellen, 362
Wilton House, Wilts., 218
Wimborne, Lord 108, 160, 565
Wintour U. F., 194, 199
Wisby, 179
*Wittersham House, Sussex, 137, 189
Women's Suffrage movement, 119
Wood, Derwent, 200
*Woodside, Chenies, 27
Woolley, Sir Leonard, 334
Worthington, Sir Hubert, 226 n.
'Wrenaissance', 103, 136
Wright, Whitaker, 61

YEATS, W. B., 233, 234
Young William, 120
*Y.W.C.A. Central Club, Great Russell St., 481

IMPERIAL DELHI
NORTH - EAS[T]

NORTH SIDE

A →

WEST SIDE